Beloved Dust

Beloved Dust

TIDES OF THE SPIRIT IN CHRISTIAN LIFE

Robert Davis Hughes III

continuum

NEW YORK • LONDON

2011

Continuum International Publishing Group
80 Maiden Lane, New York, NY 10038
The Tower Building, 11 York Road, London SE1 7NX

www.continuumbooks.com

Library of Congress Cataloging-in-Publication Data

Hughes, Robert Davis.
   Beloved dust : tides of the Spirit in the Christian life / Robert Davis Hughes III.
     p. cm.
   Includes bibliographical references (p.   ) and index.
   ISBN-13: 978-0-8264-2842-4 (hardcover : alk. paper)
   ISBN-10: 0-8264-2842-8 (hardcover : alk. paper)
   ISBN-13: 978-0-8264-2843-1 (pbk. : alk. paper)
   ISBN-10: 0-8264-2843-6 (pbk. : alk. paper) 1. Spiritual life—Christianity.
2. Holy Spirit. I. Title.

   BV4501.3.H8219 2008
   248—dc22

                                         2008023756

Ad majorem Dei gloriam

With gratitude for all my teachers,
including my family, friends, colleagues,
directees, and students.

Contents

The First Interlude

Second Tidal Current: Transfigured Dust

The Second Interlude

Third Tidal Current: Glorified Dust

Preface

The serious Christians I know want nothing more than these two things: to be agents of change in the world, and to feel close to Jesus. Yet these can strike us as mutually exclusive goals. Action can distract us from prayer, while too much attention to our inner journey can stand in the way of mission. Ultimately, this is a false problem. Unless our deeds arise out of our own experience of God's challenging love for us, they will hardly bear fruit for the kingdom. And unless our spiritual practices propel us in the direction of the neighbor, they are simply exercises in narcissism. But it is extraordinarily difficult to show how the connection between action and spiritual formation can play out in ordinary life. Put starkly, how can we have time for both?

That is the question Robert Hughes takes up in this book. In so doing, he lays out a fresh approach to spiritual theology in which action and prayer, ethics and discernment, social critique and union with Christ go hand in hand at every point. He does this by exploring the growing body of recent theological reflection on the character and role of the Holy Spirit and applying these insights to a reconsideration of what life in the Spirit means. In other words, he asks the question that the rest of us have so far neglected to ask or stick with: What is the proper work of the Holy Spirit, both within the Trinity and in the history of salvation, and what does that tell us about our spiritual journey as Christians?

Hughes's elegant answer is that the Holy Spirit brings love to its fullness by revealing its connection with freedom. Within the Trinity, the Spirit presents the Father and the Son to one another as persons whose relation is not simply given but embraced. In the economy of creation and salvation, the Spirit is continually presenting the world to the Father as something to be freely loved for the sake of the Son, through whom all things were made. But—and this is the great miracle that lies at the heart of our spiritual life—the Spirit presents us to the Father (one might say the Spirit *endorses* us to the Father) by inhabiting humankind, and, more particularly, God's covenant people and the church, in such a way as to make God's love and God's freedom something of which we become capable of ourselves, not by virtue of our own created nature but by being saturated, as it were, by the Holy Spirit resting on us. In other words, since the Holy Spirit is Christ's first gift to all who believe, our yielding to that love, however hesitant or grudging, makes us the abode of the Spirit, who sets to work immediately to transform us into saints. To use Hughes's central image, the Spirit washes over us like a tide.

What follows on this central insight is a thoughtful reconsideration of the traditional elements of Christian spiritual theology, to which Hughes brings a lifetime

ix

of scholarship and spiritual experience. The simple seeker should not be put off by all the notes at the end of each chapter. This book is for everyone, because it is shaped from beginning to end by the conviction that the Holy Spirit offers us the possibility of a holiness that is democratic and egalitarian. I also commend *Beloved Dust* to the social activist. The Spirit engaged here is the Spirit of the covenant, the prophets, and the martyrs. To be taken up into this Spirit is to enter the dazzling darkness of the transfiguration, in which, as Hughes emphatically reminds us, all our socially constructed egos lose their mooring, and our identity, inasmuch as it depends on gender, race, rank, orientation or nationality, doesn't count for much. Each of us is *beloved dust,* called to divine glory. I am grateful for this book, which calls us back to this basic Christian teaching, and invites us, through the deconstruction of our constructed selves, to become radical contemplatives and contemplative radicals. This spiritual effort (yielding to the Spirit is, indeed, an effort), and this alone, makes the church real in the world and makes our membership in the church real for ourselves.

Thomas E. Breidenthal, D. Phil.,
Bishop of Southern Ohio, the Episcopal Church

Acknowledgments

Two people have had a remarkable impact on this book, having believed in it from the start and made large contributions to it. My superlative wife, Barbara, has been much more than the reader of first resort, though she has been that; she has also pushed me to be much more inclusive in language and content and, at several points where she is credited, is the actual author. Her personal support in our life together, as well as for this specific project, has made the whole thing possible. I am a very lucky man.

Frank Oveis, retired senior editor at Continuum, miraculously "got" this book at the proposal stage and has been a great coach and cheerleader ever since. I am deeply grateful for his commitment to, and assistance with, what has emerged. If I am the mother of this book and Barbara is its midwife, Frank is the delivering obstetrician. The rest of the staff at Continuum have also been immensely helpful, including Burke Gerstenschlager, who took over from Frank the task of shepherding the book through the production process. Thanks also to Paul Kobelski and the team at the HK Scriptorium for careful proofreading that saved me from more than one howler. My thanks to all concerned.

The deans under whom I have served at Sewanee and my colleagues there have provided invaluable support, including granting needed sabbatical leaves. Special mention must be made of Christopher Bryan, editor of the *Sewanee Theological Review*, who let me work out many of my ideas in articles for that journal, some republished herein with permission, and Jim Dunkly and now his wife and assistant, Joan Blocher, who provide exactly what God meant to create in library support. Thanks also to Kit Brinson and Jamie McAdams who were my research assistants during this project. I am also grateful to the deans and faculties of the Church Divinity School of the Pacific and Seabury Western Theological Seminary for visiting scholar status on sabbaticals, as well as David Ford, John Polkinghorne, Nicholas Lash, and the principal and staff of Westcott House for an important time at Cambridge and the help I received there. I am also grateful for financial support from the Conant Fund and the Mercer Fund for these sabbaticals. Philip Sheldrake, Bernard McGinn, and Stephen Sykes have also all been encouraging and made helpful suggestions about the text; Arthur Holder gave significant help by inviting and then editing the material on the Holy Spirit in the Blackwell Companion to Christian Spirituality. Robert Boak Slocum did the same for material published in the two collections he edited in which early versions of material now in this book first appeared, *Engaging the Spirit* and *A Heart for the Future*. Deep thanks to my bishop, Thomas Breidenthal, for his willingness to do the preface. Thanks to Sam Williamson and Mary Avram; they know why.

Thanks are also due to Roy Whitten and Anne Brown for permission to make use of material (cited in the text) from the More to Life Program (formerly the Life Training Program, 1981), © K. Bradford Brown, Ph.D., and W. Roy Whitten Ph.D. Special thanks also to Reverend Mother Irina Pantescu and the nuns at the Sacred Monastery of Voroneț in Suceava, Moldovia, Romania, for permission to reproduce on the cover the icon detail of "The Throne of the Holy Spirit" from the great icon of the Last Judgment on the outside west wall of the monastery. Contributions for the support of this international treasure and the community living there may be sent to Orthodox Christian Mission Center, PO Box 4319, St. Augustine, FL 32085-4319, 1-877-463-6784, www.ocmc.org. Checks should be designated "Voroneț Monastery-Romania."

While this book could not have been what it is without these and many others, I alone am responsible for its mistakes and flaws.

Many of these flaws undoubtedly arise from the limitations of my own social location as a mostly white, mostly British-American, very privileged straight male priest of the Episcopal Church. I have tried to be sensitive to the theological claims being made by persons of other social locations but cannot pretend to represent them. Everything that follows should thus be preceded by a big, "This is the way it looks from where I stand." I hope it may be helpful to other and quite different persons, *mutatis mutandis*.

PART ONE

The Reconstruction of Spiritual Theology

1

Introduction: The State of the Discipline

The Holy Spirit is central to Christian spirituality and to any understanding of it. In fact, the word spirituality reflects the realization that the Christian life is led in the power and under the guidance of the Holy Spirit; it does not primarily designate this life as dealing with the "spiritual," in the sense of "immaterial."

—M. John Farrelly, O.S.B.[1]

These words reflect a growing Christian theological consensus that spirituality is simply about the Holy Spirit and her impact on the total lives of all human beings into whom she breathes life as its sovereign, especially those she indwells sacramentally through holy Baptism.[2] Spiritual theology is a disciplined theological reflection on the spiritual life or spirituality of Christians, and, envisioned this way, should have the Holy Spirit and her movements in those lives for its primary subject. Historically, this has included reflection on the nature of Christian life in the Spirit, life in Christ, as grounded in the gospel and the teachings of the catholic faith. It reflects on the rhythms and means by which individuals and communities grow toward their destined unity with God, and it helps to formulate principles of pastoral guidance for those on that journey.[3] As appropriate, it develops theological norms for Christian spirituality in dialogue with the lived experience of the Christian community.[4]

Any contemporary spiritual theology envisioned in this way, however, faces a challenging environment. There is, at present, a genuine concern for a shrinking world inhabited by neighbors of obviously fruitful but other faith. There is also a desire and need for interfaith dialogue, both to learn from one another and for the sake of ending religious conflicts as a major threat to world peace.[5] Often, this sensitivity makes it more difficult to establish normative claims from any one tradition. Postmodern dislike for grand metanarratives increases this difficulty. Coupled with the growing secularism in the West and the resultant disenchantment of many with the West's own religious traditions and institutions, this has produced a smorgasbord approach to "spirituality" as a desire to fulfill some inherent human spiritual capacity by drawing on an eclectic mix from all the traditions on offer. One often hears the phrase "I am not a conventionally religious person, but I am deeply spiritual." This may mean anything from a sincere if undefined quest for meaning to little more than "I hold my beliefs with a lot of intensity."[6] At its worst, it has produced the phenomenon, in bookstores, of a section on "metaphysics" (a complete misuse of that philosophical term) where one may find a book of Wiccan spells right next to the works of Saint Mechtild of Magdeburg. At its best, this consumerist phenomenon reflects a genuine hunger on the part of earnest seekers who have, in many cases, asked the churches for bread and found only stones.[7]

Until recently, the riches of the Christian spiritual tradition have not been available to the majority of people, either because mysticism was considered the province of an elite few, or because of a deep Protestant or Enlightenment suspicion of the mystical as paranormal.[8] Finally, like any contemporary Christian theology, spiritual theology must also face the "hermeneutics of suspicion" of the last two centuries and recognize the degree to which all parts of the tradition have been infected with interests and scars of class, race, gender, and personal psychological history. The Christian tradition is hardly alone in this.

It may seem odd to address this context with a bold theological claim: there is no inherent human spiritual capacity, only the materiality of human existence and the movements of the Holy Spirit within it. Although it so directly denies some of the most common assumptions of our present culture, that is, however, what I seek to do, not because I think it will be an easy sell but because I think it is true, and in the end only the truth will do. There are, fortunately, some new resources available for such a spiritual theology, thanks largely to the revival of classical Christian spirituality over the last several decades. These resources arose first from a growing desire to provide a well-prepared and restored ministry of spiritual guidance and direction for those seeking a deeper relationship with God on the Christian path, many of whom had explored other paths because the spiritual and mystical depths of the Christian way were unknown or seemed closed to them.[9] Then came an outpouring, into wide and popularly available sources, of riches from the history and literature of Christian spirituality, a trend that began with popular writers on mysticism such as Evelyn Underhill at the turn of the century and is now symbolized by the superb Paulist Press Classics of Western Spirituality series.[10] Meanwhile, contemporary mystics and spiritual writers from C. S. Lewis to Simone Weil and Thomas Merton continued the classical forms of spiritual autobiography and works arising directly from their own experience.[11] Christian traditions of all sorts continued to produce devotional literature. With the founding of the Society for the Study of Christian Spirituality and its publications, a forum was created for the serious study of precisely Christian spirituality, and a variety of scholarly approaches to the subject have emerged as a result.[12]

Theological opportunities have also been created by many movements in contemporary theology, starting with the revived Trinitarian theology of Karl Barth, Paul Tillich, and Karl Rahner, bearing new fruit in Catherine Mowry LaCugna, Elizabeth A. Johnson, Miroslav Volf, Robert W. Jenson, Kathryn Tanner, and John Zizioulas to name a few.[13] One fruit of this Trinitarian revival is a renewed interest in pneumatology, or the doctrine of the Holy Spirit. This also has roots in many of the authors just mentioned but has had a particular flowering in the works of Yves Congar and Kilian McDonnell, to name but two.[14] The uprising of new movements such as Radical Orthodoxy that critique the assumptions of modernism (which, as we shall see, contributed to the marginalization of Christian spirituality) has provided new and helpful ways to retrieve older wisdom for the contemporary world without falling into naïve repristinization, an uncritical return to premodern thinking.[15]

Spiritual theology has had a weaker and more problematic place in this revival. This is partly from a sense that the earlier scholastic models had become more limiting than helpful, and partly as a result of the somewhat dry and specialized nature of many of the classical works. There have been important works in the field dealing with foundational questions about the relationship of theology, spirituality, and lived Christian experience, notably those by Philip Sheldrake and Mark McIntosh.[16] Other books appear to be systematic spiritual theologies but represent a familiar class of Protestant authors who have discovered the helpful riches of the classical tradition and wish to make it available to their own constituency. F. P. Harton is an early Anglican example; Diogenes Allen, a recent Reformed example.[17] Special mention must be made of Simon Chan's fine *Spiritual Theology,* written from a fascinating Asian and Assemblies of God perspective, while being deeply historical and generously ecumenical.[18] Part 1 lays out a clear and helpful foundation for a spiritual theology, and part 2 is a collection of essays on important topics in the field; but in the end it is not structurally a full spiritual theology along the lines proposed.[19] On the Roman Catholic side, no serious attempt has been made since before Vatican II.[20]

I have been attempting to fill this lacuna for several years. After making a good start during a sabbatical at Cambridge, the project stalled, and I had a growing unease, a sense that something was deeply wrong with the project.[21] A helpful remark by Philip Sheldrake, that Vatican II anthropology (doctrine of humanity) had undermined the traditional way of undertaking the task, led to five articles and book chapters of my own in which I tried to come to grips with the problem and explore possible solutions.[22] A more thorough analysis of the problem is found in the next chapter, but the short version is this: traditional spiritual theologies developed as subordinate to moral theology and were located there. There were two classical formats: the first is a theology of Christian perfection for those who have largely fulfilled the commandments of obligation and are now ready to undertake the counsels of perfection; this included a theology of degrees of merit and works of supererogation (more than needed for salvation) that was a major lightning rod for Reformation criticism. The second was a looser theological reflection on three traditional stages of the spiritual life, purgation, illumination, and union, often also identified as appropriate for beginner, proficient, and perfect souls. These categories derive from Pseudo-Dionysius the Areopagite and then entered the theology of the medieval West, where the context was very different.[23] As we shall see, both traditional starting points have been invalidated by the theology of Vatican II, taken as representative of twentieth- and now twenty-first-century theology. At the same time, we can now see how the tradition of spiritual theology as a differentiable discipline arose in a modernist (Enlightenment) milieu and is deeply infected with cultural assumptions now seriously questioned in a postmodern context, such as the modernist belief in a definable, permanent, and inherently immortal human nature or essence expressed in well-defined autonomous and rational human egos.

At the same time, the need for a systematic theology of the spiritual life endures, and such a theology must have an essential role in dialogue with devotional, directional/pastoral, historical, and hermeneutical approaches, even if it is a humbler role than previously thought.[24] Too much rich wisdom about the spiritual life lies buried in the spiritual theology tradition to abandon it. The need for theological guidance in the current consumerist spiritual soup is also all too evident. A dream of re-integrating spiritual theology with the larger theological and pastoral tasks as in premodern times cannot, however, be realized by a historical romanticism. The need for a disciplined and focused treatment of life in the Holy Spirit is now inescapable and permanent, even while the enterprise must challenge some of the modernist assumptions by which the discipline was conceived. What I hope to do in this part is analyze more deeply the crisis in which the discipline finds itself, make some constructive proposals for how to restart the discipline in the face of the invalidation of its two traditional starting points, and then undertake as much as possible of a full spiritual theology on the new proposed basis.

Part 1 next presents a brief historical analysis of the rise and fall of spiritual theology as a discipline, looks at the resources for addressing the crisis, makes some constructive proposals for a way forward, and shows how each addresses one or another of the major problems that spiritual theology has encountered. Part 2 will attempt to show what a retrieved and renewed spiritual theology would look like, based on these constructive suggestions.

The constructive proposals I will be developing more fully as we proceed are as follows, in summary form:

(1) Any theology of the spiritual life should be grounded in the renewed contemporary Trinitarian theology, since the goal of the Christian spiritual life is participation in the Trinitarian life of God.

(2) The Holy Spirit is the "appropriate" author of the spiritual life, and any proper theology of the spiritual life has the movements of the Holy Spirit as its primary subject.

(3) The doctrine of the Holy Spirit (pneumatology) should be an independent theological *locus,* coming between Christology and the doctrine of the church.[a]

(4) Like Christology, pneumatology should be composed of two parts, inseparable but differentiable for theological purposes. Christology is usually divided into two parts: the first, Christology proper, focuses on the second person of the Trinity, the Word, Wisdom, Son, Child of God, and the person of Jesus of Nazareth as the fully human incarnation of the second person. The second part, soteriology, focuses on the work appropriated to the second person in the divine economy, especially but not limited to the period of the incarnation.[b] I propose that pneumatology should be similarly structured: pneumatology proper being the study of the Holy

---

a A theological *locus* is a topic in theology (usually a major doctrine), located in a particular logical place in a theological system. Since the time of the thirteenth-century Schoolmen, the traditional list of *loci* has been God (both as one and as Trinity), creation, humanity (including sin), Christ (person and work), sacraments, church, and last things or eschatology, which yields the theological number seven. In the twentieth century, Karl Rahner created a revolution in theology by suggesting that church and sacraments should be reversed. I am indebted to Herbert W. Richardson for that observation.

b All the external works of God (the divine economy as a plan for the universe) are indivisible, that is, engaged in by the entire Trinity. But they are not indistinguishable, as Robert Jenson reminds us (*ST* 1:110–14). It is traditional to "appropriate" certain functions to one person or another, such as creation to the Fount or Father, redemption to the Son, sanctification to the Holy Spirit, even though in truth the entire Trinity is involved in each. The heresy of modalism is the confusion of these external

Spirit, the third person of the Trinity, and spiritual theology being the study of the work of the Holy Spirit in the divine economy or plan for the universe from creation to final consummation. That is, spiritual theology should be to pneumatology as soteriology is to Christology. The connection is undergirded by Rahner's dictum that the economic Trinity *is* the immanent Trinity.[a]

(5) Far from remaining subordinate to moral theology as in the tradition, spiritual theology now encompasses moral theology as the study of the Holy Spirit's impact on the formation of conscience, conviction of sin, the call to and the possibility of real conversion, the discernment of the good, and the formation of character and virtue.[25]

(6) Such spiritual theology locates a theology of individual life in the Spirit in the context of the entire *missio Spiritus* (mission of the Holy Spirit), including its creative, covenantal, ecclesial, and historical/eschatological dimensions. In particular, it includes all the works in the third paragraph of the ecumenical creeds.

(7) Human beings are best conceived by as materialistic an anthropology as possible. I am proposing that we use the metaphor of dust, beloved dust, though by this I mean the stardust of creation, matter much as conceived by Pierre Teilhard de Chardin, not merely the dust of the dustbin, though even that is included. All "spiritual" qualities, including life, soul, consciousness, sociality, virtue, human spirit, and eternal life are viewed as relational terms between the dust we are on the one hand, and the Holy Spirit on the other.[26] Because of the freedom and independence the creator Spirit gives creatures as a gift, some of these emerge as universal and permanent characteristics of human being in an existential sense, but all are gifts of the Spirit.[27] This gracious gift of endurance or even permanence of some characteristics allows us to validate traditional language about the human spirit or soul, as long as its relational dependence is maintained. I do not see these human realities, however, as inherent parts of a given human nature; indeed, the abandonment of such claims removes us from the modernist "essentialism" so frequently condemned in postmodern criticism. Instead, I view human self-transcendence in its many dimensions as a resonance in the dust we are, raised by the divine self-transcendence as it becomes immanent to and in us. The *telos* (end or goal) of human being is best expressed as the resurrection of the body, the ultimate divine loving of the dust we are. Human being is thus a being confronted with a *telos* for which it has no natural capacity.

(8) The traditional insight into a threefold rhythm of the spiritual life (derived from the three stages of the spiritual life first described by Pseudo-Dionysius) is best seen not as a lawlike description of human spiritual growth but as resonances

---

appropriations with the reality of the persons within the triune life itself. Soteriology is the doctrine of the saving work of Christ.

   a The economic Trinity is the persons at work in the universe with functions appropriated as in the previous footnote. The immanent or essential Trinity is the three persons in the inner relationships of the divine life by which they constitute one another as who they are. Almost everyone quotes this for good or ill, and it is often given a mistaken, modalist interpretation by its critics. Simon Chan is an example. I take Rahner to mean simply that there is only one God, who is eternally and in Godself a triadic unity (the doctrine of the Trinity is first of all a form of monotheism), and that the economic Trinity is simply that same God encountered in God's actions in the world.

or tides in our dusty human lives raised by the Trinitarian structure of the *missio Spiritus*. I have named these tides conversion, transfiguration, and glory. As in a real ocean, these tides are concurrent, though one may predominate at any given moment in a person's life. This requires us to think and navigate in three dimensions, as it were: pitch, roll, and yaw.

(9) Human psychology is closely allied to the traditional wisdom of spiritual theology, but psychological development and spiritual growth are not the same, and the language of spirituality is not merely religious language for psychological growth. The Holy Spirit, however, never operates in a vacuum. As a result, the psychosocial history and growth of an individual is always the context or shore on which the tides of the Spirit break. The task of spiritual direction involves discerning the confluence of that human shore and the tides of the Spirit washing on it at any particular time.[28]

(10) Pastoral and theological norms for spiritual practice and direction emerge from a dialogue between spiritual theology so conceived and the accumulated wisdom of Christian communities from their historical and ongoing experience of life in the Spirit. Together, these communities make up the church catholic, and Christian "spiritualities" become Christian "spirituality" without loss of hybrid vigor.

We turn next to a deeper historical and theological analysis of the origins of the discipline of spiritual theology and the crisis in which it currently finds itself.

Notes

1. M. John Farrelly, "Holy Spirit," 492b.

2. This viewpoint, as we shall see, runs counter to many historical trends as well as some contemporary assumptions.

One must choose some pronoun for the Spirit. The biblical languages offer all three genders: Hebrew, the feminine *ruach;* Greek, the neuter *to pneuma;* Latin, the masculine *spiritus.* Without in any way suggesting that making the Holy Spirit feminine is an adequate response to gender issues surrounding the doctrine of the Trinity, I have chosen to indicate some sensitivity to the issue by doing so. See Farrelly, "Holy Spirit" 493a, 502b; Elizabeth A. Johnson, *She Who Is,* 42–60; see my "A Case for Inclusive Language by a White Male."

3. Jordan Aumann, *Spiritual Theology;* Simon Chan, *Spiritual Theology* (hereafter, *ST*), 18.

4. Mark A. McIntosh, *Mystical Theology;* Philip Sheldrake, *Spirituality and Theology;* Chan, *ST;* see also *BCCS,* 177–285.

5. See my "Christian Theology of Interfaith Dialogue."

6. Simon Chan, *ST,* 15–16; I fear AA may be partly responsible for the popularity of this mantra, though it was not what the founders intended in the twelve traditions.

7. Robert Wuthnow, *After Heaven.*

8. See chap. 2 below.

9. For example, Tilden Edwards, *Spiritual Friend;* Kenneth Leech, *Soul Friend; True Prayer;* and *Experiencing God;* Martin Thornton, *English Spirituality; Christian Proficiency; The Rock and the River;* and *Spiritual Direction;* Morton T. Kelsey, *Companions on the Inner Way* and numerous other works; also Urban T. Holmes, *A History of Christian Spirituality; Ministry and Imagination; Spirituality for Ministry.*

10. Evelyn Underhill, *Mysticism*. In English Christianity the refounding of the Anglican religious orders, beginning with the Oxford movement, also encouraged this development.

11. Lewis, *Pilgrim's Regress; Surprised by Joy; A Grief Observed;* Merton, *Seven Storey Mountain; Contemplative Prayer; New Seeds of Contemplation;* Weil, *Waiting for God.*

12. The literature is vast. Most important here at present are, I believe, Sandra M. Schneiders's many contributions, notably, "A Hermeneutical Approach to the Study of Christian Spirituality," and "Approaches to the Study of Christian Spirituality," *BCCS,* 15–33; Walter H. Principe, "Spirituality, Christian," *NDCS,* 931–38; Bradley C. Hanson, "Spirituality as Spiritual Theology," 45–51; and Philip Sheldrake, *Spirituality and History,* rev. ed., 40–64. See also the works by Sheldrake and McIntosh cited above, n. 4.

13. Anne Hunt, *What Are They Saying about the Trinity;* Karl Barth, *Church Dogmatics;* Paul Tillich, *Systematic Theology* (hereafter, *ST*); Karl Rahner, *The Trinity;* Catherine Mowry La Cugna, *God for Us;* Johnson, *She Who Is;* Miroslav Volf, *After Our Likeness;* Robert W. Jenson, *Systematic Theology* (hereafter, *ST*); Kathryn Tanner, *Jesus, Humanity and the Trinity;* John Zizioulas, *Being as Communion.* As I write, we await the publication of Sarah Coakley's multivolume systematics as a major contribution.

14. Yves Congar, *I Believe in the Holy Spirit;* Kilian McDonnell, *The Other Hand of God;* Veli-Matti Kärkkäinen, *Pneumatology;* Bernard J. Cooke, *Power and the Spirit of God;* Robert Boak Slocum, ed., *Engaging the Spirit;* John V. Taylor, *The Go-Between God.*

15. John Milbank, Catherine Pickstock, and Graham Ward, eds., *Radical Orthodoxy;* among the critical works, see Laurence Paul Hemming, ed., *Radical Orthodoxy?*

16. See n. 4 above.

17. Frederick P. Harton, *The Elements of the Spiritual Life;* Diogenes Allen, *Spiritual Theology.*

18. Also Eugene Peterson's series, starting with *Christ Plays in Ten Thousand Places;* Barry L. Callen, *Authentic Spirituality;* and Samuel M. Powell, *A Theology of Christian Spirituality.*

19. I am indebted to many of Chan's penetrating insights, however, as will be evident in the notes.

20. The one exception, Aumann, is admitted even by the author to be merely a reprise of the earlier volume written with Antonio Royo, and hence from a pre-Vatican II perspective.

21. For that sabbatical I owe special thanks to John Polkinghorne, David Ford, Nicholas Lash, the staff, faculty, and students of Westcott House, and a grant from the Conant Fund.

22. See my "Starting Over: The Holy Spirit as Subject and Locus of Spiritual Theology"; "A Critical Note on Two Aspects of Self-Transcendence"; "Procreation and Patience: The Spirituality of Parenting"; "The Holy Spirit in Christian Spirituality."

23. See Jean Leclerq, "Influence and Noninfluence of Dionysius in the Western Middle Ages," 25–32.

24. Principe, "Spirituality." I am using the term "directional/pastoral" to indicate the literature about the nature and practice of the ministry of spiritual direction.

25. I will deal with Chan's complaint that the Catholic way of doing this ignores the need for real conversion further on.

26. Genesis 3:19, and quoted in the traditional and contemporary liturgies for Ash Wednesday.

27. Indeed, I think this is the truth behind one of Rahner's most controversial and least understood concepts, the "supernatural existential."

28. Here I am indebted to and largely in agreement with Gerald May, *Care of Mind, Care of Spirit; Will and Spirit.*

2

The Rise and Fall of Spiritual Theology

Spiritual theology as a distinct discipline of theological reflection on Christian spiritual life, or life in the Holy Spirit, emerged only slowly from broader interests in theology and narrower foci on particular questions such as prayer. The story of its emergence has been well told relatively recently, and, where there is substantial consensus, can be reviewed quickly.[1] There are a few critical gaps in the story, however, that I shall try to fill; some of these are crucial to our understanding of the nature of the Western tradition of spiritual theology and how it rose and fell, collapsing as a discipline in the mid-twentieth century even in the face of a new interest in Christian spirituality as such.

There is general consensus that spiritual theology had achieved a vocabulary, a form, and a distinct place or locus in Roman Catholic theology by the time of publication of two works by the Italian Jesuit theologian Giovanni Battista Scaramelli (1687–1752).[2] These were the *Direttorio ascetico* (1752) and *Direttorio mystico* (1754). These works showed several characteristics that became typical of the genre throughout its history: (1) the division into the two areas—ascetical theology, which dealt with the practices and progress of the spiritual life through actively practiced asceticism or discipline, and mystical theology, which dealt with phenomena and later "stages" of the spiritual life from the transition to passive contemplation through mystical union, all dependent solely on grace; (2) the scholastic "manual" tone and literary form; and (3) the tendency toward artificiality and heaviness in dealing with what should be a lively subject.[3] These were all in place and would remain so until the revival of mysticism in the late nineteenth and early twentieth centuries and the "demise" of the discipline around the time of Vatican II. The tone and literary form of the discipline and its isolation as a separate subject, subordinate in the traditional Catholic curriculum to moral theology, made it seem one of the most traditional among theological disciplines. As we shall see, this appearance is misleading.

There is also substantial agreement about the prehistory of the discipline up until about 1600, and then again from 1750 to the present, although even here there are places I believe the story should be told differently from the usual accounts. The major lacuna in the stories is the early modern period from 1600 to 1750, which I will suggest gave the discipline at its conceptual heart a modernist or Enlightenment view of its subject that was disguised by its scholastic presentation in the manuals.

We will be tracing three trends during this account. *First* is a separation of spiritual theology from the main body of dogmatic theology; this echoes a decreasing emphasis on the objective content of spirituality as an account of God's presence and movement among God's people, moving toward a theology that focuses increasingly on the affective, the "interiority" of the individual, an increasing emphasis on the private sphere of life, and ultimately a kind of psychologistic or Romantic focus on personal experience to the exclusion of virtually all else. *Second*, especially in the West, is a deep ambivalence about the mystical, or the direct, personal encounter with God's presence.[a] On the one hand, as a result of the growing emphasis on interiority, there is a fascination with the mystical and with mystics. Indeed, as we shall see, the very separation of the "mystical" from other kinds of religious experience is part of this trend. The emphasis on personal, direct experience of God, however, also had a kind of democratizing effect that came to be seen as a danger to all established order: ecclesial, civil, and patriarchal. As a result, there is increasing suppression of the mystical, and subordination of it to the ascetical. This leads directly to the *third* trend: marginalization of the mystical in a small elite, preferably safely cloistered, usually female, uneducated, and easily manipulated by those in power. This is accompanied by an Enlightenment definition of the "mystical" as paranormal experience, and hence as irrational, beyond the realm of scientific knowledge; and, ultimately, the construal, in the nineteenth-and early-twentieth-century Romantic revival of mysticism, of the "mystic" as the rare "religious genius." As we shall see, despite their "conservative" appearance, crucial texts in spiritual theology embody these trends more than they resist them. A *fourth*, countervailing trend, haunts the boundaries of our discussion: the frequent outbreak of the mystical (often by other names) in popular movements, both Catholic and Protestant, that often, precisely because of a lack of appropriate theological and pastoral guidance, embody and hence re-enforce the very fears that had rendered the theology that might otherwise provide the guidance both esoteric and inaccessible.

It is generally agreed that in early patristic times there was no separation of theology and spirituality, a characteristic that remains true of Eastern Orthodoxy to this day.[4] "True theologians were those who saw and experienced the content of their theology."[5] Except for occasional treatises on prayer, such as Origen's, most of what we know about what we would now call spirituality is in dogmatic and controversial treatises, letters, sermons, and scriptural commentaries. Indeed, much (like Basil of Caesarea's *De Spiritu Sancto*) grows directly out of the dogmatic con-

---

a Bernard McGinn, *Early Christian Mystics*, 11–12, gives this definition of mysticism: "First, Mysticism is an element in the Christian religion, not a religion within the religion. Second, it is important to see mysticism as a total process, not merely some particular moments or moments in or beyond time where special contact with God is made. Mysticism is a journey, a path that almost invariably demands long preparation and whose true attainment can be measured only by the effects that mystics have upon others, both their contemporaries and their readers over the centuries." Again, in *The Foundations of Mysticism*, xv–xvi: "I understand the term by discussing it under three headings: mysticism as a part or element of religion; mysticism as a process or way of life; and mysticism as an attempt to express a direct consciousness of the presence of God."

troversies of the time. The other important genre is the collections of sayings or *apophthegmata*, from the desert fathers of the second century onward, containing stories, legends, monastic conferences, and bits of teaching embodying a growing communal wisdom about the spiritual life but in a nonsystematic fashion. Most of the theologians were also bishops with active pastoral responsibilities, and monks; as a result, dogmatic, spiritual, pastoral, and monastic theologies all grew apace and together. An early tension even in this patristic spirituality is between those who saw the spiritual journey ending in darkness (mostly the tradition of the Egyptian desert and around Sinai) and those who saw it ending in light (centered more in Constantinople).[6] Philip Sheldrake also reminds us that virtually all theologians of the time were men, and from the elite, educated classes of Hellenistic/Roman society.[7] On the Anglican side, Kenneth Kirk traces back even into patristic times the tendency for there to be two kinds of life which differ not in only in degree but even in kind: the monastic life leading to contemplation, the active life to a lower sort of salvation.[8] This problem of elitism recurs as a theme throughout the history of Christian spirituality, and Kirk adverts to it often.

One author from this period is of unique importance, probably a fifth- or sixth-century Syrian monk, known to us only as Pseudo-Dionysius the Areopagite.[9] His *Mystical Theology* gives the appearance of being the first real systematic treatise on the spiritual life, and from it come the three traditional "stages" of purgation, illumination, and union which would have so widespread an effect on later Western authors, and indeed enter spiritual theology as one of its defining frameworks.[10] It is now widely agreed, however, that in Pseudo-Dionysius these three stages do not contain a lawlike description of human spiritual growth, but emerge from his own neo-Platonic concept of celestial and ecclesiastical hierarchy as spelled out in his other works, and from the liturgical context he took for granted.[11]

In the early medieval West the monastic theme came to predominate, really right through Bernard of Clairvaux in the twelfth century; some treatises did begin to appear focusing specifically on the mystical life, but still in an overall context of monastic theology as such. While this genre continued to bear fruit in the high Middle Ages, the scholasticism of the thirteenth century brought a major shift, largely under the leadership of members of the new mendicant orders of friars (Dominicans and Franciscans) whose rule and life was quite different from the older Benedictine patterns. The establishment at this time of the great universities as the principal place of theological discourse is also surely no accident. For the first time, dogmatic, moral, and theological concerns began to be separated. Although his great *Summae* struggle to maintain a real unity of disciplines, Thomas Aquinas put most of what he had to say about the Christian life in the second part of the *Summa theologiae*, the return of all things to God, beginning a trend that would subordinate spiritual theology to moral and separate both from dogmatic theology. Thomas clearly intended the entire *Summa* to be a unified system of *sacra doctrina*, and in his own thought maintained loving knowledge of the Trinitarian God as a unity of affection and "speculation" (knowledge through intellectual abstraction).[12] But a tiny wedge had opened that would become a chasm in the subsequent tradition of Thomist manuals of the eighteenth century and onward.

Also at this time, the "mystical theology" of Pseudo-Dionysius, dividing the spiritual life into three successive stages of ascent (purgative, illuminative, unitive), re-emerged into popularity in the West, but largely taken out of the original context and often conflated with another set of three successive stages, that of the beginners, the proficient, and the perfect.[13] There was also a systematization of teaching on meditation and prayer. These three tendencies—scholastic organization and differentiation (including, ultimately, the separation of moral and spiritual theology from dogmatic and from one another), the return of Dionysian stages in a new context, and systematized teaching on prayer—had already come together in the teachings of the Canons of St. Victor in Paris (notably Richard and Hugh, late twelfth century), which came to have immense influence.[14]

These trends accompanied the emergence of a new subjective and affective piety with its own literary genres, and even very early roots of subsequent individualism. Much more attention began to be given to the inner states and affections of the individual, and there was also significant impact from what we may call the first wave of Romanticism in the courtly love tradition. Systematic treatises on the spiritual life began to emerge, including Richard of St. Victor's *Benjamin major* and *Benjamin minor*, and *The Cloud of Unknowing*, or Bonaventure's *Journey of the Mind/Soul into God*, and *The Triple Way*. Christian women from Hildegard of Bingen to Julian of Norwich contributed to the growing genre of personal theological reflection on one's own mystical experiences. The impact of the courtly love tradition is nowhere clearer than in the works of Haedewijch of Antwerp.[15] Popular works such as Marguerite Porete's *The Mirror of Simple Souls* and the *Theologia germanica*, a fourteenth-century work by a Germanic monastic knight, later admired and translated by Martin Luther, show the impact of these developments on more popular piety, just as their subsequent history, including the burning of Porete and her book, reveals the growing nervousness in the hierarchy about the spread of this new interiority. Other developments in the Rhineland School, including works by Meister Eckhart, Johannes Tauler, Henry Suso, and Jan van Ruusbroec, and later the *Devotio Moderna* in the fourteenth and fifteenth centuries, as well as the influence of Jean Gerson in France (1363–1429), deepened these trends toward an individual, often affective piety.[16] Many of these works influenced later Catholic writers; and, when Protestant scholasticism had driven the attention to personal affectivity underground, it re-emerged in Lutheran pietism, whence it passed into the Moravians and Wesley, often accompanied by one or more of the earlier texts. This backwash of Rhineland spirituality through Pietism remains a hidden "Catholic" influence in much neo-evangelical piety in our own time.

While there is some question about when the actual "modern" concept of individual subjectivity emerged from a more communal and liturgical setting, there is little doubt that this process began in the "twelfth-century renaissance," continued through the high Middle Ages, and reached a kind of peak in the fourteenth and fifteenth centuries.[17] At one level, this new sense of individual personhood and attention to the inner life of such persons was a great discovery and a great good, leading to many of the finest aspects of modern civilization, including its democracy and its psychology. But, as we shall see, the increasingly excessive focus on individual affectivity and interiority and the subsequent loss of objective theological content brought with it a host of problems that have become even more evident in a post-modern context where the certainty of individual selfhood is under question.

This late medieval period also gave birth to the philosophical movement of "nominalism" in the works of William of Ockham (fourteenth-century Franciscan theologian and philosopher) and others. The movement began by teaching that the general or abstract concepts known as "universals," which Platonism had described as the ultimately real realm of ideas, were only our names for certain aspects of experience and had no objective reference. The net effect was to turn the interest of philosophy from the known to the individual knower and his or her inner processes of knowing. Modern science is also born in this milieu, and makes use of "Ockham's razor" to eliminate unnecessary concepts and entities, often while maintaining a naive belief in external physical reality that the philosophical movement challenges as it passes into the continental rationalism of René Descartes and G. W. Leibniz, the British empiricism of David Hume, and John Locke, and ultimately to the transcendental philosophy of that strange German Pietist, Immanuel Kant (late eighteenth century). Much of the current "postmodern" or deconstructionist philosophy is actually, I believe, a playing out to its final dead end of this modernist movement rather than something new.[18] I am unaware of any full studies on the impact of nominalism on the spirituality of the time, but the increasing turn toward inner subjectivity in each case is surely instructive.[19] It is in any case within this philosophical and theological milieu that both Reformation and Catholic Reformation (a preferred term to Counter-Reformation) take place, even when they are unaware of it or seem to be deliberately appealing to earlier realist (Platonist or neo-Platonist) authors such as Augustine or Pseudo-Dionysius, or moderate realist (more Aristotelian) authors such as Aquinas.[20]

One further factor influences the spirituality and theology of the late Middle Ages: devastation. The prosperity and peace of the medieval *pax ecclesiae* (peace of the church) was brought to an end by a combination of the drama of the divided papacy, the Hundred Years' War (the War of the Roses in England), and the succession of plagues that decimated most communities. Many places were depopulated by as much as two-thirds. Economic activity slowed to a frightening degree and did not recover the strength it had enjoyed in the thirteenth century until the eighteenth.[21] Death was a grim and ever-present reality, as the new emphasis on the suffering or dead corpse of Christ on the cross makes clear in the art of the time.[22] Battles with Muslim civilization continued, culminating in the final collapse of the Eastern empire, Christian Byzantium. The divided papacy created a crisis in personal spirituality as well as ecclesial peace and discipline. If ever there was a period when life was nasty, brutish, and short, this was it.[23] Yet it is in these circumstances that one of the great flowerings of Christian spirituality and mysticism occurred. It is far too simple to suggest that the mystical turn inward was a mere reaction to these disasters;[24] we have already seen the roots of that turn in the far more optimistic twelfth and thirteenth centuries. But I do not believe the confluence of these forces is accidental: the deeper (and ultimately "darker") turn to affective subjectivity and interiority in a flowering spirituality, the skeptical subjectivism of nominalism, and the devastation in the social, political, and economic realms are surely more closely intertwined than any study to this point has made clear. The world was a very dark and dangerous place. Retreat to interiority and an increasing mysticism of darkness are surely not surprising outcomes, even if we must be careful not to overstate the case.

Then came the full Renaissance, with a recovery of a strong humanist strain that at this time remained explicitly and thoroughly Christian, even while it recovered the treasures of classical "pagan" learning.[25] While we often think of this influence as particularly keen in areas that became Protestant, most especially England, the influence was also deep in Catholic Spain and France during the critical early modern period, especially in the universities.[26] At the heart of the Catholic Reformation, the Carmelites (Teresa and John of the Cross) and the Jesuits (Ignatius Loyola) and their followers carried forth many of the medieval and late medieval themes in this more positive context. In Ignatius, the military model becomes an opportunity to make a personal choice of Christ as one's king and commander. Teresa of Avila makes the new interior self a splendid castle illuminated by the light of Christ at its center. John of the Cross faces squarely into the darkness and finds that in the end it is sheer grace, a luminous darkness. The succeeding history of spirituality is, of course, intertwined with the wars of religion and the rise of the modern state, the triumph of natural science, the passing of mercantilism over into aggressive capitalism, and the resulting "Enlightenment" in philosophy, with all that it has come to mean to modern consciousness. To make a very complicated story short, the Iberian saints and their followers, including Francis de Sales and the succeeding French school, solidified the final subjective turn of spirituality. Both personal reports of the mystics and the subsequent theological reflection on them focus on close observation of movements of individual souls, especially in the "higher" stages of spiritual development, completing the separation from academic theology and encouraging the development of a kind of personal spiritual psychologism. The Protestant focus on personal conversion and faith placed a similar emphasis on the individual consciousness and its spiritual state, even when outwardly denying the relevance of the Catholic spiritual and mystical heritage. The story of spirituality in general and mysticism in particular becomes, from this point onward, almost entirely a story of this growing interiority and affective subjectivism, right through the early twentieth century. Again, these were great and important discoveries that have given us much to celebrate. But the excessive turn to individual interiority also brought its own problems.

The most penetrating analysis of this shift is surely Michel de Certeau's in his strange *Mystic Fable,* especially section 3, "The Circumstances of Mystic Utterance," which culminates in "The Fiction of the Soul, Foundation of *The Interior Castle*" (Teresa of Avila).[27] In a postnominalist and now "humanist" universe, speaking and writing are no longer grounded in the objectivity of God's speaking, but in that of an "I" which itself will prove increasingly ephemeral as the modern era progresses. The emphasis is on *my faith* (Luther), *my decision* (Ignatius), *my ecstasy* (Teresa), *my longing in the darkness* (John of the Cross).[28] Spiritual psychologism has come to full birth and will reach maturity at the hands of the nineteenth-century romantics.[29] It will help to see what happens in the succeeding period if we put it this way: Descartes' famous *cogito, ergo sum*, "I think, therefore I am," grounding the knowing of the self in knowing its own self, is prepared by the cries of the Protestant and Catholic Reformations: "I believe, therefore I am; I decide, therefore I am; I long for a God who always escapes me, therefore I am." Or, more briefly, "I pray, therefore I am." "I believe, help my unbelief," becomes the defining text of Scripture. In each case, and indeed in Descartes, this ultimately leads to a kind of knowledge of God as the necessary ground even of the self-knowledge, decision, or longing of the "soul." But as modernity slips into the darker night of postmodernity, and the existence of God is denied, removed from Edmund Husserl's *Cartesian Meditations*, which stop at just the point Descartes turns to God, we fall inevitably into the despair of Jean-Paul Sartre's vision of "Human being is a useless passion," and the very autonomous self of Renaissance and Enlightenment humanism, which had been internally under attack since Hume, finally slips away in postmodern criticism.[30]

But that is to get ahead of our story. One additional factor in the shape of early modern spirituality needs to be mentioned here: just as the focus in spirituality shifted to an individual interiority and affectivity, a deepening suspicion of "enthusiasm" arose in the church hierarchies from the late Middle Ages on. Partly as a reaction to popular "heretical" movements claiming to bypass the sacramental and clerical structures of the church (often lumped together under the title "brethren of the free spirit") and partly as a result of internal difficulties caused by groups of similar temperament within the institution, such as the Spiritual Franciscans, the official hierarchy often reacted swiftly and brutally to suppress anything resembling such. In the transitional period of the sixteenth and seventeenth centuries, this was particularly true of the *Alumbrados,* or *Illuminati,* of Spain, who often attracted the interest of the Inquisition. As the sixteenth century progressed, the fear of illuminism became intertwined with a fear of "Lutheranism," as all Protestantism came to be called, and its claim of access to God through a personal experience of faith. And indeed there were some actual connections, as some among the *Illuminati* were attracted to Lutheran doctrines. The result was a deep suspicion of any personal mysticism, often preventing some of the brightest lights, even solid Catholics, from publishing full accounts of their own experiences. A further irony is that the established Protestants also came to suspect personal mysticism, sometimes thinking it one of those creepy Catholic things that had been abandoned in the Reform, sometimes seeing it break out in new and alarming ways among the *Schwärmerei* ("the swarmers," Luther's derogatory term for the cults of the radical Reformation) and Anabaptists. Established churches on both sides of the Reform thus came to have a deep suspicion of personal mysticism as a threat to political and ecclesial order, seeing it as a dangerous characteristic of its main opponent, *at precisely the time spirituality came to be focused almost exclusively on this psychological interior affectivity.*[31] That is, spirituality, especially the more contemplative or mystical side, is marginalized as dangerous to the forces of good order, precisely by encouraging its turn toward interior subjectivity and then becoming afraid of precisely that subjectivity, with all its democratizing possibilities.[32]

The period from about 1600 to 1750, when Giovanni Battista Scaramelli publishes, is critical, I believe, to the shape spiritual theology took from then until Vatican II; but the actual state of theological reflection on spirituality in this period is severely understudied. There are good studies on the history of spirituality of the period, which is mostly the story of the passing of energy in spirituality from Spain to France, but precious little work has been done on the theological texts concerning the spiritual life as such.[33] It is during this period that followers of the great mystics of sixteenth-century Spain and their successors, such as Francis de Sales in France, begin a more "second order" theological reflection on their illustrious predecessors as well as their own experience; their works present principles of the spiritual life in a systematic style more appropriate to academic theology.[34] The outline of the story is actually clearer if we focus less on the stellar names, such as Francis de Sales and Cardinal Bérulle, and more on three less-well-known characters who represent the birth pangs of spiritual theology as a separate discipline, and contribute to it.

(1) First is Diego Alvarez de Paz, a Spanish Jesuit born in Toledo in 1560, who joined the mission to Peru in 1584 where he became Provincial General and held other important positions, dying at Potosi in 1620.[35] His monumental work, "prolix and written entirely in Latin," is *De vita spirituali ejusque perfectione* (On the life of the spiritual man and his perfection), published in five volumes in Lyon in 1608 and running through several editions.[36] Although he quotes copiously from the fathers, the northern mystics of the fourteenth century and the *Devotio Moderna*[a] including Thomas à Kempis and Ruusbroec, also influence him.[37] More study needs to be done to trace the tension between the growing humanism in the Spanish universities of the time, the early and vigorous mystical tendencies in the Spanish Jesuits, and the fear of both in the Inquisition.[38] What we do know is that the work of Alvarez de Paz "constitutes a vast general theory of the spiritual life, in which an excessive classification by degrees gives an impression of great artificiality. But by distinguishing four degrees of prayer—meditation, affective prayer, beginners' contemplation, and perfect contemplation—he introduced a scheme that was often to be repeated after him."[39] Here we see exactly the enduring problem inherent in the discipline of spiritual theology present right at its birth: an excessively formal, scholastic presentation of the discipline, but with the subject matter viewed in the modern sense: as a description of human perfection, its degrees, and its interior states or activities. Alvarez's influence on later authors, including Scaramelli, has been widely noted.[40]

This is also an appropriate place to mention the appearance, in the exposition and publication of St. John of the Cross by Tomás de Jesús (1564–1627), of the concept of "acquired contemplation" or the development of a contemplative attitude through ascetical practice and exercises, as opposed to "infused" contemplation, which is a sheer gift of God's grace, the only form recognized by St. John. This preference for the ascetical over the mystical resonates with the fear of the Inquisition

---

a   A movement of lay spirituality, originally, in the Rhineland area in the fourteenth century, emphasizing personal devotion to the humanity of Christ. The principal text is Thomas à Kempis's *The Imitation of Christ*.

and its suspicion of mystical tendencies in individuals. At least one scholar sees it as the essential demise of the true mystical spirit.[41] This new emphasis on an "acquired contemplation" belonged more in the "ascetical" realm than the "mystical"; as it developed, the principle arose that this was indeed the more common form of contemplation, the one to which most should aspire, and the more mystical, passive, or infused kind came to be seen as increasingly rare and specialized. When combined with the analysis of interior degrees as in Alvarez de Paz, this doctrine represents a radical shift away from the more egalitarian mystical tradition in which all are called to some degree of personal union with God, but in a direction protecting later authors from the suspicions of the Inquisition. The energy in spirituality was soon to pass from Spain to France, and in Spain the seventeenth century largely saw a horde of theologians who wrote "huge and somewhat forbidding Latin treatises," "vast syntheses of mystical theology" shaped by the fear of mysticism and the effort to domesticate it, removing as much of the influence of the Rhineland mystics as they could, even to the extent of correcting St. John of the Cross's own works to "make it conform to their system." Joseph of the Holy Spirit (1667–1736) continued this trend into the era of Scaramelli.[42]

Kenneth Kirk puts it well:

> Further, they [the writers who followed the great Carmelites] tended to identify "acquired contemplation" with that meditation pure and simple which all should practice; and "infused" contemplation with those "extraordinary states" which few will ever experience and none must ever desire. By this means, though the toleration of a mystic here and there was still allowed, for the mass of Christians the vision of God—now an "extraordinary" state—became something not merely inaccessible but even taboo. They were condemned to an endless round of preludes ... and must aspire to nothing higher.[43]

Even in the earliest roots of this critical period, then, spiritual theology as a discipline is laced with internal contradictions between its traditional diction and presentation, and the modern, more subjective and psychological view of its subject matter, the growing split between ascetical and mystical dimensions of the spiritual life, and the combination of fascination with and fear of the mystical. The net result was not merely a marginalization of the mystics but actual support for the very elitism in spiritual life that the opponents of mysticism had dreaded. Indeed, the definition of mystical states as "extraordinary" not only marginalized this whole realm of Christian experience in an elite, usually confined to a strict monastic community; it also contributed to the definition in more secular realms of the Enlightenment of all such experiences as "paranormal" in the sense that would increasingly conflict with modern views of scientific "reality." What had been the common birthright of all Christians thus ends up in the same classification as E.S.P., spiritualism, and the like, where it often remains in "New Age" thinking, even in the arrangement of books in stores.

(2) These trends become even more evident in the second representative, a

French Jesuit, Jean-Baptiste Saint Jure (1588–1657), at the height of the classical "French School" of mysticism and spirituality. As Louis Cognet points out, by the nature of their mission, the French Jesuits were deeply involved in the humanism of their time;[44] though it is easy to overestimate this trend, there is no doubt that a tradition of "devout humanism" came to dominate the order, reaching a kind of climax in the works of Louis Lallemant (1587–1635).[45] In his *Spiritual Doctrine* he combines the Spanish Jesuit tendency to emphasize the mystical dimension of the Ignatian tradition with some knowledge of the Carmelites, the Rhineland School, incarnationalist views that had become common coin in France through the influence of Bérulle and the general optimism and humanism of the Society in seventeenth-century France.[46] This certainly formed the atmosphere in which Saint Jure was formed, as did conversation back and forth with his better-known contemporaries Lallemant and Jean-Joseph Surin (1600–1665).[47] It is also significant that Saint Jure is associated with the Jesuit college of La Fleche at roughly the same time as Descartes, the great rationalist philosopher. We can almost place them in the same halls at the same time. The influence is not all one way. While Cartesian "rationalism" would certainly have tremendous influence on later French theology, and indeed on Protestant scholasticism and moralism from England throughout Protestant Europe, it is also true that the French school of mysticism influenced the philosophical school, right through Nicolas Malebranche, philosopher and priest of the Oratory.[48] I do not know of an adequate study of the impact on Descartes of his Jesuit education in precisely these circumstances, and a literary and thematic comparison of his *Meditations on First Philosophy* with other such documents from Bonaventure's *Itinerarium* onward would surely be instructive.[49] Most interesting would be a comparison between Descartes' *Meditations* and the *Meditations sur les plus grandes etc.* (Paris, 1637) of his La Fleche contemporary Saint Jure. Far more work needs to be done to sort all this out. What can be asserted, I believe, is that the birthing of spiritual theology in this period is in a deep two-way conversation with the philosophical developments of the time.[50]

Saint Jure's own massive contribution to the gestation of spiritual theology is *De l'homme spirituel: les principes generaux de la vie spirituelle,* translated into English as *The Spiritual Man, or, The Spiritual Life Reduced to Its First Principles.*[51] While I know of no study suggesting a direct dependence, the resonance with Alvarez de Paz's title is striking. Part 1, treating of the human, the Christian, and the spiritual, firmly locates Saint Jure in the humanism of his time. It reflects first the nobility and grandeur of humans but only as created in the image of God, creatures of the two hands of God (Word and Spirit), ultimately above the angels, who care for them, and capable of applying their hearts to eternal things. Part 2 turns more theologically to the necessity of salvation, the true end of human beings, union with God through and in Christ, the necessity of purity of intention (or heart), the exercise of faith in every aspect of life, of continual prayer, and the place of the soul. The Dionysian three stages are used, but not in a rigid fashion.[52] Typical of Saint Jure's doctrine is the notion that the sanctified Christian is human being as perfected, *and something more.* This more, this *plus* in the perfected human, is a common theme in all Ignatian spirituality.[53] In Saint Jure it is specifically the

Spirit of Jesus Christ working tirelessly in the new humanity. Saint Jure also holds together the unity of love and knowledge.[54] Saint Jure's works, "teaching a discreet and measured mysticism, constitute a real summary of the spiritual life which was the delight of the whole seventeenth century and was warmly recommended by Bossuet [see below]. So he witnesses to the existence of a stream in the Society of Jesus which comprises and surpasses Fr Lallemant."[55] In this he does seem to lean more toward the wing of the Society of Jesus that preserved the belief in an appropriate Ignatian mysticism than that represented by the more general trend outside France represented by Alphonso Rodriguez's *The Practice of Christian Perfection,* where the antimystical trend is clear.[56] But the very balance of his work and its later approval by Bossuet bear witness to some self-imposed restraint, and Saint Jure also demonstrates clearly the other themes we have been tracing: the modern view of its subject matter in spiritual theology, deeply conversant with and influenced by the philosophical developments of the time. Despite some striking parallels to Alvarez de Paz, Saint Jure's literary form and diction are not that of late medieval scholasticism but rather bear striking resemblance to the philosophical treatises of his time. Like them, his work is not innocent of concepts and categories inherited from the Schoolmen.[57] And, he wrote in French, not Latin.

(3) Our third representative, the French Franciscan Barnabé Saladin, is even less well known, in that he has never been studied and is known only through his works.[58] He died sometime after 1702 and was a Franciscan Récollet in the province that encompasses what is now northern France and the Walloon territory of Belgium.[a] His works show no particular profundity or originality, but he is nevertheless a useful representative of what is going on during the crisis over mysticism, or the Quietism debacle of the end of the seventeenth century in France. The larger battle, between Jacques-Bénigne Bossuet (1624–1707), bishop of Meaux, against the leaders of the so-called Quietist movement, Madame Jeanne-Marie Bouvier de la Motte Guyon (1648–1717) and François de Salignac de Lamothe Fénelon (1651–1715), archbishop of Cambrai, has been widely analyzed from all sides, including a strong popularity of Fénelon among Protestant authors.[b][59] The fear of "illuminism" that had become such a brake on the Spanish developments enters France in the seventeenth century, where "the conflict was more liberal in its development but more brusque and decisive in its conclusion."[60]

It would be beyond our scope to go into detail here, except to note that Bossuet's triumph, which resulted in "making a wide sector of public opinion suspicious of mysticism for many years to come," coincided almost exactly with the publication in 1698 of Saladin's *La veritable spiritualité du Christianisme ou la haute science des saints,* "The true (or genuine) spirituality of Christianity or the high knowledge of the saints."[61] This last part is hard to capture in English, as *science* can mean knowledge in general or "science" in the more modern English sense, but generally has a

---

a The Récollets or Recollects were a reform movement within the main body of the Order of Friars Minor at this time, organized in separate houses and provinces, leading a life of more austere prayer and silence.

b The Quietists were accused of teaching the importance of a passive waiting on God's grace for infused contemplation to the exclusion of active ascetical practices or even works of charity.

meaning in between, not unlike *Wissenschaft* in German, and *saints* can refer to all seeking holiness as well as to saints in the narrower and technical sense. The title does, however, seem to reflect the concept of spiritual theology as a new and separate branch of "scientific" theology but as applying primarily to an elite class, even though its purpose is to make this knowledge available to a broader range of both religious and laity. In addition, the word *spiritualité* appears to have acquired the technical meaning of encompassing the whole field (including both ascetical and mystical as separate aspects), which would hold for nearly three centuries.[62]

Saladin's work does demonstrate the dynamism of classical seventeenth-century French spirituality and its extension to the provinces, despite the controversies. The emphasis is on spirituality conceived of as a deepening of the interior life under the influence of the Holy Spirit and as the imitation of the mysteries of Jesus, thus embodying both the more mystical school with its interiority and classical Franciscanism with perhaps a touch of Bérulle and its emphasis on the mysteries of Jesus' humanity. There are few allusions in Saladin to concrete aspects of existence, relations with others, or to the duties of states of life.[63] Saladin does appear to have been widely read. He shows a broad knowledge of the patristic authors, plus Bernard, Bonaventure, the Golden Epistle of William of St. Thierry, the *Imitation of Christ*, and among the moderns, Ignatius, Teresa, Francis de Sales, Rodriguez, Luis de Grenada, and, tellingly, Saint Jure.[64] As an interesting sidebar, relevant to some of the controversies of our own time, he concludes his work with a small office in honor of the incarnate eternal Wisdom. While he makes no particularly original contribution, Saladin shows the continuation of the streams we have been tracing: the turn toward interiority and a resulting psychologizing, the marginalization of mysticism and mystics in a secluded elite, the separation of spiritual theology as a distinct discipline, the development of the technical language of the emerging discipline itself, as well as the carrying of all these trends beyond the great universities and the metropolitan centers.[65]

This sets the stage for the appearance of Scaramelli's directories in the mid-eighteenth century. Italy had long been an active center of spirituality but without producing many remarkable works during this early modern period.[66] This continued right up to the Quietist controversy, with the introduction of many of the classical French texts of the period in translation.[67] The referral of the Quietist battle to Rome for judgment reintroduced into Italy the ambivalence toward mysticism that had shaped Spain and France.[68] This was reflected not only within the church but also in the larger culture as deism, rationalism, scientism, and the new revolutionary movements created an externally hostile environment. Or so it would seem at one level. And, indeed, few Catholic texts of great merit are produced during this period, which is mostly taken up with the manualism and moralism of Scaramelli and Alphonsus Liguori.[69]

But another current is flowing that reveals the more positive side of the ambivalence. It crops up, oddly enough, on the Protestant side, first in the preservation of much Rhineland mysticism in Lutheran pietism, whence it had been driven by Protestant scholasticism in theology, and then in two of the major figures of the Great Awakening, Jonathan Edwards and John Wesley. Wesley represents an almost direct backwash of the Rhineland tradition through the Pietists and the Moravians into William Law and hence to himself. We have learned from Albert Outler and others that Wesley was also steeped in the best patristic texts of his time, and in works such as the *Imitation of Christ*. The very word "Methodist" was at first a term of denigration aimed by their detractors at the Holy Club of Oxford, which Wesley had established as a society for those wishing to derive from the classical texts, including the Greek Fathers, an ordered method of prayer for their personal devotional lives. The literature on Wesley is vast and beyond our scope.[70] But he does embody in all that flows from his heart being "strangely warmed" at Aldersgate in 1738 the trends we have been examining. The turn toward interiority is embodied in his concept of faith of assurance as an experiential knowledge of God in one's heart, although he also establishes a countervailing trend, which will blossom again later, in insisting that this is not for an elite but for all Christians, who are all called to Christian perfection. The reaction to Wesley, however, positive and negative, demonstrates the ambivalence to anything smacking of mysticism in the culture of the time.

Jonathan Edwards is also the subject of a vast and growing literature. He is connected to Wesley through George Whitfield and the Great Awakening in America that paralleled Wesley's success with the workers in northern England and later in London. Like Wesley, many of his writings, most notably *A Treatise Concerning Religious Affections* (1746), evidence the trends we have been tracking. He wrote this treatise both to insist on the necessity of an experience of new birth in all Christians and to defend the revivals as genuine works of the Holy Spirit. It would be a mistake to read this work as the origin of a sentimental Protestant pietism. Edwards argued for a role for both the will and the intellect in the religious life, defending himself against charges of both rationalism and enthusiasm in response to the deep ambivalence of the age.[71] Edwards needs to be read, indeed, as a somewhat conservative purveyor of a heart-psychology within a long line of Puritan writers on the spiritual life.[72] Edwards's spirituality and ethics are also firmly grounded in a patristic Trinitarianism, as my colleague William Danaher has shown.[73] Indeed his religious psychology is derived principally from the psychological analogy for the Trinity rather than from a split between the immaterial and the corporeal. For Edwards, true spiritual affections are the direct result of "the indwelling and holy influences of the Spirit of God," who is clearly the third person of the Holy Trinity.[74] But a spiritual, or heart-psychology, it still is, resonating clearly with the turn toward interiority and psychologism we have been tracing since the twelfth century. Further, like Wesley in his writings and establishment of classes and bands, Edwards is chiefly concerned for what we would now call, in more traditional Catholic terms, "discernment of spirits as an essential element of spiritual direction." And, for both men, the concern grows directly out of a sense of mission, the desire that the mighty work of the Spirit in the revivals be extended as widely as possible. A third trend among Protestants is the popularity of the French Quietists among the Free Church traditions in the eighteenth and nineteenth centuries, especially the Quakers, Baptists, and Congregationalists.[75]

Both a tendency to isolate analyses of Catholic and Protestant developments from one another and the contemporary dislike for his scholastic and manualist presentation can obscure how these themes are startlingly present in Scaramelli. Giovanni Battista Scaramelli, S.J. (1687–1752), was both a missionary and a spiritual director. Indeed, despite the manual literary format, his method is not merely dogmatic but always concerned to aid directors in their conduct of souls, and his works are full of advice to directors as well as of answers to objections and difficulties.[76] In line with the ambivalence toward mysticism that we have noted, especially in the wake of the Quietist controversy, the *Direttorio mystico* (publ. 1754) had a troubled early career. There were objections to a good bit of it, which Scaramelli was instructed to alter. After some initial resistance, he obeyed. Certainly some of this conflict was a felt need by the authorities in the Society of Jesus to protect its flank against its enemies. The later composition and prior publication of the *Direttorio ascetico* may have been inspired by this caution, and it worked. The resulting balance in Scaramelli went a long way toward dispelling the hatred of mysticism following the Quietist controversy. But Scaramelli's own leanings are clear: while he did draw a line between acquired and infused contemplation in theory, it was less distinct in practice, and he deplored the fact that not enough directors properly esteemed infused contemplation, since it did not appear to be required for perfection, which consisted in charity.

The spiritual director, for Scaramelli, requires knowledge not only of dogma but also of the directee as a human being, his or her temperament, passions, desires, conditions of life, and so forth, and the ability to discern spirits in the interior movements and inclinations of the soul. While all true movement is certainly only by the gift of the Holy Spirit, the clear emphasis is on the psychology of the directee. God is seen as adapting to the nature and temperament of persons, even in the granting of mystical graces. Following the tradition of, and perhaps dependent on, Alvarez de Paz, Scaramelli distinguishes, for example, twelve degrees of contemplation and classifies a variety of mystical experiences, including visions, locutions, revelations, and so on, as well as treating the tricky issue of the active and passive purifications of senses and spirit deriving from the Carmelites. Indeed, the influence of Alvarez de Paz is also seen in the *Discerniamento degli spiriti* of 1753, which is really the final part of the *Direttorio mystico*; less surprising is the dependence on the rules for discernment of spirits from the *Exercises* of Ignatius Loyola.

It is, in short, *in spite of* his practical interests as missionary and teacher of spiritual directors that Scaramelli imposes on his work the systematic and dogmatic order that had progressively appeared in the systematizations of the Carmelite and Jesuit theologians of the mystical, in the wake of the ambivalence to mysticism within which the great Carmelite mystics had flourished. Indeed, I would suggest that in Scaramelli we paradoxically see the humanist-influenced spirituality of Saint Jure expressed in the diction of late Spanish scholastic formalism, as in Alvarez de Paz. This formalism, for which Scaramelli and the tradition flowing from him right down to Vatican II are excoriated, is, I would contend, a kind of disguise to protect their truer, promystical interests from the ambivalence of the age. Far from being purely deductively dogmatic, Scaramelli's work is highly practical in its motivation and deeply psychological in its orientation. The scholastic clothes in which it is presented allows it some protection against the hostility to mysticism, but only at the price of the separation of the ascetical and the mystical, with the latter being the more suspect and hence best limited to a specialized and ultimately marginalized elite. It also allows the discipline to fit in the new manualist tradition of Catholic theology as a separate "scientific" discipline. The disguise obscures the thoroughly modern themes of interiorization and psychologization that had been building since the twelfth century as well as the deeply ambivalent attitude toward its own subject matter in church and culture alike. The deductive method of presentation also obscures what was clearly an inductive and experiential base. Unfortunately, the disguise was increasingly successful as the history of the discipline proceeded, which became increasingly seen in its light, rather than in that of the contemporary interests the rhetoric shielded. At a deeper level there is an ironic inconsistency between the concept of the autonomous self embodied in the modernist content and the more communal and ecclesial one implicit in the scholastic form and diction. As a result, there was an inherent instability in the discipline from its birth that would be fully revealed at its "demise."

It is commonplace to note that the tradition was really set by Scaramelli and would, in one sense, become truly normative right up to Vatican II.[77] This can, however, ignore an important reversal during the nineteenth century. This has sometimes been interpreted as a true revival of classical mysticism.[78] But that is, in turn, to ignore several factors that color this revival and help determine our own present situation, an ongoing romanticism and psychologizing in the contemporary context. The first factor, then, is Romanticism, the major artistic movement of the century, which gives the "turn to the subject" its final twist. It is no accident that the century begins with the death of Wesley and the publication of Kant's third *Critique*, that of Judgment, on aesthetic knowledge, and Friedrich Schleiermacher's *Speeches on Religion to Its Cultured Despisers*, beginning the movement that would identify even dogmatic truth with human interiority. The century would end, after G. W. F. Hegel's great system uniting subject and object in a kind of dialectical pantheism and the Marxist materialist and revolutionary version of that, with the rise of Existentialism and the peak of "truth is subjectivity."[79] In the midst of all that, combined with a neo-Gothic interest in medieval ruins, there arose a new interest in mysticism indeed, but now dressing the mystic in religious garb equivalent to the Titan striding the entire century, the Great Artist. The mystic becomes the religious genius, parallel in virtually every way to the artistic genius, including the fascination with the darkly mythological, with mind-altering drugs, and with eccentricities of behavior bordering on madness. In a milder form, this persists in a popular conflation of mystical experience with aesthetic, for example, of poetic insight with mystical truth.

Nowhere is this more clearly seen than in this passage from Evelyn Underhill's classic *Mysticism: A Study in the Nature and Development of Man's Spiritual Consciousness*:

We do not call everyone who has these partial and artistic intuitions of reality a mystic, any more than we call every one a musician who has learnt to play the piano. The true mystic is the person in whom such powers transcend the merely artistic and visionary stage, and are exalted to the point of genius. . . . As artists stand in a peculiar relationship to the phenomenal world, receiving rhythms and discovering truths and beauties which are hidden from other men, so this true mystic stands in a peculiar relation to the transcendental world; there experiencing actual, but to us unimaginable tension and delight. His consciousness is transfigured in a particular way, he lives at different levels of experience from other people.[80]

Although some mystics certainly are geniuses, the danger of *equating* mysticism with a kind of religious genius becomes apparent.[81]

Grace Jantzen aptly comments as follows:

Whether or not twentieth-century writers on mysticism would subscribe to the letter of the Idealist or Romantic epistemology, or are even aware of the debt which they owe to it, the spirit of subjectivisation and with it a psychologizing of mysticism rests upon it.[82]

Jantzen proceeds to analyze Underhill in precisely these terms, noting in fairness that by the time of the 1930 edition Underhill had become dissatisfied with the psychological approach, and, were she to revise it, would pay more attention to the objective side:

But she did *not* rewrite it, and the popularity of the book helped to reinforce the appeal of the psychological approach to mysticism in contemporary thought (Underhill, 1943: 17).[83] It is precisely because mysticism is now understood in terms of a private state of consciousness that the notion of its ineffability can get a purchase.[84]

Jantzen is quick to point out the consequences for feminist deconstruction:

When these [the characterization of woman as emotional, male as rational, and the confinement of women to the private, domestic sphere] are combined in modern secularism, it has the ironic result that whereas in the medieval era the religious in general and the mystical in particular was far too important to be left to women, in the modern era mysticism and religious experience are indeed seen as available to women, but with their feminisation, they have also been marginalised. Women can be mystics only in a world where mysticism is no longer constructed as public or powerful.[85]

In language reminiscent of de Certeau, Jantzen calls the section containing this analysis "the tools of inarticulacy." Just as women are permitted to enter the field, the subject matter is defined as ineffable, enforcing yet again a kind of silence on marginalized women.

She begins the section with a critique of William James and his *Varieties of Religious Experience*.[86] She shows in a telling fashion how James identifies the mystical with the interior and the psychological (he was, after all, the founder of the school of psychology native to America as well as the middle of the three patriarchs of philosophical Pragmatism). She also points out the strong Romantic bent coloring all his work and assumptions, undercutting his own empirical leaning, even to a fascination with the paranormal and the drug induced;[87] in what follows she makes a significant connection to the theology of Schleiermacher. It is interesting to note that now religious affections have been clearly identified with feelings, while for Jonathan Edwards, for example, will and reason had been included as well. Jantzen draws the contrast with the patristic understanding, without drawing out the final irony that what would once have been a totally impossible source of knowledge (emotions) has now become the ground of the highest knowledge.[88] A similar critique of James and his Romantic inheritance, still deeply present but hidden in much contemporary neo-Evangelicalism, is found in Nicholas Lash.[89]

Though it would take different forms, this marriage between mysticism and psychology continued as a kind of love/hate relationship through Sigmund Freud's critique in *Moses and Monotheism* and Carl Jung's eclectic and uncritical embrace of it.[90] Jung has continued to have a strong following, with Jungian categories and thought strongly present in many of the authors of the current revival of spirituality, from Urban Holmes to James Arraj.[91] More common, now, is a use of neo-Freudian developmental psychology as an analytical tool in discussions of the spiritual and the mystical. The historical, theological, and pastoral issues raised by this marriage between psychology and spirituality are so salient that we will need a whole chapter to come to some resolution about them.[92] For now I note only the historic point: the trend toward interior affectivity that began in the twelfth century reached a psychologizing peak following the Romanticism of the nineteenth century, from which we have not yet recovered.[93] It is not only the odder corners of the New Age movements that are so infected but even much of the most academically respectable work on spirituality in general and mysticism in particular. While this psychologizing and the accompanying elitism and ultimate marginalization are distinct trends, they are deeply intertwined. Jantzen and others remind us that these developments are not innocent of concerns of power and domination as mysticism is made safe for the excluded by marginalizing the mystic, even in cages of supposed admiration.

A second factor in the Romantic turn is the fascination with the extraordinary phenomena of mysticism to the virtual exclusion of the ascetical disciplines or the principles of discernment by which the Christian tradition had earlier guided the deepest desires for union with God through territory mapped as downright dangerous. The Western tradition had carefully constructed the ascetical tradition as a kind of control on the potential illuminationist or enthusiast excesses that do, indeed, often afflict those on the more mystical journey, however construed.

Indeed, as we have seen, this ambivalence about mysticism and preference for the ascetical is one of the flaws in the tradition as it developed. From the Romantic movement onward, except in circles attempting to shore up the tradition, there is a major reversal, in which the worst fears of previous generations of hierarchs were now realized: the mystical impulse was cut loose from ascetical discipline, ecclesial life and supervision or direction, and now focused on precisely the most distracting and "paranormal" phenomena rather than on that union with God or *theōsis* or that perfect reign of justice and peace that had been the tradition's terminal images for the journey.[a] The culture came down with a good case of Zen sickness—loving enlightenment rather than the light, or, in Christian terms, desiring religious experience rather than God—from which it has not yet recovered. There are some hopeful countervailing trends at present we shall examine shortly; but this is the culture we have inhabited for nearly two hundred years.

Meanwhile, spiritual theology as a discipline, especially on the Catholic side, remained largely the same, at least outwardly. Manuals continued to be produced and studied, at least in some seminaries.[94] The two most notable developments prior to Vatican II were the reunification of the ascetical and mystical in a single discipline called "Spiritual Theology,"[95] and the recovery by Reginald Garrigou-Lagrange, O.P., of the doctrine that all true contemplation is actually infused and that all Christians are, at least to some degree, called to it, even in this life.[96] At a deeper level, the changing view of the subject matter can hardly have left them unscathed. The enduring scholastic presentation seemed even more necessary during the battle against Modernism in the late nineteenth century and early twentieth century; but precisely to the degree that language disguised the resonance with the Enlightenment and now Romantic tendencies, the discipline seemed increasingly irrelevant, cut off not only from the core of theology, but what now seemed the core of human spiritual experience as well. This trend increased in strength as the story of how deeply the spiritual-theology tradition at its birth had been shaped by Enlightenment concerns was suppressed by its own rhetoric. As the very meaning of the words used in the discipline took on the new Romantic reading, whatever the intentions of the authors might have been, the context in which the texts were read determined much of their meaning, when they were read at all and not simply bypassed as quaint and irrelevant at best, or oppressive to the new experiential spirit at worst. This reading still haunts, I believe, some anti-theological construals of spirituality.[97]

The theological turn represented by Vatican II is a third factor, and yet another huge subject, much studied and still studied. Certainly, it had deep roots in the *ressourcement* movement of the previous century or so in which primary sources,

---

a *Theōsis*, or being made God, is the doctrine of the Eastern church that the ultimate state of sanctified humanity is union with God that includes a sharing in the divine nature itself and incorporation into the inner life of the Holy Trinity. Translations into a more Latin English are "deification" and "divinization," but because these have misleading connotations, I prefer throughout to use the Greek word. The consideration of the third tide, glory, will examine this concept in some detail.

including Scripture and patristic texts, were once again accessed, using new critical tools. This movement on the Catholic side was actually anticipated by the two nineteenth-century Anglican movements birthed, I believe, by Wesley: the recovery of scriptural study in the Evangelical revival and the recovery of patristics in the Anglo-Catholic. The great editions of the patristic authors appeared in both Anglican and Roman Catholic circles and challenged the dominance of the manuals. Most especially, Thomas Aquinas began to be read in his own works, not in the cut-and-paste manuals that had dominated for two centuries; and, of course, under the leadership of Etienne Gilson and Karl Rahner, among others, neo-Thomism and transcendental Thomism brought Thomas into conversation with post Enlightenment philosophy in a manner that became the foundation of much the Council did.

In this new light, the tradition of spiritual theology as it had been received to that point became untenable, and it suffered a kind of demise from which it only now shows signs of resurrection. First and most obviously, its manualist deductive literary form was now outmoded in all of theology, helpfully replaced by a historical approach to primary texts that has born tremendous fruit, not least in such publishing enterprises as the Paulist Press Classics of Western Spirituality and the great histories from Louis Bouyer and Jean Leclercq to Bernard McGinn.[98] The studies that resulted began to show that "Christian spirituality" is actually a family of spiritualities, no one of which is normative for the others.[99] Ecumenical and interfaith interests of the Council also reflected the spirit of the times and, together with the loss of credibility for the scholastic manual approach, demanded a humbler and less regulative approach for whatever spiritual theology might endure.[100]

But there were deeper tectonic faults opening in the discipline, as the manner in which it had come to view its subject, as we have traced it, came under as much of an attack as did the literary form in which it had been presented. Representative of many of these new trends was Louis Bouyer, who not only contributed, as noted, to the new historical studies of the time but in a series of works also began to challenge the subjectivism, privatism, and elitism of the tradition as it had developed, using all the insights of the *ressourcement* movement. In *An Introduction to Spirituality*, Bouyer presented much of the fruits of his biblical and historical researches and showed immense impatience with excessive classifications and distinctions.[101] As in his earlier, groundbreaking *Liturgical Piety*, Bouyer also brought to bear the insights of the burgeoning liturgical renewal movement that would have such an impact on the Council, linked to the new sacramental theology of Rahner and Edward Schillebeeckx.[102] While private prayer and devotions, which had become the focus of attention especially from the seventeenth century onward, remained important, they were now once again firmly located in the context of the public liturgy of the church, especially the Eucharist; and the spiritual lives of all believers, however interior and private in one sense, were likewise firmly relocated in a corporate, ecclesial context. While Bouyer's approach may now seem a bit dated, it marks the watershed of the change in consciousness, in Catholic and Anglican circles at least, away from a privatized psychologizing of spirituality toward a more public and liturgical context.[103]

These two developments, the abandonment of the manualist presentation and the return to primary sources, would have been revolutionary enough; but there are two more developments that cut even deeper into the foundations of the discipline of spiritual theology as it had been previously conceived. There had been two traditional starting points for such a theology. The first is a theology of Christian perfection, those aspects of Christian life that come after the "commandments of obligation" (studied in moral theology and ethics) that are necessary for salvation. These involve, so it was taught, moving on to the "evangelical counsels of perfection" that go beyond salvation toward union and the beatific vision. This became the proper area of spiritual theology and involved much discussion of degrees of merit and works of supererogation. Adolph Tanquerry and Joseph de Guibert are examples of this style.[104] Needless to say, it was never acceptable in Protestant circles, as it raised a whole series of issues that had been trenches in the Reformation theological wars. But the anthropology of Vatican II also rendered this approach untenable. *Lumen Gentium*[105] clearly teaches the universal call to holiness, undercutting the elitism of the old degrees-of-merit approach. *Gaudium et Spes* in part 1 portrays the elevation of all human beings in Christ toward their divine destiny in the inner life of God, while part 2 focuses on the more ordinary means of grace such as family life, culture, and public life (social, economic, political) and the search for international order and peace.[106] The shift away from monastic elitism and excessive interiority is obvious, even if it has not yet impacted the larger culture as much as one might wish.

The second and more widely useful starting point had been a kind of theological reflection on the three "stages" of the spiritual life deriving from Pseudo-Dionysius. Various topics were then assigned to an appropriate stage. A particularly attractive representative of this style is Reginald Garrigou-Lagrange, especially since he taught the unification of ascetical and mystical theology in a single discipline of spiritual theology, recognized the universal call to holiness, and saw all contemplation as ultimately "infused," that is, dependent finally on God's grace alone. All his major works make use, in some form, of the tradition of the Triple Way. In a single telling critical essay, Karl Rahner demonstrated the fatal flaws in this approach. He argued that using the Dionysian "stages" as a lawlike description of human spiritual growth was a dreadful mistake;[107] this is especially true when this scheme is elevated to a matter of theological principle. The mistake grows larger and more dangerous when the classical stages of purgation, illumination, and union are confounded with the notion of what is appropriate for beginner, proficient, and perfect souls. This approach, he argues, does violence to the complexity of the reality of human growth.[108]

By the end of the Vatican II era, then, the tradition of Western, largely Roman Catholic, spiritual theology that had coalesced by the time of Scaramelli, had become virtually defunct. Its literary method of presentation was now out of favor in all branches of theology; its resonances with Enlightenment themes that rhetoric had obscured were now mostly forgotten; and its two traditional starting points, perfectionism and the Dionysian stages, had been rendered invalid. The only text to appear from Roman Catholic sources since the Council is, by the author's own admission, only a redo of an earlier, preconciliar text with another author.[109] There are some Protestant works that appear to be in the genre, and have often done a credible and helpful job of translating patristic and Catholic thought into useable presentations for a Protestant audience;[110] none, however, has addressed the structural ambiguities in the discipline itself. Thus the situation immediately after Vatican II was that the new interest in classical spiritual texts and methods it had inspired in a wide audience, including laity who had previously felt excluded from the deepest teaching on the spiritual life, was left without any living theological tradition to provide guidance or even reflective conversation. This need now demands to be met, but with full consciousness of the history of the discipline and the structural problems that accompanied it.

It may seem that I have told this story as if spiritual theology in its formative period was mistaken in adopting insights from the culture it inhabited. That is not so. Indeed, that is often what gave it a relevance to its own time, and allowed it to embrace new understandings of human personhood we still find invaluable. Other aspects of early modern assumptions are more problematic in the light of current postmodern criticism. But the deepest, virtually tragic, flaw was that by presenting its culturally contemporary insights in the guise of neo-scholastic manualism, historically conditioned teachings based on early modernist assumptions were made to appear as if they were timeless theological norms. As a result, when cultural understandings shifted, there was little room for the ongoing constructive criticism that we now know all theology must constantly undergo.[111] The structural separation of spiritual theology as a discipline distinct from the main body of dogmatic and even moral theology meant it did not participate in the best reflections of those disciplines on the needs of the changing historical climate. When the cultural shift had become too radical, the near demise of the discipline was the result. To provide a resurrected and sound body of theological guidance for Christian spiritual life two things are required: first, a relocation of spiritual theology back into the central stream of development in dogmatic theology, or at least theology as an integral and integrating discipline, and second, an opening up of the diction of its self-presentation so that it can embrace the best self-understandings of human being in our own culture, knowing that this very embrace will render each attempt temporally bound and conditioned and hence in need of constant revision. Only so can each age see again with its own eyes the truths perceived and recorded by its spiritual forebears, and the true wisdom of the past be accessible for present guidance.

Notes

1. Eugene Megyer, "Spiritual Theology Today"; Philip Sheldrake, *Spirituality and History*, 40–64; Mark McIntosh, *Mystical Theology*, 39–89; the standard history of Christian spirituality is rapidly becoming Bernard McGinn, *The Presence of God: A History of Western Christian Mysticism*, vols. 1–4. I am deeply indebted to Bernard McGinn for reading an early draft of this chapter and making numerous important suggestions. Errors that remain are my own doing.

2. Sheldrake, *Spirituality and History*, 53; Megyer, "Spiritual Theology," 58; Bernard McGinn, "Asceticism and Mysticism in Late Antiquity and the Early Middle Ages," 58–74.

3. Louis Cognet, *Post Reformation Spirituality*, 140.

4. At least in the classic work of Vladimir Lossky, *The Mystical Theology of the Eastern Church*; see also several works of Dumitru Staniloae, especially *Orthodox Spirituality*.

5. Sheldrake, *Spirituality and History*, 57. See McGinn, "Asceticism," for a most helpful account of the rise, especially in early Alexandrian circles, of a Christian itinerary derived from the classical *paedeia*, though thoroughly baptized.

6. Kallistos Ware, introduction to *The Ladder of Divine Ascent: John Climacus*, 56–57.

7. Sheldrake, *Spirituality and History*, 48. See also Grace M. Jantzen, *Power, Gender, and Christian Mysticism*, for a sustained feminist critique of the problems of patriarchy in the Christian mystical tradition.

8. Kenneth E. Kirk, *The Vision of God*. This is one of the classic texts in the revival of a sound interest in the mystical dimension of Christianity, which Kirk always defends as the birthright of all Christians.

9. His works are now available in a fine English translation, see n. 23, chap. 1 above.

10. For the pre-Dionysian ancestors of the "three stages," in Origen and his followers, especially Evagrius, and in Ambrose, see McGinn, "Asceticism," 63–67.

11. The discussion is nicely summarized in McIntosh, *Mystical Theology*, 44–56; see also now McGinn, *Foundations of Mysticism*, 157–82.

12. Gerald Van Ackeren, *Sacra Doctrina*. Thanks to my colleague William Carroll for bringing this to my attention, and to Walter Principe for teaching me the unity of Thomas's thought and the structure of the *Summa;* see also Principe's "Toward Defining Spirituality," for a discussion of the ambiguous use of *spiritualitas* in Thomas, sometimes meaning life in the Holy Spirit, sometimes life according to the highest capacities of human personhood, and less often in opposition to corporeity or matter; see now also McGinn, *The Harvest of Mysticism in Medieval Germany*, 11–47, for a clear analysis of Thomas's desire for unity in method and the preservation of a call to all Christians to contemplation and the vision of God, as well as the tensions built into his exposition of the spiritual life.

13. See "Triple Way," *NWDCS*, 626–27.

14. *The Twelve Patriarchs, The Mystical Ark, Book Three of the Trinity: Richard of St. Victor*, trans. Grover A. Zinn; see also "Victorine Spirituality, *NWDCS*, 631–33; *Bonaventure*, trans. Ewert Cousins.

15. The magisterial accuracy and fullness of McGinn's *The Flowering of Mysticism* in dealing with these matters makes a brief summary like this one dangerous and embarrassing, however necessary. Paulist Press editions of the works of all the figures mentioned are available.

16. See Mark McIntosh, *Discernment and Truth*, 61–62 for this period; the most judicious summary of these trends in this period is now McGinn, *Harvest*, 48–79.

17. Sheldrake, *Spirituality and History*, pp. 50–51; McIntosh, *Discernment*, 60–75; see also Caroline Walker Bynum, *Jesus as Mother*, chap. 3: "Did the Twelfth Century Discover the Individual," 82–109; note also Grace Jantzen's comment that because of this turn towards the individual, the private and the personal sphere, divorced from political and ecclesial power, it became "safe" for women to be mystics and even to write about their experiences, *Power*, 326.

18. This is a complex movement, but I refer broadly to all thinkers embracing a literary theory in which meaning is confined to texts and their interpretations. See Sheldrake, "Postmodernity," *NWDCS*, 498–500, and the bibliography there.

19. The most suggestive exception is the hints in Heiko A. Oberman, *The Harvest of Medieval Theology*, 257–65. There are also intriguing essays challenging the received approach to nominalism in *The Pursuit of Holiness in Late Medieval and Renaissance Religion*, ed. Charles Trinkaus and Heiko A. Oberman, esp. 3–102; I am grateful to David Lonsdale of Heythrop College for calling these essays to my attention. They present a much more nuanced and positive picture of nominalism, and stress continuities with the High Middle Ages as well as the impact

on Luther and early modernity. The whole question needs a great deal more study. We await the fulfillment of McGinn's promise that in his next volume he will deal with this issue in regard to Gerson; *Harvest*, 486, n. 10. In the meantime, Louis Dupré, *The Passage to Modernity* is the *locus classicus*. See "Nominalism," *NWDCS*, 462–64.

20. See especially Steven Ozment's startling conclusion: "The novelty of Luther's theology may rather lie in an unprecedented, unAugustinian merger of nominalism and mysticism." "Mysticism, Nominalism and Dissent," in Trinkaus and Oberman, *Pursuit*, 92. Ozment already recognized the significance of the *Theologia Germanica* in assessing Luther. See now Bengt Hoffman's translation of Luther's version, and the introduction to it, *The Theologia Germanica of Martin Luther*, or, perhaps better, now, the translation by David Blamires, *Theologia Deutsch—Theologia Germanica: The Book of the Perfect Life* [see Franckforter and Blamires]. When we combine Ozment's view of Luther's nominalism, the growing consensus of the influence on Luther not only of the *Germanica*, but also of many of the Rhineland mystics, especially Tauler, and the Luther who was also deeply read in the Greek fathers now emerging from the scholarship of the Lutheran Church of Finland, our traditional picture of Luther and the origins of the Reformation needs some serious re-working; see Carl E. Braaten and Robert W. Jenson, *Union with Christ*.

21. I learned these things in an economics course with Harry A. Miskimin at Yale in 1963–64. See his *Money, Prices, and Foreign Exchange in Fourteenth Century France; The Economy of Early Renaissance Europe, 1300–1460; The Economy of Later Renaissance Europe, 1460–1600*. It is all too easy for church historians to ignore things like economic realities.

22. See the famous crucifix by Matthias Grünewald in the National Gallery, for example.

23. Barbara Tuchman, *A Distant Mirror*, gives a brilliant account of this devastation.

24. See McGinn's judicious treatment, *Harvest*, 4–8. Among scholars of spirituality in this period, Ulrike Wiehaus takes serious account of these disasters: "The Medieval West," *BCCS*, 118–20.

25. R. William Franklin and Joseph M. Shaw, *The Case for Christian Humanism* is a splendid analysis and defense of Christian humanism. See also Cognet, *Post-Reformation Spirituality*, 20–25; he also traces helpfully the carrying over of many of the medieval themes; on this latter, see McGinn's argument that 1500 is not as sharp a break as it has been made out: *Harvest*, 1–4.

26. Cognet, *Post-Reformation Spirituality*, 27, and throughout the sections on France; see, for example, the comments on de Sales, 65.

27. De Certeau, *Mystic Fable*, 157–200. Obviously, I have vastly oversimplified de Certeau's penetrating analysis in this brief summary.

28. But see Rowan Williams, *Teresa of Avila*.

29. Jantzen, *Power*, 316–21. See also Denys Turner, *The Darkness of God*, 248–51; McIntosh, *Mystical Theology*, 67–69.

30. Edmund Husserl, *Cartesian Meditations*; Husserl's work is an existentialist reading of Descartes' *Meditations*; it became a foundation stone of the subsequent phenomenological movement in the twentieth century. Husserl seems to begin a project of making such an analysis of the entirety of Descartes' text but breaks off at precisely the point at which Descartes turns to God as a deeper ground of the soul's self-knowledge. Sartre's famous statement is in *Being and Nothingness*, trans. Hazel E. Barnes, 615.

31. Cognet, *Post-Reformation Spirituality*, 27–36, tells the story for Spain. See Bengt Hoffman's introduction to his edition of *The Theologia Germanica of Martin Luther* for a fine account of the developments on the Lutheran side. Henry More's *Enthusiasmus Triumphatus* (1662) is a classic text, as is Ronald Knox's *Enthusiasm*.

32. De Certeau, *Mystic Fable*, and Jantzen, *Power*, throughout, make this point about the marginalization of mysticism as dangerous to established power, Jantzen tracing especially the gender implications. I find it odd that Jantzen makes no use of de Certeau in her otherwise telling analysis. Kenneth Kirk is also a keen analyst of this "Reversal of Tradition" on Protestant and Catholic sides alike: *The Vision of God*, 414–41.

33. Cognet, *Post-Reformation Spirituality* and de Certeau, *Mystic Fable,* depending on, though critical of, two classic texts, especially for France; in English translation, these are: Henri Bremond, *Literary History of Religious Thought in France,* 3 vols.; and Pierre Pourrat, *Christian Spirituality,* volumes 1–4.

34. This is precisely de Certeau's point in *Mystic Fable.* See also "France," *DS* V, 918–54; "Espagna," IV, pt. 2, 1127–78; and "Italie," VII, pt. 2, 2141–2310.

35. His first name also appears as Iago or Jacques, depending on the language of the text.

36. Cognet, *Post-Reformation Spirituality,* 35.

37. See "Devotio Moderna" in *WDCS,* 113–14.

38. Cognet, *Post-Reformation Spirituality,* 26–35.

39. Cognet, *Post-Reformation Spirituality,* 36.

40. Cognet, *Post-Reformation Spirituality,* 140; *DS* XIV, 396–402.

41. James Arraj, *From St. John of the Cross to Us.* I am grateful to Mr. Arraj for calling his work to my attention. It is carefully documented, and much of the story as he tells it is supportive of the view taken here. But because of the very definite point of view he is proposing, an independent study confirming his work would be useful; it should be noted that Kenneth Kirk is in substantial agreement and traces the problem to precisely this period: *The Vision of God,* 431–41. A reading of Kirk would have strengthened Arraj's work. The claim that infused contemplation, not just acquired, is in the ordinary way of sanctity is made by Reginald Garrigou-Lagrange in his several works, see especially *Three Ages,* 2:547–49, 628–43, 652–54.

42. Cognet, *Post-Reformation Spirituality,* 139. See also Jean Krynen, *Mystique Chrétienne et Théologie Moderne: I. Saint Jean de la Croix et l'Aventure de la Mystique Espagnole,* especially 217–362; thanks to James Arraj for calling this work to my attention.

43. *The Vision of God,* 435.

44. Cognet, *Post-Reformation Spirituality,* 77–79.

45. Cognet, *Post-Reformation Spirituality,* 82–85.

46. Not published until 1694; there are several problems about sources and editing. See Cognet, *Post-Reformation Spirituality,* 83.

47. See Cognet's assessment of the troubled case of Jean-Joseph Surin, *Post-Reformation Spirituality,* 108–11. See also *DS* XIV, 155–56. Surin is one of the major characters in de Certeau's analysis, *Mystic Fable,* 177–187.

48. Cognet, *Post-Reformation Spirituality,* 99.

49. This was the doctoral dissertation I did *not* write when I turned to spirituality of parenting at the suggestion of Leslie Dewart. As far as I know, the work still needs to be done, and I would now add Saint Jure into the mix.

50. In the work available to me, Jean Krynen refers to two works of his, *Descartes et la spiritualité chrétienne,* which appears to be a second volume in the series with his work on John of the Cross cited above, and *L'aventure de la mystique moderne en France,* troisième partie, *Cartésianisme et spiritualité.* These works are not presently available to me. There are fascinating hints about what might be done in Dupré, *Passage to Modernity,* 82, for example, where he discusses both the relationship of Descartes to his teachers at La Fleche, and their shared nominalism and humanism.

51. It is fascinating to see continuing interest in this text into the nineteenth century. See also now the new edition and translation into Italian (with an extensive introduction): *L'uomo spirituale,* ed. M.-P. Ghielmi. My thanks to Prof. Claudio Stercal, director of the "Centro Studi di Spiritualità" for calling this new edition to my attention.

52. *DS* XIV, 155–56; much of this paragraph is my paraphrase in English of the French of that source.

53. Karl Rahner gave a penetrating analysis of the role of this more, this *magis* in Ignatian thought, "Being Open to God as Ever Greater and the Significance of the Aphorism *Ad Majorem*

Dei Gloriam," *TI* 7:25–46 at 27; see also Ignatius, *Spiritual Exercises*, trans. Kenneth Baker, S.J., 23–27.

54. *DS* XIV, 155–56.

55. Cognet, *Post-Reformation Spirituality*, 106–7.

56. Pub. 1609, Engl. trans. R. Coyne, *Christian Perfection* (Dublin, 1840); see Kirk, *Vision of God*, 436–38. Cognet takes a more balanced view of the tension among the Spanish Jesuits, *Post-Reformation Spirituality*, 34–36.

57. Étienne Gilson's early work on Descartes established this dependence once and for all; see its fruition in his commentary on *Discours de la méthode*; Louis Dupré, however, sees Descartes as more of a nominalist, *Passage*, 81.

58. *DS* XIV, 233–34 for this and much else of what follows.

59. Cognet, *Post-Reformation Spirituality*, 116–41; Kirk, *Vision*, 451–63. All the dictionaries have relevant articles on the controversy, see especially *DS* XII, 2755–2842.

60. Cognet, *Post-Reformation Spirituality*, 116.

61. Michael Richards, "Bossuet, Jacques-Bénigne," *WDCS*, 57–58. Also, *DS* XIV, 1148–50; 232–34.

62. See Lucy Tinsley, *The French Expressions for Spirituality and Devotion: A Semantic Study*, 291, for this assertion and its consequences.

63. *DS*, XIV, 1148–50, 232–34.

64. *DS*, XIV, 1148–50, 232–34.

65. Tinsley, *The French Expressions*, is the standard work tracing the linguistic developments.

66. There were, however, remarkable figures who produced a significant literature, if not of the first rank. Most notable are Paul of the Cross (Della Croce) (1694–1757), founder of the Passionists, and Alphonsus de Liguori (1698–1787), founder of the Redemptorists.

67. Della Croce was influenced by the Carmelites, Tauler, and Francis de Sales; Liguori by Rodriguez, Scaramelli, and, most tellingly, by Saint Jure.

68. It had already been introduced into Italy by the controversy surrounding, and condemnation (in Rome) of, the Spaniard Miguel de Molinos (1628–1696). See *DS* X, 1486–1514 and *NCE* 9:773. In fact, the word "quietist" appears first to have been used by Cardinal Caracciolo of Naples during this controversy.

69. Cognet, *Post-Reformation Spirituality*, 141. For Della Croce, see *DS* XII, 540–58 and *NCE* 11:34–35; for Liguori, see *DS* I, 357–89, and *NCE* 1: 307–12; for the relevant period in Italy in general, *DS* VII, 252–62.

70. Albert C. Outler (preface to *John and Charles Wesley: Selected Writings and Hymns*, ed. Frank Whaling, xiii–xvii, and *John Wesley*) is the chief Methodist scholar on these points; Cognet also recognized the main lines of this development, *Post-Reformation Spirituality*, 141.

71. *ODCC* 532–33.

72. Brad Walton, *Jonathan Edwards, Religious Affections, and the Puritan Analysis of True Piety, Spiritual Sensation, and Heart Religion*.

73. William J. Danaher, Jr., *The Trinitarian Ethics of Jonathan Edwards*, 117–56, esp. 119–24.

74. Danaher, *Trinitarian Ethics*, 124, citing the Yale edition of Edwards's works, 2:198; see also 2:201; Danaher, *Trinitarian Ethics*, 117.

75. Bernard McGinn, conversation, February 2006.

76. For this and what follows, see *NCE* XII, 724, and *DS* XIV, 397–401.

77. So Sheldrake, *Spirituality and History*, 53.

78. So Cognet, *Post-Reformation Spirituality*, 141; Arraj is particularly adamant about this.

79. See entry on Søren Kierkegaard, *Columbia Encyclopedia*. The enduring influence of Kierkegaard in contemporary spirituality is a subject that needs further study.

80. Underhill, *Mysticism*, 75–76; see McIntosh, *Mystical Theology*, 68–69, and n. 65.

81. McGinn, conversation, February 2006

82. Jantzen, *Power*, 317.

83. The reference is to Underhill's *Letters*.

84. Jantzen, *Power*, 317; Denys Turner is the other great analyst of this turn toward the psychological, of a turn from describing the negation of experience on the journey to God to a search for having negative experiences or even the experience of nothing, and hence the ineffable as such (*Darkness*, 248–51; see also McIntosh, *Mystical Theology*, 67–68).

85. Jantzen, *Power*, 321.

86. Jantzen, *Power*, 305.

87. Jantzen, *Power*, 309.

88. Jantzen, *Power*, 317.

89. Nicholas Lash, *Easter in Ordinary*.

90. On Freud, in addition to *Moses and Monotheism*, see Moshe Gresser, *Dual Allegiance*; on Jung, see such works as *Psychology and Religion* and *Psychology and the Occult*; see Robert A. Segal, ed., *The Gnostic Jung*; Harold Coward, "Mysticism in the Analytical Psychology of Carl Jung and the Yoga Psychology of Patanjali."

91. Arraj, cited above; Urban T. Holmes, see chap. 1 above, n. 9; see also Anne Belford Ulanov, *Religion and the Spiritual in Carl Jung*; and Chester P. Michael and Marie C. Norrissy, *Prayer and Temperament*.

92. See chapter 12 below.

93. A critique of this marriage between Romanticism and spirituality is a major theme in Owen C. Thomas's work, now conveniently available in *What Is It That Theologians Do, How They Do It, and Why*, 29–54, 89–116, 181–206, 263–300.

94. The chief monument of this tradition was the *Précis de théologie ascetique et mystique* of the Sulpician Adolph Tanquerry, who taught for fifteen years in the United States before retiring to France, where his *magnum opus* appeared in 1923–24. It went through nine French editions, was translated into at least ten languages, and remained a basic textbook in Catholic seminaries down to Vatican II. Antonio Royo and Jordan Aumann's *The Theology of Christian Perfection* was still in use at Weston College, Massachusetts, in the late 1960s.

95. So Joseph de Guibert, *Theology of the Spiritual Life*, 3–29.

96. Garrigou-Lagrange, *Three Ages*, 2:547–49, 628–43, 652–54; see also Kirk, as this is the whole point of *The Vision of God*.

97. This seems to be Sandra Schneiders's chief complaint; see chap. 1, n. 12, above.

98. Louis Bouyer et al., *History of Christian Spirituality*; see the various volumes of McGinn's *The Presence of God*, previously cited.

99. See especially Hans Urs von Balthasar, "Spirituality," 211–26.

100. Sheldrake, *Spirituality and History*, *Spirituality and Theology*; McIntosh, *Mystical Theology*, each propose such an approach.

101. Sheldrake, *Spirituality and History*, 55, and for his assessment of Bouyer in general.

102. See the Constitution on the Sacred Liturgy, *Vatican Council II* (Flannery), I, 1–36.

103. Sheldrake's comments on historical Anglican developments, *Spirituality and History*, 55–56, are so sympathetic and judicious I have seen no need to reproduce them.

104. See nn. 95, 96 above.

105. *Lumen Gentium* ##39–42.

106. Philip Sheldrake first called this shift to my attention in a conversation in 1998; see Eugene Megyer, "Spiritual Theology Today," esp. 65.

107. Pseudo-Dionysius never intended them to be used in this way, of course, but derived them from his theology of the celestial hierarchy. McGinn, conversation, February 2006.

108. " Reflections on the Problem of the Gradual Ascent to Christian Perfection," *TI* 3:3–23.

109. Jordan Aumann, *Spiritual Theology*, is largely an abridgement of the classic textbook, Antonio Royo, O.P., and Jordan Aumann, O.P., *The Theology of Christian Perfection*. That in turn is essentially an English translation of Royo's *Teologia de la Perfeccion Cristiana*, first published in Spain in 1954.

110. See chap. 1 above, nn. 18, 19; Chan, *ST.*

111. See Karl Barth, *Church Dogmatics*, I, *The Doctrine of the Word of God*, part 1, 15; see Barth, *Church Dogmatics: A Selection*, intro. Helmut Gollwitzer, 4.

3

Resources for Resurrection

Can these bones live?
—Ezekiel 37:3

Just as the classical discipline of spiritual theology was becoming moribund around the time of Vatican II, a renewed interest in spirituality in a broader sense was beginning to blossom; it embodied many of the more "democratic" themes of the Council but also had a life of its own. This renewed interest in spirituality owed much to the Romantic revival of interest in mysticism at the turn of the century and benefited from the strengths of that movement, including fresh interest in some of the primary texts. It certainly represented an honest seeking for a deeper relationship to the realities of the faith. It also suffered (and continues to suffer) from some of the weaknesses of the Romantic era, including excessive interiority and affectivity, a dilettantism about mysticism that resists serious discipline or ethics, and an often-naïve eclecticism in its access to the wisdom of other faith traditions. But its power and influence could not be denied. Where Christian models were not readily available, young people in the 1960s developed an interest in Eastern spirituality, often repackaged for Western consumption, and this prompted some Christians to revive teaching about classical Christian spirituality and mysticism yet again. The movement of pentecostal energy into the charismatic movement within the mainline denominations was another factor prompting a revival of classical teaching on Christian spirituality.[1] It is too soon to write the history, and it is not necessary here to provide a bibliographic essay, but it may be useful to note some highlights. There is a notable ecumenism among these trends, echoing yet another theme of the Council, especially conversations among Roman Catholics and Anglicans and Protestants, with an ever-increasing openness to the Eastern Orthodox and to the teachings of other faiths.

Early Anglican leaders included Martin Thornton, Kenneth Leech, Rowan Williams, and Esther de Waal in England, and Morton Kelsey, Urban Tigner Holmes, Rachel Hosmer, and Alan W. Jones in the United States.[2] The creation of the Shalem Institute by Tilden Edwards and Gerald May and their many publications and the founding of the Bayne Chair and the Center for Christian Spirituality at the General Theological Seminary are also landmarks.[3] Each of these shows an interest in three major trends: a revival of interest in spiritual discipline and practice in the life of the contemporary church and individuals, a new and more historically accurate access to classical texts, and a renewed interest in the ministry of spiritual direction and its relationship to other pastoral disciplines, including pastoral psychology. Among Protestant authors, Richard Foster's *Celebration of Discipline* stands out for its widespread impact.[4] The research and teaching of Baptist Glenn Hinson is a further example of the ecumenical breadth of this movement.[5]

All of these were also echoed among Roman Catholic authors, as new programs of spiritual formation and the study of spirituality arose in Catholic universities and religious orders. Highlights include the immense popularity and influence of Thomas Merton, the impact on the growing interest in spiritual direction of the "Cambridge Jesuits" and the Pecos Benedictines, and an outpouring of writing by Roman Catholic women, religious and lay, of which Joan Chittister, Rosemary Haughton, Dolores Leckey, and Joan Wolski Conn are but four examples.[6] The experience of spiritual directors, some ministering in the midst of the charismatic movement, also produced fruits, notably the works of Donald Gelpi, S.J., while serious dialogue with practitioners of other faiths is reflected in the works of Thomas Merton and David Steindl-Rast, O.S.B., for example.[7]

What began as a popular movement soon connected with academic and professional interests. The hunger for deeper access to classics of the spiritual tradition made a fruitful connection with the scholarship of the *ressourcement* movement and produced an immense output of which the Paulist Press Classics of Western Spirituality series is a useful representative symbol.[a][8] Spiritual Directors International was established as an ecumenical organization to promote training of future directors and fellowship among current ones.[9] At roughly the same time, a group of leaders established both the Society for the Study of Christian Spirituality and the Christian Spirituality Group of the American Academy of Religion.[10] A series of articles in its publication, *Spiritus,* gave early definition to a new academic field and inspired conversations attempting to define terms in a common language.[11]

From the very beginning of this movement, there has been a controversy over the place of spiritual theology as a discipline among the other possible approaches to the study of spirituality. Some have wished to exclude it, fearing its historic imperialism. Others have argued that to the degree any spirituality is Christian, it must be in serious dialogue with theological norms.[12] Taking a moderate version of this last position, several important works appeared, mapping a relationship between theology and spirituality that would be formative for each but without the perceived imperialism of the older spiritual theology.[13] These foundational works have given birth to a series of books on or within spiritual theology that contribute to the discussion, but without much serious reckoning, one way or the other, with the historical tradition of spiritual theology itself as a discipline.[14] This approach is echoed in a series of fine books by Protestant authors who mine the classical tradition, including some of the classical spiritual theologies, and point out the adaptations

---

a ˙ The *ressourcement* movement was a move away from neo-scholasticism back toward patristic sources (with much effort at providing good texts and translations) especially from 1930–1950 in France and Belgium. It contributed much to the theology of Vatican II.

needed for accessing this wisdom from within their own traditions, but again without addressing the history or structural difficulties of the discipline itself as we have inherited it in the West, especially the neo-scholastic presentation disguising what were at the time contemporary psychological and philosophical interests.[15] This latter task remains unaddressed on any side, as far as I know, and I do not believe we will have liberated all the resources of that history until it is addressed.

The possibility for a new constructive beginning for spiritual theology, in critical continuity with its past, is enriched by new resources in dogmatic and systematic theology in recent years. These developments already inform many of the foundational works just referred to and make it possible to imagine a new location and a new starting point for spiritual theology. Philip Sheldrake puts it well, "Christian spirituality exists in a framework that is Trinitarian, pneumatological, and ecclesial."[16] That is to say, Christian spirituality must exist within a theological framework that takes seriously the doctrines of the Trinity, of Christ and the Holy Spirit, and of the church. Fortunately, there have been major advances in each in the last century. Each of these is the subject of a vast literature, and many whole books have been devoted to each. Here again, for present purposes, we need only sketch some highlights.

Church

One of the most significant theological contributions of the period around Vatican II was the recovery of a strong doctrine of the church as the context for doing theology and for leading the Christian life. This was a significant reversal of several trends traced in the previous chapter, notably that of excessive interiority and privatization, as well as the concomitant marginalization of spirituality into safely cloistered elites.

Some of the documents issued by the Council in this regard have already been discussed at the end of the previous chapter. But it is important to note that the trend was already well established in Protestant as well as Catholic circles. Karl Barth fired a significant shot by naming his massive work *Die Kirchliche Dogmatik* (or *Church Dogmatics*), making it clear that theology was not an abstract discipline belonging to the academy but located within the life of the church as its lifeblood.[17] Following the outline of the creeds, after discussing the Holy Spirit (which he calls "the Spiritual Presence"), Paul Tillich turned in volume 3 of his *Systematic Theology* to a consideration of the church as an embodiment of "the spiritual community."[18] On the Catholic side, Karl Rahner's great doctrine of the church as the fundamental sacrament became the backbone of the Council's theology, while Hans Küng's *The Church* expressed well the new sense of the primacy of "the people of God" as a doctrine also embedded in the Council's ecclesiology.[19] Less well known is the degree to which many of these same concepts were anticipated within the "High Church" movement within Anglicanism in the previous century, notably in Charles Gore and William Porcher DuBose.[20] Even Protestant traditions more historically grounded in believers' individuality came to a deeper understanding of the church.

Edward Farley's *Ecclesial Reflection* and *Ecclesial Man* were groundbreaking texts, and the founding of the *Pro Ecclesia* movement within Lutheranism was a signal event. The whole doctrine has been well surveyed recently by Veli-Matti Kärk-käinen and Daniel Hardy.[21]

Several features of the new ecclesiology come together in a manner that has a major impact on spirituality, especially focused on the concept of *koinōnia*, which requires three English words to translate it: fellowship, communion, and common life.[22] This is the fundamental, underlying sacramental reality at the heart of the church's life, not merely the first gift of the Holy Spirit to the people of God but the very gift that calls, constitutes, and forms them as that covenant people. One of its chief expressions, recovered in the years before the Council, is the centrality of the public liturgy of the church as the context for all personal devotion and spiritual formation. Coinciding with liturgical reforms stemming from the historical research of the liturgical renewal movement, this produced, as we saw in the last chapter, a new sense of "liturgical piety" as prior to all individual devotion and the proper overall context for all personal prayer, even though much of that continues to take place in nonliturgical settings.[23] This reversed a trend in which more private personal devotions to the Sacred Heart or the Rosary had impinged on the public liturgy, often interfering with or replacing individual participation in it. Within the historically liturgical churches this has been a natural development that has become almost universally accepted, but there are echoes of it even within more Protestant traditions. One of the key concepts is that liturgy is essentially a public act, not a private one, and takes place in the public arena and in public space.[24] As such, it is a principal interface between church and world and the public and private spheres of life. Any true liturgical spirituality, however personally grounded, must thus have by its very nature a dialogical relationship with the larger public world of sociality, culture, and politics.

The liturgical renewal movement and the liturgical reforms of the Council also restored Baptism and Eucharist to their historic places of primacy among all the church's liturgical acts. Baptism initiates the sacramental indwelling of the Holy Spirit in the individual not only for personal sanctification but also for incorporation as a citizen in God's commonwealth, and hence in the earthly Body of Christ, the church.[25] The *koinōnia* of God's people, is, as it were, extended and rearranged to incorporate this new member, who also thereby shares with all other members in the high priesthood of Jesus Christ through participation in his death and resurrection (Rom 6:3). As a result, all ministries of the church are implicit in Baptism, which is also full initiation into church membership. Although the historical churches continue to baptize infants, the Baptism of adults is now the liturgical norm, and the theological differences between the "catholic" side and even the churches of the Radical Reformation practicing believers' Baptism have greatly narrowed. Likewise, the centrality of the Eucharist as the biblically mandated celebration of the Lord's Day (Acts 2:46) has gained wider ecumenical recognition, along with the theology that the church is itself primarily a Eucharistic assembly, constituting itself within the paschal mystery by breaking bread in fellowship (*koinōnia*).

One of the principal documents expressing this new theology is that passed by the Lima meeting of the World Council of Churches of Christ, *Baptism, Eucharist, Ministry.* This is an excellent symbol for the degree to which virtually all the churches have taken on a more ecumenical viewpoint in which they understand themselves in a variety of ways to be part of the universal church that suffers from divisions that should be overcome. Various bilateral ecumenical conversations reflect the new sacramental and ecclesial understandings and also reflect a new, more theological and less institutional, understanding of the ecumenical vision.[26] Known as the ecclesiology of a "communion of communions," in which historic church bodies will enter into full communion, or pulpit and altar fellowship, without sacrificing important historical identities, it is based on Jean Cardinal Hamer's groundbreaking *The Church Is a Communion.*[27] Here again we see the growing, common understanding of *koinōnia* as the deepest structural reality in the life of the people of God.

Indeed, the structures of *koinōnia*, the common life of the people of God, are sacramental realities provided by the Holy Spirit as the ligaments that bind together the Body of Christ as God's covenant people. These are not merely the context for any true Christian spirituality; they are its principal incarnate instruments. They are not, in principle, even at their most institutional, in conflict with the indwelling of the Holy Spirit in the individual, for it is the same Spirit who indwells and informs both. Institutional provision and personal indwelling are alike subject, unfortunately, to delusion and corruption, and hence are in need of constant discernment and reformation. But it is a dreadful and deeply romantic mistake to tell this as a story of the liberation of a good and true individual spirituality from the shackles of a confining or even wicked institution. That is the very error from which we have been seeking to recover for a hundred years.[28] The church is part of the good news not only as God's instrument for mission as both proclamation and service but also for shaping individuals for citizenship in God's commonwealth, and hence defining their personal sanctification, through those ligaments of community life that bind it together.

Particular structures include marriage and family, monastic communities, friendships formed within the life of the church community, and even the ongoing *politics* of the church at every level from prayer group through parish, larger "judicatory" such as diocese, all the way to the universal church itself, even in its current fragmented state.[29] Of course these politics are subject to corruption and can get anywhere from very annoying to absolutely deadly. But they are still the means by which the community shapes and reshapes the *koinōnia* given by the Holy Spirit as the means of formation and mission. And we must say once again, the *koinōnia* of the people of God is no *more* subject to corruption and delusion than the spiritual life of the individual, though surely institutionalized sin can be even harder to uproot than sins of individuals. Hence, any spirituality that is truly Christian will be led from within the heart of the Christian community, its fellowship, communion, and common life, its liturgy, proclamation, and even politics. This covenant community of God's people is also the source and context of the ministry of *discretio*, of discernment of spirits; spiritual directors, though called by God, are authorized by faith communities, not training programs.

The Trinity

This insight into the deepest operations of the Holy Spirit in the *koinōnia* of God's people is not, however, merely a truth about the external acts of God. Not surprisingly, it also provides us with a clue about the importance of another of Sheldrake's requirements for a restored spiritual theology: that it will be unashamedly Trinitarian; for it is the inner-relationships within the triadic unity that ground the Spirit's gift of *koinōnia* externally, and it is, as we shall see, incorporation into the inner fugue and dance of the intra-Trinitarian life that is the spiritual destiny of human beings, and thus the goal of the spiritual life.[30] Fortunately, Christian theology is in the midst of a great revival of Trinitarian thinking.[31] What had, in the West at least, become only an abstract doctrine about God's inner being, with virtually no relationship to the realities of Christian life, has re-emerged as the foundational principle of all Christian theology as such, not merely of ecclesiology, as just spelled out.

The revival certainly achieved a solid beginning with the three theological "patriarchs" of the twentieth century. Barth made a stellar beginning of recovering the Trinity as a central dogma of the church, building from a Trinitarian structure in the doctrine of revelation itself.[32] Tillich, despite some whiffs of heterodoxy in his actual presentation of Trinitarian doctrine, is committed to "Trinitarian thinking" by the creed that structures the three parts of his *Systematic Theology*.[33] The recovery of a living Trinitarian doctrine in dialogue with Orthodox thinking was a major part of Rahner's agenda.[34] Jürgen Moltmann, Wolfhart Pannenberg, and Eberhard Jüngel, among others, have continued the conversation.[35]

Most interesting has been the revival of Trinitarian thought among feminist theologians, overcoming an earlier dislike for what seemed to many the subordinationist shape of the doctrine and the masculine terminology.[36] Catherine Mowry LaCugna both came to terms with the subordinationist issue and made a passionate appeal for the relevance of the doctrine for Christian life.[37] Elizabeth Johnson reimagined the Trinity in feminist terms, beginning with the Holy Spirit.[38] Working from her theology of "gift," Kathryn Tanner has produced a Trinitarian theology in deep dialogue with the most intense feminist theory.[39]

Indeed, there is such a variety of Trinitarian theologies available, that one must simply choose one as a working basis. For a variety of reasons that I hope will become clear as we proceed, I have chosen the Trinitarian theology of Robert W. Jenson, because it embodies in a critical fashion so many of the others and also because I believe it serves the present purposes best.[40] This arises chiefly from Jenson's solution to one of the classic conundrums: the clues to God's inner life as Trinity are found in the activities "appropriated" to persons of the Trinity in their activity in creation or history, known as the divine economy; hence, the *economic* Trinity. But by the rule of *monarchē* (the rule of one), which has been dominant in the West since Augustine, the external acts of the Trinity are undivided. Jenson's solution is neat: "but not indistinguishable."[41] This allows him to make the Trinitarian interplay the key dynamic in every doctrine in his theology in a manner that I shall propose is especially illuminating for theology of the spiritual life. But before turning to that task, a special case of Trinitarian theology confronts us, the theology of the Holy Spirit, or pneumatology.

The Holy Spirit

We turn now to the third requirement Sheldrake established as defining the theological context of any Christian spirituality: pneumatology, or the doctrine of the Holy Spirit. In an earlier version of the same point, he had said "christological" rather than "pneumatological." Of course, any true Christian spirituality will be grounded in the person, life, death, and resurrection of Jesus, and thus deeply interested in contemporary movements in Christology. These have been largely characterized by a "Christology from below" that takes the humanity of Jesus with utmost seriousness.[42] But there is a growing recognition, represented in Sheldrake's change, that for us to understand Jesus' ability to impact us, or what it means for us to be "in Christ," our present focus must be on the hitherto-much-neglected doctrine of the Holy Spirit. Much Christian theology, especially in the West, has tended to suffer from a kind of "binitarianism" or "Christic monism." [43] That is, almost everything that could or should be attributed to the Spirit ends up being attributed to Christ. As we shall see, there are both good and bad reasons for this. But one solution in our time is simply to pay more direct attention to the Holy Spirit and her mission and work in the world.

Once again, the three twentieth-century theological "patriarchs" led the way. Barth certainly intended to have a fully Trinitarian theology, with a robust doctrine of the Holy Spirit included. But his overwhelming christological interests often reduced all Spirit-language to christological talk.[44] Tillich, as previously noted, following the creedal structure, devoted the entirety of volume 3 of *Systematic Theology* to the "Spiritual Presence" and its consequences for individual, community, and history. Rahner not only identified the Spirit as *The Dynamic Element in the Church*,[45] he also resisted another source of binitarianism, the tendency for "grace" to become a kind of quasi substance of its own, losing the sense that it is simply a term for referring to the direct impact of the Holy Spirit on an individual or community. This resolved a lot of the difficulties about technical terms such as "created" and "uncreated" grace and their relationships in the older spiritual theologies. Since Rahner, we are not allowed to forget that all grace is simply a name for God the Holy Spirit at work.[46]

In the aftermath of Vatican II, important works of pneumatology began to appear, of which Yves Congar's *I Believe in the Holy Spirit* became an almost instant classic. Anglican texts on the liberal catholic and evangelical sides were joined by Scots Reformed Alasdair I. C. Heron's *The Holy Spirit*, which presented a helpful survey of biblical, historical, and theological themes, concluding with a highly nuanced account of the relationship between the second and third persons of the Trinity as a clue to mending binitarianism in Trinitarian doctrine itself.[47] Orthodox works by Vladimir Lossky, Sergei Bulgakov, and Dumitru Staniloae were increasingly on the horizon.[48] Finally, serious theological works by pentecostal/charismatic and contextual theologians appeared.[49] We have already noted the place of Elizabeth Johnson's pneumatological trinitarianism among feminist theologians, and we wait, at this writing, for Sarah Coakley's first volume.

Within the last three years or so, works on pneumatology seem to be appearing more rapidly than one can catalogue them. Kilian McDonnell has given us what may be the summary of his life's work, a classic text tracing biblical and patristic themes around the tension between a "christological pneumatology" and a "pneumatological Christology," with concluding constructive suggestions.[50] Bernard Cooke has provided a helpful analysis of the Holy Spirit as power, challenging all other principalities and powers, especially violent force, in the public arena and nature.[51] We have, finally, an excellent English translation of Sergei Bulgakov's *The Comforter*, and, most intriguing of all to me, Eugene Rogers's constructive pneumatology, making positive analysis of the reticence, superfluity, and gratuitousness of the Spirit.[52]

Not surprisingly, this renewed interest in pneumatology has affected writing in theology of the spiritual life. All of the more recent works on spirituality already mentioned have some sense that spirituality is about life in the Holy Spirit. That seems a simple point, but in the light of renewed Trinitarian and pneumatological theology, it proves to be truly revolutionary. On the Catholic side, the text closest in spirit to what I am attempting here is by Portuguese/Indian Jesuit Luis M. Bermejo, who provides an excellent theology of life in the Holy Spirit but without addressing the history of the discipline.[53] On the evangelical/charismatic side, Barry L. Callen has provided a Spirit-based theological approach to spirituality that echoes many of the themes we have traced, in dialogue with the larger tradition of spirituality as a whole, but less so with the tradition of spiritual theology as such.[54]

In the light of this growing consensus, several constructive suggestions recommend themselves. As a principal means for avoiding binitarianism or christological monism, the best remedy would appear to be to provide the Holy Spirit with her own theological locus, or topic, in systematic theology, which she has hitherto lacked, usually being discussed as an adjunct to the doctrine of the Trinity.[55] In the traditional list, as modified by Rahner, this locus should come between "Christ" and "church," with "sacraments" and then "eschatology" following "church." This allows us to establish the doctrine of the Spirit precisely in the experience of *koinōnia* or communion as she rests on the Word/Wisdom within the Trinitarian co-inherence, and gratuitously provides the Word with a body, incarnational, ecclesial, and sacramental in her mission of consecration of the entire *pleroma*, at the end, as the fulfillment of all things. That is, discussion of theological pneumatology should begin with the analysis of the interplay between Word/Wisdom and Spirit in the economy of the incarnation, issuing in a pneumatological Christology and a christological pneumatology as we examine the dancing interplay between the second and third persons (eternal modes of God's being) of the Trinity from the Annunciation through the Resurrection, Ascension, and Pentecost as the climax of the paschal event.[56] This reads "inward" as the means for understanding the intra-Trinitarian relations; it reads "outward" by enabling us to see all the items in the third paragraph of the creeds—church, Baptism, forgiveness, communion of saints, resurrection, and eternal life—as belonging to the proper mission of the Spirit.[57]

This creedal analysis of the Spirit's person and work directly sets the parameters (from Baptism and church to eschaton) for the spiritual life as life in the Spirit and *hence* in Christ, the Spirit being in person the mediation of that of which Christ is the mediator.[58] This broader sense of the Spirit's *missio* therefore emerges as the ground of "spiritual theology" in the traditional and narrower sense. In particular, we can, following Rahner's proposal, make sense of the traditional language about grace; the very name of the Holy Spirit is gift and the character of the Spirit is superfluity or gratuitousness, as Rogers has emphasized.[59] Grace is the expression of God's favor as unmerited (hence superfluous and gratuitous) gift. Hence, the very definition of grace points to it being nothing more or less than the direct indwelling and activity of the Holy Spirit herself, or the impact of that indwelling on the recipient.[60]

Spiritual theology in its traditional sense of "theology of the spiritual life" is thus rescued from its exile, which started in the thirteenth century, as a topic outside dogmatics as such, related to or subordinate to moral theology. Instead, it is moved back into the heart of a Trinitarian dogmatics by being located in a new locus for the Holy Spirit coming between Christ and church. In particular, I would propose the following: Christology is usually subdivided into two co-inherent but distinguishable emphases: the teaching on Christ's person, usually called Christology proper, and that on the mission of Christ in the economy, or the work of Christ, usually called soteriology. My proposal is that the newly established locus for the Holy Spirit would have a similar co-inherent distinction: pneumatology proper would study the teaching on the person of the Spirit, especially as we see it reflected in the dance with the Word/Wisdom in the mysteries of the incarnation. Parallel to soteriology would be a subtopic on the Spirit's own mission of sanctification, that would contain, among other things, spiritual theology as teaching on the life in the Spirit, and even moral theology as the practical application of the Spirit's gift of virtue(s), character, and beatitude. This would then flow naturally into an ecclesiology of covenant, communion, formation, and mission, and hence to sacraments and ultimate eschatological fulfillment. A simpler way of putting it is this: Sheldrake's observation that any adequate Christian spirituality must be Trinitarian, ecclesial, and pneumatological does not assign to spirituality three different aspects or contexts but a unified context in which theology flows naturally from Trinity to creation to Christ to Spirit to church and beyond. The proper context for Christian spirituality is the very structure of a properly co-inherent dogmatic theology as such. Restoring spirituality to such a place within the dogmatic structure by locating it within pneumatology is thus a structural/theological move that will have immense practical applications.

I propose grounding spiritual theology not merely in a new pneumatological locus but specifically in a doctrine of the Spirit's mission as *koinōnia*—the gift to the whole created order of participation in the intra-Trinitarian relationships of *perichoresis* (co-inherence); this allows us to establish a new way of beginning spiritual theology in its traditional sense. In fact, it permits us to retrieve one of the traditional ways of getting started. The old approach of a theology of Christian perfection following on the fulfillment of moral obligation is really gone for good. It keeps spiritual theology subordinate to moral theology and both of them outside the structure of dogmatics as such, and it really does become untenable in the light of contemporary theological anthropology, which has no place for elitist notions of degrees of merit, works of supererogation, and the like. The concept of perfection will still have its uses: after all, Jesus commanded that we should be perfect even as our Father in heaven is perfect (Matt. 5:48). Classic texts in this mode may also still be mined for nuggets of wisdom.[61] But the approach itself is no longer viable.

We saw that there were also problems with the other traditional approach: theological reflection on the three "stages" that have their origin in the writings of Pseudo-Dionysius. The problem was pointed out by Karl Rahner: we cannot treat these as stages of a law-like description of human spiritual growth without doing violence to the complexity of the human reality. But something haunts us as still appropriate about this *threeness*, and its role in human spirituality. The constructive suggestions I have just made offer a way of retrieving the appropriateness of the "sense of three" without violating the human reality: locate the threeness where it belongs, on the divine side of the relationship, specifically, of course, in God's Trinitarian being. More exactly, the mission of the Spirit (*missio Spiritus*) has itself a Trinitarian structure in the economy as a whole; this arouses in human lives in the Spirit a kind of resonance of threeness that is not a law-like description of human growth; instead, it is a deeply flowing wellspring from the divine ground of human spirituality in that mission of the Spirit as she communicates the Trinitarian life to all of creation. Indeed, this way of looking at it is truer to what Pseudo-Dionysius originally had in mind than the more "psychological" use to which his categories have been put since their reimportation into the West in the Middle Ages.[62]

This Trinitarian structure of the Spirit's mission is precisely what Robert Jenson's theology of the Trinity would suggest. Each of the three persons of the Trinity has a "mission," or set of activities, within the divine economy that each has "appropriated" to it.[a] For example, the activities of creation and of summoning an original covenant people are usually appropriated to the Fount or Father.[b] But, in Jenson's theology, the Spirit and the Son each have a role in every one of those activities. Each

---

a There is some discussion as to whether it is correct to call the activities appropriated to the Fount a "mission," since the Father is not sent but is the sender. This is often out of a suspicion that excessive weight given to a *missio Dei* as such may undercut the christological ground of the gospel. Two rejoinders suggest themselves. First, in current missiology, those who send and support sending are also missionaries in the broad sense. Second, this objection does not apply to a thoroughly Trinitarian theology such as Jenson's, where the mission of each person has a fully Trinitarian structure, as the external acts of God are undivided (the entire Trinity participates in each act) though not indistinguishable. Each act is thus properly appropriated primarily to one of the persons, but the involvement of the other two is always inseparable from the character of the act.

b I have decided to use "Fount" as a gender-inclusive term for the first person of the Trinity. I certainly mean by it all that the tradition means by "Father," Jesus' "Abba," which has always included (or should have included) as well all that we humans mean by "Mother." "Fount" has the advantage of preserving the point made consistently by the Orthodox, that the Father is the Fount and source of all being, including that of the other persons of the Trinity.

Trinitarian mission, then, itself has a Trinitarian structure. In particular, the *missio Spiritus* has three dimensions: the role of the Spirit in the mission of the Fount or Father, the role of the Spirit in the mission of the Word/Wisdom, and Spirit's own proper appropriated mission (everything in the third paragraph of the creeds) in which the other two persons are also associated. Each of these aspects of the Spirit's mission raises in us a resonance equivalent to one of the Dionysian "stages" and allows us to look at the material usually associated with that stage. Insofar as we resonate with the Spirit assisting the Fount's mission, we experience what has classically been called purgation; in resonating with the Spirit's role in the mission of the Word/Wisdom, we experience what has classically been called illumination; in resonating with the Spirit's own proper mission, we experience what has classically been called union or glorification. This remains to be spelled out in greater detail and, indeed, becomes the structure of the main part of the book. But here we note a departure from the usual way of thinking about the stages:[63] precisely because we give these resonances a Trinitarian ground, they are not successive and linear stages but co-inherent in one another. And again we must emphasize, they do not derive from the human side of the relationship but from the divine.

Jenson, like Rogers and others, especially since Rahner spoke his famous maxim—the economic Trinity is the immanent Trinity—derives what can be known of the inner life of God from what we can observe of the interplay of the three in their unified missions.[64] There is, of course, no need to simply repeat Jenson's observations, though for the Spirit, in particular, I would now want to enrich them with material from McDonnell and Rogers in particular. Indeed, we shall see much of this played out from one perspective as we examine the rhythm of the spiritual life as life in the Spirit. But a brief summary of Jenson's conclusions about the place of the Spirit in the inner Trinitarian life reminds us that these relations are the source, the origin, of the relations played out in the divine economy; the finality of the creation in the Spirit (the Spirit as the ultimate goal and destiny of creation), however, also plays back, for Jenson, into our understanding of the relations of origin. For Jenson, the Spirit is liberator, the one who brings life and love precisely by providing freedom and a future:

> So we must learn to think: the Spirit is indeed the love between two personal lovers, the Father and the Son, but he can be this just *in that* he is antecedently himself. He is another who in his own intention liberates Father and Son to love each other. The Father begets the Son, but it is the Spirit who presents this Son to his Father as an object of the love that begot him, that is, to be actively loved. The Son adores the Father, but it is the Spirit who shows the Father to the Son not merely as ineffable source but as the available and lovable Father.[65]

Jenson concludes his chapter on the "Pneumatological Problem":

> Can we describe a limited set of Trinitarian relations such as the traditional "begotten" and "otherwise proceeds," that encapsulates the conclu-

sions of this chapter? Perhaps the following: the Father begets the Son and freely breathes his Spirit; the Spirit liberates the Father for the Son and the Son from and for the Father; the Son is begotten and liberated, and so reconciles the Father with the future his Spirit is. Neat geometry is lost, but life is not geometrical.[66]

Within the economy, this is reflected in the Spirit's hovering over creation, resting on the covenant people as they are called and empowered, in the womb of Mary as the Spirit prepares and then rests on the incarnate body of the Word/Wisdom. After dancing with the Word/Wisdom through all the mysteries of Christ's humanity, the Spirit is the power by which he is raised from the dead and ultimately glorified. At Pentecost, the Spirit rests on the newly forming ecclesial body of the Word/Wisdom, and the superfluous, gratuitous surprise is that this new body under the renewed covenant contains the unclean, the gentiles, thus making it a missionary society from the beginning.[67] Throughout the remaining time, the Spirit continues to rest on that body but also nourishes it and all its individual members by resting on the sacramental body, as the source of all sacramental grace. This takes place as the Spirit pursues her own mission of consecrating the entire cosmic *pleroma* in its perfect fulfillment as the sum of all individual fulfillments and more, resolving the ambiguities of life and history in the fullness of God's perfect commonwealth of justice, peace, and love. Throughout, the Spirit is the point of return to the Fount that the work of the Word/Wisdom makes possible; the Spirit is the *mediation* of that of which Christ is the *mediator*; the Spirit is not only the power of God at work in the world, the touch of God, the embrace of God, the go-between God, but is also the only means by which we have any ongoing access to either of the other two persons. The Spirit's mission throughout maintains this Trinitarian structure.[68]

In the rest of his theology, especially in his consideration of the external works of God in volume 2, Jenson uses this Trinitarian rhythm as the structure for his theological analysis. I propose to follow the same program, focusing on the Trinitarian rhythm and topics of the spiritual life, arranging the traditional content of the spiritual theology curriculum in its flow. The rhythm of the inner Trinitarian life, expressed in the missions of the Trinitarian identities in the divine economy, takes a particular form when viewed from the perspective of the role of the Spirit in each, and in the resonance raised in humans as they find and lead their lives in that Spirit within that economy.

I will be drawing out the implications of this proposal in much of what follows in successive chapters. The Holy Spirit is the power by which Jesus was raised from the dead; as Lord and life-giver, she is the source of all resurrection, the Lord and giver of all future to us and to God.[69] Hence, it is appropriate that the possibility of resurrecting spiritual theology as a formal discipline with a future should rest in its return to the structure of dogmatics as a whole precisely within pneumatology. Only the Spirit can breathe new life into these bones.[70] This reflection on mortality reminds us that while we are grounding a theology of the spiritual life in the mission of the Spirit, that mission is a mission *to someone*; the life is the life of a human creature. Before proceeding further, we must look at the human side of the relation-ship. And so, we return to dust.

Notes

1. The literature on this movement alone is vast. For our purposes it is enough to note the attention paid to the charismatic movement by Yves Congar, reflecting the welcome given by Cardinal Suenens to the movement in Belgium. See Cardinal Léon-Joseph Suenens and Dom Helder Camara, *Charismatic Renewal and Social Action*; Yves Congar, *I Believe in the Holy Spirit*. See also several works by Donald Gelpi, S.J., including *Charism and Sacrament: A Theology of Christian Conversion*. For a variety of explanations for the outbreak of interest in spirituality after Vatican II, see Sandra Schneiders, "Spirituality in the Academy."

2. Representatively, Rowan Williams, *The Wound of Knowledge*; Esther de Waal, *Seeking God*; Rachel E. Hosmer and Alan W. Jones, *Living in the Spirit*; Alan W. Jones, *Soul Making*; for the other authors, see chap. 1 above, n. 9.

3. Tilden Edwards, *Spiritual Friend, Living Simply through the Day*, and *Sabbath Time*; Gerald May, *Care of Mind, Care of Spirit, Will and Spirit*, and *The Dark Night of the Soul*.

4. Richard J. Foster, *Celebration of Discipline*, and several subsequent works.

5. E. Glenn Hinson, *Serious Call to a Contemplative Lifestyle*, and subsequent works.

6. See Thomas Merton, *New Seeds of Contemplation* and *Contemplative Prayer*, among a vast bibliography; one fruit of the work of the Cambridge Jesuits is William A. Barry, S.J., and William J. Connolly, *The Practice of Spiritual Direction*; for the Pecos Benedictines, see http://www.pecosmonastery.org and the vast output of Dove Press. Representative works of the women include Joan D. Chittister, *Wisdom Distilled from the Daily*; Rosemary Haughton, *Love*; Dolores Leckey, *The Ordinary Way*; and Joann Wolski Conn, *Women's Spirituality*, and *Spirituality and Personal Maturity*.

7. Thomas Merton, *Mystics and Zen Masters*; Robert Aitken and David Steindl-Rast, O.S.B., *The Ground We Share*.

8. See Marcellino D'Ambrosio, "*Ressourcement* Theology, *aggiornamento*, and the Herme-neutics of Tradition." The first volume in the Classics of Western Spirituality series, Julian of Norwich, appeared in 1978.

9. See their Web site, http://sdiworld.org.

10. See Web site, http://sscs.press.jhu.edu.

11. See previously cited works by Sandra Schneiders, Bernard McGinn, Walter Principe, Bernard Hanson, among others. The new *Blackwell Companion to Christian Spirituality*, ed. Arthur Holder (*BCCS*), is a good exhibit of work in this field so far.

12. See especially Sandra M. Schneiders's many contributions for the more anti-theological approach, recently, "A Hermeneutical Approach to the Study of Christian Spirituality"; for the pro-theological approach see Walter H. Principe, "Spirituality, Christian"; Bradley C. Hanson, "Spirituality as Spiritual Theology"; and Philip Sheldrake, *Spirituality and History*, 40–64. See also the previously cited works by Sheldrake and Mark McIntosh.

13. See especially Mark McIntosh, *Mystical Theology*; and Philip Sheldrake, *Spirituality and Theology*. Kenneth Leech, *Experiencing God*, is a classic attempt to show the spiritual grounds of all theology. The closest effort to what I have in mind is Yves Congar, *I Believe in the Holy Spirit*, esp. volume 2, "He Is Lord and Giver of Life."

14. William Johnston, *Mystical Theology*, is a good example. See also the massive work by Kees Waaijman, *Spirituality*, which adopts a largely phenomenological approach.

15. See Diogenes Allen, *Spiritual Theology*, which attempts to mine the past but does not offer a new synthesis. Margaret R. Miles, *Practicing Christianity*, provides a more critical frame-work. See chap. 2 above, n. 111.

16. Sheldrake, *Spirituality and Theology*, 61; see also *Spirituality and History*, 61, where "christological" replaces "pneumatological" in the later work. He reports that he is not sure why he made the change, although "the pneumatological emphasis broadens things out—and offers a space, e.g., for engaging 'the other,' not least the otherness of other faiths, as an inherent part of Christian spirituality in a global world rather than an accidental and optional extra" (personal communication, Feb. 7, 2006). If we accept Kilian McDonnell's account of the relationship between pneumatological Christology and christological pneumatology, Sheldrake's shift is less theologically significant than might be supposed.

17. Barth, *CD* 1:1, 2–3.

18. *ST* 3:162–282. Note that for Tillich "church" and "spiritual community" are not precisely coterminous but exist in a kind of creative tension.

19. Karl Rahner, *The Church and the Sacraments*; Hans Küng, *The Church*.

20. See, for example, William Porcher DuBose's statement that the church is the principal sacrament ("The Church," in *Unity in the Faith*, 98). See also Charles Gore, *The Holy Spirit and the Church*, 22–26, 52–64, 146–48. See also W. Locke's "The Church," in Charles Gore, ed., *Lux Mundi*, 305–36; Gore's own essay there, "The Holy Spirit and Inspiration," 263–302, is also significant for the theses of this book. It is important to note that the "High Church" does not properly refer to ritualist interests but to having a high doctrine of the church. As such, many "church evangelicals" claim to be "High Church" in this sense. See G. R. Balleine, *The Evangelical Party in the Church of England*; H. C. G. Moule, *The Evangelical School in the Church of England*.

21. Veli-Matti Kärkkäinen, *An Introduction to Ecclesiology*; Daniel W. Hardy, *Finding the Church*. Again, see Samuel M. Powell, *A Theology of Christian Spirituality*, 36–43.

22. "*Koinos*," *TDNT*, 3:789–809.

23. Louis Bouyer, *Liturgical Piety*.

24. See Aidan Kavanagh, *On Liturgical Theology*, 1–69.

25. Powell's account of Baptism is especially helpful on this point, *Theology of Christian Spirituality*, 49–69.

26. Anglican-Roman Catholic International Commission, several documents issued, from *Agreed Statement on Eucharistic Doctrine* to *Mary: Grace and Hope in Christ*; Lutheran-Episcopal Dialogue, *Called to Common Mission*; Lutheran World Federation and the Roman Catholic Church, *Joint Declaration on the Doctrine of Justification*; and now in particular, *The Church of the Triune God, The Cyprus Agreed Statement of the International Commission for Anglican-Orthodox Theological Dialogue, 2006*.

27. See now also Robert Jenson, *ST* 2:220–27, 234–37; J. M. R. Tillard, *Flesh of the Church, Flesh of Christ*, is a key contemporary Roman Catholic statement. See John Zizioulas, *Being as Communion*, and *Communion and Otherness*.

28. In his dialectical account of holding several creative tensions together, Samuel M. Powell does an especially fine job describing the relationship between individual and Christian community: *A Theology of Christian Spirituality*, 12, 36–43; his other "theological foundations," body and world, sin, and Trinity also resonate with the approach taken here.

29. See Jenson again on church as *polis*, *ST* 2:189–210.

30. For a through discussion of the grounding of the church's *koinōnia* in the Trinitarian relations, and the destiny of humans in that Trinitarian life, see Jenson, *ST* 2:222. See again John Zizioulas, *Being as Communion*, for what has become the classic Orthodox contribution to this discussion, grounding both ecclesiology and anthropology in the Trinitarian *koinōnia*. For the broader acceptance among Protestant authors on spirituality, see the Trinitarian ground (and even the acceptance of *theōsis*) in Powell, *A Theology of Christian Spirituality*, 45–48, Simon Chan, *ST*, 40–55, and James B. Torrance, *Worship, Community, and the Triune God of Grace*; the Trinitarian ground in Sheldrake, *Theology and Spirituality*, 75–83, 107–118, and McIntosh, *Mystical Theology*, 151–86 is less surprising.

31. For developments through the end of the twentieth century, see Anne Hunt, *What Are They Saying about the Trinity?*; Roger E. Olson and Christopher A. Hall, *The Trinity*, is also useful,

especially for the annotated bibliography, though the omission of Elizabeth Johnson, Miroslav Volf, and Jensen's *Systematic Theology* seems odd.

32. See Paul M. Collins, *Trinitarian Theology, West and East.*

33. Tillich, *ST* 3:283–94; George H. Tavard, *Paul Tillich and the Christian Message*, is still a helpful commentary.

34. Karl Rahner, *The Trinity.*

35. Jürgen Moltmann, *The Trinity and the Kingdom*; Wolfhart Pannenberg, *Introduction to Systematic Theology*, 26–36, idem, *ST* 1:259–336; Eberhard Jüngel, *The Doctrine of the Trinity.*

36. Carter Hayward, *The Redemption of God*, for example; but see Patricia Wilson Kastner, *Faith, Feminism and the Christ*, for an early countervailing voice.

37. Catherine Mowry LaCugna, *God for Us.*

38. E. Johnson, *She Who Is.*

39. K. Tanner, *Jesus, Humanity, and the Trinity*; see also *God and Creation in Christian Theology.*

40. While this approach runs throughout all of Jensons's work, the most mature expression is the two-volume *Systematic Theology.*

41. *ST* 1:110–14; I see this as the brilliant heart of Jenson's theology.

42. Veli-Matti Kärkkäinen has given us another useful summary: *Christology.*

43. Alasdair I. C. Heron, *The Holy Spirit*; Vladimir Lossky, *The Mystical Theology of the Eastern Church*; Eugene Rogers, Jr., *After the Spirit*, has a powerful analysis of this problem and shows it derives in part from the very reticence of the Spirit herself.

44. The most helpful analysis is now Rogers, *After the Spirit*, 10, 19–32, and see the references to Barth indexed on p. 244. He acknowledges his debt to Robert W. Jenson, "You Wonder Where the Spirit Went."

45. Rahner, *The Dynamic Element in the Church.* See also his first major work, *Spirit in the World* (1939); and *Experience of the Spirit.*

46. See my "The Holy Spirit in Christian Spirituality," 209–10.

47. For liberal Catholics, see J. V. Taylor, *The Go-Between God.* This is part of a long tradition, including Charles Gore's *The Holy Spirit and the Church*, volume 3 of *The Reconstruction of Belief.* For a recent collection of essays, mostly Anglican, see *Engaging the Spirit*, ed. Robert Boak Slocum. For evangelicals, see W. H. Griffith Thomas, *The Holy Spirit of God*, but there is a long tradition of writing on the Holy Spirit by Anglican Evangelicals, including Charles Simeon's four sermons: *The Offices of the Holy Spirit*; and H. C. G. Moule, *Veni Creator.*

48. Lossky, *Mystical Theology*; Sergei Bulgakov, *The Comforter*; Dumitru Staniloae, *Orthodox Spirituality* and *The Experience of God.*

49. Veli-Matti Kärkkäinen has provided another helpful survey: *Pneumatology*; his inclusion of the latter two categories is especially helpful. On the evangelical side, he helpfully gives particular weight to Clark Pinnock, *Flame of Love.*

50. Kilian McDonnell, *The Other Hand of God.*

51. Bernard Cooke, *Power and the Spirit of God.*

52. Eugene Rogers, *After the Spirit*, 33–44.

53. Luis Bermejo, *The Spirit of Life*

54. Barry Callan, *Authentic Spirituality.*

55. I agree with Rogers's caution about this—that it will not, of itself, fix the problem, and that attention must be paid to the reticence and superfluity of the Spirit herself as the source of the "problem" (*After the Spirit*, 33–44).

56. Heron, McDonnell, Rogers already provide us with this.

57. Gore and Tillich have been strongest on this.

58. McDonnell, *Other Hand*, 103–7, 112–14, etc. He helpfully makes the point that just as Jesus is the mediator of the new covenant and, hence, of the presence of the Trinitarian God to humanity and all creation, so the Spirit as the gift of God's presence is that very mediation itself.

59. Augustine, *De Trinitate* 15.18.32–19.37; Rogers, *After the Spirit*, 33–44. See also Piet Fransen, *Divine Grace and Man*; and *The New Life of Grace*.

60. Tanner's whole discussion of gift becomes particularly relevant here, *Jesus, Humanity, and the Trinity*, throughout, esp. 51–55, 60–62.

61. Especially, perhaps, Joseph de Guibert.

62. Thanks to Bernard McGinn, in conversation, February 28, 2006.

63. Though this may be truer to Pseudo-Dionysius's original intentions and resonates with Bonaventure's more subtle treatment in *De Triplica Via*.

64. Rahner, "Remarks on the Dogmatic Treatise 'De Trinitate,'" *TI* 4:78–102, at 87.

65. Jenson, *ST* 1:156.

66. Jenson, *ST* 1:161.

67. Rogers, *After the Spirit*, 85–97.

68. This paragraph derives from Jenson, McDonnell, Cooke, Rogers, Taylor, and Tillich.

69. Rogers, *After the Spirit*, 9–91, 95; McDonnell, *Other Hand*, 208–11.

70. Ezekiel 37:1–14.

4

Dust

Remember that you are dust, and to dust you shall return.
            —Liturgy for Ash Wednesday; see Genesis 3:19 and 2:7

Will the dust praise you or declare your faithfulness?   —Psalm 30:10

The Dust We Are

Our age has its own contributions to make to a revival of spirituality. These consist in the deconstructing of some of the worst examples of the oppression that arose when the tradition advocated docility and obedience to earthly authorities as religious sanction for racism, classism, and sexism. We have our own peculiar demons to face, from ideological conflict to privatistic hedonism, to say nothing of a huge reservoir of bad theology. But there are positive contributions from our time as well. Among these can be the insights of contemporary anthropology and developmental psychology, a deeper sense of the connection between holiness and liberating justice than many previous ages, and a new appreciation for sexuality and intimate relationships and family life as paths of sanctification of equal value to the celibate monastic life. We have learned much about the significance of childhood trauma and the spiritual dynamics of healing; we have a new awareness of the nature of demonic powers such as addictive disease and a variety of mental illnesses such as depression and attention deficit disorder, gaining a deeper understanding of the genetic, physical dimension even as we reach new understandings of the spiritual component of recovery. These contemporary perspectives on human dust have a prominent place here and are crucial for informing the spiritual life and the practice of spiritual direction in our time. If we do not heed them, ancient wisdom will become antiquarianism, not deeply rooted and funded gospel praxis (*praxis* is a Greek word meaning acts or practice; in English it has come to mean such acts and practices as informed by a theory or theology of action). A final gift of our age can help—the birth of a new ecumenical spirit that is especially profound, in my experience, when we are dealing with one another at the depths of our personal relationships with God. The ecumenical context allows us a chance to sift true theology from nonsense, enduring gifts of our own traditions from mere tribal badges, legitimate expressions of different perspectives and even different experiences of God from narrow partisanship and elitism. These are the tasks and opportunities *Beloved Dust* seeks to grasp.

Contemporary theology is nearly always a theology from below and, hence, must begin with theological anthropology—a doctrine of humanity, of who we are, of the subject undergoing the spiritual growth that is the topic of this book. We have seen that in spiritual theology this trend is at least as old as Saint Jure and the *Westminster Catechism*. Although I have criticized the excesses of this Enlightenment emphasis and suggested that spiritual theology must be recentered in a theology of the Holy Spirit, the human side of the relationship cannot be ignored. Life in the Spirit is the spiritual life of someone, some person or persons, and we need a theology of what it means to be human in its own right. Here there is an earthquake building around a huge theological fault-line. At the very time there is a revival of classical spirituality, the whole notion of human beings as a dualism of soul and body, part of our inheritance from the Greek thought world, is under attack from sources other than popular Romanticism and from a surprisingly broad spectrum of theological opinion.[1] More and more we are coming to believe that occult notions of a human soul or spirit have no scientific basis, that we are only a particular kind of animal assembled from the dust of the material elements that make up the universe. Admittedly this means a lot more than the dust under the bed. It is, quite literally, star dust, the dust from the great clouds born in the Big Bang, shaped and reshaped by physics and chemistry until atoms, molecules, and finally snippets of RNA and DNA emerge in organic life. As life evolves, ultimately sentient, then conscious, then self-conscious, and finally "rational" (whatever that means) creatures emerge, a process that appears to take a quantum leap in quality every now and again; but from a different perspective it is, underneath, a continuum. And it is all dust, flesh and blood, seen from the bottom up. We have no need of any occult ghostly properties to account for this emergence, even if we do need to reject a mechanistic and deterministic reductionism in favor of an open-systems analysis with room for purpose, even divine purpose.[2]

While this view of humanity appears at first glance to be devastating to a "traditional" Christianity that has had so much to say about an immortal soul separable from an earthly body, indeed based its whole hope for a redeemed life after death on such a mechanism, it really is not. From one perspective, this dualism is now at its sharpest, with a wholly material human existence portrayed on the scientific side and the wholly "spiritualist" Manichean view dominating the false mysticism of New Age sensibilities and the channeling cults on the other; but at just this time theologians are recovering a clarity that biblical thought knows no such dualism, except as it inevitably continues as an unfortunate resonance in New Testament Greek, a resonance the authors are at constant pains to combat.[3] The possibility arises, then, of a coming together of a scientific view of human being with a restored holistic view deriving from Scripture. This will have profound effects on the way we do theology of the spiritual life.

I honestly do not know how early the shift was made, but, as we have already seen, at some point in Christian history theology of the spiritual life ceased to be about what it meant to be "in Christ," to lead a human animal life indwelt by the Holy Spirit, and began to be about the cultivation and refinement of human spiritual faculties, faculties seen as different from and superior to the physical faculties of sensation.[4] Along the way, intellectual and artistic life and vocation came to be seen as superior to jobs in the material realm; celibacy was identified as better than marriage or the full exercise of sexuality in any form, which was an enemy of the spirit; and the contemplative religious life emerged as superior even to the active religious life of apostolate and service, let alone to merely secular callings.

During the early modern period in Western Europe from which the Enlightenment was born, there was a general contraction of self and spirit until self was diminished to a tiny little ghostly ego-person trapped in the head of a mechanical body of flesh, and the mystical, as we have seen, gradually became identified with rare and occult gifts and ultimately paranormal phenomena.[5] Our contemporary period, which in many quarters sees itself as "postmodern," acknowledges the shakiness and uncertainty of that sense of self and seeks to overcome the bifurcations that produced all the dualisms we have named, as well as those of race, class, gender, and sexual orientation. Two different strategies have emerged, however. One simply accepts the disappearance of a grounded sense of self as the current human condition; the other seeks to reconstruct a sense of personhood by rejecting the contraction of soul, self, and spirit that produced the problem in the first place. I have taken the second approach.

The process of psychologizing spirituality and its accompanying dualism within Christianity reached a kind of apex in the nineteenth century, when Friedrich Schleiermacher defended Christianity as true because it embodied the highest evolution of the human religious faculty.[6] Stir in a good dose of Wagnerian and Byronic Romanticism, along with a fascination for the half-understood exotica of other world religions newly encountered in a colonial context, and soon Christianity becomes only one way for realizing that potential, which is now a higher human faculty treated in isolation from any particular deity or religion. William James then identified first-hand faith with primary religious experience of the "mystical" (in the modern Romantic constricted sense) and made that so rare as to be possible only for a few charismatic geniuses.[7] Add some mood-altering drugs, a bit of Western spiritualism, a big chunk of theosophy, all while the skepticism of the scientific side about the reality of the whole "spiritual enterprise" continues to build, and eventually we arrive at the twentieth century, where the dualism became almost a multiple-personality phenomenon, the most materialistic of consumerist cultures escaping from the worst of its own self-produced horrors by wallowing in the most esoteric of nonmaterialist spiritualities.

Well, it will not do. It is time to admit it is all dust; we are all dust, flesh and blood; time to sweep out the occult and the esoteric and ask what it might be for a self-conscious bag of dust and water to have something called a spiritual life. I am afraid that means turning away, at least for a moment, from the lessons we might learn from Eastern religions, with their clear teaching that the material realm is either unreal or evil or both. We shall want to return to dialogue with these other faiths, but only when we are clear about our own.[8] One of the oddities we have produced is Westerners who adopt Eastern religions because they seem to them to handle better the material realities of daily life, when these religions have always taught more clearly than even the most spiritualized Christianity that these realities are at best beside the point, at worst illusory. In that sense, I seek to give here an account of spirituality that is more Western and Christian than has appeared in Western Christianity for some time—an account of the life of the human animal within, and indwelt by, the Holy Spirit.

Although I am going to try to maintain the focus of this work on the spiritual life, the account suggested in the previous paragraph in a sense requires a romp through all the doctrines of systematic theology. I am going to take that romp from a very particular point of view here, without spending much time arguing for it in detail. So let me just note I know there are other legitimate Christian points of view on everything I am about to say, and then get on with it, hoping the coherency of the picture may provide it some defense.

By rejecting the bifurcations and dualisms of Western modernity, this attempt at spiritual theology seeks to be "constructive" and "postmodern"; that is, to offer its own proposed solutions rather than just describing the thoughts of others, and to take some account of the contemporary critique of Enlightenment modernity. Other parts of the postmodern critique also come into play. The "hermeneutics of suspicion" that have helped the collapse of modernity are assumed to be in place. These can be conveniently thought of in three categories. The first would include Charles Darwin, Karl Marx, Sigmund Freud, and their followers, who have taught us that the relationship between consciousness and whatever we might call "reality" is complex, shaped by biology, by economic and cultural forces, and by individual psychological growth and trauma. Reality, whatever it is, never appears "raw" to human consciousness. It is always interpreted.

A second category includes the newer writings of authors from groups that have generally been oppressed by the dominant Western culture, including women, people of color, the poor, and so on. They remind us that much of what has passed for true in Western thought, including theology, has taken dominant white male experience as normative and proper. One of the things "deconstruction" means is exposing the structures by which this dominance is legitimated in institution and text. Here I want to express a cautionary note. Some thinkers act as if one could gain access to the newly privileged consciousness of the oppressed by acts of "identification." I am not so sure. This book is written by an ordained, sixty-something, academically employed White American man. I try to listen to the other voices, to heed them and take them into account. I believe in partnership and the discipleship of equals. But I cannot be a feminist, liberation, or black theologian in the strict sense of basing theology on my own experience of the oppression of women, people of color, and the poor, for I am not one of them.

Third, and closely related, is the issue of contextualization. We cannot now hide from the knowledge that all texts have an original context and sociopolitics, and a history of interpretation reflecting various shifts in those contexts right down to any present reading. This principle of deconstruction I also accept. It is important to recognize that our own context is a little bleak, characterized by what Nicholas Lash calls the *Eclipse of Word and Presence*.[9] This makes it impossible for us to speak, after Auschwitz, Hiroshima, and the other horrors of our era—including our new recognition of the scope of domestic violence and childhood sexual trauma—with any naive lack of ambiguity about God or humanity. If it seems I am doing so in parts of the book, I plead with the reader to wait for the discussion of the third current, in which the *via negativa* of theology and the spiritual life come together to undermine any such positivism (the notion that any truth, let alone theological, can be expressed unambiguously and beyond correction in propositions).

Having accepted so much of the postmodernist agenda, however, I wish to go out on a somewhat dangerous limb. Many postmodern thinkers believe that we have no solid knowledge of anything that could be called real, and no foundation *at all* for the meaning and meaningfulness of language beyond its own grammar. This is technically termed the epistemic despair of deconstructionist neo-nominalism; I doubt that its ultimately destructive relativism is finally the way out of the postmodernist dilemma of pluralism. As the culture wars between many hard scientists and the "science studies" movement have shown, hard scientists are not at all comfortable with extreme nonfoundationalism and its consequences; they really do expect the same physics to be true in the mountains of Laos and the laboratories of Yale, and they have a case. I am persuaded, along with Bernard Lonergan and others, that intellectual conversion to Christianity requires an acceptance of a philosophy of moderate, critical realism.[10] Extreme realism (idealism, the belief that abstract human concepts refer to ideas that are the most real things in the cosmos) and nominalism in all its forms (the belief that abstract nouns are only arbitrary names for convenient globs of human experience) share a denigration of either the goodness of creation or the gift of reason, or both, and are therefore ultimately incompatible with the gospel, in this view.

An expanded version of the parable of the blind scientists and the elephant is one way to envision the problem. A group of blind scientists is examining an elephant by feel, and each senses it differently—one as being like a tree trunk, another like a large python, another like a small grass snake, another like a long curved spear, and another like a large eucalyptus leaf. The traditional parable ends here. My expansion would be this: over in another corner is a group of philosophers and theologians, equally blind, listening to the scientists talk and constructing "metanarratives" of their conversation. The idealists (extreme realists) search for the governing idea of Elephant that lies behind all these fleeting appearances. The nominalists and nonfoundationalists have ceased to believe in elephants at all. Critical realists see the problems of differing perspectives (including those not in the analogy of this parable such as the distortions of consciousness caused by race, class, gender, and personal history) but persist in believing in real elephants on which there is simply no absolute human perspective. In the end, I suggest, this last is the option demanded by science and theology alike.

The view of humanity as dust, then, is also meant to be compatible with a scientific view of humanity. That does not mean it is identical to a scientific perspective, since science and theology have different points of view. John Polkinghorne, a distinguished world-class physicist turned priest and theologian, has stated that precisely for its own purposes, science trawls experience with a net which lets a large percentage of what is human slip through.[11] Whatever we mean by spiritual life, it will focus on a lot of what has slipped through that net. But it must do so in a manner that does not dictate to science that there are esoteric and occult realities it ought to acknowledge but cannot. What Polkinghorne and his biologist colleague Arthur Peacocke (also turned priest and theologian) have showed us is that an account of Christian doctrine can be given that does not in any way violate or contradict the scientific picture, but may indeed complement it.[12] That is enough to establish the reasonable possibility of our enterprise. We cannot ask science to add proof to it, since that lies outside the net with which it trawls. But as with science, we begin with the dust. As God says to Adam and Eve as they are expelled from Eden, "You are dust, and to dust you shall return," a note reechoed in the rites for imposition of ashes on Ash Wednesday, and in the Kontakion of the Dead in the Eastern Orthodox liturgy (and now that of the Episcopal Church as well). Whatever the spiritual life is, on this view, it is something that happens to an aggregate of dust.

Animated Dust

We are not just any old dust, of course, but living and self-conscious dust. We must not, however, reintroduce the mystery too soon. Science is able to account, in its own terms, for the emergence of life and consciousness out of the dust without needing to invent occult properties for matter. Even though many of us continue to believe that the question Why life? requires some kind of teleological answer, that does not mean that the question How life? does;[13] one possible exception is an acknowledgment of how fragilely well tuned the material system must be to have produced life and consciousness—which makes belief in God not "scientific" but, perhaps, from a philosophical point of view, more reasonably compatible with science than is atheism.[14] It is not the bare fact of life that requires a theological account but the quality of life as experienced by human beings. This quality of experience leads us to confess that to be alive is somehow to be "animated," to have had the breath of life breathed into dust from outside (Genesis 2), as it were. It is what humans have meant by the word "soul." And it is here we must begin to take real care, or we shall fall back into the dualist trap again.

In the first instance, by the word "soul" we mean simply the difference between a live body and a dead one. Soul is the life of a body. While the Platonist tradition came to believe this quality of soul could survive the death of the body, Aristotle was not so sure.[15] His Christian intellectual descendants, from Thomas Aquinas down to our own time in neo-Thomism, transcendental Thomism, and other forms of what is called critical realism, have always viewed "soul" as the life of a body, in the first instance.[16] As a quality of life, it does not refer to some ghostly additional thing in a human being, but more to what we mean when we say "whole person." It is what makes a bag of dust and gas and water into something unique and coherent at a higher systemic level, a higher level of complexity and organization.[17]

This personal coherency is under attack in our era, and indeed has been for some time. It really has been under attack since David Hume, and for Immanuel Kant, the transcendental ego always escapes us as an object of knowledge, but the unity of the self as the "transcendental unity of apperception" is demanded by human consciousness and thought, even though it cannot be established as an object. At a higher level the same is true for God as a regulative idea for the unity of knowledge. Postmodern critiques of the autonomous self have a long modernist lineage![18]

Christians confess the Holy Spirit as sovereign life-giver. That is, we confess that in some way life truly is *animated,* that to be alive, to have a soul, does not mean to possess an additional ghostly property in isolation, but to be in a relationship. To be embodied as souled is first to be in relationship with other embodied souls. But even that does not quite get us to where we need to be. As philosopher Jean-Paul Sartre has shown *ad nauseum,* all attempts to find in any finite other, or project with such an other, the key or ground of my being are doomed to failure, often quite gruesome failure.[19] As this dialectic plays itself out for Sartre, he finally realizes that the project of being human is the desire to be God, a necessary being—to have not just a fragile disintegrating empirical ego as a demand though never a foundation but a true sense of a grounded self-in-relation. But for him the idea of God is self-contradictory, and "man is a useless passion."[20] The alternative to this atheistic despair is to find, as did Tillich, that in God we discover the ground of our being, however paradoxical the idea of God may be.[21] To be alive, to be embodied as souled, is to be already and from the beginning in solidarity with all flesh, including animals and other creatures; indeed, it means to be in personal relationship to all other sentient and self-conscious beings, and in the deepest sense of all, in relationship to, even indwelt by, the Holy Spirit. Not the existence of life but its quality as embodied soulness demands we confess life as given, gift, grace, and hence embraced as contingent and finite. To be and make sense as a whole person, a spirited body, in the face of the disintegration of our empirical ego, is to confess thankfully a relationship to the Holy Spirit and thus the triune God as the source of life as a gift, "gift" being one of the proper names of the Spirit herself.[22] Admitting that from a purely human point of view Sartre could always be right, let's explore the happier option, which, as Barth reminds us, can only be established in the dialogue of encounter, of revelation, initiated from God's side. That is indeed the Christian claim: the demand of human being to be not only embodied but ensouled—to make sense as whole persons and participants in communities—is graciously met by God's yes, which humanity meets in the revelation of the Word of God and our ability to hear it.[23]

Spirited Dust

A second quality of the experience of human life is that of self-transcendence, which goes by the name of "spirit."[24] That is to say, human beings experience their existence as always calling them out of their present and current stature into a future in which they are somehow "more."[25] While this call varies in intensity at different stages of the human life cycle, it is constant and inexorable. At least in the fallen state in which we experience it, anxiety and guilt are its main companions. This is not, however, a call for dust to become something else, to become nonmaterial, nonfinite, nonmortal. It is a call for dust to grow, to be all that it can be, apologies to the U.S. Army. Not just in general, but in particular histories. From a Christian point of view, this call for growth into "more" is not a human drive taken in isolation but already a work of grace, of the presence of the Holy Spirit.

Some definitions of "spirit" and human self-transcendence, especially nineteenth century, obscure this dependence on grace and have led to a treatment of the spiritual life as either (1) conquering the body and material world by the soul/spirit, or (2) cultivating the higher (spiritual) faculties of reason over against the ordinary material faculties of sense and intellect.

Neither of these results in dust responding to a call to grow into "more," in the sense of more *itself*. They lead to a perversion of that call into a desire to escape the inexorable call of *self*-transcendence by becoming *something else*—a disembodied soul or spirit, free from the change and contingency, the mortality and finitude which are the marks of our historicity. Ultimately, it is a denial that to dust we shall return by seeking to possess what we mean by "spirited" as a property of ourselves instead of as an invitation from the Holy Spirit to enter precisely as dust into the heart of the great dance that is the inner life of the triune God.

The alternative I seek to present is a fully incarnated spirituality, a spirituality of whole persons in community, in relationship, dust to dust, but ensouled and enspirited, precisely because by grace human persons are already in relationship with the Holy Spirit, simply by virtue of being alive and growing dust.

"Self-transcendence" has been proposed by some contemporary writers on spirituality as a kind of inclusivist tag to give to spirituality an anthropological definition transcending religious boundaries. Bernard McGinn gives a helpful summary of the approach and of the literature reflecting this position, including Joann Wolski Conn and, to some degree and at one point, Sandra Schneiders.[26] A careful tracing back of this notion reveals roots in the theology of David Tracy and, earlier, Bernard Lonergan.[27] While this emphasis on self-transcendence as a human characteristic is useful for anthropological generalization and inclusivity, it can ignore the Christian "fact" that our self-transcendence is an element of what Rahner calls the "supernatural existential" or those universal characteristics of human existence that belong not to the givenness of human nature but to the gracious presence of God to all human beings in their concrete historical existence.[28] Our self-transcendence is, in fact, evoked in us first by God's self-transcendence, as both Lonergan and Tracy realized.[29] Human self-transcendence is ultimately dependent on being in the presence of God's self-transcendence, as Rahner so carefully argues, grounding this human self-transcendence in the self-communication of God.[30] But, of course, for Rahner, God's self-communication is the heart of the Trinitarian processions and *perichoresis,* or co-inherence, itself. Thus, human self-transcendence is not a property of human *nature*, character, or *capax* (capacity or potential) as such, in isolation from God, but a characteristic of human *existence* evoked as a kind of resonance or current by the proximity of God's self-transcendence, which is the Trinitarian *perichoresis* itself.[31] Human self-transcendence, then, is a property of human character or human being precisely as a characteristic of God mediated to humans by the Holy Spirit. This is what it means even for human beings to have a human spirit.

Indeed, characteristics, properties, virtues, moral goods, and similar attributes at stake in a theology of the Christian life as a life of self-transcendence are increasingly seen by theologians as, in the first instance, characteristics of God. In the moral realm, for example, Owen Thomas has argued, "The essence of all Hebrew-Christian ethics is the nature of God received as a demand upon the life of humanity. Thus the highest moral calling of the Christian is imitation of the outgoing love of the holy God as it is manifest in Christ."[32] In that sense, moral theology and spiritual theology alike begin with the study of such attributes of God as righteousness, holiness, and love as characteristics of God manifested in Jesus Christ. A study of the Christian life would then turn to these characteristics as mediated to human beings by the indwelling of the Holy Spirit, thereby allowing humans to be "in Christ" in Paul's sense and, hence, to participate in what are essentially divine attributes through the mystery of the *communicatio idiomatum*, the communication of the properties of each of the two natures of Christ, the human and the divine, to the one person of Jesus, without them thereby becoming mixed or confused.[33]

These "spiritual" characteristics or virtues are not attributes of human nature as such, not even as *capax,* capacity or potential, apart from the "supernatural" in Rahner's sense: the presence of human being before a gracious God as a universal structure of human existence. As I said, this is what I believe Rahner meant by his controversial concept of "the supernatural existential." In the structures of human existence, this being-in-the-presence of God as demand and *capax* is generative of all human life, not just specifically Christian life; it is always embedded and effective, but only by sheer grace and not as a property of human nature as such. Hence, there is a fundamental structure of human existence that is "supernatural" in the sense of transcending nature as such without contradicting it. It is a property of human being, but not of human nature, precisely because it is a relational, existential property, already mediated by the Holy Spirit even to those who are not fully "in Christ." It endures in human beings since God's gifts, once given, become characteristic of the recipients because of God's faithfulness as giver, not because of some abstract essentialism. It is thus meaningful to speak a language of the human soul and spirit, but only as long as we remember these are relational/existential terms, not essentialist. This anthropology of dust first presents the traditional concepts of human soul and spirit as valid only as relational terms, the other pole of which is the Holy Spirit herself. The second point is corollary: the deepest characteristic of human being is to have an end, a *telos,* for which humans have no natural capacity or potential: sharing in the divine Trinitarian life itself.[34] This is the glory and the anxiety of all human existence, which can terminate only in Sartre's despair that human being as self-transcendence is a "useless passion," or in the worship and adoration that will be perfect only in the beatific vision itself, the loving knowledge of the triune God in eternal life, that life that is only God's.

The contemporary account of human self-transcendence is also often linked to accounts of developmental psychology as applied to the spiritual life. We will deal with these in more detail when we consider psychological theories of conversion in examining that first current of the spiritual life in chapter 12. Here it might be useful, however, to sketch the relationship of dust and psyche as I envision it as a kind of paradigm for how the human sciences can aid or hinder us in the study of the spiritual life. Psychology is particularly revealing, since its root meaning is "science or talk about the soul." As we saw in the historical chapter, the modern science of psychology has deep historical roots in the rise of the individual subject in medieval Christian spirituality and theology, and in early modern observations of the movements of the human soul in response to grace. In its current, secular version, there is often a more hostile relationship to theology. There are basically three options. We can view the language of one (usually spirituality) as reducible without remainder to that of another (usually scientific psychology) so that by Ockham's razor the first language becomes superfluous, explained away by the second. Any account in which the language of spirituality appears only as religious language for scientifically describable psychological phenomena faces this danger. Sometimes the flow is in the other direction, as in New Age therapies that stir in a kind of eclectic mysticism with their psychological beliefs and techniques. A second option is to see both languages as completely separate but equal descriptions of the same phenomena, each from a valid perspective contributing its own insights but without either being reduced to the other or having any right or need to step on the other's toes. This follows a common conception of the relationship between science and theology in general.[35]

I propose a third, and, I hope, more nuanced account of the relationship: the human sciences, with no theological interference needed, describe the realities of human dust and its history from a strictly empirical point of view. The psychosocial history of any human being provides the context and concrete material out of which a spiritual life is fashioned. Other aspects of that spiritual life, however, are best accounted for as deriving, as a kind of resonance in the dust, from the Trinitarian structure of the mission of the Holy Spirit, from whom all properly "spiritual" characteristics come as gift, and hence as always relational. The Spirit never acts in a vacuum, so that all we can learn about the "dusty" properties of a human subject are vital in understanding that subject's spiritual life. But precisely its *spiritual* character and shape always derive ultimately from the Spirit indwelling that subject. This is not, by the way, a dualism. The very existence of dust, in Christian theology, derives from God as gift; it is not a co-equal and co-eternal principle. Neither is this a monistic or pantheistic view. Dust and Spirit are not two sides of the same coin. God gives creation a being of its own that is different from and separate from God's own being. The traditional Christian doctrine of *creatio ex nihilo* (creation out of nothing) is precisely meant to exclude these two errors.[36] This is, however, a properly pan*en*theistic view, in which all things are in God (where else could they be?) and God, by choice, indwells all things (or else there would be places where God is not). A human spiritual life, then, is a life describable in purely "dusty" scientific terms, *as* indwelt by the Holy Spirit and thus exhibiting resonances with God's own inner life.

Estranged Dust

It is not, sadly, quite that simple. Before we can chart the rhythms of the interaction of dust and Spirit we have to acknowledge a big monkey wrench in the works. Part of human existence as we experience it is that something is desperately wrong with this glorious picture, something that pushes it toward Sartre's despair, and that something wrong is *in* us even though it is not us by our created nature. The perversion of the call of self-transcendence just mentioned in the last section is one example. What we usually experience is not the wonderful relationship with God the Holy Spirit and others in community just described as what makes us truly human but the remnants of those relationships, now sadly deformed or even denied, from which we are alienated and estranged.

The witness to this alienation is pretty universal among human beings. In Buddhism, for example, it is the conundrum of suffering. In the Christian faith, this is expressed in the doctrines of the fall and of sin. One flaw in traditional Catholic accounts of spirituality is that this dimension often seems to be underplayed.[37] This is usually because as a theology of Christian perfection, spiritual theology always appeared in a Catholic system after the problem of sin had been dealt with. But it also gave the false impression, one that actually conflicts with Catholic dogma, that some human beings (in addition to the possible special cases of Jesus and Mary) could be free from all sin even in this life. Whatever the various doctrines of original sin may mean in their distinctness, together they bear witness to the fact that we are in a mess, that we, collectively and individually, are somehow partly responsible for the mess, that the mess is now unavoidable (and in that sense inevitable) for any human being born into the world, and that the mess has gained such power that we cannot extricate ourselves from it. Many philosophers (not all Christian by any means) and theologians point to the human reality of this experience. Rahner notes that there is a resistance not only to self-transcendence in us but to any change at all. He sees this resistance as morally neutral and the proper meaning of "concupiscence." It is morally neutral initially, because it resists the change required for the growth of evil as well as good.[38] Martin Heidegger, with whom Rahner studied philosophy, sees human being as on a quest for Being which is always somehow a failure, defining our context by guilt and anxiety. Even authentic existence is marked by dread and isolation.[39] Sartre, as we have seen, sees all human projects seeking to recover the key to our alienated being as ending in failure. The experiences (1) of our failure to heed and obey the call of self-transcendence as gift, (2) of the ego or of any form of human community to hold together, or (3) of ourselves to be truly alive and spirited whole persons may be more deeply felt by some than others, but all are enmeshed in it. Our individual lives, our intimate relationships, our community relationships, our ties to the earth, and our relationship with God are all somehow *spoiled*. This is what Tillich calls our existence or existential being, in contradistinction to our essential being.

If concupiscence is a resistance that is morally neutral, and original sin points to a mess for which we are at least partly responsible, positive sin is the willful perversion of the Holy Spirit's call to self-transcendence. And here I must tread on thinner ice, where you need not necessarily follow, and confess I agree with the teaching of the Christian tradition that when we have allowed for all that, and even the geometric growth of sin through social and systemic collusion, there is a remainder of wickedness and perversity in the picture that demands further explanation. Tradition explains it in terms of another spirit, an evil spirit who is not equal to or co-eternal with God, but from our point of view is very strong and seductive.[40] We experience our estrangement and spiritual spoilage as something from which we must be delivered.

The spiritual life thus has some aspects not merely of a quest or struggle for growth in the face of tragic estrangement but of a conflict, a battle, against parts of our own existence and even a spirit who is not our friend. On our own we are not able even to begin to fight this battle, let alone win it. Often, in fact, we are simply in denial about the problem. In that condition any growth we experience is not going to be healthy, but cancerous, at least in part, and perverted "spiritual" growth will be the sickest of all. The classical Calvinist doctrine of total depravity does not mean we are entirely bad or that "there is no health in us" but that no one is free from this mess or able to get out of it on their own (the one exception being Jesus, and, in some Catholic traditions, Mary his mother as well), and no aspect or dimension of anyone is left untainted and unscarred by the problem. If our eyes are open, we are clearly in desperate straits. We are either a useless passion, and all we can do is make the most of it with as little illusion as possible (perhaps the stance of classical Buddhism as well as Sartre), or we must look for a deliverance from the mess. We are not just dust any longer, but bogs and cesspools, all the more loathsome because the echoes of intended glory linger in a noisome perversion.

Redeemed Dust

The good news is that the same God whose Holy Spirit gives us life and calls us into self-transcendent growth does not leave us in these desperate straits but provides the deliverance not only for us but also with us. It is not just dropped down from a heavenly height as a completed package but worked out with us in our history, beginning with the call of Abraham and Sarah (or even earlier, indeed, probably from the beginning). The history of Israel, the patriarchs and matriarchs, Moses, law and covenant, some kings and prophets, the formation of a priestly people around the Temple are not just preparation or anticipation of that deliverance—they are its earliest stages, and any true spiritual life remains grounded in them.

But for Christians, the culmination of that deliverance is in Jesus of Nazareth, in whom we believe the one and only triune God has, in the (second) person of the eternal Word and by the power of the Holy Spirit (the third person), become dust in

God's own self within the womb of a human mother. The deliverance of dust from the mess is accomplished both by God and by human dust itself, in this one person.

There are many stories, analogies, and theories about exactly how this deliverance was wrought.[41] Arguing about which ones are best would be another whole book, and in any case the church has never made a dogmatic decision in favor of one against the others. Whatever their differences, all the theories bear testimony to the following: the required deliverance from the mess of sin is provided by God-in-person-as-dust (Jesus) by his very being (incarnation), by his life and teaching, by his sacrificial death for us on the cross, by God's glorious raising of him from the dead, and by a new outpouring of the Holy Spirit on all flesh. Whatever needed doing was done. The barriers of estrangement and alienation in all our relationships are cast down; we are restored to the possibility of true embodiedness, ensouledness and enspiritedness as living whole persons in true community; and even more (this is the deepest part of the good news) a new and even deeper relationship and potential are opened up by the indwelling of the Holy Spirit in those who have been joined with Jesus in his death and resurrection through the waters of Baptism. This is what Tillich means by saying that in Jesus there appears the New Being that restores us from our estranged existence to our own proper essential being, so that we may then live in the spiritual presence. It is in this death and resurrection and outpouring of Spirit that we are also given the possibility of eternal life, not something inherent in us as a property of immortality. It is important not to be too triumphalistic here: the ultimate victory is won, but the difficult cleanup continues. Christians receive this gift by faith; how it apples to persons of other faiths or no faith is another subject, too large to deal with here.[42]

There is a further mystery on which there are divergent views within the Christian family. Some of this deliverance is simply, fully, and completely given (justification); some requires our assent, cooperation, and growth (sanctification). We can simply bypass a lot of arguments about the mix by suggesting that as long as we recognize both the utter givenness of the very possibility of our deliverance and the start of its actualization on the one hand, and the free response of human beings in growth as the journey proceeds, we cannot go too far wrong. Solutions that dissolve the tension all in one direction or the other have not proved helpful over the long run. The most important thing for us to note here is that as we actually experience it, all Christian spiritual growth takes place within this vast narrative of sin, redemption, and glory.

As we have already seen, the Christian tradition has come to see this journey or growth in three successive stages, though, like St. Bonaventure and the Franciscan tradition, I shall treat them as recurring in a spiral cycle rather than as a simple ladder. In the Western tradition these stages are often called purgative, illuminative, and unitive, or the stages of the beginner, the proficient, and the perfect; but I prefer the Eastern Christian language of the cleansing of the royal image, transfiguration, and *theōsis* (being made god by participation in the triune life). Hence, the three sections of part 2, Converted Dust, Transfigured Dust, and Glorified Dust, which fall under the larger title of the book because being converted, transfigured, and glorified are all ways of experiencing ourselves as dust beloved by God.

The picture I propose is as follows: the spiritual life of any given Christian is determined by the interplay of two great narrative arcs or story lines: one is our own empirical history of creatures as dust, which can be studied by a wide variety of human and natural sciences. This is a kind of shore on which break the three great currents of the Spirit's mission, which, from the human side, can be called conversion, transfiguration, and glorification. The tides at any given point are determined by the confluence of the currents of the Spirit with the particular human shore on which they are breaking. Good discernment is thus a kind of intuitive table of the tides.

An additional aspect of self-transcendence is worth mentioning here: we have already seen that much of the current discussion derives from accounts given by David Tracy, especially in *The Analogical Imagination*.[43] Tracy (after some tidying up I have proposed) sees human self-transcendence as taking three essential forms, self-denial, self-fulfillment, and self-criticism.[a] My suggestion is that each of these is a kind of *style* that human self-transcendence takes as a resonance to one of the three great currents of the Spirit's mission. Tracy links each of these to a particular *mode* of theological understanding and discourse, proclamation, manifestation, and prophecy. As I spell out each of the currents in detail, we will be looking at how these modes and styles provide useful perspectives on the confluence of these currents with the human shores on which they break. The three great theological virtues of faith, love, and hope also characterize these three great currents in particular ways. It is important to recall, however, that the structure of the Spirit's mission is not threefold, but Trinitarian. This means that these three great movements and all their characteristics are not linearly successive but co-inherent, like the great Trinitarian *perichoresis* itself. The currents are con-current. The tide at any point is determined by all acting together, though usually one will seem to predominate at any given time.

By now it should be clear that I am writing from an unabashedly Christian point of view. It should also be clear that this book is not for generic spiritual seekers, except as they want to read something about the Christian Way to see if it might be what they have been looking for. I have tremendous respect for the spiritualities of the other great world faiths in their own integrity, but I can only write about the one I know and practice from the inside. Similarly, in my private practice as a spiritual director, I can only direct Christians; because that is the only Way I know anything about. It is not a matter of devaluing the others but of not being qualified in them. As you may have gathered, what I have little patience for is the shallow consumerist eclecticism that chooses a little from several different traditions and never undertakes the serious discipline of any.

This book then, is intended for converting and converted Christians, as an account of the journey on which we are engaged. A journey is called for, not to go somewhere else, but to be truly here as our proper selves, and it begins by turning

---

a Because of past abuse, "self-denial" is a term that needs to be used with care, to be developed in the chapters that follow. It does not mean suppression of one's true self, as we shall see. Tracy calls the third form "self-transcendence," but then goes on to admit that all three are actually forms of self-transcendence, without ever giving a proper name to the third form. For reasons that will become evident, I have proposed self-criticism as the name for this third form. See my "A Critical Note."

around. From the Latin word for turning around, we get our name for the start of the journey, conversion.

Notes

1. See now especially Nancey Murphy, *Bodies and Souls, or Spirited Bodies* for a Christian anthropology that is entirely physicalist, with helpful surveys of the philosophical and theological issues and literature. See also Owen C. Thomas and Ellen K. Wondra, *Introduction*, 135; Rahner's thought heads in this direction: "The Unity of Spirit and Matter in the Christian Understanding of Faith," *TI* 6:153–77.

2. A classic text in general systems theory is Ludwig von Bertalanffy, *General System Theory*. Its basic idea is that in organic, or "open," systems in particular, some properties emerge as properties in the system and do not derive as mere "sums" from properties of the components of the system. This allows for an analysis of purposive behavior without the need for appeal to occult or external forces. A whole book on creationism and intelligent design could be added here. Instead, see Catechism of Creation issued by the Episcopal Church's Committee on Faith, Science, and Technology (http://www.episcopalchurch.org/19021_58393_ENG_HTM.htm) and the intelligent discussion of the issues by John Polkinghorne and Arthur Peacocke, among others, in their several works. *Evolution and Emergence*, ed. Nancey Murphy and William Stoeger, S.J., provides a helpful account.

3. Samuele Bacchiocchi, *Immortality or Resurrection* is a thorough analysis from an Adventist perspective.

4. Nicholas Lash, *The Beginning and the End of "Religion,"* 164–82.

5. See Lash, *Beginning*, 132–49; Michel de Certeau, *Mystic Fable*. Much of this shift was traced in chapter 2 above.

6. There are more charitable and probably accurate ways of reading the later Schleiermacher; see Nicholas Lash, *Easter in Ordinary*, 120–29, and throughout.

7. Lash, *Easter in Ordinary*, 45–60.

8. See my "Christian Theology of Interfaith Dialogue."

9. Lash, *Easter in Ordinary*, 199–218.

10. Bernard Lonergan, *Method in Theology*, 238–40; Peter Hodgson, *Revisioning the Church*, 51–68, esp. 62–63, gives what I see as a critical realist account among what he calls *basileia*, *ekklēsia*, and the churches.

11. See John Polkinghorne, "Is Science Enough?" 12.

12. Polkinghorne, *The Faith of a Physicist*.

13. Classic texts include those by Pierre Teilhard de Chardin, whom I will discuss in the second tide. See also the previously cited works by Polkinghorne.

14. Polkinghorne, *Science and Creation*; this is the overall argument of the book.

15. *De Anima* 2.1–2 (McKeon, ed., 555–59).

16. Aquinas, *Summa Theologica*, I.75–76; Lonergan, *Method*, 95–96; Rahner, *Foundations*, 26–31; *Hearers of the Word*, 121–29.

17. See the previously cited works by Nancey Murphy.

18. Immanuel Kant, *Critique of Pure Reason*, A 106–B 158, 135–69; see also Calvin O. Schrag and David James Miller, "The Algebra of History: Merleau-Ponty and Foucault on the Rhetoric of the Person." On Kant, see Lash, *Easter in Ordinary*, 114–16.

19. Jean-Paul Sartre, *Being and Nothingness*, 363–430.

20. Sartre, *Being and Nothingness*, 615.

21. Tillich, *ST*, vol. 1; the concept is first introduced in the discussion of revelation, 106–57, and comes to the fore in the discussion of God, 163–289, esp. 235–41.

22. Augustine, *De Trinitate* 15.19; K. Tanner, *Jesus, Humanity and the Trinity*, 13–14, 53.

23. Barth, *The Epistle to the Romans*, 38–39, is the *locus classicus*. Compare Rahner, *Hearers of the Word*, 130–63.

24. Rahner, *Hearers*, chap. 8; See Tillich's great flow from the analysis of self-transcendence to the discussion of the "spiritual presence" in *ST* 3:86–134.

25. Bernard Lonergan is unique among theologians in accounting for devolution and decline as part of the life cycle, e.g., *Method* 52–55.

26. Bernard McGinn, "The Letter and the Spirit," 5–6; see Sandra Schneiders, "Spirituality as an Academic Discipline."

27. Lonergan, *Method*, 399–400; David Tracy, *Blessed Rage for Order*, 11, for example, and *The Analogical Imagination*, 429–38.

28. Rahner, "Concerning the Relationship of Nature and Grace," *TI* 1:297–317; idem, "The Eternal Significance of the Humanity of Jesus for our Relationship with God," *TI* 3:35–46, links the concept indelibly to the incarnation. Rahner's own clearest short statement of the concept and the issues it addresses is the section "III. The Existential: B. Theological," in *Sacramentum Mundi*, 2:306–7.

29. Lonergan, *Method*, 116, 243; Tracy, *Analogical Imagination*, 432. On all this and for what follows, see my "A Critical Note on Two Aspects of Self-Transcendence."

30. One can watch Rahner develop this so carefully in *Foundations of Christian Faith*, first in "Man as Transcendent Being," 31–35, then in "Man's Relation to His Transcendent Ground," 75–81, and then finally in the full-blown doctrine of the "supernatural existential" in chap. 4: "Man as the Event of God's Free and Forgiving Self-Communication," 116–38.

31. Mark McIntosh's critique of the purely anthropological approach is strikingly similar to the one just given; see *Mystical Theology*, 19–23.

32. Thomas and Wondra, *Introduction*, 100.

33. This is spelled out in detail in the definition of Chalcedon; see, for example, *BCP*, 864.

34. For an excellent analysis of this view of human being as defined by a *telos* it cannot fulfill by natural capacity but only by deifying grace, notably in Augustine, Martin Luther, and Henri de Lubac, see David S. Yeago, "Martin Luther on Grace, Law, and Moral Life," esp. 164–74.

35. This appears to have been Tillich's point of view.

36. Thomas and Wondra, *Introduction*, 111–13.

37. Simon Chan, *ST*, 59–63, and, to a lesser extent, Samuel Powell, *A Theology*, 88–92, and in the section on "the fallen world" in each chapter, provide a helpful critique.

38. See Rahner, "The Theological Concept of *Concupiscentia*," *TI* 1:347–82.

39. Martin Heidegger, *Being and Time*, 1.5.3–31, 179–82; 1.6.40, 228–35.

40. The most sensible account of this in my view is still C. S. Lewis's in *The Screwtape Letters*. See also Dorothy Marie England, *Satan Stalking*. Rollo May's account of the demonic in *Love and Will* is also instructive and will be discussed below, chap. 6.

41. See my "What a Friend We Have in Jesus," and "Justification," with Robert Jenson's reply to it.

42. See my "Christian Theology of Interfaith Dialogue."

43. See my earlier accounts of Tracy's concepts, including the "fix" to be described, in "A Critical note on Two Aspects of Self Transcendence," and "The Holy Spirit in Christian Spirituality."

PART TWO

The Tides of the Spirit

First Tidal Current:
Converted Dust

I. Conversion and Grace

5

Conversion and Early Grace

The time is fulfilled, and the kingdom of God is at hand; repent and believe
the gospel. —Mark 1:51

The First Signpost

The first signpost on the journey of human dust in the tides of the Holy Spirit is usually called conversion, an English word borrowed from Latin that means simply "to turn around." In this section we shall give the term greater depth and breadth than in many accounts, encompassing a doctrine of not one but three paradigmatic conversions, of three essential orientations in conversion, of four or five layers to any conversion, of the relationship between conversion and human dynamic and developmental psychology, and we shall develop the notion of the Christian life as one of constant conversion.

The best place to begin is with the first sort of conversion, the one most people think about when the word is used. This is a call, abrupt or gradual, *from* a previous life now experienced as sinful and defective, empty and meaningless, or badly distorted by oppression or abuse, *to* a new life as a disciple of Jesus Christ. This call comes through a variety of ways, from private reading of Scripture, one-on-one evangelization, the public preaching and worship of the church, or simply being raised in the community of faith in the midst of the struggle until at some point one chooses to claim that struggle as one's own. What is important is not so much the medium by which the call is conveyed as the recognition that the Holy Spirit is operating in all of the various media, and that in every case we are already dealing with corporate or communal experience and not merely something private. The Bible itself is already there because it has become the treasure of the Christian com-

71

munity and someone has bothered to translate, publish, purchase, and place it. So, even in what seems the most private of contexts—a lone individual being inspired by the Holy Spirit while reading the Scriptures in solitude—the Christian community is already involved. Conversion is never just a private matter.

Nor is it the beginning of the journey, let alone the end; it is only the first signpost that tells us the journey has actually begun. In that sense the journey of the spiritual life is like any ordinary journey in that it begins long before it "begins" and lasts long after it is over. A journey does not begin in one particular moment but goes through a number of stages, including noticing the possibility of a trip, deciding to go, planning the trip and taking necessary anticipatory measures such as buying tickets or prepping the car, making reservations, packing, closing up one's home, leaving home, getting in the car or other means of conveyance; then there is a magical sort of moment, different for every trip, when there is a kind of settling down into being "not at home" or even in the process of leaving it, but being *on* the trip. Conversion is like this last moment. It is the signpost that says, "Well, we've actually started this journey."

Prevenient Grace

Before we get to the first signpost, that magical moment of settling into a journey, of knowing we are committed, have crossed the Rubicon or whatever the line is for us, a lot has already happened. The decision to be a converted Christian, a disciple of Jesus, a member of the church, a follower of the Way, even when accompanied by a dramatic born-again experience, always has a long prologue. That prologue, from the standpoint of any conversion, is called prevenient grace, those gifts already given that make even the possibility of turning around a real one. It is called prevenient because it goes before, ahead of any decision or response on our part.[1] This is terribly important, because it corrects one horrible notion about God—that God is a nasty old moralistic tyrant who will not love or be gracious to us until we clean up our act. The Christian gospel is that Jesus died for us while we were yet sinners (Rom 5:8), and God has been gracious even a long time before that. In short, what we call the entire "economy of salvation" from creation through the covenant with Israel, through the Christ event, through the whole subsequent history of the church and the world to the moment we begin to notice is already filled with "grace" in two senses: the entire story is a story of God's graciousness in and toward creation, and indeed begins in the self-expression of God, the Fount of all Being in an Other, the Word/Wisdom, by the power of the Holy Spirit;[2] second, it is a story, from start to finish, of the mission of the Holy Spirit, from her first mysterious involvement in the generation of God's triadic unity to her own proper mission in the consecration and fulfillment of all things.[3] As I seek to tell the story here, most of the Spirit's activity in this first tidal current is in support of the Fount's proper mission, the things appropriated to the first person of the Trinity in the divine economy: creation and covenant. In Robert Jenson's theology, it is the Spirit who liberates the Fount to be self-expressed in an other (the Word/Wisdom), to make externally that which is not-God, to summon a people as God's own and give them the structures of community life suitable for their destiny as a priestly people.[4] In the context in which something has gone astray in that story, the Spirit, who was always the point of the great return of all creation back to the Fount, becomes the point, possibility, and call to *shuv* ("conversion" in Hebrew), to re-turn; that is the heart of repentance, healing, and liberation, the three essential forms of conversion, turning around as re-turning to the Fount from the point of the Spirit.[5] This shows again the foolishness of treating conversion as a private or merely interior affair. The whole history of the universe, from one's personal perspective, is setting the stage, establishing the community, providing the context, establishing the very possibility for our conversion. We are already and from the beginning beloved, precisely as the dust we are, along with all the rest of the dust, in a great dance by which that dust is beloved in its going forth and re-turning as a great tidal current of the Spirit in support of the eternal purposes and decrees of the Fount.[6]

Our whole life is also preparation, even those parts of it from which we may turn in disgust, fear, or rage at the time of conversion. Later in the treatment of this current we will look at some contemporary theories about how that works. We need to see that our conversion depends on several things. We must *notice* that we need conversion; we need some sense of what we are being converted *from*—called out of; we need some glimpse of what we are being called *to*, some sense, in short, of hope, or we would never get started; and some sense of *by* what or whom we are being converted, someone in whom we can have faith, someone to trust. We will be looking at each of these in more detail as the chapters about this current proceed, but what needs to be said here is the Christian message that these things are already gifts from the Great Lover, the Fount, by and in the Word/Wisdom, in the person of the Spirit, whose very essence is "gift."[7]

It is commonplace to point out that our very created being is gift. More crucial here is that all those preliminaries to conversion in our actual historical life are also gifts. This is a point the Reformers rightly insisted on—not even the beginnings of conversion can be credited to our account, as they are already gift, and thus movements of the Holy Spirit. The wounded human will is restored to a freedom in which it now has a role to play, but the fact that we wake up and notice; that we begin to experience some things as wrong, wicked, sinful, sick, oppressive, abusive; that we become ashamed, outraged, or sick and tired of being sick and tired; that we begin to glimpse a better way and a real possibility of being on it; that we have first meetings with a Beloved who will deliver and empower us for that way and accompany us on it—all these are already sheer gift. This "giftedness" is what, from our end of the stick, theology calls grace. From God's end, it is just called love, the proper name of the Holy Spirit, who is gift in person.[8] It is called "prevenient" because it comes before even my little toe starts to quiver into the right direction.

It is not just some wish of theologians to make things complicated that we have to pause here a moment. There are huge issues at stake in getting started properly, and none is bigger than recognizing that the start of the journey is God's gift and not my achievement. Indeed, in classical spiritual theologies there would, at this point, have been whole chapters of a treatise on grace, and I will be interspersing some of that as we go along. The truth is that even when we are in the early stages of paying attention, there is a real difference between experiencing grace and experiencing grace *as grace*.[9] We live in grace the way a fish lives in water, or the way we live in air. In fact, that is the power behind the metaphor that our very being as animated beings, as beings who have in them the breath of life, is already a gift of the Holy Spirit. So we do not usually notice grace *as* grace anymore than we notice our breathing unless something causes us to stop and pay attention. Worse, one of the chief mechanisms of sin is denial, which in this case means appropriating as our own properties or achievements what really is gift.

The tradition of Christian theology has done some not-so-helpful things with this notion of giftedness or grace. One is to treat it as something like silly putty, as if it were a quasi substance coming between God and us and poured into us like water (the Catholic version); another is to treat it as a mere judicial decree with little or no real impact on our concrete lives (the Protestant version). Karl Rahner has been in the forefront of theologians recently saying this idea has got to go. Grace is just another name for God at work, for the presence and work of the Holy Spirit in our lives. Insofar as "grace" refers to God's gracious loving of us, no matter what, it is what the tradition has called "uncreated grace"; its impact on us is called "created grace." Insofar as "grace" refers to the constant presence and indwelling of the Holy Spirit in our lives, it is called "habitual grace"; when we pay attention to concrete particular ways in which that presence is embodied and made available and effective for us, it is called "actual grace." But the point is it is all grace, and all grace is just a way of talking about God's loving presence to and in us in concrete dimensions of our lives.[10]

Our perceptions of these early movements of grace in our lives can have both positive and negative aspects from our point of view, and these can occur and recur in any order in individual cases. On the positive side are the joy in being alive, human experiences of love and community, and the early sense of the call to self-transcendence (that we put under the category of "human spiritedness" in the previous chapter on dust), and any sense of our own growth and accomplishment. This is already all grace, as we have seen, though we may not as yet be experiencing it *as* grace.

On what we usually see as the negative side are perceptions of our own shortcomings as sin, including self-hatred, and the beginnings of some understanding of how that is linked to something tragically wrong with the whole human world, including forces that enslave or abuse us. But this is also grace, since experiencing something *as* sin already requires grace.[a] Things are so bad we cannot even see they are bad except in the light of grace; so to begin to say how bad they are is, strangely enough, one moment in starting the journey to what is good; and the awakening of our conscience or the birth of hope in our despair is already a gift of God's love, and

---

a. I am going to use the word "sin" to cover the whole package of "wrongness" I have been describing, including not only our personal shortcomings but also those forces of evil that enslave and abuse human beings. See further, in the next chapter, the section "Evil for Which We Did Not Volunteer."

a call primarily to faith, the outcome of conversion, as we decide to trust in God's goodness, promises, and fidelity.

Recognizing this realm of prevenient grace already helps us understand some of the muddle about the once-born, in whom the turning to God is a gradual process, the twice-born, who experience a sudden irruptive deliverance and consolation, often highly emotional, and, what I believe is actually most typical, us, the many-born, who have a life characterized by a series of sharp turning points. Even the dramatically twice-born do not have their conversion drop down into no context. A lot has already been going on without their noticing it. And even the once-born have moments of awareness and decision. The many-born have these moments endlessly. It is not a difference in the quality of God's habitual grace that makes for these distinctions but only the way actual grace is shaped in relationship to a particular personality and life history. In terms of our tidal metaphor, the current of the Spirit is constant, but the human shore on which it breaks is complex and varied.

Conversion, then, is a response to prevenient grace. It requires noticing, healthy shame, hope, healing, empowerment, and falling in love. All are gifts; all are early experiences of being beloved even as sinful dust, as beings with a tragic and flawed existence but called forward into self-transcendence by some sense of an abiding true essence as gift. As previously noted, there are three movements or moments or aspects to this conversion that are traditionally studied: Conversion *from* (noticing and shame, pain, or rage), conversion *to* (hope for and growth in a new way of life), and conversion *by* (the experience of being empowered and gifted by an other). In particular life histories of conversion, these three aspects can predominate in any order. Some are first disgusted with their sins, struggle to lead a moral life, and ultimately come to Christ for forgiveness and empowerment in that battle; others, locked in false and toxic shame by abuse or neglect, may be drawn to a hopeful trust in God's compassion and faithfulness as vindicator; others may be initially attracted by virtue or the promise of a new life as a ray of hope in a desperate existence; still others are first taken with the person of Jesus and only later begin to see the depths of their own implication in, or victimization by, wickedness. Some conversions do not so much involve choosing grace instead of something "bad" as choosing the better over the good.[11] All are legitimate paths, shaped in accordance with the needs of a particular life history by the Holy Spirit. In the next few chapters, we will look at these three aspects in more detail, celebrating the presence and work of Jesus and the Holy Spirit in each. We shall do so in the classical order, with the cautionary note just taken that it can occur in a different cyclical pattern.

Notes

1. The concept of prevenient grace has a long history in the tradition. See, for example, what is now the collect for Proper 23, *BCP*, 234–45, but was formerly for the Seventeenth Sunday after Trinity Sunday, the notion that grace "prevents" or precedes us. Among Protestant traditions, the Wesleyan has placed the most emphasis on this concept; see Herbert McGonigle, *John Wesley's Doctrine of Prevenient Grace.*

2. All the recent Trinitarian theologies surveyed earlier make this point about creation being grounded in the Trinitarian processions, but it was perhaps made most poignantly in contemporary times by Karl Rahner, *Nature and Grace*.

3. Kilian McDonnell, *Other Hand of God*, Eugene Rogers, *After the Spirit*, Elizabeth Johnson, *She Who Is*, give alternative but compatible accounts of this sweep.

4. Robert Jenson, *ST* 1:161.

5. McDonnell, *Other Hand*, 99–107, and throughout.

6. The great classical portrayal of this current is, of course, the *exitus/reditus* (going forth and returning) scheme of the *Summa Theologica* of Thomas Aquinas. See Michael J. Buckley, *Denying and Disclosing God*, 65.

7. Although many of these notions are again current, their classic expression is by Augustine, *De Trinitate* XV.

8. Again, the *locus classicus* is Augustine, *De Trinitate* XV.

9. Nicholas Lash, *Easter in Ordinary*, 248–51; idem, *The Beginning and the End of "Religion,"* 166. See also Rahner, "Concerning the Relationship between Nature and Grace," *TI* 1:300; idem, "The Experience of Grace," *TI* 3:86–89.

10. Rahner, "Nature and Grace," *TI* 4:166–84. For a superb treatment of grace as the immediate presence of the Trinitarian God, see the classic by Piet Fransen, S.J., *The New Life of Grace*, esp. 24–57. Fransen also makes excellent connections to other themes we consider here, including humanism (342), matter (345), and psychology (347ff.).

11. Philip Sheldrake, *Befriending Our Desires*, 119.

6

Conversion *From*

Judgment, Repentance, and Grace

The earliest of the Gospels, Mark, begins with a double message of repentance—first from John the Baptist and then, following his own Baptism and temptation, from Jesus, "The time is fulfilled, and the kingdom of God is at hand; repent and believe the gospel" (Mark 1:15). The word *metanoia* in Greek, from which (via Latin) "repentance" comes, actually means to stand up and turn around. In the Greek context, it means a change of mind. The Hebrew word it usually translates, *shuv,* means to return (back to the covenant and the covenant community) and means mostly a change of heart. Because "repentance" has acquired so many overtones of morbid self-loathing by our time, "conversion," which means literally to turn around, may be better, even though the American revivalist tradition has put a lot of sediment on that word, too. Without suggesting that any of the more dramatic or sudden experiences of conversion are inauthentic, I do wish to use "conversion" throughout in a more general sense of being turned around, however rapidly or slowly, however dramatically or quietly.

It is important to notice that both the Baptizer and Jesus present the whole package of conversion at once, as it were. While both call the people to turn around and repent, John then invites them to a Baptism for the forgiveness of their sins, and the vision of one who will come after and baptize with the Holy Spirit. Jesus' first words are, "The time is fulfilled, and the kingdom of God is at hand; repent, and believe in the good news." There is an equal weight given to announcing what we are converted *to* as is given to calling attention to what we are converted *from.* Indeed, Mark identifies this as the gospel of God (1:15).

Accounts of conversion usually begin by discussing what we are converted *from,* because conversion is a turning around, and when we begin to turn, what we usually see first is what we are called to leave behind. I say "usually" because there are often other starting points. But we are able to see what we turn from in its true colors, and really for the first time, only because another possibility has appeared that gives us something to turn *toward.* More on that later. This new reality, the kingdom, reign, or commonwealth of God, not only gives us a new possibility, which is now present (at hand—the time is fulfilled), which makes actual turning possible; it also, and at a deeper level, casts a light on our current existence, showing us for the first time what it and we are really like. We are converted *to* something that allows us to see the truth of what we are converted *from*. Another primary aspect of the experience is that we find ourselves being turned *by* someone or something. In fact, by the time we begin to notice, all three of these aspects are in play—we find ourselves being turned by someone or something, from something, to something else. Traditional Catholic spiritual theologies did not deal much with this phenomenon, since they began after the commandments of obligation had already been dealt with in moral theology and the economy of salvation in dogmatic theology. Recent Protestant authors have rightly pointed out that this creates a distortion in our sense of the spiritual life, since it fails to take seriously the struggle with sin and evil, not only at the start of this conversion but as part of the daily reality of the spiritual life in our entire earthly existence.[1]

Until that moment when grace illuminates our current existence, we have not known sin.[a] We may have known pain, misfortune, error, disease, bad luck, all kinds of negative things, even very wicked ones. But these can be seen as *sin* only in the light of a Holiness that calls us to something else.[2] That is what Paul means when he says he had not known sin until the law appeared (Rom 7:7).[3] It does not mean it gave him a whole new list of delightfully wicked things to try out! Torah (or any attempt at discipline as a response to a call to be something better) enables us to see our wrongdoings (or the wrongs done to us) as *sin* for the first time, that is, as offenses against a personal Holiness who is the ground of our very being as animated and spirited dust and also the Heart of the universe.

That's what the real meaning of that badly misunderstood concept, the judgment of God, is really about. It is not about a fierce old tyrant writing down even the smallest faults for ample future retribution. Many classical spiritual theologies still operate on that metaphor, but it just isn't so. As good news, judgment is about the first rays of the light of divine glory (righteousness, justice, and holiness) appearing in our lives and showing us for the first time the truth about those lives. Judgment is not so much designed to get us to be good from fear of punishment as it is a wake-up call. "Wake up! Smell the coffee! Get a life." Only in this case, of course, the suggested "coffee" and "life" are offered at the same instant as the exclamation, in the sacraments. I find it very interesting that this illumination is the experience of judgment most often reported by those who have recovered from a near-death experience, though I do not make as much of that as a mystical experience as some.[4] Many such people report finding themselves in the presence of a perfectly benign being of light in whose presence they undergo a review of their entire lives. The context is not a threat of punishment but simply seeing the truth about everything with no room left for denial, equivocation, minimizing, or making excuses. What is

---

a It may be because of my own false consciousness as a "white person," but I do not know how to write about this without the metaphor of darkness and light. I can say it refers only to the common experience of day and night and has nothing at all to do with darker or lighter complexions, as African friends have reminded me.

even more interesting, this is how Jesus functions as "judge" in the Gospel of John. He just shows up here and there and things get sorted out, revealed for what they truly are, whether those present like it or not.[5]

Until this judgment comes we are in a realm of destruction and despair without even knowing it. Judgment is not bad news but the beginning of good news. That is why Amos teaches us it is not divine judgment we should fear, but a famine of the hearing of the Word of God's judgment (8:11). Among the theologians of our time, none has seen this more powerfully than Karl Barth, in his concept of God's word as *Ja und Nein*, yes and no.[6] God speaks one Word, and that Word is pure yes to human being (2 Cor 1:19). But our first experience of it is as a no because, as a yes to who we truly are and are called to be, it must first be perceived by us as a no to what we have allowed ourselves to become or what others have made of us, indeed, a no to everything that distorts human existence. From God's side, the word of judgment is all yes. It is not first judgment as no and *then* grace as yes—this is very, very, important. Judgment in this sense—the Word that makes us hear, the Light that makes us see—is not merely the beginning of graciousness but the very presence of the Gracious One, God the Holy Spirit, to and for us in our historical existence. For us in our current condition, to be out from under judgment would be to be outside the presence of God. The name for that is hell, or even worse.

This Word is not addressed to us alone. The light does not shine on us in solitude but in context. It illuminates the whole swamp in whose quicksand we are stuck. It reveals the merely human city as the City of Destruction, bordered by the Slough of Despond, as Bunyan portrayed it in *The Pilgrim's Progress*. This can be most clearly seen in one of the great conversions in the history of Israel—that of Isaiah. When he is first confronted by the personal appearance of the Holy One (note again that grace precedes judgment) he falls on his face and cries out not only "I am a man of unclean lips" but also "and I dwell among a people of unclean lips" (Isa 6:5). There is a crucial balance to notice here. It is a mistake for us to perceive this judgment as on us alone, as if we were the only or worst of sinners, and all the sins are our private affair. The same "yes-heard-as-no" is being spoken to our entire context as to us, and with the same results. Many of the "sins" we are mired in are social or institutional in their nature, and we can never get free until we see that. The even worse, and I am afraid more common, mistake, however, especially as we begin to turn away, is for us to fall into self-righteousness and begin to condemn the sin we see around us without remembering how deeply and inextricably *we* are implicated in it. Too many prophets run around without Isaiah's grasp of the truth—my personal sin and the sinfulness of the context in which I dwell are bound together with chains of steel. And the one cannot be delivered without impact on the other.

In short, when we have begun to repent, we have been addressed by the Word of God (which I believe is identical to the Wisdom of God, Logos and Sophia, masculine and feminine) and have begun to respond to it. Both our hearing of the Word and the possibility of our response are works of the Holy Spirit, the mediation of that of which the Word/Wisdom is mediator.[7] What is therefore being born in us by God's gracious presence, God the Holy Spirit, is the virtue of *faith*, the initial positive response to that Word/Wisdom, the beginning of a decision to believe in it and trust in it, and then to live faithfully in its light, our fidelity being an echo in us of God's own faithfulness, *ḥesed*, steadfast love.[8] Faith is usually born in shame, not toxic shame but the healthy shame that means that we both see the reality of our situation and acknowledge the validity of the claim being made upon us. Such shame is the sign we have begun to notice, the first recognition by dust that it is beloved.[9] This is the experience of perhaps the majority, those who will experience conversion primarily in the form of repentance. Those who have suffered demonic disease or abuse and trauma are more likely to awaken to a sense of their own pain and will experience conversion primarily as healing; those who suffer from injustice and oppression may awaken to their own sense of outrage and will experience conversion primarily as liberation. In these latter two forms, especially for those immersed in toxic shame, the first hint of being beloved may need to be an initial hearing of the yes to them, which is then a no to that which damages or enslaves them. They may first need hope in God's abiding compassion and unconditional love as a no to the blasphemy of self-hatred that has been foisted on them. But in each of the three forms, faith is born as grace helps us to notice that about which we had previously been in denial.

But notice exactly what? As long as it is only our sins, even taking in our entire context in the word "our," we have only gotten started. It is indeed usual at this point in classical spiritualities to discuss the traditional list of vices or cardinal sins. I am going to postpone that for a later chapter on the moral struggle, and, in any case, the detailed description of that belongs to an allied but different field, namely, moral theology. For spiritual theology, however, the issue is not the details about what is right and wrong in particular circumstances but the impact on the spiritual lives of persons as they are called into this struggle for the first time. At this level, the issue is not so much sins as sinfulness, my discovery that it is not simply that I do individual bad things to myself, to others, to creation itself, but that I am stuck in a mire that does not really allow me to do anything else, despite a sense of a true goodness of my being (though this is lacking and needs awakening in some of the traumatized), and that somehow I am implicated in that stuckness, even though it almost seems I just happened to be there and did not volunteer for it, which is sometimes nearer the truth. I am not only doing what I should not, I am not being who I truly am, and that is *both* because I have chosen not to *and* because I never had a chance. In fact, the mystery of the givenness of sinfulness, balanced by my implication or at least involvement in it, exactly parallels the mystery of my subsequent deliverance as solely at God's initiative, and yet also impacted by my response, which is itself prepared for by grace but is nevertheless my free response.

The World, the Flesh, and the Devil

The objective side of what we are called to turn from was classically referred to in the baptismal renunciations as "the world, the flesh, and the devil."[10] In the baptismal liturgies of the Eastern church this is very dramatic, as the sponsors literally spit at what is being renounced and physically turn from it.[11] Even though newer liturgies have often summarized these as "Satan and the spiritual forces of wickedness that rebel against God, the evil powers of this world which corrupt and destroy the creatures of God, all sinful desires that draw you from the love of God,"[12] we still need a look at the traditional terms because they have so deeply shaped much of our inherited spirituality.

In our time we must take special care with the world and the flesh, because new knowledge, including new theological knowledge, does not allow us any longer to see as true Christian spirituality a program of world rejection or flight from our very nature as flesh, as animated dust. Jesus came to die for the whole world (1 John 3) because of God's love for it, and he did so precisely in the flesh. That is where our salvation and healing were worked out and are now available—in the flesh and in the world, informed by God's Wisdom and enlightened by God's Word. A true wisdom of the flesh, a true worldly wisdom, is thus God's Wisdom. This is a necessary corollary of the doctrine of creation: the world God made is good, and the fleshly existence given human beings is also good. Salvation is not to be found in flight from world and flesh.

Further, we now know that the language of Stoic ethics, which was culturally at hand for the New Testament authors, led to some distortion of the gospel in the direction of a dualism expressed as a war between spirit and flesh—a version of what it means to be human that is not found in the Hebrew Scriptures.[13] This infected all other Hellenistic thought, including neo-Platonism and a series of mystery religions, notably the Manichaeism Augustine left behind but that leaks into Western Christianity through every seam.[a] In modern thought this was intensified by Cartesian dualism until, as we saw in the chapter 2, we ended up with the picture of a little ego-person, free in itself but locked in the head of a mechanical body governed by determinate causes and random chance only. Out of this grew spiritualities where spirit versus flesh and world became a question of mind over matter, and then of the cultivation of paranormal, antimaterialistic occult abilities. And, as we have seen, in come roaring all the howling bulls of Bashan.[14] From the perspective we are adopting here, which rejects this dualism, we can see that all sins with which *we* are concerned (angels may be another matter) are "sins of the flesh" because they are committed by beings of flesh and blood. At the same time, they are "spiritual" sins, because only flesh that is animated and spirited can *sin* as opposed to just making mistakes.

Finally, we are in the process of learning a hard truth. It is neither fair to them nor helpful to us to blame other persons or things that arouse desires, which in us are corrupt, for our consequent sinfulness. The most important place we are learning this is in the discovery of how much misogyny is the result of men blaming women for the sexual feelings aroused in themselves in the presence of women they find attractive. Well, the same is true of the flesh and the world; there are things there that do tempt us, but the problem is in the corruption of our desires not in

---

a Manichaeism was a thoroughly dualistic Persian religion of the third century C.E., with Christian roots. See *WDCS* 256–57.

the objects or persons themselves (though some of them are tainted by their own sinfulness, of course, and the tradition that the whole world is wounded by human sin cannot be ignored).[15]

Flesh

The classical name for this corruption or perversion (literally "turning aside" from their proper object) of our bodily desires is the much misunderstood word "concupiscence." It has been badly mistranslated into English as "lust" and then falsely narrowed to sexual desire, even appropriate desire for a legitimate beloved. Karl Rahner, among the theologians of our time, has been most helpful on this subject, pointing out that concupiscence is a resistance to any change. It not only resists the grace of conversion and sanctification (in which case it is sinful); it also resists change in the direction of evil and thus places a limit on it. It is, in short, a kind of inertia of our givenness, which will do pretty well as a definition of "flesh" for our purposes, especially in its more negative aspect.[16] As we begin to notice the mire in which we are stuck, part of what we see is our own self-indulgence, a tendency to pursue desires for their own sake and not for either health or salvation. From this flow all the "sins of the flesh," such as lust in the sense of cherished sexual desire for inappropriate or illegitimate partners, gluttony—the desire for more food than is good for us, including excess in drink—and so on. What we can now see is that this is not only a violation of ethical principles or God's law, a turning away from the flesh as the place of our salvation and healing; it is a denial of the flesh's very own wisdom. Smoking may be the best and most widespread example. It is not bad because it is immoral, and it is certainly not pleasure that makes it immoral; it is immoral because it is bad (for us). One of the sad things is that there is, in the constitution of the flesh of many, a mechanism by which self-indulgence becomes addictive.[17] We shall discuss this below under the "devil" but should note that the possibility is there for everyone. We can also recognize that inappropriate self-denial that brings harm to our embodied selves is also a kind of concupiscence, in that it is the pursuit of goals in opposition to the flesh and its wisdom as the place of our healing and salvation by God's grace. We have learned to recognize that there are obsessive-compulsive disorders on this denial side of the equation as well, many of which seem particularly to victimize young women, especially eating disorders and self-mutilation.[a] Even the classical tradition recognized this as a problem, called scrupulosity, an excessive fear of breaking even the smallest rules or indulging in even the smallest pleasures, which reveals a distrust of God's goodness, grace, and mercy, or an asceticism that has lost its purpose as self-discipline and become a perverse act of self-hatred.

What is called for is a balanced self-discipline, a rule of life where we make the rules for ourselves in response to God's grace; in which we seek to uncover

---

a Some forms of self-mutilation do not fit the pattern of scrupulosity, even gone amuck, but are desperate efforts to express or stop even deeper pain.

concupiscence in its merely resistive form, as well as its more explicitly sinful mani-festations, in order to rediscover our embodied lives as the arenas of God's grace. Joy and pleasure in appropriately fulfilled desires are an important part of such a discipline, as is adequate rest, recreation, leisure, and so forth. The details of what is right and wrong, appropriate and inappropriate, are better left to moral theolo-gians and ethicists, and to the application of Christian principles in specific cases by Christians and their counselors. Discernment is the most important gift of the Spirit for these ministries.[18] We need to remember in spiritual theology that it was in the flesh of Jesus that health and salvation were accomplished for all, and it is in our flesh, our embodied historical lives, that this health and salvation must be actualized for and in us, indeed that the Holy Spirit indwells us *bodily*, linking our flesh to the crucified, risen, and now glorified flesh of Jesus as our primary path to God.[19]

World

"The world" poses a similar dilemma. As the planet or the larger universe, as God's creation, the world is created good and is the arena, the historical stage-set-ting, as it were, of the drama of salvation (called technically the divine economy). It is not simply *created* good; it is also, by grace, indwelt by God as God's house in which God tabernacles with people, and it continues to be governed by God's will or providence, to use the biblical words. On both counts, the world is sacred, not in and of itself but as sacramental, as signifying and embodying God's gracious presence in it. Like the flesh, it has its own appropriate wisdom, and, like the flesh, it is the only possible place for our healing and salvation. It is, in short, the place where the reign and commonwealth of God's righteousness, justice, peace and love are being established in covenant history. As such, it includes all the institutions of human sociability, politics, enterprise, and culture as well as the natural world. There is no "otherworldly" or, in our modern sense, "supernatural"[20] place where that can happen. For these reasons, a spirituality that is world rejecting is not deeply Christian. God so loved the *world*. . . . [21]

But the same St. John and St. Paul use "world" in a different sense, meaning the powers and principalities of this world as fallen existence, not merely indiffer-ent to the reign and commonwealth of God but actually organized in opposition to it, knowingly or unknowingly. This latter is the actual condition of the world as we experience it, though the deeper wisdom and beauty of the original created grace show through glimpses that can embarrass our fallenness. Perhaps our chief expe-rience of it is in what we have come to call "systemic" or "institutionalized" evil, the ways in which society and culture have organized themselves not as means to the coming of the reign and commonwealth of God and the care for all, especially the poor, but as instruments for the satisfaction of the concupiscence of a powerful few at the expense of the oppression of the many poor. These structures tend to take on a life of their own and may continue to wreak havoc even when they no longer serve the needs of the powerful few. Concupiscence as personal resistance has a counterpart in institutional inertia: the world in the positive sense is polluted and desecrated. This social evil is particularly confusing in a culture like ours where religion and morals have been so privatized. People do not understand that even though they have no conscious racist or sexist feelings or intentions themselves, they are still responsible for their participation in racist and sexist (or classist—the whole sad litany) social institutions and in benefiting from them. It is one reason so many personally "righteous" people get upset when the church begins preaching about the social and political arena.

No theologian has shown more powerfully than John Wesley the links between personal and social sin, on the one hand, and the not only desirable but even inevitable link between personal and social holiness on the other. And he recognized the principal social institutions by which this relationship impacts the spiritual lives of individuals—money and glory.[22] The classical sins of avarice and vainglory are essentially social in their nature. The sin of avarice or greed is the desire to accumulate wealth and luxury for its own sake and at the expense of others. Vainglory is the same, and closely related to greed, but focused on social standing and reputation, often desired when we have done nothing to deserve it. In capitalist society the two are inextricably linked.

Here again, a balance is called for. The production of economic goods for the "common-wealth," that total store of goods and services that forms the foundation of the quality of material life for all, is good, and it can be part of building up the reign of God in its social dimension as divine commonwealth. The same is true of the desire to offer gifts of leadership and influence and have them recognized for effectiveness. It is no sin either to seek to have sufficient wealth and recognized influence to provide for our own care and that of our "dependents," or to fund and carry out our mission and life work. The problem arises when we pursue wealth and glory for ego-gratification, self-indulgence, and at the expense of others. On the other side, a way of being in the world that falls into quietism, rejects worldly occupation and action for the sake of God's reign, colludes in one's own victimization or indulges in a false self-deprecation that denies one's gifts and talents for the building up of the "common-wealth" of God's reign, is equally sinful. Taking myself and others as if we were *mere* dust and not also beloved (animated and spirited by relationship to the Holy Spirit) is sinful; but so is the heresy of *angelism*, treating human beings as if we were not flesh and blood, dust of this world, finite, mortal, but instead otherworldly beings of pure spirit somehow trapped here. This is Manichaeism at its worst.[23]

It is not, then, the world and the flesh that are sinful but our relationship to them. What is to be renounced is not flesh and world as God created them but our idolatrous being in and toward them. It is the world taken by us as apart from God's reign and the commonwealth of God's people that must be renounced, not the world itself. It is flesh as something other than the place of our healing and salvation that must be renounced, not flesh as God created us and other animals in it, and in which, in person, God the Word/Wisdom redeemed us. In that sense, both wallowing in the corruption of our own desires for a world and flesh we take in an idolatrous way *and* a rejection of world and flesh as if they were responsible for our corruption and sin are equally wrong. This means all the traditional catalogues of temptations and custodies, speaking as if the problem were in the objects of desire, are no longer helpful. As Pogo said, "We have met the enemy, and he is us."[24]

Devil

Well, almost. The devil is another matter. Here, the chief problem is most people no longer believe in him, and those who do make him far too powerful, falling nearly into yet another dualism, Zoroastrianism, in which the good and evil gods are coequal and coeternal.[25] There is a sense in which it is not crucial just how literally one takes the Satan myth, as long as one takes a realistic attitude toward the demonic reality to which the myth refers. This is the widespread human experience that beyond all individual human evil, beyond even the multiplication of that evil by our common collusion in social and institutional evil, there is a remainder of wickedness and perverseness of which we must take some account. Phenomenologically, we need to account for the wickedness, ubiquity, and persistence of evil, and to many of us human error does not seem a strong enough explanation on its own. There is an experience of not only being the victim of our own bad choices and of social institutions that recommend and support those bad choices but also of being actively *assaulted*. There is an experience of a resistance to our best intentions beyond anything even the deepest self- and social-analysis can illuminate (Romans 7 and 8). There is an experience of being in the grip of forces before which we are powerless and from which we need deliverance even to attempt the battle, a need for healing and liberation as out of reach as the ideals for which we strive.

Here is the abiding tragedy of human existence as we know it. When I was in seminary in the waning years of the 1960s, at what was then the Episcopal Theological School in Cambridge, Massachusetts, the great Swedish New Testament scholar at Harvard Divinity School (later dean and then bishop of Uppsala), Krister Stendahl, came to give our Ash Wednesday quiet day in 1967. He began by observing that in the traditional lectionary for Lent (the new lectionaries had not yet appeared) all the Gospels for the early Sundays were exorcisms. "What are we to make of this in our time?" he asked, then replying, "We must begin with this: we have not begun to grow up as Christians until we realize that most of the evil in this world is done by good people, with good intentions, earnestly trying to do good." I have never forgotten that. It is true despite the existence of some who deliberately set out to do evil. This experience of deep and seemingly unhealable tragic perverseness in humanity, from which no one escapes, this sense of being assaulted, enslaved, sometimes even possessed, requires some explanation.

The stories of later Judaism that introduced the concept of Satan, influenced by Persian Zoroastrianism and enhanced by later Christian apocalyptic writings, present him as a fallen angel; "Satan" refers to his role as the accuser of the faithful, the exact opposite of the Holy Spirit, who is our advocate. Once he was the archangel whose name we know not because it has been stricken from the book of heaven but whose job description was Lucifer—light bearer; we know the traditional stories about him only too well. This rebel angel who has been defeated by the angelic hosts commanded by the Word/Wisdom/Lamb and captained by the archangel Michael, defeated, and thrown out of heaven, has nevertheless been given power for a time in this world; this is the mythic answer. Of course, most of us cannot avoiding reading this myth through the lens of Milton's *Paradise Lost* and our tendency since the nineteenth century to read Satan as a Byronic hero.[26] Or we may also be influenced by the Faust legend. I am not concerned here with the overall theological adequacy of this myth as an explanation for the origins of evil. Here, our task is to delineate those aspects of the spiritual life of human beings the myth illuminates, however we take it.

First, then, there is the experience of being in the grips of what Rollo May calls the "daemonic" to distinguish it from the properly demonic.[27] The *daemonic* is any force stronger than we are that thwarts our proper growth. The *demonic* as a concept adds an element of personal malice to that force. We simply find ourselves often in the grip of natural or human forces we experience as destructive. These are very much related to the "principalities and powers" mentioned above and were usually called "elemental spirits" in the tradition. In and of themselves, they are morally neutral but may be highly destructive to us in certain circumstances. Even though these forces are not explicitly evil, we may require deliverance from them, by human, and where that fails, divine intervention. While John Polkinghorne and A. R. Peacocke have shown there is nothing in modern science to preclude God's freedom to act in this way, we must have a care here.[28] Not all who ask for deliverance get it, and in the end we all die from something. None of which makes any sense taken in isolation and out of context. Within the overall covenant history and ultimate eschatological hope, however, we can have more confidence that somehow even at this level in the end "all manner of thing shall be well." We should note that the Lady Julian of Norwich, the great fourteenth-century English anchoress and mystic who said this, was not a blind optimist by any stretch. It comes as a cry of faith and hope in a very serious section on the horrendous consequences and unavoidability of sin. "Sin is behovely, nevertheless all shall be well. . . ."[29]

On the individual front, many people experience these daemonic powers in the form of addictive and obsessive-compulsive disease. In such cases, the struggle of the individual will against the disorder is futile. This is one among many examples of a need for conversion in which healing and liberation predominate over repentance as usually understood. The recovery of health begins with admitting we are powerless over such forces but can rely on the grace of God and the companionship of fellow sufferers to restore our freedom and health. Gerald May has gone so far as to call addictive disease the "sacred illness of our time."[30] These are not private diseases, however, but "family illnesses," in that whole families become dysfunctional through sharing in the habits of mental mismanagement and delusion of the primary patient. This is the phenomenon known as codependency. Particularly when whole industries grow up profiting from the sale of the addicting substances, the result is a public health problem, not just a private one, and a whole culture can become addictive/codependent. There was a time, indeed, when it appeared the

Western democracies were actively addicted to weapons of mass destruction, an addiction now being taken up by some developing powers.

As noted above, perhaps the primary experience most people have of an evil force greater than they are is an encounter with institutionalized social evil. Individual good will is powerless over such structures, and band-aid approaches that salve individual victims and the consciences of privileged but sensitive individuals are not enough. As Karl Marx said, "Christian Socialism is but the holy water with which the priest consecrates the heart-burnings of the aristocrat."[31] I am among those who hope that is not, in the end, true, but it is true enough to remind us that relief of symptoms that does not go on to a revolutionary address to root causes will not suffice. But neither will mere human revolutions, as the results of too many of them have revealed. Reinhold Niebuhr saw clearly the tendency of well-intentioned revolutionaries to substitute their own evil for that of the system they sought to replace.[32] The social demon is not easily exorcised even by revolutionary violence. As G. W. F. Hegel saw in his analysis of the French Revolution, Absolute Freedom brings Robbespierre and the Terror, and finally Napoleon.[33] The clearest voices in our time have been Mahatma Gandhi and Martin Luther King, Jr., who have shown that with prophecy, the power of the Holy Spirit, and a commitment to real non-violence (including love of the opponent), a start can be made. And as Mother Teresa showed, it is better to apply band-aids than to do nothing at all—indeed, if you do your band-aids persistently and publicly enough, the powers that be may begin to quiver a bit at the roots.

Second, even allowing for the immensity of social evil, there is a kind of personal malice and twistedness to the evil we experience for which we must account. This wicked little remainder comes in three apparently opposite but actually intimately related forms: grandiosity, perversity, and banality. The grandiose side is most easily noticed in reference to the hard truth Stendahl pointed out—the evil done by "good people." As Ignatius Loyola taught, Satan was originally the angel of light, and when he seeks to disrupt "good people," that is how he appears. Even though his angel of light costume is in tatters and ruin, it is still enough to impress mortals. It usually appears as a kind of "sweet reason," suggesting to us that the nobility of our higher aims allows us to transcend ordinary standards of common decency and goodness and the hard job of analyzing means, ends, due proportion, and unintended consequences.[34] In short, it invites us to that false kind of heroism that infects the music of Richard Wagner (rendering it, I believe, bad for us, however gorgeous it may be) and has produced many of the horrors of the twentieth century. We miss the real horror of our time if we fail to recognize the initially positive values behind both Communism and National Socialism, a failure that is dangerous because it keeps us from seeing the same corrupting forces at work in democratic capitalism and its foreign adventures. At the more individual level, this grandiosity is behind the charismatic spiritual leaders who turn out to be sexual predators or massive embezzlers, believing their exceptional spiritual status makes such behavior legitimate for them. It shows up in the way innocent people can get sucked into the dark side of the occult through a desire to do good with white magic. It is there whenever we come to believe that the magnificence of a project of ours, however great or small, justifies cutting ethical corners. It is wishing to cast the splinter out of our neighbor's eye while ignoring the log in our own. It is even there in the ways our noble self-sacrifices turn into manipulative martyrdom and self-abuse. In our time, the structure that most keeps it in place is the rhetoric of ideological conflict.[35] It may be the most pervasive and dangerous of all the demonic manifestations, because it appeals so strongly to our nobler side.

In the end, of course, evil is never truly noble. Excessive patriotism ends in gas ovens and A-bombs. White magic and pseudo-Christian occultism lead too easily to ritual abuse. Chivalry maintains a sexism and classism that brings Camelot down. Well-intentioned revolutions lead to terror, nobility to riding roughshod over the crops and lives of peasants. In the end, as C. S. Lewis portrayed so powerfully in *Perelandra*,[36] all the seeming beauty and nobility of evil is a sham. It has no creativity of its own. It can only counterfeit and pervert what true goodness has created, and in the end it is reduced to pulling the legs off of frogs and the wings off of butterflies. It can only *spoil* goodness, truth, and beauty. Often this is because the doer has been previously spoiled by earlier brutal wounding, which perpetuates cycles of violence and abuse from generation to generation. At bottom, though, is a terrible banality. Sensuality degenerates into surfeit and then jadedness. Nobility degenerates into tyranny. It is the *portrait* of Dorian Gray that is telling the truth, and in the end it is all corruption, slime, and ashes.[37] No one has expressed this failure of all noble human aims more powerfully than Jean-Paul Sartre, though he saw no way out. Since the idea of God is contradictory, man is a useless passion, for him.[38] Indeed, but for God's grace, that is where it must end. And there is no stopping it, because at bottom, as Dante saw, hell is cold, and has no energy of its own.[39] That is the link between the grandiosity, the perversity, and the banality—the banality is always there as the underlying truth of the perversity of the grandiosity. Still, we go on, because the grandiosity is so addicting. We are not, on our own, able to escape this tragic side of existence. It is bigger than we are.

Once sin is in place, it becomes what we call "besetting." As Samuel Shoemaker pointed out, it is binding, blinding, deadening, and propagating.[40] It is *binding* in that by our own will we cannot break its grip on us. It is *blinding* because we lose the ability to understand good and evil accurately; we become deluded, and minimizing, rationalizing, and all the strategies of denial lock into place. It is *deadening* because over time persistence in evil blunts our moral sensibility, our conscience, our will, and our ability to sense and obey the movements of the Holy Spirit. It is *propagating* because it is vilely fecund, spreading like infection or cancer throughout us until no part of us is left untainted (the true meaning of "total depravity," not that there is no good left in us) and then from us to others. It grows exponentially because, as Simone Weil said, we have no way, outside grace, of dealing with the evil that assaults us except by absorbing it and sending it back bigger than when we got it.[41] Only on the cross of Christ is that infernal dialectic broken.

It is these hard truths about evil that have caused many of us to decide that the demonic must be recognized in any true account of the human predicament. While the Satan myth need not be taken literally, as myth it has a highly illuminating power.[42] Taken shallowly, it can lead to two false and dangerous conclusions. Taken deeply it reveals these falsehoods.

The first lie is "the devil made me do it!" We enter a realm of great mystery here, but even as we confess the strength of the forces of evil and how powerless we are before them, at some level we know we are also involved in our own servitude, that our will has in some way given its assent to this horror of its own bondage, even if, as in abuse, that consent is horribly coerced. No account of evil can be allowed that finally undercuts either human freedom or the goodness of God. These, indeed, are the principles that must be kept in balance with a nondeluded acknowledgment of the wickedness and persuasiveness of evil. As my old football coach said, "There are many reasons for failure, but there are no excuses." For most of us, most of the time, however big a factor the demonic may be in my life, it is no excuse. I am implicated as well as victimized. I speak in general here; this is not to deny the truth that there are situations of pure victimization where the victims bear no responsibility for the evil inflicted on them; in many cases some responsibility for how the victims respond remains, but some are too vulnerable even for that. The idea that napalmed babies are somehow responsible for their own suffering is morally repugnant. The demonic then uses these situations to enslave the victims in evil to which they may at least partly, if not freely, assent, often by becoming falsely convinced through guilt and shame that they are "bad" people because of what has happened to them. The wisdom of the Twelve Steps is helpful here. Recovering alcoholics acknowledge and make amends for wrongs committed by them even though at the time their addiction may have rendered them incapable of acting otherwise. There is, finally, a difference between guilt and responsibility. Most addicted, abused, and oppressed people do retain the freedom to seek healing and liberation at some level, though that may require the intervention of others; we may have to admit, however, that some wounding is so severe as to rob persons of even that freedom, at least in this life.[43]

The second fallacy comes from thinking that the point of hell is that we should strive to be good for fear of it, but that being bad would really be more fun. The snake already has its head in the tent with that one—the delusion is in place. A moralism based on fear of punishment will, in the end, be poisoned by resentment of the authority that threatens. It's like an alcoholic not yet fully into recovery who stays dry but resents not being able to drink and those who can do so without apparent harm. Real recovery requires embracing sobriety as a positive good and a sober life not as a consolation prize but as the grand prize. The truth is that goodness is the only way to real happiness in this life, not just in some other, and until we get that, we are not really converting.

A final aspect of the demonic of theological significance is its reminder that having a "spiritual" nature (whatever that is) is not only no protection against evil, but in fact makes it possible to be evil.[44] Once again, the dynamic of salvation is not a flight *from* flesh into something "spiritual," but the healing of the flesh; at bottom, as we have seen, even the so-called sins of the flesh are actually "spiritual" in that they are the disruption in our embodied selves as animated and spirited that is the problem, not the flesh itself. The Satan myth actually underscores this by reminding us that the prince of evil and father of lies is an angelic, spiritual being.

We need to say something at this point about demonic obsession and possession, if only because they have become so vivid in the popular imagination. There are enough genuine cases recorded, even once we have allowed that many supposed instances in the past can now be recognized as mental illnesses, that we cannot discount the possibility. But I am quite sure these extraordinary experiences are very rare and do not justify the huge investment in "ministries of deliverance" that have sprouted like weeds, leading to some parishes where there are more exorcists than lay readers. The healthiest attitude toward the demonic is represented for us in St. Athanasius's life of St. Anthony of Egypt.[45] Whenever he was beset by a demon, Anthony would say, "There are two possibilities here. One is that you have been sent by God to teach me a lesson for my own good, in which case stop wasting time and get on with it. The other is that you have not been sent by God at all, in which case you have no power over me, so be gone in the name of Jesus." And that was that, and it remains the theological truth about the demonic (except we are not so likely today to call things sent by God "demons"). It reminds us, however, that we Christians are not Zoroastrians but believe evil was never equal to good in power and has in any case been decisively defeated; nor do we practice magic dressed up as liturgy. Remembering it is faith being born in us that allows us to see evil, including the demonic, in its true colors, we will be encouraged also to remember that same faith as a trust that God has already defeated that evil on our behalf. In most cases of supposed obsession or possession, counseling, medical help, and the ordinary means of grace are enough, and must always be tried first.

Where these do not appear to suffice, special expertise, training, and gifts are required. Different faith communities have different rules about this, but on the Catholic side (Roman, Orthodox, and Anglican), the bishop *must* be called in and her or his injunctions followed scrupulously.[46] In other judicatory situations the same principle should hold. For that reason, we shall not discuss here anything further beyond recommending the ordinary means of grace, sacramental and medical, and reminding us all that one of Satan's strategies with believers is to make himself seem more powerful than he is.

In short, if denial of the demonic reality can blind us to certain features of the human condition, we must still be wary of externalizing our own sinfulness as if it could be dealt with that way. I am always somehow involved, perhaps even implicated.

Evil for Which We Do Not Volunteer

This discussion of the demonic should also, however, allow us to pause for a moment and see that not everything about the mire I notice in this new light of Word and Wisdom would go in a folder of what could be reasonably called fully self-conscious acts for which I should feel guilty, even beyond the problem of the demonic and my free or coerced assent to it. Paul Ricoeur has given a very helpful analysis of evil, showing how our post-Enlightenment limitation of it to what we have wrongly but freely willed misses several layers of more primitive experience.[47] One example is the sense of pollution, of having been slimed, by contact with what is unclean or perverse. These also cause shame in me when I notice them, even when I did not choose them at all. Survivors of rape, for example, often continue to feel shame or a deep sense of having been made unclean, even when consciously or through therapy they have come to see they bear no guilt or responsibility for what was done to them. The desire to take a shower, to get clean again, is very natural. This natural shame is an inevitable and appropriate response to rape and other forms of abuse, but guilt and toxic shame are not, not even guilt for feeling ashamed of, or guilty for, something for which I am not guilty.

There are indeed many things we are called to turn from that we do not ordinarily class as *our* sins even when evil is involved. There is the phenomenon of what Robert Capon calls "natural badness."[48] We must not be too romantic about our views of creation and nature—it is a rough place where things like earthquakes and storms and viruses seem to be an inescapable part of what it means to create a planet on which life can evolve but which can have tragic consequences for individual human beings and their projects. We may suffer from diseases and disorders that are treatable but for which we are not initially responsible. We may be oppressed or victimized in some way, and we may collude in that victimization if only by submitting to it, or we may resist it with all our might but still be defeated, or we may simply be too vulnerable to bear any responsibility. We are called in Baptism to renounce all the forces of evil that enslave human beings, including ourselves. The same Word that throws light on our actual sins also illuminates these other sorts of things for which we did not volunteer but over which we are initially powerless and from which we need to be liberated, a liberation in which we will be empowered to make our freely chosen contribution. Here again, we see liberation and healing as modes of conversion of equal importance to repentance.

Indeed, as we dig around in the swamp, we are likely to notice that some of the stuckness that swamps induce has been provided us by others, acting out of their own stuckness and ignorance. We may have been abused, or just not adequately nurtured, or damaged in other ways. We may also have been powerless victims of obsessive-compulsive disorders or addictions, as we have seen. What we must notice here is this phenomenon can provide me with a powerful temptation to stay in hell through the strategies of *blame* (blaming others, including life or God, or indeed blaming myself, inappropriately) or *denial*, which can take the pure form of ignoring it or the form of "nicing it up," or the form of pretending I can manage it on my own. These can actually prove useful in the end, however, as their failure can help us notice the dynamic that keeps us stuck.

The Dynamics of Being Stuck[49]

Being stuck begins, oddly enough, with a sense of self-righteousness, or at least of my having deserved better. Out of that I develop a series of expectations for myself, others, and life. These expectations then become demands; being unrealistic, they are never met. That leads to the direct result of my passing judgment on others, myself, or both, a judgment that is at bottom a pure no to myself, others, life, and God's yes. This is one of the things we are most clearly commanded *not* to do as Christians. This judgment is actually a very deep denial, not only a rejection of *what is* as being *what it ought not to be,* but a denial even that *it is what it is.* Delusion can become the child of disillusionment. When I have passed enough of these judgments, I make myself a person filled with resentment—not appropriate anger at real wrongs but anger stored up, cherished, and worshipped as fuel for my own hellfire. Finally, when I grow weary of that, I end up in resignation, seeming to accept life in a kind of bitter and cynical skepticism I call realistic but which has as its essence a giant middle finger raised into the heart of the cosmos. Unless something makes me notice, I shall go bumping down these stairs every time on a kind of automatic pilot. Again, this "automatic pilot" bears witness to what the tradition means by original sin and concupiscence. It is, I think, what St. John meant by "pride of life" (1 John 2:16).

The way out for most of us is once again shame, not toxic shame but healthy shame, as an approach to an appropriate humility. This is an attitude of deep acceptance of the truth about ourselves, the world as we know it, and our place in it. It goes beyond guilt, because it encompasses things for which we are somehow responsible though not willfully guilty. Shame (or "permission") is not a requirement or prelude of acceptance of the way the world and we truly are but the first symptom that acceptance has actually begun. The shame comes not because we have been scolded, internally or externally, but because loving grace has allowed us to hear clearly for the first time the disharmony between the pathetic no of our judgments and the profound yes of God's eternal Word of judgment in the sense we have defined that. This shame is not toxic because it has no sense of our diminishment in it but only a profound recognition that, to the contrary, we have been less than our true or best selves. It is not a result of being belittled but of being beloved. Faith is being born here because this shame is our initial belief and trust in God's miraculous Word of yes, that despite all the appearances we are forgiven and beloved. Any sense of belittlement is only the pain of giving up that deluded grandiosity of either hero *or* victim that got us in the mire in the first place. Faith calls forth in us the virtue of faithfulness, which is simply the concrete expression of faith in relationships. Faith calls us to fidelity to God, human others with whom we are in community (including spouses and other family, friends, colleagues, and so forth), and ourselves.

This movement from stuckness to humility takes a different shape for those who have been seriously abused or suffered deep loss or trauma.[50] Here, the lies told oneself run as follows: "I should be over this. I am making too much of my pain. I can't stop the pain, so I am really bad. Life is hopeless." In this case it is legitimate pain, grief, and rage at the abuse that is rejected as "what should not be." In this kind of stuckness, the no is oneself and one's pain, and with it a resentment forms toward oneself and others for not hearing the pain, usually resulting in deep depression.

Allowing the grief and rage to surface is the way out of this kind of stuckness, although in the case of severe trauma it may take extensive therapy before a person feels safe enough to do so. Having the safety and space to feel and express anger at the abuse as something that "should not be," at the abuser and even at God, can be an important part of spiritual healing.[51] In this way there comes an acceptance of the event, the depth of its impact on us, and our own powerlessness to handle it alone, not as in any way okay but as undeniable—the beginning of a yes. This becomes the proper attitude of humility in this case. In time, also, our complaint to God is met by the experience of God's healing, God's own yes that is heard at first as joining our no to the abuse.

Thus, it is problematic to label even as "healthy shame" the movement of insight and grace that allows people in this kind of situation to begin to feel their pain, since toxic shame is so much a part of their dis-ease. Survivors of childhood sexual abuse speak of "permission" to be where they are, a lowering of a deep, unspoken expectation that they deny their pain. It is above all a moment of compassion, within which is the revelation that it is wrong not to honor oneself and one's pain.

The shame, permission, or longing for freedom, and the acceptance they cause lead to a true humility; as we have known somewhere deep all along, this is not an obsequious self-abasement but simply a realistic assessment and acceptance of who and what we are. As Terry Holmes was fond of pointing out, it is derived from the same root as "humus."[52] Humility is a kind of earthiness, an earthiness that acknowledges and accepts that we are dust, that to dust we shall return, and that somehow and not unrelated to our own responsibility we have been slimed, and become slime that slimes others. The realistic appraisal we call humility is, oddly enough, the mother of the theological virtue of hope, because we cannot have true hope (as opposed to optimism) until we know we need something. The first great mystery of the conversion that is the first signpost on the spiritual human journey is that judgment, shame or permission, and humility give rise to hope, by grace.[53] The birth of hope, however, points us to the next topic, that *to* which we are converted.

Notes

1. See, especially, Simon Chan, *ST*, 56–75, and Samuel Powell, *A Theology of Christian Spirituality*, 43–45, and again in each chapter in the section on the fallen world; also Diogenes Allen, *Spiritual Theology*, 64–79, on the "eight deadly thoughts"; and J. I. Packer, *Knowing God*, 221–29. Recall that I am using "sin" to cover the entire range of that which is contrary to God's will, including addiction and other diseases, oppression, abuse, and other trauma, not just things for which we are morally responsible. See below, "Evil for Which We Did Not Volunteer."

2. Owen C. Thomas and Ellen K. Wondra, *Introduction*, 152–53.

3. See Christopher Bryan, *A Preface to Romans*, 45–50.

4. See, for example, Raymond A. Moody, Jr., *Life after Life*.

5. Raymond Brown, *The Gospel According to John*, 29A:954–55, with reference to John 19:31–42; 705–706 with ref to 14:8; see cxvii–cxviii in vol. 29.

6. Karl Barth, *Epistle to the Romans*, 38–39, is, again, the *locus classicus*.

7. Kilian McDonnell, *Other Hand*, 99–107, 117–20, 195–201, and throughout; John Calvin,

Institutes of the Christian Religion I.7 clearly states the role of the Holy Spirit in both the writing and reading of the Scriptures.

8. Hans Urs von Balthasar's essay on faith is especially illuminating: *Explorations in Theology III: Creator Spiritus*, 15–102.

9. K. Bradford Brown and W. Roy Whitten, the Life Training, emphasized this connection, as well as the resonance with Genesis 2, "they were ashamed."

10. The *BCP* 1549 contained language that lasted through the American 1928 edition, calling for the forsaking of the devil and all his works, the vain pomp and glory of the world, with all the covetous desires of the same, and the carnal desires of the flesh; see *The First and Second Prayer Books of Edward VI*, 244; the pre-Vatican II Roman rite called for the renunciation of Satan, all his works, and all his pride. See Philip Weller, *The Roman Ritual*, 84–85; Jean Deshusses, *Le sacramentaire grégorien*, 378.

11. This is during a threefold repetition of "Dost thou renounce Satan, and all his angels, and all his works, and all his service, and all his pride?" See Fan Sylian Noli, *The Eastern Orthodox Prayer Book*, 103.

12. *BCP*, 302; current Roman Catholic text "Rites for the Christian Initiation of Adults" allows three forms: Form A has three questions, rejecting sin, the glamour of evil, and Satan; forms B and C call for the rejection of Satan, all his works, and all his empty promises. *The Rites of the Catholic Church*, 1:157–58.

13. See Philip Esler, "Paul and Stoicism: Romans 12 as a Test Case."

14. Again, for a critique very similar to that offered here, see Nicholas Lash, *Easter in Ordinary*, the first half of the book.

15. For a sophisticated theological account of this problem and a positive view of the role of healed desire in the spiritual life, see Philip Sheldrake, *Befriending Our Desires*.

16. Karl Rahner, "The Theological Concept of Concupiscentia," *TI* 1:347–82.

17. The best account of addictive disease as an issue in the spiritual life is Gerald May, *Addiction and Grace*.

18. See Mark McIntosh, *Discernment and Truth*.

19. One of the best accounts of this is Luis Bermejo, *The Spirit of Life*, 72–121; see my "The Holy Spirit in Christian Spirituality," *BCCS*, 210–12.

20. See Louis Dupré, *Passage to Modernity*, 42–119, for a good account of the shift in the meaning of supernatural at the Renaissance and afterward. I have always been very nervous about accounts of the universe as God's body, and hence intrinsically sacred, even Sallie McFague's *The Body of God*, because of the dangers of pantheism; but at a recent meeting of the Society of Anglican and Lutheran Theologians she gave a paper in which she gave a thorough *via negativa* critique of her own concept, that like all theological language it is only an analogy, and a full account must therefore include an account of all the ways the analogy does *not* hold. She then proceeded to raise all the objections I have held! If that critique is allowed to be part of the positive account of the analogy, my objections need not stand in the way of its appropriate use. I do think, however, that a sacramental account of the universe as God's house has fewer dangers and provides all we need for a sound eco-theology.

21. The infamous John 3:16. The Greek word is *kosmos*.

22. Albert C. Outler, *John Wesley*, 31; 229–31; 238–50; see John Wesley's *Thoughts Upon Slavery*.

23. The great heresy of *The Littlest Angel* (Charles Tazwell and Katherine Evans) and a variety of popular songs such as "Teen Angel" is that dead human beings somehow become angels rather than resurrected humans. In the classical tradition, even in heaven the two orders are quite separate and distinct; humans having resurrected bodies, angels being either beings of pure spirit or of very rarified bodies. Whether or not there are angels (Scripture certainly suggests there are) the whole point is that we humans are not such. See Mortimer J. Adler, *The Angels and Us*.

24. Walter C. Kelly, *The Best of Pogo*, 163.

25. C. S. Lewis, *The Screwtape Letters*. F. P. Harton, *Elements of the Spiritual Life*, 113–20; indeed, Harton's entire chapter on the enemies of the soul (p. 120) is one of his best.

26. See C. S. Lewis, *A Preface to Paradise Lost*. But see also Stephen Sykes's critique of Milton's Arianism in *The Story of Atonement*, 20, 26–36, 146.

27. Rollo May, *Love and Will*, 121–76, esp. 121–22.

28. Of John Polkinghorne's many works, my favorites are *The Faith of a Physicist* and the three articles of "A Scientist's Approach to Belief"; for Arthur Peacocke, *God and Science* and *Creation and the World of Science* are representative.

29. Julian of Norwich, *Showings*, short text chap. 13, 148–49; see the critical edition, by Edmund Colledge and James Walsh, 1, 244–45.

30. G. May, *Care of Mind*, 159–161; see also idem, *Addiction and Grace*, throughout, where May describes the spiritual aspects of the disease and recovery, esp. 91–181. A sacred illness is an illness that in a given culture is typical of spiritual guides, shamans, and so on. Having the disease and recovering from it are often a requirement for office. See also Urban T. Holmes, III, *Ministry and Imagination*, 222–26.

31. Karl Marx, *The Communist Manifesto* III.1.a.

32. Reinhold Niebuhr, *Moral Man and Immoral Society*, 169–99.

33. G. W. F. Hegel, *Phenomenology of Mind*, 599–610.

34. *Spiritual Exercises*, Rules for Discernment of Spirits, ##329–32.

35. Herbert W. Richardson, *Towards an American Theology*, 42–48. Gayle Brown, *Feminist Rhetoric and Christological Discourse*, has shown that the rhetoric of ideological conflict has its uses, but by design it will perpetuate and even ritualize conflict rather than resolve it, short of "eliminating" one's opponent.

36. C. S. Lewis, *Perelandra*, throughout, esp. chaps. 7–12.

37. Oscar Wilde, *The Picture of Dorian Gray*.

38. Jean-Paul Sartre, *Being and Nothingness*, 363–430, 615.

39. Dante, *Inferno*, Canto XXXII–end, especially the picture of Satan frozen in ice, Canto XXXIV: 1–29.

40. Samuel Shoemaker, *Realizing Religion*, 16, phrased it thus: "It has binding power, blinding power, deadening power." *For Sinner's Only* contains the same material. See Dick B., *New Light on Alcoholism*, 2d ed., p. 42. Sam was one of the four great friends of AA at the beginning, helping Bill Wilson uncover the nature of addiction and create the Twelve Steps as a way of recovery. *Alcoholics Anonymous Comes of Age*, 38, 64, 261; *"Pass It On,"* 127ff., and see the references listed on p. 426; Dick B. also said, in a communication of 12/17/07: Howard A. Walter's *Soul Surgery*, where Frank Buchman, Walter, and Henry B. Wright collaborated and spelled out the Five C's—Confidence, Confession, Conviction, Conversion, and Conservation [later Continuance]. Walter pointed to (1) sin's binding power (Psalm 63:3); (2) sin's blinding power; (3) sin's deadening power; (4) sin's propagating power. See Walter, *Soul Surgery*, 67–75. See also Bremer Hofmeyr, *How to Change* (New York: Moral Re-Armament, n.d.), 2. Lois Wilson's notes used this same expression. Dick B., *The Oxford Group and Alcoholics Anonymous*, 194–95. Lois Wilson wrote in her "Oxford Group Notes" that "Sin blinds, binds, multiplies, deadens" (Dick B., *New Light on Alcoholism*, 546). This is p. 338 of the 1994 edition published by Good Book Publishing Co.

41. Simone Weil, *Waiting for God*, 189–91.

42. See Dorothy Marie England, *Satan Stalking*, for a powerful and sensible account; see also George B. Caird's analysis of the temptation story in *Saint Luke*, 79.

43. There are great mysteries and serious moral and theological issues at stake here. For superb treatments, see Cynthia Crysdale, *Embracing Travail*, and Flora Keshgegian, *Redeeming Memories*.

44. John Macquarrie, *Principles of Christian Theology*, 233–37.

45. Athanasius, *Life of Antony*, ## 8–10, 38–39; ## 25–44, 50–64.

46. See Martin Israel, *Exorcism*; John Richards, *Exorcism, Deliverance and Healing*.

47. Paul Ricoeur, *The Symbolism of Evil*, has an extensive account.

48. Robert Capon, *The Third Peacock,* 18–21.

49. Much of what follows I learned in events sponsored by Brown and Whitten, Life Training. I also learned a lot of this in Twelve-Step recovery. See the various official publications of Alcoholics Anonymous.

50. This and the following two paragraphs are written by my wife, Barbara Brunn Hughes. For her moving and insightful account of her own recovery from childhood sexual abuse, see her "Where Was God?"

51. See Walter Brueggemann, on the role of the lament psalms in particular in giving voice to the silenced in God's presence: *The Message of the Psalms,* 58–59.

52. See, for example, Urban Tigner Holmes, *Spirituality for Ministry,* 138.

53. Class notes, "Spiritual Theology," Weston College, spring 1969, Father William Reed, S.J. See also my "The Historic Ought-to-Be and the Spirit of Hope," 120, and several other essays in the same volume.

7

Conversion *To*

Faith is born in the first hearing and believing in the Word as a word of loving judgment that confronts us with the truth about ourselves and our society; hope as an aspect of faith is born, as we have seen, out of healthy shame or out of "permission" to feel appropriate pain and outrage, and out of acceptance of that truth about ourselves and the true humility that results. Once we have acknowledged our need, we can begin to hope that need might be addressed and trust the promise that it will. If we have been given a deep desire to turn away from a former way of life and the social forces of evil that define and support it, the first thing we need is hope that there might be something else, something better, to turn *to*. At first, we may not even see the real possibility of something better and experience it only in the forces of the turning itself. But, gradually, the strengthening of hope will bring some of the outline into the clear. In this current, hope is still an aspect of faith, which remains primary; at this point, hope is coming to believe in the covenant promises and the faithfulness of the One who promised.

Indeed, it is hope itself that provides us with the first clues about what lies ahead in our turning, returning, conversion. Here I am depending on the insights of the most significant theologian of hope of our time, Jürgen Moltmann, who recovered a proper view of this subject in his widely read book *Theology of Hope*, a theme to which he returned years later in *The Coming of God*.[1] Two main points are at stake here. The first was made by Moltmann in a talk he gave in Cambridge, Massachusetts, to students from many different theological schools in the spring of 1967. *Theology of Hope* had just been published in English and was a "hot" book. Many people had come expecting to hear about hope. But Moltmann had moved on to what would become *The Trinity and the Kingdom* and, as a good scholar, was giving us his new material, which was about the Trinity and the cross. Finally, one member of the audience could stand it no longer and said, "Thank you for the interesting talk on the crucifixion, Prof. Moltmann, but we had been hoping to hear something about *Theology of Hope*." Moltmann replied, "Well, last time I was here I discovered Americans are always confusing hope with optimism, so I thought I should talk about the cross."

If true hope is to be born in us and to bear fruit in its turn, then we must indeed carefully distinguish it from optimism, and the cross is the key. Optimism would look at the mess from which we have been called to turn and say, "Oh well, this too shall pass." The assumption would be that something inherent in us, or in life, or in the universe will automatically guarantee that things will improve. Both the quiet-ist form of optimism—"If I just wait this out things will improve"—and the activist version—"If I or we work very hard we can pull ourselves out of this mire"—are false leads. They are not hope because they are not born out of the faithful humility that comes from full acceptance of the truth but remain a kind of denial. The delu-sion becomes even more dangerous if the bootstrap by which we seek to pull our-selves up is some esoteric human property of spirituality or religiosity rather than a deep trust in the covenant promises of God (one of Moltmann's consistent themes) made available to all peoples by the cross of Christ. If we do not get this straight on the front end, we shall hopelessly misdefine the moral struggle into which we are called. The cross reminds us that the repair of sin was not even something auto-matic for God—it required a new and very costly act in history.

Moltmann's second major point is that hope does not afford us escape into mystical and mythical theophanies (appearances of God or whatever) as a retreat from the historical life of the flesh. What we have from God is promises, covenant promises, that this fleshly history in which we are engaged will, by God's grace, have a satisfactory conclusion.[2] We are not called out of life into some other occult realm but summoned to be immersed in life, history, finitude, under the discipline of covenant obedience. We identify with the community God has called together to receive the covenant promises, and we keep its laws and customs not as a means of moral self-improvement but as a way of holding God and ourselves account-able for the envisioned and promised end of our history.[3] It is our job, under the covenant and its promises, to work for that end, liberated and empowered to do so by God's grace—the presence and ultimately indwelling of the Holy Spirit. Here, we see the mission of the Spirit primarily in relation to the work appropriated to the Fount—the covenant and its promises—as the Spirit rests on the body of the covenant people, liberating them for their priestly and prophetic role, and provid-ing the point of re-turn for the lost and strayed. The Christian moral life is not about being good, and the Christian mystical life is not about having neat religious experiences. The point of both is to desire the will of God and thus live freely and faithfully under the covenant.

This is the proper interpretation (what is technically called a hermeneutical principle) of all the standard metaphors for what we are called *to*: new life, new being, new Adam (humanity).[4] All refer to a renewal of fleshly history in the cov-enant, its promises, and its people. This conversion is never just for our own sake even within that covenantal context. Scripture records many conversions, and every one of them contains a call to some particular task or role in the covenant history—Moses, Isaiah, Jeremiah, Paul, all converted from former and often sinful lives into a new existence in the Spirit of God, but in each case with a definite task. The traditional name for this task in Christian theology is "apostolate." We are all called to convert from an old life focused on whatever in the slime held our atten-tion to some task for which we are sent into the midst of the world's history as it is being shaped by covenant promise. All spirituality is apostolic spirituality, if it is Christian. All conversion is a vocation—a call to a historical task.[5]

The name for this envisioned, satisfactory end to our one and only fleshly history is the reign or commonwealth of God. This has sometimes been placed over against a more mystical version termed the vision of God, or the beatific vision, which is a loving, infused knowledge of the Trinity.[6] But it is a mistake to make that separation. The God we hope to see in the beatific vision is not a God of occult theophanies but the one whose covenant promises the perfect reign of justice and peace. All the theophanies reported in Scripture further the end of this covenant history. The God whose reign, covenant, and promises are at stake here is the Trinity, who is the subject of the beatific vision. Once, when asked about eternal life, Krister Stendahl suggested that if we inquire only about what happens to us as individuals when we die, we have missed the point of the gospel. The issue is, will there be any place to go should we have some sort of survival after death—that is, is God really bringing in the promised perfect reign of justice and peace?[7] The gospel is very clear—Jesus says the inbreaking of this reign is happening even now. That is not only the motive to repentance; it is its goal. Indeed, Jesus is the personal embodiment of that reign, fulfilling the messianic offices (*munera Christi*) of prophet, priest, and king, anointed for each by the Holy Spirit, who rests on the body of the Word/Wisdom in the incarnation, revealing her mission in support of the mission of the Word/Wisdom.

As John Wesley taught clearly, this means that in conversion we are called not merely to personal holiness but social holiness as well: justice, peace, liberation for the oppressed; it is to be on the side of whatever God is on the side of, and the liberation theologians have taught us at least one thing very clearly: according to Scripture God is always on the side of the poor and the oppressed.[8] The image of the reign of God is a profoundly *social* image. It is in the context of the covenanted society working with God to establish that reign "on earth as it is in heaven" that humans become persons and find personal holiness. The whole is greater than the sum of the parts, and it makes the parts, not the other way round.

The Holy Spirit plays an additional and often hidden role in bringing about this reign and commonwealth by resting on the ecclesial (churchly) body of the Word/Wisdom as its future. The Holy Spirit, in her own proper mission, is responsible for guiding the entire universe toward its perfect consecrated fulfillment, the notion of the sacramental *pleroma*—the fullness of all things. It is the Spirit who is "responsible" for the "already-but-not-yet" character of the commonwealth, for the reign being present and inbreaking but also still coming. Here lies the whole issue of "anticipation" and the "proleptic" in sacramental and ethical life alike, as the Spirit forms and teaches us to live as beloved and not accursed.[9]

That is to say, we are called first into the human moral struggle, but in the larger sense of that term, the fully social as well as individual sense. We may pause here to note a doctrinal truth, that of God as a Trinity or triadic unity of three co-eternal, co-equal persons. All the heresies that led to this doctrine being defined at the Councils of Nicea and Constantinople erred either by overemphasizing the distinctness of the persons to the damage of their community or by overemphasizing the community at the expense of the distinctions among the persons.[10] The classical doctrine, as developed by Aquinas, went on to define the "persons" (the word had a different meaning then in both Greek and Latin than now) as "substantial relations." That is, the community is a community of persons, but individuals are constituted as persons only through being in relationship in that community. The Fount is Father only as Father of *that* Son, for example.[11] All the heresies got that balance wrong in ways that still plague us as false notions of what it means to be a person. In the West, we have come to place too much emphasis on the private individual, while in the East there has been a tendency to overemphasize the collective. Part of the human moral struggle is to establish human personhood in this proper balance of individual and community.

Later we shall look at a traditional account of that struggle in terms of virtues and vices, gifts and fruits; meanwhile, the acknowledgment of the governing hope of God reminds us that this moral struggle is not about acquiring individual virtues as merit badges, prizes, or adornments, but about becoming good citizens of that reign, about becoming civilized for the city of God. Individual virtue is defined as a share in the characteristics of that reign—justice, peace, righteousness, love, holiness, and these are themselves the attributes of God in God's Trinitarian life as spoken and expressed in human social (covenant) history and thus experienced by individuals as a moral claim upon themselves.[12] In the deepest sense all ethics is social ethics.

The tradition does provide us, however, with a helpful sense of what we are called to as individual persons. The Eastern church calls this first current of conversion we are looking at "the restoration of the royal image." It is an essential doctrine of all Christian theologies that human beings are created in the image and likeness of God (Genesis 1). Western theologies have tended to misinterpret the Hebrew parallelism and distinguish image from likeness, the likeness being lost through sin in the fall, the image persisting, but under the condition of total depravity it is not very functional, to say the least. The image might as well be lost, for all the good it does in the more Calvinist theologies. Those theologies with a more clearly Christian humanist heritage, such as classical Anglicanism, have tended to maintain a more positive view, a "high" doctrine of humanity.[13] This often degenerates into a false optimism and, indeed, under the pressures of modernism and the Enlightenment, can become too enamored of the glories of reason on the one hand (and scarcely distinguishable from the growing secular humanism) while participating in the contraction of the "self" to the "ghost in the head of the body-machine" on the other. In general, in the West the higher the doctrine of humanity, the "lower" the Christology; the strands of Christianity with the highest doctrine of Christ and his work tend to have a low or pessimistic doctrine of humanity as totally depraved or sinful even by nature; the strands with a more humanist bent, and hence a higher doctrine of humanity, tend to play down the uniqueness and necessity of Christ and his atoning work. The exception is the non-Calvinist branches of Anglicanism (and its Methodist offspring), in which one finds a high doctrine of both.

The Eastern church, however, has tended not to overemphasize the distinction between image and likeness, or the damage done by the fall. Far from being "lost" either ontologically or functionally, the image has only been obscured, as when a mirror becomes fogged over and images in it obscured. The fog is sin and its results (and the cognates we have examined above, disease, abuse, and oppression);[14] one of the results of this first tidal current is that the mirror is cleansed and the true image of God (the royal image) in which we have been created, can shine forth again. This is the form hope takes for us as individual persons, that our true created selves may be liberated in the new Adam, the new humanity, for the reign and commonwealth of God.

As soon as we use language such as "our true created selves," however, we have a contextual problem. As we have seen, one of the symptoms of postmodernism is a loss of confidence in the "contracted self" of modernism—the tiny little ego-person reduced to a ghost in the head of the mechanical body.[15] It is not helpful to think of the "cleansing of the royal image" as some kind of ontological prop for that tattered remnant. Quite the contrary. One of the great opportunities postmodern anxiety offers a reconstructed spirituality is the recognition that the tiny little ego-person in the head is part of the fog, part of what must be rubbed off. Postmodernism itself is thus from one perspective only the last stage of modernism—the contraction of the self that has been going on for centuries finally culminates in its disappearance.[16] The faithful Christian hope (hope notice, not optimism) is that this contraction and final disappearance of the ego-self is not the end of the tale but one form of taking up the cross and dying to self (the ego-self of modernism) so that our true lives as embodied selves in the image of God, animated and spirited, might emerge.

Although this restoration of our true being in the image of God is our hope as individual persons, it is still never a purely individual hope. Christian tradition has always interpreted this image as a primarily Trinitarian image, which means individual personhood is constituted in relationship from the beginning.[17] And not just relationship to God, either. In the priestly creation story in Genesis 1 God creates humanity in God's image as male and female, as gendered and in relationship, at the same time, and apparently as equals. This means *at least* that both men and women share equally in being in the image of God, and the church fathers who thought only males were in the image of God and women in the image of men were just wrong.[18] It also means that by being created as gendered each individual is embodied in a way that makes sense only in relation to an other. The Hebrew is very explicit—men are "pronged" and women are "orificed."[a] It probably means more—that it is not any one individual, male or female, in whom the image resides, but in the community formed by the couple.

Here there has been a division in contemporary thought; Karl Barth believed the "image" referred specifically to the heterosexual couple in a marriage relationship; stirring in some not-so-good interpretation of the second (temporally earlier) creation story of woman created from the man's rib, he argued for the logical priority of men, though with virtually no content to the claim.[19] Emile Brunner and others challenged this, and asserted that only persons-in-relationship in general were the "image."[20] A couple of points are salient. First, even the second *creation* story, about Eve being made from Adam's rib, has nothing to do with the subordination of women to men (that comes later as part of the curse which is the result of sin; Genesis 2–3). The second creation story itself is about why it is not good for a human being to be alone, about God providing a fellowship of mutual help, of delight that this *fellawe*

---

a Transgendered persons who are born with mixed genitals are, of course, a special case.

creature is bone of bone and flesh of flesh, and of the origins of erotic desire (for this reason a man shall leave father and mother and cleave to his wife) (Genesis 2; also Mark 10:7 and parallels).[21] So we may conclude, the image is Trinitarian in the sense that the balance between individual and community in the constitution of friendship is maintained; men and women share equally in the image of God; and erotic friendship and a covenanted life of "one flesh" may have something to do with it.

Does that mean the image is only communitarian, and the individual not "in the image" unless in an intimate and perhaps erotic relationship? Does a fish need a bicycle after all?[22] What would that say to the many unmarried, single or celibate, gay or straight? Fortunately, the image is, as I have said, Trinitarian, and this allows us to apply the grammatical rules for talking about the Trinity by analogy. One of these is set out by Augustine in *De Trinitate*: so great is the co-equality, co-eternity, and power of the co-inherence of the three in their oneness that no one taken alone is any less than all three taken together.[23] Specifically, the divine nature (Augustine and I both speak as fools here) resides fully in each, though always with reference and in relationship to the others. So, individual humans are "in the image" taken singly, but always with reference to the full expression of the image in community. Erotic friendships covenanted as life partnerships are then a "sacrament" of that relationship but do not exhaust its possible embodiments.[24]

A major theme of Christian tradition is the teaching that only Jesus is the perfect image of God (Col 1:15).[25] In Jesus, Christians believe, God is speaking the definitive Word about what God means by "human being," of what it means to be in "the image of God, and of what it means to be God.[26] In fact, there is an important key to both faith and its accompanying hope here. If we approach the definition of the divine and human natures in the one person of Jesus at the Council of Chalcedon (451) (or its improvements at the second and third Councils of Constantinople (553 and 680–681) with preconceived notions of what "human" and "God" mean, we shall never get it. This is especially true if those preconceived notions are governed by the modernist contraction of both: the human as the ghost in the head of the machine, God as relegated to a private and specialized area of "religion." Christian faith begins with the belief that human and divine can be together in a historical person, because they have indeed been so. It then learns from that fact, given what "human" and "God" mean.

The notion of Jesus' perfect humanity is certainly linked to the traditional notion that Jesus was sinless himself though taking our sins on himself for our redemption. It is also linked to the notion that somehow Jesus is from the beginning of all creation the prototype, and in any case has now become the new Adam, the new archetype of humanity (1 Corinthians 15). We shall have more to say later about what it means to take Jesus' life as the paradigm for ours, the tradition of "the imitation of Christ." Here we take note that our *hope* is that because of him and through being in him by the power of the Holy Spirit, sharing in his death and resurrection, we shall be like him—we shall be as he is—including participating in his relationship to God (Rom 6:3–4).[27] Indeed, St. John sums up the whole of Christian hope: "Beloved, we are God's children now; it does not yet appear what we shall be, but we know that when he appears we shall be like him, for we shall see him as he is. And everyone who thus hopes in him purifies himself as he is pure" (1 John 3:2–3) This is, therefore, both a hope that here and now we may be growing into the likeness of his humanity in our flesh and history, with all the ethical implications that follow (for St. John chiefly the two great commandments of love in their relationship to one another), and also that in the end we shall be like him even in his relationship to God. Both of these maintain the Trinitarian balance of individual and community. In the flesh, Jesus is the embodiment of God's reign and commonwealth, and to be like him means to share in that (and the resulting suffering) as members of Christ's body on mission. To be like him even in his relationship to God means finally, as we shall see in the third current, to participate even in the hypostatic union itself, which is the true and deepest source of all Christians properly call "mystical."[a] Here again, personal and social, ethical and mystical can be seen as inseparable, and the key in history and for us is the crucified, risen, glorified flesh of Jesus as the Word/Wisdom among us. Christian hope is finally Christian because in every sense (including the Trinitarian) it is hope in Jesus, and in the Holy Spirit he has poured out on all flesh as the mediation of which he is the mediator.[28]

In our time especially, this has raised an important issue for women. How can the human flesh of a male be salvific for women? How can the life of a man be paradigmatic for them? Some women have turned away at this point, believing there is no way forward for them here.[29] Any man who would, on his own, suggest other possibilities is an arrogant fool. Given the issues of our time, every woman must work out in the company of her sisters (and if she chooses, some brothers as well) her own answer to this dilemma. As a man, I can suggest some answers Christian women have themselves come to that have helped me see what is at stake and have been helpful to women I know and trust. Dorothy Sayers's classic *Are Women Human* suggests that women continue to flock to the gospel, despite the mess men have made of it, because they recognize in Jesus the only man who has ever known how to treat them right and really be friends. We have already seen how she portrays women as participating fully in "the image of God."[30] Rosemary Radford Ruether suggests that, as a male of questionable legitimacy, Jesus was even lower on the social ladder than a woman, and that his prophetic office is the overthrow of patriarchy along with all other forms of oppression. Just as white racism is a problem that white folks need to deal with (it becomes a problem *for* people of color, but is not a problem *of* theirs), so only a man could overthrow patriarchy because it is a men's problem and they are responsible for it. The maleness of Jesus has meaning only in this historical economy of salvation. She also notes that feminism is largely born and sheltered in the gospel community.[31] Elisabeth Schüssler Fiorenza emphasizes Jesus as the child of Sophia God, who establishes for women and men the discipleship of equals.[32] Dorothee Sölle emphasizes the appearance of the needed nondemonic divine power of liberation in Jesus' death and resurrection.[33] Carter Heyward finds in the character and suffering of Jesus the redemption

---

a "Hypostatic union" is the technical term for the relationship between the humanity of Jesus and the person of the Word/Wisdom of God in one *hypostatis* or substantial personal being, which is itself a participation in the unity of the three persons (*hypostases*) in their co-inherence.

of God.[34] Other Christian women have found precisely within the tradition, even given a pretty orthodox interpretation, the best foundation for feminist values.[35]

We must remember it is faithful hope in the cross we are talking about here, not accomplishment. St. Paul reminds us in Romans 8 that we, like the whole creation, wait in hope for the full redemption of the flesh and the material order; we wait for the appearance of the glorious freedom of the children of God; we wait for the redemption of our bodies, since "being like Jesus" includes being resurrected as fully woman or man, fully whoever we are, not an "immortality" that abstracts from these. We wait, in short, for the fullness of God's reign and commonwealth on earth as in heaven. We are called to wait and long and hope for that which is coming and has started to arrive, something that must still be fully actualized in us, not to submit to something already finally constituted in the flesh of a dead male, however important that flesh is. Many Christian women, at least, have found hope of a way forward here, even though many struggle with masculinist language in the liturgy.

The cry of despair and victory in Romans 7 is, after all, the prelude to this glorious vision of Romans 8. That is, in the meantime we wait, not passively but in the midst of the battle by which the reign and commonwealth are being established among us and in us, which we experience together as the struggle for justice and peace, and as individuals in the struggle between virtue and vice. But before we can look at that struggle effectively we must turn to the deepest aspect of conversion—that which we are converted *by*.

Notes

1. Jürgen Moltmann, *Theology of Hope*; idem, *The Coming of God*. See my article "The Historic Ought-to-Be and the Spirit of Hope" for more implications of Moltmann's work.

2. In "The Historic Ought-to-Be and the Spirit of Hope," I link Moltmann's work to Paul Weiss's concept of the Historic-Ought-to-Be as the end of history, in both senses as goal and termination. The eschatological role of the Holy Spirit and the gift of hope are also brought into relationship with this concept.

3. See Nicholas Lash, *Easter in Ordinary*, 134–36, on the institutional element of this hope, from Friedrich von Hügel.

4. At root, *adam* is a word for human being, not the proper name of the first male of the species. It refers to human being as made from soil or dust and inhabited by God's breath or spirit (*TDOT* 1:75–87). "Earth creature" or "earthling" is a nice translation. See Susan Niditch, "Genesis," 16. As such, it is a humanity that embraces both maleness and femaleness, as Genesis 1 makes clear. I shall use "New Adam" in that sense.

5. See article on "Conversion" in *NCE* (1st ed.), 17 (*Supplement: Change in the Church*), 156–60; *NCE* (2nd ed.), 4, 231–42. Also James Fowler, *Becoming Adult, Becoming Christian*, emphasizes this vocational aspect (pp. 71–137).

6. See Antonio Royo and Jordan Aumann, *Theology of Christian Perfection*, 26–28, with references there; the whole point of Kenneth Kirk's *Vision of God* is that all Christians are called to share in this as their highest good.

7. Krister Stendahl, "Immortality Is Too Much and Too Little," *Meanings*, 193–202; see also William Temple, *Nature, Man and God*, 415–16.

8. The works of Gustavo Guttiérrez form a *locus classicus*, especially *A Theology of Liberation*.

9. See again my "Historic-Ought-to-Be"; also Kilian McDonnell, Eugene Rogers, and so forth, even Hans Küng's *On Being a Christian*, 468–78.

10. The most interesting account is still William Porcher DuBose, *The Ecumenical Councils.*

11. Wondra in Thomas and Wondra, *Introduction,* 82–86.

12. Thomas and Wondra, *Introduction,* 100.

13. See R. William Franklin and Joseph M. Shaw, *The Case for Christian Humanism.*

14. One is also reminded of Julian of Norwich's parable of the Lord and the Servant, portraying sin as a kind of disorientation that obscures a right and loving attention, Long Text, 51, Paulist ed., 267–69.

15. Lash, *Easter in Ordinary,* 90–104.

16. Lash is not so sure of this (*Easter in Ordinary,* 252 n. 75); but see Louis Dupré, *Passage to Modernity,* 250.

17. This must be based on more than the plural form of God's self-reference in Genesis 1, however.

18. Dorothy Sayers, *Are Women Human,* is the classic text; see also Phyllis Trible, *God and the Rhetoric of Sexuality*; Margaret Miles, *Carnal Knowing.*

19. Karl Barth, *Church Dogmatics* III.1, 186; III.4.

20. Emile Brunner, *Dogmatics,* 2, 60; see Thomas and Wondra, *Introduction,* 138–39.

21. Throughout most of its linguistic history, "fellow" and its earlier forms have been gender-neutral references to partnership. Only for a very limited time did this have exclusively male connotations ("For he's a jolly good fellow"), and I believe this narrow window closed with the admission of women as fellows at the historic universities at the turn of the twentieth century. As a result, I treat the term as gender-inclusive. *Fellawe* is a Saxon ancestor of "fellow" that had positive, nongendered connotations from the Saxon side, but on the Norman side came to mean "common," as in "low fellow" or "churl," that is, not a Norman.

22. In the late twentieth century, a popular feminist T-shirt read, "A woman needs a man like a fish needs a bicycle."

23. Augustine, *De Trinitate* XV.3.5.

24. Karl Rahner, *The Church and the Sacraments,* 107–12, esp. 108; that is true of all the sacraments, which are there to reveal gracefulness, not limit and confine it, as is implicit in Rahner's teaching on sacrament as intrinsic symbol (pp. 34–40); Rahner himself does not apply the sacramental principle to anything but heterosexual marriage. See, however, Bernard Cooke, *Sacraments and Sacramentality,* 93–94, where the sacramentality embodied in marriage is applied to all human friendship.

25. The Greek is *ikōn,* which leads to a whole theology of icons and indeed art, especially as expressed at the second Council of Nicea in 787.

26. Thomas and Wondra, *Introduction,* 137, 166; Richard A. Norris, *Understanding the Faith of the Church,* 197.

27. Luis Bermejo, *The Spirit of Life,* 1–70, esp. 1.

28. William Porcher DuBose is especially strong on this, including why hope must go beyond mere justification; see *DuBose Reader,* ed. Donald Armentrout, xxxi, xxxvi. For the Holy Spirit, see the previously cited works by Kilian McDonnell, Eugene Rogers, Luis Bermejo, throughout, and my "The Historic Ought-to-Be and the Spirit of Hope."

29. Mary Daly, *Beyond God the Father*; Daphne Hampson, *After Christianity*; and Carol Christ, *She Who Changes,* are among many prominent "post-Christian" women.

30. Sayers, *Are Women Human,* 47.

31. Rosemary Radford Ruether, *Sexism and God Talk,* throughout, esp. 134–38, 37–41.

32. E. Schüssler Fiorenza, *In Memory of Her,* throughout, esp. 105–54, esp. 152.

33. Dorothee Sölle, *Thinking about God,* 120–35; 183–95, esp. 187–88.

34. Carter Heyward, *The Redemption of God,* 31–59, and throughout.

35. We have already noted Cynthia Crysdale, *Embracing Travail,* and Elizabeth Johnson, *She Who Is*; Patricia Wilson Kastner, *Faith, Feminism, and the Christ,* was a very early exponent of this view; Kathryn Tanner and Sarah Coakley are more recent advocates, in the previously cited works. It should be noted that none of these authors pulls any of her feminist punches.

8

Conversion *By*

In faith we are *converted from* the life of sin, not just sins, but sin, all the powers of evil that enslave, traumatize, and oppress human beings, the mire and all that keeps us stuck there, the things that wound and oppress us and others as well as wrongs we have done or goods we have left undone. As healthy shame, "permission" for healing, or passion for liberation, and acceptance give rise to humility, hope is born, and we can glimpse what we are being *converted to*, the commonwealth or reign of God. This has at its core a community of persons in the making that image the inner-Trinitarian life of God, hence, the unity of the reign of God and the beatific vision as loving knowledge of the Trinity; the reign is the human historical expression of what the vision is about. But that reign is not simply dangled in front of us as an ideal. It is "at hand," made real by the covenant history of deliverance for that reign, and ultimately embodied in the flesh of Jesus. In both cases, what allowed us to notice, what caused us to hear and see, what empowered us to begin to turn was God's Word/Wisdom and the Holy Spirit as the point and possibility of turning and returning. This is what we are being *converted by*. If you know the Christian tradition and have been paying attention, you will already have guessed what is coming next. Being born in us as we attend to whom we are being *converted by* is the third so-called theological virtue, love, the greatest and governing virtue, though in this current of conversion, it also appears as an aspect of faith.

Life

What we are converted by first of all is *life*. God provides ordinary life with all its ups and downs as the pedagogy, school, or discipline by which we are formed as persons for the fellowship and citizenship of God's reign, the dominion of love. As long as we remain unconverted and stuck in the mire, we will continually be offered by life a series of shocks inviting us to get unstuck, to give up our illusions and delusions, resentments, judgments, and unwarranted expectations, get in touch with reality, and unleash our co-creativity with God.[1] This is not life as a "test," but a setting in which the Holy Spirit makes concrete offers for self-transcending growth. These are life's two-by-fours, as in the farmer whopping the mule on the side of the head to get his attention. One of the mysteries of the graciousness of ordinary life is that as long as we are stubbornly refusing to learn a particular lesson, we will be vouchsafed an endless series of annoying opportunities to learn it.

Many of these shocks or learning opportunities come in fairly regular patterned sequences for a variety of life choices. One of the advantages of our time is the study these patterns have received in developmental psychology. In a later chapter we shall look at how this information is used in contemporary theories of conversion. We want to notice here that the quite ordinary course of human growth, development, and life events is the primary instrument of God's shaping, of God's preparing persons for the reign/commonwealth. Life is the first way dust gets delivered the message that it is beloved.

It is important to make one qualification here. This life involves a lot of suffering and pain, some of it the result of the mire of sin, abuse, and oppression, but some of it just the price of growth. Some older theologies talked as if everything that happened in life, no matter how destructive and horrific, was sent by God to teach or punish us. For many, this deterministic approach has given a negative coloration to what I have been trying to say in the previous paragraphs. At its worst, I have heard words intended as well-meant comfort but, in context, actual blasphemy, words offered to parents of a child who died recently of a terrible accident or an aneurysm or some other tragic circumstance, words that try to make this somehow okay because it is God's will. It is really stomach turning, and I feel awful for the parents who have to smile and be polite in the face of such crap. Not everything that happens is God's will; not every event in our lives is *intended* as a learning opportunity. For one reason or another (and that's a whole different book) shit happens, and it is not sent by God to try us. We believe that by God's grace anything can *become* a learning opportunity.

Here we must face the issue of discernment, of finding helpful means to distinguish the grace of God for our growth and our good from the other things that assault us to our hurt. I like to distinguish three kinds of pain, which need to be treated very differently. First are growing pains. These really are the dues we pay to be human, the price of growing up and being in meaningful relationships with real people. If we turn aside from these, the price in lost growth and opportunity is high, and counselors and spiritual directors must be very careful not to try to rescue people from this sort of pain. An example is the stage of disillusionment in marriage, which usually happens somewhere in the first three years. We all fall in love with someone on whom we can project our ego-ideal of the opposite gender (or the same if we are inclined that way), and at some point make the terrible discovery we have married or partnered for life with a real person instead. We are supposed to be disillusioned, of course, because illusions are not really helpful to personal growth or relationships; this sudden discovery that my partner is a real person and not my ego-ideal is the opportunity to establish, for the first time, real intimacy with a person who is actually *other*. But it still hurts; many people turn back from the pain and engage in an endless and hopeless search for that ego-ideal in an other which no real person will ever be. A lot of the pain of being together in a family is of this first kind. Israel Charny has defined a family as "a cooperative for emotional development (over and above its well understood roles vis-à-vis reproduction, economic provision, etc.) which supports each member's psychological needs to grow more secure in his image and belief in himself out of his being afforded a series of provocative, stressful, upsetting experiences with those who truly love him and whom he truly loves."[2]

Or, as he puts it even more succinctly: "the goal of family life is to foster and enjoy growth through vaccinations of pain."[3] Getting through this kind of pain really is character building in the strongest sense—it is an indelible part of the way character is built.

The second kind of pain is "That's life" pain, as "Into every life a little rain must fall." This kind of pain arises from encountering difficult or even horrific life situations, some of which go beyond what should be addressed with "That's life." These encounters are not inherently valuable the way the first kind is, but if we are able to overcome them, character growth will occur. At least in life as we know it, some of this is inevitable for everyone. Some of it, indeed, is only "negative" and pain producing because of the way we have chosen to interpret it (through those infamous expectations and judgments), and by changing what we think about it our feelings alter as well, and that can be a great lesson. Death (not tragic and accidental death, but timely and natural death) can be this kind of experience. Healing pain, from medical procedures, or therapeutic pain, as we recover from even the most horrific of traumas, can be of this kind as well. My own belief is that these sorts of things are not actively sent by God to educate or discipline us but that God's gracious presence is always there to help make as much lemonade of the lemons as can be made. Ultimately, even this kind of pain can be offered to God and others as our share in making up what is lacking in the sufferings of Christ, our share in the suffering of the world, pieces of which we may be called to share with others (Col 1:24). One of the most helpful authors on this subject, Flora Slosson Wuellner, distinguishes as well the freely chosen vocation, such as working with the poor, which brings its own peculiar pain, and is life giving as long as it enriches us and does not debilitate us.[4]

The third kind of pain is demonic pain. It has absolutely no redeeming value of itself and is so destructive of personhood that even the notion it could be a learning opportunity sticks in our teeth as blasphemy. Childhood abuse is one awful example of it. Even heroic resistance to this kind of pain, however character building, also leaves remnants and scars to trouble later life. This kind of pain is the result of forces and actions clearly contrary to God's will, and people need rescuing from it, consolation, comfort and healing as much as can be. Even here, the grace of God is present to sustain us in the horror and bring about our healing, as many have experienced and testified, though it may take years of therapy before a victim can see and believe that. Remothering by the unconditional love of God may be very important here.[5] But a kindly intentioned, avuncular God will no longer do. Unless there is a God willing to do more than just empathize or help out, catch as catch can, unless there is a God with enough power to actually save and liberate and even more one willing to share fully the risk and pain of being human, then there is no God worth acknowledging, and human being is indeed a useless passion.[6] The problem, after all, is really ethical, not ontological as Jean-Paul Sartre thought. I need a God who knows what hell I am talking about first hand.

Jesus

That is why in the end Christians are not just converted by life in general (whatever that might be) or any other "ideal," not even Jesus as an ideal, but by a particular, concrete, historical life, that of Jesus of Nazareth, the Word and Wisdom of God made flesh, God sharing fully in all the risk and pain of our humanity to the point of the fear of Gethsemane and the cry of abandonment on Calvary. This is God descending on our behalf to the lowest level of things, what Galatians and Torah call "accursed" (Gal 3:13–14).[7] For Christians, anything else is Pollyanna nonsense. Christians are converted by Jesus, who is made accessible to us by the Holy Spirit.[8]

As we saw, it is one thing to experience grace, and another to experience grace *as* grace. Before we can interpret life experiences, including pain, as grace, someone has to teach us how to do so, and the language in which to do it. If we are to know Jesus, someone must introduce us; if we are to be filled with the Spirit, someone must convey it. In *Analogical Imagination*, David Tracy distinguishes three modes of theological discourse, each appropriate for different audiences at different times. I suggest the one that is native to this current of conversion is proclamation, the confrontation of a sinner or someone who needs healing and liberation with the Word and Wisdom of God in the power of the Spirit. This requires that there be a preacher or evangelist to announce the good news, or a teacher/medic to bring healing and comfort, or a prophet to decree deliverance, or all three, and in each case someone bearing the Holy Spirit in Jesus' name to those who have not received it, helping them to read their lives as grace.

Learning to read our lives *as* grace usually involves coming to some kind of insight that we are being upheld by God's love in the midst of all these life events, including the painful ones. As a result, the third theological virtue, love, enters the picture here as an aspect of faith in three important senses.

1. First, Jesus is God's ultimate declaration that the dust we are is beloved. "Beloved" is indeed the name for the Word/Wisdom, the second person of the Trinity in Augustine's Trinitarian scheme, Lover, Beloved, Love.[9] The Trinitarian Eternal Beloved is reconceived in our dust-flesh by the mystery of the incarnation, in a way that makes that dust decisively and eternally beloved even beyond the original intention of its being loved from all creation. As the Athanasian Creed reminds us, this does not take place by the taking of the divinity into the humanity, which could be temporary, but by the assumption of the humanity into the divinity, a relationship that is eternal from that point on.[10] As St. Athanasius himself puts it, echoing 1 John, the crucified, risen, ascended, and glorified flesh of the Word is the bridge we all cross to eternal participation in the Trinitarian life.[11] In the historical life of Jesus, all the burden of human history, mortality, and sin is also taken on and born on the cross to the point of utter desolation. Then, of course, Easter happens as a whole new dispensation of God's grace and power, giving us faith that nothing, not even what is worst in life, is hopeless, because nothing can separate us from the love of God in Christ Jesus (Rom 8:35–39), not even the demonic principalities and powers we discussed above or the kind of demonic pain we were just talking about.

Two theological insights from converted women among the greatest Christian mystics help us see the depth of this love and how it operates. We noted above in our discussion of sin that it is propagating because we imperfect persons (apart from the grace whose origins we are discussing) can deal with the evil that assaults us only by absorbing it and then sending it out and onward magnified, and ourselves scarred in the process. The handing-on of patterns of abuse or other familial wounds from one generation to another is an all-too-familiar and horrible example. Simone Weil was a French Jewish philosopher of the World War II era. She became a convert to Jesus but would not be baptized because God never told her to do it, and because she saw her vocation as being a sacrament to the church of what it excludes. She teaches that only when a perfect person (Jesus) arrives in history can this vicious cycle by which evil is magnified be broken; it is interrupted as Jesus is able to absorb all the evil of the world on the cross without sending any of it back at all, same size or magnified. This is symbolized by his cry of forgiveness on the cross.[12] This becomes the measure of love's commitment, of the ethic of turning the other cheek.[a] But it is not powerless. My sculptor wife, Barbara, has done an intense portrayal of the "cry with a loud voice" from the cross, expressing her belief that in that final moment of Jesus' life the absorbed pain of the centuries reached critical mass in his cry of protest and imploded into resurrection and the world's healing.[13]

Another powerful metaphor for Jesus as the embodiment of God's love is the medieval tradition of "Jesus our Mother."[14] While it appears to begin with St. Anselm, its most powerful and best-known expression is in the revelations to the fourteenth-century Norwich anchoress, the Lady Julian. In her vision, Jesus is our mother, the embodiment of God's motherhood, because as Word he gives birth to us in creation; as Jesus he gives rebirth to us on the cross and in Baptism; and as a mother nurses her child with her own substance, so also Jesus feeds us with himself in the Eucharist.[15] Modern stereotypes would also suggest that the forgiveness on the cross expresses God's mother-love as a love that loves us in spite of (or rather without regard to) what we do, contrasting it with the stereotype of father-love, which must be earned by obedience and achievement.[16] If this is our understanding of love as fathers or as children of our fathers, then this mother-love is certainly a corrective to it; but it is important to note that that is not what Julian does with it. It is the mother-love of the entire Trinity (including the first person) that is being embodied in Jesus. It is also interesting to note, given the resistance in some quarters to gender-inclusive language for God, that this striking metaphor of "Jesus our mother" appears to have caused no trouble even in an era when professional heresy hunters were on the prowl. It may be especially important to continue to retrieve this image for those who need to be re-mothered by God as a way of coming to know God's love.

Among contemporary theologians, Schubert Ogden has spoken powerfully of Jesus as the historical decisive representative and embodiment of God's unbounded love. For two reasons he wants to avoid the notion that God's love is a priori *constituted* by Jesus death, rather than being decisively *represented* by it.[b] He teaches, cor-

---

a It is a perversion of this ethic to suggest that victims of abuse or oppression should remain in their threatening circumstances, however.

b A priori in this sense means logically necessary and hence knowable independently of experi-

rectly I believe, that we must not treat the atonement as a punishment that appeases a Father-God whose love and mercy are otherwise in question. God does not wait for the appearance of Jesus to begin being gracious to people. That belief is, among other things, the heresy of Marcionitism, because it denies that there was real grace of the real God operating in the senior covenant, the one with Abraham.[a] A second point Ogden makes is that there can be other representatives of God's unbounded and eternal love in human history, even if Jesus is the decisive representative and for Christians the sacrament of that love. That would mean there could be grace and truth in other world faiths, though this cannot be known a priori; we have to engage in dialogue to find out.[17] While commending his purposes, I question a final vision in which an a priori love of God is, as it were, delivered like mail from heaven in the person of Jesus as its decisive representative. Actual grace is not first cooked up in eternity/heaven and then delivered like pizza or mail; it is constituted in history and contingency a posteriori; that is to say, it does not first come into being in God in Jesus, since God's love certainly exists from all eternity as God's very nature and as the proper name of the Holy Spirit; but in Jesus, God decisively embodies and works out that love in history. It is *constituted* historically precisely *by* being decisively sacramentally represented. That makes us nervous, because it makes the whole of our salvation and healing—which Tillich points out is of ultimate concern for us, a question of being or not-being—depend not on an a priori necessity that can be established by proof but on a historical contingency that can only be narrated. Our salvation, like our very being, is a risky contingency. That's hard to swallow, but it's the gospel.[18]

Another powerful metaphor for this love that lies at the heart of what we are converted *by* is the notion of friendship. It is easy for us as Christians to get confused about this because of a long tradition of distinguishing the four Greek words for love: *storgē*, affection, what one feels for a pet, for example; *philia*, friendship, a relationship that can exist only between persons who are roughly equal and is governed by virtues such as fidelity and honor; *eros*, love that desires intimate union with another, of which healthy sexual desire is one human expression;[b] and *agapē*, which has been treated as a special Christian form of love, disinterested, and rather Platonic in its temperature.[19] But this misconstrues *agapē*, which is not well attested in Greek before its use in Jewish and Christian writings. It usually translates (and nearly transliterates) the Hebrew *ahav*, which has about as broad a meaning as the English "love" and certainly has an erotic component. In Hebrew, *ahav* is election love, the love of passionate choosing, which is also paired with *ḥesed*, the notion of steadfastness and faithfulness in love, and both are used as technical covenant

---

ence. It does not necessarily mean temporally prior. A posteriori as we shall use it shortly is the opposite—something that is not logically necessary, but contingent, and hence can be known only through historical experience.

a Marcion (110–160 c.e.) taught that the God of the Old Testament was different from the God of love revealed in the new, and hence the church should abandon the Old Testament. See *ODCC*, 1033b–1034b

b Eros must always be distinguished from pornography, which is precisely not erotic as it does not seek intimate union with another person but only satisfaction in an object.

terms for God's choice of and faithfulness to Israel.[20] There is also a long Hebrew tradition of "friends of God" from Abraham and Moses through Enoch, perhaps derived from the common concept of "friends of the king" in several ancient Near Eastern cultures. On these grounds, *agapē* is not a disinterested, passionless positive regard but an affectionate, erotic friendship. It is not over against the other three loves but is their healing and union.

Jesus gives us a startling twist on this in John 15. The context is John's account of the Last Supper, which is marked by Jesus's washing the feet of his disciples and a lengthy last discourse, giving them the new commandment that they are to love one another as he has loved them. Soon (chap. 17) he will launch into the great "high-priestly prayer" by which he is consecrated for the coming sacrifice. After giving them the new commandment, culminating in 15:12, Jesus goes on to show what he has been trying to get across since the footwashing: "Greater love has no one than this, that one lay down one's life for one's friends." This is the measure of the love with which Jesus has loved us, with which God has loved us in Jesus. It is a self-sacrificing love not in the sense that it *seeks* death and martyrdom but in the sense that it is by nature prepared to go the whole way, to any lengths, for the sake of friends and friendship. The issue is not self-denial as that is usually understood but the love of friendship.

Jesus continues in this startling vein (especially startling in the light of the footwashing, where he assumed the role of a slave): "You are my friends if you do what I command you," namely, to love one another. "No longer do I call you servants, for the servant does not know what his master is doing; but I have called you friends, for all that I have heard from my Father I have made known to you." To the notion that friendship is a love prepared to go to any lengths for the sake of the other, Jesus adds that it is also a communion of shared moral purpose.[21] A servant merely follows orders: "Theirs is not to reason why." But you don't give orders to a friend; you invite a friend to share in a joint enterprise with a shared purpose, as an equal, a partner, a *fellawe*. Notice that being a friend is not less, but more, demanding than being a servant.

There is a third aspect to this friendship. "You did not choose me, but I chose you and appointed you that you should go and bear fruit and that your fruit should abide; so that whatever you ask the Father in my name, he may give it to you. This is my commandment, that you love one another." In images such as the vine and branches, and in the great high-priestly prayer that follows, Jesus also shows a concern for the unity achieved by love, unity of the disciples with one another, with him, and through him, with the Father. There is thus an *erotic* dimension to this friendship. The choosing is the covenant choosing of election love, *ahav*, the love of the bridegroom for the chosen bride (and we would now hope vice versa). There is the desire not only for the welfare of the other, but for intimacy and union. And the union is to be fecund; it is to bear fruit, fruit that will last. There is no hint here that this erotic dimension is sexual in nature, nor any hint that a sexual element is precluded where appropriate. Indeed, one of the more mysterious things about the Gospels in particular is how *little* they have to say about sex, either in general, or about Jesus' sexuality.[22] The point is to recognize the passionate and even erotic element in this friendship, acknowledging that whether genitalized sexuality is to be involved or not is a matter of some indifference.

There are thus three aspects to this friendship: it is prepared to go to any lengths, even death, for the sake of the other; it is a communion and partnership of equals in a shared moral purpose; and it has an erotic (but not necessarily explicitly sexual) dimension in choosing, desiring intimacy and unity, and intending fecundity.[23]

My own Christology, then, which I invite you to share, is that Jesus is the sacrament (decisive concrete embodiment, a posteriori historical constitution) of God's desire for erotic friendship (a friendship that desires union) with human dust, the concrete offer of that friendship, and the removal of all barriers to that friendship, of both inequality and sin.[24] If we take this insight seriously and borrow from both the Quakers and the Jesuits, then the church as the community of mutual love Jesus has commanded can be seen as the Society of the Friends of Jesus. This has many echoes in the Christian tradition. Gregory of Nyssa, for example, at the end of *The Life of Moses,* his great treatise on the spiritual life, says, "The only thing worthwhile is being God's friend."[25] Aelred bucked the trend in monastic life to discount and warn against particular or special friendships by suggesting they are rather the school for friendship with God.[26] Nicholas Lash, English Roman Catholic theologian at Cambridge, suggests that erotic friendship may be as close as we can get to understanding what our relationship with God and one another under the two great commandments is to be like.[27] Sallie McFague, feminist theologian now retired from Vanderbilt, believes friendship provides a particularly useful metaphor for God because of the inherent equality, which challenges the hierarchical commitments of patriarchy.[28] We can notice, for example, the application to marriage. Though it is a rather recent development, we now expect there to be a friendship at the heart of a marriage and usually consider the marriage to have failed if the friendship does not endure. That means patriarchal authoritarian structures for marriage must yield to a partnership of equals, since that is the essence of friendship.[a*]

We must wait for the section where we discuss the unitive movement in the third current of glory to examine the mystery of our partnership of equality with God in this relationship. Here we can refer back by title to the mystery of the incarnation itself: one way God makes the equality of friendship possible is by being begotten as one of us. A classic expression of this mystery is Søren Kierkegaard's parable of the king and the beggar: the king becomes a beggar to woo a beggar woman to make her his queen.[29] This is one of the ways Christians have of talking about the decisiveness of Jesus. There can be many relationships with a loving God, but friendship requires incarnation as the doorway to equality. What we shall see in the last current of this book is that it is a swinging door: as the church has taught ever since Athanasius, God became human that we might become god.

There is a further dimension of the classical notion of friendship we must

---

a See my "What a Friend We Have in Jesus," and "Procreation and Patience." The essence of this friendship as a desire for personal union, not necessarily or primarily sexual, is a salient warning in the face of the issue of sexual addiction. In this life, erotic friendships can be very hard to maintain within appropriate boundaries, and are probably not appropriate in any case where a power relationship interferes with the necessary equality.

recover, however, in the face of contemporary cheapened notions of chumminess or even hominess (as in home boy). Friendship is fulfilled in a mutual life of virtue, not just the virtue of fidelity, but all the virtues. Chief is honor; I honor my friend by treating my friend as an honorable person. I would never ask a friend to do something dishonorable nor leave unreproved a friend who seems to have acted dishonorably.[30] When I was growing up, the Sunday Funnies often included an ad for Colgate toothpaste. It was a simpler and safer era, and the dreaded social disease of the time was halitosis, bad breath. Like most ads, there was a big lie in this advertising, which was the phrase "Even your best friend won't tell you." It is a lie, because a true best friend is the person who really will tell you about faults and blemishes, telling the truth in love. This is the grand tradition of a true friend as an "alter ego," a mirror of reality in which I am called to see myself as I truly am. It is not so much my friend's reproof of me that leads to repentance and a life of virtue but the love with which that friend stays in my face. The life of virtue is not so much a precondition for friendship and love as the consequence of being so privileged to have such a friend who stays lovingly in my face always.[31]

Friendship, embodied in real concrete relationships, is the primary pedagogy of healing and forgiveness for the reign of God. The transforming and erotic dimensions of such friendship come more into focus in the next two currents; in this current of conversion we are examining, the love of friendship with Jesus and hence God is being born in us primarily in a moral sense, as a call to go to any lengths, as a call to a communion and partnership of shared moral purpose, and as a relationship with one who stays in my face with a mirror of reality in which my faults are obvious and onerous, for the sake of the love in response to that love. Where healing or liberation is more at stake than repentance, it is Jesus as the friend who defends, re-mothers, or sets us free. In this current in which faith is the principal virtue, the emphasis is love as fidelity, God's faithfulness to us under the covenant (ḥesed), which calls us to turn and re-turn in fidelity to God under that same and (re)newed covenant.

2. So far we have spoken of the love that comes into focus when we attend to what we are *converted by* from God's side, the sacramental offer in the person of Jesus of erotic friendship with God. The second major sense in which faithful love enters the picture here is in our response. Love evokes love. Once again, our virtues are resonances in us raised by the approach of a God who is righteous and loving. The experience of being dust that is beloved is intended to give birth to "loving back" in fruits that abide. Love is meant as a relationship of fecund mutuality. As a result, Jesuit theologian Bernard Lonergan describes conversion from our side as falling in love without qualification.[32] *Christian* conversion is falling in love with Jesus without qualification, and part of the ongoing place of the "penitential moment" in the recurring cycle of growth is in that phrase "without qualification." As we are more and more drawn into a loving response to being beloved, more and more of the "qualifications" we have placed on love surface. We are called upon to allow this healing and forgiving love, light, and Word/Wisdom to penetrate to all the nasty little secret places we have been holding out because we are afraid they make us unworthy, or because we take some perverse satisfaction in them and are

not yet prepared to give up, or because childhood trauma does not allow us to give them up yet. The dynamic of the moral life is not so much established by the structure of virtue versus vice as it is in the slow, painful growth by which we are called to give up the qualifications we place on our response to love and being beloved by the friend who stays in our face with the mirror of reality.

More on that purgative phenomenon subsequently. But first we can pause and enjoy the fact that conversion is falling in love, and not in general but with a real person. In our jaded and cynical time it is almost embarrassing to be in the presence of someone who is really falling in love with Jesus with real passion and enthusiasm. In fact, what one sees in others or oneself at the start often is a kind of puppy love or infatuation, with the deeper lessons of love yet to be learned. But it is no better for good "mature" Christians to put down this early stage of religious development than it is for adults to try to tell adolescents about the realities and price of real love and how it is different from our first tastes of it. What is called for is not disparagement but sound discernment and guidance. As in all early love, our own ego-ideal and other projections will be involved; but how do we know it is really God and Jesus onto which we are even projecting them?

At a very deep level we must examine in the third current, we don't *know*, not ever. But at this stage there are some helpful principles for discernment that form a kind of wisdom. Madeline L'Engle describes what she does when someone comes to tell her they are falling in love with a romantic partner. Instead of asking about that relationship, she asks about how the rest of their life is going, their work and their other relationships. If it is enriched and expanded, she believes, this is a true love; if the rest of life is being ignored, denied, contracted, or diminished, it is the "love-sickness" of infatuation and may be dangerous.[33] This is the link to what we saw in the previous section. To fall in love with *Jesus*, to have *Jesus* as a friend, means to obey the new commandment, to accept the fact that the two great commandments, to love God and neighbor, are actually one, in that one cannot love God (Augustine, *Enchiridion,* chap. 121) without loving the neighbor (1 John 4:20–21) (or, for that matter, truly love the neighbor without loving God). The result of falling in love with *Jesus* then is not a sectarian and partisan spirit of contraction, not an increase in judgmental hatefulness, or of dominant superiority, but one of true expansion of heart, of "charity" (at its deepest level of meaning, still the English form of the Latin word *caritas,* which translates the Greek *agapē*). This love always builds up ("edifies") the community of faith and does not destroy it. Here are the three classical principles of Christian discernment of spirits in Scripture: if it is a true gift of the Holy Spirit, Jesus will ultimately be confessed as Lord and as having come in the flesh; there will be an increase in actual love of neighbor; and the church (community of faith) will be built up.

Even while we make these discernments, though, it is important to let this falling in love with Jesus have room in ourselves and others. Herbert W. Richardson in *Toward an American Theology* reminds us that this means not just being grateful to Jesus for what he has done for us but taking time and energy simply to love him, to enjoy being in his presence as our friend, to delight in his person.[34] This means prayerful meditation of some kind on the fleshly life of Jesus as recorded in the Gospels *at every stage of the spiritual life*. Like fellowship with other believers, regular participation in worship and the sacraments or ordinances of the Gospel, and charity to all humans, devotion to the human life and person of Jesus is never outgrown, nor is it ever too early to start. The flesh of Jesus, and passionate delight in it, is both our anchor in reality and our hope of glory. Sitting attentively at his feet, as the Mary and Martha story makes clear (Luke 10:38–41),[35] is the one thing needful, the pearl of great price. No approach to Christianity, including Christian spirituality, can ever remove the human Jesus from the center of life, attention, and devotion.

Indeed, all the rest of "spirituality" follows from this love and friendship. Because we have fallen in love with Jesus we gladly accept the invitation to become his disciples and enter the process of "being discipled." Because we have fallen in love with Jesus, we follow him to Gethsemane and try to stay awake, and even to Calvary if need be, our own cross and suffering born for his sake. (But remember what was said above about discernment of pain and suffering.) Because we have fallen in love with Jesus we shall obey his new commandment and love one another and all our neighbors for his sake. That love will mean both serving them as Jesus our friend has served us and also inviting them into the society of Jesus's friends because that friendship is the most precious thing we have to offer them. It should be obvious that there can ultimately be no conflict, scarcely any difference in emphasis, between the "great commandments" (Mark 12:30 and parallels) and the "great commission" (Matt 28:16–20), despite efforts to divide the church along those lines. Servanthood, discipleship, apostolate, and mission and evangelism are all one loving response to commandments and commission, even if finitude means that members of the Body of Christ will specialize in particular ministries on behalf of the whole. The obedience itself, however, is not that of a slave to master, or even student to teacher, but the freely given assent to the partnership and moral communion of friendship.

Sacramental theologian Tad Guzie asks in his *Book of Sacramental Basics,* "Do you believe that the Father loved Jesus more than he loves you? Anyone who believes this does not seem to have heard the Good News."[36] In fact, Guzie is pointing out, God loves us not only as much as Jesus; God loves us all with the very same love with which God loves Jesus, with which Jesus our friend loves us, and with which he commands us to love one another and our neighbor. In Western Trinitarian theology, that love, the *vinculum caritatis*, the bond of love between Lover and Beloved (Father/Mother and Word/Wisdom) is the very person of the Holy Spirit.[37] I accept the need to take the *filioque* (the phrase, "and the son") out of the text of the Nicene Creed, because it is the text as passed by the ecumenical councils that is authoritative, and there is much to learn from the Eastern understanding of the Trinity.[a] But the Western doctrines of co-equality of persons and of the Holy Spirit as bond of love also have lessons to teach.[38]

---

a   The phrase "and the son" (*filioque* in Latin), was added to the Nicene Creed in the West by a dubious, noncanonical process; efforts to impose it on the Christian East have never been successful. The original is also in accord with Scripture, John 15:26. Whole conflicted theologies have been built up about this disagreement. The value of the Western doctrine of the "double procession," that the

3. This is how faithful love enters into *converted by* in a third way. God's very nature as love is what is being revealed by and in Jesus. Love is not something God has; it is what God is, and that is what is perfectly spoken as God's Word and Wisdom in the person and work of Jesus (1 John 4:8). I have not given an initial a priori definition of love because that is the wrong way round. We do not bring a definition of love to God and find him loving; we are *given* the definition of love in the Trinitarian life incarnated in Jesus and in the dance that weaves all creation with the economy of the Holy Spirit. We love God because God first loved us (1 John 4:19). This parallels exactly what was said in the previous chapter about the mystery of the incarnation: we do not approach it with preconceived notions of humanity and divinity, or we shall surely have problems; instead, we go to the person of Jesus to learn what "God" and "human being" mean. Ordinary life, informed sacramentally and contemplatively by the flesh of Jesus and the indwelling of the Holy Spirit, in company with other friends of Jesus, is the pedagogy, the school by which we unlearn hate and learn love, and in the process learn what love *is*.

The Holy Spirit

Herbert Richardson is helpful once more. He suggests that in the incarnation God establishes a relationship of friendship with all human beings, but in the presence of the historical Jesus that can only be actualized for a few. By taking this action, God freely undertakes the obligation to make this friendship available to everyone by the outpouring of the Holy Spirit on all flesh. What was localized in the presence of the historical Jesus is universally available, though still concretely localized in each case, in the Holy Spirit.[39] It is in fact the Holy Spirit who makes ongoing friendship with Jesus possible, now that Jesus is not only risen but ascended (gone away). A personal relationship with Jesus, however conceived, is never *immediate*, but one *mediated* by the Holy Spirit. This is the implication of the teaching about another comforter (Paraclete—Advocate) in the Gospel of John: the Holy Spirit takes the place of the historical Jesus (the first Comforter/Advocate) in the Christian community but does so by leading that community into all truth through recalling to it the person, teaching, and work of Jesus (John 14:16; 14:26; 15:26; 16:8).[40] The Holy Spirit is always also the Spirit of Christ, as is evident in St. Paul's lack of precision in defining what it means to be "*en Christo*" and "in the Spirit."[41] The lack is intended; they are in one sense the same thing. But that is because throughout the whole Gospel narrative the second and third persons of the Trinity are involved in a very delicate mutual dance, as the Word/Wisdom is conceived in history as the human being Jesus in the womb of Mary by the Holy Spirit, is consecrated as Messiah by the Holy Spirit, but then becomes the one who sends the Holy Spirit from the Fount.[42]

Holy Spirit, as the bond of love between Fount and Word/Wisdom, in some sense proceeds through both does not depend on the phrase in the creed. Many Western churches now propose to do away with the phrase in the creed, without denying the Western doctrine. The issue is that the authoritative text of the Creed is the one passed at the first Council of Constantinople.

The Holy Spirit is more than the *medium* by which divine love is delivered. The Holy Spirit, especially in Western Trinitarianism, *is* the gift of love itself, the very mediation of that of which Jesus is the mediator.[43] In Western Trinitarianism the love with which the Lover loves the Beloved and vice versa is so intense, as it were, that it itself is personal, the third person of the Trinity. The Holy Spirit is the love with which God loves God internally, the love by which the Word is spoken in creation, and then to the people and to the prophets of Israel; it is this love by which the Word/Wisdom is incarnated and commissioned as Messiah, and, if Moltmann is correct, the love that rushes into the breach opened up between Father and Son on the cross;[44] that is, the Holy Spirit is the love with which God loves the dust we are, which is not just an act or attribute of God but God in person as Holy Spirit. As gift, the Holy Spirit is also the love with which we return God's love, as the indwelling Spirit gifts us with the theological virtue of love, at root her own indwelling. Though these three moments (God loving God, God loving us, we loving God) can be differentiated, they are not divided. The love is all one, but in a complex dynamic dance of erotic friendship rather than as a static monistic ideal.[a] The mystery of the Trinity, after all, is that both unity and difference are real, that personhood is constituted by a dialectic of individuality and community.[45] The whole tide of turn and return thus begins with the self-expression of the Fount within the Trinity, then in creation, then in covenant. We see, again, that in this current the Holy Spirit's work is in support of the "mission" of the Fount, our Father and Mother.

Two bits of traditional language can be refocused in the light of this discussion. The first is the concept of the indwelling of the Holy Spirit as a "seed of God," the *sperma theou*. What is most helpful about this image is first that it corrects any lingering Manichaean notions about our having sparks of the divine trapped in a prison of flesh, or pantheistic notions of something inherently divine about humans, about our being chips off the Old Block (Ancient of Days). Christian teaching is that these images are false. There is nothing inherently divine about human beings except being created in the image of God and indwelt by the Holy Spirit as a seed of God. This protects the doctrine that by God's will and grace, all creatures, including humans, are other than God, not chips off the old uncarved block. The Holy Spirit indwelling as a kind of seed is the only spark of the divine in us as well. By our creation as beloved dust we are already animated and spirited by the Spirit; by covenant and further, even more superfluous grace, we are also indwelt by the Spirit. Two other ideas are also helpful, growth and fecundity. The idea of seed reminds us that our relationship to God and its consequence, our sanctification, is not delivered as something complete and full-grown. It has an economy of development. It grows in us and grows us to be more adequate temples in which it may grow. It reminds us again that perfection is a dynamic journey, not a steady-state accomplishment of either ours or God's. Fecundity is also helpful in the image, and we recall Hildegard of Bingen's great image of God's *veriditas*, greening power.[46] A seed gives rise to a plant that bears fruit and thus further seed. We are to manifest the fruits of the Spirit as this seed grows in us, and through those fruits other seeds may be sown in other creatures. We are also reminded by the physicality of

---

a God and reality as an undifferentiated One.

these images that the Spirit dwells in our bodies, not in our souls or human spirits alone.[47] Indeed, as I have suggested, we have souls and spirits only because of the relationship with the Holy Spirit from our creation as beloved dust.

Of course, there are problems with this analogy, as with any. One is all the sediment caused by the identification by classical biology of "seed" with the stuff in male semen that make babies; we inevitably hear the Greek *sperma* as "sperm" in the context of that metaphor for human sexuality. The mistake, of course, which could not be rectified scientifically until the discovery of human ova in the late nineteenth century, was in thinking that in bisexual animals all that makes a person or other creature was carried in the male stuff, which was then just planted in a womb construed only as passive soil. The sociopolitical deconstruction is obvious, of course. This same problem infected the notion of "begetting" in the Trinity, making the first person more exclusively male than "begetter" actually requires. With reference to the *sperma theou* concept at stake here, there are two possible solutions. One is to break the connection between seed and sperm and see the mystery as a seed of God, not a sperm. It is tempting to go this route, because it certainly guards against any creeping Pelagianism, though not creeping Manichaeism—all the important stuff is in the divine seed. That, of course, is the problem. The flesh becomes only passive ground, and the mutuality of relationship is lost. A better way, then, it seems to me, is to let it stand initially as a sperm of God, but in our newer sense, as containing half the information, the rest being provided by the flesh in which it is "planted." Pelagianism is avoided by remembering that the flesh is also given by God in creation and shaped in the image of God in humans. So the contribution of the flesh itself is also there by divine gift. On this analogy of course, the indwelling of the Holy Spirit could as well be called "the egg of God" as the "sperm," and should be on occasion to provide balance. Perhaps Hildegard of Bingen's *veriditas*, God's greening power, will do better than either. The point is to maintain the truths about bodily indwelling, growth, and fecundity.

The second bit of traditional language about the spiritual life illuminated by our discussion is the concept of that life being under "the dominion of charity." Seen thus, it has two senses. It means that the theological virtue of love in us is the governing virtue (1 Corinthians 13), the measure of all the others, the principle of discernment par excellence, to be embodied in us as both "habitual" (becoming a habit of our character—making us loving persons) and "actual" (carried out in real acts of concrete love for others). At a deeper level, it is also our confession that the Holy Spirit who gives this gift, who *is* this gift, is Lord and God.[a] The dominion of charity in life is the confession and actualization of the Lordship of God the Holy Spirit. Once again, we see the unity of the two great commandments (and, if one understands the sacrament of Baptism at all, and the role of the Holy Spirit in it, of their link to the great commission).

This is worked out in the concrete moral struggle, the life defined by the struggle of virtue with vice in us as the struggle to actualize the Trinitarian structures

a That was, of course, the point of the debates at the first Council of Constantinople. While I am sensitive to feminist dislike of "Lord," I know of no substitute that captures all the theological meaning of *kyrios*, not just sovereign, or even "sir," but of God in the biblical usage.

of the reign of God in a human life and a community as proleptic of the common-wealth. The Holy Spirit simply *is* the source of all virtue through the indwelling and infusion of faith, hope, and love. As such, it is the Holy Spirit who is the "mediatrix of all graces," not Mary. But it is through Mary's womb, pelvis, and vagina that this grace, this ultimate superfluous graciousness that is the Holy Spirit, is poured out in the Christian dispensation, and with her free (though informed by prevenient grace) consent and assent.[48] In that sense, and that sense alone, it is appropriate to call her Mediatrix of All Graces precisely as *Theotokos,* God-bearer. It is to this concrete moral struggle we must now turn, this struggle not *between* spirit and flesh, but of the Holy Spirit indwelling in the flesh as the gift of love, the growth of the seed or egg of God, the *sperma theou* in us who are dust. We return, then, to ordinary life, in the company of other friends of Jesus, in which love is learned and the seed or egg of God is nurtured for growth. We have learned that this life is the life of beloved dust, that this love comes into focus as we look at what we are *converted by*: God's sacramental offer of friendship in the person of Jesus; our falling in love without qualification with that Jesus, who then pours out on us and all flesh, all dust, the Holy Spirit who is the very gift of love as person. To speak of the dominion of charity among the virtues is to confess the Holy Spirit as Lord and God, as head teacher, principal and principle of the school for the friends of Jesus.

Notes

1. This concept of "life shock" is borrowed from Brown and Whitten, the Life Training.
2. Israel Charny, *Marital Love and Hate*, 85–86.
3. Charny, *Marital Love and Hate*, 86.
4. See Flora Slosson Wuellner, *Heart of Healing, Heart of Light,* 88; several of her other works also take a position compatible with the one outlined here.
5. Barbara B. Hughes, "Where Was God?" 98.
6. See Dorothee Sölle's recognition of this need for good divine power in her conversion to feminist liberation theology from "God is dead" theology (*Thinking about God,* 187–88).
7. Christopher Bryan in conversation helped me with this.
8. Kilian McDonnell *Other Hand of God,* 94–108; Luis Bermejo, *The Spirit of Life,* 1–10.
9. Augustine, *De Trinitate* XV.3.5; 6.10.
10. Athanasian Creed, *BCP* 864–65; this creed is later and Latin, and not by Athanasius.
11. Athanasius, *Contra Arianos* 2.62, 2.74; see Alvyn Petersen, *Athanasius,* 132–35.
12. Simone Weil, *Waiting for God,* 191–92. See Luke 23:34.
13. Barbara Hughes, "Using the Arts to Open Scripture," 142.
14. There is now a substantial literature on this. See Julia Gatta, *Three Spiritual Directors for Our Time,* 83–86; and Caroline Walker Bynum, *Jesus as Mother.*
15. Julian of Norwich, *Showings,* long text, ##57–61 (Paulist ed., 292–302).
16. See, for example, Havelock Ellis, *Man and Woman.*
17. See Schubert Ogden, *The Point of Christology;* idem, *Is There Only One True Religion, or Are There Many?*
18. See my "What a Friend We Have in Jesus," and "Christian Theology of Interfaith Dialogue."
19. The classic misuse of this distinction is Anders Nygren, *Agape and Eros,* and Dennis De Rougement, *Love in the Western World.*

20. C. S. Lewis, *The Four Loves*; see also "Love in the Old Testament," *IDB* 3:164–68. "Love in the New Testament," *IDB* 3:168–78, has the linguistic essentials but is too dependent on Nygren for my taste. See also *TDOT* 1:99–118; *TDNT* 21–55 also has much that is helpful but has a conclusion too much influenced by Nygren. See also Philip Sheldrake, *Befriending Our Desires*, 45–47.

21. I first got this from Herbert W. Richardson, in class.

22. *Pace* the *DaVinci Code* and all its sources; despite our new sense of the apostolic importance of Mary Magdalene, there is no hint of sexuality in her relationship to Jesus in the earliest texts. See Tom F. Driver, "Sexuality and Jesus."

23. This Christology of friendship has become quite popular; one major source for it is Sallie McFague, *Models of God*.

24. This obviously owes an immense debt to a variety of theologians who have seen the person and work of Christ in sacramental terms. See especially William Porcher DuBose, *Unity in the Faith*, 98; and Edward Schillebeeckx, *Christ the Sacrament of the Encounter with God*.

25. Gregory of Nyssa, *The Life of Moses*, ##319–20, 136–37.

26. Aelred of Rievaulx, *Spiritual Friendship*.

27. Nicholas Lash, *The Beginning and the End of "Religion,"* 26–48, 212–18. Again, we await Sarah Coakley's vol. 1 of her systematic theology and its discussion of a "new erotics."

28. See n. 23.

29. Søren Kierkegaard, *Philosophical Fragments*; see especially the parable of the king and the beggar woman, 32–43.

30. I learned much of this from Paul Weiss and Herbert W. Richardson in respective classes. Aristotle, *Nicomachean Ethics* VIII and IX (McKeon ed., 1058–93); and Cicero *De Amicitia* had much of it.

31. Richard Prior describes his relationship with James Brown in these terms. See my "What a Friend We Have in Jesus."

32. Bernard Lonergan, *Method*, 240.

33. Madeline L'Engle, *A Circle of Quiet*, 109–110.

34. Herbert Warren Richardson, *Toward an American Theology*, 130–31.

35. The point of the story is that Jesus has accepted Mary, a woman, as a disciple, and hence equal to the other disciples. It is not a story of submission.

36. Tad Guzie, *The Book of Sacramental Basics*, 78.

37. Augustine, *De Trinitate* XV, 6.10, 17.27–31.

38. John Macquarrie, *Principles of Christian Theology*, 330–37, is eloquent on the need to balance the two versions.

39. Richardson, *Toward an American Theology*, 143–60.

40. Raymond Brown, "The Paraclete," in *The Gospel According to John (xiii–xxi)*, 1135–44.

41. McDonnell *Other Hand of God*, 64–70; Bermejo, *Spirit of Life*, 35–71.

42. McDonnell, *Other Hand of God*, 65; see Alasdair Heron, *The Holy Spirit*, for a powerful theological analysis of this dance of coequality (157–78, esp. 170–78).

43. McDonnell, *Other Hand of God*, 104.

44. Jürgen Moltmann, *The Trinity and the Kingdom*, 80–83, but this should be read in the context of 127–90. See also idem, *The Crucified God*, 235–49, where Moltmann actually derives the doctrine of the Trinity from that of the cross.

45. As previously noted, this whole paragraph is deeply indebted to Robert Jenson, Kathryn Tanner, and the whole burgeoning literature of the new Trinitarianism.

46. Matthew Fox and Hildegard, *Illuminations*, 30–33, 111–13; Fox's interperetations of Hildegard can be excessive but seem accurate on this point.

47. Bermejo, *Spirit of Life*, 37–121, esp. 83; see my "The Holy Spirit in Christian Spirituality," 210–11.

48. See Eugene Rogers's splendid chapter on the Annunciation in *After the Spirit*, 98–134, especially the remark about our "inner Nestorius," 112.

First Tidal Current: Converted Dust

II. Conversion and the Moral Struggle

9

The Life of Constant Conversion

> *We also constantly give thanks to God for this, that when you received the word of God that you heard from us, you accepted it not as a human word but as what it really is, God's word, which is also at work in you believers.*
> —1 Thess 2:13

Spiritual theology proper exists at the interface of theological anthropology and pneumatology—that is, between the doctrine of humanity (including psychology) and the doctrine of the person and work of the Holy Spirit. It is also linked to a large field of what theologians call *praxis*, the actually experienced practice of the spiritual life and the ministry of spiritual direction, indeed, of the Christian life as a whole.

I have already been at some pains to remove spiritual theology from its customary place outside dogmatic theology and subordinate to moral theology by restoring it to a precise place in dogmatic theology as a theology of the work of the Holy Spirit. But it also has links to moral theology and Christian ethics, precisely at the point we have now reached; both study the moral life in terms of the interplay between vices and virtues. There is, however, a real difference in perspective. Moral theology studies these matters with an eye to developing a theology of the good that allows persons to decide what is right and what is wrong in particular concrete cases of moral choice; spiritual theology, by contrast, is primarily interested in how that concrete moral struggle, conversion at the moral level, as it were (and as I shall develop that further on), affects and effects spiritual growth toward communion/union with God in God's perfect reign and commonwealth. Both theologies are concerned with the formation of character, character fitted for God's reign. The moral theologian is primarily concerned with what sorts of actions and habits build such a character; the spiritual theologian focuses on the way the delicate interplay of faith, hope, and love as the impact of the indwelling Holy Spirit makes such habits and actions possible and growthful for character as a dimension of sanctification. In the tradition, a virtue is primarily a *habitus,* a habit of character, or a characteristic way of being and doing. Because these habits are themselves the response to one movement of the Holy Spirit, they can best be seen as the marks of a faithful, constant, and fecund relationship. They are personal strengths of character, but only as gifts within that relationship. Their opposite, vices, are defects or weaknesses of character.

Archbishop William Temple, echoing thoughts of Bishop Kenneth Kirk, believed that the ordinary daily moral struggle, with its interplay of grace and conscience, is *the* experience of God common to most people for most of their lives.[1] If we do not get the point about the birth of this struggle in the first appearances of faith, hope, and love in response to humility and healthy shame or liberating "permission," all as a result of the presence and indwelling of the Holy Spirit, this can become a Pelagian self-improvement course, or worse. I have been in homes where the bookshelves contain more self-help books than novels. The religious version of this is moralism, the belief that even if we cannot earn our salvation (though that belief still persists with a surprising stubbornness even in classical Protestant circles) we still ought to pull up our socks and behave, show some character and willpower. In classical spiritual theology, the distinction made between "infused" and "acquired" virtues embodied this problem in a different way; it left the theological virtues to grace, but the others could somehow be acquired by our own efforts. The position I have taken is that all real virtue is the effect in humans of the presence and indwelling of the Holy Spirit, indeed, an imparting to us of virtues that are actually resonances of God's own perfection. In the account that follows, I shall argue that the virtues that used to be thought of as acquired actually derive from the theological virtues, which, as has usually been taught, are infused and not acquired, matters of pure gift rather than anxious exercise.

That is not the end of the story, of course. The experience most of us have as virtues are given and strengthened is that they are both gift, and somehow native to us. We "ought" to have had them all along. This is because they belong naturally to a humanity created in the image of God, and their growth and development and efficacy require our free acceptance. Their existence in us as "in the image" is already a matter of the grace of creation, of course, and grace is also required to liberate us for the possibility of that free acceptance. Even beyond that, virtues and gifts that cannot be earned or acquired but only received are still meant to be trained, practiced, and exercised as they grow into habits of character, characteristic of us, habitual. This "pedagogy of contemplative practice," however, is also already addressed by grace, the presence and indwelling of the Holy Spirit, even though our own free will and initiative are always involved at the secondary level.[2] There is a very knotty mystery here, which is perhaps best solved by the doctrine of synergism:[3] once the process gets underway (and that is always purely at God's initiative), then it becomes less and less possible to separate or even differentiate God's contribution to the growth from ours. They become inextricably intertwined.

As long as we maintain a self-help or self-actualization point of view, the discipline we are likely to undertake will be an effort to subdue the flesh with spirit, given the persistent Manichaeism we have been tracking in our culture, or one of putting mind over matter, or through arcane practices to replicate peak experiences.[a] What is called for is covenant obedience in the flesh to the task of helping to build up the reign of God. That obedience is directed to the two great commandments, and in that sense we can see that virtues are the habitual disciplines of friendship with God and one another. They are the impact on us not only of the work of the Holy Spirit but of the character of Jesus our friend (the way any close friend shapes our character). They grow in the communion of shared moral purpose into which Jesus invites us.

This contemplative pedagogy of friendship builds up virtues as true habits of character, the character not of "spirit" but of animated and spirited dust. The habits called for are not merely habits of mind; they are to be imprinted in our flesh, like a kind of *over*-training in many athletic skills—you practice until the response becomes automatic and you do not have to think about it. In the ethical realm we always have to think about it, but a pedagogy of overtrained habit is still at stake, and at stake in the flesh, since it is in the flesh, in the arena of the daily life of the world, that this practice must take place, in response to the character manifested in the flesh of Jesus.[4] So quietism, waiting for God to do it all as if we had no part to play, is also ruled out. Virtues are habits of character that are freely received as gifts, not just passively received, but also actively, gifts that require training, practice, and exercise in a flesh and world indwelt by grace.

We may also note that what is called for is a life of constant conversion, not only in this first current we are now examining, which I have called "conversion," but also throughout all the dimensions and aspects of the Christian life. Here we tread on some tender ground. In the revivalist tradition, two doctrines have come together to produce a great error. The first doctrine is that all conversions, at least those marking the entrance into this first cycle of the spiritual life, are to be accompanied by an intense emotional experience of forgiveness and release, usually called the born-again experience. As I have tried to suggest, a deeper reading of the Christian tradition admits there are such experiences, and many of them are certainly authentic; but it is not necessary that all conversions be so marked, nor does any one particular kind of experience *guarantee* that what is going on is a genuine conversion, a genuine movement of the Holy Spirit and a human response to it.[5] Discernment by the fruits produced is always necessary.

The second doctrine comes from John Wesley and is usually called the doctrine of Christian perfection in the particular form of the possibility of "instantaneous entire sanctification."[6] In his truly wonderful teaching about the process of the sanctification that follows conversion and justification, Wesley states that we are all called *to go on* to perfection. As the great Wesley scholar Albert Outler points out, Wesley's own view of perfection was shaped by Gregory of Nyssa, who clearly taught that, for the Christian, perfection is the journey itself and not a state

---

a I refer here to the ordinary moral life; some self-help techniques are very helpful in a therapeutic context.

to be achieved, a notion we have seen embodied in the analogy of the seed or egg of God.[7] Nevertheless, Wesley felt compelled by his own sense of God's sovereignty to teach that it was logically possible for God to give someone entire sanctification, and hence perfection, instantaneously and at any moment, and that our prayer and hope should be colored by that possibility. From the standpoint of doctrine of God, he was right, but the consequences in practice were unfortunate. Many people began to have violent emotional experiences of being "slain in the Spirit" while Wesley was preaching, and claimed to have experienced instantaneous entire sanctification. Wesley himself did not approve of what he considered hysterical behavior and did not credit any particular claim that perfection had been reached in this life. The great question for Methodist spiritual direction in the classes and bands (small groups Wesley formed for mutual direction and supervision), and still in preparation for ordination in the United Methodist Church, was never "Have you achieved perfection?" but "Art thou going on to perfection?"

In primitive Methodist and Holiness circles the emotional experiences persisted, however, and eventually became linked to the pentecostal outbreaks of the late nineteenth and early twentieth centuries. In both the Wesleyan and pentecostal traditions, it should be noted, these experiences of instantaneous perfection are a "second blessing," subsequent to conversion and justification. The emotional power of the first and second blessings was indistinguishable for some, however, and when you stir in a literalist reading of some passages from the New Testament in some evangelical corners the notion arose that conversion/justification/sanctification/perfection/being born again were all one thing leading to a postconversion state of sinlessness.[8]

At a County Ministerial Association meeting I once attended, along with ministers and spouses of many denominations, we were having a very helpful day led by a team from the Yokefellows ministry, an evangelical group that sought to apply insights of modern psychology to Christian growth.[9] There had been a lot of deep sharing about the struggle as we experienced it, especially from some of the clergy spouses, and pretty much across denominational lines. Finally, however, one minister from a conservative pentecostal church stood up and said, "I don't know what is the matter with the rest of you! Since I accepted Jesus as my personal savior I have not had a problem or committed a sin!" It is not my job to judge the man in the context of his relationship with God, but I must condemn the teaching implied. As we shall see later when we come to consider so-called mystical experiences, one of the most dangerous and illusory of them is the sense that one has now transcended the moral struggle and is above ordinary experiences of good and evil. If it is dangerous further down the line, it is even more dangerous here at the start. Wesley was right the first time: all humans are called into a long, slow growth into perfection characterized by serious moral struggle, even if that growth is marked by one or more dramatic turning points.[10] There is no escaping the contemplative pedagogy by which virtue is formed, because virtues are not discrete packages that can be delivered and strung together like a necklace or merit badges to be hung on a sash. They are habits, and habits must be practiced in the process of receiving and acquiring them. Further, we are to be perfect not only as completed human beings but even as our heavenly Father is perfect (Matt 5:48); that calls us into an infinitude of goodness to which we cannot attain in our finitude except by grace. Wesley's theological-limit case must not be allowed to distort practice. If nothing else, we need to remember that the perfect never claim to be perfect, not even Jesus ("Why do you call me good?" Mark 10:18). In traditional Roman Catholic theology, it is actually a heresy to teach that anyone can be free from all sin, even venial sin, in this life, apart from a very rare dispensation of special grace.[11]

We are called then, to a life of constant conversion; or, if you would rather restrict the word "conversion" to an initial, born-again experience of justification (accepted and forgiven by God solely for the sake of Jesus and not our own merit), then we are all called to a life of ongoing repentance, indeed what John Booty calls the rhythm of repentance and praise, not as a *condition for* acceptance by God but *in response* to it.[12] If properly sorted out, this can be only a difference in terminology. The point is that no one escapes from the spiritual and moral struggle that is the price of growth, and to be in denial about the struggle is probably to forgo the growth. I have called us to give up both the notion of instantaneous entire sanctification and perfection on the Protestant side, and the notion of the cycles or stages of the spiritual life as a ladder defining degrees of perfection and merit on the Catholic side. When we have done so, we can build on William Temple: the experience of conscience in the moral struggle is the primary experience of God for Christians at *every* stage of their growth. Indeed, the universal testimony of all the saints is that this struggle intensifies, as does the accompanying pain and suffering, as we draw ever closer to God, not because the great saints are more sinful than the rest of us (obviously they are actually better) but because even the tiniest flaw or block which still separates them from the righteous and holy God causes deep suffering. Indeed, it takes great discernment to distinguish this deepest repentance from an unhealthy scrupulosity.

Once we have recognized that even (or especially) the great saints always continue to have an abiding sense of sin in this life as we know it, we can resolve another paradox on the Protestant side. This is Luther's great notion of *simul justus et peccator*, that we remain at every moment humans who have been freely justified by the righteousness of Christ imputed to us by grace through faith, and also still sinners since that righteousness is always Christ's and never possessed by us. Some Lutheran teaching has misinterpreted this doctrine as if it denied the very possibility of growth in virtue as a result of sanctification. Luther was seeking to protect two great truths: that all virtue comes solely as God's gift and that in this life no one is ever completely free from the power of sin.[13] The solution offered here, of constant conversion throughout life (the Benedictine *conversio moreris*), protects Luther's two principles while nevertheless allowing for growth, albeit a growth marked by fits and starts, not steady unimpeded progress. As we have seen, the growth itself is also a work of grace, even at the level of our free assent to and cooperation with it.

In the resulting *askesis,* or discipline of flesh and friendship, as we seek God's grace to diminish vice and grow in virtue, to unlearn hate and learn love, we discipline the flesh not because it is evil but because it is us. The embodied life of souled and spirited dust as flesh is who we are; the pedagogy, discipline, instruction, teaching, call it what you will, by which God the Holy Spirit shapes us as friends of Jesus for the reign and commonwealth of God is not for angels, but for human beings in the finite, historical life of the flesh, especially the flesh of Jesus. That is where virtue must become embodied by graced practice.

We cannot be reminded too often that this moral struggle, this school of charity, is not a program of self-improvement, a course to be passed and a diploma to be received and cashed in for heaven. We are called instead endlessly to engage in the struggle, experience the edge of where we are powerless in the face of evil (world, flesh, devil), and then make a series of deep surrenders of our will and lives and woundedness to the care of God.[14] We ask God to remove our defects of character and grant us such healing and virtues as God wishes for us. We make amends where we can, and seek through prayer to remain "in touch" with the grace of God (the indwelling of the Holy Spirit) in all aspects of our lives through constant self-examination and repentance. We no longer seek to *be* good or *acquire* virtue but to do God's will, and to be equipped to do it. Many will recognize the rhythm of the Twelve Steps of Alcoholics Anonymous here, and indeed it is where many of us learned that rhythm. That is because of the root and heritage of the steps in the gospel, however, not because at this point we import something foreign to Christianity.[15] It is an interesting place to learn it, because it is a program for people to recover from devastating illnesses and woundedness for which they did not volunteer. The gift of freedom that initiates recovery has the startling property of making people responsible now for what they could not be found guilty of in the past.

To say we are seeking God's will and seeking to be equipped to carry it out is not enough as bare assertion, especially if we expect to know God's will by extraordinary paranormal experiences of some kind. In one of his most famous dialogues, Plato portrays Socrates as involved in a debate about whether right actions are good because God loves them (they are the will of God) or does God love them because they are good? As is typical in the early dialogues, no verbal solution to the paradox is offered in the text; but in the dramatic action, the pious Euthyphro goes off to commit a heinous act, while the skeptical or agnostic Socrates is portrayed as the man of virtue.[16] The good is discovered not by the kinds of theoretical knowledge Euthyphro seeks but by practicing goodness in the flesh, where good theory is applied and tested and embodied. Reason and ethics have a significant part in how we do that, which is why there are not three steps in recovery programs but twelve. Full conversion requires steadfast discipling in support of the early experiences of turning and re-turning. In the specifically Christian context, the great mystic St. John of the Cross teaches that when we are trying to figure out what to *do*, we are to rely on reason and the Gospels, not extraordinary experiences, which are too hard to discern properly in the prospect of self-delusion.[17] More on that in the third current.

From a Christian point of view, a spirituality that does not result in a growth in virtue, and most especially in active love of neighbor, is not really Christian or a work of the Holy Spirit—and this means in the social and political realm as well as the personal (1 John 4:20 again, and Wesley). Growth in the Holy Spirit, the growth and fecundity of the seed or egg of God, is a transfiguring growth in God's image and expressed will (truth, beauty, goodness, love), and thus a building up of God's reign and commonwealth. Any lack of the prophetic moment of judging and noticing the truth of where we are and how far we have yet to go in the infinitude of God's perfection—that is, any existence of the "mystical" on its own without the moral—leads straight to all too real a hell, as R. C. Zaehner showed with great power in *Our Savage God,* in his analysis of the Manson family and similar horrors.[18] Obversely, the moral without the contemplative is likely to lead to moralism, rigorism, scrupulosity, and a judgmental Pelagianism.

These experiences of the moral life, of the struggle to be clothed with the virtues and cleansed of the vices, sins, or deadly thoughts that work against that, and to be adorned by the spiritual gifts and beatitudes that support and mark moral and spiritual growth, link spiritual theology to moral theology and Christian ethics.[19] We must note once more that for Christians this link is not optional but *necessary*. It is made necessary by the second great commandment from Jesus, the new commandment in John's Gospel, and St. John's teaching that the two are inextricably connected: Those who say they love God and hate their neighbors are liars (1 John 4:20). The Christian *askesis* or discipline is an unlearning of hate and a learning of love in the presence of love and empowered by love.[20] Psychiatrist Israel Charney has suggested that this is the nature of family life: it is meant to contain hatred within structures of love so that space may be created for persons to heal and grow.[21] This echoes the teaching of St. Francis de Sales that the family is a school of perfection because of the endless opportunities it affords for the exercise of fraternal charity.[22]

One more matter before we get to specifics, and that is the nature of vice. Or rather, the nonnature of vice. You might think that since most of us begin by experiencing ourselves as sinners, we are most familiar with vice, and then find virtue as its opposite and cure. One would begin, on this view, with a catalogue of vices and then introduce virtues as the remedies for them. It does not work that way, though. The Christian tradition follows a long line of philosophical thought by asserting that evil has no being of its own. It is only a distortion and depravation of something good. Indeed, as we saw in the chapter on *conversion from,* we only know vices as truly evil and sinful in the light of the birth of the virtue of faith. Once again, as St. Paul said, he did not know sin until the arrival of the grace of Torah, which showed him what righteousness looked like. Vices then, are bad habits, but we notice them only as places where good habits "ought to be" in our being as created "in the image." In a practical sense as well, only the effort to work with grace to overcome our character defects reveals to us their depth and breadth. It is just like cleaning house: clean up one mess and the next one—the one you could not see for the first one—appears.

Another way of putting this is that vices are essentially lies or grounded in lies, which is why the tradition calls Satan "the Father of Lies." These lies may be active, willfully perpetrated by ourselves, or by others on us. Or, they may be delusions caused by a variety of traumas, often strategies and beliefs that allowed us to survive childhood threats and problems but which were perhaps never really true and in any case no longer serve us well at all. These lies can be things like "I am no good" or "There is not enough good to go around in the world, so I have to grab mine while I can" or "I am never enough" or "If someone does not like me I will die" or "I am not lovable." These lies are exposed only by the appearance of at least an inkling of the truth. That is why Diogenes Allen's notion, following Evagrius, that the vices are "deadly thoughts" is so helpful. Vices are lies that obscure the virtues and prevent their practice and growth. That does not mean, however, that sin is only ignorance. It is more perverse than that, as we can so twist ourselves through practicing vice that even when the truth appears and we acknowledge it as truth, we choose the lie deliberately. That is what Platonists and most liberals do not see—the real viciousness (deliberate practice) of vice. But the truth remains that only with the appearance of the good do I have even a shot at recognizing evil for what it is, or discerning the way it affects us in the moral struggle.

For this reason, we shall adopt the classical pattern of starting with the virtues, and noticing which vices work against them, rather than vice versa. With these clarifications and qualifications we can turn to a brief consideration of specific virtues and vices and how they interrelate in the formation of character through the fleshly disciplines of friendship with Jesus learned in the school of contemplative practice (which is what the church is supposed to be).

Notes

1. William Temple *Nature, Man, and God*, 172, 195–96, 404–26; Kenneth Kirk, *Vision of God*, 470–71.

2. The phrase is from Nicholas Lash, *Easter in Ordinary*; see the references indexed, p. 310.

3. Literally, "working with or working together." See *NCE* 13, 681–82.

4. St. Paul's athletic images, such as 1 Cor 9:23–25, find their best place in relation to this notion, I believe.

5. Again, see Lash, *Easter in Ordinary*, 18–104, for the roots of this in the early modern era and William James in particular.

6. John Wesley, "The Scripture Way of Salvation," ##8, 18, in *John Wesley*, ed. Albert Outler, 275, 282; Wesley, "Thoughts on Christian Perfection," Q and A 28, in *John Wesley*, ed. Outler, 294.

7. On Wesley and perfection, see *John Wesley*, ed. Outler, 9–10, with n. 26.

8. Especially 1 John, where the early church is struggling with how to shape its discipline around the problem of grave sin after Baptism, e.g., 1 John 3:8–10; cf. 5:15–17.

9. A number or organizations use the term "yokefellow," and, in particular, I am not sure about the relationship between the group that visited us and Dr. Elton Trueblood's prison ministry; see www.yokefellowship.org.

10. See again J. I. Packer's warning about the cruelty of evangelizing anyone without warning them about the daily struggle with Satan (*Knowing God*, 121–29).

11. Venial sins are the smaller, more ordinary sins flowing from weakness of character or nature, as opposed to mortal sins, which flow from the malice of an evil will. See Antonio Royo and Jordan Aumann, *Theology of Christian Perfection*, 22–37, esp. 230 n.8.

12. Which he saw as typical of Anglican liturgy at its best; see "Word and Sacraments as Instruments of Evangelism," 23–33. As I have suggested here, healing and liberation claim equal place with repentance and pardon; see again Booty, "Healing, Pardon, Liberation."

13. The best and most succinct account of Luther's teaching on this I know is now in Robert Jenson's gracious response to my paper "Retrieving and Reconstructing 'Justification by Grace

Through Faith': Some Disturbing Questions," *STR* 45, no. 1 (2001): 51–71; Jenson's response is on pp. 72–77.

14. Recall what was said in chap. 6 ("Conversion *From*") about the enemies of the soul.

15. *Alcoholics Anonymous Comes of Age,* 253–71; and see above, chap. 6, n. 40, especially the works cited of Dick B. Of course, Twelve-Step recovery programs do not require adherence to Christianity or any other religion.

16. It was my privilege to learn to read Plato at the feet of Robert Sherrick Brumbaugh; see his *Plato for the Modern Age* for this approach to the early dialogues.

17. John of the Cross, *Ascent* (trans. and ed. Kavanaugh and Rodriguez), II.22.16–18 (185–87), II.29.15 (207).

18. R. C. Zaehner, *Our Savage God.*

19. Diogenes Allen, *Spiritual Theology;* chapter 5, "The Eight Deadly Thoughts," is a superb reading of the tradition of the (usually seven) deadly sins.

20. Alan Jones, *Soul Making,* 124–58.

21. Israel Charny, *Marital Love and Hate,* throughout, see esp. 85–87, 155–57.

22. Francis de Sales, "Counsels to Married People," in *Introduction to the Devout Life,* chap. 38, 270–81; Wendy Wright (personal communication, Jan. 14, 2008) adds the following: "The places he mentions charity as the Bond of Perfection are in the *Treatise* [*on the Love of God*], book 7, chap 3 and book 11, chap 8. He is always alluding to Col. 3:14.

"He calls friendship the bond of perfection in his famous 1604 letter to Jane (*Oeuvres* XII, Lettres 2, 262). In the *Introduction to the Devout Life* (III, 17) he calls marriage a friendship that is genuine and holy. Also see his Letters to Mdm Brulart in *Letters of Spiritual Direction,* 102–106." Wright's own selection and commentary, *Francis de Sales: Introduction to the Devout Life and Treatise on the Love of God,* serves as an excellent introduction to the principal writings. I use a lot of family examples as illustrations, not to suggest that spiritual formation can take place only in that context but because the tradition was so heavily weighted toward the monastic/celibate religious; also because it is my own experience.

10

The Theological Virtues

*And now faith, hope, and love abide, these three; and the greatest of these is
love.* —1 Cor 13:13

The next task is to develop a view of the interrelationship of the virtues (strengths of character), their relationship to the bad habits, old survival techniques now dysfunctional, and character defects that obscure them (vices), and the particular forms grace takes in supporting the growth of these virtues (gifts and fruits of the Holy Spirit, beatitudes or blessings).[1]

I have tried to make this easier by schematizing the information in the chart on pp. 134-35.[2] Caution is needed in using such a chart, however. It is important to let the scheme *reveal* the shape and contents of what we use it to look at and not *impose* itself on the material. The map is not the territory.[a] Yves Congar has very helpfully sorted out the issue of how we are to view such a scheme.[3] Until the thirteenth century, no clear distinction was made between the theological virtues and the gifts, charisms, and fruits of the Holy Spirit, a position the Franciscans under Duns Scotus continued to hold, one that was carefully *not* condemned at the Council of Trent. Philip the Chancellor and then supremely the Dominican Thomas Aquinas took the opposite view and developed the notion of very distinct and discrete packets of grace, as it were, and an elaborate theory of how they were interrelated. Congar notes that the great saints and mystics tended to the unified view, while their spiritual directors and biographers tended to the Thomist view. I propose a sort of compromise: theologically, I am on the Franciscan side—this is all one movement of the Holy Spirit, undivided in every way from that side. I have indeed harped on the notion that grace does not come in discrete packets but is just another name for the Holy Spirit at work. A scheme more like that of Aquinas, however, can be helpful in seeing the distinction (but not the division) of the human responses to that one graceful movement of the Holy Spirit; and those distinctions, if not overblown, can help us attend more carefully to the nuances of that human response. The chart that follows, then, is essentially Thomist with a few modifications, including mate-

---

a Which is another reason to be a *critical* realist, as is Bernard Lonergan (*Method*, 238–40). *Something* surprises and challenges the interpretations and even the rules of my language games with great regularity.

Table of Virtues and Vices

Vices	Gifts of the H.S. (N.T. Charisms in Italics)	Willingness: Virtues and Graces	Fruit of the H.S.	Beatitude
		THEOLOGICAL VIRTUES		
sm ical sness	Understanding, Knowledge, *Word of Knowledge* Miracles *Evangelists, Teachers, Workers of Mircacles*	**FAITH** *Conversion from* (Appropriated to the Fount) Basic Trust, Reasoned Belief	Faithfulness Truth Steadfastness	Those Who Weep or Mourn Pure in Heart
y m e	Fear (Awe) *Prophecy, Tongues, Interpretation of Tongues* Healing *Prophets, Healers Tongue Speakers Interpreters*	**HOPE** *Conversion to, Glory* (Appropriated to the Holy Spirit) Allied: Humility Proper Shame, Autonomy	Joy	Poor in Spirit
red	Wisdom *Word of Wisdom Preachers, Pastors Helpers*	**LOVE (AGAPE/CARITAS)** *Conversion by, Transfiguration* Falling in Love without Qualification (Appropriated to The Word/Wisdom) Fidelity, Intimacy, Caring Affection, Friendship Proper Eros	Peace Love	Peacemakers

Gifts of the H.S.	Willingness: Virtues and Graces	Fruit of the H.S.	Beatitude	Dan
	CARDINAL VIRTUES			
Counsel *Discernment of Spirits* *Word of Knowledge* *Teachers, Preachers, Pastors*	**PRUDENCE** Appropriated to Faith Discretio	Patience Truthful Speech	The Meek	
Piety (True Godliness) *Apostles, Administrators*	**JUSTICE** Appropriated to Love Love of Affliction (per Simone Weil) Proper Respect for Authority	Forgiveness Kindness Goodness Righteousness Piety (True Godliness) Forbearance	The Merciful	Se
Strength *Administrators* *Apostles* *Helpers*	**FORTITUDE** (Courage) Appropriated to Hope Autonomy and Industry	Gentleness Power of God	Hunger and Thirst for Justice	Au A Ina
Fear of the Lord *Discernment of Spirits* *Pastors, Preachers*	**TEMPERANCE** Appropriated to Love Proper Shame/Humility Honesty Gratitude	Forgiveness Self-Control Purity	Poor in Spirit	Glu A Ina

rial Thomas did not incorporate, especially the "hotter" New Testament charisms; but it is meant to be read in a Scotist or Franciscan manner.[4]

The virtues are presented in the middle of the chart, first the three theological virtues and then the four cardinal or moral virtues as they are called in classical tradition.[a] Allied virtues also appear there. The virtues are surrounded by supportive or related gifts and fruits of the Holy Spirit and beatitudes from the Sermon on the Mount (Matthew 5). The column with the gifts of the Spirit lists the traditional sevenfold gifts from Isaiah 11 in regular type, and the more spectacular New Testament charisms from St. Paul's writings in italics, both the prayer gifts and the ministry gifts as they are often classified. We shall have much more to examine about gifts, fruits, and beatitudes in the sections on the currents of Transfiguration and Glorification. Here we note their birth in the midst of the moral struggle and their relationship to the habits of character being forged in that struggle as defined by the theological virtues.

The outer two columns portray the vices, which oppose the virtues. As we have seen, vices are essentially lies, untruths (Allen's "Deadly Thoughts" again) and the results of believing them that block growth of the virtuous habits (healthy, life-giving, graceful). One way of combating them in prayer is to expose the lie they embody and renounce it. Both psychotherapy and the sacrament of penance can be helpful with this, as we expose the exact nature of our wrongs and those done to us and our reactions to them.[b] Here again, we confront a stubborn mystery: some of these defects we never asked for, we just have them; many, indeed, are the results of our having been wounded ourselves; some were survival techniques that have become unhealthy. Another thing we can see, and the reason they are arranged as they are, is that they form a kind of *parenthesis* to the virtue, a sort of fence that blocks and obscures it. Often vices are one side of the virtue taken to an extreme, which is one source of their seductiveness. One need not buy into a mechanical interpretation of Aristotle's notion of virtue as a golden mean between two vices to recognize that there is a tension between opposed vices within which virtues are forged.[5] Gerald May has most helpfully described virtue as a place of willingness (to be shaped for doing God's will) surrounded by two forms of willfulness—I damn well will and I damn well won't.[6] That is how I have attempted to portray the vices in this scheme. "Damn-well-won't" vices appear in the column on the left. These are the vices of negativity, the kind of negativity that ends in resignation, a bitter life of resentment, and counterfeit acceptance with a middle finger always in the air. The column on the far right is the vices of "I damn well will," of indulgence and excess, which lead ultimately to surfeit, jadedness, and a different sort of resignation.

We have already gained some familiarity with the three theological virtues

---

a The three theological virtues are faith, hope, and love; they are called theological because they are identified by Paul as the chief virtues in 1 Corinthians 13, because the tradition saw them as infused by the Holy Spirit, and because they could be distinguished from the cardinal or moral virtues (prudence, justice, fortitude, and temperance), which were known also to pagans.

b In the case of abuse and other severe trauma, this will be a delicate process of distinguishing the lies that need renouncing from the inner parts of the person that have used the lies to survive, parts that need healing.

by examining how they are born in the very beginnings of conversion, the very first stirrings of our selves in response to the Holy Spirit, the experience of being beloved, called to be friends of Jesus and made fit for the reign and commonwealth of God. Although we noted that they and the experiences of conversion from, to, and by may occur in any order in a particular case, it was necessary to consider them in sequential order, and it will be here again. Before we start, however, it is important to see at one level deeper that what is distinguished is not divided. The Holy Spirit does not have three pitchers, one containing faith, one containing hope, and one containing love, pouring into us, as it were, cocktails of different mix as life proceeds. In fact, as we have seen, there are no pitchers and no liquids—only one mystery—the indwelling Holy Spirit as person, the seed or egg of God in us. That is what grows in us, not three separate bits. In that sense, the three theological virtues are not three at all at the deepest level, but only one—three different shapes that love takes for our sake.

This co-inherence of the three theological virtues is itself a resonance of the Trinitarian *perichoresis* or co-inherence. By the Spirit's indwelling, the whole Trinity indwells. As suggested earlier, there is a Trinitarian structure to the Spirit's mission that raises in us the resonance I have identified as three concurrent currents. Each current is dominated by one of the theological virtues, though the other two also appear in each as an aspect of the dominant one. We have already seen how the virtue of faith is particularly appropriate to the Spirit's mission in support of the mission of the Fount (the Father/Mother) since the task of faith is learning to trust and believe in the fact that the Lover loves us, that we are beloved; faith in its own right appeared in the section on converted *from* as the motive for our initial (re)turning; hope as a dimension of faith came in learning to trust what we are converted *to*; love as a dimension of faith (fidelity) belonged to the realm of what we are converted *by*. Similarly, we can appropriate the virtue of love to the Spirit's mission in support of the mission of the Child/Word/Wisdom, because our love is grounded, as we have seen, in the way we can be made one with the Beloved in the flesh, within the economy of salvation leading to the reign and commonwealth of God; love thus dominates the current I have called "Transfiguration," as we learn to glimpse our Beloved in all the hidden glory of the incarnation and the way it illuminates all existence. We can appropriate hope to the Holy Spirit's own proper mission, because, as we have seen, though the Holy Spirit is Love in person, in the final current I have called "Glory" we are drawn by the Spirit to allow hope to overcome despair as we trust in her ability to bring about the promised sacramental *pleroma*, even in the teeth of the evidence. In each case, the other two theological virtues will be recognized as co-inherent in the one dominant for a particular current, just as the entire Trinity participates in each mission, even though each is appropriated to one person.

I have used the technical term, the verb "to appropriate," here (which means it is "appropriate" to make these connections) to remind us we must still avoid two heresies.[a] First, we must avoid tritheism and subordinationism by the "rule of one"

---

a "Appropriate" as a verb is the technical term by which an external operation or function of

(*monarchē*), for, as Augustine says, the external acts of the blessed Trinity are undivided. In this case, all three theological virtues are given by the whole Trinity, not just one of the persons.[7] At the same time, we must avoid the heresy of modalism by asserting that these three ways in which God is are really true of God as God, not just of our experience of God.[a] This allows us to see the Trinitarian rhythm of the theological virtues as a deep embedding in and for us of the inner-Trinitarian life of God—a theme to which we shall return. The unity and distinctness of the virtues is a reflection in our lives of the Triadic Unity of God, as expressed first in the Trinitarian character of the Spirit's *missio*. Also, as I have suggested, each is a gift to us of one of God's own perfections, and the tradition has consistently taught that the perfections of God are "simple"; that is, there is really only one perfection that arouses in us different resonances at different times.

The rest of this chapter on virtues and vices emphasizes faith, love, and hope as a Trinitarian structure from which all the others flow.[b] The four cardinal virtues, as they are called, are discussed in the next chapter. Following Gerald May, we shall examine the reconstruction of virtues as a willingness between two willfulnesses (I damn well will and I damn well won't).

Willingness and the Theological Virtues

1. Faith. In the original biblical languages, faith has three meanings, all of which are still involved in its conceptualization as a theological virtue. The first layer of meaning is basic trust, learning to rely on the faithfulness of God. This is one source of the appropriateness of connecting this virtue to the first person of the Trinity, and of using parental analogies and names for that person. As we shall see

---

God is identified with one of the persons of the Trinity, along with the knowledge that nevertheless all external acts are "undivided"—the entire Trinity participates in each. But the appropriations are, well, appropriate, and, as Barth has pointed out, do give us new theological knowledge (*CD* II.1, 322–674). We have been following the suggestion of Robert Jenson, that while the external acts of the Trinity are undivided, they are not indistinguishable.

a Modalism is the teaching that the persons in God are mere differences of appearance and function of a God who is really only One; creator, redeemer, and sanctifier are the most popular candidates. These are only the names of external functions and, hence, do not adequately differentiate the persons internally. There is, of course, a problem caused by the fact that the modern sense of the word "person" is so radically different from the classical one in use when the doctrine of the Trinity was formulated. It now suggests, wrongly, that there are three separate centers of consciousness and will in God, which would approach tritheism. Some theologians such as John Macquarrie have suggested using "mode of Being" as a replacement for "person." Since by this they mean an eternal and internal differentiation within the one Godhead, this usage is not, oddly enough, modalism. Macquarrie, *Principles*, 193; Thomas and Wondra, *Introduction*, 83–96.

b The traditional order, faith, hope, love, as found in 1 Corinthians 13, was followed in the discussion of converted from, to, and by; but here I shift to the order of the currents that each virtue dominates. Love comes in the middle because it dominates the current of Transfiguration, the current in which most Christians spend most of their lives. It is thus appropriate, under the rule of the dominion of charity, for love to predominate in this current, as well as for the specifically theological reasons given.

in the chapters on contemporary theory of conversion, faith in this sense of basic trust is first learned in the flesh when infants discover that their parents or other primary caregivers can be counted on to meet their fundamental needs in a reliable way; where such care is lacking, faith will be hard to come by. Obviously, this is also the appropriate and vital ground for including maternal as well as paternal analogies and names for God, since the mother is crucial in this development; but the father can also play a highly significant role even early on, as the growing tradition of shared parenting makes manifest.

The second meaning of faith is belief, not in the sense of mere intellectual assent to a set of dogmatic propositions, but of belief, even reasoned belief, in God's self-revelation in the covenant history and the flesh of Jesus, in the prophetic Word of judgment that reveals the truth of what we are being called to convert *from*. Its opposite is really denial, which is why trust remains at the core of this meaning as well. We should note that belief in the essential goodness of creation as the ground of the economy of salvation and sanctification is included here; it is part of God's self-revelation in Scripture and a fundamental tenant of all the religions of the Book, that the creator God and redeemer God are the same God; this is, indeed, an essential component of Christian faith over against several alternatives, including the Manichaeism whose remnants I have suggested haunt all Western thought. The latter taught that the bad creator god and the good redeemer god were quite distinct. As a result, trusting in the essential goodness and giftedness of creation as our proper and reliable home has as much place here as acknowledgment of what has gone wrong and rotten. Just as a baby learns to trust the world through the reliability of its parental caregiver, so also for us trust in God and in the goodness of the world are inextricably entwined.

The third meaning of faith in the original languages is faithfulness. Trust and belief are meant to issue as night follows day in fidelity, to God and neighbor, under the terms of the covenant. This is where the troubled relationship between faith and works that has been so tortured in the West since the Reformation finds its true resolution. Indeed, many of the classic texts that teach we saved by faith *in* Jesus Christ can also just as easily be translated as our being saved by faithfulness *to* Jesus, or even by the faithfulness *of* Jesus. At one level, it is a matter of a fine point of Greek grammar that produces the ambiguity, which may be quite deliberate, at least in St. Paul.[8] This is not even a question of both/and, of having our cake and eating it too. The point is much deeper—that trust, belief, and faithful response are one virtue, one whole cloth, grounded ultimately in the trustworthiness and fidelity of God. This helps us see that, at the deepest level, obedience to Torah in Judaism is *not* what has been condemned as works righteousness from St. Paul to Luther, when it is undertaken as covenant faithfulness; then it is justification by faithfulness, ultimately God's.[9]

Nevertheless, "works righteousness" is one of the forms the vices of "I damn well will" can take in denial of faith. This is "good" works undertaken not out of covenant fidelity but as efforts to make ourselves good or convince others we are. The issue is not the goodness of the works themselves; it is our motives for doing them, the question of whether we are trusting in ourselves and these works or allowing the works to flow from a faithful response to the God whom we trust. Allied with "works righteousness" are (1) credulity, which misinterprets faith as the abeyance of all critical questioning and even honest doubt instead of seeing that these can be modes of faithfulness;[10] (2) pietism, which identifies faith with certain intense emotional experiences and can be cut off from any sense of the necessity of concrete faithful response; and (3) fideism, which forgets that justification (our being counted as righteous before God for Jesus' sake) is caused *by* grace *through* the instrument of faith and not by the act of our believing, especially in the sense of holding certain required beliefs. This latter makes faith itself into a work of works righteousness. Faith cannot but be cast into beliefs by humans, but faith itself is never captured in those beliefs. We are called upon to believe and trust in God, not our beliefs.

One form fideism takes, especially today but in fact at all times, is what I call "theological positivism," which is the belief that theological truth about God can actually be captured in infallible propositions; this error is much the same, whether in the assertion that the words of Scripture, taken literally and in no other sense (the Protestant Evangelical version), form infallible propositions with no need for interpretation, or in the dogmatic decrees of a hierarchical judicatory or magisterium (the Catholic form). Either form sees as unfaithful any recognition that the symbols of the Christian faith have an analogous and ambiguous relationship to the truth they signify and always fail to contain it fully. Both forms neglect the reality of the historical nature of all human language and the contextuality of all discourse, which make dogmatic assertions at least as much grammatical rules for Christian discourse as claims about what is actually true.[11] Both forms of positivism are likely to turn aside at the deeper conversion offered by the dark night of the soul at the threshold of Glory, as we shall see in considering the third current; that night calls into question all claims to grasp truth. Hans Küng has shown how the incorrect notion of infallibility is better replaced by the sense of indefectibility— that the authoritative sources do not capture God's truth but do guarantee that the church as the community of believers will not fatally fall away from the gospel; but this is because of the *faithfulness of God* to the promise that the gates of hell shall not prevail, not because of any absolute human certainty in incorrigible beliefs.[12]

There are, of course, the vices of "I damn well won't" to be considered in relationship to faith. Honest doubt is one thing; indeed, it is a vital component of a living faith against which the adequacy of particular beliefs must always be tested. But a willful skepticism that, in its rejection of what it sees as shallow fideism and pietism, refuses to examine more nuanced and reasoned belief is also a vice. One suspects it may not be as bad as its opposites; as Simone Weil pointed out, when one falls out of the hand of God in search of truth one cannot fall very far.[13] But as willfulness increases, this honest doubt becomes tinged with a hypercritical spirit, intellectual pride, and ultimately a bitter cynicism and resignation that can become a chosen way of being in the world as a useless passion.

A different and more common family of vices is represented by the words infidelity and faithlessness. These tend to be sins of believers who nevertheless fail to apply their beliefs root and branch to every aspect of their lives and every relationship that defines their personhood. Simple infidelity in one's own intimate relationships is the archetypal example, but the restriction of "religion" to the privatized sphere of individual and family life also goes here, as if the gospel had no application to business and public life. Many of the common cries that "the church should stay out of politics" manifest this problem, for example.

Terry Holmes had a helpful way of speaking about this dynamic between the virtue of faith and the surrounding vices; he saw the willingness of faith as finding a place of sensibility between cynicism on the one hand (I damn well won't), and sentimentality on the other (I damn well will).[14] That is still a helpful way of looking at it. This place of sensibility, of trust, reasoned belief, and faithful response is supported and adorned by fruits and gifts of the Holy Spirit and certain beatitudes (recall how we are interpreting these gifts and blessings as distinctions in our response to grace, not as divisions in the movement of the Spirit herself).

For example, the gift of understanding from the classical (Isaiah 11) list obviously supports faith and will come into serious play in considering the current of Transfiguration. In the more "charismatic" Pauline lists, knowledge and word of knowledge (the gift of imparting knowledge through speaking) also support faith, as does the working of miracles where that is not some kind of magic-show entertainment. We might note that faith is required for a miracle to work, and faith is also required for a work to be recognized as a miracle, which need not, by the way, involve "breaking a law of nature." A miracle is simply something seen in the light of divine grace and the divine economy, as meshing with God's purposes, as increasing our trust that those purposes will prevail.[15]

The beatitudes of "those who mourn" and "the pure in heart" also support faith. Those who mourn over their own traumas will be comforted in the process of coming to faith. Those who weep for the state of the world do so in three aspects: because faith has allowed them to see the world in its true colors as it is exposed by the Word of God's judgment; because they trust in and are comforted by God's faithfulness to bring it round right; and because they are themselves determined on faithful action in service to that end. This is the prayer gift of tears, which as early as St. Symeon the New Theologian has been identified as the one gift marking the second Baptism in the Holy Spirit.[a] Purity of heart, the great virtue of the desert monastics of the early centuries, comes especially into play in the later tide of Glory but is also found here at the beginning. It is the focusing of desire on God alone, and not even particular experiences of God. It is faith because it hears the Word of divine judgment on all actual and potential idolatry, all identification of the not-God with God. It gives birth to further faith because its outcome is "to see

---

a Symeon the New Theologian was a monk and abbot in Constantinople in the eleventh century and is highly regarded in the Orthodox tradition. He taught clearly a doctrine of a second Baptism of the Holy Spirit as tears (which marked the gift for him, not tongues) of deeper repentance dissolve hardness of heart: *The Discourses*, 30, and, e.g., 336–37. Because later pentecostal and charismatic writers have used this terminology to the detriment of sacramental Baptism by water (which Simeon did not and would not do), many now prefer a term other than second Baptism, such as "the infilling of the Holy Spirit," to denote this experience. See. H. C. G. Moule, *Person and Work of the Holy Spirit*, 220–23.

God" in the glimpses of God's backside we are given in contemplation (more on that further on).[16]

The fruit of the Spirit that arises out of faith is faithfulness (Gal 5:22), which we have already seen is one of the meanings of the Greek and Latin words for faith, and resolves the faith/works dilemma by reminding us that faith is to bear fruit in covenant-faithful worship and service to neighbor. This faithfulness is embodied in and supported by the ministry gifts of teachers, evangelists, and miracle workers. Here we can also see the truth behind the otherwise false division made by some neo-pentecostal and charismatic theologians among these gifts, making them quite unrelated to one another in an effort to protect the special "supernatural" character of the charisms.[17] Faith as a theological virtue, the "hotter" charisms of faith, the ministry charisms surrounding faith, and the fruit of faithfulness are all actually a continuum of growth, grounded in the theological virtue of faith, which is also in its turn one movement with hope and love, as Paul makes clear in 1 Corinthians 13. Faith as an original gift to all believers, the intense faith of the charism, the ensuing faithfulness of the fruit, and the prayer and ministry charisms that arise out of it and support it are all one movement of the Spirit, differentiated by our response and different places in spiritual growth and by the shaping of the virtue for specific tasks of mission and ministry. Again, we see that what is usefully distinguished for purposes of understanding should not be seen as divided.[18]

2. *Love.* We have already had a good deal to say about love, sorting out the four Greek words and recognizing that love is not opposed to the desires of the flesh but is those desires healed, purified, and properly focused. We noted the priority of the two great commandments, therefore, as the governing principle for all Christian life, expressed in the "dominion of charity" so powerfully portrayed by St. Paul in the great hymn of 1 Corinthians 13, in the "new commandment" in John's Gospel, and its elucidation throughout 1 John. We have seen that love is God's very nature, expressed by the confessing of the Holy Spirit as God and as the bond of love between Lover and Beloved, and the Godhead as a whole and all creation. While the Holy Spirit is love in person, as a virtue love is best appropriated to the Beloved, in whom the Fount first loved us; thus, it belongs to the Spirit's mission in support of the Word/Wisdom in all dimensions of the incarnation. We see this as supremely the love of the Father/Mother expressed definitively in history in the person, flesh, and work of Jesus as the sacrament of God's friendship with humanity, of the fact that we are beloved as dust. We have seen the response our "loving back" is to take: friendship with Jesus empowered by the Spirit, as his disciples sharing freely in his moral purpose of serving the world, fulfilled in obedience to the second great commandment and to the great commission. Love is thus the dominant virtue in the second current of Transfiguration, in which we see Jesus, one another, and the world illumined by the first sight of glory. This is the current that will predominate in most of our lives most of the time, fulfilling in this sense the "dominion of charity." By the Trinitarian principles we have been following, however, love is co-inherent with the other virtues and appears in the other currents in which they have prime place. In the current we are currently examining, love is an aspect of faith, and hence has the primary forms of fidelity and forgiveness.

Love, too, is willingness between two forms of willfulness. Concupiscence or lust defines the "I-damn-well-will" pole. It should not be confused with sexual desire or *eros* as such; instead, it should be identified with the turning aside of any desire, including sexual, from the proper fulfillment of that desire to an inappropriate object (or proper objects to an inappropriate degree). That is what "perversion" literally means. One possible meaning of the Greek word *porneia*, from which we get "pornography," is simply indulgence in false pleasures given by objects of desire we know to be inappropriate but refuse to give up, and the external titillations which reinforce that. It is the task of moral theology to help us distinguish appropriate from inappropriate objects of desire (and notice that when we desire union with another person, they are properly an "object" of our desire in this technical language, and that does *not* mean "using" them or treating them like things, which would be perversion in the technical sense).[a] John Paul II was badly misunderstood (and ill-served by his English translators) in his teaching that one should not approach one's spouse in lust. That sounded in English like a teaching that sexual desire is so bad one should not even have it for one's husband or wife. What he meant, of course, was that one should not treat a spouse as an object in the "thing" sense, using them for pleasure apart from the deeper friendship and love marriage is meant to embody.[19]

In fact, romantic love has always been ambiguous in the tradition. All the great mystics have expressed their desire for God in romantic and even sexual terms, and from Plato to Dante to C. S. Lewis, Robert Capon, Bernard Cook, and countless others, including many poets, it has been recognized that appropriate romantic love can be a school or prelude for true love of God.[20] Of course, such romantic love must get beyond the mere infatuation stage and down to the hard work of sustaining an erotic friendship in the trials of real life with a real "other." And it is here that the traditions of courtly love can be "perverted": Lancelot falls for Guinevere and vice versa, and Camelot crumbles. That danger is always there. But even that tradition can be straightened out, as shown in the flowering of the spirituality of the *Minne-sangers* in the *Braut-mystik* (the love singers or troubadours of bride mysticism) of the fourteenth and succeeding centuries. As Robert Capon has pointed out, romantic love remains the most common invitation most people are going to receive into this mystery, and the ordinary human ways of working it out faithfully are the best schools most people can "attend."[21] The sins of "I damn well will" then are a willful insistence on continuing to desire something I should not, or in a way I should not. Ultimately, these sins desire even appropriate persons and objects but apart from that love of God that transfigures all our other loves if we will allow it. Perhaps the chief example would be wishing to impede the growth of another for the sake of our continuing to possess them securely.

The sins of "I-damn-well-won't" love tend to arise from the traumas of unrequited love and unfulfilled desire. They are born, in short, when we do not get what

---

a Special cases of obsessive/compulsive disorders around sexuality, including those stemming from prior abuse and domestic violence, children drawn into pornography, and pedophilia, require significant psychotherapeutic treatment. Neither moral counsel nor spiritual direction is likely to succeed in such cases, except as adjuncts to therapy.

we want, or do, and find it was not what we wanted. There are really three possibilities when we do not get what we want or desire.[22] One is that our wanting was unrealistic, in which case the most helpful strategy is to rethink the want and figure out a realistic goal for it. The second is that we adopted a self-defeating strategy for obtaining a realistic and legitimate want; the best recourse here is to rethink our strategy, which may involve the hard work of discovering we have literally been at cross-purposes, defeated by one or more counterintentions arising from conflicting desires or perhaps old fears and wounds, even a deep inability to love because of these old wounds that require serious healing. The third possibility is that our desire was appropriate and realistic; we acted in a thoughtful and appropriate way, and we still did not get what we want because "that's life"—sometimes one just does not. A real possibility in this case is that we should keep trying, even if that means "moving on."

The vices arise when we start resenting the fact that we did not get what we want, in the sense of choosing to store up and cherish anger about that fact. This resentment is already fed by a number of earlier vices, since it either continues to cling to inappropriate objects of desire or in seeking to demand that life be arranged for our convenience usurps the place of God and God's providence. Two unhelpful strategies offer themselves. One is denial, an attitude of "Oh, well, I didn't really want that after all." This can become a kind of cultivated indifference and apathy. This also helps us see that denial that we want or wanted something, the *repression* of desire in the modern sense, is a false asceticism. True asceticism is giving up, for a higher purpose, something legitimately and fully wanted; repression of the desire has nothing to do with it, and is in fact counterproductive, which is what is so wrong about some of the excessive language about "mortification" in earlier spiritual theologies. True mortification (entering willingly into the death of Jesus in all things, but in hope) is the sorting out of desire that we are talking about here, not its denial.

The second unhelpful strategy is to blame the object of desire, legitimate or illegitimate, appropriate or inappropriate, for our failure to get what we want or for arousing the desire in us in the first place. The result of this strategy is hatred—what I cannot love successfully I shall hate as a way of denying I love it and coping with my disappointment. It can lead to strategies that literally try to destroy the offending object or person, leading to violence and murder, or it can lead to a bitterness, cynicism, and resignation, which end in a colder and deeper indifference than the earlier denial. It is an indifference that is a kind of psychic murder.

So, denying our wants and desires is never helpful. Disciplining them is required. That means learning to love appropriately, effectively, and realistically, including acceptance of the fact that we will not always get what we want. It means purifying our desires not by denial but by an ever-deeper search for the true desire of our hearts.[23] It means disciplining our strategies for obtaining what we desire by reason, and virtues such as fidelity, practicing true intimacy and enjoyment, caring, affection, and seeking friendship and eros free of the manipulative, the dishonorable, and the pornographic (in the sense we have defined). Where necessary, it means accepting the disciplines required for healing. It means acknowledging the realities of life's outcomes and loving God anyway.

That last "anyway" reminds us again of conversion (when we pay attention to conversion "by") as a falling in love without qualification, as Lonergan put it. The vices are all ways of childishly insisting on the qualifications, of being willing to love, "if only," which then becomes "only if." It may also mean refusing the healing we need to overcome disabilities to love ingrained by trauma. Real asceticism is about facing and yielding up these qualifications, not about any denial of the reality of the desires we have because we are animated and spirited dust. That is why all sins are sins *in* the flesh (we as dust/flesh do them in the realm of the world as dust and flesh), but not really sins *of* the flesh, because the sins do not arise from fleshiness but from a perverse will and spirit that is ultimately always guided by what the tradition has called "sins of the spirit."

All this required sorting out is why the gift of the Spirit associated with the virtue of love is Wisdom, which we badly need in order to focus desire on appropriate objects to an appropriate degree, develop realistic and effective strategies for meeting those desires and disciplining them to that end, and finally the ultimate wisdom to know the difference between the things I cannot change and the things I can when I do not get what I want. Wisdom as a gift also helps us discern and cherish the presence of divine Wisdom in the beauty and order of world, in culture, even in religion.[24] The charism of "Word of Wisdom" supports this growth in wisdom in particular instances. Among the ministry gifts, preachers and teachers can help with the sorting out, while pastors and helpers can bring love to bear in concrete circumstances. The affiliated beatitude is thus "peacemakers," because they seek to unlearn the forms of willful love and desire in the midst of the ensuing conflicts, and because the blessing "they shall be called the children of God" points back to the root of the virtue of love in the fact of our being beloved ourselves in the first place. Indeed, this is empirically demonstrable—well-loved children are most likely to grow into effective lovers themselves.

The fruits of the Spirit most associated with love, then, are love and peace. This new use of "love" is not a mere repetition or tautology. It reminds us that the virtue or character-habit of love is meant to be expressed in concrete acts of love. The tradition has honored this by asserting that *habitual* love or charity—the presence of the virtue in character—can only be discerned by *actual* love or charity—concrete, visible, loving acts. "By their fruits you shall know them" (Matt 7:16). This is, as we shall see, one of the rock-bottom principles of discernment in spiritual direction. The fruit of peace is also manifested by and supportive of the virtue of love because of the link to the beatitude of "peacemakers," since peace is born as hatred and concupiscence are unlearned in a community; inner peace also flows from the wisdom coming from the threefold sorting out of desire we have described (object, degree, and outcome), damping down the inner warfare Paul portrays so powerfully in Romans 7. Finally, he (Jesus) is our peace (Eph 2:14) by taking away the barriers that have divided us and by being the Wisdom whose forgiveness enables the sorting out to occur. The way to that peace for us is falling in love with him without qualification (qualifications are sources of unpeace), in the loving company of his other friends engaged in real acts of loving service to all neighbors in the world, or at least as many as we are called to love and serve.

Finally, we can see with the mystics that "it is all love." Love is not just another virtue on the list but the very root and ground of all habits of character that respond gracefully to grace. Faith is the trust that we are loved as dust by God, passionately and effectively, a basic trust, which makes our effective loving possible. Hope is the trust that because we are beloved, the deepest and truest desires of our hearts can and will be fulfilled. The "cardinal" virtues we shall look at shortly are the habits of character needed for habitual love to be expressed in the actual.

Forgiveness and Love

In the current of conversion, love takes a particular form at the intersection between individual and community in the formation of personhood. That form is forgiveness, mutual forgiveness in the community context. Krister Stendahl has pointed out that everywhere in the Newer Testament where instruction is given for praying the powerful prayer, the one that moves mountains, within a couple of verses will be found instruction about mutual forgiveness.[25] Indeed, this notion lies at the very heart of the archetypal Christian prayer, the Lord's Prayer. From this, Stendahl concluded that *koinōnia*, the common life of communion and fellowship of the people of God, is to be grounded in mutual forgiveness, which is also the prerequisite for the community being able to pray powerfully. That is one reason we exchange the peace just before entering into the church's most powerful prayer, the consecration prayer of the Eucharist. Here again, we also see the link between love and peace, the link being mutual forgiveness.

There are some tricky bits to get over, though. First, real forgiveness itself must not be a form of denial. It never means "It didn't really matter," or "What you did was not really so bad after all," or "It's OK," and certainly never "Let's pretend it didn't happen." Above all, and particularly in abusive or oppressive situations, it cannot and must not mean "And you can do it to me again." For that reason, forgiveness may not mean reconciliation in the sense of a fully restored relationship. It may mean tough love and not being "nice."

Once we have understood those bits, however, we can see we do *not* need for the other party to "repent" in order to forgive them, though full reconciliation and restoration of relationship might require that. In fact, however, I do not really forgive the other for the other's sake, but for my own. It is, after all, my life that is poisoned by the resentments I choose to hold, and it is up to me, not the other parties, whether I choose to continue to hold those resentments. Please note it is the resentments I am most assuredly "entitled" to that are the most pernicious and the hardest to give up. Forgiveness happens when I choose not to hold the resentment any longer, whether or not the other party has repented, or reconciliation and restoration of relationship is possible or prudent, or even whether or not the other party has truly wronged me. It is also true, especially in the light of the increased knowledge available to us in our time, that in severe cases of oppression and abuse for certain, and to some degree in all cases, true forgiveness is not something that can be commanded, especially prematurely. Again, it must not be some sort of denial, permission for further abuse, or a repression of the appropriate anger and rage at what has been done. It cannot be rushed, and is often won through hard disciplines of prayer and therapy and practice. Even the willingness to begin such an *askesis* may take a long time to form, and ultimately comes as a gift. Sometimes the best we can do is pray for the willingness. In the most traumatic cases, there may be things only God can forgive, and the best we can do is ask God to forgive those who perpetrate them, to decide that we wish to hold nothing that would prevent their complete healing and restoration in God.[26] Finally, however, to refuse forgiveness in the end is a decision to stay sick and enslaved, to continue to allow one's relationship to the other to poison one's life with resentment.

The petition in the Lord's Prayer "Forgive us our sins as we forgive those who sin against us" has two possible meanings, both true. One is "Forgive others just as you have been forgiven." This means our being beloved and forgiven is what makes it possible for us to forgive. It reminds us that God forgave us before we repented or shaped up—Christ died for us while we were yet sinners.[27] The second possible reading, "You will be forgiven only to the extent you forgive," is also true, not as a threat, for, as we just said, God does not wait for anything to forgive us, but as a sort of promise. The very existence of resentments and other forms of unforgiveness in our hearts leaves less room for our taking in that we are beloved and forgiven. It literally works both ways, at the same time. Forgiveness is thus born as love and peace come together to give rise to the first fruits of actual charity. If it is willfully stillborn, actual charity will be decreased and love as a habit of character depleted. Even in the most difficult cases, however, with willingness, love begets love, and hatred and resentment are unlearned in the *askesis* of friendship in the flesh. This can be a long, hard journey, and there will be dark times in all our lives when faith and love also require hope—a deep belief that the promise of love can come true even in the teeth of evidence to the contrary (a belief that is not at all the same as denial of the evidence).

3. *Hope.* In our discussion of "converted to" we saw how hope is born out of humility, itself simply the result of seeing clearly and hearing accurately the truth about ourselves, our communities, and our world. Humility alone, as this accurate assessment, is not yet, however, hope, for it could still lead to despair, the first of the vices in the "I-damn-well-won't" column. Despair arises from our own woundedness and willfulness when we fail to notice that the accurate assessment we have just undertaken is itself already *given,* an early result of grace, of being beloved in our dust. Without some sense of how things ought to be, we could have no sense of how wrong they actually are. Despair is the failure to take seriously the positive side of this equation. For example, the experience of having an abusive, authoritarian, or just plain inadequate father or mother can make the parental language applied by tradition to the first person of the Trinity difficult for someone. But another way of looking at it is that it is only the perfection of the divine fathering and mothering that allows to see our own parenting in all its imperfection. That is the moment humility gives birth to hope. If the ideal is real, then perhaps it can be actualized

somehow, and it must be real or I would not be recognizing the imperfect for what it is.[28]

Despair that turns back from the proffered birth of hope has two forms. One is a prideful form, arising from the classical ethic of "great-souledness" or egoism, which, as Sophocles and the other tragedians before and after have shown, always leads to a disastrous end and a kind of heroic resignation and sacrifice which goes down in flames while screaming "Fuck you" at heaven. Taken to its logical conclusion via Richard Wagner [*Götterdämmerung*] and Friedrich Nietzsche, it ends up running the ovens of Auschwitz every time. It refuses the humility that would make hope possible. Its concept of tragic end reminds us that there is a vast difference between having a fate or destiny, and having a future. The name of that difference is hope.

The other form is found in those who have been so traumatized, victimized, oppressed, and wounded that they have had forced on them a kind of false humility that does not allow them to see themselves as beloved. They have been persuaded by the lie that they or their circumstances are hopelessly bad and unlovable. Toxic shame blocks the birth of the liberation or permission they need for "noticing." Often this results in patterns of false martyrdom and self-sacrifice, which can become in their turn manipulative of others. Here it is the failure to acknowledge the goodness that makes the unacceptability of the current situation manifest— which blocks hope. Sometimes these conditions require extensive counseling, and clinical depression, of course, is a disease, not a vice, and requires medical treatment as well. Both versions of despair, however engendered, are forms of hopelessness.

In a different way, so are the vices of "I damn well will." False pride, vainglory, grandiosity all lead to a kind of optimism that either covers up and denies the truth about how bad things are, or pretends they can get better on their own or with just a little good will or effort from me. Grandiosity is in some ways the worst, bordering on the delusional, in that it entertains fantasies of acknowledgment and reward in the absence of any real achievement. In all cases of false optimism, hope cannot be born because true humility never gets off the ground. Either we have turned aside from an accurate assessment of our situation or we have overestimated our ability to cope with it on our own, failing even to foresee that tragic destiny acknowledged by the despairing "great-souled" ones on the other (I damn well won't) side. All shallow programs of self-help or political liberalism share this problem of optimism and can allow all sorts of horrors to occur just because we deny they exist or believe we can manage them on our own.

Hope is born, then, when true humility catches its first glimpse of what else might be possible. It is the crack between step one and steps two and three of the Twelve Steps, as the recovering addict moves from recognition of powerlessness to belief that God can and will be of help.[29] It is the first sight of the reign of God, and even the first hint of Glory, the current in which it becomes the predominate virtue. Although its mother humility sounds like a denial of self-worth, the opposite is true; we are on the verge of discovering our true worth as beloved selves. Indeed, it is this characteristic "beloved" that truly constitutes us as self, not Descartes' *cogito.* As we saw, hope is the essence of what we are converted *to.* It can be appropriated to the third mission of the Spirit, her own proper mission. Hope is born as an aspect of faith when we come to believe that the covenant promises might just be true. It is strengthened as an aspect of love because the Word/Wisdom brings the word and light that give judgment and hope at the same time, and because the flesh of Jesus embodies the reign of God and is a healthy paradigm for our own moral and spiritual lives, helping us believe that what we love in the Beloved could become true for us as well. The cross and resurrection of Jesus also bring the overthrow of all the powers of evil that have wounded and enslaved us, and the offer of the real healing for which we long. In that new freedom and liberation, in that paradigm, in that birthing of the reign, we find the true birth in us of the virtues of autonomy and industry. In hope we discover the autonomy of those who commit themselves to the one "whose service is perfect freedom," and in hope we recover grounds for effective work under the covenant and the promise of the coming reign. In the end, however, as in the dark nights, we face the choice between despair and something else scarcely known; it is the eschatological role of the Spirit that births hope in its own right. It is the promise of the Spirit's final consecration of the universe as a sacramental *pleroma* in which all things find their fulfillment that conquers our own despair and empowers us for mission to the world. Hope, that is, gives life meaning, identity, belonging, and worth.[30]

Supporting this growth is the classical gift of fear of the Lord, which is the beginning of all wisdom and is really a kind of awe and gratitude that replaces the actual fears of our concrete historical existence and the nameless fears of existential anxiety, as it has been called in our time, the anxiety caused simply by our mortality and finitude. This fear (awe) allows us to embrace the historicity of our dust in all its limitations because there is now hope precisely in that history as the reign of God is revealed as its real "ought to be" and even "will yet be." As Karl Barth so eloquently put it, *Nicht jetzt verloren*, "Not yet lost."[31] Prophecy, tongues, interpretation, and healing all proclaim and help actualize this reign, and are embodied in the ministries of prophets, healers, tongue speakers, and interpreters, as long as these are governed by all the cautions Paul lays out in 1 Corinthians 12–14. The beatitude "Blessed are the poor in spirit" supports and is born in hope because "poor in spirit" is another way of expressing the humility that is prelude to hope. At its deepest level, it is a keen awareness of our own spiritual emptiness apart from the indwelling of the Holy Spirit through (as) sheer grace. The blessing "for theirs is the kingdom [reign] of God" refers back to the core symbol of hope—that which we are converted *to.*

Finally, the fruit of the Spirit associated with hope is joy. This deep abiding sense of praiseful gladness must, in our time, be carefully distinguished from two alternatives. The first is "being high," which can cover the gamut from pleasant chemical buzz to a severe case of ego-inflation often induced by mood-altering chemicals introduced from the outside or produced by the body itself in response to certain activities and thoughts. My own sense is that many counterfeit "mystical" and paranormal experiences, including the famous "cosmic consciousness" of Richard Maurice Bucke, Aldous Huxley, and Timothy Leary fall into this category.[32] In and of itself there is nothing wrong with the pleasure this brings; all people, however, need to beware of the potential for it to slip into ego-inflation and grandiosity, and to cause us to forget it is but a pale reflection of happiness and joy. R. C. Zaehner has most helpfully located the quasi-religious experiences of this type, carefully distinguishing them from the essence of Christian mysticism as personal communion.[33] While it may be argued that such experiences, induced or naturally occurring, prepare one for deeper levels of mystical experience and insight, care must be taken to recognize the problems just identified. For those with potential (probably genetic) for addictive disease, this path is inevitably destructive of all true happiness, joy, and personal growth and relationship. What is so confusing and seductive is that it is precisely these people, addicted or with addictive potential, who will have the most intense and colorful early experiences and seem to "handle" the drug best, as the first symptom of the disease is a build-up of tolerance for the drug. The path of being high is closed to such persons, though addiction may well be the "sacred illness" of our time, and recovery from it often is the doorway to real joy for the recovering addict.[34]

The second alternative is not really counterfeit, just limited. It is happiness, helpfully defined by Aristotle as "A life of virtue led in fortunate circumstances."[35] Particularly if one takes seriously "the life of virtue," as we are discussing it, and realizes that "fortunate circumstances" are largely outside one's own control, then there is nothing wrong with "the pursuit of happiness" at all, since it will be only a pursuit of virtue. As virtually all wisdoms teach, happiness itself cannot be pursued. It comes as pure gift, as icing on the virtue cake.

Joy, in fact, is externally distinguished from happiness only in that it abides even when fortunate circumstances never materialize or disappear (John 15:11; 16:19–24) As such, it can be associated with the Christian virtues of martyrdom and virginity, provided these are interpreted symbolically with the tradition as "the exercise of all requisite virtue under difficult circumstances" (see Jas 1:2). Joy is one way to tell true martyrdom from false. False martyrs are usually laying a guilt trip on as much of the universe as will sit still for it; true martyrs quietly go on developing a virtuous character even in the face of adversity.[36] The same may be said of virginity as a symbol for the search for purity of heart. If it flows from a fearful and negative asceticism, it will be sterile. If it flows from an ever-increasing desire for God, it will be marked by a true and fecund joy. Joy comes when we know that "to live is Christ" (Phil 1:21), and that thus we can be content in Christ Jesus in whatever circumstances we find ourselves (Phil 4:11). This is the clearest indication that joy is based not on optimism but hope. The source of a Christian's joy is to "abide" in Jesus, keep the commandments of love, enjoy being Jesus' friend, and share his sorrow, which will be turned to joy in him and us (John 15:16). It is especially connected to the indwelling of the Spirit as well (Acts 13:52; Rom 14:17), who brings us the union with Jesus. Joy, born in hope, is thus fulfilled in even deeper love.

The discipline, the *askesis*, of the Trinitarian reality of faith, love, and hope, requires embodiment in the ordinary affairs of our lives as the school and arena in which we learn and practice them. In that *praxis*, the other virtues that were known and practiced in classical paganism, and have entered the Christian canon as the "cardinal" virtues, come into play.

Notes

1. The gifts and fruits are found primarily in Paul, e.g., 1 Corinthians 12–14; Galatians 5, and Ephesians 5; the Beatitudes are in Matthew 5 and Luke 6.

2. Modified from Antonio Royo and Jordan Aumann, *Christian Perfection*, 102.

3. Yves Congar, *I Believe in the Holy Spirit*. II. *"He is Lord and Giver of Life,"* chap. 7, "The Gifts and Fruits of the Spirit," 134–41.

4. See Congar or Royo and Aumann, places cited, for the pure form with references.

5. Aristotle, *Nicomachean Ethics*, II, 5–9 (McKeon ed., 956–64).

6. Gerald May, *Will and Spirit*, throughout, especially 1–21.

7. Augustine, *De Trinitate* XV:3.5; see also the Athanasian Creed, which is actually Augustinian in theology. See also Catherine Mowry LaCugna, *God for Us*, 97–104; Nicholas Lash, *Believing in One God in Three Ways*, throughout, but esp. 117–20.

8. Christopher Bryan, *A Preface to Romans*, 62, 70–72.

9. See previous note.

10. Thomas and Wondra, *Introduction*, 207–9; Paul Tillich and James Luther Adams, *The Protestant Era*, xlv–xlvi; Simone Weil, *Waiting for God*, 69.

11. This is the essential claim of George Lindbeck's *The Nature of Doctrine*, which is saved from a dangerous relativism by a single qualification, 66, 68–69. Lindbeck's qualification, however, points to the possibility of a critical realist approach to doctrine: that it does indeed form the grammatical rules of Christian discourse, does not infallibly describe or comprehend the divine truth to which it refers, and yet can be shown to have a real reference to a referent that can be critically assessed. This seems to be Robert Jenson's position, as well as Bernard Lonergan's, though Lindbeck rejects the latter's formulation of it.

12. Hans Küng, *Infallible?*, throughout.

13. Weil, *Waiting for God*, 69.

14. Urban Tigner Holmes, III, *What Is Anglicanism?* 2–8. Urban Tigner Holmes, III, known as Terry, was dean of the School of Theology at Sewanee from 1973 to 1981, and one of the premiere pastoral theologians of his time. He had a keen interest in spirituality and its history, and the analytical scheme he developed for understanding it is still widely used.

15. See Thomas and Wondra, *Introduction*, 126–31 for a discussion of William Temple, Paul Tillich, and John Polkinghorne on miracle.

16. The biblical reference, is, of course, to Exod 33:23, where Moses sees only God's back, not God's face; the significance for this in the Christian contemplative tradition was set by Gregory of Nyssa in his classic *Life of Moses*.

17. Oon-Chor Khoo, *An Episcopal Perspective of the Gifts and Ministry of the Holy Spirit*, 29, citing Howard M. Ervin, *Spirit Baptism* (Peabody, Mass.: Hendrickson, 1987), 101, 109.

18. Hans Urs von Balthasar's section on faith in *Creator Spirit* (V.2 of *Explorations in Theology*) is highly recommended (pp. 15–102).

19. See *Familiaris Consortio* # 32; found in Michael J. Wrenn, ed., *Pope John Paul II and the Family*, 28–30 (new pagination at end of book).

20. In particular, see Bernard Cooke, *Sacraments and Sacramentality*, 79–94; on this and on the healing of desire in general, see again Philip Sheldrake, S.J., *Befriending Our Desires*, esp. chap. 4, "Desire and Sexuality."

21. Robert Capon, *Bed and Board*, 79–84; after his own personal life had taken another turn, he subsequently wrote *Exit 36* and *A Second Day*.

22. Here I am indebted to Brown and Whitten, Life Training course, "People on Purpose."

23. Sheldrake, *Befriending Our Desires*, chap. 5.

24. Paul Tillich, *Theology of Culture*; also, Simone Weil, essays on the implicit forms of the love of God, of which much more will be said in the next current, see chapters 20–24 below.

25. The primary example, of course, is the Lord's Prayer in Matt 6:8–10; Luke 11:1–3; Mark 11:15–26 (and par.) is a classic text. This is also the point about the place of concession in healing rites in James 5. Stendahl, class notes on "Early Christian Piety," Harvard Divinity School, spring 1967; see idem, *Meanings*, 115–36.

26. See again, Barbara Hughes, "Where Was God?"

27. Rom 5:8.

28. Some will recognize the Cartesian and even Augustinian form of this argument. See also Elizabeth Johnson, *She Who Is*, 193 n. 6; see Patricia Wilson Kastner, *Faith, Feminism, and the Christ*, chap. 6.

29. *Alcoholics Anonymous*, 59–60.

30. The first three are the characteristics Alexis de Tocqueville believed would be required for religion in a democracy; "worth" is my own addition, inspired by Herbert Richardson, who suggested in class that Americans believe they have found the meaning of life, but it is trivial. See de Tocqueville's *Democracy in America* and *American Institutions and Their Influence*.

31. Karl Barth, *CD IV, The Doctrine of Reconciliation*, part 3, first half, 465.

32. The belief that there is only one kind of religious experience and that it can be chemically induced is called the "Philosophia Perennialis." Richard Maurice Bucke, *Cosmic Consciousness*, is a classic text with echoes in Aldous Huxley and Timothy Leary. Important, and in my view, decisive critiques have been offered by R. C. Zaehner, *Mysticism, Sacred and Profane,* and Owen Thomas, *What Is It That Theologians Do*, 263–88.

33. Zaehner, *Mysticism, Sacred and Profane* and *Zen, Drugs, and Mysticism*.

34. For a very helpful book on this whole issue, including the notion of addiction as a "sacred illness," see Gerald May, *Addiction and Grace*. Still a very helpful basic text on addictive disease is Vernon Johnson, *I'll Quit Tomorrow*.

35. Aristotle, *Nichomachean Ethics* I.4–12 (McKeon ed., 937–50).

36. See Elizabeth Johnson, *Friends of God and Prophets*, 156, for a reminder that appropriate resistance to death is also holy and a proper fulfillment of martyrdom.

11

The Cardinal Virtues

May grace and peace be yours in abundance in the knowledge of God and of Jesus our Lord. His divine power has given us everything needed for life and godliness, through the knowledge of him who called us by his own glory and goodness. Thus he has given us, through these things, his precious and very great promises, so that through them you may escape from the corruption that is in the world because of lust, and may become participants in the divine nature. For this very reason, you must make every effort to support your faith with goodness, and goodness with knowledge, and knowledge with self-control, and self-control with endurance, and endurance with godliness, and godliness with mutual affection, and mutual affection with love. For if these things are yours and are increasing among you, they keep you from being ineffective and unfruitful in the knowledge of our Lord Jesus Christ. —2 Peter 1:2–8

The four virtues to which the tradition has assigned the title and status of "cardinal" (prudence, justice, fortitude, and temperance) have had a mixed history in Christian thought. While each is clearly commended at some point in Scripture, their traditional presentation has had more of Athens in it than Jerusalem, more of Aristotle than the prophets of Israel or of Jesus. The tendency of Catholic theology has been to see these virtues as at least partially "acquired" by practice rather than "infused" by grace as are the theological virtues, and to believe that in the "noble pagan" these acquired virtues could lead to good works with real intrinsic merit.[1] This conflicted badly with the Protestant Reformers' doctrines of justification by grace through faith alone. We might note, however, that Protestant thought was not devoid of conversation about and reverence for virtue, the personifications in John Bunyan's *Pilgrim's Progress* being one charming example. There are also many more virtues than just seven (the three theological plus the four cardinal), and we no longer feel bound by the numerology of seven. Finally, there was the problem we have traced before, that virtues seemed increasingly to be treated as collectible merit badges rather than as habits of character.

The reversal of several of these trends has brought about a new appreciation for the tradition of the virtues.[2] The number seven is now viewed only as a traditional convenience not an ontological fact. All the virtues are seen as practiced

151

habits of character that arise in response to one indwelling movement of the Holy Spirit (which is already also at work in the non- or pre-Christian) rather than as distinct collectibles, and hence this approach does not conflict with Reformation doctrine. In particular, the distinctions between infused, acquired, and imparted virtues breaks down on the new model; all is a gift of grace (the indwelling presence of the Spirit); all virtues must be practiced for habits to be "set" in character, and the "practice" itself is informed by grace at every point.[3]

Given this shift, it is still helpful to use the traditional pattern as a lens to examine this one movement of the Holy Spirit and our response to it. To avoid some of the previous problems in the traditional approach, I suggest we see each of the cardinal virtues as *deriving from* one of the theological virtues. Since we are really talking about differentiations in our response to one movement of the Holy Spirit, this also is only a kind of "appropriation." But it does reveal the dependence of the cardinal virtues on grace, and maintain the Trinitarian structure of that grace.

1. *Prudence* is the fulcrum of all the remaining virtues, in that it is the thoughtful ability (wisdom) to determine the good, and hence right action, in concrete practical circumstances. It should be clearly distinguished from prudishness, which is an "I-damn-well-will" form of prudence. Although it thus forms a bridge between habitual and actual charity (love), for example, it is nevertheless best seen as appropriated to the theological virtue of faith, from a Christian perspective. This helps resolve the Reformation problem, of course, by affirming the *sola fide* (by faith alone) right at the heart of the discussion—all good works derive from a virtue grounded in faith. The deeper reason for this appropriation, however, is that once we get rid of the "acquired/infused" binary, prudence is a kind of knowledge or understanding of that Word of judgment that we analyzed above in discussing conversion *from*. Prudence is oriented to intrinsic good, which is ultimately governed by the manifested will of God (what the tradition called "orientation to supernatural ends"). For this reason, an allied virtue is *discretio*, which means both discernment and discretion—an ability to recognize the potential for good in an actual situation calling for action, and the ability to devise an appropriate response. Finally, as a discipline of thoughtful reflection guiding action (the real meaning of "praxis"), prudence is a concrete embodiment of fidelity, of steadfast covenant obedience.

In this light, it is easy to see counsel as the classic gift of the Spirit supporting prudence, since this gift applies the knowledge and understanding of faith to concrete situations. The charisms of word of knowledge and discernment of spirits also have an obvious supporting role here, as do the administrative gifts of teachers, preachers, and pastors in their function of providing concrete counsel to the people of God.[a] These help people find the prudential mean between the polar vices. "I damn well won't" in this case is negligence, the bad habit of acting without paying attention, simply through lack of care. The "I-damn-well-will" forms are characterized by foolhardiness and impetuosity (not to be confused with appropriate sponta-

---

a "Knowledge" as a gift is having information or wisdom imparted to oneself; "word of knowledge" is the gift of a message of information or wisdom to be spoken to a faith community.

neity), where a passion for the good fails to be tempered by a careful consideration of possible outcomes and consequences, including unintended consequences, of particular actions. Scrupulosity is also a form taken by an overly zealous prudence turned hypervigilance; this is what we could appropriately call prudishness. Perfectionism as a habitual survival technique, compulsively trying always to be right or do the right thing, also fits this mold. Foolhardiness and impetuosity often manifest themselves as an overly zealous response to what is perceived as a pervasive apathy and negligence, which is a good reason for recognizing that foolhardiness is a vice equal to the apathy itself in its undesirability.

Perhaps the major contribution of our time to this discussion comes from the studies that have revealed the male tendency to think of ethics in terms of abstract principles of justice, and the female tendency to think in terms of concrete effects of actions on webs of relationship.[4] True prudence would be a just and thoughtful effort to accommodate both sorts of ethical insight, recognizing the tendency of the male taken to an extreme to be a relationship-trampling foolhardiness in pursuit of abstract principles, and of the female taken to an extreme to neglect matters of principle and the hard choices principle sometimes dictates to the discomfort of a community. This balanced prudence takes the form of appropriate *casuistry* (the application of principle to concrete case) in ethical systems based more on principle, and of community wisdom embodied in the precedents of *common law* in ethical systems based more on relationship. An ethic untempered by either will inevitably degenerate into a fanatical and dangerous moralism.

As a result, prudence is not unallied with "common sense," provided that is also informed by principle. The fruits of the Spirit associated with prudence are patience and truthful speech. Patience (you just *knew* it had to go with prudence, didn't you?) is prudence with respect to time, the knowledge that the good is not achieved in an instant, but must be born and nurtured with care. Truthful speech (telling the truth in love) is a habit coming from the prudential recognition that even "little white lies" are ultimately counterproductive. Little untruths are really not utilized to spare the feelings of others but to avoid awkward and embarrassing moments for ourselves. The "in love" qualification reminds us that impetuous blurting out of the whole truth of what we think at every juncture, especially in a brutal manner, is also not prudential. Again, the balance between principle and relationship reveals itself as essential in ethical reflection.

I suggest a change in the assignment of appropriate beatitudes to prudence and justice. The tradition assigns "merciful" to prudence, as a tempering of justice, and then "meekness" to justice.[5] That is not entirely inappropriate, but I shall argue below that mercy is not a tempering of an otherwise stern justice but its very essence. I suggest that meekness is best seen as an attitude conducive to prudence. First, it recognizes that any claim to absolute ethical knowledge or an infallible ability to discern the good, the will of God, and perform it in concrete situations takes another bite out of the fruit of the tree of good and evil—any such absolute claim for oneself is sin, and about as close to original sin as one can get. Meekness is thus a correction to a moralism of either the male or the female type, provided it is not taken as having any sort of subservience about it, but only a proper sense of one's own limitations. In this sense it is like true as opposed to false humility; taking it wrongly has been particularly damaging to women and children and the poor when imposed on them as docile obedience. Second, meekness is precisely the attitudinal balance between principle and community or relationship we have been seeking as the essence of ethical prudence, in that it refuses to absolutize either. Finally, the meek shall inherit the earth. Without a prudential meekness recognizing the claim of environment over against both principle and human community, we now know there will be no earth to inherit, or at least no one left to inherit whatever is left. At the ecological as at every other level, prudence is ultimately a proper gift of survival, a matter ultimately of being or non-being for us, and thus has a properly theological concern.

2. *Justice* in the classical sense is the habit of giving to each and all precisely and exactly what they are due.[6] If we stop there, however, we can miss the radical shift that takes place in this virtue when it comes under the covenant theology of Judaism and Christianity. Justice translates *dikaiosynē* in Greek, which in turn translates *ṣedeq* in Hebrew, which in turn is normally rendered in English as "righteousness." We really need both words (righteousness and justice), because the first has for us more of a sense of individual uprightness, while the other looks more to the establishment of justice in a social context. These are inseparable, as John Wesley so powerfully taught.

Of greater significance, I believe, is that *ṣedeq* is a technical covenant term.[7] It refers to the way the holiness and righteousness of God are embodied in God's covenant with Israel, and through Israel all humankind. It refers to God's faithfulness to the covenant, and also to the personal and communal obedience expected of us under that covenant. That is what is so misleading about the liberal reading of Micah 6:8, "What does the Lord require of you but to do justice, to love kindness (*ḥesed*—steadfast love or mercy), and to walk humbly with your God (i.e., in obedience to the covenant)." These are not three things, then, but one. Far from meaning that all one needs to do is keep a few ethical principles and dispense with institutional religion, properly interpreted this saying lays upon us the whole burden of covenant obedience as a people.

Under that covenant, much *more* is involved than giving what is due. The righteousness of God is shown not so much in wrath and punishment, which Israel and we are surely due, but in God's steadfast love and faithfulness to the covenant that maintains that covenant even when we have broken it. That steadfastness or fidelity, *ḥesed* in Hebrew, is normally translated as *elios,* or mercy, in the Septuagint (the Greek translation of the Old Testament), and that resonance carries over into the Newer Testament. God's justice is shown, not by giving people their due but by treating them as under the covenant even when they do not "deserve it." Mercy is not the "tempering" of justice; it is its very core, its fundamental attitude. If our justice is to be like God's, it will mean treating all creatures as covenant kin, which will mean far more than giving them their due. It will mean turning the other cheek, giving shirt as well as a cloak, walking a second mile, though not accepting repeated abuse.

In that light, we can see that justice is primarily to be appropriated to the theological virtue of love or charity. Justice is indeed the discipline by which love is to be applied to concrete circumstances. This sounds strange to us, because we have come to think of love and the discipline that administers justice as somehow opposed to one another. Every good parent learns this is not true, eventually. An act of discipline that is not an act of love is ultimately abuse, and an act of love not disciplined by justice ("tough love" where need be) is sentimental self-indulgence. Mercy—steadfast, faithful covenant love—is the essence of justice. It will always give others more than is due and require less of them. That is the first reason why I believe the beatitude "Blessed are the merciful" belongs here. The second is a response to Jesus' "Judge not, that ye be not judged." Only when we judge (as we inevitably must) in mercy alone can we hope for ourselves, "for they shall obtain mercy."

Once we have seen mercy as the essence of justice, we can identify the tension of the opposing vices. "I damn well won't" as the opposite of justice is the tendency to give less than is due, or not at all. Its primary form is miserliness, or a mean spirit or hardness of heart. Related are the means by which one does not give others adequate freedom or acknowledgment, including overprotectiveness, patronizing, and a spirit that sees the splinter in the other's eye while ignoring the log in one's own—the vice of being judgmental. The most extreme form is a vengeful spirit that refuses to trust in God's justice toward and discipline of those who do wrong. It should be noted that these attitudes can be turned either toward another or toward oneself, sometimes both at the same time. The vices of "I damn well will" that oppose justice are all the forms of selfish indulgence and greed, including most of those that are also violations of temperance. Here, one gives to oneself, or to another for whom one is solicitous, more than is due to an extent that is harmful. Vices of either type can lead to what we commonly mean by injustice or oppression. Allied with justice is what Simone Weil calls "love of affliction,"[8] or in this case a deep acceptance of appropriate discipline for oneself or others, delighting not in the pain but in the justice and its fruits, in the pedagogy of the reign of God; we shall have a deeper look at this in the current of Transfiguration. Allied with this is the proper respect for authority. These can turn vicious as obsequiousness and masochism on the one side, or rebellion and sadism on the other.[9]

Supporting justice is the gift of piety or true godliness. This is a sense of gratitude and filial piety toward God our Father and Mother, including an appropriate sense of adoration and religious expression; we shall also discuss "love of religion" as defined by Simone Weil in the current of Transfiguration. Here we need to note that this virtue of piety or godliness illuminates our unqualified obligation and privilege to worship and adore God because God is God and we are creatures, not because either God or we "get something out of it." To call upon and worship God is our deepest joy as creatures.[10] Piety also instills a proper respect for all other creatures, especially our fellow humans for being also created in God's image and existing as God's children and our neighbors. From this love, justice/mercy flows naturally in the form of honor—a proper respect for oneself and others. It is helpfully embodied in the ministry gifts of apostles and administrators, who are called upon to maintain justice within the community of God's people, and to send it in mission in the service of justice in the world.

It is no surprise to see righteousness and piety appear again as fruits of the Spirit—the virtue and gift appearing again later as fruit. Once the roots of justice are established in love and mercy, it is also natural to understand forbearance, forgiveness, kindness, and goodness as fruits growing from justice. They show in the deepest possible way that far from being opposed to love, justice is the form love takes as the discipline for ordering the common life of the covenant people internally and for their mission externally.

3. *Fortitude,* or courage, can best be seen as appropriated to the theological virtue of hope, for without reasonable hope what looks like courage would be mere foolhardiness. It is also the ground of that sense of personal autonomy and the virtue of industry we shall examine in the next chapter in a discussion of contemporary theories of human development. Courage is not the lack of appropriate fear in the face of adversity nor lack of an appreciation of sacrifices demanded by a situation, and it is not a denial of pain. It is realistic determination to act virtuously whatever the consequences, in spite of our fear of those consequences. Because it is called to be realistic, it also depends on the accurate humility from which we suggested hope is born. Because it is called to act in the face of adversity, courage can also give rise to "martyrdom" and "virginity" as symbols for leading a life of virtue and detachment under difficult circumstances.[a]

The "I-damn-well-won't" vices opposed to courage are led off, of course, by cowardice, which can simply be a craven lack of will. Just plain sloth is another personal vice that works against courageous action. It is important, however, that we recognize forces that can paralyze action in persons, forces for which they are not guilty in any sense. As has already been suggested and as we shall see when we look at virtue and human development, children whose parents are unable to instill in them basic trust through "good enough" infant care will have difficulty achieving autonomy or industry. Toxic shame and other forms of demonic fear resulting from abusive parenting or other forms of victimization and oppression may also paralyze someone without the assent of their will having ever been given. Courage to heal from the abuse or to challenge the oppression will be the first stirrings of courage after survival itself, even though these may look very different from what we normally identify as courage.

The "I-damn-well-will" forms of courage are foolhardiness, or audacity, and rashness. A certain kind of anger and rage also belongs here, not appropriate anger at unjust circumstances, but anger transferred from an appropriate source to an innocent substitute. This would include anger inappropriately directed against oneself as well as against innocent persons and objects. A classic example would be abusing an animal (even if the animal is dangerous and the abuse, hence, "courageous" in a false sort of way) or a child or spouse because of pent-up rage at other persons or circumstances.

The spiritual gift associated with courage is strength, often called spiritual strength. It is not a strength one claims as a personal attribute but a strength of

---

a All the cautions about these virtues from the previous chapter need to be kept in mind here as well.

relationship, a proper dependence on the Holy Spirit for the resources to carry out God's will, a dependence that paradoxically gives birth to true independence and interdependence. One form it takes is "the courage to change the things I can," while leaving in God's hands the things I cannot change. "The wisdom to know the difference" is actually a fruit of prudence, of course.[11] Among ministry gifts, apostles, administrators, and helpers have a unique responsibility for embodying and nurturing courage in the community of faith. It is not surprising to see "the power of God" emerge as a fruit of the Spirit associated with true courage. That is a fairly obvious implication of what we just said about spiritual strength as a reliance on the Holy Spirit. When we are enabled to enact that reliance, the power of God is able to mend our own powerlessness. It may be more surprising to associate gentleness as a fruit of the Spirit with courage, but true courage, as opposed to mere bluster, really is gentle. Another way to put it—only the truly courageous can afford a nonmanipulative gentleness.

The beatitude associated with courage is "Blessed are those who hunger and thirst for justice (righteousness), for they shall be satisfied." While it might seem appropriate to link this with justice, what is in focus here is the hunger and thirst as the real grounds of courage. But it is also important to note that bravado action in the service of some end less than justice is also not true courage. "They shall be satisfied" points again to hope, and indeed again back to "conversion to," where we saw hope coming into focus, because ultimately this hunger and thirst for righteousness or justice can be satisfied with nothing less than the full establishment of the reign and commonwealth of God, in which justice and peace shall kiss each other (Ps 85:10–11), and justice will roll down like waters and righteousness like an ever-flowing stream (Amos 5:24).

4. *Temperance* has gotten a bad name in some quarters because of its association with the nineteenth-century temperance movements and what some see as their moralism and prohibitionism. Even so, it is important to acknowledge the reality of the movement's concerns about mood-altering chemicals, and for the historical grounding of the suffrage movement, the abolitionist movement, and all subsequent feminist and womanist liberation in this same soil. Temperance per se, however, is not about abstinence but about the proper orientation of desire to appropriate objects and in an appropriate degree. For that reason, it is best appropriated to the theological virtue of love as that which gives desire appropriate direction and degree.

The "I-damn-well-won't" vices defining the negative pole in the tension within which temperance lies as a positive point of willingness are characterized by the denial and refusal of proper desire, even desire of proper intensity. Scrupulosity, moralism, austerity, and false mortification are thus actually vices opposed to temperance. They are a refusal to "enjoy" created life as gift, and, as the Westminster Confession reminds us, "The chief end of man is to glorify God and enjoy him forever." These negative vices ultimately lead to a mean spirit that denies even its desire for God, seeks to overdiscipline the legitimate desires of others, and above all sins against proper gratitude. Because the term "mortification of desires" has such an unfortunate prominence in the tradition, it is important to be clear at this point.

To the degree that love of Christ calls us to share in his suffering and death for love of the world, "mortification" is proper as enduring what that entails.[12] But seeking to erase legitimate desires for fear of their excess in ourselves or others is a false discipline, even an abuse. One of the first to see the necessity of tempering excess in this area was Francis of Assisi, with his concern for proper care of "brother ass," our bodies.

The "I-damn-well-will" vices forming the "warm" pole of the tension for temperance are more familiar names for excess in matters of physical and spiritual desire. The litany is well known: gluttony, drunkenness, luxury, lust, cruelty, pride, and anger, or rage, of inappropriate degree. Even to name these in our time requires a couple of cautions, however. One is that we now know there can be genetic or traumatic roots for obsessions in these areas over which the person has no control. Failure of will in these areas for such persons is not a sign of a lack of willpower, which may be quite strong in character in other areas of life. Nor will ordinary disciplines of temperance help; in some cases total abstinence must somehow be practiced (alcoholism and drug addiction) while in others (food and relationship disorders) a previously unknown moderation must be discovered as a real possibility by the sufferer. It is not blame and guilt but healing that is called for in such cases, and the appropriate discipline is not a punitive mortification but the surrender, faith, cleansing, and spirituality of the Twelve Steps.[a] I have known other programs to provide some relief, but in my experience only the Twelve-Step program and fellowship restores joy in sobriety as a positive good.

A second qualification is again about anger. There is a vice of inappropriate degree of anger, as in a marriage where "gunnysacking" hurts (storing them up) leads to the phenomenon called the "A-bomb," where things reach a critical mass and a damaging explosion occurs way out of proportion to any one of the complaints taken alone.[13] Even here, the problem arises from suppressing appropriate anger and not dealing with the little stuff as it comes up. Rage against abuse and oppression are another matter; they can be appropriate and necessary at some stage for healing and liberation, even if they must ultimately be transcended. The point is that the way to healing and liberation lies *through* the rage, not around it or in denial of it. The trick is to create safe and prudential spaces in which this rage can be experienced and expressed, though this will be more a task for therapy than for spiritual direction, at least initially. Ultimately, however, the spiritual dimension must be addressed for true healing to occur.[14]

Virtues associated with temperance include proper (not toxic) shame and liberating permission, which, as we saw in considering "conversion *from*," are the signs that we have started to notice. Closely following is rigorous honesty, which cuts through the denials and delusions with which we wrongly justify false mortification or indulgence. That honesty gives birth to an appropriate humility, which in many cases is simply an honest appreciation of our capacity to fulfill a particular desire. Faithful monogamy arises, for example, from a humble recognition that

---

a In some cases of obsessive/compulsive disorders, supervised medication may also be necessary.

however many people we might have sex with (and our very finitude places limits even on that), to be a remotely adequate *lover* to even one human being is a lifetime project requiring all the energy we have to devote to the expression of our sexuality. No denial or repression is needed, simply an honest and humble recognition of our finite capacities.

The traditional gift of the Spirit associated with temperance is "fear of God"; this has to do with awe and a proper appreciation of God as our true end rather than terror at the thought of punishment for excesses. Once again, it does not lead to a repression of desires but to their proper ordering in the light of their ultimate end. In the near field or term, this means ordering them by the two great commandments and their consequences, which is why temperance can be appropriated to love. Among the hotter charisms, "discernment of Spirits" is extremely useful, and, as we shall see subsequently, is also governed by the dominion of love. Pastors and preachers are among the ministry gifts able to nurture temperance in a community.

Self-control and purity are obvious fruits of temperance, but it is important to recognize the causal order, especially in the cases of the obsessive-compulsive disorders we have noted. We shall have much more to say of purity, especially the great monastic virtue of purity of heart, in considering the movement of Transfiguration. Like purity, self-control is a *fruit* of the grace of the indwelling Spirit, not a *prerequisite*. As a result, this initially stoic virtue takes on a different cast in the Christian context.[15] The same can now be said here of forgiveness, which is an appropriate attitude toward oneself and others in the concrete struggles for temperance, avoiding both excessive blame and rigor but also taking the wrongs of indulgence seriously. The cautions about forgiveness noted above under justice still apply and are underlined by the fact it too is a fruit and not a prerequisite of grace.

Finally, the beatitude associated with temperance is "Blessed are the poor in spirit, for they shall see God." "Poor in spirit" refers to the honesty and proper humility that ground temperance, while "for they shall see God" is a promise that the proper end to which desire is to be oriented is not so much attainable as it is receivable as gift.

The Dominion of Charity

We have just seen that the virtue of temperance is about grace shaping our wills to govern our desires by obedience to the two great commandments of love. In fact, it is traditional at this point in spiritual theologies to point out that this governance of love is the root of all virtue, in a topic called traditionally "the dominion of charity." It stems, of course, from St. Paul's great hymn to love in 1 Corinthians 13, in which he points out that all the virtues, gifts, and fruits without love are nothing, that faith, hope, and love as the theological virtues predominate, and that "the greatest of these is love," and also from the "new commandment" in John's Gospel as elucidated in 1 John.

Human faith as trust and belief in God is grounded in God's faithfulness or *ḥesed*, which is the steadfast covenant love of the Fount who is Father/Mother. Hope is grounded in a confidence in the finality God's providence, which is simply the expression of God's loving care for all creatures through God's Word and Wisdom and Holy Spirit; this loving care is expressed ultimately as incarnate in the economy of salvation, birthing the reign in history and then bringing it to a final cosmic fulfillment. As we have seen, each of the other virtues is grounded in one of these three theological virtues, and hence in the character of God. It is God who is *first* hopeful, faithful, prudent (providential—having the wisdom, will, and ability to provide the best for all creatures), righteous, brave, and temperate in character, all as expressions of the divine loving.

"Dominion of charity" is thus a manner of confessing in our lives the sovereignty of the God whose very nature (and third person) is love. The demand or attraction of this holy love of God's nature on the lives of human beings is the source of all ethics and the ground of all virtue.[16] It is also the source of hope that fidelity in this moral struggle will lead to an unimaginable consummation in love.[a]

The Virtuous Community

To this point we have followed the tradition in treating virtues as a matter of individual growth and development, of the establishment of habits of soul in the character of individual persons. This is ultimately misleading, however, in two senses. First, the very notion of virtue, as well as definitions of particular virtues, vices, gifts, fruits, and so on, is very abstract and largely devoid of content apart from embodiment in a particular culture and society and its customs and language. What is courageous in one cultural context, for example, may be foolhardy in another, while what is prudent in the second is craven in the first. What is obvious justice in one may be barbaric cruelty in another, and so on. We need to avoid a destructive relativism, however, in which virtue is simply culturally/socially defined, and in which it becomes impossible to consider a culture or society as more or less virtuous. The relationship between gospel and culture must be construed as dialectic, the gospel needing cultural embodiment to avoid abstraction, but the culture constantly needing confrontation with the gospel to discover and manifest its own truest and deepest virtue.[17]

Second, the pedagogy of covenant obedience by which such character is formed requires the context of a covenant community of faith and faithfulness.[18] Personal character is formed by a process of socialization and enculturation, not simply by the indwelling of the Holy Spirit in separate movements in one individual person after another. Indeed, the principal "indwelling" of the Holy Spirit is in the covenant community, through its common life shaping individual persons for membership in a priestly people. Individual entrance into this community (for Christians) is normatively through the sacrament of Baptism, which also, of course, engrafts one into the community of faith as a member of the Body of Christ, the church. The

---

a Again, not the same as "being good."

baptismal covenant is the address of the larger covenant of God to all of humanity in the form of a concrete community of friends. Echoing this, the gifts and fruits of the Spirit are all for the sake of the community even when given to individuals. It is, in fact, virtually impossible for these gifts and fruits to appear and flourish in a privatized context.[19] The beatitudes are all in the plural (as are the Twelve Steps). To be in Christ, in the Spirit, is always also to be in the church as a member of the people of God on mission. We cannot unlearn hate and learn love by ourselves.

It is also not sufficient to think of the virtuous community as simply a collection of virtuous persons passing on virtues to new members by individual example. As in so many other areas, the whole is greater than the sum of its parts. The *koinōnia,* or common life, communion, and fellowship of the people of God, must itself be governed by habits of character that are virtues. The community of faith as such must be faithful under the covenant; it must also be a community of hope, looking forward eagerly to the further coming of the reign of God and seeking to forward that reign in all its affairs. Ultimately, it must also identify with the Spirit's own mission of a consecrated *pleroma* of universal fulfillment. It must be a community of love, shaping its internal ministry and relationships by that principle, and deeply engaged as a community in loving service and mission to the world for which Jesus died and which the Spirit fills. The community of faith must be a prudent community, carrying habitual principle and relationship into concrete acts of internal support and external mission. It must be a community of justice and mercy, conducting its internal discipline and procedures in a just/merciful manner, and promoting justice in the larger community it inhabits. It must be a community of fortitude, prepared to risk its own well-being for the sake of its mission and not become a mere museum or defensive circle of wagons. And it must be a community of temperance, in both inner ministry and outer mission embodying and advocating a balanced life.

There are three foci for this development of communal character, or culture, which must be tended at every level: family, parish, religious community, diocese or judicatory, provincial, and national church bodies.[20] First, the culture of virtue is crucial to evangelism, seeking to establish a community that is attractive to outsiders who will be drawn into its common life and hence to faith in, and friendship with, Jesus. Second, a culture of virtue is required for its pastoral task of enabling maximum possible support for the welfare and growth of all its members; at the heart of this support will be the pedagogy of contemplative praxis of the virtuous life as a form of socialization or enculturation as its primary tool of formation.[21] Third, the church as a community must also conduct its own affairs internally and externally with the surrounding world in such a virtuous manner that when it is called upon to speak a prophetic word to the world it will have some credibility. For example, a church that wishes to preach environmental responsibility must take responsibility for its own "footprint," form its members in a solid praxis informed by sound ecotheology, and thus attract others with a similar vision who may not have seen the connection to gospel. That is, in all three areas virtues are not developed in some timeless abstract but must be carefully (prudentially) shaped around the concrete issues of a particular time and place. Communal habits of character must also be practiced in actual embodiments in history and the structures of the community of faith as it institutionalizes itself in a larger society. This embodiment is inevitable for Christianity; a dislike for "organized religion" or the "institutional church" as such reflects an ahistorical and docetic ecclesiology, a disembodied notion of community and church similar to treating Jesus as not really human.[22] As we have noted from the beginning, Christian spirituality must be pneumatological, Trinitarian, and ecclesial, and these are in the end one thing, not three.

Perhaps nothing, however, has been more responsible for the modern/postmodern sense of loss and eclipse of presence and word than the corruption of the communities of faith and authority meant to speak the Word and embody the presence of Wisdom.[23] Some of this is inevitable in the risk of being institutionalized in a society reflecting its own place in a fallen and sinful world. Too often, however, instead of struggling against that corruption, the church embraces it, shaping its internal procedures and policies by secular standards rather than radical gospel and covenant obedience in a common life of virtue; often it does not even do the secular structures justice. How often do we hear it said, for example, that the church is a far worse employer than most secular businesses, by almost every standard? How hard has it been to get all areas of the institutional church to accept the burden justice places on us in managing our investments? How much energy does the church spend defending itself as a privileged exception to laws embodying those standards? When this happens, evangelism, internal formation and ministry, and external prophecy and mission are deformed and eviscerated.

"Spiritual renewal" means more than an increase in individual fervor, piety, and virtue; it must also mean a call to the whole community of God's people to a life of radical virtue and gospel and covenant obedience for the sake of mission. The best strategy, under the dominion of love, is probably to create small communities of disciplined charity as leaven in the lump to encourage growth in virtue in their members and advocate it in the common life of the whole church. Then there will be a beloved community for the formation of beloved dust.[24]

Notes

1. Actually, in the traditional presentation there are both "acquired" and "infused" forms of each virtue. Antonio Royo and Jordan Aumann, *Christian Perfection*, 54–72; Frederic Percy Harton, *Elements of the Spiritual Life*, 30–70.

2. One of the classic texts is Stanley Hauerwas, *The Peaceable Kingdom*; See John Casey, *Pagan Virtue* (a philosophical treatment of the classical "moral virtues" of prudence, justice, temperance, and fortitude); G. Simon Harak, S.J., *Virtuous Passions*.

3. And, as the recent Lutheran/Roman Catholic agreement makes clear, all agree it is only by Christ's virtues and merits that we are justified before God.

4. Carol Gilligan, *A Different Voice*, is the classic.

5. Royo and Aumann, *Christian Perfection*, 68–69.

6. Royo and Aumann, *Christian Perfection*, 436. See Thomas Aquinas, II-II, q. 58.

7. I first learned this from Harvey Guthrie. But see *IDB* 4:81–83; *ABD* 5:725–26.

8. Simone Weil, *Waiting for God*, "The Love of God and Affliction," 117–36.

9. No one showed this more brilliantly than Jean-Paul Sartre, throughout *Being and Nothingness.*

10. I first encountered the concept of "non-provisory owing" in a lecture by Canadian sociologist George Grant; I have not been able to find a published form of that lecture, but much of its spirit is also in his writings on Simone Weil; see *The George Grant Reader*, 249–53; see also Harris Athanasiadis, *George Grant and the Theology of the Cross*, 218–42. Janet Martin Soskice also made a similar point in the Hulsian lectures at Cambridge, spring 1998, "The God of the Attributes," still awaiting publication, a far as I know.

11. The reference to "The Serenity Prayer," is, I hope, obvious.

12. See Elizabeth Johnson, *Friends of God and Prophets*, 72; when we have it, Sarah Coakley's full presentation of a new erotics will also be appropriate here; once again, Philip Sheldrake, *Befriending Our Desires,* is relevant and helpful.

13. See George R. Bach and Peter Wyden, *The Intimate Enemy*, 1–20, and throughout.

14. See Barbara Hughes, "Where Was God?"

15. See Christopher Bryan's discussion of self-control in *Preface to Romans*, 89–91.

16. Thomas and Wondra, *Introduction*, 100.

17. The resonances with Paul Tillich are strong at this point, not only with *Theology of Culture*, but also with the entire method of correlation in the *Systematic Theology*.

18. Nicholas Lash, *Easter in Ordinary*, 231–41.

19. See Harton's ecclesial grounding of the gifts, *Elements of the Spiritual Life*, 71–75; Lash, *Easter in Ordinary*, 252, and throughout.

20. Thanks to Philip Turner for the three points that follow, which I heard him make in an unpublished lecture. Many of the same insights are embedded in his *A Rule of Life for Congregations.* See also "How the Church Might Teach," esp. 143.

21. Compare Lash, *Easter in Ordinary*, 266.

22. The witness of Martin Luther King, Jr., to this aspect of the life of the church, not only in practice but in his theology (as expressed in his concept of the Beloved Community, see Kenneth Smith and Ira Zepp, *The Beloved Community*) has been immense.

23. Michel de Certeau, *Fable*, throughout, esp. 79–150; Lash, *Easter in Ordinary*, 199–218; also Owen Barfield, *Saving the Appearances,* and Taylor Stevenson, *History as Myth*; see my "The Historic Ought-to-Be and the Spirit of Hope."

24. As proposed a century ago by Charles Gore, bishop of Oxford and co-founder of the Community of the Resurrection; a helpful analysis of Gore's social teaching is James Carpenter, *Gore*, 243–68, see esp. 259 with n. 82 there; the resonances with John Wesley's classes and bands and to the Benedictine heritage should be obvious. The impact of Boston University's remnant of Wesleyanism influenced King deeply on this point.

First Tidal Current:
Converted Dust

III. Conversion, Psyche, and Theology

12

Behavioral Science and Spiritual Growth:
Psychodynamic Theories

While I hope it has been interesting and instructive to consider the classical virtues and vices and the dynamics of forgiveness in their own right, we must remember that we are not talking about discrete packets of grace as some sort of quasi substance but of one movement of the Holy Spirit and the various human responses to it. In particular, we need to recall that the virtues, gifts, charisms, beatitudes, and fruits are not badges to be sewn on a sash or jacket but habits of a character (and supports for, and results of, such habits); we are concerned with a character being shaped to the maturity of the flesh of Jesus for the reign of God. Because the process is the Spirit's shaping of our dust, the dust we are, into the flesh of Jesus, this shaping of our character into conformity with the character of Jesus' humanity has a very concrete context. Gifts of grace do not drop down from heaven as completed packages without reference to the context in which they appear. They are given in a process of growth and development of particular persons in the context of their historical lives, societies, and cultures. As Nicholas Lash puts it, "Conversion, turning, is a practical matter, a social matter, with material conditions. It cannot occur through the mere exercise of will power, or through wistfully wishing it were so."[1]

One of the most significant contributions of our age has been to create a deeper understanding of how important those concrete practical, social, and material conditions are in shaping the responses we are able to make to grace in the life of the flesh; perhaps we have gained an even deeper understanding about the Spirit's shaping of God's address to the unique concreteness of each person. One advantage of a new spiritual theology that takes account of the history of the discipline is that it need not be bound by the psychology and anthropology of earlier eras that had become embedded in the scholasticism of the discipline. Instead, we can take advantage of a number of new theories that have arisen in recent years about the nature of conversion and its relationship to other processes of ordinary human growth and interaction. These draw from developmental psychology, sociology, anthropology, the experience of many of the churches with a restored catechumenate[a] for adults (a lengthy period of preparation for Baptism), and the work of certain key theologians.[2]

Because these theories draw heavily on contemporary versions of the human sciences, it is important to get the relationship between these disciplines and theology straight from the start. The need is even more acute in the light of the previously discussed romantic psychologizing of spirituality around the turn of the twentieth century. Some scientists have wrongly deduced that once a psychological or sociological explanation has been given for something, that is all that needs to be said. This is usually called the "reductionist" view. A more reasonable position is that all human experience happens to human beings who have their own psychology and sociological place; so, of course, experience is shaped by those factors. There is also an ongoing dialectical relationship between experience and the language in which it is always interpreted; that is, there is no such thing as raw or uninterpreted experience. That does not mean, however, that these psychological, sociological, and linguistic factors are the cause, or the only cause, of the experience, so that it can be "reduced" to them.[3] So also, if conversion is to be studied psychologically, for example, that does not mean the theological language becomes superfluous, or merely a religious language game for talking about what psychology has already explained adequately in its own terms. I have proposed that conversion is a human response to a movement of the Holy Spirit, a resonance in us of the Spirit's mission in support of that of the Fount; if so, then psychology and the other human sciences have much to teach us about the nature of that human response and resonance, and even of the particular ways the Holy Spirit addresses individuals and communities. That in no way rules out the truth that the Holy Spirit remains the primary "cause" of the conversion, though the human sciences will, for their purposes, trawl with a net that lets that dimension of the experience slip through, and indeed, given the nature of God's relationship to the world, that dimension could never be the focus of objectified knowledge.[4]

On the other hand, it is also not helpful to see the language of theology as addressing only a particular realm or class of experiences, called "religious experience," as if these were merely alongside other ordinary experiences which had been or could be perfectly well explained by science—especially not if the focus narrows to paranormal or otherwise extraordinary experiences. While some conversions do entail experiences that seem to be extraordinary, not all do; and even the unusual experiences have a quite ordinary life-context in which they occur. Also, we do not want to fall back into the trap of "the shrinking God" (which not so strangely parallels the emergence of the shrunken or severed ego of modernity and postmoder-

---

a The catechumenate is an ancient practice of a rigorous, three-year preparation for adult Baptism was re-introduced into the life of the churches beginning with the publication of "Rites for the Christian Initiation of Adults" (RCIA) by the Roman Catholic Church, though with a shorter period than three years, as a rule. Other churches have followed suit.

nity) in which the divine is a mere causal explanation for phenomena science has not yet explained, a realm diminishing in size with every new scientific advance.

It is more helpful to see that there is a "limit dimension" to all ordinary human experience.[5] This is clearest in those ordinary experiences that confront all of us with the extraordinary, such as falling in love or confronting death. Human beings always at every moment stand in the presence of Holy Mystery, and stand there as self-disposed in the face of that Mystery, one way or another; that is, to *stand in the presence* of Mystery is always to *take a stand,* to dispose oneself with regard to it, and hence to all of life. This sort of mystery is especially noticeable in our relationships with other persons, who become more, not less, mysterious the better we get to know them, and this kind of personal knowing is the best analogy for our coming to know and love God in conversion.[6] The presence of Mystery is best seen in our continuing experience of human self-transcendence as we have discussed it already, as itself requiring a source beyond our own given nature; and of the way the One who might account for that resonance in us always transcends any effort we may make to explain or possess it. That which calls us to self-transcendence in its own self-transcendence always transcends any effort we can make to grasp or objectify it.

There is a potentially disclosive and converting dimension, therefore, to every human experience, however ordinary, and any such moment could become the occasion for us to wake up and notice that we stand in the presence of Holy Mystery. Two further things need to be said, however. One is that some experiences do seem more apt to "bring home" our dependence on and disposition in the face of Holy Mystery, and these do have a certain predictability.[7] The experiences of solitude, intense beauty, falling in love, having a child, facing death or the enormity of suffering in the world, and other tragedies for oneself or a loved one are commonly experienced as especially disclosive of limit dimensions of our existence, and thus offer a high possibility for noticing and conversion. Contemporary developmental psychology, for example, can help us see the patterns of life in which these events tend to occur.

Second, if a particular experience is to be disclosive of our presence to, and self-disposition in the face of, Holy Mystery, we require a community of interpretation to teach us how to talk about that experience in a way that allows us to see the Mystery and make the turn. We have already begun to notice the importance of such a community in concluding our discussion of virtues. The current point goes even deeper. A community of faith engages us in a pedagogy of discipleship that does not merely bring its stories and narratives to an experience I already have, but also in a dialectical manner actually shapes the experience I am having, though it does not "cause" it. To experience the limit dimensions of life *as* standing self-disposed in the presence of Holy Mystery, to experience grace *as* grace, requires a community of narrative and language in which such an experience can be had, noticed, and interpreted as such.[8] Contemporary theories of both social dynamics and psychological development can help us understand the forces and patterns that contribute to this shaping. Some current theologies of conversion draw on both these sources of human scientific theory, as well as some particularly apt theological concepts and the increasing experience of the churches with adult conversions and a restored catechumenate.

The point of these deliberations is this: locating a particular conversion or other "spiritual experience" in a psychological understanding of an individual's life story, and in a historical and sociological understanding of the community of faith and interpretation in which it occurred and was interpreted, can be very helpful in understanding it. But such location does not explain it or account for it as such.

William James and the Aftermath

The literature generated by scientific psychology as it studies religious conversion is immense. Indeed, it can be seen as rooted in the close attention paid to movements of the soul by the great teachers of spirituality and mysticism from the Renaissance onward, especially the Carmelites and the Jesuits. Saving only Aristotle's *De Anima*, we can go so far as to say that modern psychology is born from the religious psychology of these early modern spiritual writers. The early movements in scientific psychology often have a foundational relationship with religion: they have either a direct focus on the psychology of religion or mysticism (William James, Carl Jung), or an antipathy to religion so strong as to be itself psychologically suspect (Sigmund Freud). Most contemporary theologies of the spiritual life are heavily intertwined with some notion of human psychological development. Understanding the history of the theories of psychological development they choose helps grasp their significance.

A modern "marker event" of some accuracy and convenience in this history was the publication of William James's *The Varieties of Religious Experience*, the Gifford lectures *in* 1901–1902. Virtually everything written since must take some account, as have we, of his typology of once- and twice-born, and of the relationship of conversion to "religious experience." So much of this has entered the general culture's understanding of these matters that many evangelicals, for example, do not recognize how much of their own theory and practice derives from James and not from Scripture or classical evangelical tradition. The discussion of James alone is vast and familiar enough not to bear repeating here beyond what was said in chapter 2. It is useful, however, to note several criticisms of James that could also be applied to many subsequent "empirical" studies.[9]

First, although it is the desire of James the pragmatist philosopher to avoid, in his writings as James the psychologist, the problems of epistemology and dualism that haunted the West since Descartes, he does not entirely succeed.[a] The first evidence for how much he is trapped by the shrunken or severed ego of modernism is

---

a Epistemology is the branch of philosophy that studies the principles of human knowing. The history of Western dualism and the contraction of both the self and God have already been discussed in chapter 2.

his emphasis on a particularly delineated realm of exalted feeling as that proper to "religious experience." Conversion, then, is both one of these experiences and the result of such experiences. We have already examined the postmodern critique of this reductionism, and Nicholas Lash's reminder that we must see all experience as having a potentially revelatory character rather than delineating a special realm of religious feeling. Closely allied with this is James's individualism—conversions for him scarcely have a social context, and it is certainly individual and largely private experience that plays the dominant role.

Because of the prevalence of deism, theosophy and other forms of the *philosophia perennialis,* and transcendentalism in James's milieu,[a] his account of conversion largely seeks to be abstracted from the doctrines of any "revealed" religion, or indeed of any concrete historical faith narrative of any community.[10] The assumption is made, for example, that conversion to Christianity, conversion to Buddhism, and simply coming to some sort of cosmic consciousness are all instances of the same thing. This ignores what we had just been talking about—the manner in which the language of a historical faith community's narrative shapes the very conversion experience itself. Even the notion that conversion to Christianity and conversion to Buddhism are fundamentally similar psychological dynamics with different surface content now needs challenging. A foggy awareness of "a higher realm" that fails to provide even provisional answers to "conversion from, to, and by what?" is another matter entirely. This desire to be general and "nonsectarian" haunts all the empirical literature as a problem, though the anthropologists probably keep the highest level of concreteness.

A further difficulty haunting James's account is his identification of real conversion through a highly refined "religious experience" as a kind of genius found only in a small elite, in which the general run-of-the-mill folks share only at second hand. This reflects not only James's historic class interests and intellectual snobbery but also the echoes of nineteenth-century Romantic notions of artistic genius. Indeed, the habit of identifying the deeply religious with the refined affections of the poet-genius (often stoked with mood-altering chemicals or simple madness) was common; Walt Whitman was the American archetype as William Blake and Lord Byron were for England. Some poets certainly are genuine mystics; one thinks for example of John Donne and George Herbert, Christina Rossetti, T. S. Eliot and Gerard Manley Hopkins. But the tendency of even current books on spirituality to rely too much on any old undigested poetic insight is an echo of this flaw. The deepest layer of the flaw, of course, is the failure to take the conversions of ordinary folks seriously.

Finally, the actual empirical evidence James used, Edwin Starbuck's data on sudden and dramatic religious resolution of adolescent struggles with masturbation, has locked much subsequent empirical study into a notion of conversion lim-

---

a Deism is a philosophical belief in God apart from any religious revelation. Theosophy is a Western movement appropriating what it believed to be the teachings of the non-dualist Vedanta tradition from India. The *philosophia perennialis* is the belief that there is one archetypal human mystical experience, that of a sense of oneness with the universe, common to all religions. Transcendentalism is the earlier American philosophical movement associated primarily with Ralph Waldo Emerson.

ited to the dramatic, the irruptive, and the easily visible as a change in religious affiliation.[11] There has been precious little empirical work done on conversions that intensify commitment to a tradition one already inhabits, conversions that are slow and painful rather than dramatic and elevated, and hence no real study of that model of life as constant conversion that I am advocating as primary for Christians. The theories to which we now turn, however, seek to overcome these limitations by focusing on the contribution of the believing community and the wider culture, the place of conversion in an over-all life history, the value to be given to "ordinary" conversions of "ordinary" people having "ordinary" sorts of experiences, and the acceptance of the fact that conversion may be extended in time, filled with struggle (or not), not very outwardly dramatic, and may not entail a change of formal affiliation.

Psychogenetic Theories—Erik Erikson

Virtually all the contemporary accounts of Christian conversion rely to some degree or other on the neo-Freudian developmental psychology of Erik Erikson, notably from his *Childhood and Society* and *Identity, Youth, and Crisis*.[12] One of the most helpful accounts of this theory and related ones comes from James Fowler in *Becoming Adult, Becoming Christian*, which I find is also the most sophisticated statement of his own faith development theory.[13] The following discussion relies heavily on Fowler's account and is summarized in the "Table of Developmental Theories" on p. 172.[14] The prevalence of this theory in the theological literature parallels its wide influence in developmental psychology and sociology. It also has a particular attraction for those in the Jewish and Christian traditions because of Erikson's description of life as a series of developmental challenges engendered by an interaction of psychobiological growth and varieties of socialization around that growth. These challenges are resolved by acquiring and practicing particular virtues. In the chart in this book I have listed both the virtue as Erikson names it and the classical Christian virtues (such as we have just been examining) that I believe apply.

Before we begin the account, we must notice that there is a flow, a sublation, for Erikson. The stages build on one another, but a current challenge will retest the achievements of all the previous stages and hence provide an opportunity to repair a weakness.[a] Thus, virtues are learned most naturally and easily at roughly the times and in the sequence given, but one can go back and tidy up a weak one or even supply a missing one in response to a later stage. Also, Erikson himself realized he was describing a pattern that was a psychosocial dynamic. While the urge to grow and develop and the general pattern of the sequence were, he believed, cross-cultural and hence universal for all human psychology, the precise timings and concrete contents or pedagogy in which the challenges take shape and are resolved

---

a One stage is taken up into, or "sublated" into, the next.

Table of Developmental Theories

ber	Approximate Age	Erikson Stage	Fowler Stage	Classic Virtues	Vice
	Infancy	**Basic Trust**	Primal Faith	Faith (as Trust)	M
	2-3 years	**Autonomy and Will**	Intuitive/Projective	Hope	To:
	4-5 Years	**Initiative and Purpose**	Intuitive/Projective	Temperance	
			Continued	Justice	
	School Age	**Industry and Competence**	Mythic/Literal	Courage	I
	Adolescence	**Identity and Fidelity**	Synthetic/Conventional	Faith (as Fidelity)	C
				Love (Philia)	
				Justice	
	Young Adult	**Intimacy and Love**	Individualtive/Reflective	Love (Eros)	
	Midlife	**Generativity and Care**	Conjunctive/Paradoxical	Love (Agape)	S
				Prudence	
	Old Age	**Wisdom**	Universalizing Faith	Hope	

involve processes of socialization in particular cultures. The theory thus transcends an individualistic psychologism.

Stage one, or infancy, requires the development of basic trust as the child experiences "good enough" care from parents or other caregivers. This means emotional nurturing as well as taking care of physical needs. It is in tension with a fundamental mistrust that can result when such care is not given, or a trauma occurs from violence or abuse by others than the parents, a mistrust that can cause the personhood of the child to shrivel even to the point of death. This tension of trust/mistrust involves self, caregiving others, and the world as a whole, even though these are not yet fully differentiated from one another. From a Christian point of view, it is not hard to see this interchange as the concrete opportunity for the birth of the theological virtue of faith as the Holy Spirit seeks to act sacramentally through the love of the caregivers.

In **stage two,** the toddler from two to three is struggling to achieve a proper sense of autonomy and will in the face of toxic shame. The child develops a sense of a self differentiated from caregivers by literally standing on his own two feet and claiming her own space. The tricky job for parents at this stage is to provide the foundations for solid boundary formation without "breaking" the newly forming will. I believe discipline programs overemphasizing strong discipline for a "strong-willed" child at this stage are misleading and potentially abusive. A strong-willed child whose will is broken at this stage is likely to become either a moral vegetable or a smoldering rebel.[15] Equally unfortunate, of course, is a permissiveness that places no boundaries on the behavior of the "terrible twos" so that no space is defined. The theological virtue being born is hope, as the child learns limitations and hopes for things that transcend them.

The period of **stage three,** from four to five is, of course, the traditional time for the "family romance" issues in Freudian theory, with its Oedipus and Elektra complexes, and the supposedly attendant guilt. Even when this dynamic is well handled in a family (and it can be), a tension remains for the child between the development of virtues of industry and purpose on the one hand, and the paralysis of guilt and fear of failure on the other. The parental task is to encourage new competencies, be especially supportive and nonblaming during failures, and provide an environment of ever-new challenges that encourage nurturing of the child's resonant self-transcendence without being so demanding as to preprogram defeat; special sensitivity is needed to distinguish the child's own growing aspirations from those projected on her. The classical virtues required here are temperance, prudence, and justice: temperance as the child learns to temper emotions and desires in the service of longer-term goals, prudence as he learns to set realistic goals and develop appropriate strategies, and justice, as she learns to cope with the boundaries set to her own goals and actions by the rights of others, as well as asserting appropriately her own rights. Freud may also be fundamentally correct that issues of sexual and gender identity are formed by and during this time.

The early-school-age child, **stage four,** is plunged into an environment beyond the home, often now increasingly competitive both mentally and physically for the child, while the parents find their beloved offspring measured and evaluated by outsiders to a new degree. The child struggles to develop virtues of industry and competence in the face of feared inferiority, with the obvious classical virtue being courage, appropriately located between paralyzing fear and foolhardiness.

Adolescence was Erikson's initial area of concentration and the first extension of Freud's theory of childhood sexuality into a full-blown theory of human development. In this period, **stage five**, the child/adult swings on a pendulum from "two to twenty-five" and from dependency to counterdependent rebelliousness. This is in the service of attempting to establish a clear sense of identity in the face of a confusion caused by bewildering physical changes and mixed cultural messages. The most important virtue to be developed is fidelity—to self and certain others—largely practiced in peer relations of friendship. Erikson developed from his own clinical experience the concept of a useful "moratorium" during which a child may experiment with different values and worldviews before committing to embody them in a concrete identity. College or university, military service, and apprenticeships are common social forms that provide such a moratorium. The trick for parents and other adults is to encourage peer communities based more on true friendship than gang loyalties, where behavior can test limits without excessive danger, and to allow experiment with identity formation while encouraging positive identity formation over negative. It is also a time to discourage premature decisions (such as marriage or childbearing), which lock in responsibilities before a freely chosen identity is well formed. The classical virtues required by this stage are, first, the love called friendship (*philia*) and, second, faith in its secondary meaning of fidelity, a requirement for friendship, usually tempered by a fierce sense of justice as "fairness."

The young adult, of late or just post-college age in our culture, continues with all the education tasks but is now ready in **stage six** to turn the energy of the raging hormones into a true search for intimacy and love, which battles with isolation. Sexual intimacy in a committed relationship is the archetype, but communities of intellectual and spiritual communion are also important. Fowler notes three forms of withdrawal into isolation: insisting on rigid control of a situation of potential intimacy, withdrawal from such situations where control is not possible, or a "fusion" which is indeed closeness but at the expense of boundaries of identity and autonomy that make real intimacy possible.[16] I would add a fourth: promiscuity, or the improvident spending of the outward expressions of intimacy in relationships in which the personal dimension is ignored or downplayed. It is, I believe, especially important for institutions that still have some influence to encourage and educate young men in the direction of true intimacy and away from a prolonged adolescent gang behavior in which sexuality is more about "scoring" and always on the brink of rape. Education of males for true intimacy is a seriously missing component in our culture at present. The theological virtue seeking to be born is love as *eros*, desire for real union with an other, as opposed to the isolation that results from all the various forms of sexual concupiscence or the fears that hold one back entirely.

The adult in the large middle of life, **stage seven**, is usually struggling with vocational issues in the broadest sense, seeking to find ways of making a real contribution to a human future, however local or global. Erikson sees this as the call to "generativity," which arises from parenting and other forms of artistic and/or social creativity. The essential virtue is caring, from the Latin *caritas*, love as *agapē*.[a] This is constantly in a struggle for further growth with the inertia of stagnation. If we combine this with a Jungian sense of the midlife crisis at real middle age, when a sense of mortality hits and life begins to "run backwards" from how much time is left, we can see the sharp breaks and explosions common in our culture to "midlife crisis," as persons emotionally curved inward on themselves seek "with pseudo-intimacy, to recoup relational deficits, but without genuine giving of the self or receiving of others."[17] There is a genuine call to the "inward journey" at this time, but usually in the service of the vocational imperative or the healing of unresolved inner wounds. John Wesley's conversion at Aldersgate is a classic example. Fowler, influenced by Don Browning (*Generative Man*), sees this stage as embodying Erikson's own sense of what constitutes mature adulthood, and ultimately he derives his own sense of vocational life, which we shall examine subsequently in some greater detail, from this point. A good deal of literature also suggests this is the typical age for first experiences of a truly mystical nature.[18] Carl Jung saw it as the pivotal period for personality integration, characterized by his own observations that midlife was a crucial turning point for psychic life, including religious development.[19] As we shall see subsequently, developmental tasks described in the social theories also tend to pile up at this stage. It is no wonder this has become the typical period of conversion in our culture rather than adolescence or young adulthood.

Finally, Erikson believed that in the older adult in **stage eight** the battle is to maintain a wisdom about life in the face of despair and fear of death. This wisdom comes from a deep sense of personal integrity arising from an acceptance that though one's life has not been perfect, it has been worthwhile for oneself and contributory to larger concerns. This obviously returns to themes of fundamental hope and trust.

Where does this examination of Erikson's theories and its allies get us in terms of spiritual theology? First, it puts meat on the bones of the notion that life itself is God's own pedagogy. The Holy Spirit as sovereign God and life-giver can be seen as the source of the drive for biopsychological growth. As we just saw, Erikson's later stages show that this growth must continue even in the long period of biological decline.[20] This is a rooting internally in the flesh of the very notion of self-transcendence we have been using and borrowing from Karl Rahner. The same Spirit can also be seen as the graciousness present and met in the challenge of every developmental stage, helping to shape possible life choices as pedagogies for the virtues needed to navigate the challenge. This also is a helpfully concrete way of understanding how the virtues, discussed previously from a theological point of view, are shaped as a response required by the sequential challenges of life itself.

Second, the specific form and content this growth takes is determined by the interaction of the biological psychogenesis with a specific culture.[b] Erikson claims,

---

a *Caritas* is the standard Latin translation for the Greek *agapē*. The English word "charity" derives from it, but has now lost the broader and deeper meaning and has come to denote a patronizing almsgiving. "Charity begins at home" did not mean spend what you have on your family first. It meant that the foundation for the virtue of charity as *agapē* is learned first in family relationships.

b Psychogenesis is the birth and development of the psyche throughout the biological cycle of growth and decline.

for example, that the set of virtues he lays out must be learned in roughly that sequence in any culture.[21] It remains true, as previously noted, that virtues look different in different cultures, and indeed within a culture may look different for different groups—for men and women, for example. All the content given to these abstract forms comes from concrete pedagogies in which the challenges to the sequence of inherent growth are presented and the opportunities for negotiating them are offered. There is no school of development that transcends this contribution of the formative community; and given a dialectical understanding of the relationship among narrative and language and experience, this suggests that the growth itself is at least partially shaped and determined by these communities. The meaning of puberty, for example, varies considerably depending on the way different cultures ritualize it (or fail to by trying to ignore it).

It is no accident, then, that Erikson's account of the development of the virtues is Western, and even Christian. In his case we need not speculate overly much on his own personal religious convictions, as he has displayed some of their results in *Young Man Luther,*[22] the work in which he virtually invented the modern psychospiritual biography, of which he wrote several more.[23] This cultural specificity is no criticism, provided we understand there is no neutral culture, language, or expression of this process beyond its bare structure; there are only particular specifications of this process in specific cultures. This is one of the problems with presentations such as Daniel Helminiak's, for example.[24] Helminiak asks whether theism (in the broad, contemporary sense of any belief whatsoever in a god, not in its more restricted original sense as equivalent to deism) is required or even adds anything to a psychological account of spiritual growth; he decides it does not, and then proceeds to give what he believes to be a "religion neutral" account of such growth, only at the end finding in the gospel itself something that does "make a difference," the doctrine of the incarnation.

Two comments: first, Helminiak and those who take similar positions still labor under the false assumption that all religions are fundamentally about the same thing.[25] This is now very much questioned, the growing scholarly opinion being that the different religions (and even the word is problematic) propose quite different ultimate ends of life. Indeed, one of the great strengths of Fowler's account of the various psychological theories of development is the clarity with which he shows how they also embody a variety of interpretations about how the human good is finally to be embodied. However much they may have in common, for example, Christianity and classical Buddhism have a very different picture of the universe, very different notions of what the goal of life is, and by what process of growth that is to be obtained. In addition, they have been and continue to be very differently embodied in different cultures. At a level of abstraction at which these differences disappear, it is increasingly recognized, everything else interesting vanishes also. One of the great myths of the secular democracies, left over from their Enlightenment and deistic roots, is that there is a value-neutral stance from which all the detailed differences of "revealed religion" have been removed; in its most virulent form, it proposes that the values and beliefs of secular humanism are itself that stance. It is not fundamentalist evangelicals only who should be protesting this in educational and other public policy—it is simply true that secular humanism is only one more value-laden stance among others, all the more dangerous because of its own lack of awareness that it is such. So it is no criticism of Erikson to suggest that his account continues to have Christian and Jewish overtones, since it must have some. It is only important honestly to acknowledge them.

Second, Helminiak points somewhat unwittingly to a real issue: When we look at the process of psychospiritual growth as defined by an Eriksonian approach and ask, "Does it make any empirical difference if we ascribe this growth to some sort of internal life-force program or to the Holy Spirit?" the answer must be no, if what we are seeking is some objective empirical difference that the Holy Spirit can be seen to make as an objective force alongside other such forces. This is the deep issue of the relationship of God to the world and the difference between them that is always a crucial question for any theology. This book is not about that question, but we cannot ignore it. One of the most sophisticated accounts is Nicholas Lash's in the arguments we have already alluded to in *Easter in Ordinary*.[26] One of his deepest points is that whenever we go looking for the "difference" God makes in some element in an empirical, objective, "I-it" (in Martin Buber's sense) world, we must inevitably fail for the *theological* reason that to make such a claim would ultimately amount to idolatry, since no object in the world can be God. This is even more viciously true if the difference for which we look is restricted to a marginal or paranormal area of life. Apart from a loving surrender to the incomprehensible Holy Mystery in whose presence we stand self-disposed, within a community of narrative about that Mystery, we can never point to *any* event in growth and development and identify it *as grace*, as an experience of the true God. And, as we shall increasingly emphasize as we proceed, even such true experiences are not themselves God, nor do they comprehend God in the sense of grasping or possessing God. The only difference that will be observable empirically will be the result of the concrete pedagogy of the community that confesses in trust that this growth *is* grace, is the work of the Holy Spirit. This confession can be made only from within the faith narrative of that community, from inside the "hermeneutical circle." There is no place outside that circle to stand to make such a judgment. There is a sense in which conversion can only be recognized as such in and by a community of the converted. The weakness of the secular humanist option is that it does not see that the same is true for itself as well.

From the standpoint of pastoral care or spiritual direction, what we have gained from Erikson's scheme is an appreciation for how the opportunities for conversion always come as concrete life issues and decisions. To encourage or nourish a conversion, to develop specific narratives and pedagogies which enable that, requires us to acknowledge these life issues as well as the theological insights we hope will be learned. For example, a primary conversion occurring around midlife issues of vocation, generativity, and caring will simply look very different from conversion such as those Starbuck studied focusing on adolescent struggles with fidelity and intimacy in a battle for sexual purity as that was defined in nineteenth-century terms. In our time, with its generally permissive approach to masturbation, even adolescent conversions will look different. Perpetuating narratives and strategies derived from the nineteenth-century experience of the predominance of the latter as if they were still viable for a situation dominated by midlife conversions will ultimately be unhelpful. For example, evangelization for young adults should be addressed to fears of isolation and opportunities to develop and be educated for real intimacy, and the nurturing of what Fowler calls "the vocational dream," not around issues of personal guilt. Evangelization in midlife should focus on vocational and generativity issues, offering increased opportunities to develop and express a passionate caring in parenting or other concern for the next generation. Outreach to the older adult, in addition to ensuring meeting basic needs, should focus on the development of wisdom and its appreciation as an offer to the larger community. Fire and brimstone efforts to whip up guilt once appropriate to adolescent masturbation battles will be largely irrelevant.

Cognitive Developmental Theories: Jean Piaget, Lawrence Kohlberg, Carol Gilligan

A second set of theories derives from a well-tested set of observations about typical ages by which certain complexes of mental operations, logic, and reasoning become possible. In one way or another, all these derive from the cognitive developmental theories of Jean Piaget. Beginning with *The Growth of Logical Thinking from Childhood to Adolescence*, Piaget traced the development of thinking skills in four stages, based on a combination of brain development, cultural influence, and even the impact on the body of material being mastered.[27] These concepts have become essential in planning curricula for children in all education, including religious. Knowing them also helps a parent see why seeking to set boundaries for a child through reasoning out consequences of behavior simply will not work until the child is capable of cause-and-effect reasoning.

The four stages and typical ages at which they occur are:

1. *Sensorimotor stage*: from birth to age two years (children experience the world through movement and senses)

2. *Preoperational stage*: from ages two to seven (acquisition of motor skills)

3. *Concrete operational stage*: from ages seven to eleven (children begin to think logically about concrete events)

4. *Formal operational stage:* after age eleven (development of abstract reasoning).[28]

Piaget's theories have come to have their biggest impact on the theological enterprise, however, through their application to moral reasoning by Lawrence Kohlberg, which began with his doctoral dissertation at the University of Chicago in 1958.[29] By presenting children and adults of different ages with a series of ethical dilemmas to resolve, Kohlberg developed the following series of developmental stages in ethical thinking; it is important to note this is not a measure of how ethical a person is but of how a person is ethical, that is, of "the *ways* people perceive and reason about moral issues."[30]

Level 1 (Pre-Conventional)

1. Obedience and punishment orientation

2. Self-interest orientation

Level 2 (Conventional)

3. Interpersonal accord and conformity (a.k.a. *the good boy/good girl attitude*)

4. Authority and social-order maintaining orientation (a.k.a. *law and order morality*)

Level 3 (Post-Conventional)

5. Social-contract orientation

6. Universal ethical principles (a.k.a. *principled conscience*)

A colleague of Kohlberg's, Carol Gilligan, eventually began to have deep suspicions about the validity of this scheme raised by the data showing most women "stuck" in stage 3, the "interpersonal-concordance" or "mutual-interpersonal-relations" stage, with almost no women in stage 4, and a few in stage 5, the "social-contract-orientation" stage. Her own research indicated that women do not develop more slowly or less than men but differently, emphasizing an ethics of caring as a responsibility to a web of interpersonal and social relationships rather than an ethic of abstract principles of justice.[31] It is interesting that these two approaches also characterize, respectively, common-law and Roman-law approaches to governance and justice; the former are more typical of the ethics of H. R. Niebuhr, Martin Buber, and Anglicanism; the latter more of Immanuel Kant, Emile Brunner, Karl Barth, and classical Roman Catholicism. One result of this research has been the growing recognition of these two different approaches to ethics as equally valid and potentially complementary. Increasingly, a person of mature ethical reasoning is envisioned as making use of both modalities, of responsibility to relationship and to principle.[32] A second result has been a growing sensitivity in all developmental thinking of the typically different paths to gender identity of males and females (largely derived from different needs to identify with or differentiate from parents of same and opposite gender), which makes it increasingly impossible to take typical male experience and patterns as either normative or superior. Fortunately for the subject matter of this book, spiritual growth and wisdom about it are the areas in which women have had their say recognized by the Christian tradition, at least in principle if far from full equality; the classical "doctors of the universal church" who are women (Sts. Teresa of Avila, Catherine of Sienna) are leaders in this field, but scarcely alone.

James Fowler's Stages of Faith Development

Based largely on this material, but with some attention to other theories we will discuss further on, James Fowler of Emory University developed his theory of faith development, which has become a standard part of contemporary discussions of religious education and spiritual development.[33] In his early work, and still, as I understand it in his description of all but the last stage of development, Fowler is seeking to give a religion-neutral account of faith development. Fowler himself is never quite clear about whether he is presenting a theory of faith development as a staged growth in cognitive understanding of religious ideas, symbols, and issues, or whether he is measuring spiritual growth, or both, the one being identical to the other. The strongest voice in opposition to identifying faith development with growth in sanctity, as does Fowler, has been that of the late Gerald May, an M.D. psychoanalyst on the staff of the Shalem Institute in Washington, D.C. May has had a good bit of experience training spiritual directors for mentally retarded adults, many of whom can be discerned as having a high degree of sanctity (in the terms in which we shall subsequently discuss such discernment) despite the fact they will never be able to advance very far along any of the lines of psychological and cognitive development. May also questions Fowler's effort to develop a theory that seeks to be neutral with regard to the actual religious content of the developing faith. His challenge to Fowler is, paraphrased, "Which is more inclusive—a theory that seeks to be religiously neutral but closes off the upper reaches of spiritual growth to all but the most intelligent, or one that is tied to Christian faith but makes allowance for a saintly person of limited intellect?"[34]

This dilemma for Fowler actually reflects, as we shall see, an unavoidable paradox in the material we are examining. Spiritual growth (sanctification) and human psychosocial development are related but not identical. For most people, there will be a close relationship between the life issues of their human development and the choices and conversions marking their spiritual growth. Indeed, the very principle of the dominion of charity suggests that an increasingly sanctified person will also be increasingly effective at loving and caring relationships, which is also a measure of psychosocial maturity, especially in an Eriksonian scheme. Nevertheless, there are certainly persons who are mature and well adjusted psychologically who show little or no signs of spiritual growth as such, and there are also, as just noted, persons of limited cognitive and psychological development who are highly sanctified. There is no unambiguous resolution of this paradox. As a result, I choose to interpret Fowler as actually doing two things: in his early work and in the first six stages of faith development, he is studying and describing a cognitive development in the religious area that can be independent of faith content. In the final stage, and in his later writings about vocation and conversion, he is more focused on spiritual growth and in a much more recognizably Christian context. We shall discuss the first here, and the second toward the end of the next chapter.

One more caution is necessary. It is helpful and to a limited degree useful to line up in a chart the Erikson, Piaget, Kohlberg (with a Gilligan qualification) and Fowler stages. What is misleading is that this can give the impression these take place as parallel growth in a kind of unison lock step. Nothing could be further from the truth, as Fowler himself insists.[35] The Erikson and Piaget stages are most tightly tied to the biological clock of physical age. Moral and faith development stages are not likely to occur *before* the age at which complementary psychocognitive developments occur, but there is absolutely no guarantee they will occur at the same time or even subsequently. One can certainly think of persons who are able to do all the math and function as generative people but who are, nevertheless, for whatever reasons, still in early stages of moral or faith development. With these cautions, we can now turn to Fowler's stages.

The first few stages are in close parallel to Erikson stages. **Stage one,** or *Primal Faith,* is nearly exactly parallel to the development of basic trust in infancy noted by Erikson. The development of basic trust in the combined experience of *self-world* and its ability to balance our primal ontological or existential anxiety, and symbols for God deriving from experience of parental others mark this stage.[36]

Stage two, or *Intuitive-Projective Faith*, covers the years from two to six, and hence two Erikson stages, those developing autonomy and will and those birthing initiative and purpose. The self becomes increasingly differentiated from parents, and the acquisition of language makes symbol-behavior possible and explicit. Powerful experiences of life's joys and terrors come through strong perceptions and feelings, which are interpreted in the new language learned from home and communities, through the child's own inquisitiveness and imaginative fantasy. Where these can begin to be connected with the narratives and liturgies of a religious tradition, the possibility of providing helpful (and of course, unhelpful) powerful symbols of meaning and worth is offered.[37]

Stage three, *Mythic-Literal Faith*, typically arises during the early school years, while the child is also seeking to develop industry and competence. Fairness and rules in general become cosmic principles guaranteeing the new and more orderly world of experience. Faith is largely a fairly literal reliance on the stories, rules, and values of one's family, larger community, and perhaps religious tradition as well, and practice of a religious tradition may be well underway, marking significant life events with meaning and worth. Thinking about these matters is also colored by the Piagetian cognitive stage of "concrete operational thinking," in which regularities and rules are seen as actually embodied in the observed world.[38] The endless arguing of children about rules and "calls" in games is a familiar example.

At this point in Fowler's discussion, faith development gets increasingly unhooked from Erikson/Piaget-type development, in that growth in the latter is still fairly regular for most healthy people, while faith development may begin to "lag." Some religious communities, for example, take adherence to a mythic-literal interpretation of the contents of faith as the standard of orthodoxy, making it less likely that a member will make a transition to later stages. Persons who have had little or no personal religious faith as children are also likely to regress to this stage when religious conversion hits in adulthood. Even those who had a conventional faith commitment but have it personalized through powerful experiences of conversion and empowerment are likely to return to this stage for a time, as one can observe in certain evangelical or charismatic settings, or in *Cursillos*. There is nothing at all wrong with this, as long as room is left for subsequent growth into later stages, and for the experience of persons who already live in later stages. Good *Cursillo* teams are sensitive to this need, for example. Where such room is not provided, a believer who comes under pressure to make a stage transition in faith development will either have to suppress it or abandon a community of faith that makes no narrative space for that transition.

Stage four, or *Synthetic-Conventional Faith*, typically becomes possible in adolescence, and is often tied to the search for identity and fidelity noted there by Erikson. Fowler calls this stage "synthetic" because, in Piaget's terms, formal or abstract operations now become possible and the believer can begin to deal with the contents of faith *as* ideas, ideals, and symbols. Perspectives other than one's own come to awareness, making it possible to sense the distinction between reality and perspectives and interpretation of reality. The synthetic side comes from selecting from all the possibilities a set of personal beliefs and convictions and the beginning of meta-narratives, or "stories about stories." That is, one composes a personal narrative, for example, about why choices among the various options have been made. A personal "philosophy of life" develops. The stage is called "conventional" because typically this process is still largely dependent on content derived from significant others, which are then synthesized into an identity that is social as well as personal. It is also "conventional" in that this set of beliefs is not yet fully "objectified for [self-]critical reflection" by the person holding it. "In this stage one is *embedded* in her/his faith outlook, and one's identity is derived from membership in a circle of face-to-face relationships." Many persons also find a plateau or place of equilibrium at this stage, for many years or even for life, and the resulting sense of institutional loyalty as part of identity formation is often encouraged by religious groups.[39]

Stage five, *Individuative-Reflective Faith*, if it arises at all, will do so in late adolescence and early adulthood at the earliest. It is indeed typical of the "questing" or "searching faith" encouraged in a college or university setting.[40] Here there must be a growing sense of a self separable from social roles and expectations and even of all modes of self-expression; there is also an accompanying objectification of value for self-critical examination and choosing which is detached from social or affective components with which they were first clothed. That is, the self steps back from all inherited language and value choices and searches for its own solutions to the dilemmas of life. As Fowler notes, when this stage comes later in life, it can be very disruptive of life patterns and relationships built on earlier faith commitments. Fowler also notes that some persons carry out only half the process. They may get involved in the critical process of reflection but never develop the new sense of self that allows one to authorize personal choices amidst the alternatives. This can lead to a perpetual late adolescent skepticism. Or, they may develop the sense of self, but not carry out to the full the critical examination of beliefs and values, which may produce someone who is still affiliated with a faith community but somewhat detached or marginal to it in some ways. Fowler believes this can produce a kind of limbo between Synthetic-Conventional and Individuative-Reflective.[41]

From my own personal experience, and as one who has been privileged to hear many spiritual autobiographies as a university chaplain, parish priest, and seminary professor, I find a significant lack in Fowler at this point. He does not seem to discuss the importance for faith development of Erikson's sense of intimacy issues in the young adult. I see this in at least three specific arenas. First, one has to come to terms with personal choices in the face of inherited or previously accepted values about sexual identity and expression; this often has strong religious consequences, as any college chaplain has experienced walking across campus on a Monday, noticing the averted eyes of students embarrassed about weekend behavior. Second, individuative-reflective faith often involves a dialogue about faith with one or more beloved others with whom real intimacy is being attempted. This reaches significant proportions when commitment to a spousal relationship is possible, imminent, or in progress. The spouse's faith is always to some degree "other," and this can be very sharp when the spouse is affiliated with a very different religious community, or none at all (or vice versa: I with none, spouse with a very strong commitment). Working out what "we" believe or what "we" are going to do about "it" (religion, including commitments from and to families of origin) is a big part of this stage for many, especially since it is inevitably bound up with differentiating "us" from our families of origin even as "we" define our place in an extended family network. If it does not come into focus around marriage, it almost certainly will around children. It is also especially intense if "we" push for a genuine resolution of the tensions, a resolution that will be "ours" without one person's faith subsuming the other, and do not settle for a compromise of the inherited traditions with adolescent skepticism but engage in serious dialogue. Finally, I also find that this stage is often accompanied by definite "mystical" experiences in which intimacy with God and Jesus are a distinct focus, an intensely felt and committed and "real" relationship, the first inklings that an erotic friendship with God may be possible, even the ultimate goal of life. Even where this is not explicit, one needs to come to grips with whatever positive valuation is placed on one's own new erotic personhood in any chosen religious context, even if it is only in the rituals surrounding marriage. Particularly in the extended moratorium Western culture provides in college and graduate education, all this is often being worked through in an intense (even forced) individuative-reflective mode in a series of confusions, dramas, conflicts, and choices, along with an early commitment to vocational identity (more on this from Fowler subsequently).

Stage six is called *Conjunctive Faith* by Fowler, and normally appears first at some point in midlife. It is called conjunctive because it involves the integration in ourselves of tensions that appear to involve polarities and contradictions.[42] Things are seldom seen in black and white. Symbols are seen as "only" symbolic, as different from what they symbolize, but nevertheless as pointing to something real, indeed to what is, in some sense, *most real*. Truth is seen as complex, ambiguous, paradoxical, but there is a "second naiveté" that transcends the skepticism and reductionism of the previous two stages with a "postcritical receptivity."[43] There is also likely to be a new respect for other traditions and points of view that is not relativistic but grounded in a deep commitment to one's own tradition. Because this stage is most likely to occur not only in midlife but after what we shall call, following Alan Jones and Reginald Garrigou-Lagrange, "second conversion," this attitude is more typical of the transfigurative current, and we shall discuss it more fully in terms of Graham Greene's characteristics of the "true believer." It is enough to note here that persons in this stage are unlikely recruits for faith approaches demanding single-mindedness as proof of orthodoxy or for ideological campaigns. "They know that the line between the righteous and the sinners goes through the heart of each of us and our communities, rather than between us and them."[44]

Fowler calls his final **stage seven** *Universalizing Faith*. He sees this as typical of a very few persons of unusual sanctity who have decentered from themselves and their natural ties. They now transcend the paradoxes of the previous stage, not by a return to a single-minded literalness but by a deepening vision of God (or the equivalent in other faiths), though Fowler admits this stage raises the question whether a theistic appeal might not be required at this point.[45] God is a solid truth who calls all partial perspectives into question. In short, this stage is most typical of what we are calling the third tide, that of Glory, which follows what we shall call, following Jones and Garrigou-Lagrange, "third conversion." We shall need to wait until then to discuss fully some of the issues Fowler ultimately raises. I believe he is right that the whole process he refers to as faith development is best envisioned as a synergy between internal human growth and the presence of the Holy Spirit. This precludes a solution that sees the first six stages as merely "natural" and the seventh as a pure gift of grace. Fowler correctly sees that grace must be operative from the start. It is also the case, however, that persons who truly live in Universalizing Faith in a consistent way are not many and are very special people. The world might not even be able to bear very many of them. It is not clear to me, though, that Fowler's solution, suggesting stage six is a goal for everyone while stage seven is a special case, will do.[46] We must postpone a full discussion of this until we examine the tide of Glory. What I suggest here is that even though it is not theologically best to do so, one *can* envision the first six stages as purely "natural," while that is *impossible* for stage seven. Something else is going on, and that "else" can be discussed only in religious symbolic language. (Note it is the "else" that needs discussing, more than the "something.") I shall argue that in fact this tide is to some degree present and anticipated in all the previous stages, and is indeed the proper vocation of all human beings, *even though* only a few very special people seem to lead lives dominated by this stage, at least in this life.

This discussion, indeed, is the inspiration for Fowler's own deeper reflection on the relationship of natural development and grace as partners in the reality of vocation to which we shall return. First, we must look at two other sorts of developmental theories with a more explicit sociological bent. What we have gained up to this point is that in addition to, and to some degree in harmony with, fundamental biopsychosocial, cognitive, and moral development, there is a natural development in how one appropriates, expresses, and lives one's religious faith. Any of the stages in that development can be seen as calling for conversion and offering opportunities to make such a conversion. One can imagine, however (indeed one knows concrete instances), persons who reject the offered developmental shift, and those who accept it but with no real deeper conversion. The point about stage seven is that it is literally unimaginable except as a fruit of the deepest conversion of all.[47]

Notes

1. Nicholas Lash, *Easter in Ordinary*, 205.

2. See, for example, the *Book of Occasional Services* 1991 of the Episcopal Church, 112–40. See also Francis Eigo, ed., *The Human Experience of Conversion*; Robert D. Duggan, ed., *Conversion and the Catechumenate*; Michael W. Herriman, ed., *The Baptismal Mystery and the Catechumenate*.

3. Sarah Coakley's struggles with these issues in the light of current feminist literary theory in *Powers and Submissions* is instructive and we await more in her systematics. See also Katherine Tanner, *Theories of Culture*. Louis Dupré has shown the origins of this linking of thought and language in pre- and early modernity (*Passage to Modernity*, 102–12).

4. The trawling phrase is John Polkinghorne's: "Is Science Enough?" 12. The problem of how the transcendent dimension of experience is to be re-introduced into modern thought with its love of an objectivity that cannot be applied to the transcendent, but cannot be justified without the transcendent, haunts Dupré throughout *Passage to Modernity;* see, for example, his conclusion, pp. 249–53. In this book I must assume such a philosophical project can and must be carried out, but that is a task for another work. John Milbank, of course, would have us abjure nearly all use of the human sciences in doing theology, the whole point of *Theology and Social Theory*. I still find the most measured response to be Gregory Baum, "For and against John Milbank"; see also Owen Thomas, *What Is It That Theologians Do*, 301–10.

5. The concept of "limit dimension" is David Tracy's, *BRO*, esp. 91–119; what follows is also heavily dependent on Karl Rahner, as expounded and corrected by Nicholas Lash, *Easter in Ordinary*, 15, 219–53.

6. Thomas and Wondra, *Introduction*, 23–25; of course, as they realize, it is subject to criticism, as is any other analogy.

7. Lash, *Easter in Ordinary*, 245.

8. Lash, *Easter in Ordinary*, 248. Of course, the grace of God can break through in solitude. But the language to interpret that breakthrough must come from a community.

9. Nicholas Lash's careful critique of William James in *Easter in Ordinary* is the inspiration for much of what follows. The critique is throughout, but most intense in the first half of the book

10. On the *philosophia perennialis*, see especially Owen C. Thomas, *What Is It That Theologians Do*, 89–114, 263–88.

11. James acknowledges his debt to Edwin D. Starbuck of Stanford, later Earlham, beginning with the Preface of *Varieties*, and throughout the text, and to his research; Starbuck found that most of these adolescent conversions he studied were resolutions of the search for "sexual purity." In those days before the pill, this meant giving up masturbation or fantasies, on the whole, not actual sexual relationships. Starbuck's own commentary on James is of interest: "The Varieties of Religious Experience."

12. Erik H. Erikson, *Childhood and Society; Identity, Youth, and Crisis.*

13. James Fowler, *Becoming Adult*, 1–47; Erikson is discussed in some detail (pp. 20–30). Fowler's own discussion is itself heavily dependent on the interpretation of Erikson by Don Browning, *Generative Man.*

14. This table relies heavily on Fowler with some reference to a similar chart by the authors of the "Colorado Curriculum," "Stages of Human Development." For a related chart with more reference to recent authors, see Elizabeth Liebert, *Changing Life Patterns*, 212–14; also in Joann Wolski Conn, "Therese of Lisieux," 85; see also Joann Wolski Conn's *Spirituality and Personal Maturity.*

15. James C. Dobson, *The Strong-Willed Child*, seems a little over the top on this to me, though Dobson has a number of cautions about not allowing the corporal punishment he does recommend to fall over into child abuse.

16. Fowler, *Becoming Adult*, 25.

17. Fowler, *Becoming Adult*, 25.

18. Richard Bucke, *Cosmic Consciousness*, is a curious early work of the *philosophia perennialis* type, but, interestingly enough, he recognizes midlife as the time of most genuine "conversions."

19. Carl Jung, "The Stages of Life," esp. 395–403.

20. It is striking that among philosophers and theologians, only Bernard Lonergan really gives an account of growth that takes decay and devolution seriously (*Method*, 52–55, 243–44); see Tad Dunne, *Lonergan and Spirituality: Towards a Spiritual Integration* (Chicago: Loyola University Press, 1985).

21. Erikson wrestled with this issue in "Ego Development and Historical Change," in *Iden-*

tity and the Life Cycle, 17–50, and from his own work with American Indian children, *Childhood and Society,* 109–86.

22. *Young Man Luther.*

23. E.g., *Gandhi's Truth.*

24. Daniel A. Helminiak, *Spiritual Development.* See now also *Religion and the Human Sciences.*

25. See my article "Christian Theology of Interfaith Dialogue" for the discussion of this point and a review of the literature to that point; also Nicholas Lash, *The Beginning and End of "Religion."*

26. Lash, *Easter in Ordinary,* 219–53.

27. Jean Piaget, *Growth.*

28. The article in Wikipedia is helpful and accurate: http://en.wikipedia.org/wiki/Jean_Piaget#Major_works, as of 11/19/07.

29. Among many articles and books, a good locus is *Essays on Moral Development.* In some lists of the stages, there is a stage 0, Egocentric Judgment. http://www.xenodochy.org/ex/lists/moraldev.html has a helpful quotation and bibliography.

30. Fowler, *Becoming Adult,* 37.

31. Carol Gilligan, *A Different Voice.*

32. Fowler, *Becoming Adult,* 46. For a brief correlation of these two typologies with major figures in theological ethics, see p. 42.

33. I find *Becoming Adult* Fowler's most mature and helpful presentation of his work. The earlier volume, *Stages of Faith,* contains more of the methodology and basic raw data.

34. G. May, *Will and Spirit,* 166–71.

35. Fowler, *Becoming Adult,* 72–75, for the discussion of nature and grace; 138–41, the dialectic of conversion and development.

36. Fowler, *Becoming Adult,* 52–53.

37. Fowler, *Becoming Adult,* 53–55.

38. Fowler, *Becoming Adult,* 55–57.

39. Fowler, *Becoming Adult,* 59–62; quoted material is from p. 60.

40. The term is John Westerhoff's, starting with *Will Our Children Have Faith,* 39, 96–97.

41. Fowler, *Becoming Adult,* 62–64.

42. Flora Wuellner, lectures at Graduate Theological Union, spring 1991. See her *Heart of Healing, Heart of Light.* She believes that if a resolution is forced toward one side of a polarity, the result is demonic.

43. I believe the phrase "second naiveté" is originally Paul Ricoeur's (*The Rule of Metaphor,* 318). Bradley Morrison's "Rollo May's Psychotherapy Related to Paul Ricoeur's Language Philosophy," is helpful.

44. Fowler, *Becoming Adult,* 64–67.

45. Fowler, *Becoming Adult,* 73–74.

46. Fowler's discussion of Universalizing Faith and the problems it raises is in *Becoming Adult,* 67–75.

47. Certain authors on art therapy and spirituality have also interpreted stages that are very like Fowler's, suggesting that the great round of mandala forms also reflect stages of the inner life. See Joan Kellogg, "The Meaning of Color and Shape in Mandalas," 123–26; Susanne Fincher, *Creating Mandalas for Insight, Healing, and Self-Expression,* 144–69.

13

Behavioral Science and Spiritual Growth: Sociocultural Theories

Additional Stage Theories

Theories about the larger and more global sequences, stages, and patterns of human psychobiological growth have been supplemented in recent years with a sense of various seasons and transitions in life that also mark the rhythms and patterns by which the more global sequences are embodied in life structures in the cultures of particular societies. Indeed, these various ways of telling the stories of adult development have been something of a growth industry since the late 1960s. Most famous has been the work of Gail Sheehy, whose book *Passages,* later acknowledged to be significantly in debt to the work of her teachers, really kicked off the genre.[1]

The work with the greatest influence in the long haul, however, has been that of Daniel Levinson and his team at Yale, who originally authored *Seasons of a Man's Life,* based on longitudinal studies of the lives of some forty men, and whose *Seasons of a Woman's Life,* a similar study of the lives of forty-five women inspired by the realization they could not take men's experience as normative, only appeared in 1996.[2] Taken together, these works give a sense of the way all adults continue to grow and develop by seeking to embody more and more of themselves, and to find ever deeper personal satisfaction, in life structures that respond to fundamental psychobiological growth in a given cultural setting.

Within the large "seasons" of twenty-years' duration, marking childhood, young, middle, and late adulthood, at least in Western industrial culture, certain themes recur for men. There are major periods of change and transition between each of the double decades as individuals make decisions about how they are going to fit into the one they are entering. Then comes a period where the new structures are tested. This is often followed by a crisis in the middle (age thirty or fifty, for example) in which a decision is made to continue with the chosen structures for that season, or chuck it and adopt new ones. At thirty, a man often "dumps" previous advisors and mentors and assumes new responsibilities for his own career development. At fifty, a man is often facing the limitations of how far he is likely to get in any area of life. Following this mid-season tension, either the previous structures are affirmed or new ones are attempted. One criticism of the first *Sea-*

sons is that not enough attention was paid to domestic and family life. These events certainly loomed larger in the lives of women, as do biological events such as menarche and menopause. Recognizing the importance of mentoring for both men and women was one of the strongest contributions of these studies.

While Levinson and his team do not themselves see these patterns as necessarily involving deep intrapsychic integration and reintegration, or put any theological interpretation on the transitions, the marker events of these patterns can also provide opportunities for conversion, and conversions that take place around them will resonate with the life issues involved as well as more directly religious issues. This view of human development and its relationship to spiritual growth has been most helpfully portrayed by James and Evelyn Whitehead in their book *Seasons of Strength*.[3]

Additional theories of adult development help provide even more specific contextual information. The developmental school of family sociology, for example, has applied stage development theory to a wide range of phenomena in family life, including marriage and parenting, each of which has its own developmental rhythm.[4] Marriages go through a cycle of romance and honeymoon (in the latter, one partner or the other may have a sudden personality shift as the new social role is incorporated); disillusionment (when you discover you married a real person instead of your ego ideal of opposite gender), which leads either to dissolution or a deeper and more real marriage; the seven-year itch; the ten-year "If I don't hurry up and get out of this one I will be too old and ugly to find a nice new one"; later, clustering around year twenty-four, "the children are grown, we have grown apart or just can't stand each other, and can't stand the hypocrisy of celebrating our silver anniversary"; and, finally, enjoying the peace of late midlife, then facing together the issues of aging and death. Parenting stages, beyond the simple disruption children bring to settled structures of individuals and couples, reflect the phenomenon that as a child goes through a particular developmental stage, the parents will remember and relive their own experiences in that stage. This provides an opportunity to heal the past, but it is also important not to project the parents' experience onto the child, who may be having quite a different experience. One advantage of having two parents is that they may have had different periods of happiness and difficulty, so their own "anniversary" crises can be staggered.

Joan Aldous of Notre Dame built on the developmental family sociology tradition and developed a theory of "nested careers," which is most helpful of all.[5] She envisions adult life as composed of a structure of careers such as psychobiological, child, educational, mating, marriage, parenting, job, and so forth, each of which has developmental stages and which "nests" in different individual life structures in different ways, depending on choices and timing. Couples who do not have children, for example, will eventually experience a very different sort of marriage from even very similar couples who do. The age of the arrival of first child is also a large variable; couples who conceive in their twenties will have different life structures from those who wait until their thirties. It is impossible to schematize this simply, but it can be envisioned as a chart of rows of slide rules that can be shifted back and forth to align with timings and choices of particular people. Those engaged in a major work of healing or liberation also undergo processes that can be described in stages. The Twelve Steps of AA are probably the best-known description, but Ellen Bass and Laura Davis have also provided a useful stage-account of healing from the trauma of abuse.[6]

These theories allow us to see several pertinent things. One is the incredible variety of adult life structures. This reminds us that in spiritual direction, for example, it is not our task to locate on a chart or diagnose a directee, because no scheme could be complex enough to do full justice to an individual story. Instead, the theory of nested careers is helpful in sensitizing us to the wide range of life sources from which issues might arise to impact the spiritual life, including opportunities for conversion or other marker events.

This theory also allows us to see the way some people can experience a kind of "pile up" of developmental stages at once, which can cause a period of tremendous stress and even crisis. In a typical midlife crisis, for example, the following may all pile up:

1. Psychobiological midlife—time begins to run backwards (how much do I have left?) and the body has new limitations—to say nothing of the integration pressures the Jungians describe.

2. Aging parents may raise new concerns.

3. Children may be in a difficult teen stage, and the friends they bring home may be sexually attractive to a parent, causing a different sort of crisis (actually quite normal, though acting it out is not).

4. Marriages may be under pressure from boredom, role shifts around career choices, outside sexual attractions, and fears of sexual aging.

5. Careers may be under pressure through changes in jobs, bumping into limitations in a chosen life path, to say nothing of the economic pressure of maintaining a family lifestyle, helping aging parents, paying for children's education, and trying to save for retirement. Even the most fortunate and successful may be looking for new fields to conquer. Women who have devoted these years to child rearing may be asking, "when do I get to (re)start my career and what will it be?"

6. Education careers are more likely than ever to come into focus around issues of lifetime learning.

7. And while all this is going on, there may be new tugs in one's religious life around a deeper sense of vocation as caring and/or a deeper and even mystical sense of God, all related to a desperate need for all the rest of life to somehow be meaningful and "worth it."

Extraordinary difficulties such as death or illnesses of loved ones, debilitating illnesses of one's own, and other tragedies may intensify such pile ups to the breaking point. This is also a point in life at which repressed traumas may resurface and require healing. All these can be particularly intense examples of what David Ford writes about so sensitively as the spiritual experience of being overwhelmed.[7]

This sort of information could be used for a kind of spiritual "ambulance chasing" that would be manipulative and immoral, if we would seek to impose a particular religious tradition or spiritual experience on people undergoing such pile-ups and overwhelmings. I am suggesting instead that we use such information in pastoral care, spiritual direction, and program design to help people be aware of the connections between their spiritual/religious/theological lives and the issues of their ordinary existence, not as that hopeless project of "applying religion to life" but of learning to experience and know life as permeated by gracious presence at every turn. Developmental stages in any or several of the careers can create "teachable moments," which Evelyn Duvall described as follows: "When the time comes that body is ripe for, the culture is pressing for, and the individual is striving for some achievement, the teachable moment has arrived."[8] These teachable moments or "choice points" make conversion or other leaps in spiritual growth possible and even likely, and our care and guidance of such persons will be enhanced if we are sensitive to the whole background of what is going on.[9] Certainly such persons may well benefit from a faith community with a pedagogy that helps them make sense of these events and to name as grace the grace they find there. But the task is to listen carefully for where the Holy Spirit is supporting and calling a person at such a time in the midst of their daily lives, not to jump in with precut theories and programs. If we stay with our midlife example, we see that spiritual direction will recognize the importance of sorting out all the colliding careers that intersect at this point but will focus on the choices offered for new life, some of which will be Spirit inspired and some of which may not be. Discerning the difference is the essence of pastoral care and spiritual direction at such times. Once again we are reminded of William Temple's great dictum, "Religious experience is the total experience of a religious [person]."[10]

A Dynamic Theory of Conversion

The theories we have looked at to this point have been focused on the personal- and social-developmental background that may provide opportunities for conversion. Much of the academic psychological and sociological literature is focused much more directly on the actual process of individual conversion, and it is a vast literature, deeply shaped by the personal, disciplinary, and sample biases of the various studies and their authors, yet still having much to teach. Fortunately, the Herculean task of surveying and synthesizing this literature, along with his own broad field research, has been effectively carried out by Lewis R. Rambo in his *Understanding Religious Conversion*.

Rambo develops his own dynamic and systemic model for examining conversion to allow him to synthesize these vast amounts of "empirical" literature from psychology, sociology, and anthropology. While most of the literature focuses on rather rapid change of religious affiliation, Rambo himself sees conversion as an extended process of varying speed, which may also include intensification of commitment within the same affiliation. His is yet another "stage" theory, though he emphasizes that the stages do not occur in invariable sequence and are best viewed in a systemic rather than a linear manner.[11]

Stage one is *context*, which includes much of the psychobiological and psychosocial background we have been examining to this point. Rambo also pays a good bit more attention to social systems theory, culture, and history, with particular attention to the social, cultural, and historical setting of the religion(s) on offer to the potential convert. One is not converted to Hinduism or Christianity in the abstract but to particular expressions of those religions in a specific historical and cultural setting. That is, this includes everything we usually think of in terms of a person's "background" and all the knowledge we can bring to bear on that material.

Stage two is *crisis*, an analysis of whatever imbalance exists in an individual or culture that provides an opportunity for a new religious option. These may be individual developmental moments arising from the sorts of rhythms we looked at previously, including processes of healing or liberation; the opportunity may come from a direct religious experience or confrontation with a new religious option; all the above may be in the context of a cultural shift such as confrontation with a new culture and its religious options.

Stage three is *quest,* in which individuals engage in an active search for solutions to problems, resolution of crises, and for "meaning, purpose, and transcendence" (and I would add, worth).[12] One of the particular values of Rambo's work is his emphasis on the potential convert as, in the majority of cases, an active seeker making free choices and not a passive object of manipulation.

Stage four, *encounter,* is the critical meeting between the questing potential convert and an advocate or group of advocates (missionary) for the new religious option. This is one of the major contributions of Rambo's analysis, as he examines the personhood and context of the advocate, the significance of the advocate's missionary strategy, and the actual dynamics of interchange between advocate and potential convert. Again, a great strength is his sensitivity to the active contribution to the process made by the potential convert, as the potential benefits of conversion (meaning, emotional gratification, techniques for living, charisma/leadership, and power) offered by the advocate are weighed against the cost of leaving the old life; also significant is the recognition that both the immediate advocate and the new community of faith may be deeply changed by the encounter as well. The classic Christian example, of course, is the struggle recorded throughout Acts and Paul's epistles to incorporate gentile converts.

Stage five, *interaction,* is the process by which the new or potential convert interacts with the new community of faith beyond the advocate and begins to be incorporated into a new way of life, often during a period of encapsulation from the rest of the world, especially from a previous existence-embodiment (way of being-in-the-world). Rambo helpfully emphasizes four "R's": relationships, rituals, rhetoric, and roles, as helpful points of analysis of this interaction. He is also sensitive to the active cognitive process of adopting a new "theology" or philosophy, as well as more hidden psychological and social forces.

Stage six, *commitment,* marks the end of the probationary period (which can be of varying length) and the mutual commitment of new convert and community to each other. Rambo again emphasizes the importance of ritual, of surrender, of testimony, and of a subtle shift in personal motivation that leads not only to a new behavioral ethic but also to new inner motives for behavior.[13]

Stage seven, *consequences,* looks at the results of the conversion from several perspectives. It examines the changes for the individual in the "layers" we shall look at more intensely in the next chapter: intellectual, affective, ethical, religious, and sociopolitical. On a broader scale, Rambo recognizes that there may be social, historical, and cultural consequences of greater or smaller significance, and deals with the besetting question of whether conversion is "good" for you (developmentally progressive) or "bad" (developmentally regressive or reinforcing of *stasis*). He notes most helpfully the discrepancy between the sociological studies, which generally find a positive outcome to conversion, and the psychological studies, which generally find a negative. He finds the reason in two biases on the psychological side: a disciplinary bias that all religion, especially sudden experiences, cloaks some pathology, and a tendency for the psychologists to have studied people who have left or been extracted from religious groups, while the sociologists study those who have remained.[14]

Despite Rambo's brilliant synthesis of the empirical literature, his own position remains thoroughly nonreductionist throughout. It is worth quoting him at some length:

> What is authentic conversion to me? As will be apparent, my own approach to that question is unavoidably influenced by my sectarian past, but I see "genuine" conversion as a total transformation of the person by the power of God. While this transformation occurs through the mediation of social, cultural, personal and religious forces (as I show in this book), I believe that conversion needs to be radical, striking to the root of the human predicament. For me, that root is a vortex of vulnerability. Given my acceptance that human beings are capable of infinite self-deception and that our proclivities are often anti-God, we require change that is foundational and pervasive. Every aspect of human existence (as I have been taught to see it) is corrupted by perversity and the influences of the "world," which generally points us in the direction of evil. I believe that conversion requires the intervention of God to deliver me from the captivity that I perceive is ensnaring me.[15]

Moving Toward Theological Theories

Rambo's nonreductionist view, grounded in the midst of the empirical evidence, is pre-echoed by two scholars deeply involved in thinking through the relationship between spirituality and psychology. The first is James Fowler himself, in his own developed thought, where he comes to his own theological reflections, as a Christian, on his work in general and the paradox of his final stage in particular. The second is the late Gerald May, psychiatrist partner of Tilden Edwards in the Shalem Institute in Washington, who has some important criticisms of Fowler's approach, and much to contribute on his own.

In the second half of *Becoming Adult, Becoming Christian*, Fowler begins the process of relating the developmental theories he has set forth, including his own theory of faith development, with the norms for maturity in Christ found in the Christian story. First, he lays out his own view of "The Christian Classic and Its Narrative Structure," focusing finally on his own personal statement of belief with regard to God, creation, fall and sin, liberation and covenant, incarnation, church/community, and commonwealth of love (kingdom or reign) of God.[16] On this basis, he goes on to develop a view of what he carefully calls "the Christian understanding of the human vocation," to distinguish it from narrower concepts of "Christian" or "religious" vocation. Ultimately, he decides that the Christian view is that all human beings are called to an ever-deepening partnership with the creating and redeeming God, partnership with God's own ongoing work in the world (commonwealth, reign, kingdom, of love and liberation).[17] As his argument progresses, four concepts important to our own discussion emerge: covenant, community, conversion, and synergy.

First, Fowler takes seriously an insight of Walter Brueggemann, that the biblical perspective that sees human beings as shaped for covenantal living (covenant obedience) "transposes all identity questions into vocational questions." Vocation, says Brueggemann, is finding "a purpose for being in the world that is related to the purposes of God."[18] This leads to Fowler's own definition of the Christian view of human vocation as "*the response a person makes with his or her total self to the address of God and the calling to partnership.*"[19] The resonances with the account I have given here of faith, hope, and love in the context of conversion from, to, and by in the context of covenant obedience and community should be apparent. In order to avoid a grim works-righteousness reaction to this definition, Fowler introduces the metaphors of orchestration and dance, which become even more helpful later. He concludes this discussion by synthesizing this view of covenant vocation with the developmental theories of the first half of the book, emphasizing that vocation is not a static ideal but a dynamic reality "changing its focus and pattern over time, while continuing as a constant, intensifying calling."[20] Deepening the sense of the relationship, he concludes:

> Our life structures change and evolve over time. As we move from one season of our lives to another, in kaleidoscopic fashion the configurations that are our life structures alter in shape and complexity. A Christian view of the human vocation suggests that partnership with the action of God may be the single most fruitful way of finding a principle to orchestrate our changing adult life structures.[21]

Next, Fowler provides a discussion of the contrast between this sense of identity and the classical notions of destiny and self-fulfillment (to which we shall return in the next chapter); then, he moves on logically to the second concept, community, since, as we have seen repeatedly, covenant, like conversion, is never just an individual matter but is always with and carried by a covenant community. In his chapter on "Christian Community and Adulthood" Fowler first acknowledges this reality, and then gives an account of the way a Christian community can provide what I, following Nicholas Lash, have called a "pedagogy of contemplative praxis" in which the individual's story is integrated with the Christian story (and the story of the more local embodiment of Christianity in space and time), and a shaping of desires (affections) and virtues not unlike the account I have given.[22]

Proceeding in his effort to describe the relationship between the developmental perspectives and the Christian vision of human vocation, Fowler states his central vision, which is also the point of the present chapter, as follows:

In the present, any serious, intentional approach to helping persons and groups form their lives in accordance with the Christian story and vision has to coordinate the convergence of three vectors of meaning: (1) the dynamism and direction of their personal life narratives, (2) the web of social interchanges in time that constitute their developing life structures, and (3) the perspectives on the Divine praxis and purpose offered in the core story of the Christian faith. The word *convergence* here means to suggest a process of *interplay*, of *interaction*, of creative mutual *interpenetration* between these three vectors, which will prove transformative for persons in the direction of faithful and imaginative partnership with God.[23]

He goes on by returning to the metaphor of dance and drama to describe how these three vectors combine to shape individuals and communities, talents and gifts, limitations, encounters with evil (others' and one's own) with the graceful presence of God in partnership for the liberating commonwealth and transformation from self-groundedness to vocation.[24]

Here he finally bumps up against the reality we have been explicating throughout this "tidal current": conversion. Fowler recognizes that both the developmental theories he has examined (and we would now include the notion of developmental adult "nested careers" as well) and his own faith development theory *can* afford opportunities, teachable moments, what the scholastic tradition called "occasions," for the emergence of vocation as partnership. But he also sees that in none of the developmental schemes outlined

> . . . does one *necessarily* take a step away from self-groundedness and towards vocation. In [none of the developmental schemes] is development *necessarily* tied to the recentering of one's passion, the realigning of one's affections, or the restructuring of one's virtues. Development, as described in [these various] perspectives, *can* be a movement that simply makes an attitude of self-groundedness more sophisticated, more skillful, and more entrenched. Development can simply mean a more effective and more single-minded pursuit of one's sense of individual or group destiny.[25]

This leads Fowler to acknowledge the reality of conversion alongside that of development for the transformation toward vocation. In harmony with our own work here, he describes conversion as not simply a once-for-all dramatic experience but even more as *"an ongoing process*—with, of course, a series of important moments of perspective altering convictions and illuminations—*through which people (or a group) gradually bring the lived story of their lives into congruence with the core story of the Christian faith."*[26] He then proceeds to describe conversion in terms very much like those presented in our earlier chapters, though briefly, and reaches this conclusion about the interrelationship:

> Conversion, then, is not so much a negation of our human development as it is a transformation and fulfillment of it. It is not so much a denial of our adulthood as it is the liberation and empowerment of our adulthood towards partnership with God. Conversion does not mean the nega-

tion of our sense of specialness and destiny so much as it means a radical regrounding of both, drawing them into the movement of a much larger drama that can call forth all the potential for greatness and heroism in service that any of us has been given.[27]

This recognition finally drives Fowler toward an affirmation of the Eastern Orthodox concept of synergy, in which the human reality and God's grace interact in a manner that finally cannot be untangled. He bows to the Western caution of being ever deeply aware of the power of sin and the necessity of maintaining God's initiative in justification, and limits this sense of synergy to sanctification (though, as we have seen, that line is one we draw from our side, not a real difference in God's graciousness); he sees the requirement of maintaining our deep connection with Western "hermeneutics of suspicion," which see the potential for falsely incarnating synergy in structures of oppression. Theologically, we would add with Nicholas Lash the ultimate necessity of avoiding both blasphemy in the face of the Holocaust and idolatry, by maintaining that finally there is a difference between God and *anything* objectifiable in the world, including human growth, even (or especially) "spiritual growth." "But," as Fowler concludes, "in our present situation of confusion and ferment regarding images of human wholeness and completion, we are in *critical* need of a theory of transformation and development that takes account of the power and availability to us of the synergy of God's grace."[28] It should be noted that the "human" side of the synergy as we have described it, human beings being souled and spirited, is already the result of the "ordinary" operation of the Holy Spirit in creation. On that understanding, synergy even before justification in no way damages the principle of the divine initiative in all things.

I have discussed and quoted Fowler at some length here because I believe it is imperative that we forge the link, as he has, between development and conversion for emerging vocation and spiritual growth, for two reasons. One is apologetic: no account of the spiritual life for our time will be credible that does not take the developmental view of humanity, indeed the whole of empirical anthropology in the very broadest sense of all the human sciences, with great respect and seriousness; at the same time we must insist as I, Rambo, and Fowler have, that a reductionist, scientistic view is also not tenable.[a] The second is pastoral: the entire "pedagogy of contemplative praxis" needs to be deeply informed about both the covenant ways of God as Spirit with human dust, *and* about the concrete historical and cultural life structures and developmental growth that will shape the specific issues of converting choice for that dust in any specific space and time. Before we move on to more fully theological theories that have attempted this, however, one more corrective is necessary.

That corrective is supplied by M.D. psychiatrist Gerald May. In a series of books he has challenged certain readings of Fowler's work, including what may have been Fowler's own early reading in which not enough emphasis was given, May believes, to God's initiative and grace. As we have seen, Fowler's later, more explicitly Christian

---

a Scientism is the application of scientific findings and methods beyond the realm of material which science appropriately studies, particularly to material it deliberately excludes precisely to do its business.

reflection, has gone some way to answering this initial objection. At a deeper level, May believes it is wrong to identify spiritual growth with human development in any simplistic way. Part of his passion for this claim arises from years spent training people to be spiritual directors for mentally retarded adults, who often show evidence of quite "advanced" sanctification in certain respects. His point is that these people will never "achieve" the higher stages of any developmental scheme, yet their obvious sanctity must be respected and accounted for.[29] I think this calls for a strong caveat to Fowler's work, at the very least, suggesting that the work of the Holy Spirit, while it *is* always *within* the limitations of particular human persons (that is part of what it means to be grace) is yet not *bound* by those limitations with regard to how much loving knowledge of and union with God is possible (the other part of what it means to be grace). I shall have more to say about this in a subsequent chapter.

As a practicing clinician, May is also at some trouble to identify ways in which grace may respond to outright pathology in a manner that furthers the spiritual growth of individuals, perhaps beyond what they might have reached had they not been ill. In *Care of Mind, Care of Spirit*,[30] May walks the reader through the whole psychological diagnostic inventory, suggesting possible avenues of healing and graciousness and growth. In *Addiction and Grace*[31] he describes the principle of the "sacred illness." This is the tendency, in folk religion as well as Christian hagiography, for it to be a characteristic of "sacred" persons that they have suffered from a debilitating illness (mental, spiritual, and/or physical) and recovered.[32] May contends that obsessive-compulsive disorders in general, and addiction in particular, are the sacred illnesses of our time. I believe his case is strong, though I would suggest clinical depression and traumatic stress reaction from abuse and oppression have equal claim. What May reminds us is that, by grace, not only the struggles of growing pains but also of "stuff happens" pain and even of demonic pain can be spiritually growthful, if there is a community practicing a pedagogy of the contemplative praxis of care which can sacramentally make the healing and support available for recovery and provide the rhetoric, rituals, and relationships that will allow recovery to be interpreted as grace. Many churches strive to provide some of these dimensions, and all churches are called to grow into these sorts of communities. He preserves for us the classical insight that soul-making is forged not only in maturing in Christ in a positive sense, but also by the *via negativa* of battling the demons in the desert.[33]

May prefers to see the spiritual life as governed by four forces:

1. God's desire for us
2. Our desire for God
3. "Natural" or ordinary resistance to growth and God in ourselves and our historical, social, cultural contexts
4. Resistance at the level of the demonic.[34]

We may note that numbers 2 and 3 can be analyzed as the sort of development/ grace synergy that Fowler favors (though corrected by May's appreciation for the graceful potential of the pathological), while numbers 1 and 4 require a more explicitly theological language. On that basis, we now turn in the next chapters to examining the explicitly theological building blocks of contemporary conversion theory.

Notes

1. Gail Sheehy, *Passages*; she has written several additional works using this model, including *The Silent Passage,* and *Understanding Men's Passages*; William Bridges, *Transitions.*

2. Daniel J. Levinson et al., *The Seasons of a Man's Life*; idem, with Judy D. Levinson, *The Seasons of a Woman's Life.*

3. E. and J. Whitehead, *Seasons of Strength.* Subsequent books by the Whiteheads, such as *Shadows of the Heart* and *Wisdom of the Body,* have also made significant contributions in this interface between social psychology and spirituality.

4. A *locus classicus* is Evelyn Duvall, *Family Development.* I discussed this approach at length in *Towards a Theology of Parenthood*, 84ff.

5. Her classic work was *Family Careers* (1981). See now *Family Careers* (1996).

6. *The Courage to Heal,* 57–169.

7. David Ford, *The Shape of Living,* 43–49.

8. *Family Development,* 144.

9. See John E. Anderson, "Psychological Research on Changes and Transformations during Development and Aging," 15–16.

10. William Temple, *Nature,* 334; see Martin Thornton, *English Spirituality,* 109.

11. Lewis Rambo's own summary of his stages is *Understanding Religious Conversion,* 165–70.

12. Rambo, *Understanding Religious Conversion,* 166. My addition of "worth" is courtesy of Herbert W. Richardson.

13. Flora Wuellner makes a useful distinction between free, healthy surrender, and harmful, coerced or manipulated surrender, *Heart of Healing,* 84.

14. Rambo, *Understanding Religious Conversion,*158.

15. Rambo, *Understanding Religious Conversion,* xii.

16. James Fowler, *Becoming Adult,* 77–84; I have been compelled to do the same in various places, and indeed any honest author will be so compelled at this point. How we envision the faith narrative deeply affects the way we believe it should be embodied in a pedagogy.

17. Fowler, *Becoming Adult,* 84–92.

18. Fowler, *Becoming Adult,* 93; the reference is to Walter Brueggemann, "Covenanting as Human Vocation," 125–26.

19. Fowler, *Becoming Adult,* 95, ital. original. See the works of Letty Russell for the most sophisticated theological exposition of the centrality of partnership, esp. *Growth in Partnership.*

20. Fowler, *Becoming Adult,* 104.

21. Fowler, *Becoming Adult,* 105.

22. Fowler, *Becoming Adult,* 107–27. See also Ford, *The Shape of Living,* 51–101; and Philip Sheldrake, *Befriending Our Desires,* 101–45.

23. Fowler, *Becoming Adult,* 137, ital. original.

24. Fowler, *Becoming Adult,* 137–38.

25. Fowler, *Becoming Adult,* 139–40, ital. original.

26. Fowler, *Becoming Adult,* 140, ital. original.

27. Fowler, *Becoming Adult,* 140.

28. Fowler, *Becoming Adult,* 141, ital. original.

29. See the various works of Jean Vanier, especially *An Ark for the Poor: The Story of L'Arche.*

30. G. May, *Care of Mind,* 149–78.

31. See above, chap. 6 n. 30.

32. See again Holmes, *Ministry and Imagination,* 222–26.

33. See now especially G. May, *The Dark Night of the Soul.*

34. G. May, *Care of Mind,* 23–26.

14

Theologies of Self-Transcendence
and Spiritual Style

In the following chapters I propose to examine some contemporary theologies of conversion that make use of, or are at least compatible with, perspectives on human development and its relationship to conversion such as those just delineated. Many of them are Roman Catholic, and emerge from the experience, since Vatican II, of the restored adult catechumenate in the Rite for Christian Initiation of Adults.[1] Two theologians have made particularly significant contributions to this new theology, Donald Gelpi, S.J., and, in a magisterial work, *Christian Conversion: A Developmental Interpretation of Autonomy and Surrender*, Walter Conn.[2] Both of these assume two earlier blocks of theory from the great Jesuit theologian Bernard Lonergan, one of which is heavily mediated through the work of David Tracy; this is the concept of human "self-transcendence" as a style of spirituality. Indeed, some theologians have proposed that human self-transcendence should be taken as the focal point of the academic study of spirituality.[3] The second, to be examined in the next chapter, is Lonergan's theology of layers, or levels, in conversion. We shall look at these two pieces first, including to some extent the way they are used by Gelpi and Conn. A subsequent chapter will take a look at Conn's synthesis, suggesting two alterations in it, and a critique and extension by two Anglican authors.

Types of Spirituality and Conversion[4]

In the early pages of *Christian Conversion*, as he is spelling out the dialectical relationship between conscience and conversion, Walter Conn initiates a discussion of "responsibility" (as in H. Richard Niebuhr's sense of *The Responsible Self*) as a criterion for that vague ethical ideal of the twentieth century, "authenticity."[5] Responsibility integrates a proper regard for self and autonomy with a recognition that

> one can only be true to one's self insofar as one is true to others. One can be true to one's self, in other words, only insofar as one reaches out and goes beyond one's self in responding to the values in each human situation in a manner that is at once free and creative, critical and fitting. . . . The

criterion of human authenticity, therefore, is the very *self-transcendence* which is effected in the realization of value through critical understanding, responsible decision, and generous love.[6]

Conn notes that even "self-transcendence" needs further definition, since it is currently used in a variety of ways, "some of them quite vague and mysterious."[7] In particular, we need to note that this term, given its origins, depends on a "Catholic" sense of transcendence as derived from a solid sense of self to take a next step, rather than a more "Protestant" (or at least Barthian) sense of leaping across a great gulf toward a wholly other;[8] it must also be distinguished from a more vaguely Eastern sense of self-transcendence as a loss of ego boundaries in the face of some sort of transcendent pantheism or higher consciousness. Conn believes the first task is carefully to distinguish self-transcendence from styles of ethics, spirituality, and hence conversion based on models of both "self-fulfillment and self-self sacrifice."[9] Although Conn goes on to credit David Tracy with providing an explicit theological context for this distinction in *The Analogical Imagination*, he does not trace its origins in Tracy's earlier work.[10] I shall do so, not merely for the sake of scholarly completeness, but also because I propose to clarify the relationship between "mode" and "style" and also a completion of the model of three "modes" of the God-self relationship.

The notion of differing models of selfhood as a key to understanding different styles of theology, ethics, and spirituality began to develop in Tracy's earlier work, *Blessed Rage for Order*. He is reflecting on the similarities and differences between the modern and postmodern views of what it means to be human:

> On the one hand that [postmodern] model [of humankind] joins modernity in its rejection of a model of self-abnegation and in its demand for full-scale criticism now ordinarily described by the more radical term "liberation." On the other hand, the contemporary model reveals certain illusions in the modern model. It points out, for instance, that the "modern pagan's" struggle for rational self-fulfillment is no longer an apt ethical model for our actual situation. By and large, the contemporary model can be described as a demand for "self-transcendence," a radical commitment to struggle to transcend our present individual and social states in favor of a continuous examination of those illusions which cloud our real and more limited possibilities for knowledge and action.[11]

At this point Tracy cites Bernard Lonergan as a chief source for a clarified notion of self-transcendence, and says, "the chief alternatives [to self-transcendence] seem to be either "self-abnegation" or "self-fulfillment."[12] Tracy then continues in the main text:

> [In Nietzsche and Kierkegaard alike] . . . our primary task is not the development of a finely tuned autonomous and sincere rationalism, but the far more difficult task of becoming "individuals," of becoming a self who realizes his or her own radical limitations and possibilities and yet struggles to become a human being of self-transcending authenticity.[13]

As his overall argument proceeds, this notion is further clarified with reference to its sources. Tracy recognizes an affinity of his notion of self-transcendence with that of a neo-Orthodox expression in Reinhold Niebuhr's *The Nature and Destiny of Man*. Later, in commenting on the need of postmodern theologies, like their neo-Orthodox predecessors, to disclose the transformative powers of the central Christian symbols, Tracy cites compatible transformation models as including H. Richard Niebuhr's *The Responsible Self*, Lonergan on conversion and self-transcendence, the use of Carl Jung by many Catholic theologians, the theology of Sam Keen, and finally Don Browning's *Generative Man*.[14] Later, he acknowledges Paul Tillich's contribution in his call to move beyond both classical "supernaturalism" and secular "naturalism" by developing some form of "self-transcending naturalism."[15] In relationship to his own theological scheme, Tracy finally makes a link between this experience of self-transcendence and his own notion of "religious experience" as experience of a limit-situation in the world of the every-day.[16]

In his later *Analogical Imagination*, Tracy moves beyond fundamental theology as such to begin to provide the outlines of a systematic theology based on his notion of a "classic" and the application of "the Christian classic" to our current situation. In the process he distinguishes three interpretive models for theology, ethics, and spirituality that often compete but which he sees as ultimately complementary: The model or form of *proclamation* takes a more negative view, dialectical rather than analogical,[a] emphasizes the distinction between God, world, and self, and focuses on themes of word, judgment, and the cross.[17] The model or form of *manifestation* focuses on the immanence of the always-already gracious and present God in creation and life, and is shaped by a largely analogical method corrected by a dialectical negative that reveals the ultimate breakdown of all analogies. This model tends to focus on incarnation and sacrament. The model or form of *prophetic action*, which is to result in a liberating praxis, tends to critique the oppression and suffering in our current situation as a negative dialectic to manifestation, and emphasizes themes of covenant promise in exodus, resurrection, and eschatological fulfillment in the commonwealth/reign.[18]

One might think Tracy would identify self-fulfillment with manifestation, self-denial with proclamation, and self-transcendence with prophetic liberating action. In fact, Conn's continuing use of a three-part scheme suggests this, though his own views are more nuanced in the end.[19] But this is not what Tracy does, in fact, in the section of *Analogical Imagination* Conn cites as the theological context for the distinction. The section is a final one in which Tracy is attempting to sketch the outlines of the contents of a systematic theology based on his analysis of the three forms and the Christian classic. He is showing how the Christian classic, interpreted in these three forms, gives an account of the ordered relationships among God, self, and world. In the *locus* at issue he discusses the view of self in each form or model.[20] He does indeed identify self-fulfillment with theologies of

---

a   The "dialectical" mode begins with paradoxical opposites and differences in a kind of conversation. The "analogical" approach begins with perceived similarities, for example, between humanity and God.

manifestation and self-denial with theologies of proclamation, and at one point he seems to identify theologies of prophetic action with self-transcendence.[21] But this is misleading in two senses. One is that he has also shown how each of the first two modes issue in self-transcendence, and he then goes on to strengthen that suggestion as the argument proceeds:

> Amidst the real conflicts of Christian interpretation of the Authentic self expressed in the inevitable clash of these three classical Christian ideals for true selfhood, one fact stands out. In spite of their otherwise real and perhaps even irreconcilable ideals for the self, all three are committed to a model of radical, because graced, self-transcendence; a self always-already, not-yet free from and for this world.[22]

Self-transcendence, then, cannot be the *name* of the mode for authentic selfhood belonging to the negative social dialectics of prophetic action, precisely because it belongs to all three modes. Furthermore, as he proceeds, it is clear that Tracy sees a problem with any of the three modes taken alone and absolutized: the negative social dialectics of prophetic action is a form of self-negation subject to a *ressentiment* similar to that of the negative personal dialectics of the proclamation mode, both equally failing to achieve the agapaic ideal of self-transcendence by the event of Jesus Christ, as does also the mode of self-fulfillment stemming from manifestation, with its latent danger of narcissism.[23] Earlier, indeed, Tracy had shown how the analogical manifestation mode, when it refuses to incorporate the reality of the two negatives, ends in a sterile and uninteresting univocity, a speaking with only one voice with no nuance. He also suggests *each* of the negative dialectics (personal and social, proclamation and prophetic), when it forswears totally the positive task of theology and is left to itself, "eventually explodes its energies into rage or dissipates them in despair," leading to a dysfunctional equivocity or relativism.[24]

Because I believe this critique of the downside of both negative dialectics and the ultimate vacuity of manifestation left to itself is experientially true, I propose to clarify Tracy at this point by the following suggestions.

1. There needs to be an explicit name for the mode of ideal selfhood proper to the form or mode of prophetic action, and I shall reserve the term "mode" to refer to these three primary models as they express such an ideal. If self-denial is the mode of selfhood for the form of proclamation, and self-fulfillment is the mode of selfhood appropriate to manifestation, then I suggest the best such explicit name for the mode appropriate to prophetic action is "self-criticism."[a] This is not self-denial in the proclamation mode, and, in one sense, indeed, is a form of self-affirmation, especially for those who have been denied access to a positive sense of self for any reason. It is instead a never-finished ideological critique of the self's social location in terms of gender, race, class, sexual orientation, and so on; as such, it is an effort to transcend

---

a It will be helpful to recall what I have suggested earlier, that "self-denial" must be a term with room for personal healing and liberation as well as repentance. I recognize that the term "self-criticism" can be difficult for those struggling with their "inner critic." "Critical self-awareness" may be more helpful to such persons.

(not overcome or eliminate) the limited and even false consciousness that such location inevitably entails. That is, our perception of reality is not only limited by the finitude of our perspective; it is also actively distorted by the ideological interests of that perspective. This is a large part of the source of suspicion in postmodernist thought of all "grand meta-narratives" that claim to transcend such particularity.[a] Indeed, the chief task of "deconstruction" is to reveal precisely the finitude and ideological biases of any such text. While such criticism will call perpetrators of prejudice, oppression, and abuse to a repentance and conversion more like self-denial, it will call victims to repentance and conversion that look more like self-affirmation in the teeth of negative self-stereotypes that have been the chains of the oppression. It issues in "liberating action" in both cases. This name for the third mode preserves Tracy's sense that it is a negative or critical dialectic, but with a positive intent, and that its location is social, in contrast to the personal negative dialectic of self-denial.

2. Self-transcendence, then, is not the *name* of the third ideal of the God-self relation in the mode of prophetic action. Nor is it a fourth alternative to the other three modes of selfhood, nor even some God's-eye perspective that unifies them. It is, rather, the true *style* of each, in which each of the negative dialectics (proclamation/self-denial and prophetic action/self-criticism) moves forward to gospel affirmation, while the positive analogies of manifestation are corrected and enriched by a deep integration of the negative, the not-yet. As Tracy suggests, the corrective in each case is the fullness of the Christ event itself as incarnation-sacrament, judgment-cross, and resurrection-reign.[25] That is, self-transcendence will stand to the other three forms of self-ideal as *agapē* does to the other three forms of love, or Godhead itself to the three persons of the Trinity. It is not a fourth alternative nor a perspective that unites them by abolishing the distinctions but the deep truth putting them in proper relationship to one another. True self-transcendence is a reinterpretation of all three in a kind of Trinitarian dance step, not identical to but in resonant harmony with the dance step by which faith, hope, and love are born out of one movement of the Holy Spirit as it emerges from the intra-Trinitarian dance of the co-inherence of the Three-in-One. It is the style by which each of the modes incorporates the others in response to the Christ event, as opposed to a destructive style in which each, in isolation, pursues its program in opposition to the others and, as Tracy notes, explodes in its energies into rage or dissipates them in despair.

The Three Spiritualities and Their Fulfillment

This clarification we have just made allows us to examine each of the three spiritual modes in more depth, and then their fulfillment in the style of self-transcendence. In each case, after characterizing the mode, we shall look at what counts in each for sin and salvation, what truth is embodied in the mode, and what problems emerge when each is taken on its own in isolation from the others and without the full dialectic of self-transcendence as appropriate style. I shall take them in the

---

a   Grand metanarratives are philosophical or other systems that claim to explain everything. Hegel would be an archetypical example.

order in which they have predominated historically, and in which they occur in a "typical" life of spiritual growth, with the repeated cautions that they are all always present, and stages in which one predominates can occur in any order. Taken this way, they emerge as the appropriate modes of discourse and spiritual styles for the three concurrent tidal currents I have proposed.

1. Self-denial or the Cleansing of the Image of God

A spirituality of self-denial, self-sacrifice, or self-abnegation is empowered by the gospel in Tracy's form of proclamation. It is a negative dialectic allowing one to see the sad truth about one's self in the light of the Word, and thus it emphasizes conversion *from*—sin, and its removal. While grace is recognized, the path to and outcome of conversion are denial of self as attached to sins and sinfulness.

In this mode, sin is the violation of the moral law expressing God's will. This violation leads to death, judgment, and hell. Sin is largely conceived in personal terms, and even social evils tend to be viewed as compounded of aggregates of individual sinfulness and to be treated best by programs of individual conversion. Salvation in this mode is our deliverance from death, judgment, and hell because of the righteousness of Christ that we receive by grace through faith, which is the theological virtue emphasized in this style and is usually interpreted as right belief with a high intensity of commitment. Catholics in this mode add grace for real moral reform as well. In theory, at least the Lutheran side of Protestantism is more suspicious of any notion of progress, but popular Protestantism maintains an undercurrent of Pelagian moralism.

The deep truth embedded in this mode is that the denial of the empirical self (or the "old Adam") is necessary for the birthing of the true self in God (Col 3:1–4). Even that language can be misleading, however, and the Eastern Orthodox phrase, "the cleansing of the Royal Image," the image of God in which we were created now restored in Christ, is more helpful. It avoids the notion that there are ontologically two selves, a true and a false, and suggests instead that what is denied is not truly the self (in the Royal Image) at all but alien accretions that have smudged and obscured that image. What is denied, then, is not the self at all but only its perverse or imposed attachment to that which makes it less than itself, which prevents it from following Jesus in that love which issues in love of neighbor that is like his love for us.[26]

The dangers of this style have been well catalogued, the chief one being a viciously angry Puritanism whose own self-hatred gets projected onto the faults of others or comes out in unhealthy extremes of physical ascetical discipline. The danger coming into full clarity in our time is that this mode can be a tool of oppression when it is used to curb the legitimate strivings toward self-worth-in-God of those who have not been permitted the luxury of developing an overweening self that needs curbing. Not surprisingly, feminist and liberation theologians have been especially critical of this option. As Tracy makes clear, unless spiritualities of this mode move through self-transcendence into a deep gratitude for the self as restored and sanctified in the Word as Jesus, they will be filled with resentment and either explode in rage or dissipate in despair.[27]

2. Self-fulfillment

This second mode, although it has always been present in the tradition, is, as we experience it, largely a contemporary reaction against legalistic and rigid forms of self-denial that are perceived as oppressive. This mode is most typical of the gospel in Tracy's form of manifestation, and is sensitive to and celebrative of the always-already character of God's gracious and loving presence in creation, relationships with other humans, and mystical epiphanies. The theological virtue with which it resonates is love.[a] This love tends to be interpreted through the standard misreading of the second great commandment, "Love your neighbor as yourself," though even this maintains the true wisdom that some self-love is required before an other can be loved. The deeper truth begins to emerge from the better exegesis of the commandment, "You shall love your neighbor who is just like you, that is, created in the image of God." You love your own self and your neighbor for precisely the same reason, the image of God in you both.

The deep truths of this mode concern the sacramentality of all creation, especially in the light of the incarnation. All the positive theologies, including Christian humanism itself, are capable of expressing these truths.[28]

Sin in this context is usually seen as self-alienation and all forces that contribute to it. This self-alienation is then diagnosed as the cause of alienation from God and world and neighbor. Salvation is viewed as personal wholeness and fulfillment, psychological integration such as Jung's individuation, emergence of the true self, a proper sense of self-worth, adult relationships with others, including sexuality as graced, and a deep appreciation for the gracefulness of all creation, usually accompanied by an intense love for "nature" in the modern sense.

This mode is obviously a vital and important one for a balanced spirituality; taken in isolation, however, and apart from the negative dialectics of the other two, it is all too typical of many today who seek quite sincerely to fulfill in themselves, among other things, what they perceive as their spiritual side, as if that were the heart of all religion. The resulting potential problems have been well catalogued. It can become a secular program for the gratification of ego needs and desires of the empirical self, or a search for religious kicks, what Conn calls the self as a bag of desires which is to be affirmed and actualized by fulfilling all those desires.[29] Tracy has noted the tendency of this mode, indeed of the whole form of manifestation, toward a kind of narcissism and self-absorption when the affirmation of the always-already of this mode is not balanced with the "not-this, not-yet" of the other modes.[30] This narcissism and its unfortunate consequences have been the subject of much recent literature, including the works of Christopher Lasch, Paul Vitz, Daniel Yankelovich, and Robert Coles.[31]

Perhaps the deepest theological critique, however, is James Fowler's. He takes it on in the form of one of its most explicit expressions, the retrieval of classical "eudaimonism" in David Norton's *Personal Destinies*.[32] In this work (and Fowler

---

a The metaphor of "resonance" is meant to suggest a sympathetic connection that is not an identity.

believes, in Rollo May as well, though in a less extreme form), we are governed by the metaphor that, as in the early Greek sculpture of Silenus, each of us has inside a little golden figurine which is our true self.

Norton's message, elaborated and reiterated in his book, can be reported in his own summary: "Each person is a bust of Silenus containing a golden figurine, his daimon. The person's daimon is an ideal of perfection—unique, individual and self-identical."[33] The ethical imperative of *eudaimonism*, which Norton is willing to equate with "self-actualization," calls for a person courageously, steadfastly, and undistractedly to attend to the innately given potentiated excellence (*aretē*) seated in her/his daimon. The committed actualization of that excellence, under the adversities and challenges of historical existence, results in the enactment of a person's singular, unique destiny.[34]

This form of the classical heroism of a true and informed egotism has broad appeal, especially when filtered through its nineteenth-century versions in Lord Byron, Johann Wolfgang von Goethe, and Richard Wagner, with a touch of Friedrich Nietzsche. It is most dangerous when cut off from the sense of tragedy, the forces of evil, and inexorable fate that were its classical context; one often finds it so denuded in shallow secular versions of enlightened self-interest, including the currently popular meritocracy of liberal capitalism. But in any form, surely the horrors of the Third Reich should give us some pause as we contemplate what it can become in its most perverse form. In its more benign form, of course, it seeks to honor a similar golden daimon in all others, human and other, though the danger lurking here from a Christian point of view is a shallow pantheism. Fowler exposes the weaknesses of the individualism inherent in this position, with particular reference to Yankelovich's empirical observation that this strategy actually results in isolating its followers from relationships and larger causes that might prove firmer ground for true self-fulfillment.[35] Fowler gives his deepest critique, however, by opposing to the classical notion of *destiny* his own sense of the Christian view of human *vocation*, both of which call humans to specialness and excellence:

From the standpoint of a Christian view of the human vocation, the eudaimonist's "golden figurine within" is inevitably an idol. In the perspective of vocation, we are called to personhood in relationships. There is no personal fulfillment that is not part of a communal fulfillment. We find ourselves by giving ourselves. We become larger persons by devoting ourselves to the pursuit of a common good. From the standpoint of vocation, fulfillment, self-actualization, and excellence are by-products of covenant faithfulness and action in service of God and the neighbor. Rather than the golden figurine within, Christians see our potential as humans to be represented, as it says in Eph 4:13, "in a mature personhood that partakes of the measure of the stature which belongs to the fullness of Jesus Christ." That's the secret of our potential; that's the goal of our development. It is gift; it is by-product of faithful response to the faithful love of God.[36]

The critique, however, must not blind us to the truths expressed in this mode: most obvious is the danger of interpreting vocation in Fowler's sense in the style of self-denial, especially for the already oppressed (Fowler does not make this mistake himself). There are three other fundamental truths at stake. First is the gracefulness (and in that sense sacredness) of all creation properly celebrated in the manifestation mode's emphasis on incarnation and sacrament, and in a true *panentheism* as opposed to *pantheism*. (God is *in* all things and all things are *in* God, but God and "things" remain distinct.) A second truth is that part of the good news is, "Whosoever loses their life for my sake and the gospel's shall find it." That is, in sanctification and the eschatological community of the reign, Christians believe human beings will find real self-fulfillment. More helpful than envisioning this as the emergence of a true self, or a daimon with a destiny, however, is once again the Eastern Orthodox model. The key is transfiguration. After the royal image is cleansed, we go on to experience the same mystery Jesus did on Mount Tabor, not the emergence of a daimon which had been hidden or our transformation into something different, but the revelation and realization of who we really are and always have been and are still becoming in the light of the divine glory. Grace perfects nature in this scheme, as excellence emerges in covenant fidelity to vocation. A third truth is that this transfiguration and what lies beyond it indeed fulfills the deepest desires of our hearts, which have been perverted or cast in the shadow before the cleansing and transfiguration. When this mode of manifestation is called deeper by the dialectics of the not-yet, it also tends toward self-transcendence.[37]

3. Self-criticism in Prophetic Action

The third mode of spirituality and ethics, I have proposed, should be called "self-criticism," in the sense of "critical self-awareness." It is parallel to Tracy's theological form of prophetic action in liberating praxis. As it begins, it is also a negative dialectic, focused not on the individual self as falling short of the glory of God in an ego-ideal, but rather on the realities of society, culture, and history as falling so tragically short of the commonwealth of heaven to be established in God's reign. The emphasis is on structural sin as the context for individual wrongdoing, and in our time especially the focus is on the "isms"—racism, sexism, genderism, classism—the whole sad litany. There is a clear recognition that winning hearts and minds to a good will through individual conversions will not suffice to eradicate these evils, and also a clear sense of the extent to which all religions, insofar as they have inevitably been institutionalized in cultural structures (and this obviously includes foremost of all the Christian church), have been and remain not only supporters but often initiators of these evils. In addition to the great liberation theologies of our time, one thinks of Paul Tillich's intense perception of the ambiguities of society and history as the background to the spiritual presence and its community in part 3 of the *Systematic Theology*. One difference distinguishing this mode from the negative dialectic of proclamation/self-denial is that there is inherent in this negative dialectic an affirmation of self and self-worth that becomes a significant basis for the social protest as the same claim is recognized as valid in others.

Although the chief emphasis of the critique is social, the element of self-criticism is paramount in the desire of the converting individual to become a self as liberating servant, as one who moves with social forces seeking a closer approximation to the commonwealth/reign. Self-criticism is required to identify one's ideological location in race, gender, class, sexual orientation, and so on, in order to address the distortions of consciousness such unavoidable location inevitably brings.[38] The task is complex, as people usually cannot be labeled neatly as purely perpetrators or victims.[39] As many white feminists have learned in confrontation with women of color, for example, they may be victims of patriarchy but also perpetrators of racism and classism. While some authors speak of the possibility of overcoming ideological "false consciousness" by acts of repentance and conversion that include "identification" with the victims, I confess I am not persuaded. *Simul justus et peccator* ("at the same time justified and sinner") holds true as well for these very deep wounds, in my opinion, and the best we can do is to come to as much consciousness as we can and make an effort to correct for the distortions we have been able to identify. I believe the analogy of recovery is more helpful here than that of cure, the most powerful prophetic stance being Isaiah's: "Woe is me, for I am a man of unclean lips, and I dwell in the midst of a people of unclean lips" (Isa 6). The negative dialectics in their fullness not only remind the church it is not identical to the commonwealth/reign and is fallen far short of the glory of God; they also remind us that this is true for ourselves and all other individuals and institutions as well, even allowing for the position of epistemological privilege this position gives to the oppressed.[a] Hence, ideological self-criticism is never a finished task for any individual or group.

In this mode, sin is the social structures of oppression and any collusion with them by perpetrators or victims (though we must be very careful in speaking of collusion in victims that is ultimately forced), any profiting from it, ultimately even any failure to challenge it. Alienation is a key concept, but self-alienation is seen as derivative of social structures of alienation. Salvation is generally viewed in terms of analogies of liberation. The exodus and cross/resurrection are interpreted as liberating victory-in-vulnerability, embodied in prophetic political action on behalf of the victims of all sorts and conditions, in the name of the commonwealth/reign as a real ideal of a rule of justice and peace. As a result, the emphasis is on conversion *to*, and the virtue in focus is *hope*, hope in the covenant promise that this reign shall yet be, even in what sometimes seems the teeth of the evidence. This hope, while eschatological, is nevertheless not hope for a reward for individuals in some other order of existence, but hope for the coming of the commonwealth "on earth as it is in heaven."

The deep truth of this position is that social and personal righteousness and holiness are inextricably intertwined. Perhaps John Wesley had the clearest vision of this inseparability of any classical theologian. Any truly Christian conversion must result in liberating praxis for the coming of the commonwealth.[40] Indeed, Jesus makes it clear (the parable of the sheep and goats), as does St. Paul in his teaching about the dominion of love, or St. John's that love of God and neighbor are inseparable, that this is one of the principles for discerning true conversion,

---

a That last is the notion, common in liberation theologies, that given God's fundamental option (preferential choice) for the poor and the dynamics of the false consciousness that accompanies social class location the poor as poor have a clearer access to the truth than the wealthy and powerful.

perhaps *the* principle (Matt 25:31–46; 1 Cor 13; 1 John 2:9–11; 3:11–24; 4:7–21). Any true spirituality must have this not just as a component but also as the governing vision. Faith, hope, and love must become incarnated in contemplative and liberating praxis for the commonwealth/reign.

The weakness of this position arises when only the negative side of its dialectic is brought forward, and it can happen in three ways. The first is a failure to heed fully the "not-yet" of the proclamation/self-denial mode as a critique of one's *own* political agenda, which is then likely to be absolutized in its own self-destructive ideology.[41] At the least this can produce a self-righteous, Pelagian, do-it-yourself muscular approach ultimately doomed to failure and despair; at the worst it produces an absolutism and rage leading to the well-known phenomenon of revolutions devouring their own children.[42] The second weakness is a tendency so to emphasize the negative dialectic of the "not-yet" that one fails to recognize, bless, celebrate, and cooperate with the always-already graciousness in the world whose veneration is the strength of the form or mode of manifestation. This may lead to far more than trampling on the wildflowers when trying to save the forest or killing doctors at abortion clinics. It is likely to lead to the third sort of failure: prophetic desperation as a failure adequately to rest in and wait for the Spirit who is already at work in present graciousness; it is failure to acknowledge that hope is grounded in a commonwealth/reign that has already been founded, though not by any means finished. In the face of this despair, there is a failure of the true empowerment that requires the Spirit of love to respond to self-criticism, and the only energy available to motivate action is once again rage and drivenness.

We should note that "conversions" can be dominated by any one of these modes. Self-denial and proclamation are still very present in classical and neo-evangelical approaches; manifestation and self-fulfillment are more typical of Franciscan, incarnational/sacramental Catholic approaches, in the truth of self-help recovery movements, and in the more Wesleyan side of Protestantism; prophetic self-criticism and liberating social action bring conversion as people identify the social gospel as the best place to stand on the picket line and is typical of all the liberation theologies. Unfortunately, the stereotypes of each when it emphasizes only its favored end of the dialectic are also only too present. Too often the life of the church today seems shaped by armed warfare among several groups: angry and self-righteous puritans using swords to remove splinters from others while trying to see around the logs of their own that they deny; creation-based Pollyannas ritually grooving on sweetness and light while souls perish and cities burn; and self-appointed prophets absolutizing endless causes of special interest and determined to make everyone else miserable in the process. Pastorally, what we must try to do is enrich all three sorts of conversions in all three modes toward their reinterpretation (and hence re-conversion) and co-inherence in self-transcendence.

Self-transcendence

As I have already suggested, self-transcendence is not really another mode alongside the others, any more than *agapē* is another kind of love alongside *storgē*, *philia*, and *eros*. Just as *agapē* is the healing, fulfillment, transfiguration, and unity of the other loves, so also a spirituality of self-transcendence is not alongside the others as a fourth alternative or option but is the source of their healing, fulfillment, transfiguration, and co-inherence.[43] At its best it will affirm what is true in each of these modes while counterbalancing its dangers. It does have its own sort of content, however, as the style most appropriate to each of the modes.

Self-transcendence is fundamentally a yes to God's constant invitation to be more, constantly growing in the intellectual, affective, moral (and political), and religious spheres of life. As such, it balances the negative and positive poles of the dialectic. Growth, organic growth, at least, is always an affirmation of the basis for growth in the always-already of what is given; at the same time it is a recognition that there is a next step to be taken, a future that is "not yet" and which promises "more"; and hence there is a present reality that must be let go if that next step is to be taken. It is not surprising that this sense of transcendence as focused on the "more" as a motive to growth is particularly evident in Jesuit authors such as Hugo Rahner, Karl Rahner, and Bernard Lonergan, for this "more" is an essential component of Ignatian spirituality.[44] This honoring of the "not yet" in both personal and social life points not only to the past as something to be transcended (but not despised or obliterated) in the "more"; it also reminds us that each step into the future is not to *achieve* final integration but always to say yes to it and not no.[45]

In this style, sin is: "No, I won't grow anymore." This no can occur in any area of life and can be a refusal to acknowledge either the always-already graciousness on the positive side (growth is not possible), or the "not yet" on the negative (I am already perfect and further growth is not needed, or growth can be counted on to happen automatically through inherent graciousness). Both triumphalism and angry despair forgo true growth. The special case of the traumatized for whom growth is frightening is met first by offers of comfort and healing, assurances of being "enough." Salvation in this style is the dialogue between the call of God and our yes to it as embodied in a concrete vocation of growing repentance, healing, praise, and liberating service. A good summary of what is required from our side can be found in Lonergan's transcendental imperatives, as extended by Tracy: "Be attentive, be intelligent, be reasonable, be responsible, develop, and if necessary, change." A feminist touch might add, "be willing, be responsive, be open, be a force for healing."[46]

The deep truth of self-transcendence is that we are called to keep growing until we reach the fullness of the stature of Jesus Christ, until we become as he is (1 John 3:2), even in his relationship to God. This means sharing or participating even in what the theological tradition calls "the hypostatic union" between the human and divine natures in Christ by the grace we receive through him and the Spirit. The Eastern Church expresses this in the concept of *theōsis*, being made god by the grace of God flowing from the totality of the Christ event. We must note the caution that this is *not* the deification or divinization of our humanity as such, which would violate the rule of *non confusio naturae* ("not by confusion or mixture of the natures") of Chalcedon; rather, it is a question of relationship—our relationship to God as we are "in Christ," our flesh being united to the flesh of Jesus through the sacraments and membership in the Body of Christ. Since the God into whom we are eternally called is infinite and we are finite, this is a never-finished journey, ongoing even after death, as Gregory of Nyssa so clearly realized in *The Life of Moses*.[47] Indeed, the two major dangers are thinking we can do it ourselves because of gifts inherent in our humanity or that the grace we are currently enjoying means we have somehow arrived. But neither of these solutions is any longer truly self-transcendence.[48]

Each of the three modes has its appropriate place and time, though I agree with Lonergan and Conn that, overall, the style of self-transcendence must now be given room to be the governing style for each. We must still be careful not to oversimplify. It would be tempting, for example, to identify self-denial with the purgative stage, or tide of conversion, the style of self-fulfillment with the illuminative stage, or current of transfiguration, and the self-transcendent with the third tide, or a stage of union or glorification. In such a scheme prophetic action is likely to get lost, as it often has. It is even more tempting to use our new model and identify proclamation and self-denial with tide one; manifestation and self-fulfillment with tide two; and prophetic liberating action and self-criticism with tide three, with self-transcendence as the style appropriate in each case. The truth exposed here is that insofar as self-denial or self-sacrifice (including personal healing and liberation) has a proper place, it is likely to play its largest role in the first current of conversion; likewise, self-fulfillment will likely play its largest role in the second current of illumination and transfiguration; self-criticism is most likely to predominate in the third current, not only as a principle of prophetic action but as a guard against idolatry in mystical experience; as a result, self-transcendence will be the proper style for each mode. But the empirical truth is that all three modes are going on all the time, and persons who are chiefly at home in one of the modes can experience all three movements of the Spirit's mission in that mode. That is, as in the case of the theological virtues, we face here a fully Trinitarian resonance.

Furthermore, conversion can occur in all three modes. While conversion in the usual sense (as response to proclamation and judgment and salvation in the light of the cross), with an asceticism of self-denial as its ethic and spirituality, is most familiar, especially in evangelical circles, it is not the only way to begin. Other persons, especially those who have been made to see life in negative terms, may be converted by understanding for the first time that creation is graced and they are beloved, issuing in a mode of manifestation, celebration, and self-fulfillment. Still others find conversion in their commitment to social justice and liberating action, often precisely at the point of self-criticism where they begin to distinguish both their own ideology and that of the cause they espouse from the will of God for reign/commonwealth. Increasingly, many persons experience all three, giving new economic meaning to John Donne's great sonnet, "Batter my heart, three-personed God."

Far from being limited to the third tide, however, I have presented self-transcendence (as do Lonergan, Tracy, and ultimately Conn) as a *style* that must now govern all three modes and all three tides, currents, or movements of the spiritual life. On this basis, I suggest conversion be seen as a response to the Holy Spirit's call to self-transcendence. Self-denial or self-sacrifice is then seen only in that context, as the necessary letting go of what *was* for the sake of what truly *is* as well as what *will yet be*, of the old self for the new, of the severed empirical ego for the true self, of the denigrated self for the beloved self, of personal and ideological self-interest for the sake of the reign/commonwealth. Conn adds, correctly, that this is also letting go of all the impediments to committed service in the love of Jesus.[49] This sort of letting-go does not end with the first tide or stage of purgation; it persists through-out all three. I suggest we make the same sort of subordination of self-fulfillment or self-actualization to self-transcendence in the second movement as well, and of self-criticism in the third. And we should note again that any one of the three modes may predominate in any particular conversion.

I have come to believe that it is the theological virtue associated with each mode that rescues it from clinging unhelpfully to its end of the dialectic and thus conflict with the others. *Faith* in the mode of proclamation is called in the end not only to acknowledge the no of God's judgment, the not-yet, but also the yes of the always-already of the grace of creation, the image of God in humanity, and the prevenience of grace. Faith reveals not only human creaturely distance from God exacerbated by the alienation of sin; it is also, as Karl Barth himself came to see, faith in the "humanity of God" as faith in Jesus Christ. *Love* rescues manifesta-tion and self-fulfillment from blissful "grocking" on the always-already of grace precisely through suffering, through noticing that the beloved neighbor is afflicted by the "not-yet," and hence, so am I. Precisely as suffering love it redeems trium-phalism with a return to the cross. Hope acknowledges fully the dialectic of the "not yet" on all forms of human society in the mode of prophetic self-criticism; but precisely as hope in the covenant promises of God it turns to acknowledge the "always-already" foundation of the commonwealth in the eternal faithfulness of the God whose reign it is.[50] This Trinitarian dance of the theological virtues in each of the three major modes makes possible not a fourth position in which the three modes are overcome but a style of harmony in which all three are most truly them-selves by virtue of their co-inherence.

Self-transcendence as Precisely Transcendent

The recognition just achieved, that the three theological virtues are the key to maintaining the style of self-transcendence as the life-giving option for each of the three modes of spirituality, leads directly to the second point of critique I wish to offer. In the classic tradition, the three theological virtues of faith, hope, and love are precisely *infused* virtues. That is, they are not acquired by effort or practice but are the immediate effects of the indwelling of the Holy Spirit who has been poured into our hearts. The very possibility of the three modes of spirituality being and remaining in the style of self-transcendence thus precludes the possibility of self-transcendence being a property or capacity of human nature as such.

Rather, human self-transcendence, as many are coming to see, is the resonance aroused in us by the approach of the transcendent God whose very transcendence is precisely that self-transcendence that lies within the mystery of the Trinitarian rela-tions and their origins, the Fount being perfectly self-expressed in the Word/Wisdom through the liberation of the Spirit.[51] Once again, this is why Rahner called this resonance of human self-transcendence precisely the *supernatural* existential. It is not a property or even a *capax* of human nature as such, even though it is a universal fact of human existence. Instead, it is the existential fact that by God's initiative all human beings stand for good or ill in the midst of God's grace. The proper subject matter of spirituality as a discipline can thus never be human self-transcendence in isolation, from a Christian point of view, and any effort to make it such for purposes of "inclusiveness" will, in the end, exclude precisely the Christian perspective. The proper initial subject of Christian spirituality can only be the Trinitarian self-transcendence of God as it impacts human existence through the supernatural existential, the bare fact that in our very existence (not nature) we are confronted by a gratuitous graciousness. That is to say, the proper subject matter of spirituality as a discipline is not a human capacity, but the uncreated grace of the indwelling Holy Spirit and its impact as that Spirit makes us anew in Christ. What our previous analysis has shown is that to deny this, to focus on human self-transcendence in isolation, will lead to wallowing in the mode of self-affirmation and manifestation, to the exclusion of the negative dialectics of proclamation/self-denial and prophetic action/self-criticism which push that mode toward true self-transcendence. In short, to treat self-transcendence as a human capacity that can thus become the subject of spirituality as a discipline is to ensure that the modes of spirituality will not achieve the style of self-transcendence at all but will explode or dissipate into a style of self-destruction. Only treating human self-transcendence as a resonance in human existence of God's Trinitarian life can prevent this deterioration.

In conclusion, it is worth reiterating and completing Tracy's statement of self-transcendence as the true style of the three modes of approach to the God-self relationship:

> Amidst the real conflicts of Christian interpretation of the Authentic self expressed in the inevitable clash of these three classical Christian ideals for true selfhood, one fact stands out. In spite of their otherwise real and perhaps even irreconcilable ideals for the self, all three are committed to a model of radical, *because graced*, self-transcendence; a self always-already, not-yet free from and for this world.[52] By attempting to live that gospel call and gift of an always-already, not-yet agapaic self-transcendence, Christians realize that they cannot rest in the less radical demands of either self-fulfillment or self-negation. The *ressentiment* latent in the latter, like the narcissism latent in the former, are exposed as inappropriate ideals for the radical, agapaic ideal of self-transcendence by the event of Jesus Christ. The route to authentic selfhood for the Christian, whatever the particular focus for interpreting that ideal, remains a route of the radical discipleship of an *imitatio Christi*. The demands for real mutuality expressed in the Christian ideal and reexpressed in the *caritas* tradition, the radical self-sacrificial love disclosed in the Cross of the Crucified One are themselves expressions of the gospel agapaic gift and command to the self to live a radical equal regard for every human being, for the neighbor, not only the friend. That demand for equal regard, for concrete agapaic neighbor love, impels the transvaluation of all values by its risk of some form of a radi-

cal agapaic self-transcendence. Only that kind of self-transcendence can ultimately define the heart of any Christian attempt to become a gifted, commanded, always-already, not-yet agapaic self. The reality of God as love decisively revealed in the event of Jesus Christ is the central clue to the meaning of the self as a human self both loved and loving.[53]

Beloved Dust, that is, meets its own converting to faith, hope, and love precisely in experiencing itself as beloved, a belovedness that is both gift and demand in the face of the Beloved.

Notes

1. See chap. 12 n. 2 above.

2. Donald Gelpi in a large number of works from *Charism and Sacrament* to *The Firstborn of Many* and see especially "Religious Conversion: A New Way of Being," 175–202; also Walter Conn, *Christian Conversion*, hereafter, *CC*. See now as well Joann Wolski Conn and Elizabeth Liebert, as cited in chap. 12 n. 15 above; both follow the general line laid down by Walter Conn but add important feminist perspectives. Liebert in particular uses an expanded palette of developmental theories. See now also Peter Feldmeier, *The Developing Christian*.

3. See Sandra M. Schneiders, "A Hermeneutical Approach to the Study of Christian Spirituality"; "The Study of Christian Spirituality," esp. 2. Schneiders's position is a highly nuanced one which does not exclude, though it treats quite differently, the concerns of this book. The most helpful summary of self-transcendence in contemporary spirituality, in its philosophical, religious, and specifically Christian senses, is in Joann Wolski Conn, *Spirituality and Personal Maturity*, esp. 29–35. The Christian position as she describes it there is in accord with the position taken here.

4. Most of what follows has been published as "A Critical Note on Two Aspects of Self-Transcendence."

5. See Conn, *CC*, 274 n. 37 for additional sources.

6. Conn, *CC*, 18

7. Conn, *CC*, 19.

8. I am indebted to Herbert W. Richardson for these archetypes of transcendence.

9. Conn, *CC*, 19, and see 275 n. 38.

10. See Conn, *CC*, 275 n. 38; David Tracy, *The Analogical Imagination* (hereafter *AI*), 435.

11. Tracy, *Blessed Rage for Order* (hereafter *BRO*), 11.

12. Bernard Lonergan, S.J., *Method*, 36–40; Tracy, *BRO*, 20 n. 53.

13. Tracy, *BRO*, 11.

14. Niebuhr is similarly used by Conn, *CC*, see n. 5 above; Lonergan, *Method*, 235–37 and 267–71; Sam Keen, *Apology for Wonder*; Tracy, *BRO*, 39 n. 44.

15. Paul Tillich, *ST*, 2.5–10, 1.3–11; Tracy, *BRO*, 45.

16. Tracy, *BRO*, 117 n. 75.

17. See Wayne Whitson Floyd, Jr., *Theology and the Dialectics of Otherness*, for a different view on the tension between analogical and dialectical approaches.

18. Tracy, *AI*, 371–405.

19. Conn, *CC*, 267–68, summarizes his combination of a philosophy of self-transcendence with developmental psychology and Lonergan's notion of levels of conversion.

20. Tracy, *AI*, 432–35.

21. Tracy, *AI*, 435.

22. Tracy, *AI*, 435.

23. Tracy, *AI*, 435.

24. Tracy, *AI*, 421.

25. Tracy, *AI*, 420.

26. Conn, *CC*, 21.

27. Tracy, *AI*, 421, 433–34.

28. See R. William Franklin and Joseph M. Shaw, *The Case for Christian Humanism.*

29. Conn, *CC*, 19–20.

30. Tracy, *AI*, 432, 435.

31. Conn, *CC*, 19–20, and 275–76 nn. 39–42 for the other authors cited.

32. James Fowler, *Becoming Adult*, 98ff.; David Norton, *Personal Destinies.*

33. Fowler refers to Norton, *Personal Destinies*, 14.

34. Fowler, *Becoming Adult*, 100.

35. Fowler, *Becoming Adult*, 102; citing Daniel Yankelovich, *New Rules in American Life*, chaps. 3–5; cf. Conn, *CC*, 19 and notes.

36. Fowler, *Becoming Adult*, 102–3.

37. Tracy, *AI*, 432–33. Some uses of "higher self" in depth psychology, such as Jung's, may come closer to this

38. Gregory Baum, *Religion and Alienation, passim*, particularly 193–263, especially 201–2.

39. Cynthia S. W. Crysdale, *Embracing Travail*, esp. chaps. 1 and 2, gives a highly nuanced discussion of this dialectic.

40. This insight is perhaps most clearly expressed in the Wesleyan tradition, from John Wesley himself (see my "Wesleyan Roots of Christian Socialism," for example) to Jim Wallis, *The Call to Conversion.*

41. R. Niebuhr, *Moral Man and Immoral Society, passim*; see, for example, 199.

42. G. W. F. Hegel's section on Absolute Freedom and Terror in *The Phenomenology of Mind*, 599–610, remains a chilling critique.

43. One of the best accounts for love is Simone Weil, "The Forms of the Implicit Love of God," in *Waiting for God*, 137–215; these will be examined in detail in the second tide.

44. Hugo Rahner, S.J., *The Spirituality of St. Ignatius Loyola*, e.g., 104–5; also Karl Rahner, "Being Open to God as Ever Greater and the Significance of the Aphorism *Ad Majorem Dei Gloriam*," *TI* 7:25–46 at 27; and Ignatius Loyola, *Spiritual Exercises*, 23–27.

45. Thomas Merton, *Contemplative Prayer*, relentlessly drives home this point. See, for example, the essay on "dread," 131–38.

46. Lonergan, *Method*, 53–55; see Tracy, *BRO*, 12, 96. Feminist touch courtesy of Barbara Hughes.

47. Gregory of Nyssa, *Life of Moses*, xiii, and see the discussion on pp. 12–13 with notes and references.

48. Merton: this can lead to trying to recreate religious experience in ourselves, which leads to the total disintegration of the individual (*Contemplative Prayer*, 110).

49. Conn, *CC*, 22.

50. In *AI*, 432–34, Tracy discloses this same inner dynamic by which each mode or focus is impelled toward the end of the dialectic it tends to ignore, and hence toward self-transcendence, but without reference to the theological virtues as such.

51. See my "Retrieving and Reconstructing 'Justification by Grace Through Faith,'" 67; and "Starting Over," 95.

52. Italics added.

53. Tracy, *AI*, 435.

15

Four Layers of Conversion

The second major piece of theological structure informing contemporary theologies of conversion also derives from Bernard Lonergan's work: his notion that conversion, "the 'about face' by which a person moves into a radically new horizon" through deliberate choice taking place at three layers, levels, or dimensions of human being: the intellectual (which Walter Conn calls "cognitive"), the moral, and the religious.[1] Subsequently, Lonergan added a fourth layer, the affective.[2] Donald Gelpi, S.J., subsequently added a fifth dimension, the political, but for reasons discussed below, I choose to honor Gelpi's intentions but make political a corollary of moral conversion.[3]

The foundational notion is that conversion is a fundamental option or choice making a wholly new self-disposition of a human being in the face of the world and the Holy Mystery who haunts that world. It thus causes a shift in the horizon, boundary, or limit of that world as personal to that individual, in a manner that affects and effects him or her in every dimension of life; these dimensions embrace the classical faculties of the affections or desires, the intellect, and the moral will, thus bringing conversion to bear in affective, intellectual, and moral areas of life. For some good philosophical reasons, Gelpi has difficulties with this notion of "horizon."[4] He prefers "frame of reference" or "perspective." While there are important issues at stake, for our purposes the fundamental point is the same: conversion is a chosen (and empowered) shift in the fundamental relationship between self and world that changes everything. Because it is a self-disposition before God, it also takes place in a religious dimension or layer that restructures not only the relationship to God, but through that to all the rest of reality as well.[5] Because Lonergan has spelled out his own views so thoroughly, and Conn and Gelpi have given such helpful commentary and expansion, I shall not repeat that in detail, but summarize the gist and importance of each dimension and show its importance for our present task.[6] I shall do so in the order in which they tend to predominate in an individual's spiritual life, though again they can actually occur in any order in any given instance, and all are actually going on all the time in any conversion.

Affective Conversion

Affective conversion in the classical sense is the reorienting and reordering of the appetites, desires, and emotions. In the more contemporary sense it includes a decision to take adult responsibility for the appropriateness and health of this emotional side of our lives. Affective conversion thus moves us from an infantile omniverousness and rage and emotions wounded by trauma to adult responsibility for our feelings and the actions flowing from them. It is thus a liberation and healing of our desires, passions, enthusiasm, and liveliness for their true "object."

In many experiences of conversion, especially those shaped by an evangelical-revivalist tradition, the affective dimension may first refer to a strong emotional aspect of a conversion experience itself; but even then its deeper meaning is a slow growth toward letting our emotional life be shaped by grace. The strong initial emotions are caused by the sudden turn of the appetite away from inappropriate or lesser objects and toward God. The deeper shift in our feelings comes as we find our emotional life increasingly shaped by a graced orientation to appropriate and greater objects of desire, above all, God, a shift that requires prayer, meditation, and, for many, therapy. The call of this deeper shift is one of the reasons it is a terrible mistake to order a spirituality around perpetuating the emotions of initial conversion; that only blocks the further growth and development that conversion was meant to initiate and the attachment to appropriate objects as God wills. It will also block recognition of the second and third currents of grace, to be discussed later, and thus impede the process of learning to live in this new love proficiently and without qualification. Since the postconversion feeling-shift is not only natural but in accordance with God's will in most cases, it will simply occur. Faith communities with no language or guidance for this shift are likely at this stage to lose persons who become discouraged, or, worse, encourage them to recreate the initial religious experiences in themselves. As Thomas Merton points out, all such attempts to produce any sort of religious experience in ourselves leads inevitably to the complete moral and personal disintegration of the persons involved.[7]

From a merely human point of view, the attempt to preserve the emotional content of initial conversion may also block the deeper task of seeking to take adult responsibility for our emotional life. It also has occasioned in some Christians suspicions of human disciplines that can assist in this task, such as psychotherapy, pastoral counseling, and other sources of healing, including healthy intimate relationships, all of which should be welcomed and integrated into one's life as a Christian. Some theorists and practitioners of these disciplines have contributed to this suspicion, of course, by a hostile attitude toward religion on the one hand, or a kind of New Age fuzzy eclectic spirituality appropriated into their therapeutic practice on the other. My own sense is that Gerald May provides the best overall guidelines for an appropriate relationship between spiritual direction and the therapeutic professions. I heartily endorse his suggestion that when looking for a therapist, an old-fashioned practitioner of a secular therapeutic discipline who also happens to be a believing Christian is a better bet than someone who claims to stir a variety of spiritual practices into their technique.[a][8] Twelve-Step and other self-help groups are also often of greatest benefit, as long as Christians receive guidance *from their*

---

a Some Christian therapists have successfully incorporated knowledge and practices of spiritual disciplines into their work. This can be particularly helpful when certain healing courses reach the need for spiritual healing, but care must be taken to distinguish therapy from spiritual direction.

faith community beyond what can be expected or demanded of the self-help community itself—guidance that: (1) it is perfectly all right for them to be quite sure that they know their "Higher Power" is the "Abba" of Jesus Christ, indeed the Trinitarian God, and (2) it is also all right to let other persons have a different sense of who their Higher Power might be for the sake of the program.[9]

There is a stronger link between intellectual conversion and affective conversion than might be thought at first. This arises from the knowledge, suggested by rational emotive therapy and other similar schools of thought that, apart from traumatic, neurotic, or pathological situations, our emotions are not caused by what happens to us but by what we think about what happens to us—our beliefs.[10] Intellectual critique of our beliefs can be one of the most helpful tools to emotional maturity, provided we understand it is not to be used to eliminate or repress feelings but to reshape them. Walter Conn also reminds us of the many schools of humanistic psychology that now stress the cognitive dimension of our emotions and passions, and the contribution they make to human identity and knowledge.[11]

For Christians, the governing virtue of affective conversion is love. It is a healing and refocusing of our natural desires.[12] Conn also finds helpful the work of philosopher Robert Solomon, with his analysis of our passions and emotional lives as constitutive of our identity. This passionate identity culminates in a love that can be romantic but is no longer the naiveté of "innocent love" and the hopeless task of endlessly recapturing that early fervor; in maturity it becomes reflected love, which is self-aware of its choices, resulting commitments, and the behavioral standards they imply.[13] While Solomon recognizes the internal commitments of loving choice, he denies the appropriateness of commitments to future love (loving a particular person for years into the future), a stance challenged by theologian Rosemary Haughton in a series of works linking more clearly the healthy development of romantic love to covenant commitments and a theological context.[14] Out of all this, Conn develops a notion of affective conversion as a transformation of the whole person that marries intuitive passion to deliberate commitment.[15] None of these elements can be ignored, nor the various sorts of love set over against *agapē*. What emerges is a vision of affective conversion in which passions arise and are then (1) "'signed' in the other-centered transformation of feeling effected by symbols and guided by reflection;[a] (2) 'sealed' in the deliberate decision of commitment to love; and (3) 'delivered' in the action of loving service."[16] That, of course, links affective conversion to moral conversion. The hope that there might be a desirable world to share and co-inhabit with the beloveds of one's life establishes a link to the political dimension of the moral as well. Spiritualities of self-fulfillment, self-denial, and self-criticism play an appropriate role at various stages of this process. Enjoying a fulfillment of all legitimate desires, denial of sinful distortions (including the healing of wounded emotions), and critique of ideologically based appetites have an obvious place in affective conversion.[b]

---

a As I have previously noted, this requires a foundation of a positive regard of one's own self. One must have a self before one can donate it in a relationship.

b Objects of ideologically based appetites include the symbols and perks of gender, class, or racial preference.

The key to affective conversion remaining solidly in the mode of self-transcendence, however, ultimately lies in a link to religious conversion. The search for the monastic virtue of purity of heart is the ultimate expression of affective conversion even in nonmonastic life.[17] The exercise of this purity of heart discovers God and God's perfect reign in the commonwealth of heaven as the deepest desire of our own hearts. This helps us honor appropriate "penultimate" desires without needing to repress or deny them; at the same time it helps us let go of desires that are actually "qualifications" that we place on our love for God, or ideological barriers (such as class, race, and gender interests) to loving action in the service of the commonwealth/reign. This love is learned and practiced in the primary relationships of the human individual in her or his affective development (again, "charity begins at home"); as a result, the developmental theories previously discussed can illuminate the human contents of the occasions and opportunities for affective conversion.[18] But affective *conversion*, as opposed to simply affective development, also requires a breakthrough enabled by grace; to be experienced as such, such a conversion requires, in the long run, contemplative pedagogies of faith communities to provide appropriate symbolic interpretation and moral guidance. There is much more to affective conversion than emotional health.

Intellectual Conversion

Intellectual conversion is what St. Anselm so succinctly described as "faith seeking understanding."[19] Faith is indeed the virtue appropriate to this layer, as we seek to come to grips with the doctrinal content of the Christian Scriptures and theological tradition. It is, however, by no means a "fideism" by which the mind simply surrenders to some external authority as a result of an emotional outburst. Even where that happens in the face of an overpowering affective conversion, there will still be homework to do, often called "discipling." Catholic tradition has recognized this with the development of a long preparation for Baptism called the catechumenate, now restored in the practice of several denominations, which also nurtures conversion at the other levels as well.

Many thoughtful contemporary people, however, begin with intellectual problems with what they have thought was Christian doctrine, and their conversion will be nurtured only as their questions are taken seriously and they are helped to find answers that really satisfy them. Some are purely intellectual, raised, for example, by commitment to scientific culture; some are raised by the lived realities of trauma, abuse, and oppression.[20] Simplistic or authoritarian approaches, or appeals to "just believe harder" and forget the questions, are unlikely to bear fruit in such instances. In terms of faith development, such persons in Fowler's stage four (individuative-reflective) or John Westerhoff's "questing faith" will be highly resistant to emotional appeals to return to a mythic-literal approach to faith, which they will accurately see as pressure to regress in their own growth. Instead, they need to be nurtured in the questions, with the hope they will eventually grow into the second naiveté of Fowler's stage five.[21]

My own experience in a variety of contexts suggests that the number one problem, the most common source of resistance to both evangelization and spiritual growth in Christian terms, is the angry, punishing father-god of patriarchal oppression. It is something of a mystery to me that this God concept, so foreign to the actual contents of the gospel and Jesus' picture of his Abba, should be assumed by so many to be what in fact Christianity offers, and the degree to which it remains embedded in Christian literature and art. Furthermore, I find this problematic image deeply infecting all "brands" of Christianity, from the most anti-ecclesial charismatic/evangelical to Catholic to liberal. I do not mean they all deliberately teach it, but rather that all are somehow infected by it, one way or another, indeed have embraced it, even in rejection of it. Many have abandoned or rejected Christianity because their affective and intellectual development has rendered this notion of God intolerable, and they do not know and indeed often cannot imagine that Christianity has something else to offer. Intellectual conversion will mean, as Shug says to Celie in *The Color Purple*, first, you gotta get that angry old white man out of your head.[22] It will then mean finding truer images of God in the tradition itself.[23] For most of us this will obviously also include some psychological sorting out of our own family/childhood issues.

In any case, and at any stage of faith development, the task is not intellectual submission to authority but faithful use of the mind and reason, within the limits of one's abilities and interests, to harmonize one's interpretation of all of life with the gospel, until some kind of *modus vivendi* is achieved. For most contemporary people, this will mean a critical reappraisal of their thoughts about the gospel and the Christian tradition, their thoughts about reality in general, and their thoughts about the relationship between the two. This conversion also has an additional link to affective conversion, as it develops tools of reason, including therapy as needed, to sort the true from the false even in the face of emotional attachments and the constant background of "mind-static." There is also a strong link to moral conversion, particularly its sociopolitical dimension, as we develop tools of ideological criticism to uncover the false or limited consciousness resulting from our location in class, gender, race, and so forth. The link to religious conversion is a deep falling in love with reality and a commitment to banish as much illusion, especially cherished illusion (which from the point of view of this layer of conversion is idolatry), as one can. Intellectual conversion is a commitment to a life-long process of being dis-illusioned.

Lonergan describes this conversion as a turning of the mind from myths about reality to a critical realism.[24] For him, this has a very specific form called "transcendental Thomism" (a philosophy that marries the tradition of Thomas Aquinas's use of Aristotle to insights of modern philosophy from Immanuel Kant to Martin Heidegger). Lonergan shares this perspective to some degree with Rahner and others, and it is part of the common heritage of many contemporary Catholic thinkers, including Tracy and Gelpi, even where they depart from earlier versions of that tradition. Obviously there are deeply intellectually committed Christians who do not adopt this specific option, and many others who are not of a temperament to pursue the details of these philosophical questions; but it is worth pausing to note the usual alternatives and critical realism's own general outline in order to establish some criteria for discernment, even though such an account must be grossly over-simplified. The argument remains, as it always has, about the relationship among language, ideas, perceptions, and whatever reality may be.[25]

A. Myths about Reality

1. The tradition called "realism" comes in two forms: first, a popular naive realism, which simply assumes that language refers accurately to ideas that involve perceptions, which in turn accurately portray external reality; "realists" simply remain blissfully ignorant about the problems with this view unless some crisis causes painful doubts to arise. Lonergan analyzes this myth as believing that "knowing is like looking, that objectivity is seeing what is there to be seen and not seeing what is not there, and that the real is what is out there now to be looked at."[26] The second form is philosophical idealism, a long tradition stemming from Plato, which treats language as referring to a realm of perfect ideas (in the Christian version, in the mind of God) that are the truly real, while what we ordinarily call "reality" is simply an ever-shifting realm of change that most imperfectly reflects this ideal realm. There is, for example, an idea of perfect "chairness" that real chairs embody only fleetingly. Because Platonism itself may derive from earlier Hindu philosophy, there are strong links to what many see as "Eastern" thought, though that is another complex subject.

A special case in our time is fundamentalism, as that term has come to be used, or theological positivism, as I prefer to call it, which is present in nearly all religions and is found in all versions of Christianity. It simply takes all the authoritative texts of a particular tradition as if they literally and without error describe all reality with no further ado. The result is often a mind-destroying anti-intellectualism. On the other hand, scientism is a "fundamentalist approach to science." It fails to note that science's most powerful tool, mathematics, is derived from a pure world of ideas, whose relationship to "reality" is at least an interesting problem. The intelligibility, or transparency, of the universe to reason is a great mystery, which a narrowly scientist point of view simply ignores.[27]

2. Subjectivism is a family of views treating human language and knowledge as referring only to events in the consciousness of an individual person. The relationship of such interpreted human experience to any external or truly other or objective reality is problematic. Existentialism is the most common form of this view today, but, when painted with a very broad brush, it would include as well Kant's notion that all our ideas, to which language refers, are essentially made up of an interaction between subjective perceptions and structures of human reason or consciousness, all of which may or may not apply to anything that could be called objective reality—the thing in itself. "Chair" is the name of a mental object made up of some particular perceptions and governed by a set of concepts that derive from the human mind.

3. Skepticism begins by seeking a knowledge supported only by empirical obser-

vation, and doubting or discounting everything else. In its various forms, however (from David Hume's early version through logical positivism, the language-game philosophy of the later Ludwig Wittgenstein, deconstructionist theory in its various literary and political incarnations, etc.), it has been unable to escape the problem that human experience provides no certain empirical basis for believing in external or objective reality. Hence, in this view, language is only about perceptions, or, later, only about language games themselves, with no reference beyond the communication itself, not even to a self or subject. The effort to verify everything "scientifically" ultimately results in undercutting the reality of science's object. "Chair" is just a group of perceptions I customarily lump together, or is just a noise I learn to use properly in various language games to which it belongs.

B. Critical Realism

In its various forms, critical realism seeks to establish a more solid relationship among language, ideas, perceptions, and objective realities than the alternatives just listed. It is "realism" in that it affirms both "objective reality" and the notion that sense perceptions *and* the concepts of human ideas and language actually refer to that reality, even if the relationship is complex. It is a *critical* realism, however, because it recognizes all the problems and subtleties about how language, thinking, and perceiving relate to one another and to "reality." It acknowledges, for example, that language is historical and changes, that the meaning of a word is determined as much by the "grammar" of the language in which it functions as by anything to which it might refer. It distinguishes literal pointing language (which has its own problems) from symbol, poetry, analogy, and myth, and it knows that all symbolic language is "multivalent," that is, possessed of many layers of meaning. It recognizes that reason, imagination, and consciousness, including the previously discussed "false consciousness," make their own contributions to the picture we have of reality, and that indeed, for humans, reality is always already interpreted in the act of being experienced; it never comes to us "raw." At the same time, it affirms that through all that, reality is nevertheless truly being truly known, albeit imperfectly and partially. There are real objects, which are truly "chairs" and known as such; but "chairness" exists only in those real objects *and* in the human concept by abstraction from them, not in some ideal realm.

The classical form of this view comes from Aristotle, passes through Aquinas, and in that form extends to the "neo-Thomists" of our era such as Etienne Gilson and Jacques Maritain. When it seeks to account as well for the specific criticisms of the German school from Kant to Heidegger, it is the transcendental Thomism previously discussed, in which Karl Rahner has been a leading figure. Other and quite different options include versions of American pragmatism that remain close to Charles Saunders Peirce, the metaphysics of Paul Weiss, and the "scientific realism" of a thinker like John Polkinghorne.[28] They all recognize that the relationship among world, thoughts, and language is complex, that symbols are multivalent. But each affirms the essential goodness of world, senses, mind, and word by asserting that real knowledge of a real reality, however partial and imperfect, does reliably occur.

That is the issue for Christians. The alternatives all denigrate creation, human reason, or both. As Lonergan puts it: "Only the critical realist can acknowledge the facts of human knowing and pronounce the world mediated by meaning to be the real world; and he can do so only inasmuch as he shows that the process of experiencing, understanding, and judging is a process of self-transcendence."[29] A Christian realist position believes that engagement with reality is a difficult and complex ongoing task. Through study, work, and prayer (three balanced elements of the Benedictine Rule), the Christian engages reality in a careful exploration of the relations among the mind of God, the world, and our mind and experience, using all the best tools we have. I shall have more to say in the next "tide" about the spiritual value of intellectual and scientific work; the point for now, as we examine the role of the intellect in the first tide of conversion, is at the end of Lonergan's sentence: the disciplined struggle for true knowledge is itself one form of the human self-transcendence that I have described as a resonance in us of God's own self-transcendence. All true knowing is both a letting go (of old ideas and commitments) and a turning toward (new knowledge), and hence participates in the tide of conversion. That many who are deeply engaged in intellectual pursuits do not see this is largely due to the failure of the church to provide the contemplative pedagogy to assist persons in seeing grace as grace in this arena. Anti-intellectualism in all its forms does no service to the gospel or its spread. We can also note that for those in the "healing" mode of conversion, intellectual conversion involves a deep falling in love with reality in the face of the delusions offered by the illness or outgrown survival strategies; these may need intellectual critique as well as affective therapy. For the oppressed, there is an important task of ideological critique and affirmation that also requires a firm commitment to the real world if it is not to expire in utopian explosions.

One of the implications of intellectual conversion and critical realism is a historical/critical approach to Scripture. Myth is understood as myth, an analogical/poetic narrative means for expressing some truths, which cannot be conveyed in any other way. As a result, myths are neither taken literally nor discounted as nonsense, simply treated critically and affirmed as myths, poetry as poetry, apocalyptic as apocalyptic.

C. Thinking with the Church

One of the great insights of postmodern thought is that language is a social and historical reality. Discourse and interpretation arise from *communities* of discourse and interpretation, and some such community is where we all learn to speak and think. Christian intellectual conversion means choosing the church, in the broadest sense, as one of one's primary communities of discourse and interpretation. It means to choose to think of things not slavishly *as* the church but always *with* the Christian covenant community as part of its ongoing conversation by which it seeks to understand itself, the world, and God.[30] This means not submission to, but respect for, tradition, which will also be *critically received*. That is, all the documents of tradition will be interpreted with some sense of their historic setting and linguistic context. Such an approach excludes the possibility of any naive "simple Bible teaching," which always turns out to be the special interpretation of some particular group unwilling to look at the distortions of its own historical and social location. It means neither "free thinking," critical or uncritical, nor a lapse into fideism and anti-intellectualism, but ultimately the willingness to undertake the hard job of personal theological work in the context of membership in a community of theological discourse. Even when thinking "outside the box" is necessary for a time, as in feminist, womanist and liberationist theologies, in the end this is still most fruitful when anchored in the covenant community as one of its self-critical acts. It means learning a language, a tradition, and a rigorous discipline, to the extent one is able.[31]

D. Thinking with the Holy Spirit

The Christian tradition has also generally taught that thinking accurately and truly about virtually anything requires grace. There is, of course, the grace already present in the interaction between a creation given as intelligible and a human reason created to understand it. But sin creates various problems in addition to the unavoidable limitations on our perspective deriving from our finitude. The intellect must be healed (including by therapy when needed) and enlightened to understand anything truly, but most especially the hidden mysteries of God; this is one of the tasks of the Holy Spirit—to recall to us the words of Jesus and lead us into all truth (John 16:13). There is a long tradition supporting this need for divine illumination in human knowledge from Augustine to Bonaventure in the West; one of the odd results of the critical realism stemming from Aquinas was to limit illumination to understanding mysteries only, giving reason about creation a greater independence. As noted in chapter 2, this opened the door for the ultimate idolatry of the light of human reason as an independent entity in the Enlightenment. I have come to believe that true understanding of anything requires intellectual *conversion* and, hence, grace, the activity of the Holy Spirit. Knowledge of God is the case par excellence, since knowledge of God and love of God are inseparable. The goal is loving knowledge, as Aquinas teaches, or the prayer of the mind in the heart in the tradition of the Eastern Church.

E. Doubt and Spiritual Growth

If we have gotten this far in our understanding of intellectual conversion, we can now have a proper sense of the role doubt plays in spiritual growth. This is especially critical when so many are tempted to blame all the perils of modernity on Descartes and his method of universal doubt.[32] Honest doubts as they arise are not the enemy of faith, but its friend, the call of self-transcendence to the intellect.

As Tillich points out, honest doubt is not opposed to justification by faith, but is enabled by it.[33]

There are two sins, two impediments to spiritual growth, not in our having doubts but in our willful approach to them. Denial of doubt is one—not good faith, but actually bad faith because untrue. A doubt not faced actually points to a lack of faith, a lack of hope that the doubt can be answered. This is "I-damn-well-won't doubt." "I-damn-well-will doubt," of course, is a willful skepticism, a decision not to work through doubt but to cherish it for its own sake (which Descartes certainly did not do!). This also is a kind of despair, a refusal to see the doubt through. Urban Holmes used to talk about "sensibility" as the position of willingness between the two willfulness of "sentimentality" and "cynicism."[34] The relationship among denial, honest doubt, and skepticism is similar. We should note that this does not refer to the "inner doubter" encountered in many psychologically wounded persons; this is not a source of true intellectual doubt but the voice of one of the inner parts needing integration. It is especially important to acknowledge honest doubts in the flow of the third current, as I shall suggest later, since doubt is the motive to give up some final idols.

In all conversions, the goal is for the Christian to enter a process of growth into the fullness of the stature of Jesus. In intellectual conversion, faith is informed by hope, which allows us to avoid sentimental affirmation of partial knowledge as absolute in denial of all doubt, on the one hand, as well as the intellectual despair of cynical skepticism on the other. It is informed by love to let the mind be in the heart, to understand intellectual fidelity as a response to the command to love God with all our heart, soul, *mind*, and strength. It is the earnest prayer that this mind may be in us as it was in Christ Jesus.[35]

Moral Conversion

Moral conversion, as Lonergan puts it, "changes the criterion of one's decisions and choices from satisfactions to values."[36] As such, it builds on or sublates affective conversion, in that moral conversion is a conscious, chosen redirection of appetites and desires from personal satisfaction to the Good.[37] As we have seen, this may require therapeutic healing or liberation of wounded desires from oppression, addiction, depression, and the like. Moral conversion also builds on intellectual conversion, in that it remains dedicated to the truth as a value but goes on to values in general—a broader range. Since "values" is, in a sense, a morally neutral term (Hitler had values—just bad ones), moral conversion must ultimately be expressed in a particular set of values that manifest an apprehension of the Good. Christian "values" derive ultimately from the just and holy nature of God perceived as a demand upon and invitation to us for self-transcendent growth. Christian values are expressed in the two great commandments and the great commission and are finally the values of God's commonwealth or reign, those Jesus expressed in the Sermon on the Mount (Matt 5). Gelpi thus describes Christian conversion as mediating between affective conversion and moral conversion.[38]

Moral conversion has its own rhythm and stages. Following the work of Lawrence Kohlberg, as reinterpreted by John Gibbs, Conn sees these stages as occurring in two major groups—natural stages in which most persons are converted to some understanding of conventional morality as expressing the needed shift from satisfaction or self-denigration to value, and postconventional or critical morality, which is manifested not so much in natural stages as critical existential choices. Far fewer people, Conn believes, move into this second range of morality.[39]

A. Cleaning Up Our Act

1. The moral dimension of conversion usually begins directly out of a new consciousness or conviction of sin. It is a first awareness of how short we have fallen of the justice and holiness of God, and therefore of our own inner drive toward true self-transcendence, as discussed in chapter 6. It usually entails immediate effort to clean up the grosser stuff that obviously separates us from God and neighbor; as noted previously, this will involve repentance, healing, and liberation in different proportions for different people. For those involved in personal sin, it will mean repentance; for those with a self shattered by trauma or abuse, it will mean finding a sense of self as beloved; for those suffering under oppression, it will mean finding strength in a passion, even a "blessed rage" for their own liberation. The tools available are more than likely to be the wisdom embodied in the conventional morality of the faith community with which we are affiliating, as well as its own resources for healing and liberation, which may well connect to a larger base of support. Care must be taken that this does not include support for ongoing submission to abusive relationships or compulsive, codependent "doing for others." For Christians, however, the primary resource is the two great commandments of love for God and neighbor, the great commission, the Ten Commandments, and the other ethical teachings of Jesus as well, mediated in the historical and social understanding of a concrete Christian group.

2. Even here, one may experience challenges that go beyond mere programs of self-improvement. In particular, those who suffer from addictions and obsessions will discover they cannot deliver themselves from these forces of moral distortion, but that God can and will if asked;[40] they are then confronted with the strange paradox that although they are not morally responsible for having the addictions or obsessions, recovery and health depend on taking responsibility for their consequences in action through self-examination, confession of some sort, resolution to amendment of life, and, where possible, restitution and forgiveness. Where powerful forces of this nature are at work, therapy, support groups, pastoral counsel, and sacramental confession all have a role to play. Because of the distortions of will and consciousness such forces bring with them, a tested conventional morality is actually probably the safest guide until a person has grown strong enough in discipline to be ready for a critical, postconventional morality. In a liberation mode, the moral community will be the base community of resistance, not the dominant culture.

B. Searching for the Good

For many persons, however, whether suffering from the more demonic forces or not, a second moment occurs when the stables have been swept out, as it were, and it is now time to see what should be put in them. Here one must begin to wrestle with the positive side of morality, the claims of vocation we have discussed in looking at Fowler. As Jesus points out, once the demons are cast out, it is vital to *choose* something to put in their place lest worse demons occupy the newly renovated space (Luke 11:24–26).

This is a point at which there is a right use of idealism, especially as a source of a sort of youthful moral enthusiasm. Lives of the saints, examples of current heroines and heroes of the faith, fellowship with companions in the struggle are all helpful. Ongoing moral guidance from a good pastor, in either the confession or counseling mode, can be of particular help in finding balanced and sensible approaches and in avoiding the normal pitfalls of scrupulosity, discouragement, and a growing threat of self-righteousness or works-righteousness. Good counsel can remind us, for example, of our obligation to affirm and take proper care of ourselves, even to enjoy God and life. It can and should gradually move the motivation for ongoing moral reform from fear and sorrow to gratitude and love. For many people this guidance can remain conventional and need not develop a fully self-critical edge.

C. The Experience of Moral Failure

Some persons, however, perhaps more than our current pastoral practice allows us to see, eventually bump into a wall that makes continuing in a precritical, conventional morality somewhere between frustrating and impossible. This may be a large, life-shattering event requiring a difficult moral choice. It may be the result of ongoing intellectual and educational development. It may come from a deepening sense of the perspectival limitations from which all conventional moralities suffer, including the biases stemming from locations of gender, race, and class. For many, it is simply an abiding sense of moral failure despite real growth and progress, failure not necessarily in huge things but in confronting the demands of the everyday. It is a common experience of persons in recovery from addictions and obsessions, for example, that God seems to remove the "elephant," often quite suddenly and dramatically, but leaves the "fleas." This is the experience of our besetting sins, as the tradition calls them, whose problem is not their size but their besettingness. It is the countless small ways we fail every moment to live up to that endless call of self-transcendence in the face of the Spirit, including, for some, patterns of destructive self-negation.

Where and when this becomes a deep and abiding sense, a transition to the second current, transfiguration, may well be being indicated—a transition to be looked at later. But for anyone who begins to take the "fleas" seriously, it means the end of any easy, naive moralism, for oneself or others. It means, in fact, the onset of true Christian adulthood as one wrestles with that great Lutheran reality, *simul justus et peccator*, "at the same time justified and sinner." One sees oneself as part of both the problem and the solution, always and everywhere, with no escape. Where there is support for nurturing "second" conversions, as we shall define that in the chapter 17, or support for serious, ongoing intellectual conversion, the opportunity exists for a conversion to an ethic of critical principles, deep care for community and its webs of relationship, and a universalizing faith[41] that transcends and critiques even the best conventional morality.

D. Searching for the Will of God

Face to face with one's own abiding imperfections, demons, and failures, and a deepening sense of the limitations of one's own, and indeed, any conventional morality, the converted Christian is driven to an endless prayerful search for the will of God and the power to carry that out. This requires substantial growth in humility as we face our own personal shortcomings and our own implication in social evils; but the ultimate virtue required here is hope, hope that focuses on our own final sanctification in the beatific vision *and* fellowship with all of humanity in the healing of the world in the commonwealth/reign of God. Just as the endless longing for God in prayer will be the ultimate outcome of religious conversion in the life of prayer for this life, so also in moral conversion it will be the longing to see right prevail, the beatitude of those who hunger and thirst for righteousness. This deep search for God's will and the power to carry it out, indeed the moral courage to act when none of that seems clear, is the outcome of moral conversion and the task of keeping on doing the next right thing.

E. Political Conversion

Gelpi has added political conversion, a conversion from my own interests first to the common good and ultimately to the commonwealth of God, as a fifth sort of conversion. He has done this because he sees so many people who seem to have "gotten it" in their personal lives but not in this public realm, because he thinks it is so badly needed, and because he thinks it is important to distinguish the differing ethical demands in managing one's personal affairs, interpersonal institutions, and impersonal institutions.[42]

I choose not to make it a fifth category as Gelpi does, though I honor his imperatives for doing so. This is because, like John Wesley, I believe personal and social holiness are absolutely inseparable, even at a precritical level. It is not that one *should* not have one without the other, but that one *cannot*. If one adopts any philosophical option beyond modern subjectivism/nominalism in its various forms, the inherent social dimensions of affectivity, intellectuality, and morality emerge clearly. As Gelpi himself puts it,

> The moral inevitability of social-political conversion flows from the fact that without it one cannot live a fully responsible life even in one's interpersonal dealings with others. Those who have experienced an integral,

personal conversion seek authentic self-understanding at an affective, intellectual, moral, and religious level. All self-understanding, however, employs symbols whose significance and connotations have been determined in important ways by social institutions, including large, impersonal ones. We live in a racist, sexist, individualistic, capitalistic culture. Anyone who deliberately ignores that fact or refuses to deal with the massive institutionalizations of moral perversity that surround us will hardly escape their taint even in private dealings with others. Think, for example, of what sexism, individualism, and capitalism have done to family relationships.[43]

The disagreement with Gelpi is small, however, as what is shared is the passion that the social and political dimension must not be missed: "If you will, then, call sociopolitical conversion a second moment within the total process of moral conversion, but a moment so sufficiently distinct as to require a conversion in its own right."[44] That is certainly true for the vast majority of persons—there often is a specific moment when their converted moral consciousness breaks through the privatistic cultural assumption that religion and morality are only personal matters. I would only add in balance that many passionate social reformers have a complementary moment when they realize that their social and political commitments require a previously lacking attention to personal sinfulness and reform, if only for the sake of critiquing the false consciousness of their own agenda and its motivations.

The parallel in the two forms of moral conversion is exact—from personal satisfaction (or excessive negation) to the Good and then to the will of God in the personal dimension—from self-interest or oppression (individual or group) to the common good and then to the commonwealth of God in the sociopolitical. The moral bankruptcy of our current situation is revealed equally by the omniverousness and hedonism encouraged in consumerist society's approach to personal life, and in an ethics of special interests and national self-interest in public life. It is marked by the degree to which the public acquiesces in the notion that national self-interest is in fact an adequate public morality. It is particularly tragic that those nations that had a high and idealist ethic in domestic and foreign policy, having experienced some of the limitations of the naive version of that approach, have not gone on to a fully critical social morality but have retreated to a stage of nonconversion governed by rather unenlightened self-interest.

Either Gelpi's position or mine allows us to see political conversion as the social dimension of moral conversion, but only if we acknowledge the necessary sociopolitical dimension in the other layers of conversion as well. The personal/political dialectic is better seen as the tension between the terminal images of beatific vision and commonwealth/reign, which inform all the conversions. The former reflects the personal dimension of loving knowledge (love informed by faith); the latter reflects the social dimension of covenant commitment to the reign (love informed by hope). A conversion at any level or layer that does not issue in political conversion is thus defective in hope. This is clearly visible in theologies that split off religion into a personal realm that has little impact on business or politics, where there is literally "no hope" that Christian vision and virtue could really apply. It can also be seen in the failure of more liberal Christians to acknowledge the need for appropriate evangelism and world mission, since religious belief is seen as a purely private matter. A failure to have a public dimension is a sign of incompleteness at any level of conversion.

Religious Conversion

Religious conversion is ultimately turning from idolatry to God. It begins in this first movement with being confronted by God alone as the ultimate concern in which all other concerns are judged and prioritized, leads to learning to live in loving delight in God's presence in all of life, and "ends" in the third tide, as we shall see, with critiquing everything else in the world or experience as ultimately "not God." Lonergan describes it beautifully:

> Religious conversion is being grasped by ultimate concern. It is other-worldly falling in love. It is total and permanent self-surrender without conditions, qualifications, reservations. But it is such a surrender, not as an act, but as a dynamic state that is prior to and principle of subsequent acts. It is revealed in retrospect as an under-tow of existential consciousness, as a fated acceptance of a vocation to holiness, as perhaps an increasing simplicity and passivity in prayer. It is interpreted differently in the context of different religious traditions. For Christians it is God's love flooding our hearts through the Holy Spirit given to us. It is the gift of grace.[45]

In this first tide of conversion, the religious dimension is a cutting loose from worldliness as either attachment or oppression; when healthy, this leads not to an ignoring or despising of the world but to detachment with love. In the second tide, it will be the experience of God in what Simone Weil calls the implicit forms of the love of God in religion, beauty, affliction, and friends and neighbors. In the third tidal current, it is the birth of explicit experiences of loving and being loved by God, the entrance into the mystical life as such through the purifications of the second of the "dark nights." Or, I might put it this way. If religious conversion is a "falling in love without qualifications," then the first movement is about *falling* in love, the second is about falling *in love*, and the third is about falling in love *without qualifications*.

Religious conversion at every stage is thus a centering on God as the ultimate concern of the other three layers: love of God is the core of affective conversion; faith in God as truth is the core of intellectual conversion, and hope in the vision and commonwealth of God is that of moral conversion. As such, as Gelpi puts it, religious, specifically, Christian conversion is the transvaluation of all the other conversions.[46] Indeed, he suggests this occurs precisely by the infusion into the other conversions of the theological virtues of faith, hope, and love. Although he identifies hope with affective conversion and love with moral, while I have done the opposite, this only serves to remind us, I believe, that we are dealing with one movement of the Holy Spirit; hence, all the theological virtues are involved in the transvaluation of each layer of conversion in a fully Trinitarian fashion. Gelpi helpfully reminds us that the transvaluation of sociopolitical conversion (or of the political moment of moral conversion) is the search for social justice as reflective of God's justice in the commonwealth/reign.[47]

Lonergan says something of the same in retrieving the classical distinction between operative and cooperative grace:

> Operative grace is the replacement of the heart of stone by a heart of flesh, a replacement beyond the horizon of the heart of stone. Cooperative grace is the heart of flesh becoming effective in good works through human freedom. Operative grace is religious conversion. Cooperative grace is the effectiveness of conversion, the gradual movement towards a full and complete transformation of the whole of one's living and feeling, one's thoughts, words, deeds, and omissions.[48]

Translating into Gelpi's terms, cooperative grace is equivalent to the transvaluation of affective, intellectual, and moral conversions by the infusion of the theological virtues

Fitting Them Together

Three final points need to be made on how these various layers of conversion fit together:

1. The first is a reminder that all are modes of self-transcendence. Affective conversion is to God and God's reign as the deepest desire of the heart by affectional self-transcendence. Lonergan continues:

> Intellectual conversion is to truth attained by cognitional self-transcendence. Moral conversion is to values apprehended, affirmed, and realized by a real self-transcendence. Religious conversion is to a total being-in-love as the efficacious ground of all self-transcendence, whether in the pursuit of truth, or in the realization of human values, or in the orientation man adopts to the universe, its ground, and its goal.[49]

2. Second is a sense of the structural relationship among these layers. Lonergan sees them as building on one another in a sublation that results from their being modes of self-transcendence, in which each deeper layer

> goes beyond what is sublated, introduces something new and distinct, puts everything on a new basis, yet so far from interfering with the sublated, or destroying it, on the contrary needs it, includes it, preserves all its proper features and properties, and carries them forward to a fuller realization within a richer context.[50]

In that sense, some sorting out of our thoughts and feelings and their relationship in affective conversion is necessary before reason can be freed for its own proper task. Intellectual conversion moves beyond affective by being concerned with truth as well as sanity or health, without losing interest in them, since it depends on them. Moral conversion moves beyond the value truth, to incorporate values generally, but still requires dedication to truth in its need to keep hold of reality. Religious conversion moves beyond value to a being-in-love-without-qualification that transvalues all values, but in no way denigrates or abolishes them, even as it takes them to a new dimension and horizon.[51]

Two structural points: the first, as Lonergan insists, is that despite the fact they build on one another in this fashion, these layers of conversion are not successive moments in any simple sense, going from affective to religious. Indeed, from a causal point of view, one begins with God's love and runs through them the other way round.[52] I believe this helps us see these are not types of conversions to be arranged in a hierarchy or successive order but *layers of succeeding depth,* all of which are present in any genuine conversion. This becomes even clearer when we come, second, to recognize a familiar Trinitarian logic. Just as *agapē* is not an alternative alongside *storgē, philia,* and *eros,* but their fulfillment and healing, and self-transcendence is not an alternative form of ethics and spirituality to self-denial, self-fulfillment, and self-criticism but their own proper style, so also religious conversion is not so much an additional conversion to affective, intellectual, and moral, but their transvaluation in a love that transcends the horizons of this world.

3. Finally, Lonergan gives us the chilling reminder, "Besides conversions there are breakdowns."[53] These can begin as a series of negations in a proper critique of the affectivity, beliefs, values, and religion of a current position, and where correct can be a reforming effort to offset decline. But these same negations "may be false, and then they are the beginning of the decline." They can occur at all these layers of depth in individuals and cultures, and Lonergan's apocalyptic vision of a society in such decline, where the eliminations, distortions, and mutilations caused by such negations are hailed as progress, has an all-too-relevant sound.

The Christian terminal images require conversion at all levels. The beatific vision of God as loving, transfigurative knowledge of the triune God involves affective conversion (loving), intellectual (knowledge), moral and political (loving and transfigurative), and religious (of God). Kingdom, commonwealth, or reign involves affective as a discipline of desires to that end; intellectual as understanding how to promote it and critique opposing ideologies, including one's own; moral as directing all action to that end; and religious as the recognition that all other moral and political utopias are not *it* and are thereby relativized.

Each of these layers will be present in any genuine conversion, though some may emphasize one or more over the others. Indeed, a large part of the pastoral task in nurturing conversions will be identifying and supporting the *underemphasized* or neglected dimensions. For example, a person expressing a dominantly affective conversion might be encouraged to add to a fervent outpouring of devotion a commitment to study, the work of service in the world, and more contemplative forms of prayer, while a "black belt" contemplative might need reminding of the efficacy of devotion to the sacraments and Christ's humanity, of the study of doctrine, and of loving service and political action. This, I believe, is the chief heuristic value of this concept of layers of conversion for spiritual direction and other pastoral care.

With the psychological and theological pieces in place, it is now time to look at how they may come together in a consistent account of conversion.

Notes

1. Walter Conn, *CC*, 112.

2. The *locus classicus* for the first three is *Method in Theology*, 103, 131, 189, 216–19, 235–36, 237–43, 250; the addition of affective dimension comes in "Natural Right and Historical Mindedness," 140–41; also "Reality, Myth, Symbol," 36–37; see Conn, *CC*, 112 and 310 at n. 16; and Donald L. Gelpi, S.J., "Religious Conversion," 175 and 201 n. 2.

3. Gelpi, "Religious Conversion," 175 and 201 n. 2.

4. Gelpi, "Religious Conversion," 176.

5. Conn, *CC*, 112; Lonergan, *Method in Theology*, 237–38, 131.

6. See Conn, *CC*, 310–11 n. 16 for a helpful listing of critical literature.

7. Thomas Merton, *Contemplative Prayer*, 88, 104.

8. Gerald May, *Care of Mind*, 14–15, 199–203. May's distinction was even stronger in the first edition.

9. EMDR is another such treatment modality that has shown great clinical promise. See Francine Shapiro and Margot Silk Forest, *E.M.D.R.*

10. The literature is substantial, as any search for Albert Ellis as an author will reveal. For present purposes, a helpful work is Albert Ellis, *Reason and Emotion in Psychotherapy*. Again, the Wikipedia article on Albert Ellis is helpful (accessed 11/25/07).

11. Conn, *CC*, 136–39.

12. Sam Keen, *The Passionate Life*. See Conn, *CC*, 322; also Philip Sheldrake in *Befriending Our Desires*, and David Ford in *The Shape of Living* hold similar views.

13. Conn, *CC*, 139–43. Robert Solomon's classic text is *About Love*.

14. Conn, *CC*, 143–47; of Rosemary Haughton's many works, *Love* is a classic. For her views on what we have called the tide of conversion, see *The Transformation of Man*.

15. Conn, *CC*, 148.

16. Conn, *CC*, 150. Numbers and punctuation added for clarity.

17. John Cassian, *Conferences*; Norman Russell, *The Lives of the Desert Fathers*; Benedicta Ward, *The Sayings of the Desert Fathers*; see Harriet Luckman, Linda Kulzer, eds., *Purity of Heart in Early Ascetic and Monastic Literature*.

18. Conn, *CC*, 150–53, notes especially the helpfulness of Erikson's concept of *caritas*, and Kegan's transition from the stage of the Institutional Self to that of the Inter-individual self.

19. Anselm, *Proslogion*, preface.

20. See again, Barbara Hughes, "Spiritual Questions of Sexually Abused Children."

21. See Marianne H. Micks, *Loving the Questions*; Sewanee's Education for Ministry program is a Christian pedagogy taking intellectual questions of participants with great seriousness.

22. Alice Walker, *The Color Purple*, 166–73.

23. Among the many feminist theologies engaged in this task, Elizabeth Johnson's *She Who Is* is one of the most apt.

24. Lonergan, *Method*, 238–40.

25. For a pneumatological approach to these issues, see my "The Historic Ought-to-Be and

the Spirit of Hope." I found W. Taylor Stevenson's discussion in *History as Myth* especially helpful. Owen Barfield, *Saving the Appearances*, is an Anglican classic.

26. Lonergan, *Method*, 238.

27. John Polkinghorne, "Is Science Enough?" 14–16.

28. See Charles Saunders Peirce, *Collected Papers*; Paul Weiss, *Modes of Being*; John Polkinghorne, *The Faith of a Physicist*.

29. Lonergan, *Method*, 239.

30. Ignatius Loyola, "Rules for Thinking with the Church," *Spiritual Exercises*, Paulist ed. 211–14. See also Hugo Rahner, *Ignatius the Theologian*, 214–28. See also Philip Endean, "The Same Spirit Is in Everything: Towards a Contemporary Theological Reading of Ignatius' Rules for Thinking with the Church," 509–23.

31. See Fredrica Harris Thompsett, *We Are Theologians*.

32. Descartes began his philosophical reflection by doubting everything he believed, in order to discover what was absolutely certain. Critics from William Temple, *Nature, Man and God*, 57–81, to C. Fitzimmons Allison, *The Rise of Moralism*, 204–5, as well as those within the philosophical tradition, have questioned whether this is either desirable or possible.

33. Paul Tillich, *The Protestant Era*, xiv–xv; see Thomas and Wondra, *Introduction*, 208.

34. Urban Tigner Holmes, *What Is Anglicanism?* 2–8.

35. Phil 2:05

36. Lonergan, *Method in Theology*, 240.

37. See Lonergan, *Method in Theology*, 241–42. This is a similar sublation to the one we saw in the psychologies of development, where one stage takes up and builds on the results of the previous stages.

38. Gelpi, "Religious Conversion," 184.

39. Conn, *CC*, 105–57, esp. 107–16.

40. *Alcoholics*, 60. The content of the "Twelve Steps" is recognizable in what follows.

41. See the previous discussion of Fowler and Kohlberg, as modified by Gilligan.

42. Gelpi, "Religious Conversion," 180–84.

43. Gelpi, "Religious Conversion," 182.

44. Gelpi, "Religious Conversion," 181.

45. Lonergan, *Method* in Theology, 240–41.

46. Gelpi, "Religious Conversion," 184, 190ff.

47. Gelpi, "Religious Conversion," 201.

48. Lonergan, *Method in Theology*, 241.

49. Lonergan, *Method in Theology*, 241. It is important to recall our previous cautions about self-transcendence as applied to those whose selfhood has been shattered by abuse or oppression.

50. Lonergan, *Method in Theology*, 241.

51. Lonergan's similar account is *Method in Theology*, 242.

52. Lonergan, *Method in Theology*, 243.

53. Lonergan, *Method in Theology*, 243.

16

Bringing It Together

Synthesis

One of the marks of contemporary thinking about conversion and its relationship to spiritual growth has been the effort to synthesize the elements we have been discussing—developmental theories, the modes of God–self relation, and the dimensions of conversion—into a coherent theology of Christian conversion. On the Roman Catholic side in particular, this has been associated with the new experience of adult conversion through the reformed Rite for the Christian Initiation of Adults and a restored catechumenate or period of preparation for Baptism. While there have been several collections of essays along these lines, the first major synthetic work was Walter Conn's *Christian Conversion*.[1] Conn combined "biblically grounded theological reflection, a philosophy of self-transcendence, and the perspective of developmental psychology" into what he saw as a multidimensional but normative theory of Christian conversion.[2] He then proceeded to illustrate and support the theory by using it to provide an insightful spiritual biography of Thomas Merton, tracing affective, cognitive, moral, and finally religious (and specifically Christian) conversions in his life. These successive conversions were closely linked to stage transitions in Merton's life, illuminated by the various developmental theories.

Conn states his core methodology as follows:

> Within this pattern of personal development (moral and faith as well as cognitive and affective), I specified conversion as a vertical shift in structure (in contrast to a horizontal change of content) from a spontaneously instinctive to a reflectively personal orientation toward truth, value, and love. Moral, cognitive, and affective dimensions of conversion in this sense of structural shift in orientation were located at key developmental points—the conscious counterparts of unconscious stage transitions and crisis resolutions.[3]

In making this very close link between developmental stage transitions and conversions of spiritual growth, Conn sometimes seems even to identify them as if Christian conversion were little more than a religious interpretation of the stage transitions, despite what he had earlier said about a more nuanced sense of the interrelationship between development and conversion.[4] Even so, it is unfair to see him as making religious conversion merely an unnecessary interpretation of what is really psychodynamic. On the contrary, he suggests that secular developmental theories need to acknowledge that human development actually *requires* conversion in its "higher" stages such as universalizing faith and postcritical moral thinking; he recognizes that conversion always occurs within a developmental process. Even here, though, Conn does not give a clear sense of the operation of grace in conversion, and the word "grace" does not appear in the index.[5] At various points Conn does seem actually to identify a conversion with a stage transition: true moral conversion with the transition to Lawrence Kohlberg's postconventional morality, for example.[6] His concluding defense makes clear the intimacy of the connection he envisions:

> Indeed, the criterion of both religious conversion and the development of personal autonomy is self-transcendence. Justice, universalizing faith, generativity, and interindividual intimacy all insist on mutuality as the norm of authentic autonomy. Only the inauthentic notions of absolute autonomy and self-fulfillment are contradicted by the self-transcending love of religious conversion. Christian religious conversion is not the antithesis but the completion of personal development toward self-transcending autonomy.[7]

As we have seen, it would not be fair to critique Conn by suggesting he has simply sold out the religious dimension to the developmental. His claims that some stage transitions require conversions and that all conversions occur within a developmental context seem unexceptionable and were a major contribution to the understanding of the relationship between spiritual and psychological growth presented here. But problems remain at two levels. First is an empirical problem we have noted before—there seem to be some individuals who "successfully" negotiate even the "highest" developmental stage transitions without any explicit experience of a religious dimension or indeed of anything they would call "conversion." On the other hand, we are faced with persons of obvious and very real sanctity who are deeply flawed or neurotic if judged by psychosocial developmental standards, at least as those are usually interpreted.

The second, deeper problem, however, is a hidden kind of elitism. All the empirical developmental theorists, including James Fowler (but with the possible exception of Erik Erikson), acknowledge that as the stage transitions proceed, fewer and fewer people are still on the train, as it were. Only a few can reach the heights of postcritical principled morality and universalizing faith; indeed, the developmentally challenged or even those who die young simply do not stand a chance. This ultimately locks us into the same trap we saw in William James—real religious experience is the domain of a heroic and privileged few, and the ordinary folks just trail along at second hand.

Challenge

This undercurrent of elitism in linking conversion too closely to psychosocial development had its most passionate critic in Romney M. Moseley.[8] Afro-Caribbean by birth and culture, Moseley began his career as a firm developmentalist, seeking to provide in his research empirical verification for the categories of stage development in the theories of Kohlberg and Fowler. Indeed, for some time he was a colleague of Fowler at Emory. He describes, however, an occasion of cognitive conversion for himself, when he heard a woman's narrative of heroic struggle with a painful part of her life assigned to a very low stage of faith development. This led him eventually to a recognition that developmental theories needed a severe ideological critique, with much more attention paid to the metaphorical character of the theories, to the hard edge of paradox, and the narratives of oppression and suffering. I quote him at some length, because frankly, it would be unfair to the passion his prose contains to paraphrase it:

> An analysis of metaphor and paradox prevents us from settling for a closed system of moral and religious development. Closed systems of moral and religious development fail to appreciate the hard paradoxes of faith as evidenced in the struggle to affirm meaning in the face of meaninglessness, doubt, suffering, and despair. Locked in a tunnel vision of linear progression and hierarchical stage, the moral life and religious faith fall victim to progressivism and triumphalism.

After describing the occasion of his "conversion," he continues:

> It is not difficult for theories of moral and religious development to succumb to the distortions of triumphalist ideologies and to relegate faith from the underside of history to the lowest levels of development. Triumphalist ideologies ignore the history of suffering and the eschatological hope for divine justice and freedom maintained by victims of oppression.

He continues with a biting analysis:

> Given the North American [I would suggest broadly Western] obsession with triumphalism in its many forms, it is not surprising that pragmatism and its ally developmentalism are attractive hermeneutical strategies for charting moral and religious transformation. Both thrive on the myth of progress—in the case of pragmatism, a myth steeped in the American ethos of a Promethean individualism; in the case of developmentalism, a neo-Hegelian myth of autonomous reason. In either case, morality and religion are filtered through a value system in which the hard paradoxes of faith are overcome by advancing through hierarchically ordered stages of moral and religious development.[9]

Moseley begins by critiquing the Jamesian pragmatist tradition about conversion in much the same way as we have—its ultimate picture of real religion being experienced only by the heroic elitist vanguard.[10] Moseley then gives a critical reading of Fowler, which does not abandon faith development theory but seeks to expose its unsuccessful marriage between empiricist and idealist models by showing its inevitable but unacknowledged realist claims. He insists that any faith development theory take seriously the metaphorical (or I would argue, analogical) character of the concept of stage, and that more space be given to paradox and the previously excluded experience of the oppressed. Moseley seeks to accomplish this first by correcting Fowler's developmentalism with a psychology of dialectical transformation in which "the transformation of the self is a response to multiple arenas of conflict and ambiguity" and not just the result of simple stage transitions.[11] In this section he draws on the personalist philosophy of Stephen Toulmin, the ethics of H. Richard Niebuhr, and the feminist critique of Fowler's work by Carol Gilligan.[12] He then introduces the concept of paradox, as a counterweight to the notion of stage transitions as achieving integration or equilibrium:

> It is very easy to see religious conversion as the resolution of conflict— moral, emotional, or spiritual. The metaphor of the paradoxical self goes against such victory. It signals that transformation is unfinished. The center of gravity is not the resolution of conflict but the paradox—the paradox of struggle and surrender, fulfillment and emptiness, *pleroma* and *kenosis*.

Later, he identifies this paradox with the tension between "always-already" and "not-yet," which I discussed in the dialectic of self-transcendence:

> Faith is always more than its empirical stages. This "more than" quality, the "surplus of meaning," has to do with the paradox of seeking the eternal in the temporal. Whatever is identified as a stage is and is not yet. If there is any normativity to stages of faith, it is this paradoxical quality. This "is and is not yet" quality takes us into the realm of theology and ethics.[13]

Moseley proceeds to develop this concept of paradox in two ways. First comes a chapter on archetypal transformation, in which he gives a helpful analysis of Carl Jung's approach through the archetypal "conjunction of opposites."[14] This provides a useful "hook" for retrieving the vast amounts of literature using Jungian categories as a lens on spirituality. He preserves his sense of paradox, however, and corrects Jung's own view of the possibilities of integration (which depend on downplaying a realistic doctrine of evil); he does this with Robert Dorran's notion that some of the oppositions Jung recognizes are of contraries, which can indeed be integrated, while others require a hard choice between true contradictories.[15]

Not surprisingly, Moseley turns next to the master of paradox, Søren Kierkegaard, and draws a helpful distinction between mere recollection as a remembrance of the past, and true liturgical *anamnesis* as a repetition toward the future; this dangerous memory maintains the tension between the "always-already" and the "not-yet," of the eternal in the temporal, of the incarnation itself. It is not so much in successive integrations but in constantly and faithfully living in the face of this paradox in the midst of life's hard struggles, choices, and suffering that we become authentic selves before God.[16]

Moseley's own solution is to develop a spirituality and theology of self-emptying (*kenosis*) and suffering that responds to God's suffering and self-emptying love on behalf of the world.[17] I will not caricature it by too facile a summary. My one critique is anticipated by Moseley's own defense of the concept of *kenosis* against liberation criticisms as unhelpfully recommending repentance and forgiveness to the oppressed, of reinforcing stereotypes of the subservient slave. He is surely correct that this is a terrible caricature of kenotic spirituality that fails to recognize the power in vulnerability.[18] But it seems to me Moseley's anxiety to correct the immanentism of the developmental model has led him to emphasize exclusively the negative, "not-yet" sides of the self-transcendence dialectic: self-denial and self-criticism.[a] Pastorally, the positive "always-already" of the manifestation, self-fulfillment mode is still needed, not least for providing the most ground-down people a place to begin. But his cautions against ideological triumphalism and elitism in the developmental model are only too telling.

Reconstruction

Oddly enough, Moseley does not mention or discuss Conn's work. From his perspective, however, Conn's strong ties to developmentalism would be a serious problem.[19] This is in addition to criticisms I have made, that Conn treats dimensions or layers of conversion as successive stages, even though Bernard Lonergan warned against that, and that he makes the relationship between conversion and progressive stage-shifts too simple. At the same time, Conn's fundamental claim, that the "higher" stages of secular developmental theories really demand conversion (and I would add, grace, and operative grace at that, as well as cooperative grace), and that all conversions take place in a developmental context, remains unexceptionable as well as pastorally useful.

As we have seen in his critique of progressive developmentalism, Moseley has felt so obligated to emphasize the negative, "not-yet" dimension of conversion in self-denial and self-criticism (even to the point of embarrassment at one juncture) that he eliminates the "always-already" which is the primary experience of so many, and so necessary where an adequate sense of self has not been allowed to develop. How are we to find a way forward?

My own synthesis seeks to affirm the truth of Conn's work while avoiding the triumphalist pitfalls Moseley delineates by:

1. Not treating the three stages of the classic Way as successive, hierarchical steps on a ladder of ascent but as three concurrent tidal currents always under way in a complex, Trinitarian rhythm. These tides form a complex dance in which the

---

a Immanentism is the emphasis on God as immanent in the world and human growth rather than as transcending them.

theological virtues of faith, hope, and love are being born in a convert through a single movement of the Holy Spirit. The metaphor of the three channels of the inner ear tracking pitch, yaw, and roll can again be helpful here.

2. I have also proposed a more nuanced approach to the connection between developmental theories and spiritual growth. Growth in sanctity is not defined as human developmental growth informed by a religious conversion, in a hierarchical, progressivist fashion. Instead, developmental and other theories are used as lenses to illuminate the life issues that provide the human *context and content* in a conversion, a series of possible occasions or "teachable moments" for conversion, without linking a particular conversion necessarily to a particular developmental stage. The complexities of adult development are also recognized by adding the theory of "nested careers" (as described in chapter 13) to the more basic psychobiological and cognitive models. A religious interpretation of a developmental-stage transition does not necessarily equate with a genuine religious conversion or with spiritual growth. Room is left to recognize the sanctity of persons whose natural endowment or environmental circumstances do not allow the later stages of hierarchically interpreted developmental schemes to occur.

3. I likewise treat the three forms of the self/world/God relationship—self-denial, self-fulfillment, and self-criticism—not as hierarchically sequential but as three modes that may predominate in different persons and different times; they are best seen as dialogically related, most helpfully in a style of self-transcendence, which is not a fourth mode but the proper mode of each of the three in their healthiest dialogical (Trinitarian) interrelationship.

4. I have also suggested interpreting the layers of conversion (affective, intellectual, moral and political, and religious) as dimensions of depth present in all conversions and hence also not as hierarchical stages. Religious conversion in its Christian form is indeed not so much a fourth kind of conversion as it is the transvaluation of the other three.

5. All of this amounts to avoiding the "Chinese menu fallacy"—the bifurcations typical of Western patriarchal thought are overcome by means of an implacable Trinitarian logic that has emerged from the material itself: the three theological virtues and the three stages of the classic Way as one movement of the Holy Spirit in three concurrent currents; the three forms of self-relation as dialectically related in self-transcendence; three dimensions of depth of conversion as transvalued by Christian religious conversion.[20] Most important has been to see the energy behind the spiritual growth, the tidal currents, as coming from the Holy Spirit, with the human developmental and similar material being useful ways to map the shore.

Two points are worth noting about this Trinitarian logic: the first is that there are not three concepts in each set, but four, though in each case the fourth is not a fourth alongside the others (forming a quaternity) but the substance which the three express in common each in its own way. Similarly, divinity or godhead (*divinitas* or *deitas*) is not something over-against or alongside the Three, but the substance they express in common, each in its own particular relational way, and which does not exist except in that expression. As such, "*De Deo Uno*" (the doctrine of God as one) cannot be envisioned or discussed except as a dimension of the Trinitarian *peri-*

choresis or co-inherence.[21] Eastern theologians would remind us that this "Fount of being," even the divine being, is not to be thought of at all as an impersonal fourth thing but within the Trinity is relationally attributed to the Father/Mother (though most Eastern theologians would not add Mother, I suspect).

A second point requires us to keep the Eastern and Western doctrines of the Trinity in balance. The Eastern doctrine reminds us that there is a normal, perhaps even normative economic order in the mission of the persons; this order may well be reflected in the most usual occurrence of the steps of the Threefold Way, the birth of the theological virtues, some progression through the three modes of self-transcendence and the dimensions of conversion, perhaps even in the thrust of human development itself. But the Western insistence on the co-eternity and co-equality of the Three and on the rule of *monarchē* (the external acts of the Blessed Trinity are undivided—that is, where one acts, all act) prevents us from identifying an economic order of normal temporal sequence with a hierarchical ascent.

The simultaneity of virtues, currents, modes of self-relation, and layers of depth allows us to maintain a sense of vocation and growth, while acknowledging the truth of *simul justus et peccator*, of an endless rhythm of confession and praise, of turn and return. It allows us to acknowledge the sanctity of the simple as well as the epistemological privilege of the oppressed, and the hard, irreconcilable paradoxes of faith, while still recognizing the structures of human growth and development as the normal shape of the banks of life issues within which the energies of conversion flow; this is especially evident when those developmental theories are themselves treated with a nuance that acknowledges the complexity of adulthood's "nested careers" and the impact of race, class, and gender on how the common developmental flow is structured and expressed.

Pastorally, this approach reminds us that all the stage-like conceptual lenses are there to aid in discerning issue-content and direction of movement, not in a diagnosis in relation to a hierarchical norm. Christian spiritual directors are not engaged in diagnosis but in listening to help directees discern the concrete Word of God calling them into the next step of their lives. Placing directees in a hierarchical map has little to do with that and will probably impede it. Progress as such, to the degree it can be observed at all, remains under the dominion of charity, the increase in actual loving action as covenant faithfulness to the two great commandments and the great commission. The sequential schemes help us exegete the human context for that faithfulness; they must never be allowed to become identified with it. Larger questions of context and of the specific dynamics of any particular conversion are illuminated by Lewis Rambo's systemic approach to the complex interaction of personal, historical, psychological, and social factors.[22] Finally, the approach I have taken here allows us to take account not only of growth but also of regression and struggle, and even decline and dissolution.

Perhaps the most important protection against the progressivist triumphalism of the developmental perspective, however, is in the concept of Beloved Dust itself. Whatever spiritual growth is, it is not the internal development of characteristics, such as spirit and soul, which belong substantially to human "nature," or to any human being as achievements or accomplishments, and which somehow transcend or contradict our material, fleshly nature. Soul and spirit are treated as wholly relational terms, pointing to God's gift and initiative in our "beloving" as well as our dusting, to the priority of operative grace over cooperative, however necessary the latter. The cure for the pride of triumphalism is what it has always been—reconversion to the cross, and "Remember you are dust, and to dust you shall return," but heard in the sure and certain hope that the dust we are is always and already being beloved into the reign of God which was, and is, and is to come. Even at the grave we make our song, Alleluia, Alleluia, Alleluia.[23]

A Theology of Three Conversions

This concludes our discussion of the first movement of conversion in the rendering of Dust as Beloved. If we are left with only a series of interpretive lenses to increase our pastoral sensitivity to the complex factors shaping individual conversions, that may not be bad. We live in an age deeply suspicious of grand unified theories and universal metanarratives, rightly suspicious since all too often these have elevated the particular experience of a favored class to universal stature. I hope to have avoided that, while still providing pastoral tools for discernment, interpretation, and encouragement. There is one further use of "conversion," one additional theological theory, however, that we must now examine; it is not so much a theory about the flow within this first tide we have been describing but one about marker events that delineate a transition from the predominance of one tide in the Triple Way to another. In the metaphor I am using, these can be envisioned as the slack between tides. There is a period, called "slack," between ebb and flood tides in the ocean, when the "tide is turning." Here the water seems still and motionless unless troubled by weather and other currents. It can feel like nothing is going on. But experienced SCUBA divers know that the slack between ebb and flood is the best time to schedule a dive leaving from the shore.[a] Classically, these slacks are the realm of the "dark nights" of St. John of the Cross, painful times when it can seem like nothing is going on. But these, too, can be the most fruitful periods of exploration of the depths of God and self. We shall explore these slacks in chapters devoted exclusively to them. There is a sense, however, in which each of these transitions is a new upwelling of the conversion tidal current. This aspect of the journey has been most helpfully expounded by Alan Jones, based on work of the French Dominican spiritual theologian Reginald Garrigou-Lagrange, as a theology of three fundamental types of conversion.

In *Soul Making: The Desert Way of Spirituality*, Alan Jones presents what I find as his most personal and powerful portrayal of contemporary issues in the spiritual life. As he seeks to find a way to believe "that is passionate, intelligent, and honest," he uses the metaphor of desert spirituality as embodied for him in his visit to Fr. Jeremiah of the Coptic Monastery of St. Macarius in Egypt.[24] The three imperatives

---

a The last of the ebb helps carry you out to the dive site; you dive during the slack, and catch the start of the flood to carry you back in.

of the desert life: "Look! Weep! Live!" provide a field for reflection on a number of issues, which culminates in a doctrine of conversion not dissimilar to the one I have been suggesting.[25] This is conversion, not as a single event but as a life-long process of "unlearning hate and learning love."[26] "To be human, from the believer's point of view, is to be in a continual process of conversion. St. Paul writes, 'I am in travail with you . . . until you take the shape of Christ' (Gal 4:19)."[27] And again,

> Conversion is not a once and for all event, but a way of psychological and spiritual formation that takes a lifetime. Often the great and first step is confused with the whole lifelong process. Conversion experiences, life changing though they may be, are but the first step on a long journey.[28]

Jones next describes two perspectives on continuing conversion to Christ. The first is the long tradition of the imitation of Christ, which does not mean a slavish, lock-step duplication of Jesus' life or any other, but rather that over the course of our lives, we shall recapitulate the rhythm of Jesus' life, even as he recapitulated in his the fullness of human life.[29] "Everything that happens to Christ also happens to us."[30] The connection of this concept to the tradition of the Threefold Way can be seen in a fine quotation Jones makes from Aelred of Rievaulx's Second Sermon for Pentecost:[a]

> Contemplate Christ in three stages, as it were, planned by his wonderful kindness, not for his benefit but for ours. First he was baptized, then he was transfigured, finally he was glorified. He was baptized in the Jordan, transfigured on the mountain, and glorified at length in heaven. At Christ's baptism the Holy Spirit was shown as a dove, at his transfiguration as a cloud, but after his glorification as fire. Take these three stages to represent three stages in the soul's progress: purification, probation, and rewarding. Christ's baptism represents our purification, his transfiguration our probation, and his glorification our rewarding. We are purified by confession, we are proved by temptation, and we are rewarded by the fulness of charity.[31]

The second, and related way of understanding this continuing conversion, is to reflect on the experience of Jesus' first followers and to recognize that we are called on to repeat that experience in our own way as well. This experience also has three critical stages: the initial call, the experience of betrayal at the crucifixion, and the sense of absence in the period from Ascension to Pentecost. An important exponent of this in the twentieth century has been the French Dominican Reginald Garrigou-Lagrange:

> . . . beginners in the spiritual life must, after a certain period undergo a second conversion, similar to the second conversion of the Apostles at the

---

a Aelred is a twelfth-century Anglo-Norman monk and spiritual writer of note.

end of our Lord's Passion, and that, still later, before entering the life of perfect union, there must be a third conversion or transformation of the soul, similar to that which took place in the souls of the Apostles on the day of Pentecost.[32]

What Jones develops from these two related schemes is a further sense of conversion, not simply as the initiation of the spiritual journey but as the critical moments of transition marking the entrance to each of the three stages:

> The first crisis is one of meaning. [I would add, "and worth."] "What shall I do with my life? To whom should I surrender my obedience?" The twelve apostles [I would add "and the women"] "forsook all and followed him" because in Jesus they found new meaning and direction in their lives. [I would add, "and the ground of their worth in his loving them."]
> The second crisis is one of betrayal. "The one whom I am following is making his way to meaninglessness and destruction. Does he know what he is doing? Where is a way of escape?" It is easy to follow Jesus while all is going well; but when he sets his face steadfastly towards Jerusalem, the disciples are gripped by fear and they all abandon him. [I would add, "or stand helplessly by," to include the women's experience.]
> The third crisis is one of absence or emptiness. "We have experienced new life in the Risen Lord, and now he is going to forsake us again." The disciples meet the Risen Lord and he tells them that he is going to leave them, and this time for good (in both senses of the word) . . . in mature faith, the believers have to do without the direct presence of Christ and learn to live in the stretching, demanding experience of Christ's hidden yet pervasive presence through the gift of the Holy Spirit.[33]

The connection to the Triple Way becomes helpfully explicit at this point:

> At each stage or crisis of conversion, the drama or gospel has to be reinterpreted. An open view of conversion will take into account all the stages in the journey home. In classical Christian mysticism, this journey has three distinct phases.[34]

He recognizes the problems with overly schematizing the Way (an intellectual move technically called "reifying," treating an explanatory concept as if it were a thing), which has caused Protestant objections in particular:

> The trouble comes when people take this threefold model and use it as a yardstick by which to measure themselves. Following Christ then becomes a *work* that is never finished, rather than a life that is never ending. The Christian life becomes burdensome and exhausting. The simple way of following Christ easily becomes overlaid and embellished with degrees, gradations, and steps. The way to God degenerates into a struggle up a

ladder or progress by degrees. At each stage of the way we stop to take our spiritual temperature.[35]

Similar to my suggestion of three tidal currents defining the motion of growth in which all three "tides" of the Way are going on all the time (concurrent currents), though one may predominate at any moment, Jones also solves this problem by treating this path of soul-making as spiral.[36] He then describes the first conversion briefly, in terms very compatible with what has been said here of the tide of conversion:

> As we saw right at the beginning, the most basic and true thing about each one of us is our unique and inalienable dignity. The sinner knows that he or she is loved, and weeps. Who would not weep when we realize just how far we have trivialized and trampled on our own true worth? Appreciation of our true dignity and worth initiates the process of purgation because true self-knowledge brings with it an awareness of the discrepancy between what we are now and what we are meant to be.[37]

In the narrower sense, then, "conversion" means this first movement of entry into the spiritual Way of Christ, with all the rich dynamics we have traced to this point in its relationship to life issues and psychological and cultural forces, as well as the movement of the Holy Spirit birthing in us the theological virtues and their companion virtues, gifts, and fruits. But in a broader sense, "conversion" must also be taken to mean those critical moments marking the transitions to periods of our lives when the second and third movements of transfiguration and glory will predominate for a time. Pastorally, as we support and nurture a conversion, it can become crucial to understand which of the three tides is currently at issue, or if a directee is in a "slack." As we shall see in the next part, attempting to force back a person who is in the midst of a second-conversion transition into the second current into the mold of a first conversion can be very damaging. But we need have no fear of abandoning the fundamental themes of this first movement, for it does not cease. As we repeat the spiral of growth into the future, we shall revisit each of these movements, including this first, many times. Repentance (accompanied by healing and liberation) remains a theme of constant conversion to the end, though it will have a different character from the perspective of each new turn on the spiral. What is most important, we never leave behind our need to be anchored in the humanity and flesh of Jesus.

Conclusion to the First Tidal Current

In the course of examining this tide of conversion, we have examined the theological significance of what we are converted from, by, and to. We have looked at the Trinitarian dance of the three theological virtues in the formation of character through the human experience of moral struggle. We have looked closely at the relationship between human biological, psychological, and social development on the one hand, and spiritual growth on the other, determining that the former describes the shore on which the tides of the Holy Spirit's Trinitarian mission break, producing the confluence that is human spiritual growth. We have developed a theology that relates this model to modes of conceiving the relationship between self and God in the style of self-transcendence, and incorporated Lonergan's tracing of four layers of depth to the tide of conversion.

Following Lonergan, I have described conversion and the spiritual growth flowing from it as a "falling in love without qualification." This first tidal current of conversion we have been examining is about Dust "falling," falling into its own belovedness and falling in love with its Lover; the second movement, to which we now turn, is about the hard work of being "in love" and the way Dust is transfigured and illumined by that work and being worked on; and, as we shall see later, the third movement is about "without qualification," about the *kenosis*, the emptying, the letting go of qualifications, the embracing of absence, which is the prelude to Dust sharing in the divine glory itself. Governing this process is a rhythm of imitating and following Jesus, governed by the dominion of love in his great commandments and commission. Dust is never finished with conversion but is always faced with the paradox that the end of conversion is the call to further conversion, indeed, to a covenant and rule and contemplative pedagogy of perpetual conversion. The slack we feel at the "end" of the conversion tide, in which we come to see the necessity of "perpetual conversion," is the gateway to the second tide, transfiguration.

Notes

1. On the Rite for the Christian Initiation of Adults and the catechumenate, see above, chap. 12 n. 2. See chap. 14 above for my initial analysis of Walter Conn's work. Note also the continuation of this approach, albeit with some additional cautions, in the work of Joann Wolski Conn and Elizabeth Liebert.

2. Walter Conn, *CC*, 267.

3. Conn, *CC*, 267–68.

4. Conn, *CC*, 156–57.

5. To be fair, "God" is indexed and appears frequently.

6. Really throughout, but see Conn, *CC*, 128–34 especially, and 156.

7. Conn, *CC*, 268.

8. Romney Moseley, *Becoming a Self before God*.

9. Moseley, *Becoming a Self*, 2. I would argue that Charles Saunders Peirce's pragmatism is not as subject to this charge as the later work of William James and John Dewey, but that is a different project.

10. Moseley, *Becoming a Self*, 19–37.

11. Moseley, *Becoming a Self*, 14.

12. Moseley, *Becoming a Self*, 59–72.

13. Moseley, *Becoming a Self*, 68.

14. Moseley, *Becoming a Self*, 73–87.

15. Moseley, *Becoming a Self*, 82–83. See Robert Doran, *Theology and the Dialectics of History*.

16. Moseley, *Becoming a Self*, 88–106.

17. Moseley, *Becoming a Self*, 107–31.

18. Moseley, *Becoming a Self*, 118.

19. *Mutatis mutandis*, this would also apply to Joann Wolski Conn, Elizabeth Liebert, and Peter Feldmeier.

20. "Chinese menu fallacy" is my term for the common structural theological error Karl Rahner identified in "The Order of Redemption within the Order of Creation," in *The Christian Commitment*, 35–74. It consists in assuming all tensions can be expressed as opposing dyads, lining a series of these up in two columns and then seeking further wisdom by choosing one from column A and one from column B, hence, Chinese menu. Among theologians, Anders Nygren and Matthew Fox tend to think this way. See Nicholas Lash, *Easter in Ordinary*, 131–77, for Trinitarian logic as a corrective to bifurcation.

21. Thomas and Wondra, *Introduction*, subordinate the traditional topics of *De Deo Uno* to those of *De Trinitate*, 67–108.

22. See the previous discussion in chap. 13 n. 11 above.

23. The *kontakion*, or song for the dead, from the Eastern Orthodox liturgy; now in the *BCP 1979*, 499.

24. Alan Jones, *Soul Making*, 6.

25. Jones, *Soul Making*, 22.

26. Jones, *Soul Making*, 159. The reference is to W. H. Auden's "Psychology and Art Today" (1935).

27. Jones, *Soul Making*, 162.

28. Jones, *Soul Making*, 164.

29. Irenaeus, *Adversus Haereses* V.19–21, Richardson ed., 389–91.

30. Jones, *Soul Making*, 164.

31. Quoted by Jones, *Soul Making*, 159.

32. Quoted by Jones, *Soul Making*, 174; Garrigou-Lagrange, *Three Ways*, 29.

33. Jones, *Soul Making*, 166–67.

34. Jones, *Soul Making*, 166.

35. Jones, *Soul Making*, 168.

36. Jones, *Soul Making*, 169.

37. Jones, *Soul Making*, 170–71.

The First Interlude

17

The First Slack, or "Second Conversion"

The second conversion comes as a terrible shock to believers of long standing and wide experience.[1]

As far as I know, there is no logical reason why the Christian life at this point could not be a simple transition from the dominance of the first Trinitarian current of the Spirit's *missio*, conversion, to the second, transfiguration; so the flow of events is in most lives, though even the order is not uniformly necessary.[2] One can only say that the tradition teaches that in our fallen existential circumstances, there is a dark interlude in the midst of the transition that calls for a "second conversion" and a deeper renunciation; and most people experience something like that at this point in their pilgrimage. This is the tradition of the classic "dark nights" of St. John of the Cross, helpfully described for us in this developmental context by William Johnston and Gerald May.[3] In terms of the primary metaphor I am using, between the two great tides of conversion and transfiguration, there is a "slack," a period when nothing, or at least nothing "positive," seems to be moving or happening. Only in retrospect can we see such periods as times of grace-filled growth.[4]

There comes a time of disillusionment in every intimate, life-shaping relationship of significant duration, a time when the illusions of our projections on the other are smashed to bits by the sheer reality of their otherness; and both we and they stand revealed, warts and all, trying to decide how to go forward, if at all. This is a familiar stage in the development of a marriage, for example, when we discover we have made a dreadful mistake and married a real human being instead of our ego-ideal of opposite (or, perhaps, same) gender. It is at that point that falling in love ends and the real work of being in love begins; and it cannot really begin until we suffer the necessary disillusionment—the taking away of our illusions and even delusions about the other, ourselves, and the real nature of our relationship. People who are unable to go through this disillusionment and carry on with the hard work of love, always retreating behind some romantic ideal of themselves and a perfect other, will be doomed endlessly to repeat the early stages of courtship with a succession of partners; they will never know the pain and glory of sustained loving faithfulness to one real person. The moment of disillusionment in a marriage may come as early as the first day of the honeymoon (or earlier in contemporary courtship patterns), or may be delayed for a few years, but come it surely must. It need not mean the ending of romance in the relationship, only of the romantic illusion. It is the gateway to the long work of love that is the only true path to real consummation.[5]

It is no accident that the language of erotic attraction, courtship, betrothal, marriage, and consummation has been used by Christian mystics through the ages to describe our relationship with God; it is one of the best analogies in human experience for that ultimate relationship.[6] It is so not only on the lighter, more pleasant and ecstatic side, but also on the heavier and more devastating side. There comes a time, then, when anyone seriously pursuing the Christian Way will bump up against realities that challenge the early romance-like fervor of first conversion. These realities may include our own ongoing failure to live up to the new life we have been given: the fact that though we are entirely dependent on grace, there seems still to be a lot of work left for us to do; the recognition that the leaders and institutions that brought us the gospel are not only imperfect but often downright corrupt; and the experience that God is a good deal scarier and more inscrutable and sometimes distant than we had thought; or that this new life is going to cost a lot more than we expected. This moment of religious disillusionment, it turns out, is an invitation to enter the second great movement, or current, of the spiritual life, transfiguration; but it is usually experienced as a rather rough shifting of gears, especially where no community of covenanted, contemplative praxis exists to interpret this shock as our second conversion. Without such support, we may have difficulty escaping the two great temptations at this stage: to give up, or, worse, endlessly to seek ever-jazzier means to recreate in ourselves the emotional kick and fervor of our first conversion. Like the serial polygamist in romantic relationships, religious people may run from one offered experience, group, or even cult to another, never digging into the hard work of any one spiritual path.

That is, the enthusiasm of initial conversion and birthing into the life of the faith by the Spirit usually begins to cool, and we can make the tragic errors of trying to re-ignite it or replicate it in ourselves. When this fails, as it always does, even Christians of long standing and great faith can be surprised by the desolation that follows, especially when there is no teaching in the community that this is to be expected, and is the birth of a deeper intimacy with God.[7] We are usually brought face to face at this time with the ways in which we have not lived up to our new calling, and are discouraged by our ongoing battles with the demons of possessiveness and despair. This crisis initiates in us what St. John of the Cross called "the dark night of the senses." It is both a last gasp of the style of self-denial and also our initial letting go of it, as we face the deepest layers of our own self-betrayal.

At a much deeper level, that which is usually called the passive purgation of the senses, this is not an act on our part at all but a deeper upwelling of the Spirit in her indwelling. "This dark night is an inflow of God into the soul which purges it. . . ."[8] Johnston also likens this first dark night to the experience, in Jungian terms, of beginning to come to grips with our own shadow.[9] God is no longer teaching us indirectly through the exterior senses but directly through the upwelling of the

Spirit. God the Mother is weaning us from the milk of children that we may begin to walk on our own in her presence.[10]

At the end of the previous chapter, we noted the suggestion of Reginald Garrigou-Lagrange, O.P., that the conversions marking the transitions to three stages of the classic Way (or, I would say, a new emergence into prominence of one of the three tidal currents of the Spirit's mission), reflect not only the rhythm of Jesus' life in the Holy Spirit, manifested in Baptism, transfiguration, and glorification, but also in the experience of Jesus' first disciples of their initial calling, then of their failures at the cross, and finally of coping on their own after the Ascension.[11] Because the second conversion is so unfamiliar, Garrigou-Lagrange dedicates most of the smaller book to its description, which he sees foreshadowed scripturally in the call to further conversion in childlikeness in Matt 8:2, and in a reference to Peter's postbetrayal second conversion in Luke 22:31.[12] While he finds the teaching clear in many saintly teachers of the church, including Johannes Tauler, Henry Suso, and St. John of the Cross, it is in chapters 60–63 of Catherine of Siena's *Dialogue* that he discovers the most explicit and helpful reference.[13]

The archetype of this second conversion is the experience of St. Peter in his threefold denial of Jesus, his subsequent repentance when Jesus looks at him on the way out of the trial at the high priest's house, his flight from the cross, and his ultimate conversion by the resurrection.[14] St. John and the women have a different experience—after fleeing at first, St. John stays with Jesus through the trial and is ultimately drawn with the women (Jesus' mother first among them) to the cross, nevertheless standing by helplessly; despite the experience of helplessness and powerlessness, that cross and Jesus' words and perseverance lead to their second conversion, even if that conversion, too, must be consummated by the resurrection experience. There are thus four moments in this conversion: betrayal, a noticing that leads to a falling apart of the old self, a process of letting go, and resurrection.[15] This fourfold event introduces us to the stage of illumination, of understanding, of proficiency in prayer and service, of the hard work of being in love, of transfiguration. As noted, a lot is going on under water during this "slack."

Betrayal and Failure

The first aspect of this experience can come from either of two directions, and often from both at once. Sometimes we have a sense of God's having abandoned us or taken us in a direction we had not bargained for, and we feel betrayed by God. Wrenching healing or dearly bought liberation may not bring all the new freedom we had expected. It was easy enough to follow Jesus during the Galilee period, preaching, teaching, and healing, with seemingly few setbacks. But when Jesus sets his face to go up to Jerusalem, risking suffering and death for himself and us, too, things appear quite different. At any sign of increased cost or suffering we may feel that God has somehow not kept the deal we made at first conversion and has let us down. Perhaps most common at this time, God often seems to withdraw from us the sense or awareness of God's presence to which we have become accustomed;[16]

we feel left to our own devices, deeply missing the feelings that had consoled us for the sacrifices required at first conversion. Our reaction to this emotional dryness frequently reveals a self-interest and egoism in our love of God, showing that we had loved God only because of the many benefits and consolations of our new life in Christ. It is this egoism we are called to surrender in this second conversion.

Where first conversion has been the work of healing or liberation from trauma, abuse, or oppression, the language of "egoism" may not be as appropriate, especially at first glance. The first wave of healing and liberation has brought a much-needed restoration and development of the crushed or annihilated ego, a process that continues to be a challenge in all the currents. Here the besetting negative behaviors are the survival strategies that were created to cope with violence. Now such skills as avoiding people or rituals of self-abuse have become destructive habits. It usually takes substantial therapy for abused or oppressed persons to reach the point where they are able to let go of these "old tapes." Even with God's grace and healing, these defects persist, often as permanent scars, not unlike those on the resurrected body of Jesus. This is when falling into God is the only open door. The disillusionment in this first slack in such situations involves coming to grips with the fact that no amount of healing or liberation will make the abuse or oppression OK, that some pain and other consequences may, like scars, be permanent, even as the remaining lies, such as "I am bad," can be surrendered here. There is also a possible realization that survivors have abused themselves and others. Here, too, there is a kind of false empirical ego that still overlays and covers up the true self that the Spirit is birthing in Christ.[17]

We also find that if God has not lived up to our expectations, neither have we. We may, in the face of this sense of abandonment, turn back from the Way in anger or fear in a major betrayal like Peter's. More commonly, however, and often apart from any sense of abandonment by God, our egoism is revealed in an ongoing battle with what are called besetting sins.[18] These are not the gross, deadly sins from which many of us were called at first conversion, and which are often quite dramatically removed. Instead, these are the naggingly persistent expression of our abiding character defects, with which God so often seems to leave us alone to battle. As we probe them more deeply, we often discover they stem from parts of our lives that we are not yet willing to surrender, even habitual dimensions of our character that seem tied to our very sense of self-identity, "positive" or "negative." Cherished resentments, for example, deeply tied to our personal life histories, can be particularly virulent causes and symptoms of these defects. Old survival strategies, as we have just seen, may play a similar role for survivors of abuse or oppression. Often these besetting sins are also the defects preventing us from being of real service to the reign of God and our neighbor. Although the sins we are led to commit by defects of this sort are relatively "small," if left unattended they can break out in a major episode.

Sometimes what appears to be character defects or symptoms of them is the emergence of previously repressed or suppressed aspects of ourselves that we have failed to integrate into our sense of self-identity. These include the orectic or monstrous and our fascination with it;[19] certain of the deepest aspects of our sexuality; repressed traumas in our personal history; and everything making up what Jungians call "the shadow." Care is needed here, as some of this material is unintegrated parts of ourselves that need re-incorporation; other bits of it may be real demons that need renunciation and exorcism. Discernment is key, and the help of a spiritual director or a therapist may be prudent or even required. It is, oddly enough, our very personal and spiritual growth that usually allows these hidden aspects to emerge, since the layers that covered them have been removed or become transparent. This is, indeed, a common experience in the practice of meditation or even early stages of contemplation, where the "distractions" that surface are actually the negative bits from the self that need to be exorcised or reintegrated. We have now grown enough so we can deal with these things, and thus they emerge, much like cleaning up the first layer of mess in an untidy house allows us to notice deeper layers previously hidden. A growing consciousness of our own inevitable and inescapable immersion in social and institutional evil is also often part of the picture at this time. We finally realize we can't be part of the solution until we *know* we are part of the problem, since it is the very culture that has shaped our identity that has also embodied these evils.

In either case, the least helpful strategy is ongoing denial and repression. Besetting sins arising from denied character defects will simply keep cropping up until they amount to a real disaster. Similarly, turning aside in further denial from repressed or damaged parts of ourselves will only leave undisciplined a lot of psychic energy which is also likely in the end to afflict us and others, especially the ones we love most, in major ways. The grace of God at this time is engaged in burning out some of our remaining egoism, or the false negative ego of the survivor of abuse or oppression, and unless we co-operate with that grace, asking God to remove all our defects of character, especially those we cling to as part of our self-definition, that egoism will remain, locking away our true selves in our false empirical ego and poisoning our own lives and those of others. All the means of grace at our disposal may be used in faith and gratitude, from sacraments and prayer to therapy, and the one we most resist using is probably God's chosen scalpel for the needed surgery. Birthing the true self means surrendering the false self, and the first step is telling the truth about that false self. Turning away from our own shadow and defects, then, is like turning away from the cross. Ironically, this passing by the cross is supported by the deism rampant in our culture that desires to relate directly to God, usually the Father alone, without "passing by the way of Christ crucified, because they have no desire to suffer."[20] Real Christianity lets neither God nor us off the hook at this point.

Falling Apart

At the deepest level, we are being purged of what St. Catherine calls the "mercenary love of God" for the sake of ourselves. Up to this point we do not so much love God as we love what God has done for us and continues to do for us. Gratitude is essential, but only the beginning of love. We stick with it only as long as our consolation in God continues. We are tempted to turn back when we meet such difficulties, or when we don't get what we think we want and deserve because of our discipleship, or when the sense of consolation in prayer is withdrawn, which it usually is at this time. Our supposed love for God is revealed at its root as mixed with a deep and selfish and inordinate love of ourselves (perhaps in desperate circumstances where that has been a necessary first step) and a pride in our just-begun relationship with God.[21] If we turn aside at this point, we will find we cannot ever really get back to the naive joys of the first conversion. As Garrigou-Lagrange says:

> Just as the child who does not grow does not merely remain a child but becomes an idiot, so the beginner who does not enter upon the way of proficients when he ought to, does not merely remain a beginner, but becomes a stunted soul. It would seem, unhappily, that the greatest majority of souls do not belong to any of the three categories of beginners, proficient, or perfect, but rather to that of stunted souls![22]

As we begin to experience the awful truth about even our redeemed selves, we run smack into Luther's great truth of *simul justus et peccator,* "at the same time justified and sinner." Far from having been rendered sinless by the grace of our first conversion, we have been given a new sense of how far we have fallen short of the glory of God and the life God intends for us, even in the face of some real moral reform and an abiding sense of being forgiven.[23] As our cherished illusions about ourselves, our culture, our new life, our healing and freedom, and even God (the chief place of disillusionment about God is, after all, the cross) emerge to an awful consciousness, everything starts to come unstuck. Our entire view of the world fragments, including our newly won sense of assurance we know what God is up to in the divine economy of salvation. Most frighteningly, our very sense of who we are, to the degree it has been based on that false empirical ego, is shattered. Since God seems to be absent or at least to have become incomprehensible and inscrutable, there is literally nothing to cling to, nothing. For the first time, then, we experience the *nada,* the nothing, as an element in the graceful structures of the spiritual life. And I don't mean, here or elsewhere, that we should seek to cultivate delightful esoteric experiences of nothing.[24] It is also to be distinguished from inflicted experiences of evil and the not-God. This no-thing is a frightening abyss over which we hang when everything, including our selves and our relationship to God as we understood God, falls apart, an abyss that in truth is our own spiritual poverty.[25]

Letting Go

We are called upon to let go and fall into that abyss, which, it turns out, is not hell but the darkness of God's brilliant ineffable light. Blessed are the poor in spirit, oddly enough, for theirs is the kingdom of God. Every effort to escape this letting go will involve clinging to a chunk of lead to avoid drowning, at the expense of hanging on to one of the lies on which our false self has been constructed. The experience of this letting go is what St. John of the Cross has called the dark night of the senses—the frightening entrance into a new relationship to self and world.[26] It is also called the passive purgation of the senses because it is not a housecleaning we do, as in first conversion, but a falling apart and letting go in which we remain nonactors while we are being reshaped and reborn yet again.

Saint John, following Johannes Tauler, listed three signs of the entrance into this period of purgation, which have become classic marks of discernment at this point:

> The soul finds no pleasure or consolation in the things of God, but it also fails to find it in anything created. . . . The second sign . . . is that ordinarily the memory is centred upon God, with painful care and solicitude, thinking that it is not serving God, but backsliding because it finds itself without sweetness in the things of God. . . . The third sign is that the soul can no longer meditate or reflect in its sense of the imagination. . . . For God now begins to communicate Himself to it, no longer through sense, as he did aforetime, by means of reflections which joined and sundered its knowledge, but by an act of simple contemplation, to which neither the exterior nor the interior senses of the lower part of the soul can attain.[27]

This process of learning proper detachment from the sensible and created world, from our experience of God as opposed to God, from any remaining false sense of our own worthiness and usefulness (including a toxic belief in our own unworthiness), and from accustomed methods of prayer and devotion does not mean *rejection* ("cold" detachment) of world, self, or experience of God. Instead, it means letting go of the bonds that had enmeshed our empirical ego in possessing these things, so that in freedom we may come to love them properly ("warm" detachment).[28] In our time it is also crucially important to distinguish such predictable and growthful periods of aridity from clinical or chemical depression, since the emotional feel can be quite similar. As Gerald May has pointed out, the key to discernment is in the rest of the person's life and relationships.[29] During true dark nights, they are not only unimpaired—they are often more fruitful than usual. In the case of depression, the opposite is true.

Alan Jones cites Graham Greene's three marks of the true believer, which, I believe, are closely associated with the three classic signs just listed from John of the Cross. "Perhaps, truthfully, we can count on nothing more than the divided mind, the uneasy conscience, and the sense of personal failure."[30] These are not the characteristics of the fervor of first conversion, of course, but of the believer undergoing the second, whose divided mind prevents unambiguous commitment to any thing or cause in this world, and whose ongoing uneasy conscience and sense of personal shortcoming cause that believer to identify with all of sinful humanity, and thus to be "an unlikely candidate for totalitarian seduction."[31]

The third sign, inability to meditate using either the physical or mental senses is often more baffling and even a bit trickier. The tradition is very strong that what we are being offered is an entry into the first darkness of a contemplation of God which transcends the senses, and wise spiritual directors are likely at this point to recommend abandoning more externalized devotion in favor of centering prayer or other forms of quiet waiting, always taking into account the natural proclivities of different personalities.[32] At the same time, long experience has shown the need to stay hooked to the flesh of Jesus as our anchor in reality during such periods, which means that the ordinary disciplines of attending community worship and sacraments, daily scriptural prayer (Daily Office in the traditions that have it), and keeping on with the normal demands and opportunities of one's vocation, service, and family life are crucial. Drawing into a shell of moping instead usually immerses one in the classical sin of acedia (*accidia*), which is a kind of spiritual slothfulness and self-indulgence typical of those who have become, even if temporarily, what Garrigou-Lagrange calls stunted or tepid souls.[33]

Where there is no clear teaching about the classic spiritual path of the Christian Way and its manifold conversions, we are sorely tempted to turn back at some point in facing these difficulties. As we have already noted, there are two possibilities. The first is that persons become discouraged and decide that the Christian Way is a dead end. They may at this point remain in the Christian community, but as stunted or retarded souls; they may seek a better way in other religions and spiritual disciplines; or, perhaps most commonly in our time, they drift into a generic secularism and abandon the spiritual quest entirely. The tragedy is that the difficulties they faced were signs that they had made real progress on the Way; but with no one to show them the map they could not know that.

The second kind of turning back is a desperate effort endlessly to find again the emotions and fervor of our first conversion. In the end, this means falling into the trap of trying to recreate religious experience in ourselves, which, as Thomas Merton wisely noted, "leads ultimately to the total moral and psychological collapse of the individual."[34] It can mean rushing from one renewal exercise or meeting to another, much like the addict seeking again that first high after tolerance for the drug has set in. Or, perhaps worst of all, it can mean faking the behavior of enthusiasm so others in our faith community will not know we have been backsliding. All of these involve, tragically, clinging to the very religious experiences God has now withdrawn from us for the sake of our own further growth in grace. What looks like piety is actually resistance to the movement of the Holy Spirit in us.

Alan Jones puts well the need for spiritual counsel from the tradition at this point:

> If more of us knew about these three stages we might save ourselves a great deal of needless pain and anxiety and thus use our energy for the real work of soul making. It might help to know that, when things are hard and we feel abandoned, we are going through a well-documented process and traveling a path that many have covered before us. Soul making has its solitary side, but it is not a solitary thing. We stand in a great tradition. We have companions. The testimony of the survivors of spiritual conflict are there to assure us that there is glory through struggle; and this gives hope to those who are waiting in the dark on the edge of the second conversion.[35]

Resurrection

At some point, the dawn begins to break, or, better, our eyes become accustomed enough to the light that we can begin to see it is not darkness at all, only that we have been blinded by it. Instead, as we have seen, it is a new upwelling of the Spirit. Two points are crucial: the first is that we do not first climb out of the pit of the second conversion's abyss of aridity and then experience light and relief. That could give the false impression we should be struggling to get out of the pit, when what is called for is willingness to stay where God has put us and see it through. No, the dawning light is experienced *in* the pit, at the very bottom, and indeed is what shows us the truth that causes us to weep with the deeper repentance of this stage—for our besetting sins and for the sin of all humanity in which we also are hopelessly mired.[36] It is as if the first tide of conversion has one last burst before the transition. The pit of second conversion is not an obstacle to get over to go on with the real journey but one of the primary schools of the Way. And when we find ourselves by grace finally climbing out, it is Mount Tabor, the mount of the transfiguration, that we find we are climbing.

Another mistake we can make also looks at the dark night as a kind of interruption and believes we come out of it untouched, as we were before, or perhaps deeply and totally healed. We forget that the body of the risen Christ could be recognized precisely because the prints of nails and spear and thorns remain tangibly in it. The reality for us is that *simul justus et peccator* remains. We emerge deeply changed, and for the better, but bearing the scars of the fearsome struggle. Personally, I find in the recovery model the best description of the exit from the pit. We emerge with a deeper acceptance of exactly who we are, defects and all, scars and all, ready to live as recovering people (alcoholics, addicts of all kinds, racists, sexists, self-indulgers, perpetual victims or martyrs, truly wounded and abused, and so on). We emerge determined and empowered to go on despite these things, or even because of them, scars and all, hoping to correct defects in our behavior flowing from them, longing for an ultimate healing we know lies only in ultimate glory, seeking to be of use and to keep growing in the meantime. We give up the false hope of a healing in this life that would leave us as if we had never been afflicted and defective, knowing that believing we have had *that* kind of healing will only lead us back into the snares from which we have just been delivered. "We claim spiritual progress, not spiritual perfection."[37]

As the dawn breaks, we begin to experience the three "motives which must inspire the second conversion," as Garrigou-Lagrange lays them out: a love for God alone and a desire to be of service; a deep appreciation and contemplation of the mysteries of salvation and the *price* God has paid in the blood of Jesus for our redemption; and a deep love of all our neighbors, a wish they might share in the journey of salvation, and a determination to be of service to that end.[38] These three motives respond to the three signs that marked entrance into the second conversion: first, creation, which we now experience in a loving detachment for God's sake, is given back in love for its salvation/sanctification in the divine economy; second, our scarred (wounded but now healed) selves are given back as vessels of loving service; and third, prayer returns as grateful contemplation of the mysteries of the divine economy and of the light of divine glory now illuminating the world and ourselves.

"After the crisis of betrayal comes illumination."[39] The Easter dawn begins to break—was Peter glad at first? Were the Mary's? Why could they not at first recognize Jesus? Why were Peter, James, and John so bedazzled by the transfigured Jesus, and so confused about what they were supposed to do? Why does Jesus speak to them of the necessity for his suffering on the way down to where an epileptic boy remains to be healed? Some of these mysteries begin to become clear for us as we walk out of the pit and up Mount Tabor. Many scholars have noted the link between the transfiguration and the resurrection, to the point where some have claimed the transfiguration is only a misplaced resurrection appearance. I do not think that, though clearly the three disciples are seeing Jesus proleptically in the light of resurrection glory.[40] But the point of the story, of course, is that we cannot now remain in that splendor but must walk back down into the valley filled with epileptic boys, the building of the commonwealth of God's reign, and ultimately the cross. There is no shortcut, no staying in booths on the mountain. The light we have seen there is now meant to be seen in the midst of the real world, with all its beauty and agony.

It is also important to note that Jesus is not *changed* by the transfiguration. What happens is not transformation but the illumination of Jesus by the light of divine glory, in the power of the Spirit, which reveals to the disciples the truth about who Jesus has been all along.[41] In the same fashion, our own beginning transfiguration in that same light is not a transformation into something else, but the revelation and birthing of our own true selves. In the light of Mount Tabor, what we see first is our own betrayal of our Master, but as our eyes adjust and the light strengthens, we begin to see ourselves and all creation revealed in our true existence as sacramental vessels of the Holy Spirit's presence, and of the economy by which God is making all things well.

For myself, when I am still in what feels like the dark pit, I have always found great comfort in two of George Herbert's magnificent poems: first, "Love bade me welcome," which has helped so many, including Simone Weil, who will appear in a later chapter:

Love (III)

Love bade me welcome: yet my soul drew black,
　　Guilty of dust and sin.
But quick-ey'd Love, observing me grow slack
　　From my first entrance in,
Drew nearer to me, sweetly questioning,
　　If I lacked anything.
A guest, I answer'd, worthy to be here:
　　Love said, You shall be he.
I the unkind, ungrateful? Ah my dear
　　I cannot look on thee/
Love took my hand, and smiling did reply,
　　Who made the eyes but I?
Truth Lord, but I have marr'd them: let my shame
　　Go where it doth deserve/

And know you not, says Love, who bore the blame?
>   My dear, then I will serve.
You must sit down, says Love, and taste my meat:
>   So I did sit and eat.[42]

And also, "The Dawning":

Awake sad heart, whom sorrow ever drowns;
>   Take up thine eyes, which feed on earth;
Unfold thy forehead gathered into frowns:
>   Thy Savior comes, and with him mirth:
>   Awake, awake;
And with a thankful heart his comforts take.
>   But thou dost still lament, and pine, and cry;
>   And feel his death, but not his victory.
Arise sad heart; if thou dost not withstand,
>   Christ's resurrection thine may be:
Do not by hanging down break from the hand,
>   Which as it riseth, raiseth thee:
>   Arise, arise;
And with his burial linen dry thine eyes;
>   Christ left his graveclothes that we, when grief
Draws tears, or blood, not want an handkerchief.[43]

Notes

1. Alan Jones, *Soul Making*, 176.

2. See John of the Cross, *Dark Night* 1.14.5; W. Johnston, *Mystical Theology*, 219.

3. Johnston, *Mystical Theology*, 211–34. See also G. May, *The Dark Night of the Soul*.

4. See previous chapter for a more complete definition of "slack."

5. See below, chap. 24, for a more complete analysis of marriage and similar relationships in the current of transfiguration.

6. Simone Weil, *Waiting for God*, 171–72: "The longing to love the beauty of the world in a human being is essentially the longing for the incarnation. It is mistaken if it thinks it is anything else. The incarnation alone can satisfy it. It is therefore wrong to reproach the mystics, as has been done sometimes, because they use love's language. It is theirs by right. Others only borrow it."

7. Jones, *Soul Making*, 159–84.

8. John of the Cross, *Dark Night* 2.5.1; Johnston, *Mystical Theology*, 220. I have followed Johnston in seeing the first night as that of the senses, active and passive, and the second as that "of the soul," active and passive. An alternative is to see the first night as both active nights, the second as both passive nights. I do not believe this a theoretical difference but an empirical one; that is, in some persons it occurs the way Johnston describes it, in others, the alternative is more accurate. Note that R. Garrigou-Lagrange also sees this transition as a second conversion, marked by the passive night of the senses (*The Three Ages of the Interior Life*, 2.21–64); the use of Catherine of Sienna, Suso, and Tauler is particularly apt.

9. Johnston, *Mystical Theology*, 218.

10. John of the Cross, *Dark Night* 1.1.2; Johnston, *Mystical Theology*, 216–17.

11. See Jones, *Soul Making*, 164; also Eugene Rogers, *After the Spirit*, several chapters on the christological mysteries, 75–207. On apostolic experience, see Garrigou-Lagrange, *Three Ways*, 48–49; Jones, *Soul Making*, 165–66.

12. Garrigou-Lagrange, *Three Ways*, viii.

13. A good and widely available edition is Catherine of Siena, *The Dialogue*.

14. Garrigou-Lagrange, *Three Ways*, 31.

15. Jones, *Soul Making*, 174–81.

16. Garrigou-Lagrange, *Three Ways*, 35; Catherine of Sienna, *Dialogue*, 63; Jones, *Soul Making*, 177.

17. I am grateful to Barbara Hughes for many of the insights in this paragraph.

18. Garrigou-Lagrange, *Three Ways*, 32.

19. U. T. Holmes, *Turning to Christ*, 134.

20. Garrigou-Lagrange, *Three Ways*, 37; Catherine of Sienna, *Dialogue*, chap. 75.

21. Garrigou-Lagrange, *Three Ways*, 32.

22. Garrigou-Lagrange, *Three Ways*, 34. See also p. 76. The reference to mentally challenged children would now be considered unfortunate, of course.

23. Antonio Royo and Jordan Auman, *Christian Perfection*, 230 and n. 8, on how no one in this life is free from at least venial sin. Claims to the contrary usually arise from a simplistic reading of 1 John.

24. Again, see Denys Turner, *The Darkness of God*.

25. Susanne Fincher, *Creating Mandalas*, makes the connection to what she calls "the void" in the great round of healing (pp. 144–83, esp. 153–54).

26. See citations in n. 3. Also, Garrigou-Lagrange, *Three Ways*, 75; and in Christian *Perfection and Contemplation According to St. Thomas Aquinas and St. John of the Cross*, 6; *Three Ages*, 2.21–64, 353–421. In general, Garrigou-Lagrange assigns both active purifications to the work of conversion—the passive night of the senses to the entrance into the illuminative way, and the passive night of the soul to the entrance into the unitive way. He explicitly calls these transitions second and third conversions.

27. Dark Night I, chap. 9; Garrigou-Lagrange, *Three Ways*, 35, see also 75; Jones, *Soul Making*, 178.

28. Thanks to Barbara Hughes for this distinction between two forms of detachment.

29. G. May, *Care of Mind*, 102–12.

30. Graham Greene, *The Portable Graham Greene*, 587; Jones, *Soul Making*, 117–20.

31. Jones, *Soul Making*, 118.

32. The contemporary classic on this question has been Chester P. Michael and Marie C. Norrisey, *Prayer and Temperament*, a largely Jungian account. Anne T. W. Harvey has suggested an alternative approach to "spiritual style" less dependent on the Jungian categories: "Spiritual Style in the Work of Urban T. Holmes and Beyond."

33. Garrigou-Lagrange, *Three Ages*, 1.456–70.

34. Thomas Merton, *Contemplative Prayer*, 88.

35. Jones, *Soul Making*, 179.

36. Jones, *Soul Making*, 179.

37. *Alcoholics Anonymous*, 60; actually, as Albert Outler has shown, both Gregory of Nyssa and John Wesley actually define perfection as a journey of progress. See *John Wesley*, ed. Albert C. Outler (New York: Oxford University Press, 1964), 9f., esp. n. 26.

38. Garrigou-Lagrange, *Three Ways*, 41–47.

39. Jones, *Soul Making*, 179.

40. See the next chapter for a fuller discussion of the exegetical issues.

41. See Rogers, *After the Spirit*, 172–99, for some superb work on the Spirit's role in transfiguration.

42. George Herbert, *The Country Parson, the Temple*, 316.

43. Herbert, *The Temple*, 233.

Second Tidal Current:
Transfigured Dust

I. Charting the Second Tide

18

Transfiguration:
The Second Tidal Current

He who has been set in motion by the Spirit has become an eternal move-ment, a holy creature. For when the Spirit has come to dwell in him, a man receives the dignity of a prophet, of an apostle, of an angel of God, whereas hitherto he was only earth and dust.[1]

The second "movement" or tidal current in the spiritual life, parallel to the stage of illumination or proficiency in Western Christian tradition, is called "trans-figuration" in Eastern Christian theology. This has a number of advantages. First, it reminds us that the light of "illumination" is not a "natural" one, neither some natural light of human reason or spirit, nor some inherent light in the created world of nature, but rather the very glory of God illuminating world and self, as they are also illumined from the inside, as it were, by the Holy Spirit indwelling them. Second, tying this light to a mystery of the life of Jesus grounds it christologically, reminding us that for Christian faith all illumination is not only from God, but through the Incarnate second person of the Trinity, the Eternal Word and Wis-dom of God, who "is the true light which enlightens every one who comes into the world" (John 1:9). It also reminds us that this divine light is not abstract, but has been made flesh in the concrete life, teaching, death, and resurrection of Jesus of Nazareth; as Christians experience it, this light is the glory radiating from the face of Christ (2 Cor 4:6). Third, because the event in question is the transfiguration, which occurs in the midst of Jesus' active ministry, between Peter's confession and the final trip to Jerusalem, it teaches us to look for this light now, in the midst of life, and to wait for resurrection and glorification in our own experience, even though this light anticipates them. Fourth and finally, as noted at the end of the previous chapter, transfiguration is not transformation, not a magical change of something into what it previously was not, but rather the illumination by the light of God's glory of what has always been and remains true.

Scriptural Account

The primary source for this analogy, of course, is the scriptural accounts of the transfiguration itself. If we are to understand this second movement or current of the Holy Spirit in our lives, it will be helpful to pause and look at this biblical mystery. Here, the work of Arthur Michael Ramsey, late archbishop of Canterbury, *The Glory of God and the Transfiguration of Christ,* holds up remarkably well from a theological point of view, even if there is much new to be said from a biblical-critical perspective since he wrote.[2] In the first part of the book, Ramsey gives a careful analysis of the concept of God's glory, *kabod* in Hebrew (and the closely related, but not identical, rabbinic concept of the *shekinah*), and *doxa* in the Greek of both the Septuagint and the Newer Testament. "*Kabod* denotes the revealed being or character of Yahveh, and also a physical phenomenon whereby Yahveh's presence is made known; and scholars have not been agreed as to the priority in time of one or the other of these uses."[3]

To summarize a long development: a concept perhaps originally tied to a storm theophany becomes increasingly universalized. In First Isaiah, the concept of God's glory is linked to holiness and righteousness; Second Isaiah makes clear that this is the glory of the one and only God of the entire universe; and Third Isaiah "pictures Jerusalem as the scene of the shining-forth of the glory of Yahveh to the nations."[4] In the later priestly tradition, the paradox develops that while it is indeed the one universal God who is truly present in the local theophanies of Sinai and the first tabernacle and temple, it seems clear the *kabod* has not again become manifest in the postexilic temples, despite their importance. That remains a future hope. The rabbinic concept of *shekinah*, the dwelling of glory in the cloud over the tabernacle, places further respectful distance between the transcendent God and God's presence in history and covenant community; but the notions of *kabod* and *shekinah* are recombined in the Septuagint use of *doxa*, which then carries over into Christian usage. In the process, one of two original meanings of *doxa* ("opinion") disappears, and the other, "distinction or reputation," is transformed by the link to the concepts of *kabod* and *shekinah* it now translates.[5] At roughly the same time, the relationship of glory to the expected Messiah as the future hope for nation and temple increases, and (though Ramsey does not discuss this), the character of Wisdom also gets stirred into the pot.

All of this conceptual and verbal history becomes, in the Newer Testament, a lens for interpreting the person, life, work, death, and resurrection of Jesus. Of course, the messianic link is obvious, but further reflection would go deeper. In Paul and the Synoptic Gospels the primary emphasis is on the full revelation of the divine glory in the risen, ascended, and eschatological Christ, though as that reflection deepens, it is seen by anticipation in the whole Christ event, from birth through the passion.[6] There is also a growing sense of participation by Christians in this proleptic (anticipatory) reflection of final glory because of their unity with Christ and one another in the Holy Spirit, especially in St. Paul.[7] In the Gospel of John and the subsequent Johannine literature, this presence of glory throughout is paramount, from the Word's participation in creation right through the final consummation.[8] Ultimately, we reach the following pinnacle of Christian faith:

> It is often hard to determine which aspect of the glory is present in a particular passage, and indeed the different aspects melt into one another in the New Testament as in the Old. But in every aspect of the glory the person of Jesus Christ becomes the dominant fact. In so far as *doxa* means the power and character of God, the key to that power and character is found in what God has done in the events of the gospel. In so far as *doxa* is the divine splendour, Jesus Christ *is* that splendour. And in so far as a state of light and radiance awaits the Christian as his final destiny, that light and radiance draw their meaning from the presence and person of Christ. Hence new possibilities of language emerge: such is the place of Jesus Christ in relation to the divine glory that it is possible to speak of *the glory of Christ* and by those words to mean no less than the glory of God Himself.

Ramsey continues with an important reminder to view the divine economy in a holistic manner:

> It follows that the word *doxa* both reflects and expresses the pattern of God in creation, in nature and in the history of Israel; it has as its centre the glory of God in the birth, life, death and exaltation of Jesus, and as its goal the participation of mankind and of all creation in the eschatological glory of the Messiah. Creation, redemption, eschatology form a single pattern; and to separate them is to render each of them unintelligible and to distort the theology of the apostolic age.[9]

Matthew, Mark, and Luke solidly embed this concept of glory in the person and work of Jesus in the midst of the gospel in the story of the transfiguration; it is to that story that Ramsey turns, as shall we, though from a slightly different point of view. The biblical scholar must wrestle with such issues as "Is this mere legend, a misplaced resurrection appearance story, a subjective but historical 'mystical experience' of Jesus and/or the three disciples, or a still more objective event, which is credible if Jesus is indeed the one envisioned in the Christology of the evangelists and other early witnesses."[10] If, as Schubert Ogden asserts throughout *The Point of Christology*, as Ramsey also seems to accept and as I believe, it is this earliest Christology that is the raw material for theology and not a reconstructed "historical Jesus" behind that Christology, then we can prescind from some of these questions.[11]

Perhaps even more clearly than did Ramsey we may now recognize that this story, especially in Mark, is intimately placed in its setting. It is tightly connected to the events at Caesarea Philippi, especially Peter's confession of Jesus as Messiah, by the phrase "after six days." Only in the passion narrative is this temporal exactness duplicated.[12] The link to the events at Caesarea Philippi is even tighter if Ramsey is correct that the historical site is not the traditional Tabor but Mt. Hermon.[13] The theological theme, then, is Jesus' identity, not merely as Elijah or the Prophet, but as Peter confessed, the Messiah, the Christ. The injunction to the three disciples not to tell about the transfiguration duplicates exactly the similar injunction to the twelve after Peter's confession. Once we see the place of the prophecy of the passion that follows each and the clear teaching about both the cost of Jesus' messiahship and that of accepting it, which is intermingled with these prophecies, the import becomes clear. Jesus is acknowledging that he is indeed the Messiah but asks that it be kept quiet since his messiahship is going to be very different from what is expected. In this light, the voice and cloud echo not only the themes from the Older Testament and apocalyptic messianic literature usually cited but also look back to Jesus' anointing as Messiah and Son of God at his Baptism, and perhaps these contrast with the darkness that fell at the time of his death. The appearance of Moses and Elijah do indeed herald the presence of the messianic age and the testimony of the Law and the Prophets to Jesus as the expected one, the new Moses, the Prophet who was to be like Moses and in his succession (as was Elijah);[14] but in this context they appear specifically as confirmation of the prophecies of the passion and the validity of the sort of messiahship Jesus was embodying.

The cloud, voice, and actual transfiguration of Jesus insist he is also, even beyond Messiah, the very Son of God (the point of Mark's Gospel), and the child and embodiment of the Divine Wisdom. Perhaps a parallel to Solomon's prayer in Wisdom 9 is not far-fetched, given that the theme of Booths, or Tabernacles, is about to appear. Indeed, the booths Peter wants to build recall the feast of Tabernacles (just as a new living out of Passover and Pentecost is about to be enacted) and all the themes of the *kabod* of God tabernacling with Israel. As Ramsey notes, following Ernst Lohmeyer and contrary to what is often taught and preached, Peter's remark is far from stupid.[15] In fact, he grasps the theological significance of the event perfectly in terms of the imagery available to him as a Jew. He was wrong only in thinking that the reality of God tabernacling with Israel (and all humanity) in Jesus could be or needed to be made permanent in this way; instead, it was to come to full fruition only through what was yet to come but which had already been prophesied. Jesus' response to the question about Elijah (that John the Baptizer has fulfilled that prophecy) also firmly places his story (and that of his cousin) in the larger context of God's history of presence with the covenant people. That story can never be frozen; it now leads down the mountain to heal an epileptic boy, and soon on to Jerusalem, where the prophecy will come true and Jesus' messiahship will be enacted in his death and affirmed in his resurrection, by which he is indeed declared both Lord and Christ.

The major themes, then, are the continuity of Jesus with the entire previous scriptural and liturgical tradition, the affirmation, nevertheless, of his shocking version of messiahship for this age and in the age to come, and its crowning with the sonship affirmed by the voice, with a possible reference to the embodiment of

Wisdom as well, and the illumination of all this as true by the light of the divine glory itself.

The Tabor Tradition

Early in the formation of the tradition of the Eastern Church, transfiguration became not only a significant celebration of an important event in the life of Jesus but also an important symbol of the nature and goal of the spiritual life. This development reached its peak in the writings of St. Gregory Palamas, fourteenth-century Eastern monk and archbishop and last of the great Byzantine theologians. We shall take him as our guide for this "current" (though he does not distinguish the second and third tidal movements as clearly as we shall try), not in spite of, but precisely because of the manner in which this tradition in Orthodoxy has always made the Western Church nervous.

The main theme of Palamas's writings is grounded in the universal teaching of the Eastern Church (stemming from at least as early as Athanasius) about the significance of the incarnation.[16] John Meyendorff puts it this way: "The living God is accessible to personal experience, because He shared His own life with humanity."[17] This experience includes more than the Western notion of a personal relationship with Jesus. Resonant with other Eastern authors from Athanasius and the Cappadocians through Pseudo-Dionysius or Denys, Pseudo-Macarius, John Climacus, and Symeon the New Theologian, Palamas describes experiencing, in body and mind (but in a manner that transcends both), the light of divine glory itself; the phenomenon is focused on the experience of the transfiguration of Jesus on Tabor, but now illuminating us in a manner transfiguring us into the likeness of Christ, and ultimately deifying us as we come to share in his union with the Father, traditionally called the "hypostatic union" (the union of the divine and human natures in the one hypostasis [person or subsistence] of Jesus Christ). This movement of deification, or *theōsis* in Greek, will be treated later as the essence of the third movement in the spiritual life. The Eastern Orthodox use and theology of icons also grow out of this insight—the gold illumination in them represents the light of Tabor.

Insofar as it is conscious, this experience of illuminating transfiguration is certainly what we would call "mystical," and is easiest to see in the great monastic and contemplative saints; it is not, however, esoteric, reserved to isolated religious geniuses, "but is, in fact, identical with the Christian faith itself, and, therefore, offered to all members of the Church, in virtue of their Baptism."[18] Because our first entry into this experience is often perceived as darkness when we are overwhelmed by it, many Orthodox writers (including Gregory of Nyssa) emphasize the darkness as the core of the experience. For Palamas, the emphasis is all on the light, though he knows of the other: "there remains an unknowing which is beyond knowledge; though indeed a darkness, it is yet beyond radiance, and, as the great Denys says, it is in this dazzling darkness that the divine things are given to the saints."[19]

This is not a generic mystical experience of illumination, but specifically an experience of *Jesus* as the personal presence of the divine light of glory: "for He is

Himself deifying light."[20] The advantage of using the transfiguration for the analogy, rather than a mystical perception of the risen, ascended, and glorified Christ, is that it anchors the picture in the fleshly life of Jesus. One of Palamas's most urgent themes, argued against his Westernized opponent Barlaam, is that this process of transfiguration in us, as in Jesus, is not only in the mind and spirit but also includes the whole person, not leaving out the body.[21] It is on this basis, and the notion of the body as a temple of the Holy Spirit, that Palamas defends the physical practices of the Hesychastic monks,[a] to which he belonged, in such practices as the breath prayer or Jesus prayer, and of including the body in contemplation by "circumscribing the mind in the body," in the prayer of the mind in the heart.[22] This approach suggests that spiritualities that emphasize "out-of-body" experiences are suspect;[23] it links our salvation and sanctification to that of the whole created order through the incarnation; it also moves the goal of impassability or passionlessness (*apatheia*) away from a more rigid and neo-Platonic stoicism.[24] Indeed:

> Impassability does not consist in mortifying the passionate part of the soul, but in removing it from evil to good, and directing its energies towards divine things . . . and the impassible man is one who no longer possesses any evil dispositions, but is rich in good ones. . . .
>
> But if one uses [the powers of the soul] properly, then through the knowledge of created things, spiritually understood, one will arrive at knowledge of God; and through the passionate part of the soul which has been oriented towards the end for which God created it, one will practise the corresponding virtues. . . .[25]

Indeed, without a properly ordered rather than "killed" passionate part of the soul, one would have no momentum for spiritual growth. While this ordering is certainly easier for the monastic contemplative, it is not at all impossible for those who live in the world. "Thus one must offer to God the passionate part of the soul, alive and active, that it may be a living sacrifice."[26]

This reaffirmation of the whole person, of the body, of the healthy and properly ordered passions has a distinctly modern sympathy. But it should by no means be concluded that Palamas thinks there is some natural faculty by which we receive this divine transfiguring light, let alone that it is a natural light itself.[27] Instead, for Palamas it is only by the gift of the indwelling Holy Spirit that we are able to perceive and receive this transfiguring light.[28] One could imagine the first tidal current of the spiritual life as a natural development (though it would still be a mistake to

---

a Hesychasm was a movement in Eastern Orthodox monasticism with possible roots in the Sinai tradition as early as the sixth century, coming to full flower in the monasteries of Mt. Athos by the fourteenth century. The mental and prayer disciplines of these monks were accompanied by physical practices including yoga-like postures and the use of the breath prayer, or Jesus prayer, to aid the practice of "the mind in the heart." The tradition is best known to Westerners through the Russian folk classic *The Way of a Pilgrim; and, The Pilgrim Continues His Way*, translated from the Russian by Olga Savin; foreword by Thomas Hopko (now Boston: Shambhala, 2001). It was made even more popular in J. D. Salinger, *Franny and Zooey* (Boston: Little, Brown, 1961).

do so); but the second and even more the third tide cannot even be *conceived* as anything but sheer grace, specifically the grace of the glorified and transfigured Jesus as Word and Wisdom, seen and apprehended by us only through the indwelling Holy Spirit who also is, in one sense, the divine light radiating from the face of Jesus. There is not even a "natural" faculty by which we are *capable* of receiving this great gift, not even the process of a natural detachment or negation.[29] Instead, the Spirit must by grace create even the capacity in us by her indwelling.

Palamas insists, in another of his major themes, that it is not the divine essence we see, but the divine energies, which are themselves uncreated and hence God, though God transcends them, as he also transcends essence and even godhead, and is thus "God beyond God."[30] This is not the place to examine all the arguments for and against this classic Eastern position, but it is important to probe the meaning being protected: God certainly transcends all our experience of God.[31] Indeed, that will be the theme of our third movement. But that transcendence does not mean that what we experience as immanent in us is not God. We are not experiencing a movement within ourselves that is fully natural, even if enabled by grace, nor some grace that is a quasi substance but not itself God. The spiritual life instead is the experience of the movement and gifts of the very Holy Spirit, who is God, and who transcends any experience we may have of that movement. Both these truths must be protected: that it is truly God moving in us that we experience, and that God transcends anything we apprehend in any experience. If we choose to put it differently from Palamas, we must honor these boundaries.

In a most helpful footnote, Nicholas Gendle points out an important corollary: even the self-transcendence humans experience at this point is not capable of being interpreted as a characteristic of human nature, nor, I would add in contemporary terms, as a naturally occurring structure of human existence. The self-transcendence we experience in ourselves is *evoked* by the transcendence of the immanent God: "The divine light *is* God insofar as he is knowable, yet God remains transcendent even in His self-manifestation, evoking *ecstasis,* self-transcendence, in those to whom he appears."[32] This is the ultimate reason why, in Christian terms, the human experience of self-transcendence cannot by itself be the defining ground of spirituality. It is not a human property at all, properly speaking, but is only evoked by the self-revelation of its transcendent object, friend, and lover. Again, I think this balance is what Karl Rahner is trying to protect in his difficult concept of the "supernatural existential": there is a universal and inescapable characteristic of human *existence*, that of being addressed by, and capable of responding to, the Word of God; but that "existential" is "supernatural" in that it is itself already from God and not an inherent characteristic of either human nature or existence taken in isolation.

From Servant to Friend

Biblical and patristic tradition offers us yet another way of looking at this second movement, or tidal current, of the spirit, especially in transition from the first. It is, in a very real sense, a shift in our vocation, or, perhaps better, a deeper insight into our vocation. It is focused helpfully in Jesus' startling statement in John 15:14, "I no longer call you servants, but friends." In the surrounding material, Jesus gives two very explicit distinctions between the two vocations. A servant merely obeys orders without question. By contrast, what one seeks in a friend is cooperation based on a communion of shared moral purpose. And, as Jesus says, he has told his friends everything the Father has told him. The second difference strikes even deeper: "Greater love has no one than this, to lay down one's life for one's friends." A friend, indeed, only a friend, is someone "to die for." This puts a unique spin on Rom 5:8, "While we were still sinners, Christ died for us." God is our friend before we are ready to be God's friends in return.

Palamas and others, such as Gregory of Nyssa, as we saw at the end of the last chapter, help us to see that the three movements or tidal currents of the Spirit evoke in us three different self-definitional senses of our relationship with God in Christ through the Spirit. In the first movement (the midst of it, once we have begun to respond) we experience ourselves primarily as called to be God's faithful *servant*.[a] In this second tidal current, we experience the great mystery of being called to be God's *friend*. In the third current, we find ourselves called, indeed wooed, to be God's *spouse*. But remembering the nature of the model we are using, that of concurrent currents, to be called to spousehood and friendship does not abandon servanthood—it intensifies it.

There is a strong stream of "friendship theologies" from the past up to some of the most contemporary.[33] There is an important link here to the concept of transfiguration in this second movement. Friendship, *philia*, requires at least a rough equality between the parties to the relationship, as we have known since Aristotle.[34] A free person cannot really be friends with a slave (which Aristotle meant in a manner that could be seen as condescending, but from a Christian point of view is one of the most powerful arguments against slavery); nor can human beings be friends with animal pets. In both cases, what we feel is *storgē*, affection. As we shall see, the spousehood of the third movement also has an erotic component that goes beyond *philia* to a desire for consummation. In the best theologies, these three loves are not over against *agapē* but appropriate forms *agapē* takes in particular relationships.[35]

The friendship between us and God that is evoked in this second movement requires at least the beginnings of a rough equality. As Simone Weil pointed out, it requires a distance that respects the autonomy and freedom of each other.[36] But the necessary equality is not in us—that would be blasphemy. We cannot ignore Karl Barth's warning: nothing a creature does can turn it into its own creator.[37] So the required equality must come from God. Theologians from the Greek Fathers to Søren Kierkegaard have seen the incarnation as itself the God-chosen and given means for this to occur, as God takes on humanity and raises it to divine glory.[38] Indeed, I believe establishing this friendship is the real reason for the incarnation, to which "fixing the sin problem" is only prelude.[39] In a systematic theology, it leads

---

a People in situations of abuse or oppression may experience themselves in this first movement as called first to be God's beloved child. Here the "service" would initially be the work of their own healing and liberation; later, it becomes acting out of self-respect (as opposed to violent self-negation) and helping others to heal.

to a Christology and soteriology of Jesus as the sacrament of the friendship between God and humanity, as in his person and work he manifests the friendliness of God while making it possible for humans to grow into their vocation of "friends of God."

As William Porcher DuBose so often points out, however, it is not enough that this be externally so in Jesus.[40] Both incarnation and atonement must also become real in us if God's purposes for the covenant commonwealth are to be realized. The budding equality/friendship between humanity and God is gifted to us in the transfiguration, as we are illuminated by the same light of divine glory as Jesus, because we are friends of that Jesus who turns out to be that very glory and light itself, in partnership with the Holy Spirit. To be in Christ is to be God's friend, as what was localized in Jesus becomes a universal offer in the outpouring of the Holy Spirit in the (re)new(ed) covenant.

What This Means

On the devotional side of spirituality, this suggests that the life shaped by a primacy of the second tidal current can be conceived as cultivating friendship with Jesus. Through prayer, meditation on the Gospels, and especially in the Eucharist, the sacrament in which we share table fellowship with our risen friend and rabbi (and also, as we shall see later, participate in the messianic banquet, the supper of the Lamb), we enjoy his presence and our relationship to him (and through him, with God) even as we are evermore deeply recruited into that moral communion where we share his purposes for the reign, the covenant commonwealth. We are called in friendship with God, through the mystery of transfiguration, to nothing less than a "praxis of the incarnation," co-working with God by the power of the Holy Spirit to make the flesh of Jesus ever present in our flesh and in the matter of the world as we look in hope toward the fulfillment of the commonwealth of God's reign. Indeed, all the virtues now become not so much matters of moral reform as the habitual discipline of friendship with God in the flesh of Jesus; the dominant theological virtue here (remembering the Trinitarian logic that governs these virtues, however) is love, as in our persons and our work we act under grace as if the commonwealth for which we hope were already fully realized in the outpouring of God's love in the present, through the Spirit whose proper name is "Love" and "Gift." This is the awesome nature of seeking to grow into that maturity measured only by the stature of Christ, the awesome nature of the "proficiency" that is to characterize this tide of the Spirit.

This means that theologically speaking we are in the mode David Tracy calls "manifestation." The mode of human self-transcendence (still evoked by the self-transcendence of God) is self-fulfillment. While our present culture has all too often given this a shallow "bootstrap" (and hence Pelagian) meaning, it need not be so. In the mode of manifestation and governed by the dynamics of transfiguration, "self-fulfillment" no longer means the self fulfilling *itself*, nor even primarily, having its own natural capacities fulfilled. Instead, it means celebrating the Divine

Wisdom and Word in all things and ourselves, and, more deeply, beginning to see and celebrate ourselves and all things in the Logos/Sophia, which we can now see by the light of Tabor. As F. D. Maurice says, "The Transfiguration has lived on through ages and shed its light upon all ages. . . . In the light of that countenance which was altered, of that raiment which was white and glistening, all human countenances have acquired a brightness, all common things have been transfigured."[41]

Ramsey specifies three transfigurations in Christian experience that manifest the glory in the transfiguration of Jesus. First, our suffering is transfigured by the suffering of Jesus on the cross. Second, knowledge of the world is transfigured from "the service of man's pride and man's destruction . . . for the unfolding of God's truth and the enlarging of God's worship." Third, the world itself is transfigured as the historic arena of divine judgment and divine renewal.[42] The transfiguration of pain, the transfiguration of knowledge, the transfiguration of work—to this we shall add one more—the transfiguration of relationships and community as the indelible link between love of neighbor and love of God becomes manifest in the quest for the just commonwealth of God's reign. This link is not abstract, of course, but the very third person of the Trinity herself.

In subsequent chapters we shall explore this current of transfiguration in the modes of manifestation and self-fulfillment by examining Simone Weil's teaching on the forms of the implicit love of God: affliction and justice, the order and beauty of the world, religious practices, and love of neighbor consummated in friendship. But before leaving the larger picture, we must note with Ramsey, himself borrowing insight from C. H. Dodd, the particular relevance to our postmodern time of the *attitude* of transfiguration as defined by Arnold Toynbee:

> Analysing the possibilities open to those who are aware they live in a "declining civilization" Dr. Toynbee distinguishes four principles: archaism, futurism, detachment, transfiguration. *Archaism* is the yearning for a past golden age; futurism is a phantasy of a new age utterly unrelated to that which now exists, and the quest of it is often pursued by violent means; detachment (for which "escapism" would be a better word, since Christians know detachment in a good sense) is escape into contemplation;[43] but *transfiguration* is a faith whereby "we bring the total situation, as we ourselves participate in it, into a larger context which gives it new meaning."[44]

In a paragraph that anticipates H. Richard Niebuhr's *Christ and Culture* that would follow three years later, Ramsey insists on the peculiar relevance of transfiguration for our time in words that still call our shallow liberal-conservative analysis into question:

> Confronted as he is with a universe more than ever terrible in the blindness of its processes and the destructiveness of its potentialities mankind must be led to the Christian faith not as a panacea of progress nor as an other-worldly solution unrelated to history, but as a gospel of Transfigura-

tion. Such a gospel both transcends the world and speaks to the immediate here-and-now. He who is transfigured is the Son of Man; and, as He discloses on mount Hermon another world, he reveals that no part of created things and no moment of created time lies outside the power of the Spirit, who is Lord, to change from glory into glory.[45]

Jesus is the personal event by which God condescends to us, and his flesh is the door by which we ascend to God. The Holy Spirit is thus, finally and especially in the third current, the "means" of *theōsis*, the mediation of that of which Jesus is the mediator.[46] But the Holy Spirit's first act is not *theōsis* as such. We are not taken directly into participation in God's nature and glory, but first converted and then transfigured in a manner that heals and then illuminates our human createdness and earthly history with the glory of God radiating from the face of Christ. This means our creatureliness and history are not left behind in *theōsis* any more than the flesh of Jesus is left behind in his final glorification. Rather, the very path to *theōsis* passes through the illumination of animated and converted dust with the light of glory. In the meantime, there is work to do and life to enjoy.

The remaining task of the commentary on this "movement" or tidal current of the Spirit is dedicated to spelling out what this manifestation looks like in concrete terms. How are our true selves fulfilled through illumination by the light of Tabor? How is that light manifested in the world, and how are our lives to be shaped around our perception of that light illuminating the world as it and we tremble on the threshold of being changed from glory into glory? Before we examine the way these questions are played out in "the forms of the implicit love of God" in Simone Weil, we pause briefly to spend some time with one of the great apostles of dust illumined by glory, Pierre Teilhard de Chardin.

Notes

1. Pseudo-Basil, *c. Eun.*, 5, PG 30:769 B; cited in Gregory Palamas, *Triads*, III, i, 36, *Gregory Palamas, the Triads*; gendered language of the translation left unaltered.

2. Arthur Michael Ramsey, *The Glory of God and the Transfiguration of Christ*. See now Dorothy Lee, *Transfiguration*, esp. 122–38, where she gives her theological conclusions, which are highly compatible with the approach taken here; also John Paul Heil, *The Transfiguration of Jesus*. See also Christopher Bryan, *A Preface to Mark*, 101–2.

3. Ramsey, *Glory of God*, 10.

4. Ramsey, *Glory of God*, 14.

5. Ramsey, *Glory of God*, 23ff.

6. Ramsey, *Glory of God*, 29–45. Matthew and Luke both see the glory anticipated in Jesus' birth, while Luke traces it back even to his conception in the mystery of the Annunciation. See also Eugene Rogers, *After the Spirit*, 172–99, for a brilliant discussion of the role of the Holy Spirit at this point, and an account of the theological consequences very much in harmony with the approach here and in subsequent chapters; see esp. 172 for transfiguration as the work of the Spirit.

7. Ramsey, *Glory of God*, 46–56.

8. Ramsey, *Glory of God*, 57–81.

9. Ramsey, *Glory of God*, 28.

10. There is really no reason to assert the "mere legend," as would many "Jesus Seminar" members, unless one had already decided, which most of them have, on what are actually (I think bad) theological grounds that Jesus cannot have been the sort of person to whom such things happened, so that all miraculous and unusual events are excluded from historical reality. The misplaced-resurrection-appearance view was commonly held by early form critics and is well discounted by Ramsey, but later and thoroughly by C. H. Dodd, in "The Appearances of the Risen Christ," 121–22; see also Adela Yarbro Collins, *Mark*, 417–27; the connection is there of course—the glory glimpsed on Tabor becomes more fully manifest at Jesus' resurrection and will be fully revealed at the *parousia*. The subjective view was apparently espoused by Evelyn Underhill, who sees it as principally a vision of the disciples, and Ramsey has some sympathy for it, though he opts in the end for a more objective view of a Maisie Spens, who argued it was also part of Jesus' experience (Ramsey, *Glory*, 106–8).

11. Schubert Ogden, *The Point of Christology*; Ramsey, *Glory of God*, 106.

12. Noted in Ramsey, but now more clearly in Christopher Bryan, *A Preface to Mark*, 101–2.

13. Ramsey, *Glory of God*, 113.

14. Ramsey, *Glory of God*, 114–15; see Christopher Bryan, "The New Moses and the Heavenly Man"; and Dale C. Allison, Jr., *The New Moses*.

15. Ramsey, *Glory of God*, 110, referring to Ernst Lohmeyer's *Gospel of Mark*.

16. Alvyn Pettersen, *Athanasius*, 109–35.

17. *Gregory Palamas, The Triads*, 1.

18. *Gregory Palamas*, ed. John Meyendorff, 8. Note agreement with Kenneth Kirk and the analysis of de Certeau in chapter 2 above.

19. *Triads* I, iii, 18, *Gregory Palamas*, ed. Meyendorff, 36.

20. *Triads* I, iii, 5, *Gregory Palamas*, ed. Meyendorff, 33.

21. *Gregory Palamas*, ed. Meyendorff, 6.

22. For this whole paragraph, see *Triads* I, ii; *Gregory Palamas*, ed. Meyendorff, 41ff.

23. *Gregory Palamas*, ed. Meyendorff, 44.

24. *Gregory Palamas*, ed. Meyendorff, 41–42, 50–52.

25. *Gregory Palamas*, ed. Meyendorff, 51.

26. *Gregory Palamas*, ed. Meyendorff, 55, see also 111.

27. *Triads* III, i, 26–27; *Gregory Palamas*, ed. Meyendorff, 82–83.

28. *Triads*, I, iii, 17–18; *Gregory Palamas*, ed. Meyendorff, 34–35, also 37–38.

29. *Gregory Palamas*, ed. Meyendorff, 34–36.

30. See *Gregory Palamas*, ed. Meyendorff, 93–111, and 20–22.

31. Robert Jenson, for example, believes Palamas is absolutely correct in asserting that that vision of God includes our physical (if transfigured) eyes, but sees the doctrine of God's ultimate unknowability, even in God's self-revelation, as the disaster of Orthodox theology. *ST* 2.358, 342–45; *ST* 2.152–53.

32. *Gregory Palamas*, ed. Meyendorff, 131 n. 6.

33. We have already looked at Gregory of Nyssa and Gregory Palamas. See also R. Garrigou-Lagrange, *Three Ways*, 38–39, with reference to Catherine of Sienna, *Dialogues*, 60. The late medieval Western tradition of "the Friends of God" was expressed in the text by the unknown "Franckforter," possibly a fourteenth-century member of one of the military monastic orders, that came to be known as the *Theologia Deutsch* or *Theologia Germanica*, a work later approvingly translated and used by Martin Luther. On a more contemporary front, this is a central theme of Herbert W. Richardson, *Towards an American Theology* (New York: Harper & Row, 1967), and it is from Richardson, as my teacher, that I first became aware of the importance of this concept. It is also an important theme in Sallie McFague's works, including *Metaphorical Theology* and *Models of God*. See also Elizabeth A. Johnson, *Friends of God and Prophets*.

34. Aristotle, *Nicomachean Ethics*, VIII and IX (McKeon ed., 1058–93); and Cicero *De Amicitia*; Simone Weil, *Waiting for God*, 204.

35. The classic text is, of course, C. S. Lewis, *The Four Loves*.

36. Weil, *Waiting for God*, 204-5; see 214–15 for the source of "something of equality" between us and God in precisely "liberty of consent."

37. See Karl Barth, *CD* 3.3.49.3, 159. The whole section (154ff.) would seem to be relevant.

38. From Athanasius's treatise on "The Incarnation of the Word" to Søren Kierkegaard's *Philosophical Fragments*, again the parable of the king and the beggar woman, 32–43. See also the essays in *Theōsis: Deification in Christian Theology*, ed. Stephen Finlan and Vladimir Kharlamov.

39. Again, I wish to acknowledge having first learned this from Herbert W. Richardson, and it is a dominant theme in his *Towards an American Theology*.

40. William Porcher DuBose, *Reader*, xxxi, citing *High Priesthood and Sacrifice*, 161, 217.

41. *The Gospel of the Kingdom of Heaven*, 157, quoted by Ramsey, *Glory of God*, 144–45.

42. Ramsey, *Glory of God*, 145.

43. The infused contemplation that begins in this current and is consummated in the next is indeed escapist if we seek it only in the self, or without reference to kerygma and manifestation. Indeed, it is not to be sought in itself at all but only as a byproduct of yearning for God.

44. Ramsey, *Glory of God*, 146.

45. Ramsey, *Glory of God*, 147; H. R. Niebuhr, *Christ and Culture*.

46. Kilian McDonnell, *Other Hand of God*, 104ff.

19

The Divine Milieu: Hunting the Manifest in Teilhard de Chardin

Today it is not nearly enough to be a saint, but we must have the saintliness demanded by the present moment, a new saintliness, itself also without precedent . . . [capable of blending the love of God] and filial piety for the city of the world, for the country here below which is the universe.[1]
— Simone Weil

. . . by virtue of the Creation and, still more, of the Incarnation, nothing here below is profane for those who know how to see.[2]
— Pierre Teilhard de Chardin

We seek, then, to trace the tidal current of the second movement of the Spirit, the transfiguration of the world and ourselves, the illumination of beloved dust by the light of that divine glory that is one of the uncreated energies of God. We seek it as manifest, as shining forth in the *via positiva;* and, as children of our time, we seek it not in a Manichaean dualism opposing matter to spirit but looking for a new holiness in which love of God and love of earth are not merely compatible but inescapably intertwined. In finding a contemporary understanding of transfiguration and manifestation we may take as our guides two great exponents of such a new saintliness, both "liminal" French "saints," Pierre Teilhard de Chardin and Simone Weil. Both are liminal saints in the sense that they dwelt on the boundaries of the Christian community, both geographically and intellectually (Weil more clearly so than Teilhard); certainly neither has been officially recognized as a saint in the technical sense. Each, however, was possessed by a vision of the immanence of God in the world, manifest as transfiguring illumination of life and creation; each was determined to convey this passion in ways honoring both the gospel and the Catholic faith on the one hand, and the best of secular wisdom on the other; both have proved immensely attractive to many like themselves on the edges or outside of the Christian community. Despite flaws, their works bid fair to become Christian classics of our time.

Our first liminal saint, Pierre Teilhard de Chardin, was, at one level, more centrally located in the church. He was, after all, a priest and a Jesuit. His scholarly vocation as a paleontologist, however, committed him to loyalties and ideas that at the time seemed to conflict with Catholic orthodoxy.

He was born May 1, 1881, in Sarcenat (Orcines, Puy de Dôme), France, and prepared at the Jesuit College of Mongré, entering the Society of Jesus in 1899. After the usual philosophical and theological studies, he was ordained in 1911, and, in 1912, began his study of paleontology at the Museum of Paris. His studies were interrupted by serving as a stretcher bearer in World War I, but he took his doctorate at the Sorbonne in 1922. Most of his professional life was spent in China as a consultant to the Geological Survey, simply as a working scientist. He participated in the discovery of *Sinanthropus* ("Peking Man"). From 1946 until his death on Easter day 1955, he spent time in France and New York developing his scientific/philosophical/theological anthropology and cosmology in works published mostly after his death. Because of their mixed type, these profound works have raised both adulation and critique in all three academic areas, including a *monitum* from the Holy Office in 1962 warning not to adopt all his theories uncritically. But even his critics acknowledge he played a profound role in the shift in Catholic consciousness that led to Vatican II.[3]

This tension between what seemed two worlds, the theological and the scientific, the City of God and the City of the Earth, was "resolved" for him in a growing vision of the presence of God in the earth, loving it, sanctifying it, divinizing it. He gained a mystic's vision of "holy matter," recorded for us in a variety of texts.[4] He reflected on all his knowledge in a series of works, which, as we have noted, are not science, theology, or philosophy in separation, but rather a coherent vision informed by all three. And, in one classic text, *The Divine Milieu*, he spelled out the implications of that vision for spiritual life in our time. The work is written neither for the wholly unconverted nor for the firmly established Christian, but for "the waverers, both inside and outside. . . ." It seeks to answer the dilemma of "those whose education or instinct leads them to listen primarily to the voices of the earth, [and hence] have a certain fear that they may be false to themselves if they simply follow the Gospel path."[5] Three paths of resolving this tension he rejects: abandoning and rejecting the world to focus only on the religious and spiritual; abandoning the counsels of spiritual perfection to seek to lead what seems "a complete and human life"; or simply and most commonly, giving up the struggle, and seeming to serve two masters without belonging wholly to either, leading a double life.[6] He concludes:

> There is, without possible doubt, a fourth way out of the problem: it consists in seeing how, without making the smallest concession to "nature" but with a desire for greater perfection, we can reconcile, and provide mutual nourishment for, the love of God and a healthy love of the world, a striving towards detachment and a striving towards development.[7]

Teilhard proceeds, in a manner fully consistent with his Jesuit heritage of "contemplation in action," to delineate a psychology and theology of the spiritual life in this mode of transfiguration/manifestation;[8] he does so by looking at two aspects of human existence, what we do, or our activities, and what we undergo, or our passivities, and finding each to be "full of God." In sketching our own map, we shall first look at Teilhard's concept of "The Divinisation of Our Activities," and, on that basis, examine, in the next chapter, some finer detail in Weil's four forms of the implicit love of God. Next, we shall look at some traditional topics that belong here—love of neighbor and study, contemplation of the beauty of the world, vocation and work; religious practices, especially sacraments and other positive means of grace, and the usual forms of active prayer; and finally what is tradition-ally called "states of life," but is now better seen as intimacy and sociality ordered to sanctification. Then, we shall turn to the darker side, a side less often given full and adequate attention in this mode: the divinization of our passivities, what we undergo. This will provide us with the start of the second transitional "dark night," which is the bridge to our consideration of the third tidal movement, glorification itself, the movement of union.

The Transfiguration of Our Activities

What we have called transfiguration, Teilhard calls divinization—since what he means is not yet full *theōsis*. As we have seen, he makes the explicit connection to the transfiguration, and, as in Gregory Palamas, the line between transfiguration and *theōsis* is not clear. This transfiguration in which we find all things full of God should not be seen as the illumination of our lives and the world by divine glory, as it were by a spotlight shining from the outside on them; it is rather the mani-festation of God present in and to them as they are illuminated from within. The presence of God the Holy Spirit, the interior illumination by divine glory, and the shining forth of the true nature or character of things and persons form a whole we have seen focused in the light of Tabor, the light radiating from the face of Christ in the mystery of the transfiguration. We might also note here that, consistent with the French piety that formed him, Teilhard is very Christocentric, making no clear distinction between Christ and the Holy Spirit, and, indeed, when he uses the word *esprit*, he usually means the human spirit.[9]

Teilhard begins with a problem: in what sense is the committed Christian committed also to an earthly vocation? Is the commitment to the latter whole-hearted or only provisional? What does it mean to say, "the general influence and practice of the church has always been to dignify, ennoble, and transfigure in God the duties inherent in one's station in life, the search for natural truth, and the development of human action"? First, he rejects one easy solution—that our earthly work is blessed by the obediential intention with which we do it, an intention that will find its meaning and fulfillment in another realm. In spite of the truth in this position—the initial and basic role of intention—this is not enough for Teilhard:

> The divinisation of our endeavour by the value of the intention put into it infuses a precious soul into all our actions; but *it does not confer the hope of resurrection upon their bodies.* Yet that hope is what we need if our joy

is to be complete. It is certainly a very great thing to be able to think that, if we love God, something of our inner activity, of our *operatio*, will never be lost. But will not the work itself of our minds, of our hearts, of our hands—that is to say, our achievements, our products, our *opus*—will not this, too, in some sense be "eternalised" and saved?[10]

Teilhard's solution is a syllogism, cast in soul-language not too difficult to translate into the terms I have offered of soul as a relational term between the body of dust and the Holy Spirit:

Major premise: "At the heart of our universe, each soul exists for God, in our Lord." Here Teilhard traces the precise links between the Incarnate Word and us. These links are communal, since the *pleroma*, the fulfillment of all things in Christ, is also the communion of saints. He already finds in "the strengthening and puri-fication of the reality and urgency contained in the most powerful connections revealed to us in every order of the physical and human world" the reality of mysti-cal union: "by virtue of the powerful Incarnation of the Word, our soul is wholly dedicated to Christ and centered upon Him."[11]

Minor premise: "But all reality, even material reality, around each one of us, exists for our souls." I would say, for the nurturing of the relationship of the dust-we-are to God through the Spirit of God. But the conclusion is impeccable: our fulfillment in relationship to God, the self-fulfillment/self-actualization that is the mode of self-transcendence in the movement of manifestation, does not lie else-where, but in the earth and our earthly life:

> We hardly know in what proportions and under what guise our natural faculties will pass over into the final act of the divine vision. But it can hardly be doubted that, with God's help, it is here below that we give our-selves the eyes and the heart that a final transfiguration will transmute into organs of a capacity for adoration and beatification special to each one of us.[12]

Although Teilhard is in many senses a modernist, he adumbrates in his argument the postmodern sense of self as relational:

> . . . we must not forget that the human soul, however independently cre-ated our philosophy imagines it to be, is inseparable, in its birth and in its growth, from the universe into which it is born. In each soul, God loves and partly saves the whole world which that soul sums up in an incom-municable and particular way.[13]

This truth, this summing up or synthesis of self-world-God, is not given from the start.

> It is we who, through our own activity, must industriously assemble the scattered elements. . . .
> Thus every man, in the course of his life, must not only show himself obedient and docile. By his fidelity he must *construct*—starting from the

most natural zone of his own self—a work, an *opus*, into which something enters from all the elements of the earth. *He must make his own soul*
throughout all his earthly days; and at the same time, he collaborates in
another work, in another *opus*, which infinitely transcends, while at the
same time it narrowly determines, the perspectives of individual achievement: the completion of the world. . . . Beneath our individual strivings
towards spiritualisation, the world slowly accumulates, starting with the
whole of matter, that which will make of it the heavenly Jerusalem or the
New Earth.[14]

The conclusion of the syllogism is: ". . . all sensible reality, around each one of
us, exists, through our souls, for God in our Lord."[15] Here we reach Teilhard's great
"organic" vision, that "everything forms a single whole."[16]

. . . the power of the Incarnate Word penetrates matter itself; it descends
into the deepest depths of the inferior forces. And the Incarnation will
be complete only when the part of chosen substance contained in every
object—spiritualised first of all in our souls and a second time with our
souls in Jesus—has rejoined the final Centre of its completion. . . .
    It is through the collaboration which He stimulates in us that Christ,
starting from *all* created things, is consummated.[17]

Teilhard here and elsewhere can still sound a bit Manichaean, though he is at
some pains to purge Christian thought of the very Manichaean flaw we have previously identified. If the above paragraph and others like it are given a substantial
reading—that there is some peculiarly spiritual element in each bit of matter that
is somehow saved and transfigured by the process of Christogenesis, the problem
remains. But if, as I have suggested, we treat it relationally, there is no such problem.
All matter, including the dust-we-are, is saved, transfigured, spiritualized because
of its relationship to God in Christ through incarnation and consummation in the
final commonwealth, all as the work of the Holy Spirit. There need be no introduction of occult metaphysical properties—there is still only matter and the Spirit; and
matter is holy matter only because it is indwelt to its greatest depth and built into
the history of the New Jerusalem.
    Because of the incarnation and the intended consummation, "Each one of our
works, by its more or less remote or direct repercussion upon the spiritual world,
contributes to the perfect Christ in His mystical totality." Teilhard's great passion
is satisfied: not merely our intention, but our work itself is saved and transfigured
—all work. Not by importing some purpose above and beyond the work itself, but
in the very "will to succeed, a certain passionate delight in the work to be done."[18]
Thus, in our work, precisely by immersing ourselves fully in it, not by a divided
mind in which we also contemplate "higher things," "we have the utter joy of discovering His presence once again." This is also the crowning fruit of the mode of
self-transcendence appropriate to this movement, namely, self-fulfillment or self-

actualization. Just as later one word to the Christian will be, "First, develop yourself,"[19] so also here:

> Hence, whatever our human function may be, whether artist or working-man or scholar, we can, if we are Christians, speed towards the object of our work as though towards an outlet open on the supreme fulfillment of our beings.[20]

In all this, an awesome collaboration is established in which our work is God's work and our means of both self-fulfillment and sanctification. We are indeed illumined, but by a light which is interior, not just to us, but also to all things, even though it is the light of divine glory and not a ghostly property of things or ourselves. As a result, God does not distract our gaze from our actual work to another realm. The divine illumination does not blur the details of our earthly work. Again, it is worth quoting Teilhard's own words at some length to convey his vision, since this truth is something that must be *seen*:

> God, in all that is most living and incarnate in Him, is not withdrawn from us beyond the tangible sphere; He is waiting for us at every moment in our action, in our work of the moment. He is in some sort at the tip of my pen, my spade, my brush, my needle—of my heart and of my thought. By pressing the stroke, the line, or the stitch, on which I am engaged, to its ultimate natural finish, I shall arrive at the ultimate aim towards which my innermost will tends. Like those formidable physical forces which man contrives to discipline so as to make them perform operations of prodigious delicacy, so the tremendous power of the divine attraction is focused on our frail desires and microscopic intents without breaking their point. It sur-animates;[a] hence it neither disturbs anything nor stifles anything. It sur-animates; hence it introduces a higher principle of unity into our spiritual life, the specific effect of which is—depending upon the point of view one adopts—either to sanctify human endeavour or to humanise the Christian life.[21]

Teilhard then proceeds to develop both perspectives. One can already see from what has been said that human endeavor is sanctified, indeed is the very means of sanctification through the duties of our station in life.[22] Teilhard exhorts Christians to "continue to immerse yourself in God":

> If your work is dull or exhausting, take refuge in the inexhaustible and becalming interest of progressing in the divine life. If your work enthralls you, then allow the spiritual impulse which matter communicates to you

---

a This notion of sur-animation is one of Teilhard's crucial concepts. The Spirit animates and indwells from below, from within, in full union with the created nature and character of things, not as something foreign imposed from without. For the Spirit is Lord and life-giver.

to enter into your taste for God whom you know better and desire more under the veil of His works. Never, at any time "whether eating or drinking," consent to do anything without first of all realising its significance and constructive value *in Christo Jesu,* and pursuing it with all your might. This is not simply a commonplace precept for salvation: it is the very path to sanctity for each man according to his state and calling. . . . [23] Right from the hands that knead the dough, to those that consecrate it, the great and universal Host[24] should be prepared and handled in a spirit of *adoration.*

The second perspective, the humanization of Christian endeavor, is necessary to counter the charge that Christianity, through its teaching of detachment, makes its adherents inhuman, that it renders them only half committed to human tasks, that it "creates deserters and false friends."[25] Any time this is true of Christians, Teilhard declares, they have not understood what has just been said about the sanctifying character of human work as such. Here, he bears his own personal testimony to his secular colleagues:

As though for us as for you, indeed far more than for you, it were not a matter of life and death that the earth should flourish to the uttermost of its natural powers. As far as you are concerned (and it is here that you are not yet human enough, you do not *go to the limits* of your humanity) it is simply a matter of the success or failure of a reality which remains vague and precarious even when conceived in the form of some super-humanity. For us it is a question in a true sense of achieving the victory of no less than a God.[26]

He continues:

As much as you, and even better than you (because of the two of us, I alone am in a position to prolong these perspectives of my endeavour to infinity, in conformity with the requirements of my present intention) I want to dedicate myself body and soul to the sacred duty of research. We must test every barrier, try every path, plumb every abyss. *Nihil intentatum* [Nothing ventured]. . . . the Incarnate God did not come to diminish the magnificent responsibility and splendid ambition that is ours: *of becoming our own self.* Once again, *non minuit sed sacravit.* [He did not lessen, but sanctified.][27]

I have dwelt with Teilhard at such length on this topic because it is crucial to what follows. When, in the next chapter, we turn our attention to Weil's account of the forms of the implicit love of God, we must see them as truly *implicit,* as the discovery of a God we can love and who loves us in the very warp and woof of things, not as an imported foreign element distracting us from this life. We must have this perspective as we turn to consider states of life, means of grace, forms of prayer, all the usual topics of this part of the spiritual theology syllabus, or we shall fall back into that Manichaean dualism that makes double-minded Christians a scandal to the honest doubters in a world of humanity come of age. Even now, this perspective is far from having won the day in Christian circles. In particular, in academic and other research circles, the principle of academic freedom is demanded, an open search for truth with an open mind in an open society. Only the most minimal and necessary prudential limits on this freedom of inquiry, those that protect the learning environment itself, can be imposed, or we betray the true Christian vision and increase the scandal. Above all, perhaps, we must maintain this perspective here, or we shall totally misunderstand the third movement and tidal current that follows.

The Transfiguration of Our Passivities

Even at this point, Teilhard notes, "we are still only half way along the road which leads to the mountain of the Transfiguration."[28] We have only looked at the divinization of our active lives—we must still examine the passivities of growth and diminishment, which Teilhard does subsequently, and we shall also at the conclusion of this current as it moves into the second "slack," or dark night. And there, as Teilhard says, "the arms of the Cross will begin to dominate the scene more widely." But there is one more element that must be identified here, the true and deep renunciation and detachment that lie at the very heart of a sanctified human endeavor or humanized Christian endeavor, the essence of detachment through action which is the ground of the Ignatian practice of contemplation in action: "... there is nothing so distinctly human in the Christian . . . as his detachment."

There are three sources of, or dimensions to, this detachment through action. First, there is an endless call to self-transcendence in the creative act itself:

> To create, or organise material energy, or truth, or beauty, brings with it an inner torment which prevents those who face its hazards from sinking into the quiet and closed-in life wherein grows the vice of egoism and attachment. An honest workman not only surrenders his tranquility and peace once and for all, but must learn to abandon over and over again the form which his labour or art or thought first took, and go in search of new forms. To pause, so as to enjoy or possess results, would be a betrayal of action. Over and over again he must transcend himself, tear himself away from himself, leaving behind him his most cherished beginnings.[29]

That is, at the very heart of human endeavor, of both self-making and "external" work, there is an implicit structure that rubs our noses in the inescapable fact that self-fulfillment and dedication to work are both forms of self-*transcendence* at every moment of this tidal current. Indeed, self-actualization or fulfillment degenerates into the narcissism of shallow and self-congratulatory self-help precisely when this drive to self-transcendence, which is inherent in them as their true character, is covered over and ignored. Also, in the theology presented here, this self-transcendence, like all other, is evoked in us by the self-transcendence of the divine other through the approach and indwelling of the Spirit. Thus, all true human work is a field of inevitable encounter with the Holy Spirit.

The second source of detachment is the realization that this renunciation behind self-transcendence in work is not merely the placing of a new object in front of an old, but an enfolding of ourselves and our work in the "marvelous mounting force contained in things." This is a further expression of Teilhard's great vision that the whole universe in all its elements is moving from the Alpha of creation to the Omega of consummation by a mighty evolution of Ontogenesis and Christogenesis. He discusses this in the section on "the spiritual power of matter," and it is the essence of his other works such as *Mass on the Earth* and the *Phenomenon of Man* (which we would now certainly translate as "the human phenomenon").[30] That is, the principle of self-transcendence as a structure to creative work resonates with a principle of upward evolution in the very stuff with which we work, so that we strive not just for the new but for the "higher ideal."

These first two principles of renunciation are so implicit in self-making, creation, and work as such that all are called to them, regardless of theological vision. The third requires a Christian, or at least a theistic, seeing:

> It is God and God alone whom he [the Christian] pursues through the reality of created things. For him, interest lies truly *in* things, but in absolute dependence upon God's presence in them. The light of heaven becomes tangible and attainable to him through the crystal of beings. But he wants only this light, and if the light is extinguished, whether because the object is displaced, surpassed, or displaces itself, then even the most precious substance is only ashes in his sight. So that in himself and in his most personal development, it is not himself that he is seeking, but that which is greater than he, to which he knows he is destined. In his own view he himself no longer counts, no longer exists; he has forgotten himself in the very endeavour which is making him perfect. It is no longer the atom which lives, but the universe within it.[31]

It is vital to be clear here. This is not the false renunciation that comes from a dualism where matter and flesh are opposed to spirit. It is not even the same as the renunciation called for in the previous penitential current of conversion. It is rather a detachment that comes precisely from loving things perfectly in our work, from actualizing ourselves toward perfection of our true selves. It is a detachment implicit in the very heart of transfiguration and manifestation, of the *via positiva*. Self-fulfillment is only complete when we give up being in love with our own enlightenment and plunge into the ecstasy of falling wholly in love with the light, one of the many names of the Holy Spirit.

As we celebrate the tangibility of this light in the crystal of beings, we can now turn to appreciate some finer detail in Simone Weil's account of the forms of the implicit love of God.

Notes

1. Simone Weil, "Last Thoughts," in *Waiting for God*, 99, second half, 175; see *Waiting for God*, 8, where Leslie Fiedler makes the connection.

2. Pierre Teilhard de Chardin, *The Divine Milieu*, 35.

3. For helpful accounts of Teilhard's life, the relationship between his scientific work and his spiritual theology, and a judicious evaluation of his influence, see now Thomas M. King, S.J., *Teilhard's Mass*; the article by Boné in *NCE* 13, 977–78 also provides the facts and a judicious evaluation.

4. A complete bibliography with standard abbreviations is now available in King, *Teilhard's Mass*, 169–70. Particularly relevant for our purposes are "The Mass on the World," and "Hymn of the Universe."

5. Teilhard, *Divine Milieu*, 11.

6. Teilhard, *Divine Milieu*, 20–21.

7. Teilhard, *Divine Milieu*, 21.

8. See, for example, Teilhard, *Divine Milieu*, 40, for transfiguration.

9. King, *Teilhard's Mass*, 60.

10. Teilhard, *Divine Milieu*, 23.

11. Teilhard, *Divine Milieu*, 26.

12. Teilhard, *Divine Milieu*, 29.

13. Teilhard, *Divine Milieu*, 29.

14. Teilhard, *Divine Milieu*, 29–30.

15. Teilhard, *Divine Milieu*, 25.

16. Teilhard, *Divine Milieu*, 30.

17. Teilhard, *Divine Milieu*, 30–31.

18. Teilhard, *Divine Milieu*, 32.

19. Teilhard, *Divine Milieu*, 70.

20. Teilhard, *Divine Milieu*, 32.

21. Teilhard, *Divine Milieu*, 33–34.

22. Teilhard, *Divine Milieu*, 34–35.

23. Teilhard, *Divine Milieu*, 35–36; recall James Fowler's thoughts on vocation in *Becoming Adult*, throughout, discussed above; we shall return to the concept of vocation in a subsequent chapter.

24. A fundamental concept in *"The Mass on the World,"* where Teilhard links Eucharist and the sanctification of the whole world; see King, *Teilhard's Mass*, 59–90.

25. Teilhard, *Divine Milieu*, 38.

26. Teilhard, *Divine Milieu*, 38–39.

27. Teilhard, *Divine Milieu*, 39.

28. Teilhard, *Divine Milieu*, 40.

29. Teilhard, *Divine Milieu*, 41.

30. Teilhard, *Divine Milieu*, 81–87; the original French of the last named is *Le Phénomène Humain*.

31. Teilhard, *Divine Milieu*, 42–43.

20

The Implicit Love of God in Simone Weil

One of the great mystics and prophets of our time is Simone Weil, whose essays on the four forms of the implicit love of God constitute one of the most brilliant ever expositions of this second tidal current of transfiguration in the mode of manifestation. We can learn much from briefly reviewing these four forms and suggesting their significance for our task, as we shall in subsequent chapters. For those who have not read them, of course nothing can replace enjoying the originals.

But first, for those who do not know this remarkable woman, a short biography.[1] She was born in Paris, February 3, 1909, into an agnostic Jewish family. Given her later negative attitude toward biblical Israel (classical Rome shared her dislike of military brutishness) and subsequent "conversion," it is important to note she neither practiced nor knew much about religious Judaism. Although she always felt overshadowed by the brilliance of an older mathematician brother, she excelled in her studies of philosophy, especially under Alain (Émile Auguste Chartier) at Collège Henri IV, and took her degree at *L'Ecole Normale Supérieure* in 1931. She entered upon her career of teaching philosophy at girls' secondary schools, interrupted by periods of illness (apparently migraine headaches and depression), and spent one stretch working in a Renault factory to share the lot of workers. She had already adopted her habits of looking as unattractive as possible (she appears never to have had a romantic relationship, wore dowdy clothes that emphasized her gawkiness, and either had an eating disorder or fasted a lot, depending on your perspective). She thus earned for herself the nickname "The Red Virgin," and, in 1936, she left her work to express her solidarity with the Republicans (Marxists) in the Spanish Civil War and to share their suffering. In the process she injured herself, apparently by stepping in a cooking pot.

Although she states in her spiritual autobiography that she had always seen herself as within the Christian community in terms of culture, values, and ethics, though not dogma or worship, she then had three powerful spiritual experiences that changed her life. Her long-suffering parents took her to Portugal to recover from her illness after the factory period; in a poor, small village there she observed a popular ceremony of the fishwives. It had a profound effect on her, which she described as a reverse twist on Friedrich Nietzsche: "There the conviction was suddenly borne in upon me that Christianity is pre-eminently the religion of slaves, that slaves cannot help belonging to it, and I among the others."[2] In 1937 she had two marvelous days at Assisi, having fallen in love with St. Francis, and there for the first time fell to her knees. In 1938 she made her way to Solesmes—the great Benedictine Abbey known for the restoration of Gregorian Chant—just to hear the music, from Palm Sunday to Easter Tuesday. The Holy Week liturgies spoke to her own suffering from awful headaches. She also met a young English Catholic boy whose face was transfigured after going to communion, and he introduced her to the English metaphysical poets.[3] Reciting George Herbert's famous "Love Bade Me Welcome" (quoted at the end of chapter 18 above) became frequent solace during her bouts of suffering, and finally, during one such recitation, "Christ himself came down and took possession of me," and she became Christ's most surprised, reluctant, and skeptical mystic. She always emphasized that she had never previously read any of the mystics, though she later found a kindred spirit in both John of the Cross and the *Bhagavad-Gita* (the most monotheistic of the Hindu texts).

Her life was indeed changed, this new relationship to Christ becoming its center. Yet she would never be baptized, despite some pressure from Catholic friends, because she saw herself as a sacrament to the church of that which it excluded, including her own intellect, and, quite simply, because God did not tell her to seek Baptism (unless one gives credence to reports of a deathbed Baptism). It was another five years before she actually prayed, beginning, after some intensive study, a daily recitation of the Our Father. Meanwhile, World War II began to have a local impact, and the Nazi danger in France led her family to relocate to Marseilles, where she joined a Catholic agricultural colony under the leadership of Gustave Thibon, and formed her deep friendship with Fr. J. M. Perrin, O.P., himself later superior at Montpelier and then a hero of the Resistance. Her letters to Fr. Perrin and her other writings, which she left with Thibon, are her literary legacy. In 1942 she followed her family to New York for further safety, but responded to a call to return to England to serve with the Gaullists. She would eat only what she imagined her compatriots in the Resistance were eating, and finally, exhausted and starving, she died at a sanatorium in Ashford, Kent, August 29, 1943.

As Leslie Fiedler puts it, "Since her death, Simone Weil has come to seem more and more a special exemplar of sanctity for our time—the Outsider as Saint in an age of alienation, our kind of saint."[4] By "outsider" we now mean not only her profound sense of loneliness and of being a misfit, but also the intellectual skepticism and integrity that never allowed her to choose simply to give in and belong, her agnosticism, her political passion, and even her character as anti-hero, including the klutziness and probable anorexia. What is remarkable is that it is from this unlikely saint that we get not only some of the most moving theological reflection on suffering of our time but also some of the most original theological thought, the first person account of perhaps the first postmodern mystic, and, for our present purposes, the splendid essays on the four forms of the implicit love of God, which have so much to teach us about this current of transfiguration/manifestation.[5]

The indirect or implicit forms of the love of God are the appropriate mode of the soul's attention to the hidden or secret presence of God in the world before "God comes in person to take the hand of his future bride."[6] Weil analyzes these in terms of four proper objects or loves: love of neighbor, love of the order and beauty of the world, love of religious practices and ceremonies, and friendship, which is related to, but distinct from, love of neighbor.[7] Different temperaments and circumstances result in one or more of these loves being dominant in each individual, but proficiency in all four is probably required before the soul is ready "to receive the personal visit of its master." The implicit loves do not disappear when God's love becomes explicit but, indeed, become stronger. In fact, one should be deeply suspicious of those who claim a kind of detachment in which these implicit loves disappear.[8] There is also a deep connection to the vision, common in the current of transfiguration and already evident in what we have seen in Teilhard, that all these implicit loves have a sacramental character, each having the virtue of a sacrament in itself, pointing to contact with God in friendship as the true sacrament.[9]

No summary or analysis can substitute for the brilliance of Weil's own presentation of these four loves. In this chapter I wish only to give a brief definition and characterization of each, drawing connections to the layers of conversion derived from Bernard Lonergan, and connecting each to an aspect of the Benedictine Rule: study, work, prayer, and community. In subsequent chapters we shall be exploring, within the framework of the four implicit loves, several of the topics traditionally treated in spiritual theology within the stage or theme of illumination.

Love of Neighbor

Love of neighbor, of course, is the second half of the summary of the law, as Christians usually call it, "Hear, O Israel: the Lord our God, the Lord is one; you shall love the Lord your God with all your heart, and with all your soul, and with all your mind, and with all your strength." The second is this, "You shall love your neighbor as yourself." There is no other commandment greater than these (Mark 12:29–32 and parallels).[10] Weil's insight that these are not really two loves but one is echoed throughout 1 John: "Those who say, 'I love God,' and hate their brothers or sisters, are liars; for those who do not love a brother or sister whom they have seen, cannot love God whom they have not seen" (1 John 4:20). Indeed, in the end it is God in us who is loving the neighbor.[11]

For Weil, love of neighbor is focused primarily on the issues of justice, including proper punishment and charity. Both are modes of dealing with affliction and the afflicted, and require a particular creative attention to the "other" precisely in his or her own person, not in the abstract or as a means of doing good. This creative attention is a kind of renunciation, imagining an equality in a relationship that does not, in fact, exist.[12] In this it is like the fundamental restraint and renunciation God shows in creating beings less than Godself who are autonomous. Generosity and compassion are inseparable.[13] The proper attitude for the duly punished or the afflicted one who receives charity or the autonomous creature who receives being is gratitude, and the dialectic between generosity and gratitude becomes, in a kind of genius, a form of friendship (thus linking us to Weil's fourth love).[14]

The rather harsh section on punishment and the positive treatment of affliction must give us some pause. Weil's conception of truly just punishment as itself a kind of creative attention to the criminal is certainly true if there is to be, as there must, a penal system; but there is a kind of coldness to the analysis that makes one wonder about this area of her own psyche and its relationship to her eating disorder. The earlier essay, "The Love of God and Affliction,"[15] in which she insists that affliction is not the same as simple suffering, casts a deeper light. As Fiedler notes, there is really no good English translation for *malheur*. My own sense, especially in the light of the conclusion of that essay, is that Weil is attempting to find a redemption of all suffering in the desolation mystics report experiencing in the dark nights. While this is a profound theological insight at one level, at another it may not provide an adequate basis for the struggle against unjust or demonic suffering, an area in which Weil herself is open to criticism. That said, the insight can stand, especially side by side with the demand that justice and charity both demand creative attention to the afflicted.

At first glance it may seem odd to connect this love with "study" in the Benedictine Rule. The kind of creative attention Weil calls for, however, requires significant knowledge of ethics, law, politics, and social analysis of the conditions that produce the afflictions being addressed. A well-intentioned ignorance will not do, most especially not the desire to be "doing good" that is motivated more by our own ego needs than attention to the other. What is required is an inner knowledge that allows us to imagine the contrafactual equality in the relationships and an external knowledge of circumstances and law. Plus, as we have seen, the whole point of school studies, according to Weil, is to train a person in precisely the kind of attention that is required for true justice and charity. In Lonergan's terms, this means second conversion reaches not only the affective and moral levels, but also the intellectual, if we are to both manifest and perceive the glory of God in the dialectic of neighbor love.

We are all, of course, the recipients of God's justice and mercy, and, as a result, "God is, moreover, our real neighbor."[16] In this current of our spiritual lives we need to develop a deeper gratitude for the justice and mercy shown *us* in the first current than was possible when we were in it. One dimension of the "spiritual awakening" in AA and allied programs is a sense of gratitude not merely for the deliverance from the pain of the disease but for the positive good of the sober life itself. We become *grateful* recovering alcoholics. This requires a deep acceptance of the dynamic of the repentance (or healing or liberation) of the first current, including its attendant suffering, that is not possible from within that current itself. I still do not accept a theology that God caused the suffering that we might learn and grow. But what is certainly true is that now we can see the glory of God in the unexpected mercy, charity, and justice that we experienced in the teeth of the suffering. The resulting gratitude becomes a solid base for developing the virtues and habits needed for active expression of love of neighbor in this second current.

Love of the Order and Beauty of the World

According to Weil, the love of the order and beauty of the universe is the "complement of the love of our neighbor." Creating a universe that operates according to its own laws of necessity and chance requires the same kind of renunciation on God's part as the creation of autonomous rational creatures. Even though we do not have the power God has renounced, we imagine that we do, placing ourselves at the center of the universe. This too must be renounced as the proper detachment called for in this love. As a result, "By loving our neighbor we imitate the divine love which created us and all our fellows. By loving the order of the world we imitate the divine love which created this universe of which we are a part."[17] I believe Weil has caught perfectly the core of the dark night of the senses, passive and active: a liberation of ourselves from a false attachment to the world as if we were its center and purpose. The issue is coming to terms with the universe and our place in it in a thoroughly realistic manner, and we might note how this eschews all doctrines such as creationism or intelligent design that find too easy an access to God's providence in the evidence:

> To empty ourselves of our false divinity, to deny ourselves, to give up being the center of the world in imagination, to discern that all points in the world are equally centers and that the true center is outside the world, this is to consent to the rule of mechanical necessity in matter and of free choice at the center of each soul. Such consent is love. The face of this love, which is turned towards thinking persons, is the love of our neighbor; the face turned toward matter is love of the order of the world, or love of the beauty of the world which is the same thing.[18]

This detachment, in other words, does not lead to despising the world but to respecting the distance between it and us. We have seen that at the heart of love of neighbor is a creative attention to that neighbor's autonomous personhood, who, like us, is created in the image and likeness of God. Similarly, love of the order and beauty of the world is creative attention to the autonomy with which God has gifted it as it operates according to its own laws. This requires study, of course, but even more, we engage in the beauty and order of the world through work, as co-creators with God. Thus, work, the second pillar of Benedictine life, governs this love, and we shall consider it in some detail in its own chapter. In the current of transfiguration especially, it is not enough merely to appreciate; we are called also to co-operate, literally, to work with God on an *opus* that is truly ours, and our engagement with the world in its order and beauty, even as we accept its resistance to our plans. It is thus odd that "the beauty of the world is almost absent from the Christian tradition. . . . How can Christianity call itself catholic if the universe itself is left out?"[19]

The beauty of the world is also one of the most common means of grace by which people are brought to see God:

> Just as God hastens into every soul, and immediately it opens, even a little, in order through it to love and serve the afflicted [love of neighbor], so he descends in all haste to love and admire the tangible beauty of his own creation through the soul that opens to him.

But the contrary is still more true. The soul's natural inclination to love beauty is the trap God most frequently uses in order to win it and open it to the breath from on high.[20]

"The beauty of the world is not an attribute of matter in itself." It is a peculiar relationship to human sensibility that God has willed, through a co-operation of the divine wisdom in creation:

The beauty of the world is Christ's tender smile for us coming through matter. He is really present in the universal beauty. The love of this beauty proceeds from God dwelling in our souls and goes out to God present in the universe. It also is like a sacrament.[21]

In this language, so reminiscent of Teilhard, Weil shares a vision of the Holy Spirit praying in us, in and through us, both in our contemplation and in our work, thanking and praising the Fount and Word/Wisdom for the beauty of the world. But only universal beauty can be the means of this proper adoration. Any particular beauty may lead us to this proper contemplation, but when it does not, we have been seduced into idolatry. In particular, the sins of greed and concupiscence arise from failing to acknowledge that beauty exists for its own sake, indeed, is "the only finality here below."[22] Failing to respect the autonomy of the universe and aim at its entirety, its very universality, leads to greed, vanity, excessive luxury, and the lust for power, imposing our own ends on what must be its own end.

Art and science, in contrast, are meant to be forms of work coming from a true creative attention to universal beauty and order. All true works of art reflect the beauty of the whole universe, and hence the glory of God:

Every true artist has had real, direct, and immediate contact with the beauty of the world, contact that is of the nature of a sacrament. God has inspired every first-rate work of art, though its subject may be utterly and entirely secular; he has not inspired any of the others. Indeed the luster of beauty that distinguishes some of those others may quite well be a diabolical luster.[23]

Science is a creative attention to the order of the world, in a theoretical construction that is always in relation to "the mental, psychic, and bodily structure of man." It is a serious error for scientists to believe that any methodology can free them from this "existential" orientation. The incarnation itself dictates what we may broadly call a "humanist" orientation to science: "The object of science is the presence of Wisdom in the universe, Wisdom of which we are the brothers, the presence of Christ, expressed through matter which constitutes the world."[24] This is precisely what Teilhard celebrates in his Mass, of course.

Labor, especially as experienced by the poor, has its own special privilege: "Physical work is a specific contact with the beauty of the world, and can even be, in its best moments, a contact so full that no equivalent can be found." The weary laborer "bears the reality of the universe in his flesh like a thorn. The difficulty for him is to look and to love. If he succeeds, he loves the Real."[25] One of the major injustices of our culture is that workers are not taught this kind of looking. Indeed, everything seems to conspire against their seeing and loving. Weil's own time spent working in a Renault factory is her ground for making this claim.

The final arena Weil addresses is that of carnal love and the desire for pleasure. These also have the beauty of the world for their proper object; indeed, because of the chance for reciprocal love, finding the beauty of the world in another person is the most satisfactory of all. But "the longing to love the beauty of the world in a human being is essentially the longing for the Incarnation. It is mistaken if it thinks it is anything else."[26] Weil believes, "That is why sins in this area are so serious" because they are distracted by a desire for pleasure from the search for universal beauty, and hence God, in this particular person. She appropriately nails the essence of the worst sins in this area from rape to seduction to pornography: "the more or less complete determination to dispense with consent. To be completely determined to dispense with it is perhaps the most frightful of all crimes. What can be more horrible than not to respect the consent of a being in whom one is seeking, though unconsciously, for an equivalent of God?"[27] That is, by treating the other in whom we find beauty as something to possess for any end of our own, even or especially pleasure, we impede their own incarnation for us as autonomous selves and defeat our own desire to be incarnate and find God in incarnation.[28] Creative attention to appropriate autonomy is again the key to active love. Any relationship in which mutual physical love is to aim at the high goals Weil sets will require also a lot of work.

As a result, all human work participates in the beauty of the world, and hence in what I have called the current of transfiguration:

> However it may be, in every kind of human occupation there is always some regard for the beauty of the world seen in more or less distorted or soiled images. As a consequence there is not any department of human life which is purely natural. The supernatural is secretly present throughout. Under a thousand different forms, grace and mortal sin are everywhere.[29]

Finally, in each instance, it is the necessity we find in matter and the freedom in thinking beings that require from us both a creative attention and a renunciation of our own willfulness that is the essence of love. As that formed the essence of neighbor love, here it allows us to love the world as our home, our country, because: "It is real; it offers resistance to love."[30] This resistance is always its own autonomy—necessity in matter, freedom in other persons. It is these that resist our illusions of using them for our own ends and require of us the creative attention that is the essence of love, or drives us to the crimes by which we deprive others of the opportunity to learn such attention that "should wring tears of blood from us."[31] Obviously, respecting the autonomy of the material world also has implications for environmental ethics as well. Work thus involves more than affective conversion. Intellectual and moral conversion, including political, are also required.

The Love of Religious Practices

> The love of institutional religion, although the name of God necessarily comes into it, is not itself an explicit, but an implicit love of God, for it does not involve direct, immediate contact with him. God is present in religious practices, when they are pure, just as he is present in our neighbor and in the beauty of the world; in the same way and not anymore.[32]

In these words Weil stakes out her position on the love of religion as a form of the implicit love of God, equal to but not above the other three. The context in which she writes is perhaps more apparent in this section than any other, as she deals with the problems of secularism, pluralism, and totalitarianism in ways that remain startlingly relevant. She begins by noting that we live in an age in which some persons have developed "a hatred and contempt for religion because the cruelty, pride, or corruption of certain of its ministers have made them suffer." Others have simply been raised in an atmosphere in which institutional religion is despised or discounted, as has become so automatic for the educated young in our time. Weil expresses a hope we may share, that in such cases love of neighbor and love of the beauty of the world will be enough to awaken such souls.[33]

The fact of religious pluralism then takes a good bit of her attention. She certainly believes that there is some truth and even salvation in all the great religions, and could be accused of being a pluralist, despite her own commitment to Christ. Of course, the more nuanced typologies of this question have emerged since she wrote, and it is possible that if she wrote now, she would opt for an inclusivist or dialogical position.[34] In any case, several points qualify her seeming pluralism. First, not all religions are equal. In Weil's mind, for example, the state religion of Rome "can scarcely be said to deserve the name of religion at all."[35] Where an unsatisfactory native religion, or hostile life circumstances do not prevent, however, Weil believes one should stick to one's native religion. True "comparative religion" is very difficult, because it requires certain sympathy for other faiths, and this in turn requires adherence to one's own but in a generous way. Because her argument for this is also so deeply applicable to the issue of friendship that is to follow, it is worth quoting at length:

> This [the sympathetic understanding of the inner core of another religion] scarcely ever happens, for some have no faith, and the others have faith exclusively in one religion and only bestow upon others the sort of attention we give to strangely shaped shells. There are others again who think they are capable of impartiality because they have only a vague religiosity which they turn indifferently in any direction, whereas, on the contrary, we must have given all our faith, all our love to a particular religion in order to think of any other religion with the high degree of attention, faith, and love that is proper to it. In the same way, only those who are capable of friendship can take a real heartfelt interest in the fate of an utter stranger.
> In all departments of life, love is not real unless it is directed toward a

particular object; it becomes universal without ceasing to be real only as a result of analogy and transference.[36]

Weil's next major point is that the virtue of religious practices is "due to a contact with what is perfectly pure, resulting in the destruction of evil."[37] As we saw in the previous section, only the total beauty of the universe is perfectly pure; since that is beyond most of us, religion expresses that (in accordance with the discussion of particularity just given) in finite tangible things that are pure, not in themselves, but by convention, almost a kind of transubstantiation. Where "faith and love do not fail," these are usually expressed in the form of beauty, though at the center of the Christian faith is something devoid of all beauty, the morsel of bread in the Eucharist, itself symbolic of the crucified body of Christ, also stripped of all beauty. "The virtue of the doctrine of the real presence lies in its very absurdity."[38]

This leads to a powerful discussion of the atonement, which seems at first like a digression but is actually a portrayal of how in the Christian religion purity overcomes evil. As finite beings, however pure, we are incapable of reacting to evil (which Weil defines as sin plus suffering, or, rather, a common root of both) except by transferring evil from ourselves to others, who then transfer it back to us.[39] Each adds to the evil in this exchange. The cycle of escalating violence is very like what Weil describes in more universal terms. Only an infinite being of perfect purity in human form is capable of absorbing evil without becoming defiled and hence sending it out magnified. This is exactly what happened in the incarnation and the crucifixion, as all the evil in the world was transferred to Christ: "In a mysterious manner this transference constitutes the Redemption."[40] Finite souls find redemption by turning their attention to the being of perfect purity and thus transferring some of the evil safely to it.

Thus, Weil's core concepts of purity and attention come together in her assertion that "looking is what saves us," as we gaze at Christ like the bronze serpent in the wilderness.[41] This leads to a series of conclusions that describe what can only be called a beginning of true (technically called "infused") contemplation, though it must be noted that all this is from meditating on the real presence in the Eucharistic bread, not a direct apprehension of God. First is a description of what sounds like a dark night as the perfect opportunity for such gazing, with a thorough description of the resistance, illusions, and lies that plague us at such times. The effort to reject the illusions and lies is almost violent, yet unlike anything else we call "effort," since the will is not involved:

> The effort that brings a soul to salvation is like the effort of looking and listening; it is the kind of effort by which a fiancée accepts her lover. It is an act of attention and consent; whereas what language designates as will is something suggestive of muscular effort.[42]

This looking, attention, and consent that is the essence of contemplation (Weil does not use this term) is passive and obediential. We do not find God by our efforts. "If however we look heavenward for a long time, God comes and takes us up."[43] This leads to a sharp contrast between a futile secular morality based on effort of will, and religion, which is based on desire. Weil is not a quietist. Waiting for the good is passive, but keeping away evil is active and involves the will. The passive waiting is, however, "more intense than any searching." Thus, "Attention animated by desire is the whole foundation of religious practices."[44] We should recall the earlier emphasis on consent as well.

Weil concludes with a list of "veils" that come between us and perfect purity, all of which resonate with traditional teaching about the spiritual pitfalls of the current of transfiguration, most of which involve a kind of "Zen sickness" in which we are in love with our own enlightenment rather than with the Light. These veils include fascination with states of the soul, joys, and consolations; focus on a particular person or a social group; or, worst of all, our own imagination of "the divine perfection religion invites us to love. Never in any case can we imagine something more perfect than ourselves. This effort renders useless the marvel of the Eucharist."[45]

Poignantly, "The trap of traps is the social trap."[46] The feeling of social solidarity and belonging to a like-minded group is a dangerous counterfeit of faith. It would be easy to critique Weil's privatism and failure to appreciate the communal and covenant aspect of Christianity at this point; it is indeed true that she has hardly any ecclesiology, though the next essay on friendship ameliorates this somewhat. But it is clear what she sees as the real demon: "Under present circumstances, it is perhaps a question of life or death for faith that the social imitation should be repudiated." Clearly she is thinking of ideological commitment to something like National Socialism as the demonic counterfeit of faith, a point that is still preeminently valid in our time, even when the commitment is to the values of liberal capitalist democracy or "the American way of life."

By contrast, true mission becomes taking Christ, the opportunity to gaze on the bronze serpent, "into those places most polluted with shame, misery, crime, and affliction, into prisons and law courts, into workhouses and shelters for the wretched and the outcast."[47] That is, love of religion and love of neighbor become combined in mission (Weil does not use the term). "Christ should not be absent from the places where work or study is going on."[48] Most ultimately, religion should not be seduced by the social trap into claiming to be anything other than this looking which is attention animated by desire and culminating in consent. It should not claim a larger place in society than that "which rightly belongs to supernatural love in the soul." Neither for our looking, nor for our attention to our neighbor, should we claim too much:

> Love should always be accompanied by modesty. True faith implies great discretion, even with regard to itself. It is a secret between God and us in which we have scarcely any part.[49]

That is, at bottom, the love of religious practices, by the very love and desire for God that animates its loving attention and consent to perfect purity, requires a kind of humility. Focus on the impersonal piece of bread at the heart of the Eucharist aids this, reminding us that there is something impersonal in our love of God until God comes in person. One of Weil's greatest strengths, however, is the way she shows how outward religious practice leads intrinsically to contemplation, at least of God "in secret." As such, love of religious practices is not yet fully "religious conversion" in Lonergan's sense; that will only come in the third tidal current. What we have here is a religious intentionality implicit in the core of affective, intellectual, and moral/political conversion.

Liturgical prayer, in the Benedictine model, is actually work; hence the traditional name for the daily round of psalms and Scripture that is the "daily office": *opus Dei,* the work of God. Although Weil focuses on the Eucharist, the other great center of daily liturgical prayer, the point is that all true religious ritual practice should lead in one direction toward contemplative fulfillment, which in the Benedictine model is prayer. Perhaps most important, however, is to see already the ways in which attention, looking, desire, purity, and consent run as constant threads through all of Weil's analysis of these first three loves. The other main point is thus that all true religious practice is also intrinsically related to love of neighbor and of the beauty of the world, and hence leads to service and mission as well as contemplation. Since all these are the result, not of people searching for God, but of God searching for them, what is developing is a powerful theology of *vocation.*

Friendship

These threads come together in a kind of denouement in friendship, which is not so much a fourth love, as the culmination of the first three in a relationship between human persons:

> There is however a personal and human love which is pure and which enshrines an intimation and reflection of divine love. This is friendship, providing we keep strictly to the true meaning of the word.[50]

Attention, desire, consent, and purity remain strong elements in Weil's analysis of friendship, to which she adds an important further concept—distance. She begins by distinguishing friendship from that charity which is love of neighbor. The latter is more universal, available to all in affliction, and is given a particular focus only when there chances to be a particular "occasion there for the exchange of compassion and gratitude."[51] Friendship, in contrast, by its nature focuses on one particular person, in whom we seek some good or whom we need. There follows a keen analysis of the dialectic between good and necessity, with an understanding of how what was desired as good can transmute to a need in an addictive process.[52] Even the desire for a good for ourselves in a relationship, though it does not contradict desire for good for the friend as well, keeps friendship from fulfilling all its requirements as "a supernatural harmony, a union of opposites."[53]

When there is any degree of need, of necessity, there is only constraint and dominion, making it impossible to desire good for the other without ceasing to desire it for ourselves. The problem arises for Weil, in a description that again reminds us of Sartre's keen analysis,[54] because the chief good to which I must pay attention and also desire for myself and an other is autonomy, free consent:

> The central good for every man is the free disposal of himself. Either we renounce it, which is a crime of idolatry, since it can be renounced only in favor of God, or we desire that the being we stand in need of should be deprived of this free disposal of himself.[55]

That is, the ultimate good I seek for myself and a friend, autonomy, makes any necessity problematic. This is why a relationship based purely on necessity, without wishing for any good for the other, "is a fearful thing. Few things in this world can reach such a degree of ugliness and horror. There is always something horrible whenever a human being seeks what is good and only finds necessity."[56] Because this dialectic between good and need is so universal, "The human soul possesses a whole arsenal of lies with which to put up a defense against this ugliness and, in imagination, to manufacture sham advantages where there is only necessity. It is for this very reason that ugliness is an evil, because it conduces to lying."[57] This aspect of denial in the face of need, of constructing delusions, is only too familiar to anyone recovering from addiction or working with addicts. Indeed, what Weil is moving toward is that loving detachment we saw as the chief lesson to be learned in the dark night of the senses. Affliction comes about, she says, when need "is imposed so harshly that the hardness exceeds the capacity for lying of the person who receives the impact."[58] That is why, oddly enough, good and pure people suffer the most, because they have the greatest capacity to renounce the lies.

Weil agrees with Jean-Paul Sartre that this dialectic between good and necessity cannot be resolved by any natural means: "When a human being is attached to another by a bond of affection which contains any degree of necessity, it is impossible that he should wish autonomy to be preserved both in himself and in the other." But she goes where Sartre could not: "It is, however, made possible by the miraculous intervention of the supernatural. This miracle is friendship."[59]

The essence of this miracle is equality. "Friendship is an equality made of harmony. . . . There is equality because each wishes to preserve the faculty of free consent both in himself and in the other. . . . There is no friendship where there is inequality." Further, real friendship requires reciprocity. There can be, as it were, no unrequited friendship. If I desire friendship with another who does not want that relationship with me, I must renounce it out of respect for their autonomy; if another desires a friendship with me that I do not, I must renounce it out of respect for my own. No compromise with this respect for autonomy is really possible, ruling out both the desire to please and the desire to dominate. This respect for autonomy requires a detachment Weil defines as "distance":

> The two friends have fully consented to be two and not one, they respect the distance which the fact of being two distinct creatures places between them. Man has the right to desire direct union with God alone.

> Friendship is a miracle by which a person consents to view from a certain distance, and without coming any nearer, the very being who is as necessary to him as food.[60]

This distance or detachment, this attention to the autonomy of the other, is what links friendship with love of neighbor: "Through this supernatural miracle of respect for human autonomy, friendship is very like the pure forms of compassion and gratitude called forth by affliction."[61] This distance requires that there be something in a friendship like indifference, something that preserves impartiality. There is also something in this very particular love that pushes toward the universal love we should like to have for each member of the human race. This universality also derives from the "consent to preserve autonomy within ourselves and others." Once we move from the particular to the universal by desiring the autonomy of everyone, "we cease to arrange the order of the world in a circle whose center is here below. We transport the center of the circle beyond the heavens."[62] Then comes a key point that addresses all forms of friendship, even that which should be at the core of a marriage:

> Friendship does not have this power if the two beings who love each other, through an unlawful use of affection, think they form only one. But then there is not friendship in the true sense of the word. That is what might be called an adulterous union, even though it comes about between a husband and wife. There is not friendship where distance is not kept and respected.[63]

When bonds of affection are not supernaturally transformed into friendship through this distance of mutual consent to autonomy, what results is not love but hatred and revulsion: "We hate what we are dependent upon. We become disgusted with what depends on us."[64]

Weil concludes her discussion of friendship with a discussion of John 15: "When Christ said to his disciples: 'Love one another,' it was not attachment he was laying down as their rule." The bonds of affection among them, from their common life, had previously been expressed in terms of servanthood, which does not yet have in it the fullness of equality or consent to full autonomy. "[H]e commanded them to transform these bonds into friendship, so that they should not be allowed to turn into impure attachment or hatred."[65] Jesus now invites his followers into a new relationship with one another and himself that has nothing in it of compelled obedience, but becomes a communion of shared moral purpose. As a result, "pure friendship, like the love of our neighbor, has in it something of a sacrament." Christ indicates this by his promise to be in the midst of any two or three gathered in his name (Matt 18:20). Weil concludes with a deep theological insight that pushes (in a manner we shall see is intrinsic to this second current) deep into the third tide of glory:

> Pure friendship is an image of the original and perfect friendship that belongs to the Trinity and is the very essence of God. It is impossible for

two human beings to be one while scrupulously respecting the distance that separates them, unless God is present in each of them. The point at which parallels meet is infinity.[66]

What began as one individual having affection for another has now also expanded to become a vocation, embracing all our intimate relationships and radiating out through communities into the whole world. For Christians it has a particular focus on the *koinōnia*, the common life of the covenant people, the church. Here also what appears to involve primarily affective conversion must also be informed as well by the intellectual, the moral/political, and ultimately, the religious. In the Benedictine life this *koinōnia* is the essence of community, expressed in the vow of *stability*. In that tradition, there has been a long struggle about the place of "special friendships" in the community and spiritual growth. Caution is appropriate for all the reasons laid out by Weil: the danger of obsessive need creating not love but hatred and repulsion is all too real. But embodied in at least one great English Benedictine saint, Aelred of Rievaulx, we find Weil's insight that by supernatural grace the particular is meant to be a school for the universal.[67]

The Vocation to the Four Loves

Weil has several important points to make about all four loves. First, it must be obvious that they exist beyond any limitations of covenant or church in both space and time. Second, they are in some sense absurd: "So long as the soul has not had direct contact with the very person of God, they cannot be supported by any knowledge either in experience or reason."[68] Once God has come in person, however, the four loves are not abandoned, but now have become "a movement of God himself, a ray merged in the light of God." This experience belongs more to the third tide, and we shall return to it there. In fact, we should be deeply suspicious of any who claim to have had direct contact with God that causes the disappearance of the implicit loves.[69]

Most important, perhaps, is the clear sense that a call into the third tide is part of the experience of this second tide. To see ourselves and the world illumined with the glory of God radiating from the face of Christ is powerful in its own right, but it creates a hunger for the glory itself. The implicit, despite being good in itself, longs for the explicit, and it is a grave error to deny this:

> In the period of preparation the soul loves in emptiness. It does not know whether anything real answers its love. It may believe that it knows, but to believe is not to know. Such a belief does not help. The soul knows for certain only that it is hungry. The important thing is that it announces its hunger by crying. . . .
>
> The danger is not lest the soul should doubt whether there is any bread, but lest, by a lie, it should persuade itself that it is not hungry. It can only persuade itself of this by lying, for the reality of its hunger is not a belief, it is a certainty.[70]

This actually becomes material for the third conversion, or the slack between the second and third tides, as Weil herself comes to realize, and we shall consider it more thoroughly there.[71] Just as in the first conversion and tide we saw that it was cruel to evangelize someone without warning of the daily struggle with Satan, so in this second conversion and tide it is dishonest to downplay the truth that even in the life of illuminating grace, most of what we shall find is a more intense hunger, a desire that only becomes deeper the more it is fulfilled. In the meantime, the testimony of those who have been immersed in the third tide about the realities of the second must reassure us. God is "the reality inspiring all the indirect loves, the reality of which they are the reflection."[72] God, who is the true subject of all religious ceremonies and practices, is also our real neighbor, perfect beauty, and our true friend.[73] Even as we realize this, the themes of attention, consent and autonomy, equality, and distance remain. The result: "In fact, contact with God is the true sacrament."[74]

Thus *theōsis*, the reality of the third tide, which is only glimpsed in the second by reflection, the reality of becoming God's friend and, hence, in some sense God's equal, is driven both by our desire for God and God's desire and movement within us.[75] We long for a union with God that is only possible with an equal, a friend. The equality that is the essential motive of distance and detachment thus lies at the heart of being God's friend, from both sides. It is always, however, a miracle, not the evolutionary fulfillment of a capacity of our own. Only the reality of Christ's flesh from incarnation through the fire of Pentecost can make it real.

In the meantime, until God comes in person to make love explicit, we are given the vocation of "waiting for God," an active waiting animated by the imperative by which the implicit loves drive us into relationship, community, and the world itself, in service and friendship. We can enjoy this period of grace, as long as we do not deny the still-underlying and growing hunger. Alan Jones puts it well:

> The second conversion brings not only a new awareness, but also a new energy and power. The light warms and heals and makes strong as well as shines in the darkness. It is thus that souls are made. It is thus that we grow in discipleship. We move from an initial burst of enthusiasm, through a period of humbling, to a bracing yet relaxing enjoyment of grace. We become less the victims of mood and emotion. We learn that feelings come and go. [Affective conversion.] We move in the light from a vague and unfocused faith to a living conviction. But the desert believer knows that this is not the end of the story. There is a third conversion, deeper and more devastating and more wonderful than the second. We have to be born again and again.[76]

Before we face third conversion, this second slack between the tides, the dark night of the soul, we can pause and notice how the implicit loves allow us to make sense, in Tabor's light of transfiguration, of several practical topics traditionally dealt with in what was formerly called the stage of illumination.

Notes

1. Three quite different perspectives are given in *Waiting for God*: a cleaned up family version which replaces that of her friend Fr. J. M. Perrin from the French original, Leslie Fiedler's comments in his introduction, and Weil's own autobiographical letters to Fr. Perrin. For a substantial bibliography on Weil, see "Simone (Adolphine) Weil: (1909–1943) Biographies, Criticism, Journal Articles, Work Overviews."

2. Weil, *Waiting for God*, 67.

3. Fiedler notes the appropriateness of this skeptical saint being grasped by two deeply Christian art forms that have appealed even to the anti-Christians of our irreligious times—Gregorian chant and metaphysical poetry (*Waiting for God*, 23–24).

4. Weil, *Waiting for God*, 3. The claim of Weil's saintliness should not be accepted without criticism, especially in the light of her own silence on the atrocities of anti-Semitism raging around her. See the thoughtful assessment of Jillian Becker, "Simone Weil, A Saint for Our Time?"; if I agree with Fiedler and not with Becker in her final analysis, it is only because I do believe even great saints can have tragic blind spots and great flaws. And, of course, Weil died young in both years and her faith; until the fullness of the commonwealth, we shall not know what more grace-filled history might have made of her. What is remarkable is the enduring value of what she did accomplish and leave behind, despite her flaws and short life.

5. Of course, one also thinks in this context of Anne Frank and other Holocaust survivors, of Dietrich Bonhoeffer; and we recall again Weil's failure to speak to the suffering of the Jews of her time and her own troubled relationship with her own Jewishness.

6. Weil, *Waiting for God*, 137; the concept of contemplative attention is key in Weil's thought and correlates with her belief that knowledge is a kind of looking. See the essay "Reflections on the Right Use of School Studies with a View to the Love of God," in *Waiting for God*, 105–16.

7. Weil, *Waiting for God*, 138.

8. Weil, *Waiting for God*, 214.

9. Weil, *Waiting for God*, 138, 214.

10. Jesus is, of course, following a common rabbinic tradition based on Deut 6:4–5 and Lev 19:18.

11. Weil, *Waiting for God*, 151.

12. Weil, *Waiting for God*, 147–49.

13. Weil, *Waiting for God*, 145–46. Weil also connects the same generosity to the passion.

14. Weil, *Waiting for God*, 146–48.

15. Weil, *Waiting for God*, 117–36.

16. Weil, *Waiting for God*, 213.

17. Weil, *Waiting for God*, 158.

18. Weil, *Waiting for God*, 159–60; see also 176: "Those who think to discern special designs of Providence are like professors who give themselves up to what they call explanation of the text, at the expense of a beautiful poem." There is here also perhaps a possible ground for criticism of excessive focus in much deconstructionist thought on another kind of "explanation of the text."

19. Weil, *Waiting for God*, 161.

20. Weil, *Waiting for God*, 163.

21. Weil, *Waiting for God*, 164–65.

22. Weil, *Waiting for God*, 166.

23. Weil, *Waiting for God*, 169.

24. Weil, *Waiting for God*, 169.

25. Weil, *Waiting for God*, 170.

26. Weil, *Waiting for God*, 171.

27. Weil, *Waiting for God*, 172.

28. Jean-Paul Sartre has a superb analysis of this in *Being and Nothingness*, 361–433, only for him, of course, there is no God and hence no resolution (p. 615).

29. Weil, *Waiting for God,* 175.

30. Weil, *Waiting for God,* 178.

31. Weil, *Waiting for God,* 180–81.

32. Weil, *Waiting for God,* 181.

33. Weil, *Waiting for God,* 182.

34. See again my "Christian Theology of Interfaith Dialogue."

35. Weil, *Waiting for God,* 183.

36. Weil, *Waiting for God,* 184.

37. Weil, *Waiting for God,* 186.

38. Weil, *Waiting for God,* 187.

39. Weil, *Waiting for God,* 190.

40. Weil, *Waiting for God,* 191.

41. Weil, *Waiting for God,* 192–93; John 3:14, 12:32.

42. Weil, *Waiting for God,* 193.

43. Weil, *Waiting for God,* 194.

44. Weil, *Waiting for God,* 197.

45. Weil, *Waiting for God,* 197.

46. Weil, *Waiting for God,* 198.

47. Weil, *Waiting for God,* 198.

48. Weil, *Waiting for God,* 199.

49. Weil, *Waiting for God,* 199.

50. Weil, *Waiting for God,* 200.

51. Weil, *Waiting for God,* 200.

52. Weil, *Waiting for God,* 201.

53. Weil, *Waiting for God,* 202.

54. *Being and Nothingness,* the whole section on pp. 361–413; Sartre saw no way out of this conflict precisely because he did not believe in the possibility of the miraculous, God- grounded possibility of friendship that animates Weil. But they agree on the problem.

55. Weil, *Waiting for God,* 202.

56. Weil, *Waiting for God,* 203.

57. Weil, *Waiting for God,* 203.

58. Weil, *Waiting for God,* 203.

59. Weil, *Waiting for God,* 204.

60. Weil, *Waiting for God,* 205.

61. Weil, *Waiting for God,* 205.

62. Weil, *Waiting for God,* 206

63. Weil, *Waiting for God,* 206–7.

64. Weil, *Waiting for God,* 207.

65. Weil, *Waiting for God,* 207–8.

66. Weil, *Waiting for God,* 208.

67. See Aelred of Rievaulx, *Aelred of Rievaulx's Spiritual Friendship;* and John R. Sommer-feldt, *Aelred of Rievaulx on Love and Order in the World and the Church.*

68. Weil, *Waiting for God,* 209.

69. Weil, *Waiting for God,* 214–15.

70. Weil, *Waiting for God,* 210.

71. Weil, *Waiting for God,* 211.

72. Weil, *Waiting for God,* 213.

73. Weil, *Waiting for God,* 213–14.

74. Weil, *Waiting for God,* 214.

75. G. May, *Care of Mind,* 23–24.

76. Alan Jones, *Soul Making,* 180.

21

Love of Neighbor, Vocation, and Study

You shall love your neighbor as yourself.
—Matt 19:19 and par.; Lev 19:18

In the tide of transfiguration, the life of virtue takes on a new character. It is no longer primarily a counter to vice or a set of constructive habits to be acquired for a good character. It now becomes more obvious that all real virtue is what the tradition has called "infused," our participation in God's perfections through the indwelling of the Holy Spirit.[1] The virtuous life is no longer primarily a response of faith to proclamation; in the Trinitarian dance of the three theological virtues of faith, hope, and love, in this tide *love* emerges as the dominant virtue, in response to the manifestation of God's glory in this world, the essence of transfiguration. Love of God and love of neighbor are revealed as two sides of one coin, and thus not only should not be separated but also *cannot* be separated. Love of neighbor leads to a kind of zeal that results in both mission and work, and hence the realities the tradition has called *vocation* and *charism* or gift.[2]

In this tide, with its style of self-transcendence as self-fulfillment or self-expression and its mode of manifestation, love of neighbor grows from an initial impulsive affectivity to being habitual, active, and effective. Love of neighbor is increasingly detached from our own narrow agendas, even our need to "do good"; it flows increasingly from our love for God and God's for us and others; indeed, our love (*caritas*, Latin for *agapē*, "charity" or "care" in English) becomes a response to seeing Christ in others, to perceiving God's love for them, and perceiving them in the light of God's love. We are able to fulfill the promises of the baptismal covenant regarding others only "with God's help." If this loving care is to be sufficiently detached from our own agendas, discerning of God's will, and truly attentive to the other's personhood, good intentions are not enough. Knowledge, wisdom, and prudence are all needed, and each is first a gift of the Holy Spirit and then also a virtue to be grown in our character through exercise. In particular, we recall here Simone

Weil's assertion that *study* is required for love to be effective, that indeed the whole real point of school studies is to acquire the habits of attention necessary to engage in the implicit forms of love of God in a way that is both conscious and effective.[3]

In the traditional spiritual theologies, this material is often treated in a deeply scholastic cataloguing of virtues, gifts, means of grace, and degrees of prayer that most people no longer find very edifying. But there are some essential themes that require notice here. These include the relationship between love of God and love of neighbor with the concept of friendship as key; the "dominion of charity" among the virtues in this current in both personal and social arenas; the grounding of vocation in this overflow of love, and hence of mission. These themes lead to a consideration, in the next chapter, of work and the beauty and order of the world, a topic often left out of the traditional treatises. Then follows a chapter on "the means of grace" and religious practices. This section then concludes with Weil's fourth implicit love by returning to the theme of friendship as embodied in intimate relationships and community, including marriage, parenting, and the monastic or religious life.

Love of God and Love of Neighbor

As we saw in the last chapter, Simone Weil teaches that love of neighbor flows solely but naturally from love of God, that is, both God's initial loving of us and our initial response of love to God. In this relationship, the possibility of friendship with God opens up a potential to be extended to fellow humans and other creatures. Indeed, Weil saw clearly that in the end we love others with God's own love for them, just as the one appropriate love for ourselves is to participate in God's love for us.

This profound connection between love of God and love of neighbor has deep roots in Christian tradition. We have already cited its scriptural ground in the great commandments or summary of the law, John 15, and much of 1 John in particular; its appearance in patristic literature, especially Gregory of Nyssa; and in the "Friends of God" movement that impacted Martin Luther, as well as its retrieval in several contemporary authors.[4] This theme of friendship with God also appears, however, in a surprising place in traditional spiritual theology, in the discussion of the life of virtue in the illuminative stage, which I am now re-imagining as the current of transfiguration. Reginald Garrigou-Lagrange, for example, after a lengthy discussion of all the virtues in the moral edifice of illumination, comes to a much more enlightening discussion of the three theological virtues (faith, hope, and love) as "infused," that is, as participation in God's own parallel perfection(s) by the gracious indwelling of the Holy Spirit. First, *faith* is a simple participation in God's wisdom by which "we believe at the same time in God revealing and in God revealed."[5] As such, it is a gift of God, aided by the charisms of wisdom and understanding. It belongs to the same order as eternal life, is given by the divine indwelling (of the Holy Spirit and hence of the whole Trinity), and is the root and ground of the movement toward contemplative prayer that begins in this current.[6]

Second, the infused virtue of *hope* is also a tending toward eternal life, a confidence in God that our desire and love for God will ultimately be fulfilled by God's gracious gift of union. We do not rely on ourselves or on our own effort but on God our helper "according to His mercy, His promises, His omnipotence."[7] Hope is aided by humility in that it reminds us of our total dependence on God's graciousness.[8] We cannot hope for something until we admit our own need and inability to meet ourselves; hence humility is the mother of hope. But the ultimate ground and motive of hope is God's own graciousness and fidelity.[a]

Finally, Garrigou-Lagrange's treatment of charity, *caritas, agapē,* or infused *love,* a participation in that love which is God's own nature in the inner life of the Trinity, has a title that does not seem promising in contemporary terms: "The Love of Conformity to the Divine Will."[9] But it is precisely at this point that his discussion takes a surprising turn: it is grounded in a discussion of the notion of becoming, in this current, one of the "friends of God," with helpful support from Thomas Aquinas.[10] Every true friendship has three characteristics, all forms of "philial" love (*philia* is the Greek word for love as friendship): benevolence, wishing for the other's good; mutuality, or the reciprocity of the relationship (and here is where Weil's concepts of attention and distance become so critical); and community of life (*convivere*).[11] This love of friendship with God is pure gift because we have no capacity as creatures to be friends with our creator without the gift of an equality that does not otherwise exist. Even our natural inclination to love God cannot be efficacious without healing from sin. But even more, God gives us the gift of what the tradition calls "mutual benevolence" precisely as a gift of grace, through the indwelling of the Holy Spirit by Baptism, in a manner that establishes a *koinōnia*, a *convivere* with God that ultimately demands the permanent union of the third current as its fulfillment.[12] It is pure gift, and even the predisposition to receive it is gift.[13]

What initially sounds so stultifying, "conformity to the divine will," has its roots in a much more exciting notion—transfiguring union. That is, as we grow in union with God, whatever virtue we have comes more and more to be a participation in God's own perfection(s). This is like the effect of friendship with a truly great human person whose excellences of character "rub off" on us. But we have also seen, as Jesus taught in John 15, that friendship is a communion of shared moral purpose. Thus, our will becomes increasingly aligned with God's will, not from compulsion, but through love, *philia* as transfigured in *agapē*.[b] The love of God for us and our love of God for God's own goodness become increasingly the ground and motive of all other virtues. This includes, naturally, loving also that which our great Friend loves, and hence loving one's neighbor in God and God in one's neighbor. Thus, love of neighbor, what the tradition has called "fraternal charity," flows naturally, directly, and inevitably from love of God.[14] Indeed, because love of God cannot be seen reliably, the only visible measure we have for someone's progress in the spiritual life is an increase of effective love for the neighbor.

---

a Those in recovery programs will recognize the rhythm of steps one and two—after admitting our own powerlessness and unmanageability (humility), we come to believe "that a Power greater than ourselves could restore us to sanity" (hope).

b Again, the recovery community will recognize here the ground of step eleven.

In short, everything that now sounds so unpalatable in the traditional phrases, such as "progressive conformity to the will of God" or "docility to the Holy Spirit," is still resonating primarily with the first current and themes of submission, sub-ordination, and obedience, which we have seen can be pastorally ambivalent even there.[15] In this second current, however, the focus shifts to the growing, loving communion of shared moral purpose between friends, resulting in a transfigura-tion of character and ultimately an increasing (by grace) equality that will issue in the *theōsis* of the third current.

Before that becomes dominant, however, the overflow from love of God to love of neighbor creates in each of us the reality of *vocation*. In the first current, vocation was primarily experienced as the general call to leave behind the world of sin (as personal wrongdoing or as the abuse or oppression from which we are liberated) and follow Jesus. Now, in the transfiguring experience of friendship with God as a communion of shared moral purpose, each of us is called to a particular "piece of the action"; as our natural endowments and inclinations interface with the needs of neighbor and world, we are given gifts for work to do on behalf of the up-building of the commonwealth, work that can cover a gamut from physical labor to theoreti-cal physics. Work as charism will be a primary focus of the next chapter. Here we note that as we grow into our particular calling, the will of God is mediated to us by the gift of wisdom that helps shape us for our vocation, and also by life events, "some of which are painful and unexpected."[16] The indwelling of the Holy Spirit and the events of our personal life-history slowly shape us into something useful for God's commonwealth.

This can sometimes be a painful process; just as in a marriage we make prom-ises, "for better, for worse; for richer for poorer; in sickness and in health," so it is in our friendship with God. We must learn to love in affliction as well as prosperity.[17] We are called to love God in travail as well as triumph; indeed, given the circum-stances of the human world as we know it, perhaps more often in travail. Eventually we come to love this very travail and even the suffering that can accompany it, not because God has sent it for our education, but because, whatever its source, God is able to trump it with a grace that transfigures it for our formation.[18] Of course, everything said previously about demonic pain must be reiterated here. Choosing to suffer with Christ on behalf of the world is far different from giving in to abuse or oppression. Ultimately, we face here the scandal of the cross—Christ's and ours.[19] We are not to seek suffering for morbid reasons, or because it builds character, or because God sent it; but, mysteriously, being willing to suffer some things with Christ for the world does sometimes have a miraculous ability to expand love. It is certainly the best we can do with those things that must unavoidably be suffered anyway. Sometimes, the final sacrifice of friendship is life itself.

> We should, therefore, deem as nothing all that we give to obtain the price-less treasure of the love of God, of ardent love. He alone gives to the human heart the interior charity that it lacks. Without Him our hearts are cold; we experience only the passing warmth of an intermittent fever.
>
> When we give our love to God, He always gives us His.[20]

This reveals, in the sharpest terms, a point that is dear to Garrigou-Lagrange's heart—the union of the ascetical and the mystical. From the standpoint of this divine friendship (of transfiguration leading to *theōsis,* of the third current as already implicit in the second), love of conformity to the divine will, the passive love of participation in the divine life, and active charity in love of neighbor are not three separable realities to be assembled in some hierarchical ladder of growth in merit; instead, they are but three different aspects of the end of the spiritual life in the ordinary way of grace.[21]

As a result, divine love, as both God's first love for us and then our love for God, overflows inevitably into active and effective love of neighbor. God desires the same *koinōnia, convivere* with other humans as we have come to enjoy; it becomes our passion to expand this community of love indefinitely until it embraces the whole human race, and indeed, as appropriate, the whole material creation. As 1 John in particular makes clear, we cannot truthfully claim to love God without also loving our neighbor, habitually, actively, and effectively (3:10–24). Because love of God is the ground and motive of "fraternal charity," agapaic love of neighbor is the extension of *philia* to all God's children; because love of God and love of neighbor are indeed actually one love, true love of neighbor is far different from codependent "doing for others" and greater than liberalism and its connection to a natural inclination to benevolence, or even to justice.[22] We love our neighbor because we first love God, and hence our friendship with God dictates that we love all God's children, even our enemies, beyond the bounds of all natural inclination.[23] In particular, this deep connection requires that we desire for all neighbors the greatest happiness a human can enjoy: being in Christ and hence in God, as a temple of the Holy Spirit. If we have come to believe that this is our own greatest good, true love of neighbor, real friendship, cannot but desire this also for others.[24] As a result, the concept of vocation that has emerged here, as grounded in and motivated by *caritas,* includes not only loving service but also *evangelism.* No particular methodology of evangelism is privileged by this insight, but the obligation to help our neighbors discover the good news of their destiny in Christ and hence in God is clear. Anyone filled with love of God and hence of neighbor will have a zeal for both the material and spiritual well-being of all neighbors, and thus a call to some "apostolate," some sense of mission, of being sent into the world to do work that both serves the earthly needs of others and helps them find their destiny in God.[25]

Each one of us will need to discern our particular "piece of the action," and the methods best suited to our temperament, gifts, and context; but the vocation to mission and evangelism is universal, precisely because it is implicit in love of neighbor as grounded in love of God and God's own love. Study will be required for us to understand ourselves, our own gifts and motives, and the unique shape of our own particular call. Study is required, as we have seen, to learn the habit of attention to our neighbors and their own unique context. Study is required to understand our neighbor's life story. Study, of Scripture and of the human reality, is required for effective evangelism. In the metaphor I have developed here, evangelism is any means by which we stand with others on their promontory of the human shore, and, as the tides of the Spirit break on their beach, with sensitivity to their story and context, say, "There, that is grace." This will require our own conversion at all levels, including the political, as we work with our neighbors to build an earthly commonwealth that resembles as much as possible that of God's reign. So crucial is this "study" for making love effective that some will find here their work also, in vocations as scholars and teachers.[26]

For those of us within the body of the church, the vocation to effective love means helping to shape its *koinōnia* to be evidently a communion of minds and hearts, illumined by the divine glory that Christ seeks to share with us all.[27] It must be carefully distinguished from an *esprit de corps* of groupings that form only by natural affinity, including loyalty to a common citizenship. These can be merely a collective egoism, a sense of "we" that excludes others or wishes to leave them behind.[28] The love in which the *koinōnia* of the church is grounded requires openness and attention to all neighbors.

Vocation and Mission

The traditional accounts of the illuminative life usually continue at this point with a further cataloguing of the "lesser" virtues, mostly focused on the interior cultivation of character under the dominion of charity. While there is still much that could be learned from these texts in our time, there is a more urgent task in our context. This task is restoring a deep sense of vocation and mission that leads naturally from study to work, to establishing the kind of *opus* as the product of our lives in God that Teilhard suggested requires no less than the resurrection of the body. This sense of vocation as work, service, and mission generally received some attention in the older theologies of the spiritual life under the topic of apostolate, but it acquires a new urgency in our time.[29] Focus on vocation or apostolate breaks the assumptions by which we locate the spiritual life in individual interiority and demands not only affective, intellectual, and moral conversion but also a deeply *political* conversion, focused now on the *polis* par excellence, the city of God. In this light, the spiritual life can be seen as embracing our entire embodied existence, inner and outer, individual and communal, as we recognize our individual spiritual growth as an aspect of vocation, which is always a call to serve as God's friends in the up-building of the commonwealth, as co-creators with God in the perfecting of the universe. The new humanity does not exist only for itself, but for the sake of the world.

The traditional spiritual theologies also grounded the apostolate in the imitation of Jesus and his immediate followers, and this remains a fruitful topic.[30] But it can be misleading if we think only in terms of imitating a past life or lives, of merely extending the *missio Christi* in time and space. The pneumatological focus I have proposed for re-founding this whole enterprise becomes critical at this point. The power by which Jesus was raised from the dead is still with us, not only indwelling us and decorating us with virtues for our salvation and individual perfection; the Holy Spirit who is Lord and life-giver also calls us into her own Trinitarian *missio*, offering opportunities to work in concrete projects for the final end or perfection of all creation and history, even while shaping us into a community (the Body of Christ with all the dimensions of its *koinōnia* as gifts of the Spirit) that is both the sacramental anticipation of the final commonwealth and *pleroma*, and God's chief incarnate instrument for bringing them about. Surely one of the great weaknesses of the earlier literature was its neglect of this great theme, by which we see all our individual lives of virtue and character flowing directly from love of God to love of neighbor, to love of the world in God, equipping each of us and all of us together for the vocation and mission of up-building that commonwealth. Instead of a catalog of virtues at this point, then, what is called for is a missiology, a pneumatological theology of mission.[31]

In most contemporary literature, while mission in its broadest sense is any outreach of love of neighbor, it has become a term focused on such outreach as it crosses significant boundaries, usually cultural. That is, it is an extension of love of neighbor beyond a natural definition of "neighbor," inspired and mandated by the parable of the Good Samaritan. Crossing a cultural boundary to extend love of neighbor beyond its natural limits may require actual travel, but it is also possible such boundaries may lie across the street, or within one's own home. This reach across boundaries exists in a historical context that now includes all the issues of the collapse of colonialism and the growing encounter among the world religions. In our time, then, we join the search for a postcolonial theology of mission, or missiology, a way to embody the gospel of Jesus Christ across cultural boundaries, in full acknowledgment of the sins of imperialism and a real desire not to import them again.[32] In this search, there has been an increasing tendency to ground missiology in a Trinitarian base.[33] Like the revival of pneumatology traced here in chapter 3, efforts in this direction draw on the revival of Trinitarian theology from Catherine Mowry LaCugna and Elizabeth Johnson to Kathryn Tanner and Sarah Coakley, from David Cunningham to Robert Jenson.[34]

Even the new Trinitarian missiologies tend to move from the *missio Dei* (the mission of God) to the *missio Christi* (the mission of Christ) and then to the *missio ecclesiae* (the mission of the church) in a manner typical of the functional binitarianism of Western theology we have already noted. Indeed, as a professor teaching this material in an ecclesiology class, I have myself been guilty of this approach. Because of the imperial imagery often used to describe Jesus in the tradition, it is difficult for such a presentation not to sound hierarchical and thus resonating with colonial rather than postcolonial contexts. Missing in such an account is a serious consideration of the *missio Spiritus* (the mission of the Spirit) as coming between the *missio Christi* and the *missio ecclesiae*. This is not only an error in Trinitarian thinking but also a lost opportunity to ground a new postcolonial missiology.

Before developing a Spirit-based missiology, however, we can pause and note the postcolonial implications of Trinitarian missiology even so far. The linear model of *missio Dei, missio Christi* requires us to then insert *missio Spiritus* and only then come to the *missio ecclesiae*. We are learning to emphasize that the Holy Spirit is the mediation of all that of which Christ is the mediator, and hence *missio Spiritus* is the mediation of the *missio Christi* to the *missio ecclesiae*.[35] The church is found in the third, or Holy Spirit, paragraph of the creed, and is born on Pentecost, not as a separate event but precisely as the climax of the paschal mystery. The power by which Jesus was raised from the dead is still with us, forming us into a community which is his postresurrection body on earth. In particular, the church cannot be understood properly without an account of the manner in which the Spirit, in precisely her superfluity, gratuitousness, and reticence, unexpectedly gifts the Word/Wisdom with a body—incarnational, resurrected, ecclesial, and sacramental.[36] The contemporary theologies of the church focused on the concept of communion, and the ecumenical goal of a "communion of communions" in particular, must be grounded in an account of *koinōnia* (common life, fellowship, communion) as ligaments graciously provided by the Spirit as sheer first gift to the covenant people.[37]

Here there are already immense *missio*logical implications. From the very beginning, or near it, the Spirit rests on the new community, creating its *koinōnia* as the sacramental reality that is the body of the risen Christ; the surprise is that this new body is going to include the unsavable other, the gentile.[38] We should note that in Acts it is precisely the Spirit who drives this radical inclusiveness, from the phenomenon of tongues at Pentecost, right through the conversion of Cornelius and his entourage, to the apostolic council of Jerusalem. So, even this linear model proposes an important postcolonial principle: a radical hospitality and inclusivity that welcomes the Spirit-filled but previously unsavable other precisely in his or her radical otherness. That is, from its very inner core, this pneumatological ecclesiology funds a missiological basis:[39] the ecclesial body with which the Spirit gifts the Word/Wisdom surprisingly and in principle contains gentiles, Samaritans, the illegitimate, the eunuch, the unclean, the unrighteous sinner, the tax collector, the prostitute, the unsavable other. There are huge implications here for both interfaith dialogue and even the sexuality issues currently facing the churches.[40] But we also find here a first principle of postcolonial missiology grounded in the Spirit—the recognition of a *koinōnia* and hospitality that demands radical inclusivity of the confronting and strange other, not simply as an ethical demand for praxis but as a theological principle at the heart of what it means to be church in its very pneumatological and therefore sacramental/missiological ground. This is also an appropriate foundation for addressing what I see as the besetting issues of contemporary missiology: the appropriate approach to persons of other faiths and the desire to find development programs that do not lead to new slavery.

A more constructive proposal along the lines already developed in previous chapters joins the call for giving the Holy Spirit her own theological *locus*, coming between Christ and church in the post-Vatican II list of the *loci*. At the same time, we must honor the reticence and gratuitousness of the Spirit herself as a reason this has not yet happened.[41] The purpose is not merely to allow for a study of the Spirit in her own right but to recognize all the items in the third paragraph of the creeds as the work of the Spirit in her own mission. In particular, we can continue to follow Jenson's suggestion that the external works of the Trinity are undivided, but not indistinguishable; it then becomes clear that the Trinitarian structure of the Spirit's *missio*, which up to this point has been the ground for the three tidal currents of the spiritual life, also resonates in the activities we call "mission."

The first Trinitarian aspect of the Spirit's *missio* is thus completion of the work or mission of the Fount in creation and covenant. In the rhythms of the spiritual life, I have called this tide "conversion." In missiology, this is the discourse of evangelism. But in a Spirit-based missiology, before we present the kerygma, the gospel proclamation, as we know it, we are called on to listen to the other and discern where the other and the other's culture already embody the Spirit as the point of return, of *teshuvah*, of *metanoia* and *metamorphosis*. It is not simply that this will be the point of leverage for the return or conversion of the other to the covenant and the Fount who is its ultimate author, but rather that the desired turning is not toward us and our gospel but internally to the point of re-turn already present in the context of the other, which our kerygma may help reveal. I have also suggested that this tide of conversion includes *healing* and *liberation* equally with what we have classically thought of as repentance and conviction of sin. Such an approach provides a wider perspective on the possibility of fruitful dialogue with persons of other faith than one that is christological only (though, following Kilian McDonnell in particular, we must recognize that just as any proper Christology is pneumatological, so any proper pneumatology is ultimately christological).[42] The Spirit is both the means of access to the other persons of the Trinity and the point of "return" to the Abba-Fount through the Word/Wisdom that is the consistent call of Scripture.[43] We need not, however, begin with the classic presentation of repentance as leaving behind an old identity as sinful in the act of repentance, and then submission to Christ the King dressed in the imperial robes of the missionary culture. Instead, we recognize the Spirit already at work in the other and the other's culture, always and already the point of return to the Fount via the Word/Wisdom. That means a couple of things. In the postcolonial context, in fact, it is probably best to discern, precisely in the Spirit-as-point-of return already present in the other, the opportunities for mission in service of healing and liberation. Indeed, when the moment of conviction of sin and the time for repentance finally come, it will not result in a repentance by the other for what we perceive as his or her otherness, but for those things present in the other and the other's culture that alienate them from the point of return already embedded in themselves and their context.

Because the second aspect of the Spirit's mission is support of the Word/Wisdom in the *missio Christi*, we can note, with McDonnell and Eugene Rogers among others, the complex dance these two Trinitarian persons weave in the mysteries of the incarnation.[44] A particular theme gives the name and character to what I see as the second tide of the Christian life, transfiguration. In the classic tradition the light of divine glory shines on Jesus on Mt. Tabor and reveals to the three disciples the truth about who he has been all along, with Moses and Elijah representing the testimony of the Law and the Prophets to that truth. The glory radiating from the face of Christ (Paul in 2 Cor 4:3–6) also reveals for us and in the other the deepest truth of who we are, and this also is the work of the Spirit as love and light. This dimension of the *missio Christi* can result in mission activities that serve directly the cause of illuminating the gracefulness already present in the other, including the other's culture and religion. It may call for healing and liberation; but in addition it will also involve celebration and activities of manifestation. Ultimately, Christians will want to name the name of Jesus in this celebration. But (1) the point of return and the light of Tabor are already present in the other and the other's culture; (2) as we have seen, in the end all true pneumatology is also christological, the Spirit herself bearing witness to the Word/Wisdom as incarnate Lord. As a result, we can trust the always-and-already-present Spirit to identify the christological opportunity precisely within the life of the other. It is not something we need to import from the outside. We can also trust the Spirit to give the discernment of when the time has come within the dialogue to name the Name, to call glory, Glory, and to identify the gracious life as precisely one lived in grace.[45]

A third theme in the emerging pneumatological consensus is the importance of the Spirit's role in eschatology.[46] This is the third aspect of the mission of the Spirit, the Spirit's own proper mission that is, in turn, supported by the Fount and the Word/Wisdom, to sanctify the entire cosmic *pleroma* by sacramentally consecrating it as the gift of return to the Abba-Fount in and by the Word/Wisdom. In the process, all things are not merely redeemed but resurrected and fulfilled. Not only our intentions, but our work, our *opus* has a place in the final *pleroma*. As Teilhard indicated, this requires nothing less than the resurrection of the body, and here we note again the emphasis in current pneumatology on the Spirit as the power by which the Fount raises Jesus from the dead.[47] Not only humans but, somehow and beyond all hope, all beings are included in the *pleroma*. This allows a broader sense of mission in a postcolonial situation in that it enables mission not only as "bringing to Christ," but also as enabling all peoples and things to be gifted with their own proper fulfillment and ultimate destiny. Thus, a pneumatological perspective on mission provides a new way of addressing the besetting issues of economic development and environmental stewardship that plague contemporary missiological praxis. Pneumatological development must respect the critiques of, for example, ecofeminist theology, even while it seeks to find ways of fostering economic development that do not re-enslave peoples to the multinational corporate monsters. This pneumatological approach also allows for a mission of "discernment of spirits" to identify and support movements of the Spirit in a highly contextualized fashion, opening up avenues of service that are genuinely Christian without being imperialistic or triumphalist. Mission can be seen not only as *kerygma* but also as manifestation and prophecy in the service of that healing and liberation by which the Spirit prepares and rests on the gratuitous body she gives to the Word/Wisdom.[48]

Continuing to make use of the analysis of David Tracy and Robert Jenson here yields some additional thoughts, taking this construction deeper into a fully Trinitarian dialectic:

First, the Trinitarian structure of the Spirit's *missio* provides a distinguishable but unified sense of mission:

The Spirit's mission in completion of the Fount's mission yields a missiology of proclamation, of conversion to covenant redemption for repentance, healing, and liberation. As we have seen, this involves Spirit as the point of return to the Abba-Fount. As the Spirit liberates the Fount to be the God of strangers, she liberates us, strangers all, to be the people of God through the theological virtue of faith.

The Spirit's mission in support of the Word/Wisdom's is in the mode of manifestation or transfiguration, supporting a missiology of loving service to the neighbor and a celebration of divine immanence and incarnation (pan*en*theism). As the Spirit liberates the Word/Wisdom to be the child of the Abba-Fount and also the head of an earthly body, she liberates us to be the organs of that body in completion of the mission of the Word/Wisdom in service of the virtue of love. The cross is, of course, the decisive expression of that love in history.

In her own proper *missio*, the Spirit is the eschatological Spirit of hope, bringing the entire material cosmos to the fulfillment of its finality and ultimately glory, liberating the other two Trinitarian persons and the cosmos for this unforeseeable future. Both prophetic self-criticism for liberating action and infused contemplation of the glory that shall be belong to this current.

Second, the dialectics of the Trinitarian missions support one another. As we have previously seen, Tracy suggests that the negativities of the outer two, proclamation and prophecy, by themselves will degenerate into rage or despair; the positivism of the middle, manifestation, by itself collapses into a Pollyannaish optimism. Only in a Trinitarian balance do they together point toward true hope. This provides a theological basis for critique of all one-dimensional missiologies: missiologies of proclamation alone or of prophetic criticism alone are likely to become exhausted in despair or explode in rage, as Tracy predicts. A missiology of service alone, however, will collapse under the weight of its own unmitigated optimism, failing to address the serious issues of evil and transcendence. Only when the three are held together in tension do we find a balance, with each dialectic enriched by the others. Practical missiology thus involves *study* so that neighbor-love may be effective beyond its usual boundaries. This will involve not only the study of the historical, cultural, linguistic, and religious context of the other, as well as considerable study of our own reactions and agendas, but also of theological missiology in order that our plans and actions may have this proper Trinitarian balance. So important is this study that some will find in it their own particular vocation.

Understanding these three tides of conversion, transfiguration, and glory as concurrent currents of the Spirit's *missio* allows us to see each mission situation in its own context, discerning the point of entry suggested by the Spirit's current activity *in loco*. While eventually all modes will need to come to bear in a fully Trinitarian dialectic, any particular situation may call for a different starting point. In particular, in a postcolonial approach to persons of other faith, we may want to go beyond co-operation in loving service to a real mutual perception of the unimaginable future of the *pleroma*, paying principal attention to the Spirit's own proper *missio* as the ground on which to introduce later, in a fully dialogical diction, our witness to covenant and incarnation. As such, we can begin not only with healing and liberation but also with all activities that bring persons and other beings to greater fulfillment of their pleromic finality. This can mean healing and liberation from the forces that work against that fulfillment, and, in the context of a pneumatological/Trinitarian theology of the diversity of world religions, co-operative work with persons of other faith.[49] In this way, love of neighbor does indeed overflow out of God's love beyond the natural definition of "neighbor."

In a missiology grounded in the *missio* of the Spirit, we can see the appropriateness of this approach and the required postcolonial humility. In the power of the Spirit we can manifest in healing, service, and prophetic liberation the tip of the Trinitarian iceberg, trusting the Spirit herself to do the work and make apparent when and if the moment of proclamation has arrived, and knowing then it can be in a fully dialogical context (beyond exclusivism, inclusivism, pluralism). In accordance with this missiology, the most important gift for missionary work is thus the charism of discernment or *discretio*.[50] This charism allows us to listen to the other with an ear not only for how the Logos/Sophia is already enlightening the others (John 1) but also how the Holy Spirit is already seeking to bring them to their destined perfection in the *pleroma*. On that basis we not only have the possibility of a non-imperialist conversational response in which we might also learn something; we also can design mission strategies that minister to the flow of the Spirit in the others as we and they have mutually discerned it. As Christians we are confident that in the end all pneumatology is christological, as all Christology is pneumatological. This approach is thus not a betrayal of the kerygmatic imperative but fidelity to Jesus' own usual first question to an other, "What is it you want me to do for you?" This provides a general ground for all Christian vocation; but some may find their lives shaped by a call to this specific kind of activity as a way of life. Others will be called to work in a broader context, but in some fashion all real work will contain some element of this love of neighbor, some sense of participation in the Spirit's mission.

Notes

1. Part of the exercise of this book is to translate wisdom from the older generation of spiritual theologies into a structure and language that is useful in our context. In this chapter and chapter 23 in particular, I am doing that with reference to Reginald Garrigou-Lagrange's *Three Ages of the Interior Life*. I will be citing particular passages occasionally but wish to note here a deeper dependence on that text than the footnotes may convey. Garrigou-Lagrange's work is among the most attractive of the "old school" for a variety of reasons. It is very much in the French tradition of embracing what were then contemporary humanistic concerns; it takes a very clear position on the unity of ascetical and mystical theology and life; struggles to find a less hierarchical relationship of spirituality to moral theology; and it agrees with Kenneth Kirk that infused contemplation, as a foretaste of the beatific vision, belongs in at least some measure to the ordinary life of grace of all Christians. See especially the epilogue and addenda on these issues in *Three Ages*, 2.628–54. He gives us the first clear sense of the dark nights as additional conversions and adopts the scheme I have repeated of seeing the night of the senses, active and passive, between purgation and illumination, that of the soul between illumination and union. See *Three Ages*, 2.21–64 for his description of this second conversion and first night (what I have called "slack"). Nevertheless, Garrigou-Lagrange's work is very much of its time, in a pre-Vatican II scholastic diction (though the references to Aquinas are often very helpful), envisioned as a certain and universal theological science, highly monastic with little application to the life of laity in the world or even "secular" (nonmonastic) clergy; it is also deeply imbued with other characteristics of French Catholic piety of the time that are direct descendants of the seventeenth-century movements discussed here in chapter 3, many of which now strike us as quaint rather than helpful. Translation is needed, but much wisdom is retrievable. This chapter is highly dependent on *Three Ages*, 2.65–248.

2. Like James Fowler in *Becoming Adult*, I thus see vocation as linked to the human psycho-

logical stage of generativity and the virtue of caring=*caritas*=*agapē*=love of neighbor as it flows from love of God; see p. 93.

3. See especially the brilliant essay "Reflections on the Right Use of School Studies with a View to the Love of God," in Weil, *Waiting for God*, 105.

4. See previous discussions of friendship theology in chap. 8 above.

5. Garrigou-Lagrange, *Three Ages*, 2.72–167, for the discussion of virtues; 2.169 for the quote.

6. Garrigou-Lagrange, *Three Ages*, 2.169–70.

7. Garrigou-Lagrange, *Three Ages*, 2.179. Here as elsewhere, he gives fulsome citations, especially of Aquinas.

8. Garrigou-Lagrange, *Three Ages*, 2.118–22.

9. Garrigou-Lagrange, *Three Ages*, 2.187–98.

10. Garrigou-Lagrange, *Three Ages*, 2.188–92; the primary reference to Aquinas is IIa IIae, q. 23, a.1, but see additional references on p. 189 nn. 5, 6.

11. Garrigou-Lagrange, *Three Ages*, 2.188–89.

12. Garrigou-Lagrange gives a highly significant footnote at this point, *Three Ages*, 2.193 n. 15, in which he defends the doctrine that infused or mystical contemplation "proceeds from infused faith illumined by the gifts of wisdom and understanding" in the ordinary life of grace through the gifts of the Holy Spirit. He decries the romantic error that locates the mystical in certain natural qualities of a select few "who are more emotional and poetical than others"; he also critiques the opposite error of identifying the mystical life with extraordinary phenomena. Both of these are excluded by the teaching of St. John of the Cross and St. Teresa that the true mystical life is not to be confounded with either sentimentality or extraordinary phenomena.

13. Garrigou-Lagrange, *Three Ages*, 2.192; see n. 12 with reference to Aquinas, IIa IIae, q. 24, a.3 and Ia IIae, q. 109, a. 3 and a.4.

14. Garrigou-Lagrange, *Three Ages*, 2.191, 199.

15. Garrigou-Lagrange, *Three Ages*, 2.193, 223–40.

16. Garrigou-Lagrange, *Three Ages*, 2.193–94. These are what Life Training (Brown and Whitten) calls "lifeshocks."

17. Again we are reminded of Weil's essay, "The Love of God and Affliction," in *Waiting for God*, 117–36.

18. On the concept of travail and its link to the cross, see Cynthia Crysdale, *Embracing Travail*.

19. Garrigou-Lagrange, *Three Ages*, 2.195; and for the important issues raised here for feminist and other liberation theologies, see again Cynthia Crysdale, *Embracing Travail*.

20. Garrigou-Lagrange, *Three Ages*, 2.196.

21. Garrigou-Lagrange, *Three Ages*, 2.197–98, with important reference to John of the Cross and writers that were contemporary with him. This is a keystone of his proposal for the restructuring of spiritual theology as a unified discipline.

22. Hence, Weil was correct to subordinate justice to love of neighbor, to show that true justice is indeed a form of love of neighbor (*Waiting for God*, 139–57).

23. Garrigou-Lagrange, *Three Ages*, 2.200; again, there is a helpful reference to Aquinas, IIa, IIae, q.23, a.1, ad 2um, strikingly derived from the concept of friendship.

24. Garrigou-Lagrange, *Three Ages*, 2.201–3, with reference to Aquinas, IIa, IIae, q.25, a.1. Note that proper esteem for our own selves as animated or souled bodies is included in this neighborly benevolence flowing from love of God.

25. Garrigou-Lagrange has a whole chapter on the classical concept of zeal and its relationship to mission or apostolate (2.213–22).

26. The classic work on this vocation remains Jean Leclercq, *The Love of Learning and the Desire for God*.

27. Garrigou-Lagrange, *Three Ages*, 2.212, with reference to John 17:22ff.

28. Garrigou-Lagrange calls this "nosism," and links it to chauvinism as opposed to true

patriotism (*Three Ages*, 2.205). Indeed, this failure of fraternal charity is the glaring weakness of the whole "left behind" phenomenon.

29. Garrigou-Lagrange, *Three Ages*, has a chapter on it, but in the section on the stage of union, and it is a bit perfunctory, though we shall return to it later (2.489–96). The topic scarcely appears in Antonio Royo and Jordan Aumann.

30. Garrigou-Lagrange, *Three Ages*, 2.490–94; on Thomas à Kempis's *Imitation* itself, see 2.272–78; Garrigou-Lagrange's argument there that the way of the *Imitation* supports his claim that infused contemplation and union with God "are in the ordinary way of sanctity" remains an important statement.

31. What follows is drawn from a longer treatment first delivered as a paper, "The *Missio Spiritus*: An Underexplored Ground of Post-Colonial Missiology and Praxis."

32. Ian T. Douglas and Kwok Pui-Lan, eds., *Beyond Colonial Anglicanism*.

33. See, for example, Titus Presler, *Horizons of Mission*.

34. Catherine Mowry LaCugna, *God for Us*; Elizabeth Johnson, *She Who Is*; Kathryn Tanner, *Jesus, Humanity and the Trinity*; David Cunningham, *These Three Are One*; Robert Jenson, *ST*. Again we await the first volume of Sarah Coakley's systematics.

35. Kilian McDonnell, *Other Hand of God*, 105–6, and several other places noted under "Spirit-as-mediation," 258.

36. I am following Eugene Rogers here, *After the Spirit*, 85–97.

37. Jenson has a good discussion of this, *ST* 2.220–27, 234–37.

38. Following Rogers again, see n. 36 above.

39. See also Steffen Lösel, "Guidance from the Gaps: The Holy Spirit, Ecclesial Authority, and the Principle of Juxtaposition."

40. See again my "Christian Theology of Interfaith Dialogue"; Rogers obviously intends this connection to the sexuality issues, given his personal and scholarly commitments. See his *Sexuality and the Christian Body*.

41. Rogers, *After the Spirit*, 23–29, 45–47. The list of the *loci* would then read God, creation, humanity and sin, Christ, Holy Spirit, church, sacraments, last things.

42. McDonnell, *Other Hand*, 88, and throughout.

43. McDonnell, *Other Hand*, 95, and throughout.

44. McDonnell, *Other Hand*, 88, and throughout; Rogers, *After the Spirit*, 75–212, and throughout.

45. Nicholas Lash, *Easter in Ordinary*, 242–53.

46. See my "The Historic Ought-to-Be and the Spirit of Hope."

47. Pierre Teilhard de Chardin, *Divine Milieu*, 29ff.

48. I again follow here David Tracy, *The Analogical Imagination*. For a full statement of the relationship of my project to Tracy's, see my "A Critical Note on Two Aspects of Self-Transcendence."

49. Veli-Matti Kärkkäinen, *Pneumatology*; and idem, with Amos Yong, eds., *Toward a Pneumatological Theology*, esp. 191ff.; idem, "How to Speak of the Spirit among Religions"; also, idem, *Trinity and Religious Pluralism*; Amos Yong, *Beyond the Impasse*.

50. See now Mark A. McIntosh, *Discernment and Truth*.

22

Love of the Order and Beauty
of the World and Work

God so loved the world (kosmos).   —John 3:16

The love of the order and beauty of the world is thus the complement of the love of our neighbor.

It proceeds from the same renunciation, the renunciation that is an image of the creative renunciation of God.   —Simone Weil[1]

As we have already seen in chapter 20, one of the most startling omissions in traditional Christian spiritualities, according to Simone Weil, is the neglect of the beauty of the world as "the tender trap God most frequently uses."[2] This is, perhaps, even truer in our time, as the numbers of people who experience God primarily through the hunger and peace they experience in encountering "nature" increases apace with "civilization and its discontents." Both Pierre Teilhard de Chardin and Weil have taught us that our primary engagement with the world, in appreciation for its beauty and order, is through the second of the Benedictine principles, *work*. Thus conceived, work is the vocation from God to create and leave as an inheritance an *opus*, a body of work that is the product of our lives as co-creators with God. It is also startling, therefore, how few works of spiritual theology devote any serious attention to this subject.[3] Those that mention it at all treat it only as an unfortunate necessity for the maintenance of human physical existence, or as part of the discipline that can aid toward the true end of human being, which is contemplation. The idea of work as an essential aspect of being human, as an end in itself, as itself a positive spiritual practice, would seem almost foreign to the Christian tradition.

Fortunately, other voices have joined the fundamental insight derived from Teilhard and Weil that this is a serious lacuna that must be closed; this is especially important in a time and culture such as ours where work has achieved nearly obsessive status, its attitudes and practices often driving even our practice of leisure. The principle guide for us here will be Miroslav Volf, *Work in the Spirit: Toward a Theology of Work,* with some reference also to a succeeding and somewhat complementary work by Armand Larive.[4] I shall first mine from these works principles that are most relevant to work as a spiritual practice in the tide of transfiguration; following the hints in Weil and Teilhard, sections on physical labor, science, and art follow, concluding with a brief consideration of labor for ecojustice as the crown of this love in our time.

Work in the Spirit

Volf sees the traditional teaching of Catholic theology, at least until recently, as hampered by a view that work is not an end in itself for human spirituality but only a means to that end by providing human sustenance and as a kind of *askesis* or discipline that can be conducive to contemplative prayer.[5] On the Protestant side, actual work is viewed as a specific external vocation (*vocatio externa*) that expresses the universal call of God to all people (*vocatio spiritualis*) in a specific work determined by one's state of life and profession. This improves on the medieval view Martin Luther was critiquing, by giving work a higher value and freeing the active, working life from subordination to the contemplative.[6] Even this vocational view has several problems, however. It fails to deal with the issue of the alienation of workers; it cannot deal with conflicts between the universal call (*vocatio spiritualis*) and actual states of life and employment; it provides no basis for ideological critique of dehumanizing forces in the workplace; it can deal neither with the contemporary experience of *diachronic plurality of employment* (holding several different jobs over a lifetime), or *synchronic plurality of employment* (multi-tasking, having several different "jobs" at the same time); and over time it became enmeshed in limiting the notion of work to gainful employment, which ignores the value of all work that does not receive financial compensation, including "house work."[7]

Volf suggests a radical shift in the theology of work toward a pneumatological approach, which is highly consistent with the pneumatological approach to spirituality I am proposing. This shift has two fundamental aspects. First, although work remains co-operation with God in creation, the emphasis shifts from a *protological* approach in which we essentially conserve what God has created, to an *eschatological* approach; in this latter, all human labor is work in the Spirit, co-operating with God in establishing the new creation in Christ that eventuates in the *pleroma* and ultimately the fullness of God's commonwealth or reign.[8] In that light, Volf's second constructive proposal is to keep the concept of the universal call, the *vocatio spiritualis*; but instead of having that expressed only as a static vocation shaped by state of life or profession, it now becomes expressed as *charisms*, or specific gifts, both natural endowments and more directly divine gifts; that is, at the level of work *charism* replaces vocation.[a][9]

---

a Larive helpfully points out that a fully Trinitarian structure gives an even richer view of work, preserving the protological dimension of God as creator in *homo conservans*, focusing the eschatological on Christ and *homo artifex*, the human being as able to do new things, and the equipping of humans for these tasks by the Spirit (*charisms*) in the emergence of *homo viator*; see *After Sunday*, 73–126. He already takes account of, and adds helpful material to, Volf's arguments. My own scheme would suggest a synthesis of the two views: Volf is correct to see a fundamentally pneumatological approach to work, which can account for Larive's Trinitarian richness by noting the Trinitarian structure of the Spirit's *missio* as has been consistently carried out here. This would suggest that all work is work in the Spirit, some in assisting the Abba/Fount in creation and covenant (protological), some in assisting the

This double shift has several consequences that resonate well with seeing work as pneumatological in both senses: eschatological and charismatic. First is an ethical theme that runs through Volf's proposal. A pneumatological doctrine of work dictates three ethical principles: attention to the dignity and freedom of individuals, "satisfaction of the basic needs of all people, and the protection of nature from irreparable damage."[10] Note the way this fulfills precisely Weil's notions of attention and renunciation at the heart of love of neighbor and love of the order and beauty of the world.

Second, this approach demands an eschatology, a vision of the final end, that is *transformative* rather than *annihilationist*. It requires, that is, a view of the *pleroma* that subsumes human work on behalf of the new creation, rather than merely replacing it. This is true not only of the work of human individuals but of the "human project" as a whole, and, indeed, calls for a place for human work even in a glorified world.[11] This resonates with Teilhard's claim that the salvation of our *opus* requires the resurrection of the body and also with the position taken here that locates work primarily in the tide of transfiguration, looking back as it does to creation and forward to glory.

Third, and as a direct consequence, work refers to self-fulfillment as the spiritual style of this tide. Volf sees our own personal development through work, including the work of co-operating in making ourselves (which involves more than work, as we shall see, since leisure as worship is also required), as the appropriate form of self-fulfillment and self-expression.[12] Indeed, the theological understanding of human destiny in the concepts of *theōsis* and beatific vision require this expression of self-transcendence as fulfillment and personal growth and development.[13] Human self-transcendence, however, is also a ground for something as "practical" as the dynamic (or expanding) character of human needs, including product-needs in the economy.[14] The limits on the expansion of product-needs also derive from a recognition of human needs that in turn spring from human self-transcendence.[a] These are the needs for communion with God, solidarity with nature, the commonwealth of care for one another's well-being in the Body of Christ, and the need for ongoing human growth and development. In short, the ultimate requirement for work is to serve the universal need for "the new creation, which is the kingdom of freedom."[15] Ethical attention to these needs in a theology of work helps resolve the issues of alienation and ideology, partly through appropriately embracing the cross and suffering on behalf of the world, and ultimately gives birth to activities of liberation and the construction of a humane political economy.[16] Volf gives a helpful summary of his vision:

> Since human beings were created to live on earth as God's co-workers in anticipation of the new creation, the Spirit imparted to them various gifts to accomplish that task. These gifts form part of their personality that they

---

Word/Wisdom in incarnation and redemption (*artifex* as incarnational), and work directly in service of the New Creation, the fully eschatological dimension of the Spirit's own proper mission of consecrating the *pleroma*. Working this out in detail would take a book on its own.

a A reminder again that human self-transcendence is not a property of human nature but of the gracious dimension of human existence as a resonance of God's Trinitarian self-transcendence.

are responsible to respect and develop, both because of the intrinsic value of their personalities as integral parts of the new creation, and because the more they are developed, the better they can anticipate the new creation through their work. Since human beings should strive to image the new creation in the present world as the good that God ultimately desires for them, their personal development is, to use Kantian terminology, a command of morally practical reason, not merely a counsel of technically practical reason.[17] Which of the many aspects of their personalities they should concentrate on developing depends on what gifts they have received from God and what tasks they have been called to accomplish. The duty not to treat other people (and oneself) as a means only and the responsibility to perfect oneself provide important criteria for diagnosing alienation and give direction to efforts to humanize work.[18]

I would also add that we see here, in work as such, a source of the drive for personal development in gifts and virtues sadly neglected in most spiritual theologies. We develop gifts, talents, and virtues not only *by* work (as an *askesis* for contemplation), but also *for* work as itself one of the ends of human being in service of the new creation, and therefore itself a positive spiritual practice, at least potentially. This view of work as spiritual practice helps undo the false identification between "spirituality" and the "inner life" that has plagued Western spirituality, by giving the *vocatio externa*, now interpreted as the exercise of charisms in support of the new creation, its own value as both practice and end.[19]

In particular, if a Christian theology and spirituality of work are to contribute to nonalienating and increasingly humanized work, it must insist on three foci: the call of God (which implies, as we shall see at the end of this chapter, worship as a leisure activity that limits work); discernment of individual gifts or *charisms*; and care for the common good. This common good includes the welfare of others, a political economy that meets the basic needs of all, a culture that promotes human dignity and autonomy in loving the order and beauty of the world, and solidarity with nature itself.[20] In short, as any good charismatic theology would insist, true *charisms* are inherently edifying not just of the individual but also of the body, the commonwealth.[21] Work that truly expresses such gifts will also help build the new creation almost by definition. Volf concludes with a helpful reminder of the way work as self-expression, as a true expression of graced self-transcendence, ultimately leads to the kind of self-forgetfulness that leads to glory:

> To state that neither work nor the product of work should be a mere means but should also be ends in themselves is to maintain that every good worker goes out of herself and loses herself in her work. Without such "self-forgetfulness," in which the inborn egoism that twists everything into means for our ends loosens its grip on us, there is no true joy in work.[22] The opposition between the self-forgetfulness in work and self-realization in work is only apparent. Just as "everything else" will be added when we seek the kingdom of God (Matt 6:33), so will self-realization be added to us when

we seek good work, when we serve others by self-forgetful, enjoyable work that does not violate our personhood.[23]

Physical Labor

The Elixir

Teach me, my God and King,
  In all things thee to see,
And what I do in anything,
  To do it as for thee:
  Not rudely, as a beast,
  To run into an action;
But still to make thee prepossest,
  And give it his perfection.
  A man that looks on glass,
  On it may stay his eye;
Or if he pleaseth, through it pass,
  And then the heav'n espy.
  All may of thee partake:
  Nothing can be so mean,
Which with his tincture (for thy sake)
  Will not grow bright and clean.
  A servant with this clause
  Makes drudgery divine:
Who sweeps a room, as for thy laws,
  Makes that and th' action fine.
  This is the famous stone
  That turneth all to gold:
For that which God doth touch and own
  Cannot for less be told.[24]

These famous lines of George Herbert catch both the essence of a theology of labor and the dilemma: how to maintain what is true in it without succumbing to being religious support for an oppressive ideology of inhumane work.

Brute physical labor is, perhaps, the archetype of all work, the most direct confrontation between the autonomy of human beings and the hard, mechanical necessity of the material world. Originally, and still predominantly worldwide, labor is a direct confrontation with nature for survival and subsistence; in modern industrial societies it was more often an experience of mindless, repetitive mechanical production on an assembly line, though this is being altered again by the shifts typical work is undergoing in the "information age."[25] Weil, we may recall, viewed physical labor in almost romantic terms:

Physical work is a specific contact with the beauty of the world and can even be, in its best moments, a contact so full that no equivalent can be found elsewhere. The artist, the scholar, the philosopher, the contemplative should really admire the world and pierce through the film of unreality that veils it and makes of it, for nearly all men at nearly every moment of their lives, a dream or stage set. They ought to do this, but more often than not they cannot manage it. He who is aching in every limb, worn out by the effort of a day of work, that is to say, a day when he has been subject to matter, bears the reality of the universe in his flesh like a thorn. The difficulty for him is to look and to love. If he succeeds, he loves the Real.[26]

It would be easy to interpret this, as it would Herbert's poem, as a kind of upper-class romanticism about labor, if we failed to recall Weil's own decision to work in a Renault plant for a time to have this experience for herself. I had a similar experience in a teenage summer job, unloading boxcars of green lumber and cement blocks at a building supply yard. I remember well the experience of physical exhaustion, of thirst, of hunger, which did produce a strange kind of satisfaction at the end of the day. Many spiritual retreats involve periods of physical labor, usually agricultural, as part of the schedule, and to good effect. Even so, there is a vast difference between those like her or me who engage in such labor voluntarily and only for a time, as a learning experience, and those whose life is circumscribed forever and involuntarily by poverty and toil. It is of extreme importance that a spirituality of work not put itself in the service of an ideology of oppression and servitude but seek rather to give both just compensation and real dignity to physical labor. Weil is not unaware of the dilemma:

> That is the immense privilege God has reserved for his poor. But they scarcely ever know it. No one tells them. Excessive fatigue, harassing money worries, and the lack of true culture prevent them from noticing it. A slight change in these conditions would be enough to open the door to a treasure. It is heart-rending to see how easy it would be in many cases for men to procure a treasure for their fellows and how they allow centuries to pass without taking the trouble to do so.[27]

Even in the "information age" it is difficult to imagine a human society in which all hard physical labor can or should be eliminated. As Christians we are obligated to create the conditions in culture and economy where physical labor may also be humane work. That will require not only economic justice but also a culture that celebrates the encounter of human autonomy with natural mechanical necessity in physical labor, so that it may be undertaken in love for the beauty and order of the world as much as any other work. The social status of janitors, maids, garbage collectors, and agricultural workers will perforce change. It may also be the case that all who are physically able should take some share in this labor during at least some time of their lives, for both the sake of justice and also their own spiritual growth.

Science and Art

Science and art are the archetypal human intellectual and creative work by which humans encounter the order and beauty of the world. It is tempting to say that the very possibility of engaging in them rests on someone else's more directly "productive" labor, yet that would misread what we can know of ancient civilizations where folklore, proto-science, and early art seem as ancient as what we know of labor itself, often as part of what we usually think of as "religion," at least for *homo sapiens*. Weil seems to have an implicit grasp of this.[28] Indeed, one of the conditions for creating a culture and a political economy that makes physical labor humane will be the deeper recognition of the art, science, and *charisms* that often lie hidden in much of what we think of as "mere" manual labor. Some types of manual labor, such as carpentry and other construction professions, make this obvious, but it is inherent in all labor insofar as it is human, let alone humane.

Nevertheless, we usually think of science and art in the more limited sense as the realm for "the gifted," even for those with genius, though it is important to note that, even in these disciplines, genius-level insight bears a more direct relationship to hours of hard scut work than is often acknowledged. Nor need every participant in these enterprises be a world-class genius in order to make a real contribution—that is one of the illusions of Romanticism. The violin concerto needs the last-desk player in the second violin section as well as the soloist up front, and art, including music, may be pursued as spiritual practice by anyone, including those who will never seek to contribute at the professional level. Science as culture needs everything from the genius theorist to engineers to lab assistants to amateur inventors, and even "staying up" on the latest developments can be a spiritual practice for an informed layperson. Once we have freed "work" from the bonds of "gainful employment," it can become hard to draw a sharp line between work and leisure when science and art are pursued as avocations. My own sense is that it is still "work" when some shared product, process, or performance is in view, "leisure" when it is pursued for merely personal ends. This would, for example, bless the work done by a volunteer community chorus at rehearsal for a public performance as "work," even though many in the chorus consider it a leisure activity.

Science begins by seeking to understand the order of the world and may end in contemplating its beauty in a kind of love, as Weil saw clearly:

> Science has as its object the study and the theoretical reconstruction of the order of the world—the order of the world in relation to the mental, psychic, and bodily structure of man. Contrary to the illusions of certain scholars, neither the use of telescopes and microscopes, nor the employment of the most unusual algebraic formulae, nor even a contempt for the principle of noncontradiction will allow it to get beyond the limits of this structure. Moreover it is not desirable that it should. The object of science is the presence of Wisdom in the universe, Wisdom of which we are brothers, the presence of Christ, expressed through matter which constitutes the world.

This resonates clearly, of course, with Teilhard's passion for his own vocation. Weil continues:

We reconstruct for ourselves the order of the world in an image, starting from limited, countable, and strictly defined data. We work out a system for ourselves, establishing connections and conceiving of relationships between terms that are abstract and for that reason possible for us to deal with. Thus in an image, an image of which the very existence hangs upon an act of our attention, we can contemplate the necessity which is the substance of the universe but which, as such, only manifests itself to us by the blows it deals.

Then comes the profound turn from order to beauty:

We cannot contemplate without a certain love. The contemplation of this image of order of the world constitutes a certain contact with the beauty of the world. The beauty of the world is the order of the world that is loved.[29]

Teilhard is only one among many scientists who have fallen in love with the beauty of the order of the world. Indeed, for many who, unlike him, are atheists, this becomes, I think, the outlet for their natural religious passion and even a kind of faith.[30] Particularly potent testimony is the role of a kind of aesthetical and ascetical principle in science: the equation that is simplest and most beautiful is most likely to be true.[31]

Art, by contrast, begins in the contemplation of beauty, seeking to express, extend, or even create it; but in the very act of seeking to mold a finite quantity of matter into an expression of universal beauty, the artist encounters the hard reality of the mechanical necessity of the natural order.[32] This is as true in music and the performing arts as in the visual arts. Whether in a lump of clay, a musical instrument, or one's own body, the world with its order is there to be wrestled into something that points to beauty, even if only by being "ugly," as is often done in art that supports a cause of social justice.[33] Like science, art's contemplation of the world is not direct but "is a relationship of the world to our sensibility, the sensibility that depends upon the structure of our body and our soul."[34] Nevertheless, all art, whatever its proximate intentions, aims ultimately at that universal beauty that is itself an attribute of God, rendering art, like science, a kind of sacrament.[35] That is, art requires the Holy Spirit to *be* art, and many artists have an at least implicit sense of the call to self-transcendence in their discipline.[36] Where art fails to aim at this sacramental reference to universal beauty, it ultimately fails as art.[37]

Essential to both disciplines, if they are to be true to their vocation, is that they should move from the focus on the particular (a particular scientific problem, a particular work of art under construction) to the universal, as only universal beauty is truly sacramental.[38] In this light, each is pursued as an end in itself (*ars gratia artis*). This is the source of their inspiration. Oddly enough, it is precisely when pursued most purely for its own sake that, as Christian vocations, each is in the service of the new creation finally embodied in *pleroma* and commonwealth.[39] More proximately, but also as work, each can be a tool for healing and social justice and may contribute to the creation of a culture and technology that increases the possibilities for all human work to be more humane;[40] there are also additional vocations in applying science and art to the needs of culture and technology, with, perhaps, different charisms from those pursuing the pure disciplines. Thus, art and science as such are archetypal for all the "arts and sciences" of human intellectual endeavor.

Ecotheology, Ethics, and Human Ecology

In our time especially, science, art, and contemplation of the order and beauty of the world come together in a unique way as work that is caring directly for the world as nature, that is, in its own right. This goes beyond the previously noted requirement that all humane work must avoid irreparable damage to nature, though some of the work to which we now turn will be in the service of ensuring precisely that. But there is also other work that is in direct care of the world of nature, repairing the damage previously done, as well as exercising ongoing stewardship of natural resources in a manner that seems more faithful to the intentions of Genesis 1 than ever before. At Sewanee: The University of the South, where I teach, the various natural resources and environmental sciences majors in the College of Arts and Sciences are burgeoning, expressing the hope of the young people engaging in them that their personal ethical passions will also find gainful employment.

Volf puts succinctly the relationship between work and the ecological crisis we now face:

> It will suffice to note that all explanations of the ecological crisis (even the population explosion theory) intersect at the point where *human beings intervene in nature through their work*. By definition, ecological problems are problems arising "as a practical consequence of man's dealings with nature"[41]—"nature" being understood as the nonhuman environment in which human beings live. It is safe to claim that human work is *the* cause of human ecological problems.

The need, then, is for human beings "to learn how to work in a way that is cooperative with, and not destructive of, their nonhuman environment."[42]

Further on, he devotes some time analyzing the relationship among Spirit, work, and nature.[43] He sees the crisis as uniquely grounded in the body/soul dichotomy we have inherited from Plato through Descartes. The result is a theology that has "stripped the human spirit of everything corporeal and emptied corporeality of everything spiritual."[44] Volf's arguments that this is neither sound nor biblical echo much of what has been said here, especially in chapter 4. Odd as it may seem to those unfamiliar with his pneumatology, John Calvin is a countervailing voice that emphasized the presence of the Holy Spirit in nature as the source of "essence, life, and movement."[45] Human beings must care for nature because they are both in it and of it, and hence in solidarity with it. Creation as nature is at least partly an end in itself, and must be respected as such. This does not preclude its ongoing use for human purposes; but its claims to value and worth are not limited to human usefulness. God has "a distinct soteriological relation to nature (which is, however, not separable from God's soteriological relation to human beings)."[46] As a result,

"All work must have not only a productive but also a protective aspect. Economic systems must therefore be integrated into the given biological systems of ecological interdependence."

But this protective dimension of work is not in and of itself enough. It remains, says Volf, too static and focused on the past:

> An adequate concept of care for nature must have a dynamic, future-oriented dimension. It must take into account that there is *history of nature* that necessarily accompanies the human encounter with nature. The question is not simply how to preserve the environment in the state in which it presently exists, but *how to preserve the naturalness of nonhuman nature that is subject to change because of the human relation to it.*[47]

There is, in particular, a deep responsibility to our fellow human beings for the state of the home we all share. This is inherent in the gift of *dominium terrae*, the dominion or stewardship over the earth, which we cannot now abdicate even if we should wish to. It is not a gift to us as needy, rapacious individuals, but as a human community being shaped by the Holy Spirit for "the glorious liberty of the children of God," for the commonwealth we shall all inhabit. "Human beings, therefore, have to exercise *dominium terrae* in *responsibility to the whole human community, the global community in the sequence of generations.*"[48]

This goes beyond conservation or even art focused only on the present moment to a real care for the future of the earth not merely in its human instrumentality but in what Weil called the ultimate finality of its own beauty. At the deepest level of "natural resources management," art and science will need to intersect at the cross-roads of love of neighbor and love of the order and beauty of the world to develop disciplines we do not yet envision, disciplines that might fulfill our true stewardship to "tend the garden" for the sake of its own ultimate place in the *pleroma*, intertwined as it is with our own place, both practically and theologically:

> We should not think of the worker only as imposing order on a recalcitrant nature, but also as engaging "in a sort of dialogue with her material," by which "she lovingly coaxes it into revealing its potential."[49] The point of this dialogue is to help nature in a small and broken way to grow into ever greater correspondence to the state into which it will be transformed. In this way we will be able to pass on a better earth to future generations.[50]

Although I have focused to this point on what we might call natural ecology, we have already seen the role human ecology (as care for the structures of the human community) plays even in this enterprise. It has its own claim as a principle of both a human work ethic and an environmental ethic. In addition to caring for the earth directly, there are vocations in art, science, and politics that focus on the enrichment of human culture as such. In a culture that also meets the ethical challenges of providing humane work, the claims of the nonhuman environment cannot be left out, as we have just seen. Indeed, that the two are intrinsically intertwined can be seen in one of the ultimate sins against ecojustice, the dumping of construction and toxic wastes in communities inhabited by the human poor. What I wish to note here is that in addition to a spirituality of caring for the earth as such, there is also a spirituality of working directly for social justice, and a series of methods, gifts, and vocations that apply to that enterprise.[51] Both sets (natural- and human-ecological), if Christian, involve work in the Spirit in service of the new creation groaning to be born that will ultimately be fulfilled only by the resurrection of the body as the entire human *opus*, embracing the earth as its home and partner.

Leisure as Limit

Volf also points out that human development requires more than work; it also requires Sabbath as both rest and leisure.[52] Indeed, human development requires that work be limited by leisure, not just to avoid burnout but because all humans receive more charisms than can possibly be expressed in one mode of gainful employment or even in several over a lifetime. True leisure must also be distinguished from recreation, which is those activities such as exercise that we engage in to restore our bodies and minds to the state needed for effective work.[53] Leisure as such is the time we have left when even our needs for recreation have been met. Volf, responding to the human need and gifts for communion with God, focuses on worship as the ultimate leisure activity, a theme that will be the focus of the next chapter. Before leaving the consideration of work and turning to that pinnacle of leisure, however, note should be taken of other dimensions of leisure that need to serve in some kind of balance as a limit to work.

Both avocations (which, as I just suggested, can be a kind of bridge between work and leisure) and sheer play are needed for human development. *Homo viator*[a] needs *homo ludens* (human being at play) for complete fulfillment, which suggests that there will be aspects of play as well as work in the final consummation of the new creation.[54] Sport, for example is an important consideration.[55] It can, of course, hone skills needed for some kinds of work. It can also, as professional, become the appropriate work of some in order that it might become leisure for spectator "fans." There are also gifts and vocations within the recreation and leisure industries that provide helpful support to others in their recreational and leisurely activities. But we see precisely what goes wrong in turning leisure to work when all sport aims at professionalization; this is evident not only when college sports become minor leagues for professional teams but when even the play of children is coopted as possible preparation for sports careers. The link to ecojustice is clear when the pressure is especially intense on poor children who see prowess in sports as the only way out of miserable conditions. There is an intrinsic human value in games played strictly for fun. Play is also a means of experiencing and expressing love and enthusiasm for the order and beauty of the world, and any proper spirituality must make room for it. If there is godly work, there is also godly play.[56]

---

a Human being "equipped to take on the work ahead and is on his or her way according to the eschatological promise."

Notes

1. Weil, *Waiting for God*, 158.
2. Weil, *Waiting for God*, 163. It might be helpful to reread the material in chap. 20 before proceeding, as I shall not repeat it but do presume it here.
3. It is not found in R. Garrigou-Lagrange or in Antonio Royo and Jordan Aumann, despite the tradition of papal reflection on work and economic justice expressed in a series of encyclicals beginning in the nineteenth century; but see the early classic by M.-D. Chenu, O.P., *The Theology of Work*. It is more surprisingly absent from such work as Samuel Powell's (though he does have important things to say about caring for creation, which we shall acknowledge later); Simon Chan has a few paragraphs (*ST*, 131–32, 142) sketching a possible theology of work, but only as part of an *askesis* to open us to prayer, not as a positive spiritual dimension or practice in its own right. Ann Loades has some helpful reflection on spirituality of work in "Sacramentality" in *BCCS*, 260–62.
4. Miroslav Volf, *Work in the Spirit*; Armand Larive, *After Sunday*.
5. Volf, *Work*, 69–74.
6. Volf, *Work*, 105–6.
7. Volf, *Work*, 106–9; Volf points out that on the Catholic side this was recognized in *Gaudium et Spes*, but that this insight has not been expressed in a consistent theology of work (pp. 104–5).
8. Volf, *Work*, 79–102.
9. Volf, *Work*, 103–22.
10. Volf, *Work*, 15–17, and consistently throughout.
11. Volf, *Work*, 88–102.
12. Volf, *Work*, 131–38; everything said here so far also reminds us that this work will include ongoing conversion as repentance, healing, and liberation.
13. Volf, *Work*, 137–38.
14. Volf, *Work*, 150.
15. Volf, *Work*, 152–54.
16. Volf, *Work*, 157–201; see also now Kathryn Tanner, *Economy of Grace*. There are some interesting resonances between Tanner's work and Volf's on the question of what a humane political economy might look like, not surprising given the centrality of the notion of gift for both.
17. Here Volf notes (n. 50) Immanuel Kant, *The Metaphysics of Morals*, A387. Note again the attention to autonomy that resonates with Weil.
18. Volf, *Work*, 173.
19. For a devastating critique of identifying interiority and spirituality, see Owen C. Thomas, "Interiority and Christian Spirituality," *What Is It That Theologians Do*, 183–205.
20. Volf, *Work*, 194, 199.
21. Volf, *Work*, 190. Larive helpfully points out that charisms bring not only skill but also rapport, as part of equipping human beings for work that is truly on the way to the new creation (*After Sunday*, 112–26).
22. Volf here notes (n. 168) Dorothee Sölle, *Lieben und Arbeiten: Eine Theologie der Schöpfung* (Stuttgart: Kreuss, 1985), 132.
23. Volf, *Work*, 201.
24. George Herbert, *The Temple*, 311–12.
25. Volf, *Work*, 25–68; he returns to these themes in considering the possibilities on nonalienating work, 179–86.
26. Weil, *Waiting for God*, 170.
27. Weil, *Waiting for God*, 170.
28. Weil, *Waiting for God*, 171.
29. Weil, *Waiting for God*, 169–70.
30. Arthur Gibson, *The Faith of the Atheist*, is still a classic theological assessment of this phenomenon.

31. John Polkinghorne, "Is Science Enough?" 14–16.

32. Weil, *Waiting for God*, 168.

33. See Robin M. Jensen, *The Substance of Things Seen*, 6–10.

34. Weil, *Waiting for God*, 164.

35. Weil, *Waiting for God*, 165; cf. Jenson, *ST* 1.225–26, 234–36, and his eloquent vision of God as a great fugue (what else could a Lutheran say?) and *ST* 2.369, where the final shape of the commonwealth of the redeemed is like a New England singing society in which the redeemed sing the fugue that God is. Dare I extend the metaphor and suggest that they must be singing a "fuging tune" of the kind beloved by such singing societies? On music as spiritual practice, see Don and Emily Saliers, *A Song to Sing, a Life to Live*. On art as spiritual practice, see Barbara Hughes, "Using the Arts to Open Scripture"; Robin M. Jensen, *The Substance of Things Seen*; Catherine Kapikian, *Art in the Service of the Sacred*; Michael Sullivan, *Windows into the Soul*. On philosophy of art, see Paul Weiss, *Nine Basic Arts*; *Religion and Art*; and *The World of Art*.

36. Barbara Hughes, "Using the Arts," 140.

37. Weil, *Waiting for God*, 169.

38. Weil, *Waiting for God*, 165.

39. On the role of art in a culture of social justice, for example, see John W. De Gruchy, *Christianity, Art, and Transformation*.

40. Barbara Hughes, "Using the Arts," 152–53.

41. Volf here cites J. Passmore, *Man's Responsibility for Nature* (London: Duckworth, 1974), 43.

42. Volf, *Work*, 42.

43. Volf, *Work*, 141–48.

44. Volf, *Work*, 143.

45. Volf, *Work*, 144, citing John Calvin, *Institutes of the Christian Religion* (ed. McNeill), 138.

46. Volf, *Work*, 145, grounding this insight especially in Romans 8; as I write, this insight is a source of serious contention among American evangelicals.

47. Volf, *Work*, 146.

48. Volf, *Work*, 147, citing *The Oxford Conference (Official Report)*, ed. J. H. Oldham (Chicago: Wallet, Clark, 1937); *Rights of Future Generations—Rights of Nature: Proposal for Enlarging the Universal Declaration of Human Rights*, ed. L. Vischer, Studies from the World Alliance of Reformed Churches, no. 19, 1990; and John Locke, *Two Treatises of Government* (Cambridge: Cambridge University Press, 1966), I, §24ff.

49. Citing here Nicholas Wolterstorff, "Evangelicalism and the Arts," *Christian Scholars Review* 17 (1988): 449–73, at 466; with other secondary references as found in n. 94 (Volf, *Work*, 220).

50. Volf, *Work*, 146, citing here Sir F. Catherwood, "Christian Faith and Economics," in *The Year 2000*, ed. J. Stott (Downers Grove, Ill.: InterVarsity, 1983), 126–45 at 128. Although I have chosen for my own purposes to focus on Volf here, mention should be made of Samuel Powell's magnificent chapter "Works of Love: Caring for Creation" in *Theology of Christian Spirituality*, 188–206; while placed in the context of his own theological scheme, it seems to me utterly compatible with what I have done here following Volf.

51. Simon Chan is especially helpful on this (*ST*, 185–89).

52. Volf, *Work* 131–40.

53. See n. 55 below; and Neil H. Cheek, Jr., "Toward a Sociology of Not-Work."

54. On *homo viator*, see Larive, *After Sunday*, 106; For Larive, this equipping is precisely the work of the Holy Spirit as giver of all gifts, 107–26. On *homo ludens*, the *locus classicus* is Johan Huizinga, *Homo Ludens*. See also Jürgen Moltmann et al., *Theology of Play*.

55. See Paul Weiss, *Sport*. For helpful commentary and Weiss's more mature reflections, see *The Philosophy of Paul Weiss*, 637–79.

56. This is, of course, the name of a particular approach to Sunday School curriculum. See the articles in *STR* 48, no. 1 (2004).

23

Love of Religious Practices and Prayer

The third form of the implicit love of God, according to Simone Weil, is love of religious practices, institutional religion itself.[1] When we examined her thoughts in this area we noted that true religion is also a kind of attention, in this case to true purity, animated by desire and leading to consent.[2] It issues in service and mission as well as leading ultimately to contemplative prayer for an individual. Weil's thoughts at this precise point are focused not only christologically, but specifically on the Eucharist. This implicit love, then, though it also refers to the other three (neighbor, beauty of the world, friendship), finds its focus in the Benedictine element of *prayer*, both liturgical and contemplative. There is a vast literature on both, and so I shall not try here to reproduce the tracts on sacramental devotion and the practice of prayer that are widely available elsewhere. What is needed is a recasting of the theological framework in which these subjects have been treated in the older spiritual theologies, since nowhere is the shift to a very different religious consciousness since Vatican II more evident. This can be seen under two significant lenses: first, Miroslav Volf's understanding of worship as the archetypal form of leisure, and hence as a limit to work; and, second, the sacramental theology and liturgical renewal at the heart of the Vatican II "shift." We conclude this chapter with a look at the consequences for personal prayer and the birth of contemplation.

Leisure and Worship

For Volf, leisure is a limit on work because it is an activity that is an end in itself, meeting certain needs of the participant but not focused on meeting other, more basic needs either of the participants or their fellow creatures.[3] Leisure is a limit to work because "In that the Spirit liberates human beings from slavery to their own selves and opens them for the reality of God's new creation, they become free, not only to work, but also to worship and to play."[4] Leisure and work are polar opposites on a kind of continuum but are not mutually exclusive.[5] As we saw in the last chapter, many activities, such as amateur singing or woodworking as a hobby, combine elements of both. Indeed, the closer work approaches leisure, the more humane it becomes.

Volf sees leisure as meeting several fundamental human needs beyond those of sustenance: "[e]njoyment of the beauty of nature, delight in the exercise and development of one's own skills, and appreciation of fellowship with one another (especially relations between the sexes)."[6] The analysis of sport in the last chapter is only one example of the way leisure reflects Weil's other forms of the implicit love of God, and friendship and sexuality will be in focus in the next chapter. But Volf sees a further human need for leisure, the one on which he chooses to concentrate: "to delight in communion with God."

Even if the essence of human being is God's relationship to us, with the Spirit leading us as partners into the new creation, the question arises whether working to do God's will is worship enough or whether we also need something more:

> . . . God did not create human beings simply to be servants but above all to be God's children and friends. As much as they need to do God's will, so also they need to enjoy God's presence. In order to be truly who they are they need periodic moments of time in which God's commands and their tasks will disappear from the forefront of consciousness and in which God will be there for them and they will be there for God—to adore the God of loving holiness and to thank and pray to the God of holy love.[7]

For Volf this goes beyond a change in self-perception, liberation from sin with a resulting new ethical orientation and even "an anticipatory transformation into a new creation." At the heart lies something deeper, "the union of human beings with the Son of God through the Spirit," that is, the mystery of union with God that the Eastern Church calls *theōsis*. After discussing Paul's metaphor of "being made to drink of the Spirit" (1 Cor 12:13), Volf continues:

> When Christians commune with God in worship, they come to drink from that fountain their very life as Christians and hence their identity as human beings depends on. At the same time, in worship they anticipate the enjoyment of God in the new creation where they will communally dwell in the triune God and the triune God will dwell in them (see Rev 21:22; Jn 17:21).[8]

In consequence, not all charisms are given for work; some are given for leisure, and, specifically, for worship. As a limit to work, leisure demands space and time as an alternating activity with work, with neither subordinate to the other.[9] Indeed, they are not only *alternating* activities but also *interdependent* ones. It is, of course, in the theology and practice of the Sabbath in Judaism that leisure, worship, and communion with God come together most organically.[10] The Sabbath commandment liberates people, especially in countries dependent on subsistence agriculture, from enslavement to work. But even where work is not so all consuming, Sabbath provides "the context of meaning that gives work ultimate significance," by anticipating the eschatological shalom, "inspiring people to do their work as creative activity in the service of God's new creation. And most significantly, the presence of God in worship transforms people so that they can advance through work 'that transfiguration of the whole universe which is the coming of the Kingdom of God.'"[11] That is, worship and work share a common eschatological purpose. In Weil's terms, every proper work requires sustained attention to that purity religion reveals as the sacramental dimension in the other loves. In the terms developed here, it is worship that locates work firmly in the tide of transfiguration; worship ensures that work's ultimate agenda is the Spirit's *pleroma* and not a narrower one of our own; and ultimately worship enables the gift of contemplation in action. For, as we have seen, all true worship also leads to work, at least of service and mission. When work and worship achieve the kind of balance that the model of alternating, interdependent activities suggests, "A Christian does not work out of an experience of the Spirit that belongs in the past (a Sunday experience). She works through the power of the Spirit that is now active in her. She works *in the Spirit*."[12] Worship as leisure thus does not merely enrich work; it liberates it to be truly humane work by being attentive to its true end and deepening the "presence of the Spirit in the life of a Christian."[13] Achieving the proper balance between work and leisure (including all its modes and activities as Volf laid them out), especially worship, is thus not merely an ideal to be embodied in a rule of life for the good of one's soul as a kind of extra; it is demanded by the very theological nature of work itself. If work is to be worshipful, Sabbath is not merely desirable but intrinsically necessary. Worship, then, is foundationally sacramental, since it engages and reveals the sacramental character of the other loves.

The Ecclesial and Liturgical Ground of Prayer

We have reached a point where one of the most obvious differences emerges between the traditional spiritual theologies and one that seeks to make sense on our side of the Vatican II theological divide. In the traditional theologies, liturgical worship, usually focused solely on participating in the Mass, is treated very much as a personal devotion, in the service of fostering contemplative prayer or of building Christian character.[14] The major shifts in sacramental theology that characterized Vatican II are not in evidence.

The shifts in sacramental theology around Vatican II go hand in glove with the reforming practices of the liturgical renewal movement. Although both this theology and practice seemed "new" to many who had grown familiar with the texts and norms established at the time of the Protestant and Catholic Reformations of the sixteenth century, in fact they were largely guided by the enriched biblical and patristic scholarship of the "*Ressourcement* movement" in the Roman Catholic Church, anticipated in Anglican circles, for example, by the evangelical and Anglo-Catholic renewals of the nineteenth century.[15] Increased ecumenical contact with Eastern churches also played a significant part for both Roman Catholics and members of the World Council of Churches of Christ and its national counterparts, many of which had members from the Eastern churches. What looks new, therefore, often has a firmer biblical and patristic basis than what had become familiar in the West since the Reformation. This is not always transparent to those who see themselves as "traditionalists."

While several of the basic concepts of the new sacramental theology and its concurrent liturgical reforms were anticipated by Anglican theologians such as Charles Gore and William Porcher DuBose some fifty years before Vatican II, and on the Roman Catholic side have deeper roots in the *Nouvelle Theologie*, it is probably in the theology of Karl Rahner that they became most influential on the Council and best known to most Christians, spurring a host of works following in the same track.[16] As previously noted in chapter 2 above, Louis Bouyer's *Liturgical Piety* had also begun to convince many that the public, sacramental, and liturgical life of the people of God was primary, and formed the context for all personal devotion. Protestant appreciation for this shift may be found in such works as Edward Farley's *Ecclesial Man* and the document *Baptism, Eucharist, Ministry,* issued by the World Council of Churches.[17] The impact of this movement is well documented in several chapters of *The Blackwell's Companion to Christian Spirituality,* for example, and in *The New Westminster Dictionary of Christian Spirituality.*[18]

Among the foundational and constituent concepts of this shift may be included:

1. Sacramentality, the ability of certain signs to convey sacred reality, is a foundational concept of Christian theology, grounded in the self-expressive love of the Holy Trinity in both the inner divine life itself and the works of God *ad extra.*

2. Creation itself is sacramental in character and is revealed as such in the tide of transfiguration. This sacramental character of creation is foundational for any theology of the particular sacraments and is the theological ground for how material symbols can convey grace.

3. The most intense sacramental relationship is the incarnation and the hypostatic union of the divine and human natures in Jesus Christ. The flesh of Jesus becomes the chief sacramental sign.

4. After the incarnation, the "fundamental sacrament" is the church constituted as the Body of Christ by the Holy Spirit.

5. The particular sacraments derive their efficacy as acts of the church expressing her fundamental sacramental character.

6. Sacraments are celebrated by the whole people of God. Officiating clergy preside as authorized, but as leaders and representatives of the people, even when they act or speak *in persona Christi.*

7. Baptism and the baptismal covenant (the promises made at Baptism) are foundational for both ecclesial life and mission and personal life and vocation.

8. The church is primarily a Eucharistic community, grounded in the paschal mystery from the passion of Christ to the outpouring of the Holy Spirit.

9. Personal spirituality for Christians is thus indelibly grounded in ecclesial, baptismal, Eucharistic existence.

10. The end of human spirituality is the incorporation of the church as a sacrament of the entire human race into the inner Trinitarian life from which the sacramental dynamic began. This is commonwealth or kingdom of God, beatific vision,

and cosmic *pleroma* all at once. The means of this incorporation is the sacramental dynamic itself as carried forward by the Spirit into the new creation.

Understanding this sacramental dynamic helps us see that from a Christian point of view, the claim "I am not really religious, but I am deeply spiritual," is highly problematic. As we have seen, there is no "spiritual potential" native to human nature apart from the operation of the Holy Spirit. While it is certainly true that the Holy Spirit can and does operate beyond the boundaries of the covenant community, it is this same Spirit who proceeds as love from the Trinitarian heart,[19] hovers over the water of creation, sanctifies the covenant people and anoints their officers, enables the incarnation of the Word in the womb of Mary, is the power by which Jesus performs his works and is raised from the dead as well as the power that makes the sacraments "work"; it is the same Spirit who binds the people of God together in a common life in union with Christ as his body, as the sacramental sign of the coming commonwealth of God that is the social expression of the *pleroma* that is the Spirit's own ultimate mission. It is this ecclesial community in which *charisms* enabling humans to work their share toward that end are transmitted and trained.[a] Ultimately, true Christian spirituality can thus bypass neither the flesh of Jesus nor his ongoing earthly body.

Another way of seeing the ecclesial ground of spirituality would be this: Weil, as we have seen, points out in each of the other three implicit loves that what each has as the focus of its attention is a kind of sacrament, in the sense of a vehicle of God's presence, a source of grace for the one paying attention, and a thrust into love and service on behalf of the new creation. It is in the sacramental life of the church, including the church itself as the fundamental sacrament, that we are given the gift of seeing the sacramental dimension in the other loves, and, to use Nicholas Lash's terms, in the church's pedagogy of contemplative praxis we are given the language with which to make that identification. It is also within the household of faith, especially in the common life we share with others whom we did not choose, that we are meant to learn the depth and breadth of love of neighbor, of work, and of friendship. This love of religious practices is no more optional than any of the other loves; indeed, it is the ground by which we are enabled to see the others for what they are, to experience grace as grace. The covenant people of God as a community of biblical interpretation not only teaches us the Christian faith; it is also called upon to be the community of our spiritual formation, through all the structures of its common life (*koinōnia*), most especially the particular sacraments.[20] The whole point of the "liturgical piety" movement is that personal prayer and contemplation are grounded here rather than the personal dimension being primary and liturgical life adjunct to it. It is also the deepest reason why language about the "inner life" or "interiority" as the essence of spirituality is less than accurate: Christian spirituality is *first* grounded and expressed in what is external, public, and social, essentially ecclesial, and only *then* bears fruit in personal life.[21] In the General Thanksgiving in Anglican tradition we give thanks for "the redemption of the world by our Lord

---

a Obviously, not all churches offer this opportunity, and some persons who have been turned off by institutional religion had good reasons to be so.

Jesus Christ, the means of grace, and the hope of glory."[22] The love of religious practices, at its core, is gratitude for the visible means of grace. Chief among these, after
the church itself, are the "particular sacraments," chief among them the two great
sacraments of Baptism and Eucharist.

The Particular Sacraments and Life in the Spirit[23]

A marker for this shift in the place of sacramentality in spirituality is the
restored centrality of holy Baptism. In the classic spiritual theologies, Baptism seldom, if ever, appears.[24] They presume it has occurred, but as pursuit of the counsels of perfection, spirituality was seen to move beyond Baptism and conversion.
Throughout a widespread variety of churches and denominations, this is no longer
desirable or even possible. Instead, Baptism and conversion (initial and ongoing)
have become central features of Christian spirituality, a trend I have followed by
suggesting that the first "tide of the Spirit" is conversion.[25] Baptism is the sacrament
of full initiation, by which a new member is engrafted into the *koinōnia* of the Body
of Christ and raised from the death of sin into new life by the indwelling of the Holy
Spirit (Rom 6:3–5).

While one's own Baptism probably does belong primarily to early childhood or
a period shortly after initial conversion, contemporary sacramental theology sees
an ongoing role for Baptism in the spiritual life in at least three areas. First, baptismal fonts are now often located at the door of the church, where all who enter may
be reminded of and participate in Luther's great declaration, "I am baptized," either
visually, or, in many traditions, by "taking the water" with the sign of the cross
on the way in.[26] Second, holy Baptism is now usually a public liturgy, on Sundays,
major feast days, or the occasion of the bishop's visit. It is particularly associated
with and celebrated on the feasts of Christ's Baptism (First Sunday of Epiphany),
Paschal Vigil, Pentecost, and All Saints (November 1). Each feast reminds us of one
of the grounds of the spiritual practice of Baptism: Jesus' own Baptism as entrance
into his life of mission; our participation in his death and resurrection (the paschal
mystery) in Baptism; the indwelling of the Holy Spirit and her gifts in Baptism; and
the binding together of the church as the covenant people of God and the Body of
Christ in the *koinōnia* (communion, common life, fellowship) of saints. Third is
the new emphasis on the ongoing role of the "baptismal covenant," the promises
and vows made at Baptism, in the spiritual and moral life of all believers, often
now renewed in services of holy Baptism and on the four great feasts just listed.
Increasingly and normatively, the sacrament of Confirmation is restored to the rite
of holy Baptism, or theologically linked to it. Baptism and the *koinōnia* it extends
are thus the ground of all Christian life in the Holy Spirit and, hence, in Christ
Jesus, and renewed liturgical practice signifies this in a variety of ways. All three of
these emphases can come together by participating in the catechumenate, or preparation of new candidates for Baptism, as a sponsor or a teacher.[27]

In the most ancient liturgies, preserved in the Eastern tradition and now
renewed in many Western churches, Baptism, Confirmation, and first Eucharist

form one unified sacrament of initiation.[28] Baptism and Confirmation are normally administered only once to each member, but the Eucharist as a family meal continues as the ongoing nurturing of life in Christ by the Holy Spirit on a regular, perhaps even daily, basis. There are great shifts in liturgics and spirituality here, as well. First, the Eucharist is now, in an increasing number of Christian church families, normative as the context for the other sacraments and the chief act of worship on Sundays and major feasts. It is a public, corporate, communal, family act, which all celebrate together. In most families of churches it is normative for a bishop or presbyter to preside, but roles for deacons and laity have been given new emphasis. This is no longer the Mass as a private devotion but the family meal of the people of God, renewing, restoring, and reinvigorating the *koinōnia* we share with one another in the Holy Spirit and hence with Christ as the head of the body we are and are becoming. The new emphasis in many liturgies on "passing the peace" reflects this deepened sense of *koinōnia* as mutual forgiveness and reconciliation among the people of God. Previous instructions in traditional spiritual theologies about preparation, devotion during the celebration, and thanksgiving afterward may often still provide personally helpful suggestions, but never now at the price of interfering with our participation in the public, familial, corporate acts of liturgy.

Second, Eucharistic *koinōnia* as common life and fellowship celebrated in the public liturgy is now more clearly the ground for that *koinōnia* that is individual reception of the consecrated bread and wine as communion of the body and blood of Christ. Such individual communion has become much more frequent as older requirements for preparation that insisted on sacramental penance (see below) have been relaxed. An appropriate penitent heart is still an ideal for receiving communion, but the newer rites include corporate acts of repentance, except where liturgically inappropriate, and there is an increased realization that the Eucharist is itself, in the power of the Spirit, a bearer of forgiveness of sins and a medicine for sinners, not a reward for the already purified. As a result, in many church families it is now normative for all the baptized present to receive at every Eucharist.

Third, there has been a great expansion of understanding of the sacramental symbolism of the Eucharist. The connection to "the Last Supper" and the tradition that in the Eucharist we "show forth the Lord's death until he comes" (1 Cor 11:25–27) has not been lost; but new dimensions have been uncovered. These include the offering of the bread and wine by all in fulfillment of the priesthood of Adam and Eve common to all humanity;[29] solidarity with the people of the senior covenant in the mystery of Passover; the traditional meals eaten by Jesus and his disciples throughout his ministry with them and their extension to the crowds in the feeding miracles; table fellowship with the risen Lord after his rising from the dead; and, most significant of all, participation by anticipation in the supper of the Lamb, the "heavenly" messianic banquet attended by all the angels and redeemed humanity with Christ as host.[30] Eucharistic piety is not now so much focused on the older penitential disciplines and devotions as on our entrance together as a priestly people into the heart of these great mysteries.

Fourth, there is a renewed recognition of the literal truth of the root meaning of Eucharist—thanksgiving. Life in the tidal current of transfiguration is most particularly grounded in gratitude, primarily for "the redemption of the world by our Lord Jesus Christ, the means of grace, and the hope of glory." Most Eucharistic prayers in the liturgical churches now reflect this fundamental reality of giving thanks.

Fifth, there is a deeper appreciation of the role of the Holy Spirit in the Eucharist, symbolized by the restoration to most Western rites of the *epiclesis*, a prayer invoking the presence and action of the Holy Spirit on the elements being consecrated; it has become contemporary "best practice" for the Spirit to be invoked also on the gathered people.[31] This renewed understanding of the Holy Spirit's role in sacramental consecration has helped develop nonmagical approaches to the doctrine of Christ's real presence in the Eucharist: the Spirit indwells us, each individual and the people as a whole, as the source of our *koinōnia*, and also, as always, indwells the human flesh of Jesus, now risen and glorified. By indwelling also the bread and wine the Spirit makes them literally "means of grace," a material link of our common flesh to the flesh of Jesus as our way of being "in Christ" and Christ in us, and hence our being drawn into the fullness of the Spirit's intended *pleroma* (new creation) and the fullness of the Trinitarian life itself. The Spirit also gifts us as individuals and community with the theological virtues of faith, hope, and love that make it possible for us to "receive" this ultimate gift. For many, this moment of invocation of the Spirit has become a principal focus of Eucharistic devotion.

Sixth, the emphasis on the Spirit's *pleroma* reminds us that the Eucharist is not only for the nourishment of the church and its members but also for their empowering for mission and work. A Eucharist that fails to "send us out to do the work you have given us to do" is not an authentic Eucharist.[32] In the Eucharist we are called together to renew our *vocatio spiritualis* and the charisms given by the Spirit that shape our individual and corporate work and mission, and also loving service to those in the household of faith as well as those neighbors beyond it. In the Spirit whose very name is Love we are thus nourished, in the Eucharist, for all the other loves.

Sacraments of Restored *Koinōnia*

Once we move beyond the two great sacraments of Baptism and Eucharist, the use of the term "sacrament" becomes more contentious. Certainly these two great sacraments hold a unique place in any list, but the difference between "sacrament" proper and "sacramental" rite grows less as we are more deeply formed by patristic theology and the Vatican II theology of Karl Rahner. The issue of "dominical institution," whether or not Jesus left explicit instructions about a particular action, has been subsumed by our understanding of his institution of the church as his Body and hence fundamental sacrament. Any act that is an official act of the church, expressing her fundamental sacramental character in a manner that is somehow decisive for a recipient, is thus a sacrament. This embraces the other five sacramental rites in the traditional Western list of seven, and now expands to include other rites that are sacramental in character as well. I propose to treat a total of nine, but the list need not stop there.

The next three sacraments restore *koinōnia* as fellowship, common life, and communion when it has become impaired or broken. Sin, illness, and death all have this unique, alienating character, alienating us from one another, from the material universe that is our home, and from God. The rites of Reconciliation of a Penitent, Unction of the Sick, and Burial of the Dead all deal with restoring communion in the face of these realities. In each case, the new theology suggests that we do not bring a new grace of forgiveness, healing, or eternal life in the communion of saints to someone who previously stood outside such grace; instead these rites are now much more celebrations of the grace, the operation of the indwelling Spirit, already at work in the recipient. At the core these also are corporate sacraments, not acts of individual devotion, and the officiating ministers are there not because God cannot act directly on a believer without a priestly intermediary but because they function as officers and representatives of the human community, the covenant people, with whom fellowship has been impaired and is now being restored.

Sin, as we saw in the last current, is the theologically ultimate alienating force. In all the tidal currents it still makes its appearance (the truth of Luther's famous *simul justus et peccator*, "at the same time justified and sinner"), bringing new upwellings of the current of conversion. In the new sacramental theology, however, reconciliation is not a juridical process by which the damned are restored to grace, but a celebration of the Spirit's gift of forgiveness of sins by the blood of Christ that has already been impacting the life of the penitent.[33] The laying-on-of-hands has been restored as an action in many of the renewed rites, symbolizing the fact that the forgiven sinner is now "back in touch" with the Christian community and with God. For penitents leading lives dominated by the current of transfiguration, the focus of reconciliation is usually no longer the huge, gross sins that kept us entirely outside the community of grace, though should they arise again, they must be dealt with; now our attention is on those remaining besetting sins that hinder our fellowship, our prayers and our usefulness. Forgiving others as we are being forgiven is also a restored focus. "Making one's confession" is now practiced less often even in Roman Catholic circles, with greater emphasis on community repentance, though occasional personal confession is still called for. As a result of this change in frequency, "the confessional" is less often now a location for spiritual direction, and rather an adjunct to it, with the confessor often being a different person from the director. Moral guidance is still important for the spiritual life of Christians in all the tides, but insisting on a return to the kind of penitential sorrow that might have been appropriate to first conversion, even on the part of those living primarily in other tides, is no longer helpful. Instead, direction can focus on the battle with sin in the new context, and always in the context of a forgiveness in which we are already living. Restoring the sacrament to its ecclesial context also reminds us of the mutual forgiveness that lies at the heart of *koinōnia* and is necessary for a human heart to take in while being forgiven.

Illness also isolates us and puts us out of touch. Since the Epistle of James there has been a close connection drawn between sin and sickness, forgiveness and healing. The teaching that illness is punishment for sin is neither helpful nor what is at stake here. Instead, the state of mutual reconciliation of the praying community is a precondition for its praying the powerful prayer that will heal.[34] The oil, a common medicine in biblical times, symbolizes as always the inner anointing by the Holy Spirit who is giver of life and health, including eternal life when healing terminates in death rather than ongoing earthly life. The laying-on-of-hands also puts ill persons "back-in-touch" with their faith community, from which illness often isolates them. There is expectation that real healing will occur, even though we do not dictate the form that it takes. Now that unction is no longer "extreme," no longer only a final rite for the dying, it is once again becoming much more frequent in the Western church families. Flora Wuellner has suggested that healing should be as common as confession, since most of the evil we do comes from our wounds not from deliberately chosen sin.[35]

In the end, we all die. Death is temporally and physically the ultimate alienating force. Communion, in the sense of common life and fellowship as we have known it as *convivere* with a loved one, is not merely impaired but broken. The sacramental character of the Burial of the Dead is manifold: a reverent disposal of the remains of an image of God in the context of our grief over our loss of that person; an entrusting of a loved member of the Body of Christ to the ongoing care of God; and the sacramental assertion, in the very teeth of death, of the communion of saints, the ongoing fellowship with the faithful dead through the gift of Christ's resurrection and hence ours; all these occur in the power of the Spirit by which Jesus was raised from the dead. Both the realities of death and grief, and the "sure and certain hope" of the people of God need to be held in liturgical tension, without either one being suppressed by practices of denial or sentimentality.[36] Someone is really dead and gone, *and* in Christ, by the power of the Spirit who raised him from the dead; somehow *koinōnia* with them is not ended but continues as part of the total *koinōnia* of the people of God as the Body of Christ.[37]

The Ordering of *Koinōnia*

Another family of sacraments or sacramental rites gives order and structure to the common life of the people of God by blessing certain offices and relationships. These used to be considered under a rubric of "states of life," but, as we saw in Volf's analysis of work, this concept of external vocation is too static. Like work, these are now better understood in relationship to charisms, gifts of the Holy Spirit to individuals, enriching the personality that was their first gift with new calls and abilities. Some of these may call for permanent embodiment; others may be exercised for a time before moving on to the practice of new charisms. Vocations to ordained ministry in later life are a good example. The sacrament of Order is what we shall consider here. Because they embody particular forms of friendship, Weil's fourth implicit love, holy Matrimony (with a consideration of family and parenting) and the taking of monastic vows, will be discussed in the next chapter.

As a result of the Vatican II shift we have been tracking, it is now more common to identify this sacrament of "Order" as the total ordering of the common life of God's people for worship and mission than to focus on the rites of ordination to individual ministries, though these still occur and have sacramental significance for those being ordained as well as for the whole church.[38] All the ministries of Jesus Christ are recognized as gifts already given to the whole church in Baptism; as a result, any baptized member is in principle eligible for any office and already shares in the priesthood of all believers (not each believer); the rest is a matter of prudence and discernment. Through the sacrament of Order the church as a community examines its needs for mission and ministry and structures its common life to meet those needs, distributing tasks and functions among various members in the light of their discerned natural abilities and charisms. In churches of the catholic tradition this will include selection of persons for the ordained ministries of bishops, priests, and deacons, as well as laypersons gifted for liturgical, service, educational, artistic, and missionary ministries.

Those called and ordained to the three traditional ministerial orders, as a body of people belonging to those orders and carrying out the functions assigned to them, constitute the outward and visible sign of the sacrament. They show forth in the life of the church the apostolate, the sentness of Jesus, and the unbroken eyewitness testimony to his resurrection (bishops); the priesthood of Jesus in his vicarious sacrifice for the world and his pastoral care for the flock of God (priests or presbyters); and the servant ministry of Jesus to the sick, the prisoners, and the needy of all kinds (deacons). Those who are ordained to embody these ministries are no longer seen as taking these ministries away from the people as a whole but embodying them in and for the people, to awaken, recall, and enable these ministries in the whole people. This puts a very different spin on what has usually been seen as the "hierarchical principle" in the church. Office is based on the discernment of charism, and all leadership is at heart servant leadership grounded in Baptism. Dynamics of leadership, "followership," authority and obedience remain as issues of church order; but the older, rigid, monarchial structures are now usually replaced with conciliar models in which all "orders" participate appropriately.[39] Indeed, the more top-down authoritarian style, though still all too common, is less and less suitable for church life. The life of the ordained itself is a life of obedience before it is a life of leadership. This is expressed in the series of vows and promises that give a particular shape to the baptismal covenant as appropriate to each order. Other sacraments of "state of life" have this same characteristic as a life regulated (lived under a rule) by vows.

This more functional definition of Order need not deny the particular sacramental grace of ordination, not even the traditional teaching that the rite conveys an "indelible character" of ontological significance to the ordained. At the lowest level, all this means is that once one is ordained to a particular order, one is not re-ordained to that order again no matter what life events may have suspended the exercise of a ministry. Baptism, Confirmation, and perhaps Matrimony are the other sacraments that bestow an indelible character in this sense. Form follows function, but it does follow, however, and there is a grace (a movement of the Spirit) in ordination that awakens the charisms in the ordinand for service in the ministry of the order he or she is joining. This grace, coupled with the actual exercise of the appropriate ministry, does create a process of formation by which apostolic, priestly, and diaconal character are formed in ordained individuals as a particular shaping of that sanctification that is common to all the baptized. As Karl Rahner points out, the success of the mission of the church requires that at least some of her ministers be holy, and so grace is given to guarantee that this happens.[40] There is no magic here, however, and thus no guarantee of sanctity in any one particular member, and all remain *simul justus et peccator* and hence vulnerable to temptation and character defects, even while growing in the grace and sanctity appropriate to office. Even this shaping of character and sanctification, however, is not primarily for the sake of the ordained individuals but for the ordering of the common life of the people of God for worship, service, and mission.

This latter principle, grounding ordination in the ministries of the whole people of God, helps address the phenomenon of clericalism and its most virulent form, sacerdotalism. In the circumstances in which the church developed, especially in the West in late antiquity as the empire decayed under barbarian onslaughts, it was natural for the ordained to assume governmental powers beyond those dictated by their ministries as such and to become the repository of literate learning. It was this ability to read and write that caused them, like lawyers, to be identified as "clerks" and, hence, clergy. In the context of an increasingly literate and educated laity, the prerogatives that derived from this monopoly on learning and the assumption of extraministerial powers of governance are no longer appropriate. Instead, clergy now need to be educators sharing the fullness of the faith and its tradition with laity, and leaders practicing shared servant leadership. While this decreases the phenomenon of clericalism, if anything it deepens the demand for an educated body of ordained ministers. At the level of personal spirituality, one additional consequence of the newer view is that it is "lay spirituality" or the spirituality common to all the baptized that is primary and normative for all; the spirituality of the ordained is a special set of that, not the other way round, as older tradition tended to put it.

Sacerdotalism is the mistake of an ordained person losing the distinction between *ex officio* and *in propria persona*, what one has by way of office from what belongs to one's own personhood. When this occurs in the ordained, at the least it produces a cloying piety that is generally off-putting rather than enabling of others; at its worst it falsely sanctifies egotistical agendas and power trips and can lead to the final disaster of immoral acting out because one has become convinced that the ordinary rules of right and wrong no longer apply to one's exalted state. The history of the church is unfortunately replete with such disasters. The renewed emphasis on the grounding of all ministry in the ministries of Jesus as a gift to the whole community of the baptized is one help in preventing such disasters, as is a process of education and formation that constantly reminds everyone involved that despite the grace of ordination, *in propria persona* we who are ordained remain *simul justus et peccator*, just like everyone else. This is the proper ground of humility in all the ordained, so that they might be as sacramental signs for the people, good shepherds, troubadours of transfiguration, and wardens of worth.

Koinōnia and the *Opus Dei*

In addition to celebration of the sacraments, the people of God join the entire creation in a daily round of praise to God the Fount, through the Word-Wisdom, in the Spirit. Stemming from Jewish prayer practice, in the Catholic tradition still practiced in several church families, there exists alongside sacramental worship those daily devotions of psalms, Scripture reading, song, and prayers that make up what tradition calls the daily office, or the *opus Dei*.[41] While different church families embody this tradition slightly differently, it usually contains the elements just listed, in the well-known services of matins or morning prayer, and evening prayer, evensong, or vespers, and the increasingly better-known noonday prayers and compline at the end of the day. This represents a simplification of the monastic tradition of prayer seven or even nine times per day, and some return to the even earlier "cathedral" tradition of daily prayers that emphasized matins and vespers.

The exact form is not of theological or spiritual significance. Three principles, however, are: (1) This is first and foremost objective prayer, a way of engaging in that prayer which all creatures owe their creator. (2) This is still prayer in common, liturgical prayer, a joining in the prayer of the whole church, indeed of the whole creation. Even when said alone, the daily office is not a personal devotion as such, though its regular practice, in community or in solitude, can have a profound impact on one's personal life in the Spirit. The daily office, like the relationships in the *koinōnia* of the people of God, is sandpaper by which we are being formed as suitable blocks for the temple of God. (3) The essential ingredient is daily confrontation with the word of God written, on a regular basis, including rules that require one to read the bits one would rather avoid. In cases where someone does not belong to a church family that has this tradition as part of its own, such daily scriptural prayer, accompanied by Bible study, will have much the same effect, especially if there is some community with others in doing it.[42] Once prescribed for clergy in Roman Catholic, Orthodox, and Anglican families, the practice of the daily office, sometimes in simplified forms, is growing among laity as well. When practiced regularly it not only strengthens the ligaments of *koinōnia*; it also forms the individuals praying in "habitual recollection," leading a life with an increasingly sustained consciousness of God's presence throughout. Practices such as Ignatian scriptural meditation, *lectio divina*, and "centering prayer," especially when done in groups or community, form a kind of bridge between liturgical and personal prayer.[43]

Personal Prayer and the Birth of Contemplation

Practicing "the presence of God" requires personal, private prayer as well as liturgical prayer, of course. The theological shift since Vatican II has indeed changed the order of priorities—personal prayer is now seen as derivative of and grounded in ecclesial life and liturgical prayer, rather than the public liturgies being reduced to private devotions. This does not decrease the importance of personal prayer to the individual, however; it simply grounds it in a way that gives it the possibility of greater depth and breadth.

The older spiritual theologies usually have sections on prayer at this point that list various types and degrees of prayer and other spiritual practices that are seen as aids to the soul in coming to that perfection which is the unitive life of glory.[44] Quite often these included detailed instructions on particular preferred methods. There is still much wisdom in these texts, but most of what can be retrieved belongs in books on practical counsel for the spiritual life rather than the theology of it. There are now a great many such books on prayer and the life of prayer available, so, while it may seem odd to devote so little space to a topic that has traditionally occupied so much, I wish here to note only a few essential theological points about the personal life of prayer.[45]

First, prayer as a life activity, a fundamental act and choice, is prior to any and all methods and techniques. Indeed, prayer is the fundamental act defining us as human; "we are the praying animals," the ones whose very being is constituted by being addressed by God's Word and Wisdom.[46] Only through a prayerful attention to that address do we have any opportunity for self-knowledge, for confronting the foundational restlessness of our hearts that Augustine identified in the *Confessions*. Only as practicing members of the church as primarily a "*koinōnia* of prayer," as deeply embedded in the sacramental and liturgical life of that community, are we enabled to shape our personal life of prayer in a manner that reflects God's divinizing address to us and the response the Spirit makes within us at any particular time.[47] The question of methods and techniques is usually not a matter of theology (I suppose there could be some methods so out of tune with Christian doctrine as to be unsuitable for any Christian on theological grounds); rather, it is a question of prudence, based on discernment of the personality, charisms, history, and spiritual style of the individual, as well as a discernment of how the Spirit is seeking to lead that person now.[48] The issue is prayer, not prayers.[49]

Second, prayer is primarily enjoying the presence of God, of spending delightful time in the presence of one who loves us. It is a kind of dalliance, an ongoing flirtatious conversation, with God doing most of the flirting, and it comes to fruition in the erotic descriptions of the third tidal current that we shall examine in turn. It is, however, meant to become an increasingly honest conversation in which we lay bare our own personal selves with all their desires, virtues, and character defects, ask that we be continually transfigured by our friend and lover, and listen for and await God's response. As in any relationship, there will be difficulties, and there will be periods of dryness and desolation, as there will be increasingly times of great intimacy and joy. The relationship is no less secure in the more difficult times, however, and the lament psalms in particular encourage us to make the conversation with God at such times honest, even brutally honest.[50]

Third, all the other usual classifications of prayer are simply an analysis of the response of our hearts to this friendship. Further contrition, thanksgiving, praise and adoration, supplication and intercession, all become part of a natural conversation with our friend. Intercession is perhaps the trickiest. Suffice it to say it begins with a duty to join Christ as he sits at the right hand of the Fount making intercession for us, specifically "to make intercession for those who cannot so address him [as 'Our Father'], with words and with the Eucharistic embodiment of words."[51] Every true Christian intercession, grounded in Christ's own as the Spirit prays in us and unites our prayer to Christ's, must thus end with "Nevertheless not my will, but yours, be done." It is not a matter of giving God instructions on how to accomplish our agenda but rather a sharing of our desires and concerns as a means of identifying ourselves with God's agenda, including, I have come to believe, God's own sorrow for the things that do not work out as originally hoped, even as we take new hope and even confidence that somehow, "All shall be well."

Fourth, and implicit in what has already been said, at its deepest level personal prayer is an attentive joining in the prayer the indwelling Spirit is already praying within us, even, or especially when we do not know how to pray (Rom 8:25–27). Our most personal prayer turns out to be a participation in God's own inner Trinitarian conversation.

Prayer thus begins from the depths of our ontological constitution by God's divinizing address as praying animals, dust that prays; it becomes grounded by our ecclesial existence in salvation history and the Trinitarian inner conversation and outpouring; and it finds its deepest personal expression in the *convivere*, the dalliance with our great friend and lover, that forms the ground of our transfigured life, as we join the prayer the indwelling Spirit is already praying within us. It is here that we will, perhaps with help, discern what we really need in order to make choices among types and methods from moment to moment, and in the presence of this Fountain of living water, all the discussions of degrees of prayer appear a little lifeless.[52]

All that said, nevertheless, there is often a shift in prayer in this current of transfiguration. Indeed, as we saw in the first slack or interlude, the entrance into this current is marked by a kind of darkness or dryness that makes our previous forms of prayer seem like they are not working. One of the most important aspects of the *askesis* (discipline) we learn in the church as a "*koinōnia* of prayer," through its "pedagogy of contemplative praxis," is that we should not cease praying even when difficulties arise. Indeed, staying faithful to a rule of life and the practices it recommends can be crucial under difficult circumstances. When we emerge from that transition and begin to live predominantly in this tidal current of transfiguration, we largely enjoy our life together with God by seeing God's glory illuminating our own being and everything around us, including our neighbor, our work, our worship, and our intimate relationships. Prayer is the enjoyment of this transfiguring light and becomes a means of grace in support of that ongoing transfiguration. As our life continues in this tide, however, we begin to turn from what is illuminated to the light itself, first contemplating it in its enlightening of others and ourselves but ultimately desiring to know the light in person. This is the shift the Orthodox describe as the move from "natural contemplation" to the prayer of stillness, the prayer of the "mind in the heart."[53] It is the birth in us of what the Western Catholic tradition identifies as "infused contemplation," that is, an increasing desire for loving knowledge of, and union with, God motivated by the gift of the Holy Spirit itself.[54] It is the point at which that friendship with God that Gregory of Nyssa identifies as the culmination of the spiritual life takes on an increasingly erotic dimension, going beyond dalliance to serious courtship. These are really the signs of entrance into the third current, and we shall have a second dark night or tidal slack to navigate before we get there. In the meantime, there is a fourth love to examine, one in which we learn the skills and virtues this shift will evoke in us— the practice of actual friendship and its loves in concrete relationships and communities. We turn to those intimate relationships in which we learn the essence of *convivere*, and by which are formed in the arts and virtues of conviviality.

Notes

1. Simone Weil, *Waiting for God,* 181–200.

2. See above, chap. 20.

3. Miroslav Volf, *Work,* 133–34.

4. Volf, *Work,* 133; on leisure as a limit to work, see 138–39.

5. Volf, *Work,* 134.

6. Volf, *Work,* 136.

7. Volf, *Work,* 137.

8. Volf, *Work,* 137. Volf refers here to R. H. Gundry, "The New Jerusalem: People as Place, Not Place for People (Revelation 21:1–22:5)," *Novum Testamentum* 29 (1987): 262; and J. Moltmann, *Der Weg Jesu Christi: Christologie in messianischen Dimensionen* (Munich: Kaiser, 1989), 353.

9. Volf, *Work,* 138–39; and see reference to Nicholas Wolterstorff, *Until Justice and Peace Embrace* (Grand Rapids: Eerdmans, 1983), 147.

10. The many writings of Rabbi Abraham Joshua Heschel are classics on this subject, beginning with *The Sabbath;* for an application to Christian spirituality, see Tilden Edwards, *Sabbath Time.*

11. Volf, *Work,* 140, citing Evelyn Underhill, *Worship,* 18.

12. Volf, *Work,* 141.

13. Volf, *Work,* 140–41.

14. For example, R. Garrigou-Lagrange, *Three Ages,* puts it between chapters on the discernment of spirits and devotion to Mary (2.241–71) focused on personal participation in the prayers of the Mass and the practice of communion. Chapters on contemplative prayer follow. In Antonio Royo and Jordan Aumann, the chapter on sacraments (pp. 345–63) comes first in a section called "Positive Means of Spiritual Growth," which is otherwise a series of chapters on the virtues. The chapter on the sacraments deals only with Penance and Eucharist, largely as a matter of personal devotion. Where there is some theological content, it clearly reflects a pre-Vatican II world.

15. See n. 16 below.

16. William Porcher DuBose's remarkable thought is best studied in *A DuBose Reader,* ed. Armentrout; see esp. xxxv, 21–47, 186–98; Charles Gore's most relevant text is *The Holy Spirit and the Church,* esp. 108–50. On the scholarship of the *Ressourcement* movement, "back to the [original] sources," see Marcellino D'Ambrosio, "*Ressourcement* Theology, *Aggiornamento,* and the Hermeneutics of Tradition"; for Karl Rahner, see his *The Church and the Sacraments,* which serves as a *locus classicus* for this topic; important subsequent texts include George S. Worgul, *From Magic to Metaphor*; Bernard Cooke, *Sacraments and Sacramentality*; Tad Guzie, *The Book of Sacramental Basics*; James F. White, *Sacraments as God's Self Giving*; and Alexander Schmemann, *Sacraments and Orthodoxy.*

17. Edward Farley, *Ecclesial Man.*

18. David J. Lonsdale, "The Church as Context for Christian Spirituality"; Ann Loades, "Sacramentality and Christian Spirituality"; and Susan J. White, "Ritual Studies," in *BCCS*, 239–53, 254–68, 387–400, with accompanying bibliographies; see Susan J. White, "Spirituality, Liturgy and Worship," *NWDCS*, 44–48, and the bibliography there. The entry on "Liturgical Spirituality" in the older *WDCS*, 248–49, reflects an earlier consciousness of this same shift.

19. Recall again the several references already made to theology of interfaith dialogue, especially in chapter 21.

20. See David Lonsdale, "The Church as Context for Christian Spirituality," *BCCS*, 244–48; Jean Cardinal Hamer's *The Church Is a Communion*, is a classic that has been deeply influential on ecumenical discussions of the church; John Zizioulas (Metropolitan of Pergamon), *Being as Communion*, is well on its way to becoming such a classic; see now also his *Communion and Otherness*; for an example of its impact on recent ecumenical discussions, see International Commission for Anglican-Orthodox Theological Dialogue, *The Church of the Triune God*.

21. Owen Thomas, "Interiority and Christian Spirituality," in *What Is It That Theologians Do*, 181–205.

22. From the Anglican "General Thanksgiving," *BCP* 86, 101.

23. The analyses of the particular sacraments that follows is highly influenced by years of teaching the works listed in n. 16 above, without being dependent on any one of them, except as noted.

24. Neither Royo and Aumann nor Garrigou-Lagrange has so much as an index reference to Baptism. *WDCS* did not have an entry on Baptism; *NWDCS* has a lengthy one, 140–42.

25. On the Protestant side, see Simon Chan, *ST*, 34, and indexed references to Baptism on 293; and Samuel M. Brown, *A Theology of Christian Spirituality*, 49–69, 86.

26. See, for example, Luther's discussion of Blandina's claim of Baptism to foil Satan in "The Babylonian Captivity of the Church," *Luther's Works*, 2.222–23.

27. See chap. 12 n. 2 above.

28. Guzie, *The Book of Sacramental Basics*, 67; see throughout for much of what follows on the Eucharist; also idem, *Jesus and the Eucharist*; Sam Powell has an excellent chapter on worship, *Theology of Christian Spirituality*, 100–121, focused on the centrality of the Eucharist.

29. See Robert Farrar Capon, *An Offering of Uncles*.

30. As I was taught by Krister Stendahl in class, Harvard Divinity School, spring of 1967, this is the true meaning of "give us this day our daily bread." A better translation may be "the bread that is coming," or the messianic bread, the bread of the messianic banquet. See entry *epiousios*, *BDAG*, 376–77.

31. Eastern Orthodox rites have always contained this prayer and their theologians have stressed its significance. For many of us, Alexander Schmemann's *Sacraments and Orthodoxy* was a classic source enabling this recovery of patristic sacramental theology. See also his *The Eucharist—Sacrament of the Kingdom*. More recently, Kallistos Ware, "The Holy Spirit in the Liturgy of St. John Chrysostom."

32. *BCP*, 366; for a classic on this subject, see Regis A. Duffy, O.F.M., *Real Presence*.

33. Guzie, *The Book of Sacramental Basics*, 87–88.

34. Stendahl, *Meanings*, 115–36.

35. Flora Wuellner, *Heart of Healing*, 58.

36. *BCP*, 501; 1 Corinthians 15.

37. See David Babin, *The Supreme Festival of Life and Death*; Alexander Schmemann, *O Death, Where Is Thy Sting?*

38. One of the best analyses of this new theology of Order is Robert Farrar Capon, "Ordination of Women: A Non-Book."

39. "Followership" is a term coined by Guy Fitch Lytle, III, in a series of unpublished papers and sermons in the 1990s.

40. Rahner, *The Church and the Sacraments*, 99–103.

41. An excellent essay on the daily office and its ground in the Eucharist and the *koinōnia*

of the church can be found in Society of St. Francis, *Celebrating Common Prayer*, 677–85. This use of *opus Dei* to refer to the daily round of prayers is older than the current Roman Catholic sodality that bears that name.

42. See Dietrich Bonhoeffer, *Life Together*, 40–75.

43. See "Ignatian Spirituality," *NWDCS*, 355–56, with associated references and bibliography. Joseph de Guibert, S.J., *The Theology of the Spiritual Life*, has an extensive section of several chapters on mental prayer that is, not surprisingly, Ignatian in orientation and includes detailed instructions (pp. 189–254); *lectio* is a Benedictine practice for prayerful reading of Scripture; see entry, *NWDCS*, 403-4; centering prayer is the practice of nondiscursive meditation or prayer of quiet closely associated with the work and teaching of Thomas Keating, of which *Open Mind, Open Hearts* is generally considered the *locus classicus*.

44. See, for example, Garrigou-Lagrange, *Three Ages*, 2.265–341; Royo and Aumann, 499–614; de Guibert as in n. 43 above and 305–67; by contrast, Simon Chan, *ST*, 125–224, has an excellent section on prayer that is firmly grounded in ecclesial and liturgical life.

45. Two of my favorites are Anthony Bloom, *Beginning to Pray*; and Kenneth Leech, *True Prayer*.

46. Robert Jenson, *ST* 2.58–59, 76.

47. Jenson, *ST* 2.227.

48. Anne T. W. Harvey, "Spiritual Style in the Work of Urban T. Holmes and Beyond."

49. I hope it is clear this is not a criticism of the use of written or set prayers. That usually arises out of confusion between liturgical and personal prayer, especially in worship traditions where liturgy is dominated by one person saying personal prayers out loud.

50. Walter Brueggemann is superb on this, of course, especially in *Praying the Psalms*.

51. Jenson, *ST* 2.227.

52. Contemplative journaling, various forms of meditation, art, and movement are all possible and helpful choices here. See Ira Progoff, *At a Journal Workshop*; Catherine Kapikian, *Art in the Service of the Sacred*.

53. See Kallistos Ware, "The Holy Spirit in the Personal Life of the Christian," 152–55. This article also gives a succinct Orthodox view of many of the aspects of the pneumatological approach to spirituality presented here.

54. Perhaps Garrigou-Lagrange's greatest contribution is his insistence that this is the normal and normative end of the spiritual life of all Christians. See above, chap. 21 n. 13. Of course, on the Anglican side, this was also the thrust of Kenneth Kirk's argument in *The Vision of God*.

24

Love of Friendship and
Life in Community

According to Simone Weil, the fourth form of the implicit love of God is friendship, that unique relationship that lies at the heart of all human community. In chapter 20 we looked at those things Weil considered essential to friendship: purity, attention, and a kind of distance that keeps the two persons separate even in their most intense intimacy. This distance in friendship is opened up by a dialectic between need and respect for the autonomy of both persons, and that requires real equality between them. Weil believed that this tension could be overcome only by something like a miracle, and concluded:

> Pure friendship is an image of the original and perfect friendship that belongs to the Trinity and is the very essence of God. It is impossible for two human beings to be one while scrupulously respecting the distance that separates them, unless God is present in each of them. The point at which parallels meet is infinity.[1]

We have seen that the source of the perfect friendship in the Trinity, as well as the cause of the Trinitarian God indwelling each of us, is the Holy Spirit; thus what is called for at this point is a pneumatological theology of friendship. Since all proper pneumatology is also christological, Jesus' teaching about friendship in John 15 and his role both as our friend and as the sacrament of God's offer of friendship with the human race also come into play. Jesus invites us into a *koinōnia* of shared moral purpose by calling us no longer servants but friends. He then establishes friendship by laying down his life for us, even as we are commanded to love one another as he has loved us, that is, with a like friendship. His first act as risen Lord is to gather his friends and pour on them the gift of the Holy Spirit by which he was raised from the dead, thus binding them together in his ecclesial body with himself as head, while by the same Spirit feeding them with his sacramental body.

Parish churches are actually very good places to make friends, or, at least they should be. It has certainly been the experience of my wife and me as we travel that the surest source of new friendships is our connections with others in churches and recovery groups. Such ecclesial settings offer us rare opportunities for friendship with others with whom we may not share a natural affiliation, even persons we find initially troubling or even repugnant. Of course, not all friendships are directly and obviously ecclesial. If Weil is right, however, there is a miracle in all friendships that, if followed to its logical conclusion, would find a place in that eschatological commonwealth of which the church is also a sacrament. In the incarnational interplay with concrete realities of actual cultures and societies, the Spirit gives the ecclesial *koinōnia* of friendship specific forms. This chapter will examine the traditional ones of personal friendship in general, religious community (including consecrated celibacy), and marriage (including parenting); it concludes with reflections on friendship with God as that moves toward the third tidal current of glory through the emergence of the more erotic dimensions of that friendship.[2] Because friendship is also a kind of communion of shared moral purpose, I suggested earlier that it requires a life of virtue in each friend that is honored by the other(s) as part of the distance, part of the respect for autonomy that is essential to the miracle friendship requires. Honor, integrity, fidelity, and respect for the autonomy of each are primary ingredients of this life of virtue. We have already seen how the work of Erik Erikson confirms this view in his research on developmental psychology.

We often think of theology of friendship as a contemporary concern;[3] we should note, however, that friendship has its place in the classic texts of spiritual theology as well.[4] Aelred of Rievaulx's great work on friendship is the classic text on the spiritual or sacramental theology of friendship;[5] Thomas Aquinas lists three qualities essential to a true friendship: benevolence, by which we wish the highest good for another; mutuality (the friendship is reciprocated); and community of life or *convivere*.[6] It is in such community as vivified by the Holy Spirit, and in healthy particular friendships within that community, that we learn the virtues of what the tradition has called true "fraternal charity." This concrete form of charity (*caritas, agapē*) is both an outcome of love of God and an efficacious sacrament of it. "Charity begins at home" means that it is precisely in our domestic relationships, however configured, that we have a school for learning the love that is essential to our common life and our relationship with God. By no means does it mean that love is to be limited to our domestic relationships; indeed, such a limitation would indicate an unhealthy love.

While all human friendship has this sacramental potential as a school of charity, Christian tradition has normally envisioned adult life as led in one of two primary forms of friendship: celibate religious community and marriage and family. Especially in the West these came to be seen as mutually exclusive, although today there are an increasing number of religious communities that are mixtures of celibate and married (or covenanted) members. Such communities generally do not interpret chastity as celibacy in the case of the married, but as fidelity.[7] In the context of this tide of transfiguration, we are less concerned with the ways these structured relationships are cures for and bulwarks against sin than for their sacramental character, the way they embody for us the gracious indwelling of the Holy Spirit. These two archetypal structures of fraternal charity have been privileged as sacramental, and are both characterized by a discipline, an *askesis*, shaped by vows that constitute the way of life and determine its structure. For this reason they are both sacraments of Order, in my view, particular structurings of ecclesial *koinōnia* as a means of sanctification.[8]

Religious Community and Celibacy

The phenomenon of monasticism as a primary expression of ecclesial community grew rapidly from the fourth century onward, largely in response to the end of persecution after Constantine's legalization of Christianity and the resultant decline in the opportunity to express spiritual heroism in martyrdom; other scholars recognize precursors in the desert tradition that predate the legalization of Christianity or even Christianity itself.[9] While the eremitic (hermit) tradition is older, eventually the coenobitic (community) tradition became more predominant, and it became standard practice that even one desiring to be a hermit should train in a community first. This reminds us that even a solitary monk or nun is enmeshed in the ecclesial *koinōnia* and is called upon to embody it. Celibacy came to be a predominant virtue of this formal "religious life," and, given the ascetical character of the time, was viewed as superior even to chastity as fidelity in marriage. In the East, at least, the taking of monastic vows came to be seen as a sacrament.[10] Western orders have a particular root in the foundations and rule of St. Benedict, and in Eastern and Western churches alike, monastic life came to be seen as the spiritual ideal and monastic spirituality as normative.

The Vatican II shift discussed in the last chapter has had significant impact on this situation. First, it is increasingly recognized that a decision to enter the monastic or religious life should be based on a careful discernment of vocation and personal charisms, not on a desire to win merit by choosing a higher spiritual way.[11] Together with a deeper understanding of the *askesis* of marriage, this has led to seeing the two paths as increasingly equal alternatives determined by individual call and gifts. Just as lay spirituality has replaced clerical as normative, so the spirituality of the celibate religious is now normed by lay spirituality, or at least seen as an equal to it. Second, while celibacy continues to be the dominant pattern of monastic life with regard to sexuality, except for the newer mixed communities where monogamous marriage is also practiced, this is now seen as an expression of sexuality rather than as a suppression or repression of it.[12] Third, the practice of fraternal charity in community within the religious life as an essential means of formation now includes a much greater openness to the appropriate place of healthy "special friendships," in contrast to an earlier time when the dangers of such friendships were so feared that they were all but forbidden.[13]

The formal structure of the religious life is determined by an interplay between vows and rule, while the material structure is determined by local circumstances and concrete relationships. The monastic vows usually include some mix of poverty (from simplicity of life, to communal ownership, to real Franciscan sharing the lot of the poor), chastity (celibacy for the unmarried), obedience (to rule and community authorities, ultimately to God), and, for some, stability and constant conversion of life. The various rules, whether the more informal conferences of the

East or the more legislative of the West, usually determine some appropriate mix of the four Benedictine aspects we have been examining as embodiments of the four loves: study, work, prayer (liturgical and personal), and community. These rules often give a particular shape or flavor not only to the common life of the community but also to the spirituality it seeks to embody. In the Western church in particular this gives rise to a variety of schools of spirituality associated with the major religious orders, such as Benedictine, Franciscan, Dominican, Carmelite, and so on. Regional variations also occur, as in Eastern (Christian) spirituality or "Celtic" spirituality.[14] A given local community is likely to develop its own particular history and style through an interplay of these formal elements with the material factors peculiar to its location and history. We can now see all these spiritualities as concrete embodiments of the ecclesial *koinōnia* of the Spirit's gifting. It has become increasingly popular, for example, to refer to each particular spirituality in terms of unique charisms. While nearly all church families that foster celibate religious communities have seen a decline in the number of vocations, many communities that have a vowed, celibate community at the core now include in their extended family large numbers of associates, companions, "Third Order" members, and oblates, as nonmonastic clergy and laity find such associations supportive of their spiritual lives led in the world. If I devote more space to marriage and parenting in this chapter, that is not to denigrate the vowed religious life but only because it has been largely the focus of attention until recently.

Soul Friendship and Spiritual Direction

One special form of friendship in ecclesial life is that of the *anamcara*[a] or soul-friend, the companion on the path who provides godly conversation and guidance.[15] In present usage, this term tends to describe a relationship of mutuality and equality, while other terms such as "spiritual director" or "elder" (*gerōn* in Greek, *starets* in Russian, often translated as spiritual father or mother) imply a relationship that is more one-way and even professional.[16] It is important that both parties be clear about the nature of the relationship so that responsibilities for boundaries and other ethical issues are maintained. In a spiritual friendship, there is mutual accountability for the boundaries, while in the more directive relationships the director or elder is responsible.[17] Theologically, however, the essence is the same: a friend or director who listens both to us and to the Holy Spirit at the same time, seeking discernment, guidance, and direction for our life in Christ by the Spirit, is a kind of sacrament, an embodiment of God's gracious presence to us, a pneumatophoric or Spirit-bearing figure.

At the human level, such a companion provides an objective sounding board for our expressions of our spiritual state, and, if well trained, will have available not only a sensitivity to us and the movement of the Spirit at the moment but also a

---

a Irish for soul friend. See the entry "Direction, Spiritual," NWDCS, 243–45 and the bibliography there.

deep grounding in his or her own spiritual life and practice and in knowledge of the tradition and its general principles for discernment: anchoring in the human flesh of Jesus, increase in "actual charity," and edification of the faith community. But the chief requirement is the elder's or director's own discernment of the movement of the Spirit in this particular person at this particular time.

While education and training are helpful, even essential, this is not a vocation to which one can aspire by such training. Rather:

> The elder, whether man or woman, is a prophetic or "charismatic" figure, in the sense that he or she is not appointed an elder by a superior author- ity, nor ordained to the ministry through any liturgical rite, but is revealed to the Christian community through the direct action of the Holy Spirit. Normally, there is no act of formal appointment; all that happens is that, in the continuing life of the Church, it becomes clear to the people of God that a particular person has been endowed with the gift of spiritual father- hood, and to this person others turn in ever-increasing numbers.[18]

That is, spiritual directors or elders are not made but discerned by the ecclesial community. You know you have been called to this ministry when people begin to ask you for it. At that point training becomes not only essential but also an act of appropriate humility, more necessary for a ministry of spiritual direction than for an occasional relationship with a spiritual friend. The most important thing of all, however, is one's own life in the Holy Spirit, and to that end the general rule that all directors need to be in direction themselves is pertinent. In our time of greater pub- lic accountability it is also appropriate that there be some kind of supervision plan, now often carried out in a peer group.[19] This training is essential to the director's own formation and the store of wisdom from which he or she may draw, but it can- not replace the essentially charismatic nature of the ministry:

> Spirituality is not taught, but caught; the spiritual father [or mother] is the infectious person, who has the disease himself and is able to transmit it to others. He teaches his children not so much by what he says as by what he is. . . . The elder's message is communicated, not so much through words of instruction as through his compassionate love and intercessory prayer. Without this love, without this prayer of intercession, no one can be a true *starets*. Love is above all the quality that marks him.[20]

That is, even in the more unidirectional forms, this relationship is governed by the theological virtue of love as a gift from the Spirit whose proper name is Love, and the boundaries necessary to the relationship are dictated by the distance that is the loving attention to the autonomy of the other, which Weil discerned at the heart of the love of friendship. As such, it is one sacramental form of the ordering of friendship within the ecclesial *koinōnia*. As with any ministry, its exercise outside a rooting in the community of faith is an anomaly.[21] There can be no such thing as generic spiritual direction any more than there is generic spirituality. Directors can guide only on the paths they themselves tread, and it is intellectually and perhaps spiritually dishonest (again, a sin against humility) to claim to be able to direct persons on other spiritual paths. That is not the same as saying the ministry cannot be offered to those who at present have at best a tenuous relationship to the church, or that one cannot learn from the wise of other faith traditions; it is to say that even to those persons one must be clear, "This is the path I follow and for which I can be some kind of guide."

One of the major instruments of church renewal in our time, I believe, is the ongoing recovery of the ministry of spiritual direction in the Western churches, which has accompanied the recovery of classical spirituality previously noted. The ecumenical Shalem Institute, the program of the Cambridge Jesuits, the publication of the code of ethics by the Pecos Benedictines, and the formation of Spiritual Directors International are key examples of this recovery.[22]

Marriage and Parenting

Marriage, like the formal religious life, is a form of vowed friendship. It is specifically the normative form that the *koinōnia* of friendship takes when an erotic dimension surfaces in the relationship. Marriage as an institution and a sacrament is designed to be a structure by which such an erotic friendship can be expressed appropriately and shaped with regard to both physical love and the building of the common life of a household. This insistence on a friendship at the heart of a marriage has generally replaced the economic and dynastic concerns of an earlier time. Because the energy is fundamentally erotic, this friendship is characterized not only by the other aspects of friendship already treated, such as benevolence and *convivere* but also by a desire for union and some focus on the possibility of fecundity, whatever form that takes. It is also a well-established principle of Christian spirituality that for married Christians marriage is the principal means of daily formation. What is less often expressed is that parenting is also a principal means of formation for the parents. Again, a home is a school of perfection because of the endless opportunities that it affords for the exercise of fraternal charity. That is, the give and take of normal family life is the primary school for learning the virtue of agapaic love, the proximate goal of all Christian spirituality. This is the principle of the "dominion of charity," laid out so clearly in 1 Corinthians 13 and throughout 1 John, the fact that love of God is practiced primarily in the form of love of neighbor, as we have been exploring throughout this tidal current of transfiguration. As we have seen, the two loves are not merely morally inseparable but are in fact one love, which is God's very own nature and the proper name of the Spirit who sanctifies us.[23]

From the standpoint of Christian theology, marriage is a form of vowed common life for the sanctification of the couple—and hence a sacrament, or a sacramental.[24] Indeed, in Karl Rahner's theology a marriage and the family that gathers around it is the church in miniature.[25] This has led Bernard Cook to describe marriage as the archetypal sacrament, expressing as it does a relationship of friendship and intimacy pointing to the eschatological destiny for all human beings, the desired outcome of all spirituality in union with God in the perfect commonwealth of peace and justice.[26] If this were something imposed on marriage from outside, it could feel like a kind of invasion, but when we understand marriage as an ongoing project expressing the intertwining of the intentionalities of the couple, then we can see that the sanctifying sacramental grace is the fulfillment of nature, not its denial or eradication. This also allows us to see the place of parenting in the larger marriage project as a whole. In what follows, I will be discussing the relationship that has undoubtedly been, and still is, the Christian sacramental norm: a faithful, monogamous, heterosexual marriage with children born to the couple. However (and this is the way post–Vatican II sacramental theology works), *mutatis mutandis,* the same grace operates in shaping other intentionally covenanted relationships, including those of adoptive and single parents and, I believe, same-sex couples, as instruments forming Christian character and hence means of sanctifying grace. Indeed, it would help us focus some of the current debates if we acknowledged that the real issues should be around precisely what is required by *mutatis mutandis* in each case.[27]

The project of marriage has been well described by both existentialist philosophy and at least two clinical psychologies of marriage in dialogue with such thought. The marriage project is a dialectic of overcoming the inevitable tragedies and negativities of love's actual history in a fallen and imperfect world within a framework of transcendent love. The deepest intentionality in human sexual love is not ultimately a satiation of a desire for pleasure, but rather the discovery of being-in-the-world as a being-with-others (*Mitsein,* as the inevitable form of *Dasein,* in the language of German phenomenologist Martin Heidegger).[28] With his usual Gallic acerbity, Jean-Paul Sartre showed how this project combines with enfleshed sexual desire in a series of projects by which I seek to recover the key to my being in that of specific others. He envisions this as a hopeless alteration between sadism, in which I seek to compel an other to yield the key to my being, and masochism, in which I seek to seduce an other into providing that key. Of course, for Sartre, this is all hopeless and always ends badly.[29] Given his atheism, that is probably the only possible conclusion for him: in this as in all existence, human being is a useless passion.[30] Marriage, particularly when undertaken as a sacrament, is an effort to close this dialectic of negativity by the free formation of a "we" in the face of the world and its tragedy and alienation, a "we" carved out of the realities of the world and its history, not in idealistic or romantic isolation from it. This "we" is covenanted, defined, and bounded by the vows that establish it as they are lived out in a subsequent history. This helps us to see the importance of accepting "marriage as an institution" as the proper form for the ideal love of the couple. Failure to do so produces a kind of disincarnate romanticism that never comes to grips with the task of writing a real concrete history in which love's project can be embodied in the world. On the other hand, resignation to the tragic circumstances of love in a fallen world, and abandonment of the project of forging a true "we" in the face of the world, is the opposite way of giving up.

Ironically (given the failure of his own engagement), of all the philosophers,

Søren Kierkegaard saw this dialectic most clearly, despite his inability to actualize it in his own personal life. In the speeches of Judge William in "The Aesthetic Validity of Marriage" in *Either/Or*,[31] Kierkegaard shows how first, or romantic, love requires an inner history in which it acquires itself and the virtues necessary to it, in patience, precisely in the form of a marriage in which the daily negativities threatening that love can be transmuted into challenges to further growth. "When patience thus acquires itself in patience, we have inward or interior history."[32] In this context procreation as an expression of marriage's inner project is an almost perfect embodied symbol or sacrament: the desired baby and the real one that results are at once an embodied expression of the love of the couple and a threat to it by the introduction of a third (and very demanding) person into the relationship. But the more-or-less successful navigation of the difficulties of parenting is precisely the kind of challenge that marriage must constantly undertake and integrate into itself as project in order to acquire itself in patience and thus write the inner history upon which its being depends. Procreation (by which I mean the whole process of parenting, not just the physical acts of conception and birth) as an end of marriage is not imposed from outside but from within marriage's own deepest intentionality.[33] Its relationship to marriage as a project is thus intrinsic rather than extrinsic. Marriages that do not include procreation in this most common sense will need to find other ways, equally challenging, to write their history as a "we" in the face of the world and its tragedy.[34] Some of the best psychological reflection on these matters underlines the same fundamental points. My personal favorites are Israel Charny and Rollo May.

In his famous *Love and Will*, Rollo May described what he saw as the "sickening of Eros," particularly as focused on the repression of the procreative power of sex.[35] Eros, for May, is what causes us "to seek union with the other person in delight and passion, and the procreation of new possibilities of experience which broaden and deepen the being of both persons."[36] The drive toward procreation is thus an intrinsic part of our yearning for union and wholeness, even as it pushes us toward self-transcendence.[37] Thus, the project of eros, including that of procreation, is a key expression of the intentionality of human being in general.[38]

> It is thus correlated with freedom. *We participate in the forming of the future by virtue of our capacity to conceive of and respond to new possibilities, and to bring them out of imagination and try them in actuality.* This is the process of active loving. It is the eros in us responding to the eros in others and in the world of nature.[39]

May is not in romantic denial about the reality of the resulting dialectic. He understands fully the conflict and negativity at its heart, indeed, of the embrace of the negative within the dialectic of the project if the positive outcome is to be possible.[40] Thus, flight from the ontological procreativity of sexuality is a denial of the tragic element in sexuality that can lead only to banality.[41] Hence, the dialectic by which the personalities of the partners are enriched and fulfilled in their common history is intrinsically—and sacramentally, we might say—linked to procreation:

The most powerful symbol imaginable for this is *procreation*—the fact that a new being may be conceived and born. By new being I mean not simply a literal "birth," but the birth of some new aspect of one's self. Whether literal or partly metaphorical, the fact remains that the love act is distinguished by being procreative; and whether casual and ephemeral or faithful and lasting, this is the basic symbol of love's creativity.[42]

If May helps us see the intrinsic connection between the truly erotic project of sexuality and marriage and the agapaic demands of procreativity, Israel Charny makes even clearer the need to embrace the "negative" within the heart of the positive in the dialectic by which love acquires itself in patience in a more concrete history. The title of his classic *Marital Love and Hate* on its own catches the spirit of the dialectic to this point: the incorporation of the negative into the positive intentionality of love.[43] Charny begins a chapter titled "Family Life as a Crisis Co-op for Becoming Self-Regarding People" as follows:

All of which [the title of the chapter] dictates an entirely different concept of family life from our traditional Western picture of the family as a
haven
fortress
island of security
oasis
refuge
warm hearth
tender bosom.
Rather, we suggest that we consider the family as a cooperative for emotional development (over and above its well understood roles vis-à-vis reproduction, economic provision, etc.) which supports each member's psychological needs to grow more secure in his image and belief in himself out of his being afforded a series of provocative, stressful, upsetting experiences with those who truly love him and whom he truly loves.[44]

While recognizing the difference between desirable, growth-causing pain and unbearable, debilitating pain (which may be most destructive in situations of domestic violence), he nevertheless asserts that "the goal of family life is to foster and enjoy growth through vaccinations of pain."[45]

One Saturday morning when our children were about twelve and ten, my wife Barbara and I had wearily plopped down for a second cup of coffee after the boys had gone off to play. She observed: "It's too bad our children didn't get grown-ups for parents." What I have learned is that no children get grown-ups for parents, but children will teach us to be the adults that they need if the crises they engender are taken as graced opportunities for our own personal and spiritual growth. As with all true pearls, the price will be high but eminently worth it.

We do have some knowledge of the psychology of parenting, though it is still understudied in comparison to child psychology and the impact of parents on children; such a psychology can provide further insight into the way the procreative aspect of eros functions as a means of grace and sanctification. First, we may agree with the developmental neo-Freudian school, deriving from the work of Erik Erikson, that real parenting over the life-cycle of a child (as opposed to an act of conception taking no responsibility for the consequences) is the normal and primary expression of human generativity.[46] Generativity is Erikson's sixth developmental stage and the one that James Fowler deems the dominant theme of most of adult life.[47] Recalling what was said in chapter 12 above, each Eriksonian stage presents a challenge to be overcome and a virtue to be practiced and "acquired." In the case of generativity the challenge to be overcome is stagnation—that the intimacy established in the previous stage (which has usually resulted in some form of life-partnership) will stagnate and stop growing. This stunts the growth not only of the relationship but also of the parties to it. Generative activities take the couple outside of themselves and their own "two-ness" or subjective "we-ness" into further projects for a broader future, projects in which they can practice and acquire the virtue of care, Latin *caritas* (the primary meaning of the English "charity"), which is the biblical *agapē*. It is this stage that is most clearly a school of perfection in its opportunities for the exercise of charity.[48] The procreation and nurture of children is not the only means of embodying this generativity, though it is the most common, and, when actual children are present, they make the challenges of this stage unavoidable. Other activities fulfilling this stage need, in any case, to involve taking some personal responsibility for the generations to follow. Generalizing, the challenges and tasks of each developmental stage in life offer choices. Some of these choices will be choices for God, and some will not. The omnipresence of the Holy Spirit assures us of the grace to make choices for God, even though the gift of freedom means that we may not. In general, the choices that are "for God" are also most likely to produce the virtue marking the successful traversal of a particular stage, which virtue will also be in part a gift of the Spirit. This is preeminently true of that agapaic love that, as an "infused" virtue, is at root a participation in the divine nature itself through the indwelling of the Holy Spirit whose proper name is "Love."

As we saw in chapter 12, the complexity of adult development exceeds the scheme presented by Erikson. There have been many efforts to fill in the blanks.[49] The most helpful scheme I have found is one that emerges from developmental family sociology, as in the works of Evelyn Duvall and Joan Aldous.[50] This school of thought envisions human development as a nest of overlapping careers—biological, child, education, job, and so on, including an adult subset relating to family: mating and intimacy, marriage, and parenting. Each of these has its own describable developmental rhythms for those who undertake them, and the different careers can be overlaid in many different ways. For example, forty-year-old parents having their first child after many years of marriage are embodying a very different pattern of adult life from a couple who married in their late teens and were already expecting, all of whose children will be grown by the parents' early forties. Adoptive parents, single parents, and blended families produce their own unique rhythms. Still, some generalizations are possible about the development appropriate to parenting as such.

First, the rhythm of parental development is always in harmony with the life of a particular child (or potential child). Its stages from conception (or planning it) onward are marked by the ages and developmental stages of the children. Specifically, parents of, let us say, a ten-year-old child will devote a lot of their own inner lives to reliving their own memories of being ten. This shows up most clearly in the clinical phenomenon known as anniversary crisis: when a child of yours reaches an age that was difficult for you, you will have a crisis, even though the child may be doing just fine. If parents approach this phenomenon with a healthy sense of present reality and a reflective and prayerful "inner" life, they have an opportunity to redo that difficult part of their lives and to heal the memories. But they must do this as their own "inner" work even while immersed in the "outer" work of caring for the child. It is a dreadful mistake—with sad consequences for both parent and child—if the parent demands that the child carry the burden of this reliving. It is equally a mistake if the parent "acts out" inappropriately as a result of this dynamic. A common example is seen with the presence of an adolescent child, which usually means the presence of friends in the house who are attractive at some level to one or another of the parents (at least at the level of the teenage self that they are remembering). A desirable outcome is the rekindling of the romance between the parents. Less happy is a decision to dump the family for a romance with someone else. Also less fortunate, at this or any stage, is the strategy of blaming the child for the unacceptable feelings aroused in the adult parent and resulting anger productive of toxic shame in the child. Does it need to be said that this kind of blaming and shaming is not a good strategy for disciplining even behavior that may really need it? Worst of all is any acting out with one of the children—one's own or their friends. It is also possible, where good spiritual direction is available, to make increased erotic energy available to a growing relationship with God. We might also note here one advantage of having two parents—they may not have had difficulties in the same stages of childhood, so that the one who had an easier time at a particular age may assume most of the parenting of a child of that age while the other parent does the more difficult "inner" work.

A second phenomenon is that parents may well learn to have their own excessively high or even moralistic standards loosened up a little (and I don't mean to the point of "anything goes"). One year, my wife and I had plans to attend my tenth college reunion in New Haven. Having just taken "Parent Effectiveness Training" (a good thing, although our boys figured it out in about ten seconds), we offered them a choice between two young couples to stay with them while we had a trip.[51] One couple was engaged, and the other was recently married with no children as yet. Our children knew and liked both couples, but our elder son, then about nine, thought for a minute and said, "You know, the trouble with people who don't have kids is that they expect kids to be too good."[52] He and his brother came on the trip, and we spent a lot of time in the museum looking at dinosaurs.

Children provide a constant reality check, testing all our assumptions and values. In addition to compelling us to relive parts of our own developmental history, including those we would prefer to leave in shadow, they also test the virtues that we are to have learned in the process. For example, a five-year-old deep in the "family romance" stage will profoundly test the bond between the parents, even though the child's worst fear is that it will succeed in splitting them apart. Again, a successful outcome for the parents will be a strengthening of their relationship. The most disastrous is any sexualizing of the child.

What needs noticing at this point is that it is precisely the way in which our children discomfit us that leads to new opportunities for growth in grace. As my younger son put it in a remarkable insight for one then so young: "You don't understand! My purpose in life is to bug you!" It is this very discomfiture that is the challenge of the parental stage, making the growth in the requisite virtue of *caritas* possible as well as necessary. Our children teach us to be the adults that they need us to be. It is also my own experience and observation of others that parents who are able to manage their own inner dynamic of parenthood do a pretty good job of raising their children. The art of parenting has more to do with managing our own parenthood than managing our children.

A third phenomenon is a combination of the first two with a specific focus. Becoming a parent requires us to come to terms with the "inner parent" that we incorporated when we were at the age of the child that we are now parenting. The most obvious phenomenon is the way in which we all say and do the things that our parents did—and we swore we would not—in dealing with our own children. Here again is an opportunity to mend broken object relations with the inner parent, or to reconcile with actual living parents where appropriate. This desired outcome is the equally common phenomenon of suddenly understanding our own parents and their wisdom in the light of our own parenting. The undesirable outcome, of course, is the perpetuation of generational cycles of violence, abuse, and dysfunction.

A fourth phenomenon is what I have called "the reverse flow of freedom." New babies are wholly dependent on their parents for everything. In truth, all the freedom is in the parents, and very little yet in the child. But there is already a paradox here, the paradox of love of neighbor as Martin Luther portrays it, because these seemingly *free* parents are ineluctably *bound* by the needs of the new infant—more bound than at any other stage. In fact, for parents to navigate this period there needs to be a world-shattering revolution in their own consciousness, a kind of switch that gets thrown, turning on the parental perspective. I remember consciously experiencing this myself when I saw my first child for the first time—I could literally feel the boundaries of my world shift. Previously, the world had been mine or maybe "ours," my wife's and mine. Suddenly, it was his, and my behavior had to change.[53] A generation later it was a great joy to watch the same switch get thrown in that son's own consciousness as in his own turn he became, overnight it seemed, a very fine father to his new daughter, our granddaughter. This paradox, there from the start, establishes a dynamic in the parenting process of a flow of freedom from parent to child. The older the child, the more freedom the child must have, and the less the parent will have, but for what is now a substantial portion of the lives of many people, parents and their adult children can enjoy a rough equality of freedom. This relationship between parents and adult children is ideally one of deep friendship.

This is the true *telos* or end of parenting, just as being friends with God is the true end of the spiritual life. In many cases, however, the dynamic ends with an elderly parent being increasingly dependent on a child. Theologically, this recapitulates God's creativity as "letting be," to use John Macquarrie's terms.[54]

Closely allied to this experience of a shift in the boundaries of the world is that of an almost unbearable sense of the risk of love. Already acute in the decision to marry, it becomes even keener with the arrival of a child. One's happiness—indeed, the key to one's very being and the being of the world as one knows it—is now in the tiny hands of an infant who is weak, vulnerable, and totally dependent on the parent whose happiness is now at stake. The pathological breakdown of parents who abuse or kill their infants, as well as the almost universal horror at such acts, provides a kind of ghastly testimony to the power of this frightful risk. At the deepest level it is a sharing in God's risk in creation, so well described by John Macquarrie.[55]

Even beyond this, I am happy to say from both theory and experience, one of the joys of *grand*parenthood is that you get to do it all over again, but without so much desperate intensity. There is also a whole range of uniquely "domestic" virtues, some of which are so crucial to the *koinōnia* of any community that they have also entered the vocabulary of the Benedictine life.

Friendship is thus at the heart of parenting as its final desired outcome, as well as at the heart of a marriage, with erotic elements also emerging as an enrichment of *philia*, not its destruction. When handled appropriately, by all the *askesis* of the vowed life that marriage shares with the monastic life, this new erotic dimension actually moves *philia* and *eros* together toward their fulfillment (not cancellation) in *agapē*, in particular structures of love of neighbor as *koinōnia* that make the household, monastic or family, a church in miniature. Two of the "domestic" Benedictine virtues are essential for living these lives of disciplined love. One of the essential virtues by which these forms of community embody *caritas* is hospitality, the welcoming of the stranger with warmth and care into the *koinōnia* of the household. In the case of children or other new members, this is a permanent welcome; in the case of sojourners, it is more temporary but still vital; it can be an important way by which a family or monastic household functions as a sacrament, an effective sign of the grace of ecclesial *koinōnia* to a world that hungers for it.[56] That is, hospitality is a kind of evangelism. The second virtue is the final Benedictine vow, stability. Deep-gifted friendships and communities require a commitment to permanence, to the community in the monastic life, "until death do us part" in marriage, which is also implicit in the commitment to parenthood. *Convivere* requires time, extended time. This stability commits us to endure the growthful (not abusive) vaccinations of pain as the means of grace by which we are shaped as sacraments to one another in a consecrated friendship. Hospitality and stability are both incarnations of the attention that Weil identified as the essence of all love of neighbor.

For Christians, there is an intentionality in these relations of communities of structured friendship that points beyond themselves to an even more deeply evoked self-transcendence. The Holy Spirit lies at the heart of each form of *koinōnia* structured as friendship and community, especially as a life under vows. In the Trinitarian structure of her mission, the Spirit liberates us from the attachments of sense and ego that prevent us from paying the appropriate kind of attention in our relationships; in the incarnate structures of vowed life as *askesis*, the Spirit supports the autonomy of the individual participants and helps maintain the distance required for true friendship, even while gifting us with the intimacy for which we long; and finally, the Spirit is the true miracle Weil said was necessary for real friendship to exist: by indwelling consecrated relationships the Spirit makes each one a sacrament of the commonwealth and the *pleroma*, and hence a means of grace for us who participate and for the world. That is, each friendship so consecrated shares in the deepest sacramental character of the church and is an expression of its mission.

There is even more. In the end, as Gregory of Nyssa taught, we are called and gifted to be the friends of God.[57] It is also the Spirit who makes this miracle possible as the most profound intentionality of consecrated friendships. As we move from implicit love of God to explicit, as we turn from the transfigured, illumined world to the light of glory itself, Christian tradition uniformly treats of this as a coming together of friendship and desire, *philia* and *eros*, in a yet deeper intimacy characterized by both union and fecundity as well as *convivere*, in a new tidal current of our relationship with God. Before we arrive at this glory, however, glory that is the mystery of our participation in the hypostatic union of Christ's two natures and hence in the very inner life of the Trinitarian God, tradition also teaches that there is a second "slack," a deeper dark night and desert, and a third major conversion to undergo.

Notes

1. Simone Weil, *Waiting for God*, 208.

2. See what was said about Jesus and friendship in chapter 8 above, and my article "What a Friend We Have in Jesus."

3. See, for example, Isabel Anders, *The Faces of Friendship*; David B. Burrell, C.S.C., *Friendship and Ways to Truth*; Paul J. Wadell, *Becoming Friends*.

4. Even Antonio Royo and Jordan Aumann have a sensible if brief account, *Christian Perfection*, 591–93. It is somewhat dominated by the concern for dangerous friendships, but even here the symptoms listed that mark an unhealthy friendship (not unlike an infatuation in the erotic realm) are pertinent: exclusivity, possessiveness and jealousy, and an obsessive character to the relationship.

5. See again Aelred's *Spiritual Friendship*; *Aelred of Rievaulx's Spiritual Friendship*; and John R. Sommerfeldt, *Aelred of Rievaulx on Love and Order in the World and the Church*; see also the entry "Friendship," *NWDCS*, 316–17.

6. Aquinas, IIa IIae, q.23 a.1; cf. R. Garrigou-Lagrange, *Three Ages*, 2.188, in the context of discussing friendship with God.

7. The Community of Celebration is one such example within the Episcopal Church. They are headquartered in Aliquippa, Pa. See Rob Moll, "The New Monasticism."

8. Wendy Wright expresses similar views in *Sacred Dwelling*; see especially "A Vowed Life," 139–51,

9. Derwas J. Chitty, *The Desert a City*, is a classic; see also Columba Stewart, "Christian Spirituality during the Roman Empire (100–600)," *BCCS*, 84–87; Robert Hale, "Monasticism," *NWDCS*, 444–45.

10. See Nicholas Palmov, *The Assumption of the Religious Dress in Monasticism*. This view is not universal, however. See Paul Evdokimov, *The Sacrament of Love*, 68.

11. For a particularly striking discussion of the church as a school of discernment, see David Lonsdale, "The Church as Context for Christian Spirituality," *BCCS*, 246–48.

12. The classic text is Donald Goergen, *The Sexual Celibate*; see also Edward Schillebeeckx, *Celibacy*; Heinz-Jürgen Vogels, *Celibacy, Gift or Law*; Adrian L. Van Kaam, *The Vowed Life*.

13. See the entry "Religious Life," *NWDCS*, 537–38, with the excellent bibliography; also the entry on "Relationships," 536–37.

14. But see the cautionary entry "Celtic Spirituality," *NWDCS*, 182–84, in contrast to the same entry, *WDCS*, 83–84.

15. See Kenneth Leech, *Soul Friend*; Tilden H. Edwards, *Spiritual Friend*; Martin Thornton, *Spiritual Direction*; Margaret Guenther, *Holy Listening*; the standard text on how to conduct this ministry remains William A. Barry, S.J., and William J. Connolly, S.J., *The Practice of Spiritual Direction*.

16. See Kallistos Ware, "Personal Life," 161–64, for a concise description of Eastern Orthodox theology on this subject.

17. Thomas M. Hedberg and Betsy Caprio, *A Code of Ethics for Spiritual Directors*.

18. Ware, "Personal Life," 162; elsewhere he refers to spiritual mothers as well as fathers.

19. The Shalem Institute in Washington, D.C., has pioneered both the training of directors and the practice of mutually accountable peer groups (http://www.shalem.org).

20. Ware, "Personal Life," 163.

21. Thomas and Wondra, *Introduction*, 306.

22. For Shalem, see n. 19 above; the Center for Religious Development was founded by William Barry and William Connolly and others in 1971; much of the energy of that project now resides at the Campion Center (http://www.campioncenter.org); for SDI, see http://www.sdiworld.org.

23. Augustine, *De Trinitate* XV. See also Martin Luther, "The Freedom of a Christian," esp. 301–16; and C. S. Lewis, *The Four Loves*; for a keen analysis of the household as a school for the formation of Christian character and virtue, see also Thomas Breidenthal, *Christian Households*. Wendy Wright, *Sacred Dwelling*, is also a very fine contribution to the literature on family spirituality.

24. Karl Rahner, *Foundations of Christian Faith*, 420–21; *Theological Investigations*, 10.212–18.

25. Rahner, *Foundations*, 421.

26. Bernard Cooke, *Sacraments and Sacramentality*, 79–94.

27. See my brief statement in "Dogma and Freedom"; Breidenthal makes much the same point (*Christian Households*, 116–37). In the case of single people who are neither called to nor gifted for the celibate religious life, for example, the discussion is often too focused on whether or not they should have sex. The deeper question is how they are to experience intimacy and faithfully embody friendship and *koinōnia* as well as express the *caritas* that is essential to their generativity.

28. Martin Heidegger, *Being and Time*. These are fundamental concepts that run throughout the book. Much of the analysis of this section was first carried out in my doctoral work: see Robert Davis Hughes III, "Towards a Theology of Parenthood."

29. Jean-Paul Sartre, *Being and Nothingness*, 363–430.

30. Sartre, *Being and Nothingness*, 615.

31. Søren Kierkegaard, *Either/Or*, 2.5–129.

32. Kierkegaard, *Either/Or*, 2.99.

33. One of the chief conclusions of my doctoral research was that the word "procreation," especially as it describes an "end" or purpose of marriage (though no longer, in Anglican thought, the primary purpose—see the development in the documents of the Lambeth Conference from 1930 to 1958: for example, *The Lambeth Conference 1930*, 41–45; and especially "The Family in

Contemporary Society," *The Lambeth Conference 1958*, 141–50; regarding the purposes of marriage in the rite of solemnization, see *BCP*, 423) best applies to the whole process of parenting, nurturing, and educating children for the lifetime of all involved, and not merely to their physical generation. This expansion allows for the broader understanding of the arena in which parenting may be experienced as a means of grace and sanctification, as suggested here.

34. See also Charles Levy, "The Experience of Married Love We-ness."

35. Rollo May, *Love and Will*, 46, 116–17.

36. May, *Love and Will*, 73.

37. May, *Love and Will*, 74, 77.

38. May, *Love and Will*, 78.

39. May, *Love and Will*, 91.

40. May, *Love and Will*, 145–47.

41. May, *Love and Will*, 115, 117–20.

42. May, *Love and Will*, 311. For an argument making much the same point, see Breidenthal, *Christian Households*, 138–58.

43. Israel W. Charny, *Marital Love and Hate*.

44. Charny, *Marital Love and Hate*, 85–86.

45. Charny, *Marital Love and Hate*, 86.

46. The *locus classicus* is Erik H. Erikson, *Childhood and Society*; also see his *Adulthood*.

47. James Fowler, *Becoming Adult*, 14–36. My discussion above is based heavily on Fowler's exposition of Erikson. See also Don S. Browning's classic, *Generative Man*.

48. See also Breidenthal, *Christian Households*, 148–49.

49. Gail Sheehy's work, *Passages*, is the more popular example. A different and more nuanced approach is Daniel J. Levinson et al., *The Seasons of a Man's Life*, and *The Seasons of a Woman's Life*; for an application of virtually all the lessons of developmental psychology to Christian spirituality, see now Peter Feldmeier, *The Developing Christian*; Feldmeier wrestles throughout with the relationship between human and spiritual growth, between holiness and wholeness, and reaches conclusions very similar to those I have advocated.

50. Evelyn Millis Duvall, *Family Development*; Joan Aldous, *Family Careers*.

51. Thomas Gordon, *Parent Effectiveness Training*. What ultimately worked best for us was the Adlerian family council approach; see Rudolph Dreikurs and Vicki Soltz, *Children: The Challenge*.

52. See J. Bradley Wigger's hilarious description of the reaction of seminary classmates without children to the stickiness of his own parenting experience in "Face to Face: A Spirituality of Parenting," 18.

53. Daniel Aleshire describes his own experience of this phenomenon in "Family Life and Christian Spirituality," 212.

54. John Macquarrie, *Principles of Christian Theology*, 211–35.

55. Macquarrie, *Principles*, 211–35.

56. See entry "Hospitality," *NWDCS*, 347–48, and the bibliography there; Dolores R. Leckey, *The Ordinary Way*; Esther De Waal, *A Life-Giving Way*.

57. Gregory of Nyssa, *Life of Moses*, ##319–20, 136–37.

The Second Interlude

25

The Dark Night of the Soul

You will do well to pay attention to this as to a lamp shining in a dark place, until the day dawns and the morning star rises in your hearts.
—2 Peter 1:19

At the conclusion of the second tide, that of transfiguration, we recognized in the erotic desire for union and fecundity expressed in marriage and parenting a means for forming Christian character, making them sacramental relationships. We saw there the hints of glory to come, to which we begin to turn our attention; I also suggested that there is a dialectic with the negativities of growth in a sinful world that require radical restructuring of ego and personal psychological life if real intimacy is to be possible. As we turn from the enjoyment of the world and our human relationships as illumined and informed by glory to the very Fount of Glory, toward the actual third tidal current of glory itself, most of the traditional literature begins to express this desire for union and fecundity as erotic, and uses, as we shall see, erotic images of the spiritual espousal and the spiritual marriage to describe the ineffable; but all speak of encountering first a desert or a dark night.

Our deepest engagement with the realities of the most personal and erotic human relationships surfaced the need to incorporate the negative aspect of the human dialectic; just so, precisely in this slack between the tidal currents of transfiguration and glory, a second dark night appears, traditionally called the dark night of the soul, active and passive. As our friendship with God turns from the implicit forms of love to the explicit, and a more openly erotic dimension emerges, the same sort of dynamic arises as in human intimacy. Just as marriage and parenting required us to dig down deep into the psychology of our own broken object-relations, so the turn toward the Fount of Glory itself requires a similar spiritual digging into the depths of our soul, already in itself a relationship with God. At one level, this is a new upwelling of the current of conversion, for it appears as a kind of "third conversion." At an even deeper level, it is a further upwelling of God's love in us, of the current of transfiguration as an expression of God's desire for us, as we learn to love ourselves as illumined by glory.[1] At the deepest level it is an upwelling of the current of glory itself, in the mode of hope, which is the theological virtue, with its eschatological overtones, that will dominate the third current, at least in

358

this life. Because our eyes are not used to this splendor, it appears to us at first as darkness, but a luminous darkness. The first dark night required us to embrace the gift of detachment of our egoism from the world and the things of the world so that we might see the glory in them; this second dark night requires us to embrace the gift of detachment from our very selves, even as they have been related to God to this point, not so that our selves may be annihilated but so that they may be ravished by the glory that awaits, for which our restless hearts long, for which all our being awaits in hope.

So, before we turn to the tide of glory, we have a second "slack" (a space between the tides) to examine—a second dark night, called by St. John of the Cross the dark night of the soul. Indeed, this is the true night, of which the night of the senses was merely a foretaste.[2] In this second night, we learn loving detachment from ourselves and all the fondly held structures of our egos, even our relationship with God as we have conceived it to this point. At first, this feels like a new upwelling of the tide of conversion, a "third conversion."

Third Conversion

The biblical typology developed by Reginald Garrigou-Lagrange to express the three conversions, as analogous to three dimensions of apostolic experience, continues to be helpful. The first conversion, entrance into what I have called the current of conversion per se, is like the original call of the disciples from being fishermen or tax collectors to following Jesus; the second is the experience of betrayal, abandonment, and powerlessness at the crucifixion. That is ultimately relieved by the experience of the resurrection, which marks the entrance into a period dominated by the current of transfiguration and illumination as we enjoy the presence of our risen Lord and the world around us as illuminated by the glory radiating from him.[3]

Though this current of transfiguration can be the tide dominating most of our lives, eventually it fades. In terms of apostolic experience, Garrigou-Lagrange suggests, we are faced with the reality of the Ascension. Jesus goes away—at least that is what it feels like from our perspective, however much we develop a theology of the Ascension that makes Christ more universal.[4] We know the biblical story and its liturgical celebration—soon after the Ascension comes Pentecost as the climax of the paschal feast, when we receive another advocate, the power by which Jesus was raised from the dead, and which now rests on us to make us his body. But there is an interval, a space between Jesus and the Spirit that opens up a time and a space for human history, a history that is not opposed to the *theōsis* of human beings but is rather its sacramental enactment and celebration.[5] That is, we live for a time in an interval between resurrection/transfiguration and the fullness of the Spirit as she takes us deep into empowerment and glory itself. This interval is the slack we are examining—a dark night in which we mourn the loss of immediate contact with our Lover even while we wait for consummation. In this interval we suffer more than the purification of our senses, the painful detachment of our egoism from the things of this world; now we experience a complete blank in which God seems to be absent, or at least in which our intense desire for God seems unfulfilled.[6]

In this space, this interval, this tidal "slack," we are first confronted with the fact that many imperfections remain in us, a kind of "rust deep down in the spiritual faculties of the soul," that represent an attachment to the structures of our empirical egos still standing between us and full union with God.[7] Here we experience the paradox of the great saints, who seem to others to be models of perfection, but decry themselves as still great sinners; whatever unrefined dross remains as a barrier to full union with God, however objectively small, becomes subjectively most painful. The closer we grow to God, the more intensely we experience the love of God and the desire for God that awakens in us, the more painful become all those defects of character to which we still cling because they are part of our self-definition; this includes even our definition of ourselves in relation to God as we have experienced that to this point. We are now called not merely to detachment of worldly things from our egoism but the very giving up of those structures of self that we believe have defined us as persons. It is for this reason that I have suggested we call the third style of self-transcendence, as in David Tracy's analysis, "self-criticism."[8]

Self-criticism is different from self-denial, even as we gave that a more positive interpretation in the analysis of the tide of conversion. There we examine ourselves and confess the major flaws, sins, wounds, oppressions that have prevented any relationship with God. Self-criticism assumes that work has been done, indeed that we have also spent some time in the style of self-fulfillment, enjoying the way in which our newly converted and purified selves are illumined by transfiguring glory. But now this light penetrates deeper, beyond our attachments to the world and the things of the world, to the very structures of our selves insofar as they harbor resentments, character defects, and outgrown defense mechanisms that now impede our growth. Now we must let go not only of our fondnesses but also of our very selves. It feels like annihilation of self in some cases, but that is a dangerous word, especially for the abused and the oppressed, who may have a very different experience. As Beverley Lanzetta points out, St. Teresa did not experience annihilation of that new beloved daughter-self she had discovered in Christ, but rather had to unsay or unknow all the definitions of herself as woman that had been imposed on her. This becomes archetypal for Lanzetta's analysis of this dark night of the soul for women as the "dark night of the feminine" in which many women at this point in their spiritual growth must let go of the construction by patriarchal society of their selves as feminine and woman.[9] While this points first to what may be a unique configuration of the night for many women, at a deeper level it reveals a dimension of self-criticism that is universal and can, perhaps, be clearly seen only in our time: the need to deconstruct our social selves, the very relationships that have made us "persons" up to this point, insofar as those relationships ground our self-definition in social realities that embody institutionalized evil.[10]

This night, then, faces us again with the inadequacy of interpreting spirituality only as "inner work" at a personal or psychological level.[11] There is certainly a lot of that which needs to happen. But now it is also deeply engaged with social deconstruction and self-criticism, as we confront the distortions of consciousness that inevitably accompany our own social location in terms of race, gender, class, sexual orientation, and so on;[12] it also encompasses the ways these aspects of our social location inevitably infect us with sin (as perpetrators, victims, or bystanders), sin for which we did not volunteer, but which is a kind of rust or dross that tarnishes the very forces that made us who we are. If for women in an oppressive patriarchal context this means a deep "unsaying" or unknowing (deconstruction) of "woman" even as this has defined their very self-understanding, for example, so also for men in the same context there must be a deep unsaying, unknowing, or deconstruction of "man" at the level of self-definition.[13] This kind of ideological self-criticism (the Marxists had the right idea at least) is needed for the new erotic intimacy to which we are called. The deconstruction of gender I have been using as an example is surely necessary for any real deep intimacy between wife and husband in our time. The entire critique of the sinful rust in our social location is necessary for the new intimacy with God into which we are being invited, which has traditionally gone by the name of "infused contemplation" insofar as it refers to a personal dimension of the life of prayer. But the same critique is needed if we are to be empowered for real liberating prophetic action, apostolic ministry, and mission. Indeed, we often see these two, the contemplative and the apostolic, in the same persons. Lanzetta's portrait of St. Teresa certainly includes both, and in our time a Mother Teresa or Desmond Tutu also expresses a unified spirituality of deep prayer and prophetic, apostolic action. Of course, there is more to this night than ideological self-criticism, and not all such self-criticism belongs to the night. But the second night will require that we face such issues.

Gerald May relates a number of other contemporary issues to this night—again, not that every confrontation with such issues is truly the night nor that every night will confront any or all of these issues. He merely observes that in our time they are often commingled. These include depression, which can, in some cases, be distinguished from the night by its clinical symptoms, and should always be treated;[14] recovery from addiction, as one needs to move beyond the idols of recovery to a larger life of service to a God who is now more than merely a rescuer;[15] issues of personality and gender much as Lanzetta has discussed;[16] and the confrontation with institutionalized, social evil.[17] He also has some sage advice about spiritual direction in this night.[18]

What surfaces in this second and deeper night, then, is the dross, the rust in our ego-structures that impedes both intimacy and apostolic or prophetic effectiveness, and it is the same rust that impedes both. While this rust is still expressible as personal character defects, we now see that these structures are also deeply embedded in social constructs that themselves are infected with institutionalized evil. In short, we are now faced with what Teilhard de Chardin called "the divinization of our passivities" as a deeper purification than the "divinization of our activities" that had characterized his approach to the first night. It is not only what we do that must be purified, but what we undergo, and who we are.

Teilhard and the Divinization of Our Passivities

Teilhard's first point is that the realm of our passivities, that which we undergo, though conceptually half of human experience, is actually much wider and deeper than the other half, our activities. Indeed, our passivities always accompany our activities but also extend beyond these limits. The beam with which we know ourselves and the world illumines only a very small circle, and "beyond lies impenetrable darkness, though it is pregnant with presences—the night of everything that is within us and around us, without us, and in spite of us."[19] Further: "everything beyond a certain distance is dark, and yet everything is full of being around us. This is the darkness, heavy with promises and threats, which the Christian will have to illuminate and animate with the divine Presence."[20]

Teilhard then distinguishes between the passivities of growth, "which sustain our endeavour and lead towards achievement," and the passivities of diminishment, which seem at first to be hostile powers obstructing our development.[21] These correspond, at the highest level, to the realities Teilhard distinguished in "The Mass on the World" as the growthful aspects of evolution, and the suffering. Over the first, Christ says "this is my body"; over the latter, "this is my blood."[22]

The Passivities of Growth: This Is My Body

The passivities of growth, then, encompass all the gifts we have received from God that make up our life and its possibilities. Some of these are internal, inherited, personal gifts; some come from the milieu into which we are born and the positive assets that milieu embodies; but some come from the sheer overwhelming discovery of the Fount of the turbulent current of our life as sheer gift, completely beyond our compelling: "In the last resort the profound life, the fontal life, the new-born life, escape our grasp entirely."[23] Attempting to return from the abyss of this discovery, Teilhard experiences next, in the web of surface life as such, a deep fragility of the Providence that must undergird any possible successful world:

> After the consciousness of being something other and something greater than myself—a second thing made me dizzy: namely, the supreme improbability, the tremendous unlikelihood of finding myself existing in a world that has survived and succeeded.[24]

This double realization, that the Fount of life is outside myself and beyond my grasp and that the favorable circumstances of history are as well, leads to a kind of existential despair as we contemplate our finitude and contingency, crushed by the number of living things and the stars. "And if something saved me, it was hearing the voice of the Gospel, guaranteed by divine success, speaking to me from the depth of the night: *ego sum, noli timere* (It is I, be not afraid)."[25] Teilhard concludes his reflections on the passivities of growth with a prayerful meditation on the two hands of God, one shaping us inwardly and the other shaping us through outer history and circumstances. While he does not do so, this could be linked to the tradition of the two hands of God as Word and Spirit, though I am reluctant to identify them with inner and outer. But the main point is that at the bottom of the personal abyss that gives us life, as well as in the darkness of being overwhelmed by the course of the universe that shapes us, we find, perhaps unexpectedly, the presence of God:

> By their very nature, these blessed passivities which are, for me, the will to be, the wish to be thus and thus, and the opportunity to realise myself according to my desire, are all charged with Your influence—an influence which will shortly appear more distinctly as the organising energy of the mystical Body. In order to communicate with You in them in a fontal communion (a communion with the sources of Life), I have only to recognise You in them, and to ask You to be ever more present in them.[26]

In the light of our analysis, "the organising energy of the mystical Body" is the Holy Spirit, who forms the church as the Body of Christ, brings the reality of his Eucharistic Body to the faithful, and finally, if Teilhard is right, in an inconceivable end redeems both "souls" and history as the universe itself becomes the risen Body of Christ.[27]

Again we face the existential choice: exploring either the source of the inner flow of our lives or the outer history and circumstances, we face our own contingency, our own failure to be necessary beings, the ground of our own being, the object of the ontological proof. Either we learn to let go of that anxiety in the two arms of the loving God who is Fount, savior, and fulfiller, or we accept ourselves as " a useless passion." The night is either totally dark and empty, or it is full of Being. And when we are in it, we are not always sure which, despite any previous faith.

The Passivities of Diminishment: This Is My Blood

It is a naïve and inaccurate view of the world that focuses only on the passivities of growth, "the inner and outer forces which animate our being and sustain its development."[28] Though there is some challenge even here, it becomes easy enough to trust God in the forces of life. But can we also trust God in the forces of diminishment we must undergo, culminating in death? It is surprising how few theologians have actually wrestled with this problem head on. In addition to Teilhard, another Jesuit, Bernard Lonergan, has done so.[29] Teilhard is clear that the internal passivities of our diminishment, both those that lay in wait for us from the beginning and those that appeared later on, "form the blackest residue and the most despairingly useless years of our life."[30] Death is the ultimate evil, physical and moral, and we can only overcome it by finding God *in* it. We do so by embracing the cross and resurrection of Jesus, through which alone we can face reality without a false sense of optimism or a false sense of resignation and detachment.[31] Teilhard considers three basic topics under this rubric: our struggle against evil, our defeat and its transfiguration, and the nature of true resignation, surrender, or acceptance.

In the struggle with evil, God is our constant ally, divine Providence "concerned throughout the ages with the prevention and tending of the wounds of the

world." If we are to avoid the failures that result from simple laziness or impru-
dence, we must struggle against evil to the end, with all our heart, mind, soul, and
strength and "make no peace with oppression."[32] We must not run to embrace suffering that can in any way be avoided or fail to battle against the suffering of others.
The *via negativa* of martyrdom is open to us only when all other options that can
be undertaken with integrity fail us. Even at the end, we do not surrender to the evil
but to God. To surrender to anything less than God is idolatry.

But in the end, we all do fail. We are not strong enough to undertake the battle
against evil on our own, and, in the end, we all die, the final diminishment. Even
here, there are three levels of failure: one that directs our attention to better and
higher ends, and a second that has no intrinsic value of its own, but strengthens the
one undergoing it for a deeper success. But then there is the third kind of diminish-
ments, the most common of all:

> which utterly disconcert our wisdom. At every moment we see diminish-
> ment, both in us and around us, which does not seem to be compensated
> by advantages on any perceptible plane: premature deaths, stupid acci-
> dents, weaknesses affecting the highest reaches of our being. Under blows
> such as these man does not move upward in any appreciable direction;
> he disappears or remains tragically diminished. How can these uncom-
> pensated diminishments, which are death in its narrowly mortal form,
> become a good for us?[33]

Most especially, I suggest, we experience this darkness when we confront the
intractable dimensions of our own personality that bind us to evil and diminishment, especially those deeply rooted in institutionalized, social evil over which we
are largely powerless, which we can transcend by no conceivable human means. At
such times, especially when God seems to be silent or absent, we seem to be facing
a darkness not only within ourselves but in God as well.[34]

At this point, there is no relief except in a resurrection that is the one and
only gateway to an eschatological hope. Like Teilhard, we need to come to see the
redemptive activity of God as something more than we have experienced to this
point: "But he will do still more for, as a result of his omnipotence impinging upon
our faith, events which show themselves as pure loss will become an immediate
factor in the union we dream of establishing with him."[35]

What is required is a final surrender, not to evil but to God, our supreme Lover,
with whom we desire final and ultimate union. The initial detachment from our
egoism that leads to spiritual growth is not yet "the critical point of our ex-centra-
tion, of our reversion to God. There is a further step to take: the one that makes us
lose all foothold within ourselves—oportet illum crescere, me autem minui [I must
decrease, that he may increase]."[36] If true union requires a kind of death, which the
mystics describe as "an annihilation in the other [which] must be more complete
the more we attach ourselves to something greater than ourselves, then we cannot
set limits to the sacrifice required of us on our journey to God."[37] What feels at
times like self-annihilation of our empirical ego turns out to be something quite
different—the discovery of that which God loves in us, the highest of the four loves

described by Bernard of Clairvaux, as we surrender ourselves into the arms of our great Lover, faults, failures, and all, in a final act of communion. Indeed, one of the most potent experiences arises from God using the parts of ourselves we loathe the most as tools in his mission, turning our very flaws inside out to expose an unknown virtue that lurked within. But before turning to that theme, it is good to recall Teilhard's caution about true resignation.

Teilhard's point, that a misunderstanding of resignation as passivity in the face of evil becomes a principal source of hatred for the gospel, is felt even more keenly in our time on the part of those who have suffered wicked, abusive, and oppressive diminishment in the social sphere.[38] Indeed, some earlier Christian piety can be justly criticized as "a perverse cultivation of suffering and diminishment." This largely comes about when surrender *as such* is valorized above surrender to God. Teilhard is clear that we are never free to abandon the struggle against evil. We are entitled to unite ourselves to the will of God only at the point at which all our strength is spent; even then, we struggle no less valiantly than the pagan hero with his stoicism. The difference is a belief about what lies beyond failure, not an excuse to give into it:

> Unless I do everything I can to advance or resist, I shall not find myself at *the required point*—I shall not submit to God as much as I might have done or as much as he wishes. If, on the contrary, I persevere courageously, I shall rejoin God across evil, deeper down than evil; I shall draw close to Him; and at that moment the optimum of my "communion in resignation" necessarily coincides (by definition) with the maximum fidelity to the human task.[39]

It is for this reason that we are to be wary of acedia, *accidia*, the sin of spiritual sloth that tempts us to abandon the struggle in the depths of the night. It is this same principle that calls us to be willing to be in the night as long as God wills us there, until we have reached the point Teilhard describes. In a letter to a friend, Fr. Auguste Valensin, Teilhard gave a helpful clarification and summary:

> To sum up, *complete* Christian endeavour consists, in my view, in three things:
> 1. collaborating passionately in the human effort in the conviction that, not only through our fidelity and obedience, but also through the *work* realized, we are working for the fulfillment of the Pleroma by preparing its more or less immediate material,
> 2. in the course of this hard labour, and in the pursuit of an ever widening ideal, achieving a preliminary form of renunciation and of victory over a narrow and lazy egoism,
> 3. cherishing the "hollownesses" as well as the "fullnesses" of life—that is to say its passivities and the providential diminishments through which Christ transforms directly and eminently into Himself the elements and the personality which we have tried to develop for him. . . .[40]

At this same point Teilhard also recognizes the overflow of grace, especially in the third stream, in both prophetic apostolic action and mystical annihilation: "Within the Church there are St. Thomas Aquinas and St. Vincent de Paul side by side with St. John of the Cross."[41]

For Teilhard, as for Paul Tillich,[42] this embrace of spiritual darkness is possible only because of a deep faith in the final parousia of Christ and the *pleroma* of the Spirit, in which God preserves, transfigures, and ultimately incorporates all good, even that which seems to have been lost in the forces of diminishment.[43] This vision remains to us even while we struggle with doubt in the night itself. In the end,

> We must try everything for Christ; we must hope everything for Christ. *Nihil intentatum.* [Nothing ventured. . . .] That, on the contrary, is the true Christian attitude. To divinise does not mean to destroy, but to sur-create. We shall never know all that the Incarnation still expects of the world's potentialities. We shall never put enough hope in the growing unity of mankind.[44]

The Birth of Erotic Intimacy

Precisely at the point Teilhard describes, where struggle does not cease but faces one's inevitable failure and one hopes, with deep and even doubtful longing, for a consummation it can barely envision, as we surrender to the great Lover in whom we hope for that consummation, the dark night takes on an erotic dimension in which mystical union and apostolic fecundity coincide. There is now a tendency to ascribe this language only to the historical phenomenon of bridal mysticism (*Brautmystic*), in which the soul experiences itself as bride to Jesus the bridegroom, flavored by the courtly love tradition in the Middle Ages.[45] Instead, I suggest, following Simone Weil's comment that the language of eroticism belongs first and naturally to the mystic and only derivatively to human lovers, that this birth of eroticism at precisely the point of proper resignation, acceptance, or surrender is inevitable and appropriate.[46] In the actual poem *Noche Oscura* (Dark Night), in verses that did not get commentary in the unfinished prose teaching, St. John of the Cross turns naturally to erotic imagery.[47] Indeed, the flow at this point in the commentary, as it breaks off abruptly, drives us into his version of the classical use of the Song of Songs as a mystical text, in *Cantico Espiritual.* This is because, as it turns out at the very bottom, in the darkest pit of the night, this very night is a new upwelling of God as love in the soul:[48]

> This dark night is an inflow of God into the soul, which purges it of its habitual ignorances and imperfections, natural and spiritual, and which contemplatives call infused contemplation or mystical theology. Through this contemplation, God teaches the soul secretly and instructs it in the perfection of love without its doing anything nor understanding how this happens.[49]

That is, great teachers before and after the Carmelite mystics see the birth of what can only be described as an erotic longing for union and fecundity precisely at this point. The tradition of using the Song of Songs as symbolic of Christ's union with both bridegroom and the church is as old as Origen in the third century, and hence predates both the courtly love tradition of the thirteenth and the Romantic movement of the nineteenth, though both have indelibly affected the way we are now able to read these texts, requiring some caution.[50] Most of the writing using this image to express mystical union and the night that precedes it has been produced by celibates, with little or no personal experience of the physical reality of "two in one flesh." The result is that just as that reality has sometimes, in Christian tradition, been virtually despised, so its positive use has been excessively idealized or romanticized. As José de Vinck pointed out at the time of *Humanae Vitae*, most celibates writing on marital sexuality underestimate the hard work and asceticism that are required to keep a faithful married sexual relationship alive and well, and also seem totally ignorant of additional dimensions of the experience, such as the ridiculous.[51] In the previous chapter I attempted to give a more realistic view of marriage in both the mode of union and the mode of fecundity, but we have just begun to develop a deep literature of married spirituality, which is largely yet to be written.[52]

The Space Between Espousal and Marriage

As I suggested above, another difficulty in appropriating the texts of bridal mysticism is that the practice of abstinence between the time of betrothal and the consummation of marriage seems to be an ever-scarcer commodity in our culture, though some of us are old enough to have experienced it or remember it, and occasionally one still meets young couples who come to marriage chaste in the older sense. Yet, whether we deal with St. Teresa, St. John of the Cross, Jan van Ruusbroec, or any of the other great mystics of this erotic tradition, the dark night is specifically this period of time between the spiritual betrothal, when we and Christ commit to one another "for time and eternity," and the consummation of the relationship in the ecstasy of the "spiritual marriage," which again has two phases—the honeymoon-like foretastes possible in this life and the enduring union in resurrected, eternal life.[53] Indeed, the very essence of the dark night is a deep erotic longing for one with whom one is now totally in love and to whom one is totally committed but as yet not fully joined, with a Lover who seems to be absent. Even those who have tastes of the spiritual marriage in this life report this ever-increasing longing and desire as the principal experience, along with a transformation of ourselves, the bride, into the glorious equal partner with our groom, the Incarnate Word, as he gifts and decks us with virtues that turn out to be his own.

It all begins with falling in love without qualification, as Lonergan puts it, a falling in love that is the essence, as we saw, of what he calls "religious conversion," and which we discover, as the process proceeds, is grounded first in God's love for us:[54]

To be in love is to be in love with someone. To be in love without qualifications or conditions or limits is to be in love with someone transcendent. When someone transcendent is my beloved, he is in my heart, real to me from within me, supreme in intelligence, truth, goodness. Since he chooses to come to me by a gift of love, he himself must be love.[55]

In the first instance, the bridegroom, the beloved Lover, is Jesus, the Word Incarnate, and the love is very personal and very explicit.[56] This very erotic explicitness in the mystics has been deeply embarrassing to some, and the prevalent homophobia of our time, especially among men, makes it difficult for us to read a text like St. John of the Cross's *Canticle*, although it would be as big a mistake to read it as a gay text as to pass by it in fear. The soul is the bride, in a man, a woman, or the church as a whole, and, after all, the erotic language, however explicit, is only an analogy of the reality of the spiritual union, though it also points to the actual physical reality of human unions in sacramental relationships. And, in the end, union does not stop with the Word Incarnate. By virtue of the hypostatic union of the two natures in his one person, we are invited into the full depths of the Trinitarian life of union itself, as participants, in some sense now equal by gift (as *philia* and *eros* both require), but never identical in nature or number, in one sense annihilated in our Beloved, in another enduring and not absorbed, in true interpersonal communion. All this is a gift of the Spirit, in Christ, as we are prepared for our place in the final *pleroma*. In the night, in the period of the betrothal, we have just enough of a glimpse of this glory to become dissatisfied even with the reflections of that glory that previously delighted us. Now we become entranced, enchanted by glory as God's own self, satisfied with nothing less, in this interval fed only by a deep hunger and an ever-growing desire, while we are slowly and unconsciously bedecked with the finery of our marriage garment.

Here again, the style of self-transcendence appropriate to this interval, this slack, reveals itself as the exercise of self-criticism in the service of love. Every part of our being that makes us unequal to and unworthy of Jesus and union with him becomes increasingly painful. That is the negative side. On the positive side, the longing love for God for God's own sake now begins to lead to learning to love ourselves for God's sake (Bernard's final love), to discover ever more of our own inherent goodness and beauty as now transfigured by our Lover and bedecked with his own virtues. We learn, in darkness and the fire of desire, not of unrequited love but of not-quite-consummated love, through Christ to love ourselves in God and God in ourselves, in the power of the Holy Spirit who is the flame that consumes and yet is finally painless.[57]

In most of the classic texts of Christian spirituality, the emphasis at this point is on union and infused contemplation, not fecundity and apostolic action. This does not adequately reflect the tradition, however. If it did, this would be a matter of serious concern, as we recall from the previous chapter what Rollo May had to say about the suppression of the procreative power of sex.[58] In fact, as William Johnston has pointed out, the procreative fecundity of eros at this point has been manifest in the actual lives of the mystics who have experienced this night of longing and tastes of the subsequent ecstasy. In a section on "Birth of the Child," Johnston states that the mystic undergoes the purification of the night "not just for self-purification, but for the purification of humankind," with particular reference to the problem of social and institutional sin we have noted here.[59] Thus, "The mystic, then, plays a central role in the life of the world. . . . And mystics are creative." This is true even of contemplatives who lead little or no active life, in their prayerful concern for the growing reign of God and the state of the poor. Many of the greatest contemplatives have born obvious fruit; Teresa and John in their reforms of the Carmelite order, for example, or the missionary efforts of Ignatius Loyola and his followers. In a later return to the theme of mysticism and social justice, Johnston makes particular reference to one of the great mystics of the twentieth century, Thomas Merton, who also evidenced a deep passion for social justice.[60] Within the classic texts, perhaps Ruusbroec best embodies this balance between contemplation and action, union and fecundity.[61]

The Luminous Darkness and the Deep Desert

Contemplative prayer is, in a way, simply the preference for the desert, for emptiness, for poverty. One has begun to know the meaning of contemplation when he intuitively and spontaneously seeks the dark and unknown path of aridity in preference to every other way. The contemplative is one who would rather not know than know.[62]

These words of Thomas Merton remind us that the night has its own importance, not just as a prelude to a dawn, and that the task of the contemplative is to stay in the desert, in the night, and find grace there. The darkness is real, and in the process of unknowing we lose our grip on what we thought we knew of ourselves and what we thought we knew about God. It is important to note that spiritual direction is absolutely necessary during such times in order to help sift the real from the self-delusionary. Also, it is critical to maintain the ordinary disciplines of life, especially liturgical prayer and participation in the sacraments. This is serious stuff, and one needs all the resources at one's disposal to get through it.

But it is a strange kind of darkness. It is, as Teilhard said, full of Being. The desert has an unexpected fecundity that happens only when we are not paying attention to it but are willing to remain precisely where God has put us for the moment, filled with a deep, longing desire for a Lover who seems to evade our grasp or even be absent. Though there is some alternation between mysticisms of darkness and light in the tradition,[63] the eventual consensus is that the dark night is a luminous darkness, parallel to the "eloquent silence" the prophet Elijah experienced on Mt. Horeb (1 Kgs 19:9–18).[64] Ruusbroec is very clear that the luminous character of the night is the Son of God, the coming bridegroom, in whom we become capable of seeing and contemplating eternal life. This luminosity in the night itself is that glory which is God's own self, as the contemplative spirit "ceaselessly becomes the very resplendence which it receives."[65] It is important to note that at least in this life we are not talking about a dawn that succeeds the darkness but rather the luminous character of the night itself. Christian contemplatives do not chase false lights; they remain in the darkness until it itself is experienced as luminous.

In fact, the darkness is itself light, which we perceive as darkness for three reasons: the weakness of our "eyes" and understanding, which cannot take in so great a light as God's glory, but are at first blinded by it; this weakness is compounded by the ongoing experience of self-criticism as a fear of giving in to temptations we may not even fully understand; and, most of all, the experience of the light of glory as a luminous darkness is simply an effect of the immensity of the light itself.[66] Again, while we are in this period, though we may hope against hope for an ineffable dawn, desire and long for a consummation of love, while we are in the night itself, or the deep desert, we do not go chasing after what seem to be heralds of that dawn or the edge of the desert. Instead we wait in the darkness and dryness until it in itself becomes for us luminous and fertile by God's grace. Otherwise, we may be tempted by efforts of what remains of our old ego to anticipate the dawn and imitate "the effects of such regeneration." In our relationship with God, this is disastrous: "To falsify our inner truth under pretext of entering into union with God would be a most tragic infidelity to ourselves, first of all, to life, to reality itself, and of course to God. Such fabrications end in the dislocation of one's entire moral and intellectual existence."[67] These stern words remind us of the need for spiritual direction in the night and a guide in the desert, as well as the counsel always to choose darkness and unknowing until the dawn does not so much break as something different from the night but emerges in us without our knowing as the luminosity of the night itself. From our side, the night is illumined as the spiritual gift of understanding begins to expand our natural faculties beyond their created capacity in the process of unknowing; the desert is made fertile by the gift of tears as a prayer gift, in which our tears find their place in God's own sadness at the state of the world.[68] If we move on to the subjects of the next and concluding chapter, it can only be in fear and trembling, after a terrible but awesome waiting.

Notes

1. William Johnston, *Mystical Theology*, 220.

2. Johnston, *Mystical Theology*, 220–27.

3. Johnston, *Mystical Theology*, 218–20.

4. Reginald Garrigou-Lagrange, *Three Ways*, 48–65; on a theology of the Ascension and Pentecost, see Eugene Rogers, *After the Spirit*, 200–207; on the Ascension as such, see Douglas Farrow, *Ascension and Ecclesia*.

5. Rogers, *After the Spirit*, 204; see also my "The Historic Ought-to-Be and the Spirit of Hope."

6. Garrigou-Lagrange speaks of this sense of abandonment, which echoes John of the Cross, *Three Ways*, 49–58; this may be more typical of men, as Beverley J. Lanzetta points out that St. Teresa did not experience abandonment but a rather different kind of pain (though, as we shall see, the dynamic is actually the same) (*Radical Wisdom*, 119–36, esp. 129).

7. Garrigou-Lagrange, *Three Ways*, 58.

8. See my "A Critical Note on Two Aspects of Self-Transcendence."

9. Lanzetta, *Radical Wisdom*, 133–36.

10. Johnston, *Mystical Theology*, 211–12.

11. Thomas, *What Is It That Theologians Do*, 181–205.

12. My first encounter with the concept of social false consciousness was in class with Gregory Baum, in 1973; see his *Religion and Alienation*, throughout, p. 75, for example.

13. Lanzetta, *Radical Wisdom*, 133–36.

14. G. May, *The Dark Night of the Soul*, 155–59; this represents some change from his earlier view in *Care of Mind, Care of Spirit*, where depression was helpfully distinguished from the dark night in that other aspects of life are still going well for one in the night, where depression darkens everything. This criterion still holds, but May now believes that often an experience of the night and a battle with depression overlap. What remains constant is that symptoms of clinical depression require treatment, night or no night, and that appropriate medication does not interfere with spiritual growth. His final considered opinion, then, is that the battle with depression is one form the content of the dark night can take for some people. Not all depression is the night, however, and not all night involves depression. Discernment is key to make sure that clinical depression does not go untreated.

15. May, *Dark Night*, 159–64; I am less happy about his acceptance of relapse as a possible part of this journey—too many relapses are final or fatal for such a view to be appealing.

16. May, *Dark Night*, 164–68.

17. May, *Dark Night*, 174–80.

18. May, *Dark Night*, 168–17.

19. Pierre Teilhard de Chardin, *Divine Milieu*, 46–47.

20. Teilhard, *Divine Milieu*, 47.

21. Teilhard, *Divine Milieu*, 47.

22. Thomas King, *Teilhard's Mass*, 97.

23. Teilhard, *Divine Milieu*, 48–49.

24. Teilhard, *Divine Milieu*, 49.

25. Teilhard, *Divine Milieu*, 49–50; Teilhard is quoting the frequent words of Jesus, especially the risen Christ when he makes his appearance, such as Matt 28:10.

26. Teilhard, *Divine Milieu*, 50.

27. This is the great conclusion to the *Divine Milieu*, the "Epilogue, In Expectation of the Parousia," 133–38.

28. Teilhard, *Divine Milieu* , 52.

29. On Lonergan, see *Method*, 52–55, 240–43; see Thomas Aquinas Dunne, S.J., "Lonergan on Social Progress and Community."

30. Teilhard, *Divine Milieu*, 53.

31. Teilhard, *Divine Milieu*, 54–55.

32. Teilhard, *Divine Milieu*, 56; *BCP*, 260.

33. Teilhard, *Divine Milieu*, 59–60.

34. See again Denys Turner, *The Darkness of God*, 226–51, on John of the Cross, dark nights, and depression, and his final cautionary assessment on 252–72.

35. Teilhard, *Divine Milieu*, 60.

36. Teilhard, *Divine Milieu*, 61, reference is to John 3:30.

37. Teilhard, *Divine Milieu*, 60.

38. Teilhard, *Divine Milieu*, 63.

39. Teilhard, *Divine Milieu*, 65–66.

40. Teilhard, *Divine Milieu*, 67.

41. Teilhard, *Divine Milieu*, 67.

42. Paul Tillich, *ST*, vol. 3, notes the way the discourse on the spiritual presence as the source for resolution of the ambiguities of human life includes culture, and then the whole discussion moves to the relationship between the kingdom of God and the end of history. I have also grappled with this in "The Historic Ought-to-Be and the Spirit of Hope." William Johnston does

an excellent job of suggesting a new vision of the essential unity between contemplative mysticism and truly prophetic engagement with social issues in *Mystical Theology*, 345–64.

43. Teilhard, *Divine Milieu*, 133.

44. Teilhard, *Divine Milieu*, 138. This sense of the relationship between contemplation and apostolic action is evident in the Ignatian tradition of contemplation in action, but one also finds it earlier, in, for example, the exquisite balance in *John Ruusbroec, The Spiritual Espousals and Other Works*; see especially James Wiseman's introduction (pp. 12–22).

45. *NWDCS*, 155–57; Sasika Murk Jansen's entry is itself a fine piece of work, but the volume refers "Marriage, Spiritual" only to that entry (p. 422), which would be unthinkable in a more traditional Catholic presentation.

46. Simone Weil, *Waiting for God*, 171–72.

47. The turn is at stanza 4 and continues through the balance of the poem, *Collected Works*, 711–12.

48. Johnston, *Mystical Theology*, 220, is excellent on this.

49. "Dark Night," 2.5.1, *Collected Works*, 335.

50. Origen, *The Song of Songs*, see esp. prologue, 29.

51. José de Vinck, *The Virtue of Sex*; also Sydney Callahan, in *Beyond Birth Control*, presents throughout a realistic view of marriage in opposition to both antisexual and romantic interpretations; the personal accounts collected by Michael Novak in *The Experience of Marriage* bear out this more realistic view.

52. Johnston, *Mystical Theology*, 277.

53. Johnston has two excellent chapters on what must here be compressed in a few paragraphs (*Mystical Theology*, 235–77).

54. Johnston correctly begins here (*Mystical Theology*, 236–37).

55. *Method*, 109; see Johnston, *Mystical Theology*, 251, for this use of Lonergan.

56. Lanzetta notes that the gender relationships are sometimes reversed in the tradition, with Jesus as the motherhood of God or the Word appearing as Lady Wisdom (*Radical Wisdom*, throughout, esp. 58–59).

57. Johnston, *Mystical Theology*, 264–71; St. John of the Cross, Canticle, 36:5, *Collected Works*, 547; May, *Dark Night*, 100; Canticle, 39:14, *Collected Works*, 562.

58. See the previous chapter, nn. 36–40.

59. Johnston, *Mystical Theology*, 231–33.

60. Johnston, *Mystical Theology*, 345–64; the discussion of Thomas Merton and other examples is on pp. 346–48. Merton's own contribution at this point in the discussion can best be savored in his last and fiercest book, *Contemplative Prayer*; see esp. 112–16 where Merton wrestles with the issue of the relationship between contemplation and social justice.

61. Jan van Ruusbroec, *John Ruusbroec, The Spiritual Espousals*, see n. 44 above, esp. pp. 21–22.

62. Merton, *Contemplative Prayer*, 89.

63. Kallistos Ware, introduction to *The Ladder of Divine Ascent: John Climacus*, 56–57.

64. Harvey Guthrie was the first one to suggest to me the translation "eloquent silence," Old Testament class, Episcopal Theological School, spring 1967.

65. Ruusbroec, *John Ruusbroec, Spiritual Espousals*, 3.1, p. 147.

66. See Garrigou-Lagrange, *Three Ages*, 2.384–91.

67. Merton, *Contemplative Prayer*, 88.

68. A. Jones, *Soul Making*, has a wonderful chapter on tears as a gift of the Holy Spirit (pp. 82–106). Among the fathers, Symeon the New Theologian has some of the clearest teaching about the gift of tears as a gift of the Holy Spirit, indeed, as the sign of the "second Baptism," and precisely at this point—the deeper conversion of the night of the third conversion; see *The Discourses*, 16–18, with references there.

Third Tidal Current: Glorified Dust

26

Waves of Glory

And all of us, with unveiled faces, seeing the glory of the Lord as though reflected in a mirror, are being transformed into the same image from one degree of glory to another; for this comes from the Lord, the Spirit. Therefore, since it is by God's mercy that we are engaged in this ministry, we do not lose heart. . . . For it is the God who said "Let light shine out of darkness," who has shone in our hearts to give the light of the glory of God in the face of Christ. —2 Corinthians 3:18–4:1; 4:6

His divine power has granted to us all things that pertain to life and godliness, through the knowledge of him who called us to his own glory and excellence, by which he has granted to us his precious and very great promises, that through these you may escape from the corruption that is in the world because of passion, and become partakers of the divine nature. —2 Peter 1:3–4

I wish I had more to say about glory, the third great tidal current of the Spirit. I mean that in two senses: first, I wish it were possible to say more about it; the witness of all those who have tasted it, however, is that it cannot really be spoken but only alluded to by analogies and art, especially poetry. After all, it is God's own glory that is at stake here, whether belonging to his essence or only to the uncreated energies.[1] Eye has not seen, ear has not heard, and we seek to speak here the unspeakable. Even St. Paul is shy about revealing his own experience (2 Cor 12:2). But like all the figures in the great tradition who have sought to speak or unspeak it, there is in me a deep desire to communicate what I know of it. After all, this third tidal current of the Spirit is the deepest (most profound) and, even if transfiguration is the tide in which most of us will spend most of this life, glory is the current in which we shall live eternally. Structurally, from a theological point of view, the consideration of this tide should be at least as long as that of the other two.

Which leads directly to the second reason I wish I had more to say: I know precious little of it. To this point in the book, right up to the dark night itself, I can attest to the validity of the general line of teaching in the Christian tradition either from personal experience or from working with directees. I have known glory by reflection in the second current, especially from the face of Christ and the indwelling of the Spirit, and in touches of the darkness, but I wait in longing for the promised consummation. While it has been my privilege to be in the presence of persons of great sanctity, I have not been the spiritual director of any such, though I have been fortunate to have wonderful directees showing substantial growth. So precisely at this point I can rely only on the tradition itself, trusting that because it has proved reliable to this point, it will continue to do so. In any case, the best way into this current of glory is to read the primary texts of those who have tasted it, such as John of the Cross's *Cantico* and *Llama* or Teresa's innermost mansions, or Julian's deepest *Showings*.[2] Much of the classical literature of spiritual theology failed us at just this point, with dry treatises on grades of prayer and analyses of mystical phenomena or extraordinary graces. What should have been the most exciting part of the discussion of Christian spirituality becomes the most boring or voyeuristic. So, the best way to get even an initial apprehension of the third tidal current, that of glory, is to read the primary texts themselves. Here we "see" the way in which the Fount and Word/Wisdom now assist the Spirit in bringing each of us, the entire human race, and the whole cosmos into the destined *pleroma* of final consecration and eschatological fulfillment.

Nevertheless, some things must be said in order that there be a little more than silence. Guidance is still needed here. We remain, in this life, at the same time justified and sinner, so self-criticism continues. We remain finite and subject to self-delusion: indeed, in the last chapter I noted Thomas Merton's stern warnings against imagining ourselves at this dawn before we really are (that is a danger I know only too well). So, some theological principles are still important not only to complete a theology of the spiritual life but also as guidance to pilgrims and their directors. We never outgrow our need for direction; indeed, the need increases the closer we grow to union with God.

Extraordinary Phenomena

Let's get this one out of the way first, because it can be the biggest temptation to the kind of fabrications against which Merton warned, as noted in the previous chapter. Let me begin with a personal story.

During my freshman year at Yale, 1962–63, I was part of the outbreak of what *Time* called "blue tongues," an irruption of charismatic phenomena in the Yale chapter of Inter Varsity Christian Fellowship, including speaking and singing in tongues and other gifts. Indeed (and this is part of the story that has no relevance here), I was partly responsible for it.[a] We were all caught up in the glorious reality of the gifts, filled with joy, and dutifully reading 1 Corinthians 12–14 to one

---

a I had been given a copy of the *Logos* magazine of the Blessed Trinity Society, an early, ecumenical charismatic organization. It featured an article on Harold Bredesen, at that time pastor of First Reformed Church, Mt. Vernon, New York. As a result of my sharing the magazine with members of the IVCF chapter, Pastor Bredesen was invited to come speak to us.

another on a regular basis to avoid the pitfalls. The chaplains at the time (and they were very good—this was the Bill Coffin era) were bemused and unhelpful, and the evangelist who had brought us the infilling had gone home. We were without guidance. Perplexingly, everything St. Paul predicted could go wrong promptly did. It started with trying to incorporate in our community the experience of members who had deeply desired the gifts but apparently received none, while those of us who had been more skeptical were happily singing in the Spirit (I now know this is not unusual). It ended with deep divisions in our little community over points of doctrine and what the consequences were for mission.

I was confused and perplexed by the undeniable reality of the experience and the contradictory outcome. Having had a wonderful time of retreat at the motherhouse of the Society of St. Francis in Dorset the previous spring, what came to me was that I needed a monk. While visiting an old schoolmate then at Harvard, it occurred to me that there was a house of the Cowley Fathers in Cambridge, and I set out walking up the Charles River to find it one Saturday. I did indeed find it, and knocked on the door, and must have said something really bright like, "I'm a freshman from Yale and I need some spiritual direction." God bless whoever opened the door, because he took me seriously, and soon I got an hour with one of the wisest of the brethren, Fr. Pederson.[3] He listened carefully to my story, let me know that he had spoken with others who had experienced charismatic phenomena, and then said something to this effect: "Robert, I have no doubt that what you have experienced is an authentic movement of the Holy Spirit in your life. But I must share with you the universal teaching of all the great catholic doctors of the spiritual life, that whenever we have had any extraordinary experience of God in our lives, what are meant to do is give thanks for it, and then get about our business." The rest, one might say, is history, including the passion that has led to writing this book.

Of course, Fr. Pederson was basically citing St. John of the Cross's teaching in *The Ascent of Mt. Carmel* 2.1–31, especially chapter 10:4, where, after distinguishing true, dark contemplation from all seeming particular knowledge of God in mystical phenomena, he says "The dark and general knowledge (contemplation, which is imparted in faith) is of one kind only. We have to lead the soul to this contemplation by guiding it through all these other apprehensions, and, beginning with the first [visions] divesting it of them."[4]

And, apart from voyeuristic temptations, that is about all that needs saying. Extraordinary phenomena are beside the point. Some are from God; some are from the evil spirit; some are self-delusional; and we have little direct wisdom that does very much good in sorting all those out in any given case.[5] Even a wise director can only look for growth in charity and edification of the faith community in its pleromic mission, not anything intrinsic in the experience. Even extraordinary graces that truly come from God can be a distraction at this point, as our attention focuses on the gift, not the giver, whereas in the end (and we are nearing the end) the desire of the soul must be for God alone and not any particular experience of God. Fascination with extraordinary experiences is at best a distraction, at worst a delusion or temptation from the evil one. In any case, it will do no harm to thank God for it, and then get about our business. And that saves the usual several dozen pages on extraordinary phenomena. Should you have any, see your spiritual director. If you do not have one, find one. If you are having trouble finding one, ask for one in your prayers. Direction is absolutely essential under such circumstances, as all too many cases of spiritual delusion and error make clear.

Discernment and True Contemplation

True contemplation, that which the tradition calls "infused" and is the ordinary outcome of any true spiritual life, has a typical flow to it.[6] It begins almost naturally in the second current of transfiguration, though even this beginning is a new gift of grace. In each of the four implicit loves, as we followed Simone Weil's analysis, there is a sacramental experience of reflected glory that creates in us a hunger for glory itself. The ultimate sin is to deny that we are hungry. True contemplation, as we saw, does not come to despise these implicit loves but rather takes them up into itself, as the love of God becomes explicit. As the attention turns to glory itself, or, better, as our attention is turned by glory to itself, the initial experience is of blindness, luminous darkness, deeper hunger and longing, as we saw in the last chapter. All true touches of contemplation follow this route, and its features can be used as principles of discernment (not despising the implicit loves but continuing to grow in actual, effective charity, preference for the way of darkness and unknowing over distracting phenomena). Weil certainly experienced the explicit herself, as have other great mystics; sometimes the irruption of this explicit love is dramatic and sudden, while at other times it is accompanied by phenomena one is tempted to interpret in post-Enlightenment terms as "paranormal." But the three most important criteria for discernment for Christians are growth in actual charity; the building up of the community of faith precisely in its role as a mission society that is a sacrament of the coming commonwealth and *pleroma*; and a continued focus on and confession of the flesh of Jesus and its embodiment in the common life of the church, especially the sacraments. Particularly when we get to the point where what the world calls "mystical" enters the picture, the flesh of Jesus and the call to the practice of effective love grounded in the community of faith are the soul's anchor in reality.[7] The tradition provides us with two intertwined descriptions of the end the soul is now approaching as union with God: friendship with God and the more erotic description of spiritual marriage. Both emphasize that this is a union of communion, not of absorption; each of these helps us see important aspects of this third current, if only glimpses in the darkness.

Things Pertaining to Friendship

In the previous consideration of friendship in chapter 24, four features of friendship emerged that are helpful in understanding the importance of the venerable picture of the end of the spiritual life as being friends with God:[8] moral communion, *convivere*, reciprocity and commitment, and the dialectic between equality and distance at the heart of true intimacy.

As the classic texts all emphasize, the desired union with God is ultimately a transforming union, a union in which we are changed into God's likeness even beyond the restoration of the royal image in us, even beyond ecstasy.[9] While we are dealing with the ultimate reality that Bernard Lonergan calls religious conversion, each of the other "layers" is affected. The first dimension of this transformation is moral. We saw in chapter 24 that in John 15 Jesus defines the new relationship of friendship with his disciples as a communion of shared moral purpose. This is a deepening and perfecting of the moral conversion that began in the first tide as the Christian turned from sin and sought to lead a new life in faith. This moral life was further deepened in the second tide of transfiguration, as the more mature Christian found motive for virtue not in "moralism" but in delighting and loving the goodness revealed in the world and oneself by the reflected light of God's glory. Emphasizing the continuity of moral development in this third current with what has gone before helps protect against the false mysticism that can lead to the delusion that one now transcends good and evil and the belief that ordinary rules no longer apply; this demonic combination often leads to monstrous acting out.[10] In this third current, by contrast, the human will is drawn into an ever more perfect harmony with the divine will. Although this has often been viewed as submission or surrender, it is more helpful, I believe, to see it as the perfection of the moral communion of shared purpose that flows from any true friendship. It is a deep expression of the benevolence St. Thomas saw as one of the characteristics of friendship.

In step eleven of the Twelve Steps of Alcoholics Anonymous, we are taught to pray only for God's will for us and the power to carry that out.[11] That is a fearsome description of the final *askesis* of self-criticism. The first part of the step focuses on the degree to which we are still distracted by agendas of our own, whether selfish or altruistic. It points clearly to the development of harmony between our will and that of God as one of the aspects of growing union. But the real self-criticism comes in the second part. Beyond even the battle with our remaining besetting sins (*simul justus et peccator*—and it is also Catholic teaching that in this life no one achieves a state of sinlessness), beyond the cleansing of the image of God in us in the first tide, even taking account of the transfiguring of our characters in the light of Christ, humility demands a final admission: even so we do not in ourselves have the power to carry out the will of God perfectly. Our only hope—hope born of humility and becoming the dominant dance partner of the three theological virtues in this tide—is that God will give us this power.

This usually leads to a discussion of the heroic degree of the virtues that no longer seems very helpful, but a couple of threads in that tradition still resonate at this point.[12] First, because we now realize how great are the forces arrayed against us in our work for the *pleroma*, both in ourselves and in the world, because we now understand only too well our own debilitating weaknesses; and because we now understand the immensity of the task, we know that this can be no bootstrap affair, no perfecting of our own inherent strengths. Indeed, by this time we have also probably experienced God's annoying tendency to make good use of what we think of as weaknesses and character defects. What humility teaches us here is a new degree of what we learned in accepting justification as a gift in the first tide: only God has the power to carry out God's will. That was hard enough to swallow as we turned from sinfulness and woundedness toward health and moral reform. It was still annoying when we experienced besetting sins and character defects even as illumined by transfiguring, reflected glory; but now we are "at our best" and still inadequate. The miracle here, described by all the great saints, is that as an act of love our divine Lover now begins, beyond all hope except this new infused hope against hope, to clothe us with what are indeed God's own perfections, all our strength and virtue becoming a participation, in Christ and by the power of the Holy Spirit, in God's own moral character.[13] This is the very essence of heroic virtue, and most of the succeeding catalogues merely spell out what that looks like in the case of each virtue in the list, which I shall not do here. Here we see the first characteristic of what the Eastern Church calls *theōsis*, the way in which humans are increasingly divinized by participation in the divine nature itself, always because of the hypostatic union of the two natures in Christ and as a result of our being in him by flesh in the sacraments and the gift of the Spirit.[14] This first characteristic is a *moral* participation, arising from the moral communion of shared purpose at the heart of friendship as it now begins to flow from the *communicatio idiomatum* (communication of the particular characteristics of the two natures to the one person of Jesus) in the hypostatic union itself.

A second feature of this first dimension of moral communion is worth noting, however. Often at this point the beatitudes re-enter the discussion, and there is a description of how each of the new heroic virtues is focused on only the things of God.[15] What comes most deeply into play here is that virtue of all virtues sought by the desert fathers: purity of heart.[16] This is a simple and constant focus of "the mind in the heart" on God our friend and God's will for us, increasingly freed from all distractions, interior or exterior. That is, it is especially "Blessed are the pure in heart, for they shall see God" (Matt 5:8) that comes into focus. Purity of heart is a prayerful way of describing this gift of moral harmony between our will and God's, an increasing freedom of all our desires and attention for God alone. Precisely this beatitude also reminds us that this purity of heart is the necessary gift for entrance into one expression of our ultimate hope: to see God, the beatific vision, intellectual, loving, participatory knowledge of the Trinitarian life of God's own self. It represents the culmination of both the affective and intellectual layers of conversion as Lonergan spelled them out. This purity of heart is, in my view, the best peg on which to hang all the traditional discussions of purity in general, and chastity and virginity (the latter one of the traditional heroic virtues) in particular.[17] These discussions all end up sounding moralistic and antisex, even when they do not mean to, and all that is beside the point (though as we have said, following Weil, sexual sin is very serious), which is the gift God gives in this third tide: purity of heart, of will, of intention, and of attention, along with the other gifts necessary to carry out that will.

The second dimension of friendship in view is what the tradition, as we saw, calls *convivere*—the establishment of a common life together with God. This has two expressions, one christological and one pneumatological. Each is a gift of contemplation as loving to spend time in God's presence, as just plain "hanging out" with God for no other reason than that we both enjoy it. First, this is a deepening of our "philial" love for Jesus, as Christ, as Word, as Wisdom, as a beloved companion who has chosen us as his friend. In sacramental as well as private prayer we are gifted simply to spend time with Jesus, and as we do, we indeed discover "what a friend we have in Jesus."[18] The thanksgiving of the previous tides turns into pure adoration of him for his own sake, not for any agenda of ours, however noble.[19] This lack of other agenda than *convivere* itself is another expression of purity of heart and of deep affective conversion. The pneumatological dimension of this reality is that it is by the indwelling of the Spirit that we can be in Jesus' presence and he in us, as promised. It is, as we have seen, the Spirit who gifts us with the *koinōnia* that we share with one another because we share it with and in Christ. Because it is also in the Spirit and through Jesus that we are being drawn back to the Fount, the ultimate reality is Trinitarian, with the whole Trinity indwelling us; thus, at the deepest level all friendship with and in God is a resonance of the divine *perichoresis* or Trinitarian co-inherence. And all this flows from, as it were, setting up housekeeping with Jesus as our friend. There is a further dimension of *theōsis* at the heart of *convivere*, namely, God's desire that this friendship as life-in-common never end. The result is the gift of eternal life, which, as I have suggested following Teilhard, cannot be a property of immortality in ourselves but must be the resurrection of the body by the Spirit who raised Jesus from the dead if our work and the history of the world are truly to be redeemed.[20] The point, however, which may have been at the heart of the patristic doctrine, is that only God is immortal. Hence, the only means by which we can be gifted with eternal life is to share in the divine nature itself. Only as beloved can dust live at all, let alone live in eternity.

The third dimension of friendship that is helpful in unpacking friendship with God as a terminal image for the spiritual life is reciprocity and commitment. This is primarily loyalty or fidelity, measured by Jesus' own standard in John 15: "No one has greater love than this, than to lay down one's life for one's friends," as, of course, he was just about to do. Here, the other classical heroic virtue comes into play, martyrdom. This is not and must not be choosing suffering as good for us out of some sort of pride or fear, but only a loyalty to our friendship with Jesus in any and all circumstances, even those that are life threatening. Traditionally it involves not only fortitude as a subordinate virtue but also prudence, in knowing which ditch to die in;[21] the motive is not suffering itself nor desire for the martyr's crown (even St. Francis had to be taught that), but only that loyalty flowing from our deep friendship with Jesus in the Spirit, so that we are gifted with the strength not to betray him, but always to bear witness to our friendship in all we do. Anyone who has been through the *Sturm* of adolescent friendships with any reflective consciousness knows exactly what the issues are.

The fourth dimension of friendship as a terminal image for the spiritual life is that fine dialectical dance between equality and distance that we saw at the heart of Weil's description of true intimacy. Here is the key to understanding two vital points about the teaching on *theōsis*. First, we are given equality with God as a gift, not for our own glory, but for the sake of the friendship between us, which can only occur between at least rough equals. And so the Word became flesh that we might become divine, sharing, by the power of the Spirit, in his flesh and hence in the hypostatic union itself, including the *communicatio idiomatum*, not by the divinizing of our human nature as such but by our being caught up in God. The only way we can be "equal" to God is to share in God's nature, which we can never do on our own, but only by gift, the ultimate gift of friendship, as Christ adorns us with his own virtues and wisdom through the indwelling Spirit. But there is also distance. Because this is a friendship, a moral communion, we never become numerically identical with God. The creature does not become the creator; our human nature is not divinized in itself, as if it were fulfilling some inherent characteristic of its own. Pantheism does not sneak in through this door. *Theōsis*, union with God, is never ontological absorption, however much we lose ourselves in God and God loses Godself in us in love. Such an absorption does not embody true friendship or love, but a kind of egoism that is absent from both God and us at this point. We desire the distance between us even as we desire the equality, because the love of true friendship demands both. All the language about mystical "self-annihilation" needs to be read in the light of this critical principle. Indeed, as we turn to the great mystery of the spiritual marriage, it is important to recall Simone Weil's words that an error here, precisely as friendship takes on an erotic dimension, can be disastrous.[22]

Things Pertaining to Spiritual Marriage

As we turn to the emergence of an erotic dimension to this "philial" relationship, the tradition uses at this point the image of the spiritual marriage. The union we had desired begins to be experienced in bursts of ecstasy, though these are brief, unpredictable, and not to be sought for their own sake. This is not at all unlike the reality of human marriage itself, as we discover that even the first taste of honeymoon consummations only begins the hard work of building a lifetime of "two in one flesh." Happiness is a byproduct of this effort, not to be sought for itself. Since, as we have seen, a deep friendship is now an essential ingredient to a healthy marriage, everything we have just said about friendship still applies but now takes on a new dimension. Not all human friendships have this erotic dimension, and not even all that do are appropriate for marriage itself, which, as we saw in chapter 24, desires both union and fecundity. Nor, of course, do all erotic relationships have, at their core, this deep friendship. But true marriage, be it between humans or the spiritual marriage itself, requires the confluence of *eros* and *philia*.[23]

As friendship takes on this erotic dimension, the reality of *convivere* deepens to a desire for full union, a kind of consummated dance between desire and afterglow, which again requires both equality and distance as ingredients of *theōsis*. This is because the equality at issue here is an equality of love.[24] It is hard to find a more certain affirmation of *theōsis* than this passage from St. John of the Cross's *Flame*:

Having been made one with God, the soul is somehow God through participation. Although it is not God as perfectly as it will be in the next life, it is like the shadow of God. Being the shadow of God through this substantial transformation, it performs in this measure in God and through God what He through Himself does in it. For the will of the two is one will, and thus God's operation and the soul's is one. Since God gives Himself with a free and gracious will, so too the soul (possessing a will the more generous and free the more united it is in God) gives to God, God Himself in God; and this is a true and complete gift of the soul to God.

As a result, there is a christological dimension to this mystery that completes the mystery of the atonement:

It is conscious there that God is indeed its own and that it possesses Him by inheritance, with the right of ownership, as his adopted son, through the grace of the gift of Himself. Having Him for its own, it can give Him and communicate Him to whomever it wishes. Thus it gives Him to its Beloved [Jesus], who is the very God who gave Himself to it. By this donation it repays God for all it owes Him, since it willingly gives as much as it receives from Him.

There is also a pneumatological dimension, completing the Trinitarian picture:

Because the soul in this gift to God offers Him the Holy Spirit, with voluntary surrender, as something of its own (so that God loves Himself in the Holy Spirit as He deserves), it enjoys inestimable delight and fruition seeing that it gives God something of its own which is suited to Him according to His infinite being.

It is this reciprocal giving, in which the soul gives back to God that which it had received from God, God's own self in the Word and Spirit, that St. John likens to a marriage:[25]

A reciprocal love is thus actually formed between God and the soul, like the marriage union and surrender, in which the goods of both (the divine essence which each possesses freely by reason of the voluntary surrender between them) are possessed by both together.

Indeed, the soul "loves through the Holy Spirit, as the Father and the Son love each other," completing the Trinitarian doctrine at the heart of *theōsis*:[26] the love with which we love God is a participation in the love of the Trinitarian *perichoresis* itself, in and through the person of the Holy Spirit in her proper name of Love. First, we notice that this union of *theōsis*, which was first a moral union, is now a deeply affective and intellectual one as well. Memory, understanding, and will are all equally involved in the mutual self-giving. Second, this is the apex of human growth, the fullest extent of dust becoming beloved, and at this point we can see precisely why the destiny of beloved dust must lie outside its own natural character-istics in a further gift of God. But, third, we should note that however exalted this sounds, it is a gift God wills to give every human being and lies in what the tradi-tion calls the ordinary way of sanctity. That is, even at this most exalted point of the spiritual life, there is no ground for the elitism that had crept into tradition. This point is clearly argued precisely at this point by Garrigou-Lagrange and the sources he cites.[27] The highest spiritual gifts are intended for all people, at least to whatever degree possible, in this life.

Most of the spiritual theologies, when considering spiritual marriage, focus their attention on the life of union and infused contemplation.[28] But, as I have been suggesting since the analysis of marriage in chapter 24, real eros not only desires union but also implies a new fecundity, a procreative power that has an ever-deeper ground in the harmony of the human and divine wills. More than our motiva-tion for apostolic service is involved; the deeper relationship with God entails gifts that strengthen ministry, not in ignorance or negation of, nor in competition with, natural gifts but transcending them as they now participate in God's perfection and power. We receive the gift of the power to do God's will, which is God's own power, and which itself is essentially "missionary."

In contemporary theologies we are more likely to see increasing attention to this phenomenon of fruitfulness and fecundity, with the approbation of figures such as Desmond Tutu, Martin Luther King, Jr., Dorothy Day, or Mother Teresa of Calcutta, linked together as symbols of the passion for justice and heroic action for the poor and oppressed that dominates our age. It is important to notice that in each case there is also testimony to a deep life of prayer out of which the social wit-ness grows. Indeed, those who have experienced some of the purification leading up to contemplation and the spiritual marriage bear a *more* effective social witness because their hearts are more deeply purged of their own agendas and counter-intentions. Thus, the prophetic, liberating action that David Tracy sees as the fruit of self-transcendence in this third mode or tide is something qualitatively different from the more sophomoric efforts of those espousing causes without the benefit of real self-criticism. At its very best this true prophetic action is an expression of God's own perfection, especially justice and love; these become demands on human society as it is called to grow sacramentally into the commonwealth of God within the destined *pleroma*. We have already noted the role of the church as the people of God in this economy, as the effective sign or sacramental anticipation of that commonwealth. This reminds us that effective actual charity must inevitably have a social dimension. The recognition of this kind of socially conscious heroic sanctity and an insistence that it find its proper place in the communion of saints, even in the pantheon of those recognized as such, may be one of the major contributions to be made by a renewed spiritual theology of our time. This emphasis does not alter the traditional teaching that in this tide even apostolic action is subordinate to contemplative union;[29] on the contrary, it is the flow of this apostolic action from the "deeper well" of transfiguring union that makes it so powerful in immediate as well as prophetic and sacramental effect. What our age would have more difficulty accepting is any claim to heroic sanctity that did not include this prophetic dimension in some significant degree.

As in the image of spiritual friendship, there are christological, pneumatological, and Trinitarian dimensions to the teaching about spiritual marriage. On the christological front, we are guided by the previously noted use of the Song of Songs from Origen through St. John of the Cross's *Cantico Espiritual.* The spiritual marriage is first and foremost a consummation of the spiritual espousal between Jesus the bridegroom and the soul and/or the church. This link is hallowed by Jesus' own use of bridegroom language for himself, surely catching up in itself all the language in the Older Covenant in which God is the suitor and ultimately bridegroom of Israel. We have already noted, with Beverley Lanzetta, that there is sometimes some gender bending in this relationship, the Word often appearing as Lady Wisdom when appropriate, and at several crucial points in thoroughly orthodox tradition; nevertheless this image of Christ as the principal form of the divine spouse has been central in the tradition at least since the composition of Ephesians 5. If I insist on this, it is because I myself have witnessed, in communities deeply devoted to Christian social action, a reluctance to allow people to "just be in love with Jesus," a kind of judgmental embarrassment in the presence of such love, as if it conflicted with a Christianity of justice and inclusion. As I suggested in the last paragraph, if it is the real Jesus we are in love with, the values-overturning rabbi from Nazareth, then not only is there no need to suppress love for Jesus in favor of social action but the healthiest and most effective social action will grow directly from a deep, contemplative love of Jesus. The ultimate eschatological symbol for all this, of course, is the marriage supper of the Lamb who was slain and has been raised (Rev 19:8–10; 22:17).

In this tide of glory, the Holy Spirit appears primarily as pentecostal fire. In that light, the pneumatological dimension of this marriage is probably best portrayed in St. John of the Cross's *Llama de Amor Viva, The Living Flame of Love.* I have just quoted extensively from the commentary above, but the dimension of erotic friendship probably comes most clearly into view through reading the poem itself:

Pues ya no eres esquiva,
Acaba ya, si quieres;
Rompe la tela de este dulce encuentro.

Since now you are not oppressive.
Now Consummate! If it be your will:
Tear through the veil of this sweet encounter![30]

Note especially the lack of coercion here.[31] And, in the commentary on the last verse, the christological and pneumatological emphases come together in a fully Trinitarian consummation, which can be quoted at length:

But in this awakening of the Bridegroom in the perfect soul, everything that occurs and is caused is perfect, for He is the cause of it all. And in that awakening, which is as though one were to awaken and breathe, the

soul feels a strange delight in the breathing of the Holy Spirit in God, in which it is sovereignly glorified and taken with love. Hence it says in the subsequent verses:
And in Your sweet breathing,
Filled with good and glory,
How tenderly you swell my heart with love!

At this precise point, where we learn the truth of St. Paul's great teaching about the Holy Spirit praying within us and reaching to the very depths of God (Rom 8:26–27), even St. John feels the same reticence I have expressed, as he goes on to describe this marriage of good and glory, the moral and the mystical, the intellectual with the affective:

> I do not desire to speak of this spiration, filled for the soul with good and glory and delicate love of God, for I am aware of being incapable of doing so, and were I to try, it might seem less than it is. It is a spiration which God produces in the soul, in which, by that awakening of lofty knowledge of the Godhead, He breathes the Holy Spirit in it in the same proportion as its knowledge and understanding of Him, absorbing it most profoundly in the Holy Spirit, rousing its love with divine excellence and delicacy according to what it beholds in Him. Since the breathing is filled with good and glory, the Holy Spirit, through this breathing, filled the soul with good and glory, in which he enkindled it in love of Himself, indescribably and incomprehensibly, in the depths of God, to Whom be honor and glory forever and ever. Amen.[32]

What we can and must say theologically is that this ultimate consummation is profoundly pentecostal, in three senses. First, at the experiential level, following Garrigou-Lagrange's typology of apostolic experience, what follows the grief of losing the presence of the risen Christ at the Ascension is finally the fiery indwelling of the "other comforter." The spiritual marriage, though it is with the bridegroom Jesus, the Incarnate Word and Wisdom, is nonetheless a profoundly pentecostal and pneumatological reality.[33] It is sacramental in the precise sense that human marriage as such is sacramental. In addition to a christological blessing, both require an *epiclesis*, an invocation of the Holy Spirit, who creates the common life that makes both possible, by her own indwelling.

Second, Pentecost is the culmination of the paschal mystery in all its Trinitarian glory: the power by which the Fount raised Jesus from the dead now establishes the common life of the people of God in Christ as its head, as the context by which the kind of personal intimacy described by St. John of the Cross can be nurtured. It is in the pentecostal/pneumatological dimension that a true apprehension of the Trinitarian mystery is born.[34] It is not the Spirit in isolation but precisely the pentecostal Spirit who consummates the paschal mystery in missionary fervor and power who is the *"living flame."* Union and fecundity are one at the deepest level of the Trinitarian well, and it is no accident that Pentecost leads naturally to a celebration of the Triadic Unity of God as a whole and to a world of mission. It is also at this juncture that the most significant reason for my proposal to reground spiritual theology in pneumatology proper emerges: spiritual theology is to pneumatology as soteriology is to Christology precisely because at the deepest level of the third current of glory we encounter the pentecostal Spirit as our entrée into the Trinitarian ground of the paschal mystery itself.

Third, the Spirit is the Spirit of hope, the eschatological Spirit, who sanctifies the work we examined in chapter 22 through the power of resurrection by which even our *opus*, as well as our selves and our intentions, is taken up into the totality of the universe as a sacramentally consecrated *pleroma*. This resurrecting and consecrating work of the Spirit presents the meaningful *past* of the covenant (especially the incarnation and the cross) to the *present* as a *future* ideal; this is a historical ought-to-be that is both effectively present in the Spirit's own indwelling person but also still to come as final *pleroma* and commonwealth.[35] The church, warts and all, as the fundamental sacrament with all its particular sacraments, crowned by *epiclesis* and the communion (*koinōnia*) of saints across space and time, is itself a sacramental instrument by which the Spirit is bringing about this *pleroma*. From this perspective, we now see clearly the deepest ground of John Wesley's insistence that personal holiness and social justice not only *should* not be separated but *cannot be*, a truth both left and right in today's church need to take more seriously. The ground is the ultimate unity in the Spirit's final consecrated *pleroma* of both the beatific vision and the commonwealth or reign of God, not merely as inseparable realities but as two sides of the same coin, individual and social/corporate perspectives on the same fundamental reality. If we are experiencing a conflict here, it is the result of our sin, not of any defect of the Spirit's resting and wresting. Further, each individual is called, through contemplation, to approach as closely as possible to the beatific vision, even in this life, even while the resulting mode of theological speech, liberating, prophetic praxis, seeks to bring present human society as close as possible to the destined commonwealth.[36] The commonwealth is the social context in which the beatific vision is the experience of each individual, as the ground of our now universal *koinōnia* is revealed as the *perichoresis* or co-inherence of the Triadic Unity; that Trinity we will then see, together, with our own eyes, as the ultimate expression of not only Truth and Goodness, but now most especially, Beauty, and praise with one accord, forever:[37]

> Glory to the Father (Fount),
> And to the Son (Word/Wisdom),
> And to the Holy Spirit;
> As it was in the beginning,
> Is now,
> And ever shall be,
> Even unto the ages of ages. Amen.
> *Doxa soi, Kyrie, doxa soi.*

Conclusion

That final doxology is where any decent work on spirituality would simply end, of course. This is not a primary spiritual text, however, but a constructive proposal for a re-founded spiritual theology. As a result, we must end with a look back at the journey we have taken to see if a case has been made. In the first part of this book, I traced the decline of the traditional discipline of spiritual theology, assessed its current moribund state, and examined resources available for its resurrection. The constructive proposal was that we turn back from the descent of spiritual theology to a kind of spiritual psychology with us as the subject, subordinate to moral theology as a discipline distinct from dogmatics. Instead, I proposed, the proper subject of spiritual theology is the movement of the Holy Spirit in the divine economy in her mission, which has a Trinitarian rhythm to it: first, the Spirit in her hovering, firing, and resting aids the Fount in creation and covenant; then engages with the Word/Wisdom in a complex *pas de deux* (actually *de trois*) around all the mysteries of the incarnation, most especially the paschal mystery and its aftermath; and then works with the other two of the Trinity to fulfill her own proper mission of the final sacramental consecration of the universal *pleroma*. The rest of this book has been an experiment at reinterpreting the classic Trinitarian rhythm of the spiritual life as resonances in us of the Trinitarian structure of the Spirit's mission, as if three resulting concurrent tidal currents were breaking on a human shore, understood in the fullness of its own complexity, but in a thoroughly material manner, as dust. The miracle is that the dust finds itself unexpectedly beloved, with a precious and costly love.

In the first tidal current of conversion, we find our dusty selves enlivened by the Spirit as the life-giver in creation and then bound together as the people of God and the community of faith in the covenant, as the Spirit does her part in the mission of the Fount. This awakens in us the theological virtue of faith, through which we understand both our finitude and our sinfulness and woundedness (in the only history we know), and also the will of God that trumps both, given to us in the theological mode of proclamation as the Spirit confronts us with truth. A primary mechanism of this confrontation is the Spirit's inspiration of both author and reading community of the Word written; but a second is the Spirit's own co-operation (as life-giver) with the forces of human psychosocial development and the occasions that become teachable moments. These call us to share the apostolic experience of an initial Galilean conversion, experiencing the call to self-transcendence that is a further gift of the Spirit beyond our created natural capacity, in the style of self-denial (or healing and liberation), as we turn away from the enemies of the soul, including our own empirical egos, toward the promises of God. In this current, we experience the Holy Spirit primarily as life and life-giver.

In a slack between the first two tides, we are called to a second conversion, sharing the apostolic experience of betrayal or powerlessness at the foot of the cross, realizing that we are not living up to the new life we have been given. This slack carries with it what the tradition has called the dark night of the senses, as we are called to detach not from the world but from our enmeshments in it.

In the second tide, transfiguration, the Spirit aids the Word/Wisdom's mission by resting on every mystery of the incarnation, including most especially the resurrection, as she is revealed as the power by which the Fount raises Jesus from the dead and makes him still present among us as, quite gratuitously, the head of a new body that now includes the unsavable other, the gentile. We are called to share the apostolic experience of table fellowship with the risen Christ, united to his risen flesh by the sacraments, especially of bath and table, by which the Spirit binds us to him and to one another as his body and the renewed Israel of the covenant. The theological virtue of love is awakened in us by the theological mode of manifestation, as the glory of God, reflected from the face of the transfigured Jesus, illumines the world and ourselves in it. The style of self-transcendence in this current is thus self-fulfillment, but it is the Spirit whose proper name is Love who now fills the self and illumines it, so that self-fulfillment is indeed to have a full self, but not to be full of self. As the Spirit confronts us with the goodness of God in ourselves and the world, we experience the sacramental dimension of the forms of the implicit love of God expressed in the Benedictine virtues: love of neighbor and study; love of the order and beauty of the world and work, especially our participation in the church's mission; love of religious practices and ceremonies, especially prayer, personal and liturgical, sacrament and office; and friendship governed by stability or loyalty as we engage in the dialectical dance of equality and distance that lies at the heart of true intimacy. Especially as expressed in human marriage (though in a different way in consecrated celibacy), the erotic dimension of this friendship emerges and pushes us on toward the third current as we turn from glory reflected toward glory itself.

But as we do, we encounter a second slack as we share the apostolic experience of the Ascension, which the tradition calls the dark night of the soul. Here we enter a desert and even a desolation in which we seem to lose touch with Jesus and indeed all our previous ideas and experiences of God, as we are called to detach even from them and learn to desire, with an ever-deepening hunger and longing, Christ's own person and God's own self alone. Oddly enough, as the Spirit rests with us in this slack, we find that the darkness is itself luminous, the silence eloquent, and the longing contains in itself the odd assurance of espousal at the level of engagement, but we learn this only as we are willing to live in the darkness as long as God wills it, as the entrance to both contemplation and a prophetic apostolate.

Then, glory, truly unspeakable glory itself, as we begin to experience the resonance in us of the Spirit's own proper mission of the sacramental consecration of the entire universe in the final *pleroma*. We take with us from the longing of the second night the theological virtue of hope, hope against hope for this already but not yet promised consummation of ourselves and the world's history. Sharing the apostolic moment of Pentecost, we experience the Holy Spirit in this tide as fire, the fire of love, in the theological mode of prophecy that points to the final conflagration as a true, and beyond all hope, desirable end for ourselves and the world. The Spirit is also the power that resurrects us from all inability to know and do the will of God, even as we enjoy the presence of our lover and the ecstasies of being ultimately *beloved* dust. The style of self-transcendence to which we are now called is that of self-criticism, criticism of all that still separates us from our final union in and with God, including ideological criticism of the false consciousness caused by our own social location in class, race, and gender. The other side of this self-transcendence is *theōsis*: being, by the Spirit and her sacramental union of us with the flesh of Jesus, so deeply in Christ that we come to share in the hypostatic union itself, participating even in the mystery of the *communicatio idiomatum*. The Spirit, as a dower-gift from our espoused, begins to deck us with God's own virtues and power, preparing us for a penultimate union of erotic friendship that is also fecund with apostolic effectiveness, a taste in this life of both beatific vision and common-wealth as aspects of the final *pleroma*. In the end, then, we are ravished by beauty, God's own, as now fulfilled in us and the world with all its history.

But the currents are concurrent. Even when our lives are touched by glory itself we remain here *simul justus et peccator*, always with further need to swim in conversion. There is also always more study, work, and prayer to do, so the implicit loves of transfiguration also re-emerge constantly; but underneath is always, even from the very beginning, a deep glory calling us from one degree of glory to another, holding up to the "always" a deep "not yet" that keeps us swimming in hope.

Whether this account has succeeded sufficiently to establish the constructive proposal that spiritual theology be relocated in dogmatics, specifically in pneumatology, I cannot say. Where it is right, may God be glorified; where it is wrong, may God enlighten my critics.

Poi si tornò all'etterna Fontana.[38]

Come, Holy Ghost, our souls inspire.
And lighten with celestial fire.

Veni, Creator Spiritus. Amen

Notes

1. That is itself a huge argument that I have no intention of trying to resolve here. But see R. Jenson, *ST* 1.152–53; 2.342–43.

2. *Collected Works*, 393–565, 569–649; Teresa of Avila, *The Interior Castle*; Julian of Norwich, *Showings*.

3. Father Alfred Lowell Pederson, S.S.J.E., died in 1976: email communication from Brother Eldridge Pendleton, S.S.J.E., 07/10/07.

4. *Collected Works*, 131. See also *Ascent* 2.32, 213, *Flame*, 2.21, 602. See Reginald Garrigou-Lagrange, *Three Ages*, 2.594–95.

5. There is some wisdom, and some experiences have a higher degree of reliability; if you insist, see Garrigou-Lagrange, *Three Ages*, 2.575–627; Antonio Royo and Jordan Aumann, *Christian Perfection*, 617–74: "we . . . have attempted to hold fast to the principle that no phenomenon should be attributed to a superior cause if it can be explained by an inferior one" (p. 674).

6. Again, following Garrigou-Lagrange and Kenneth Kirk here.

7. Recall here all our suspicion of the term "mystical," following Michel de Certeau and Nicholas Lash.

8. See esp. Gregory of Nyssa, *The Life of Moses*, ## 319–20, 136–37.

9. Garrigou-Lagrange, *Three Ages*, 527–72; Royo and Aumann, *Christian Perfection*, 556–60. I have not said much about ecstasy as such, the experience not of the negation of reason but of reason in a style of self-transcendence under the influence of the Spirit. One of the best treatments is Paul Tillich's, *ST* 1.111–14; 3.112–20; for a fine account from a biblical scholar's point of view, see now Edith M. Humphrey, *Ecstasy and Intimacy*, throughout, but with a good definition of ecstasy on pp. 13–14.

10. Two texts of Robert C. Zaehner bring this point out strongly: *Mysticism, Sacred and Profane* and *Our Savage God*; see my article "Zen, Zurvan, and Zaehner." All too typical examples of such acting out are pastors who engage in inappropriate sexual relationships believing their spiritual status somehow makes these licit.

11. See Alcoholics Anonymous, *Twelve Steps and Twelve Traditions*, 96–105.

12. Garrigou-Lagrange, *Three Ages*, 2.441–79.

13. See, for example, Garrigou-Lagrange, *Three Ages*, 2.442–43.

14. There is a renewed interest in *theōsis* in all branches of Western theology: see especially Andrew Louth's entry, "Deification" in *NWDCS* 229–30, and *Theōsis: Deification in Christian Theology*, ed. Stephen Finlan and Vladimir Kharlamov. The discussions of renewed interest in *theōsis* in Lutheran and Reformed circles are especially important for the contemporary scene. See most particularly the chapter by Myk Habets, "Reforming *Theōsis*," in *Theōsis: Deification in Christian Theology*, 146–67, with a fine discussion of Thomas F. Torrance; for the origins in Clement of Alexandria, see Bernard McGinn, *The Foundations of Mysticism*, 107.

15. Garrigou-Lagrange, *Three Ages*, 2.442, 443.

16. See the references under the entry "Apatheia," in Bernard McGinn, *The Foundations of Mysticism*, 489, also the entry in *NWDCS*, 520–21.

17. So Fr. William Reed, Weston College, class, "Spiritual Theology," spring 1969.

18. See my article by that title. The reference is, of course, to the old evangelical hymn by Joseph Scriven; see above, for the previous discussions of friendship theology and some of its proponents.

19. H. W. Richardson, *Toward an American Theology*, 130–31.

20. Teilhard, *Divine Milieu*, 23, and, strangely, Samuele Bacchiochi, *Immortality or Resurrection?*, esp. 249–301; also, William Temple, *Nature, Man and God*, 461–68; Karl Rahner, "The Resurrection of the Body," *TI* 2:203–16.

21. Garrigou-Lagrange, *Three Ages*, 2.448, for example.

22. Simone Weil, *Waiting for God*, 172.

23. This is the point, I think, of C. S. Lewis's most difficult but intriguing novel, *Till We Have Faces*.

24. See Garrigou-Lagrange, *Three Ages*, 2.546, citing an article by Fr. Gabriel of St. Magdalen (*Angelicum*, 1937, fasc. 1–2), here p. 275; there the citation is to St. 3, par 89–91, but this appears as quoted here in the *Collected Works* as pars. 78–79, 641.

25. Surely what George Herbert intended when he said, "And the cream of all my heart I will bring thee," "King of Glory," *The Country Parson, The Temple*, 270–71.

26. St. John of the Cross, *Flame, Collected Works*, par. 82, 642.

27. Garrigou-Lagrange, *Three Ages*, 2.547, citing again the article by Fr. Gabriel of St. Magdalen, and 547–68, where Lagrange simply reproduces an article by Fr. Alexander Rozwadowski, S.J., from *La Vie spirituelle* (January 1936). It is, of course, Lagrange's most fundamental claim, to which he returns on pp. 628–54, and is consonant with the conclusions of Kenneth Kirk, as previously described. Thus, at lest in these significant figures there is accord between Roman and Anglican Catholics.

28. As usual, Garrigou-Lagrange is something of an exception, as he includes a brief and helpful chapter on the apostolic life and contemplation in his consideration of the state of perfection, though it has an exclusively monastic and clerical tone. He does include preaching, teaching, and missionary endeavor (*Three Ages*, 2.489–96).

29. See Garrigou-Lagrange, *Three Ages*, 2.491–94.

30. John of the Cross, *Collected Works*, 717.

31. Recall, following Weil, that we saw a deep respect for the freedom and autonomy of the other in the dialectic and dance of equality and distance, for any consummation that is not to be rape. Note that this erotic friendship need not be experienced in explicitly sexual terms, as the transition from the *Canticle* to the *Flame* makes particularly clear.

32. John of the Cross, *Collected Works*, 649.

33. Garrigou-Lagrange, *Three Ways*, 62–65; *Three Ages*, 2.423, 511–18; perhaps the new pentecostal theology of Veli-Matti Kärkkäinen and Amos Yong, to which I referred in chapter 23, grounded as it is in the new Finnish understanding of Luther's doctrine of *theōsis*, may yet provide us with a powerful link between denominational pentecostalism and the Catholic tradition at precisely this point. See Barry Callen, *Authentic Spirituality*; and Eugene Rogers, *After the Spirit*, 200–207.

34. Again, as I write, we await volume 1 of Sarah Coakley's systematic theology on this point.

35. See again my chapter "The Historic Ought-to-Be and the Spirit of Hope"; the debt I owe Jürgen Moltmann, W. Taylor Stevenson, and Paul Weiss is more fully acknowledged there.

36. Of the many works now making this point, one of the finest is the chapter by Miroslav Volf, "The Final Reconciliation: Reflections on a Social Dimension of the Eschatological Transition"; also, Flora Keshgegian, *A Time for Hope*, throughout.

37. Keshgegian, *A Time for Hope*, 184–86; see also Alejandro Garcia-Rivera, *The Community of the Beautiful*; and, of course, Jenson, *ST*, 1.234–36, 2.369.

38. "And so she (Beatrice) turned back to the eternal Fount" (Dante's *Paradiso*, Canto 31, l. 93; the climax of C. S. Lewis's *A Grief Observed*, 60).

Abbreviations and Bibliography

Abbreviations

AI   David Tracy, *The Analogical Imagination.*

ABD   David Noel Freedman. *The Anchor Bible Dictionary.* New York: Doubleday, 1992.

ATR   *Anglican Theological Review.*

BCCS   *The Blackwell Companion to Christian Spirituality.* Edited by Arthur Holder. Oxford: Basil Blackwell, 2005.

BCP   *The Book of Common Prayer.* Unless otherwise noted, this is the American edition of 1979.

BDAG   *A Greek-English Lexicon of the New Testament and Other Early Christian Literature.* Third edition. Edited by Frederick William Danker. Chicago and London: University of Chicago Press, 2000.

BRO   David Tracy, *Blessed Rage for Order.*

DS   *Dictionnaire de spiritualité ascétique et mystique, doctrine et histoire, publié sous la direction de Marcel Viller, S.J., assisté de F. Cavallera, et J. de Guibert, S.J., avec le concours d'un grand nombre de collaborateurs.* Paris: Beauchesne, 1937–1995.

CC   Walter Conn, *Christian Conversion.*

CD   Karl Barth, *Church Dogmatics.*

IDB   George Arthur Buttrick. *The Interpreter's Dictionary of the Bible: An Illustrated Encyclopedia Identifying and Explaining All Proper Names and Significant Terms and Subjects in the Holy Scriptures, Including the Apocrypha, with Attention to Archaeological Discoveries and Researches into the Life and Faith of Ancient Times.* New York: Abingdon, 1962.

NCE   *The New Catholic Encyclopaedia* (second edition, unless otherwise noted). Detroit: Thomson/Gale; Washington, D.C.: Catholic University of America, 2003–.

NDCS   Michael Downey, ed. *The New Dictionary of Catholic Spirituality.* Collegeville, Minn.: Liturgical, 1993.

NWDCS   *The New Westminster Dictionary of Christian Spirituality.* Edited by Philip Sheldrake. Louisville, Ky.: Westminster John Knox, 2005.

ODCC   *Oxford Dictionary of the Christian Church.* Edited by F. L. Cross. Oxford/New York: Oxford University Press, 2005.

ST   For Tillich and Jenson, *Systematic Theology;* for Simon Chan, *Spiritual Theology;* for Pannenberg, *Systematic Theology.*

STR   *Sewanee Theological Review.*

TDNT   Kittel, Gerhard. *Theological Dictionary of the New Testament.* Translated and edited by Geoffrey W. Bromiley. Grand Rapids: Eerdmans 1964-.

TDOT   G. Johannes Botterweck and Helmer Ringgren. *Theological Dictionary of the Old Testament.* Translated by John T. Willis. Grand Rapids: Eerdmans, 1977.

TI   Karl Rahner, *Theological Investigations.*

WDCS   *The Westminister Dictionary of Christian Spirituality.* Edited by Gordon Wakefield. Philadelphia: Westminster, 1983.

Bibliography

Ackeran, Gerald Van. *Sacra Doctrina: The Subject of the First Question of Summa Theologica of St. Thomas Aquinas.* Rome: Officum Libri Catholici, 1952.

Adler, Mortimer J. *The Angels and Us.* New York: Macmillan, 1982.

Aelred of Riveaulx. *Aelred of Rievaulx's Spiritual Friendship: A New Translation.* Translated by Mark F. Williams. Scranton: University of Scranton Press; London/Cranbury, N.J. Associated University Presses, 1994.

―――. *Spiritual Friendship.* Cistercian Fathers Series 5. Kalamazoo, Mich.: Cistercian Publications, 1974.

Aitken, Robert, and David Steindl-Rast, O.S.B. *The Ground We Share: Everyday Practice, Buddhist and Christian.* Edited by Nelson Foster. Boston: Shambhala; New York: Random House, 1996.

Alcoholics Anonymous: The Story of How Many Thousands of Men and Women Have Recovered from Alcoholism. New York: Alcoholics Anonymous World Services, 2001 (first edition, 1936).

Alcoholics Anonymous World Services, Inc. *Alcoholics Anonymous Comes of Age: A Brief History of A.A.* New York: Harper, 1957.

―――. *"Pass It On": The Story of Bill Wilson and How the A.A. Message Reached the World.* New York, 1984.

―――. *Twelve Steps and Twelve Traditions.* New York, 1981.

Aldous, Joan. *Family Careers: Developmental Change in Families.* New York: Wiley, 1978.

―――. *Family Careers: Rethinking the Developmental Perspective.* Thousand Oaks, Calif.: Sage Publications, 1996.

Aleshire, Daniel. "Family Life and Christian Spirituality." *Review and Expositor* 86, no. 2 (1989): 209–14.

Allen, Diogenes. *Spiritual Theology: The Theology of Yesterday for Spiritual Help Today.* Cambridge, Mass: Cowley, 1997.

Allison, C. Fitzimmons. *The Rise of Moralism: The Proclamation of the Gospel from Hooker to Baxter.* New York: Seabury, 1966.

Allison, Dale C., Jr. *The New Moses: A Matthean Typology.* Minneapolis: Fortress, 1993.

Anders, Isabel. *The Faces of Friendship.* Cambridge, Mass.: Cowley, 1992.

Anderson, John E. "Psychological Research on Changes and Transformations during Development and Aging." In James E. Birren, ed. *Relations of Development and Aging.* Springfield, Ill: Charles C. Thomas, 1964.

Anglican-Roman Catholic International Commission. *Agreed Statement on Eucharistic Doctrine.* Introduction by Julian W. Charley. Bramcote : Grove Books, 1972.

―――. *Mary: Grace and Hope in Christ.* Harrisburg, Pa.: Morehouse, 2005.

Anselm, Saint, and Thomas Williams, and Gaunilo. *Proslogion: With the Replies of Gaunilo and Anselm.* Indianapolis: Hackett Pub, 2001.

Aquinas, Thomas. *The Summa Theologica.* Translated by Fathers of the English Dominican Province. Benziger Bros. edition, 1947. Available online at www.ccel.org. All references to Aquinas are to this work, unless otherwise noted.

Aristotle, and Richard Peter McKeon. *The Basic Works of Aristotle.* New York: Random House, 1941.

Arraj, John. *From St. John of the Cross to Us: The Story of a 400 Year Long Misunderstanding and What It Means for the Future of Christian Mystics.* Inner Growth Books, 1999. Available online at http://www.innerexplorations.com/catchspmys/fromst1.htm;

Athanasiadis, Harris. *George Grant and the Theology of the Cross: The Christian Foundations of His Thought.* Toronto: University of Toronto Press, 2001.

Athanasius, and Robert C. Gregg, trans. *The Life of Antony and the Letter to Marcellinus.* Classics of Western Spirituality. New York: Paulist, 1980.

Aumann, Jordan. *Spiritual Theology.* London: Sheed & Ward, 1984.

B. [Burns], Dick. *New Light on Alcoholism: God, Sam Shoemaker, and A.A.* Kihei, Maui, Hawaii: Paradise Research, 1998.

———. *The Oxford Group & Alcoholics Anonymous: A Design for Living That Works.* Kihei, Maui, Hawaii: Paradise Research, 1998.

Babin, David. *The Supreme Festival of Life and Death.* Cincinnati: Forward Movement, 1972.

Bacchiocchi, Samuele. *Immortality or Resurrection? A Biblical Study on Human Nature and Destiny.* Biblical Perspectives 13. Berrien Springs, Mich.: Biblical Perspectives, 1997.

Bach, George R., and Peter Wyden. *The Intimate Enemy: How to Fight Fair in Love and Marriage.* New York: Morrow, 1969.

Balleine, G. R. *The Evangelical Party in the Church of England.* London/New York: Longmans, Green, 1933.

Balthasar, Hans Urs von. *Explorations in Theology III: Creator Spiritus.* Translated by Brian McNeil, C.R.V. San Francisco: Ignatius, 1993.

———. "Spirituality." Pp. 211–26 in *Explorations in Theology I: The Word Made Flesh.* Translated by A. V. Littledale with Alexander Dru. San Francisco: Ignatius, 1989.

Baptism, Eucharist, and Ministry. Faith and Order Paper 111. Geneva: World Council of Churches, 1982.

Barfield, Owen. *Saving the Appearances: A Study in Idolatry.* London: Faber & Faber, 1957.

Barry, William A., S.J., and William J. Connolly, S.J. *The Practice of Spiritual Direction.* New York: Seabury, 1982. Currently published by New York: HarperCollins.

Barth, Karl. *Church Dogmatics.* New York: Scribner; Edinburgh: T. & T. Clark, 1936–1969.

———. *Church Dogmatics: A Selection.* Introduction by Helmut Gollwitzer. Translated and edited by G. W. Bromiley. New York: Harper Torchbook/Harper & Row, 1961.

———. *The Epistle to the Romans.* Translated by Edwin C. Hoskins from the sixth edition. London: Oxford University Press/H. Milford, 1933.

Bass, Ellen, and Laura Davis. *The Courage to Heal: A Guide for Women Survivors of Childhood Sexual Abuse.* New York: HarperCollins, 1992.

Baum, Gregory. "For and against John Milbank." Pp. 123–39 in Robert C. Cully and William Klempa, eds. *Three Loves: Philosophy, Theology, and World Religions: Essays in Honor of Joseph McLelland.* Atlanta: Scholars, 1994.

———. *Religion and Alienation: A Theological Reading of Sociology.* New York: Paulist, 1975. References are to this edition; new edition Toronto: Novalis; Maryknoll, N.Y.: Orbis Books, 2007.

Becker, Jillian. "Simone Weil, A Saint for Our Time?" *The New Criterion* 20, no. 7 (March 2002): 15–23. Also available at http://www.newcriterion.com/archive/20/mar02/weil.htm.

Bermejo, Luis M. *The Spirit of Life: The Holy Spirit in the Life of the Christian.* Anand, Gujarat, India: Gujarat Sahitya Prakash, 1987; Chicago: Loyola University Press, 1989.

Bloom, Anthony. *Beginning to Pray.* New York: Paulist, 1970.

Bonaventure. Translated by Ewert Cousins. New York: Paulist, 1979.

Bonhoeffer, Dietrich. *Life Together.* New York: Harper, 1954.

Booty, John. "Healing, Pardon, Liberation." *STR* 34, no. 4 (1991): 69–72.

———. "Word and Sacraments as Instruments of Evangelism." *STR* 34, no. 4 (1991): 19–33.

Bouyer, Louis. *History of Christian Spirituality.* New York: Desclee, 1963.

———. *Liturgical Piety.* Notre Dame, Ind.: University of Notre Dame Press, 1955.

Braaten, Carl E., and Robert W. Jenson, eds. *Union with Christ: The New Finnish Interpretation of Luther.* Grand Rapids: Eerdmans, 1998.

Breidenthal, Thomas E. *Christian Households: The Sanctification of Nearness.* Cambridge, Mass: Cowley, 1997.

Bremond, Henri. *Literary History of Religious Thought in France.* 3 volumes. London: S.P.C.K.; New York: Macmillan, 1929–1937.

Bridges, William. *Transitions: Making Sense of Life's Changes.* Reading, Mass.: Addison-Wesley, 1980.

Brown, Raymond, *The Gospel According to John (i-xiii)* and *(xiii-xxi)*, Anchor Bible 29–29A. Garden City, N.Y.: Doubleday, 1970.

Browne, Gayle Hansen. "Feminist Rhetoric and Christological Discourse: Conflict or Conversion." M.A. thesis, Sewanee: University of the South, 1993.

Browning, Don. *Generative Man*. Philadelphia: Westminster, 1972.

Brueggemann, Walter. "Covenanting as Human Vocation." *Interpretation* 33, no. 2 (1979): 115–29.

———. *The Message of the Psalms A Theological Commentary*. Augsburg Old Testament Studies. Minneapolis: Augsburg Publishing House, 1984.

———. *Praying the Psalms*. Winona, Minn.: St. Mary's Press, 1982.

Brumbaugh, Robert Sherrick. *Plato for the Modern Age*. Lanham, Md.: University Press of America, 1991.

Brunner, Emil. *Dogmatics*. Philadelphia: Westminster, 1950.

Bryan, Christopher. "The New Moses and the Heavenly Man: An Essay on the Theology of St. John's Gospel with Special References to Chapters 1–2." Ph.D. thesis, University of Exeter, 1983.

———. *A Preface to Mark*. New York and Oxford: Oxford University Press, 2000.

———. *A Preface to Romans: Notes on the Epistle and its Literary and Cultural Setting*. New York: Oxford University Press, 1990.

Bucke, Richard Maurice. *Cosmic Consciousness: A Study in the Evolution of the Human Mind*. Many editions since 1901, including New York: E. P. Dutton, 1962.

Buckley, Michael J. *Denying and Disclosing God: The Ambiguous Progress of Modern Atheism*. New Haven, Conn.: Yale University Press, 2004.

Bulgakov, Sergius. *The Comforter*. Translated by Boris Jakim. Grand Rapids: Eerdmans, 2004.

Bunyan, John, and James Blanton Wharey. *The Pilgrim's Progress from This World to That Which Is to Come*. Oxford: Clarendon, 1960.

Burrell, David B., C.S.C. *Friendship and Ways to Truth*. Notre Dame, Ind.: University of Notre Dame Press, 2000.

Bynum, Caroline Walker. *Jesus as Mother: Studies in the Spirituality of the High Middle Ages*. Berkeley: University of California Press, 1982.

Caird, George B. *Saint Luke*. Philadelphia: Westminster, 1977 (1963).

Callahan, Sydney Cornelia. *Beyond Birth Control: The Christian Experience of Sex*. New York: Sheed & Ward, 1968.

Callen, Barry L. *Authentic Spirituality: Moving beyond Mere Religion*. Grand Rapids: Baker Academic, 2001.

Calvin, John. *Institutes of the Christian Religion*. Library of Christian Classics 20–21. Philadelphia: Westminster, 1960. Also, edition edited by J. T. McNeill. Philadelphia: Westminster, 1977.

Capon, Robert Farrar. *Bed and Board: Plain Talk about Marriage*. New York: Simon & Schuster, 1965.

———. *Exit 36 A Fictional Chronicle*. New York: Seabury, 1975.

———. *An Offering of Uncles: The Priesthood of Adam and the Shape of the World*. New York: Sheed & Ward, 1967.

———. "Ordination of Women: A Non-Book." *Anglican Theological Review* 2 (1973), 68–78.

———. *A Second Day: Reflections on Remarriage*. New York: Morrow, 1980

———. *The Third Peacock: The Goodness of God and the Badness of the World*. Garden City, N.Y.: Doubleday, 1971.

Carpenter, James. *Gore: A Study in Liberal Catholic Thought*. London: Faith, 1960.

Casey, John. *Pagan Virtue: An Essay in Ethics*. Oxford: Clarendon, 1990.

Cassian, John. *Conferences*. Translated by Colm Luibhéid. Introduction by E. Pichery. Classics of Western Spirituality. New York: Paulist, 1985

Catherine of Siena. *The Dialogue*. Translated by Suzanne Noffke. New York: Paulist, 1980.

Catholic Church. *The Rites of the Catholic Church as Revised by Decree of the Second Vatican*

Ecumenical Council and Published by Authority of Pope Paul VI. Collegeville, Minn: Liturgical, 1990.

———, and Jean Deshusses. *Le sacramentaire grégorien, ses principales formes d'après les plus anciens manuscrits.* Spicilegium Friburgense 16. Fribourg: Éditions universitaires, 1971.

———, and Philip T. Weller. *The Roman Ritual.* Milwaukee: Bruce, 1964.

Certeau, Michel de. *The Mystic Fable: Religion and Postmodernism.* Chicago: University of Chicago Press, 1992.

Chan, Simon. *Spiritual Theology: A Systematic Study of the Christian Life.* Downers Grove, Ill.: InterVarsity, 1998.

Charny, Israel W. *Marital Love and Hate: The Need for a Revised Marriage Contract and a More Honest Offer by the Marriage Counselor to Teach Couples to Love and Hate, Honor and Dishonor, Obey and Disobey.* New York: Macmillan, 1972.

Cheek, Neil H., Jr. "Toward a Sociology of Not-Work." *The Pacific Sociological Review* 14, no. 3, Sociology of Leisure (July 1971): 245–58.

Chenu, Marie-Dominique. *The Theology of Work: An Exploration.* Translated by Lilian Soiron. Chicago: Regnery, 1966.

Chittister, Joan. *Wisdom Distilled from the Daily: Living the Rule of St. Benedict Today.* San Francisco: HarperSanFrancisco, 1991.

Chitty, Derwas J. *The Desert a City: An Introduction to the Study of Egyptian and Palestinian Monasticism under the Christian Empire.* Oxford: Blackwell, 1966.

Christ, Carol. *She Who Changes: Re-Imagining the Divine in the World.* New York: Palgrave Macmillan, 2003.

[Episcopal] Church Hymnal Corporation. *The Book of Common Prayer.* New York, 1979.

———. *The Book of Occasional Services.* New York, 1991.

Climacus, John. *The Ladder of Divine Ascent.* Translated by Colin Luibheid and Norman Russell. New York: Paulist, 1982.

Coakley, Sarah. *Powers and Submissions: Spirituality, Philosophy, and Gender.* Challenges in Contemporary Theology. Oxford, U.K.: Blackwell, 2002.

Cognet, Louis. *Post Reformation Spirituality.* Translated by P. Hepburne Scott. New York: Hawthorn Books, 1959.

Collins, Adela Yarboro. *Mark.* Hermeneia. Minneapolis: Fortress, 2007.

Collins, Paul M. *Trinitarian Theology, West and East: Karl Barth, the Cappadocian Fathers and John Zizioulas.* Oxford/New York: Oxford University Press, 2001.

Colorado, Bishop and Diocese of. "Stages of Human Development." (Chart). 1981.

Congar, Yves. *I Believe in the Holy Spirit.* Milestones in Catholic Theology. New York: Crossroad, 1997.

Conn, Joann Wolski. *Spirituality and Personal Maturity.* Integration Books. New York: Paulist, 1989.

———. "Therese of Lisieux: Far From Spiritual Childhood." *Spiritus* 6, no. 1 (Spring 2006): 68–89.

———. *Women's Spirituality: Resources for Christian Development.* New York: Paulist, 1986.

Conn, Walter E. *Christian Conversion: A Developmental Interpretation of Autonomy and Surrender.* New York: Paulist, 1986. New edition, Eugene, Or.: Wipf & Stock, 2006. Page references are to earlier edition.

Cooke, Bernard. *Power and the Spirit of God: Toward an Experience-Based Pneumatology.* Oxford: Oxford University Press, 2004.

———. *Sacraments and Sacramentality.* Mystic, Conn.: Twenty-Third Publications, 1983.

Coward, Harold. "Mysticism in the Analytical Psychology of Carl Jung and the Yoga Psychology of Patanjali: A Comparative Study." *Philosophy East and West* 29, no. 3 (July 1979): 323–36.

Crysdale, Cynthia S. W. *Embracing Travail: Retrieving the Cross Today.* New York: Continuum, 1999.

Cunningham, David S. *These Three Are One: The Practice of Trinitarian Theology.* Challenges in Contemporary Theology. Malden, Mass.: Blackwell, 1998.

Daly, Mary. *Beyond God the Father: Towards a Philosophy of Women's Liberation*. Boston: Beacon, 1973.

D'Ambrosio, Marcellino, "*Ressourcement* theology, *aggiornamento*, and the Hermeneutics of Tradition." *Communio* 18 (Winter 1991): 530–55.

Danaher, William J., Jr. *The Trinitarian Ethics of Jonathan Edwards*. Louisville and London: Westminster John Knox, 2004.

Dante Alighieri. *The Divine Comedy*. Translated by Charles Eliot Norton. Great Books of the Western World 21. Chicago: Encyclopædia Britannica, 1955.

De Gruchy, John W. *Christianity, Art, and Transformation: Theological Aesthetics in the Struggle for Justice*. Cambridge/New York: Cambridge University Press, 2001.

De Waal, Esther. *A Life-Giving Way: A Commentary on the Rule of St. Benedict*. Collegeville, Minn.: Liturgical, 2000.

———. *Seeking God: The Way of St. Benedict*. Collegeville, Minn.: Liturgical, 1984.

Dobson, James C. *The Strong-Willed Child: Birth through Adolescence*. Wheaton, Ill.: Tyndale House, 1978.

Dodd, C. H. "The Appearances of the Risen Christ: An Essay in Form Criticism of the Gospels." Pp. 102–33 in *More New Testament Studies*. Grand Rapids: Eerdmans, 1968; originally pp. 9–35 in Dennis E. Nineham, ed. *Studies in the Gospels: Essays in Memory of R. H. Lightfoot*. Oxford: Blackwell, 1955.

Doran, Robert. *Theology and the Dialectics of History*. Toronto: University of Toronto Press, 1990.

Douglas, Ian T., and Kwok Pui-Lan. *Beyond Colonial Anglicanism: The Anglican Communion in the Twenty-First Century*. New York: Church, 2001.

Dreikurs, Rudolph, and Vicki Soltz. *Children: The Challenge*. New York: Duell, Sloan, & Pearce, 1964.

Driver, Tom F. "Sexuality and Jesus." Pp. 118–32 in *New Theology* 3. New York: Macmillan, 1966.

DuBose, William Porcher. *The Ecumenical Councils*. New York: Christian Literature Co., 1897.

———. *High Priesthood and Sacrifice*. New York: Longmans, Green, 1908.

———. *Unity in the Faith*. Edited by W. Norman Pittenger. Greenwich, Conn.: Seabury, 1957.

———, and Donald S. Armentrout, *A DuBose Reader*. Sewanee, Tenn.: University of the South Press, 1984.

Duffy, Regis A., O.F.M. *Real Presence: Worship, Sacraments, and Commitment*. San Francisco: Harper & Row, 1982.

Duggan, Robert D., ed. *Conversion and the Catechumenate*. New York: Paulist, 1984.

Dunne, Thomas Aquinas (Tad), S.J., "Lonergan on Social Progress and Community: A Developmental Study." Ph.D. diss., Univ. of St. Michael's College (Toronto), 1975.

Dupré, Louis. *The Passage to Modernity: An Essay in the Hermeneutics of Nature and Culture*. New Haven: Yale University Press, 1993.

Duvall, Evelyn. *Family Development*. Fourth edition. Philadelphia/New York/Toronto: Lippincott, 1971.

Edwards, Tilden. *Living Simply through the Day: Spiritual Survival in a Complex Age*. New York: Paulist, 1977.

———. *Sabbath Time*. Nashville, Tenn.: Upper Room Books, 2003.

———. *Spiritual Friend*. New York: Paulist, 1980.

Eigo, Francis, ed. *The Human Experience of Conversion: Persons and Structures in Transformation*. Villanova, Pa.: Villanova University Press, 1987.

Ellis, Albert. *Reason and Emotion in Psychotherapy*. New York: Stuart, 1962.

Ellis, Havelock. *Man and Woman: A Study of Human Secondary Sexual Characters*. London: Walter Scott, 1904.

Endean, Philip. "The Same Spirit Is in Everything: Towards a Contemporary Theological Reading of Ignatius' Rules for Thinking with the Church." Pp. 509–23 in *Encounters with the Word: Essays to Honour Aloysius Pieris SJ*. Edited by Robert Crusz, Marshal Fernando, and Ashanga Tilakarine. Colombo: Ecumenical Institute for Study and Dialogue, 2004.

England, Dorothy Marie. *Satan Stalking*. Cincinnati: Forward Movement Publications, 1993.

Erikson, Erik H. *Adulthood: Essays*. New York: Norton, 1978.

———. *Childhood and Society*. New York: Norton, 1964 .

———. *Gandhi's Truth: The Origins of Militant Non-Violence*. New York: Norton, 1969.

———. *Identity and the Life Cycle*. New York: Norton, 1980.

———. *Identity, Youth, and Crisis*. New York: Norton, 1968.

———. *Young Man Luther: A Study in Psychoanalysis and History*. New York: Norton, 1962.

Esler, Philip F. "Paul and Stoicism: Romans 12 as a Test Case." *New Testament Studies* 50 (2004): 106–24.

Evdokimov, Paul. *The Sacrament of Love: The Nuptial Mystery in the Light of the Orthodox Tradition*. Crestwood, N.Y.: St. Vladimir's Seminary Press, 1985.

Farley, Edward. *Ecclesial Man: A Social Phenomenology of Faith and Reality*. Geneva: World Council of Churches, 1982.

Farrelly, M. John, O.S.B. "Holy Spirit." *NDCS*, 492–503.

Farrow, Douglas. *Ascension and Ecclesia: On the Significance of the Doctrine of the Ascension for Ecclesiology and Christian Cosmology*. Grand Rapids: Eerdmans, 1999.

Feldmeier, Peter. *The Developing Christian: Spiritual Growth through the Life Cycle*. New York/Mahwah, N.J.: Paulist, 2007.

Fincher, Susanne. *Creating Mandalas for Insight, Healing, and Self-Expression*. Boston: Shambhala, 1991.

Finlan, Stephen, and Vladimir Kharlamov, eds. *Theōsis: Deification in Christian Theology*. Eugene, Or.: Pickwick, 2006.

The First and Second Prayer Books of Edward VI. Everyman's Library 448. London: Dent; New York: Dutton, 1910, and many subsequent editions.

Floyd, Wayne Whitson, Jr. *Theology and the Dialectics of Otherness: On Reading Bonhoeffer and Adorno*. Lanham, Md.: University Press of America, 1988.

Ford, David. *The Shape of Living: Spiritual Directions for Everyday Life*. Grand Rapids: Baker, 1997.

———. *Self and Salvation: Being Transformed*. Cambridge and New York: Cambridge University Press, 1999.

Foster, Richard, J. *Celebration of Discipline: The Path of Spiritual Growth*. San Francisco: Harper & Row, 1978.

Fowler, James W. *Becoming Adult, Becoming Christian: Adult Development and Christian Faith*. San Francisco: Harper & Row, 1984. Second edition, San Francisco: Jossey Bass, 2000; page references are to the first edition.

———. *Stages of Faith: The Psychology of Human Development and the Quest for Meaning*. San Francisco: Harper & Row, 1981.

Fox, Matthew, and Hildegard. *Illuminations of Hildegard of Bingen*. Santa Fe, N.M.: Bear, 1985.

Francis de Sales, Saint. *Introduction to the Devout Life*. Translated by John K. Ryan. New York: Doubleday, 1982.

———. *Treatise on the Love of God*. Translated and revised by Vincent Kerns, M.S.F.S. Westminster, Md.: Newman, 1962.

———. and Jane Chantal. *Letters of Spiritual Direction*. Translated by Peronne Marie Thiebert, V.H.M. Selected and introduced by Wendy M. Wright and Joseph F. Power, O.S.F.S. Mahwah, N.J., 1988.

Franckforter, and David Blamires. *The Book of the Perfect Life: Theologia Deutsch: Theologia Germanica*. Sacred Literature Series. Walnut Creek, Calif.: AltaMira, 2003.

Franklin, R. William, and Joseph M. Shaw. *The Case for Christian Humanism*. Grand Rapids: Eerdmans, 1991.

Fransen, Piet. *Divine Grace and Man*. Translated by Georges Dupont. New York: Desclee, 1962.

———. *The New Life of Grace*. Translated by Georges Dupont. London: Chapman, 1969.

Freud, Sigmund. *Moses and Monotheism*. Translated by Katherine Jones. New York: Vintage Books, 1967.

Garcia-Rivera, Alejandro. *The Community of the Beautiful: A Theological Aesthetics* Collegeville, Minn.: Liturgical, 1999.

Garrigou-Lagrange, Reginald, O.P. *Christian Perfection and Contemplation: According to St. Thomas Aquinas and St. John of the Cross*. St. Louis/London: B. Herder, 1937.

———. *The Three Ages of the Interior Life: Prelude of Eternal Life*. Translated by Timothea Doyle. St. Louis/London: B. Herder, 1946, 1948.

———. *The Three Ways of the Spiritual Life*. Rockford, Ill.: Tan Books, 1977, original 1938.

Gatta, Julia. *Three Spiritual Directors for Our Time: Julian of Norwich, The Cloud of Unknowing, Walter Hilton*. Cambridge, Mass.: Cowley, 1986; now reissued as *The Pastoral Art of the English Mystics*. Eugene, Or.: Wipf & Stock, 2004.

Gelpi, Donald L., S.J. *Charism and Sacrament: A Theology of Christian Conversion*. New York: Paulist, 1976.

———. *The Firstborn of Many: A Christology for Converting Christians*. Milwaukee: Marquette University Press, 2001.

———. "Religious Conversion: A New Way of Being." Pp. 175–202 in Francis Eigo, ed., *The Human Experience of Conversion: Persons and Structures in Transformation*. Villanova, Pa.: Villanova University Press, 1987.

Gibson, Arthur. *The Faith of the Atheist*. New York: Harper & Row, 1968.

Gilligan, Carol. *A Different Voice: Psychological Theory and Women's Development*. Cambridge, Mass., Harvard University Press, 1982.

Gilson, Étienne. *Discours de la méthode / Descartes*; avec introduction et notes par Étienne Gilson. Paris: J. Vrin, 1961.

Goergen, Donald. *The Sexual Celibate*. New York: Seabury (Crossroad), 1975.

Gordon, Thomas. *Parent Effectiveness Training: The No-Lose Program for Raising Responsible Children*. New York: Wyden, 1970.

Gore, Charles. *The Holy Spirit and the Church*. Volume 3 of *The Reconstruction of Belief*. New York: Charles Scribner's Sons, 1924.

———. *Lux Mundi: A Series of Studies in the Religion of the Incarnation*. New York: United States Book Company, 1889.

Grant, George. *The George Grant Reader*. Edited by William Christian and Sheila Grant. Toronto: University of Toronto Press, 1998.

Greene, Graham . *The Portable Graham Greene*. Edited by Philip Stratford. New York: Penguin Books, 1977.

Gregory of Nyssa, Saint. *The Life of Moses*. Translated by Abraham J. Malherbe and Everett Ferguson. Preface by John Meyendorff. Classics of Western Spirituality. New York: Paulist, 1978.

Gregory Palamas, The Triads. Translated by Nicholas Gendle. Edited and introduction by John Meyendorff. Classics of Western Spirituality. New York, Ramsay, N.J./Toronto: Paulist, 1983.

Gresser, Moshe. *Dual Allegiance: Freud as a Modern Jew*. Albany: State University of New York Press, 1994.

Guenther, Margaret. *Holy Listening: The Art of Spiritual Direction*. Boston: Cowley, 1992.

Guibert, Joseph de. *The Theology of the Spiritual Life*.Translated by Paul Barrett. New York; London: Sheed & Ward, 1953.

Gutiérrez, Gustavo. *A Theology of Liberation: History, Politics, and Salvation*. Translated and edited by Sister Caridad Inda and John Eagleson. Maryknoll, N.Y.: Orbis Books, 1973.

Guzie, Tad W. *The Book of Sacramental Basics*. New York: Paulist, 1981.

———. *Jesus and the Eucharist*. New York: Paulist, 1974.

Hamer, Cardinal Jean. *The Church Is a Communion*. Translated by Ronald Matthews. New York: Sheed & Ward, 1965.

Hampson, Daphne. *After Christianity*. Valley Forge, Pa.: Trinity Press International, 1996.

Hanson, Bradley C. "Spirituality as Spiritual Theology." Pp. 45–51 in *Modern Christian Spirituality: Methodological and Historical Essays*. Edited by Bradley C. Hanson. American Academy of Religion Studies in Religion 62. Atlanta: Scholars, 1990.

Harak, G. Simon, S.J. *Virtuous Passions: The Formation of Christian Character*. New York: Paulist, 1993.

Hardy, Daniel W. *Finding the Church: The Dynamic Truth of Anglicanism*. London: SCM, 2001.

Harton, Frederic Percy. *The Elements of the Spiritual Life: A Study in Ascetical Theology*. London: SPCK, 1932.

Harvey Anne T. W. "Spiritual Style in the Work of Urban T. Holmes and Beyond." S.T.M. thesis, Sewanee: The University of the South, 2002.

Hauerwas, Stanley. *The Peaceable Kingdom: A Primer in Christian Ethics* Notre Dame, Ind.: University of Notre Dame Press, 1983.

Haughton, Rosemary. *Love*. London: Watts, 1970.

————. *The Transformation of Man: A Study of Conversion and Community*. Springfield, Ill.: Templegate, 1967.

Hedberg, Thomas M., and Betsy Caprio. *A Code of Ethics for Spiritual Directors*. Pecos, N.M.: Dove Publications, 1992.

Hegel, Georg Wilhelm Friedrich. *The Phenomenology of Mind*. Translated by J. B. Baillie. New York: Harper & Row, 1967.

Heidegger, Martin. *Being and Time*. Translated by John Macquarrie and Edward Robinson. New York/Evanston: Harper & Row, 1962. Page references are to the English edition.

Heil, John Paul. *The Transfiguration of Jesus: Narrative Meaning and Function of Mark 9:2–8, Matt 17:1–8 and Luke 9:28–36*. Rome: Editrice Pontificio Istituto Biblico, 2000.

Helminiak, Daniel A. *Religion and the Human Sciences: An Approach via Spirituality*. Albany: SUNY Press, 1998.

————. *Spiritual Development: An Interdisciplinary Study*. Chicago: Loyola University Press, 1987.

Hemming, Laurence Paul. *Radical Orthodoxy? A Catholic Enquiry*. Heythrop Studies in Contemporary Philosophy, Religion, & Theology. Aldershot, England: Ashgate, 2000.

Herbert, George. *The Country Parson, the Temple*. Edited by John N. Wall, Jr. New York: Paulist, 1981.

Heron, Alasdair I. C. *The Holy Spirit: The Holy Spirit in the Bible in the History of Christian Thought and in Recent Theology*. Foundations for Faith. London: Marshall, Morgan & Scott, 1983.

Herriman, Michael W. ed. *The Baptismal Mystery and the Catechumenate*. New York: Church Publishing, 1990.

Heschel, Abraham Joshua. *The Earth Is the Lord's; And the Sabbath* [expanded edition]. Cleveland: World, 1950.

Heyward, Carter. *The Redemption of God: A Theology of Mutual Relation*. Washington D.C.: University Press of America, 1982.

Hildegard of Bingen. *Scivias*. Translated by Columba Hart, and Jane Bishop. Classics of Western Spirituality. New York: Paulist, 1990.

Hinson, Glenn, E. *Serious Call to a Contemplative Lifestyle*. Philadelphia: Westminster, 1978.

Hodgson, Peter, *Revisioning the Church: Ecclesial Freedom in the New Paradigm*. Minneapolis: Fortress, 1988.

Holmes, Urban Tigner, III. *The Future Shape of Ministry; A Theological Projection*. New York: Seabury, 1971.

————. *A History of Christian Spirituality An Analytical Introduction*. New York: Seabury, 1980.

————. *Ministry and Imagination*. New York: Seabury, 1976.

————. *Spirituality for Ministry*. San Francisco: Harper & Row, 1982.

————. *Turning to Christ: A Theology of Renewal and Evangelization.* New York: Seabury, 1982; reprint, Cambridge, Mass.: Cowley, 1994.

————. *What Is Anglicanism?* Wilton, Conn.: Morehouse-Barlow, 1982.

Hosmer, Rachel, and Alan W. Jones. *Living in the Spirit.* New York: Seabury, 1979.

Hughes, Barbara Brunn. "Using the Arts to Open Scripture," *STR* 50, no. 1 (2006): 138–53.

————. "Where Was God? Spiritual Questions of Sexually Abused Children." *STR* 48, no. 1 (2004): 87–108.

Hughes, Robert Davis, III. "A Case for Inclusive Language by a White Male." *Religious Education* 80 (1985): 616–33.

————. "Christian Theology of Interfaith Dialogue: Defining the Emerging Fourth Option." *STR* 40 (1997): 383–408.

————. "A Critical Note on Two Aspects of Self-Transcendence." *STR* 46, no. 1 (2002): 112–32.

————. "The Historic Ought-to-Be and the Spirit of Hope." Pp. 109–20 in *A Heart for the Future: Writings on Christian Hope.* Edited by Robert B. Slocum. New York: Church Publishing, 2004.

————. "The Holy Spirit in Christian Spirituality." Chap. 12 in *BCCS*, 207–22.

————. "The *Missio Spiritus*: An Underexplored Ground of Post-Colonial Missiology and Praxis." Delivered at a session of the Christian Systematic Theology Section at the annual meeting of the American Academy of Religion, November, 2006; subsequently published as "After the Empire: Mission in the Power of the Spirit." *STR* 50, no. 3 (2007): 430–39.

————. "Procreation and Patience: The Spirituality of Parenting." *Sewanee Theological Review* 48 (2005): 391–406.

————. "Retrieving and Reconstructing 'Justification by Grace through Faith': Some Disturbing Questions." *STR* 45, no. 1 (2001): 51–71.

————. "Starting Over: The Holy Spirit as Subject and Locus of Spiritual Theology." *ATR* 83, no. 3 (2001): 455–72. Reprinted, pp. 85–102 in *Engaging the Spirit: Essays on the Life and Theology of the Holy Spirit.* Edited by Robert B. Slocum. New York: Church Publishing, 2001.

————. "Towards a Theology of Parenthood: The Place of Procreation among the Ends of Christian Marriage." Ph.D. diss., University of St. Michael's College, Toronto, 1980.

————. "Wesleyan Roots of Christian Socialism." *The Ecumenist* 13 (1975): 49–53.

————. "What a Friend We Have in Jesus: Theological Reflections on the Atonement." *STR* 35 (1992): 247–63.

————. "Zen, Zurvan, and Zaehner: A Memorial Tribute to the Late Spaulding Professor of Eastern Religions and Ethics, Oxford." *Studies in Religion/Sciences Religieuses* 6 (1976/77): 139–48.

Huizinga, Johan. *Homo Ludens: A Study of the Play-Element in Culture.* Translated by R. F. C. Hull. Boston: Beacon, 1955.

Humphrey, Edith M. *Ecstasy and Intimacy: When the Holy Spirit Meets the Human Spirit.* Grand Rapids/Cambridge, U.K.: Eerdmans, 2006.

Hunt, Anne. *What Are They Saying about the Trinity?* New York: Paulist, 1998.

Husserl, Edmund. *Cartesian Meditations—An Introduction to Phenomenology.* Translated by Dorian Cairns. The Hague, Netherlands: Martinus Nijhoff, 1960.

Huxley, Aldous. *The Doors of Perception.* New York: Harper, 1954.

Ignatius Loyola. *Spiritual Exercises.* Translated by Kenneth Baker, S.J. New York: Herder & Herder, 1965.

International Commission for Anglican-Orthodox Theological Dialogue 2006, Mark Dyer, and John Zizioulas. *The Church of the Triune: God, The Cyprus Statement.* London: Anglican Communion Office, 2006.

Irenaeus, Saint. *Adversus Haereses.* Excerpts in Cyril Charles Richardson, ed. *Early Christian Fathers.* Philadelphia: Westminster, 1953.

Israel, Martin. *Exorcism: The Removal of Evil Influences.* London: SPCK, 1997.

James, William. *The Varieties of Religious Experience: A Study in Human Nature.* London:

Longmans, 1903. A good critical edition is the one introduced by John Smith. Cambridge, Mass.: Harvard University Press, 1985.

Jantzen, Grace M. *Power, Gender, and Christian Mysticism.* Cambridge Studies in Ideology and Religion 8. Cambridge: Cambridge University Press, 1995.

Jensen, Robin M. *The Substance of Things Seen: Art, Faith, and Christian Community.* Grand Rapids/Cambridge: Eerdmans, 2004.

Jenson, Robert W. *Systematic Theology: I, The Triune God, II, The Works of God* New York: Oxford University Press, 1997–99.

———. "You Wonder Where the Spirit Went." *Pro Ecclesia* 2 (1993): 296–304.

John of the Cross. *The Collected Works of St. John of the Cross.* Translated by Kieran Kavanaugh and Otilio Rodriguez. Washington, D.C.: Institute of Carmelite Studies, 1979. Page references in text are to this edition.

Johnson, Elizabeth. *Friends of God and Prophets: A Feminist Theological Reading of the Communion of Saints.* New York: Continuum, 1998.

———. *She Who Is: The Mystery of God in Feminist Theological Discourse.* New York: Crossroad, 1996.

Johnson, Vernon. *I'll Quit Tomorrow.* San Francisco: Harper & Row, 1980.

Johnston, William. *Mystical Theology: The Science of Love.* London, HarperCollins, 1995.

Jones, Alan W. *Soul Making: The Desert Way of Spirituality.* San Francisco: Harper & Row, 1985.

Julian of Norwich. *A Book of Showings to the Anchoress Julian of Norwich.* Toronto: Pontifical Institute of Mediaeval Studies, 1978.

———. *Showings.* Translated by Edmund Colledge and James Walsh. Classics of Western Spirituality. New York: Paulist, 1978.

Jung, C. G. *Psychology and the Occult.* Bollingen Series. Princeton, N.J.: Princeton University Press, 1977.

———. *Psychology and Religion.* The Terry Lectures. New Haven: Yale University Press, 1938.

———. "The Stages of Life." Pp. 387–403 in *The Structure and Dynamics of the Psyche.* Collected Works 8. Princeton: Princeton University Press, 1969.

Jüngel, Eberhard. *The Doctrine of the Trinity: God's Being Is in Becoming.* Grand Rapids: Eerdmans, 1976.

Kant, Immanuel. *Immanuel Kant's Critique of Pure Reason.* Translated by Norman Kemp Smith. London: Macmillan; New York, St. Martin's, 1963.

Kapikian, Catherine. *Art in the Service of the Sacred.* Edited by Kathy Black. Nashville: Abingdon, 2006.

Kärkkäinen, Veli-Matti. *Christology: A Global Introduction. An Ecumenical, International, and Global Perspective.* Grand Rapids: Baker, 2003.

———. "How to Speak of the Spirit among Religions: Trinitarian 'Rules' for a Pneumatological Theology of Religions." *International Bulletin of Missionary Research* 30 (2006): 121–27.

———. *An Introduction to Ecclesiology: Ecumenical, Historical and Global Perspectives.* Downers Grove, Ill.: InterVarsity, 2002.

———. *Pneumatology: The Holy Spirit in Ecumenical, International, and Contextual Perspective.* Grand Rapids: Baker Academic, 2002.

———. *Trinity and Religious Pluralism: The Doctrine of the Trinity in Christian Theology of Religions.* Aldershot, Hants, England: Ashgate, 2004.

———, and Amos Yong, eds. *Toward a Pneumatological Theology: Pentecostal and Ecumenical Perspectives on Ecclesiology, Soteriology, and Theology of Mission.* Lanham, Md.: University Press of America, 2002.

Kastner, Patricia Wilson. *Faith, Feminism and the Christ.* Philadelphia, Fortress, 1983.

Kavanagh, Aidan. *On Liturgical Theology.* New York, Pueblo Publishing, 1984.

Keating, Thomas. *Open Mind, Open Heart: The Contemplative Dimension of the Gospel.* New York: Continuum, 1992.

Keen, Sam. *Apology for Wonder.* New York: Harper & Row, 1969.

———. *The Passionate Life: Stages of Loving*. San Francisco: Harper & Row, 1983.

Kellogg, Joan. "The Meaning of Color and Shape in Mandalas." *American Journal of Art Therapy* 16 (1977): 123–26.

Kelly, Walter C. *The Best of Pogo*. Edited by Mrs. Walt Kelly and Bill Crouch, Jr. New York: Simon & Schuster, 1982.

Kelsey, Morton T. *Companions on the Inner Way The Art of Spiritual Guidance*. New York: Crossroad, 1983.

Keshgegian, Flora A. *Redeeming Memories: A Theology of Healing and Transformation*. Nashville: Abingdon, 2000.

———. *Time for Hope: Practices for Living in Today's World*. New York: Continuum, 2006.

Khoo, Oon-Chor. "An Episcopal Perspective of the Gifts and Ministry of the Holy Spirit: A Workshop for Parish Renewal." D.Min. thesis, Sewanee: The University of the South, 1993.

Kierkegaard, Søren, *Either/Or: A Fragment of Life*, vol. 2. Translated by David F. Swenson and Lillian Marvin Swenson with Walter Lowrie. Princeton, N.J.: Princeton University Press; London: H. Milford, 1944.

———, and David F. Swenson, Niels Thulstrup, and Howard Vincent Hong. *Philosophical Fragments, or, A Fragment of Philosophy*. Princeton, N.J.: Princeton University Press, 1962.

King, Thomas M., S.J. *Teilhard's Mass: Approaches to "The Mass on the World."* New York/Mahwah, N.J.: Paulist, 2005.

Kirk, Kenneth E. *The Vision of God*. New York: Harper & Row; Harrisburg, Pa.: Morehouse, 1991; and Attic Press, 1977 (new impression edition).

Knox, Ronald. *Enthusiasm*. New York and Oxford: Oxford University Press, 1950.

Kohlberg, Lawrence. *Essays on Moral Development*. San Francisco: Harper & Row, 1981.

Krynen, Jean. *Mystique Chrétienne et Théologie Moderne: I. Saint Jean de la Croix et l'Aventure de la Mystique Espagnole*. Toulouse: Presses universitaires du Mirail, 1990.

Küng, Hans. *On Being a Christian*. Translated by Edward Quinn. Garden City, N.Y.: Doubleday, 1976.

———. *The Church*. Translated by Ray and Rosaleen Ockenden. New York: Sheed & Ward, 1967.

———. *Infallible? An Inquiry*. Garden City, N.Y.: Doubleday, 1971.

LaCugna, Catherine Mowry. *God for Us: The Trinity and the Christian Life*. San Francisco: HarperSanFrancisco, 1991.

The Lambeth Conference 1930. London: SPCK; New York: Macmillan, 1930.

The Lambeth Conference 1958. "The Family in Contemporary Society." London: SPCK; Greenwich, Conn.: Seabury, 1958.

Lanzetta, Beverley J. *Radical Wisdom: A Feminine Mystical Theology*. Minneapolis: Fortress, 2005.

Larive, Armand. *After Sunday: A Theology of Work*. New York: Continuum, 2004.

Lash, Nicholas. *The Beginning and the End of "Religion."* Cambridge: Cambridge University Press, 1996.

———. *Believing Three Ways in One God: A Reading of the Apostles' Creed*. London, SCM, 1992; Notre Dame: University of Notre Dame Press, 1993.

———. *Easter in Ordinary: Reflections on Human Experience and the Knowledge of God*. London: SCM, 1988.

Leary, Timothy Francis. "The Religious Experience: Its Production and Interpretation." *The Psychedelic Review* 1 (1963–64): 324–46.

Leckey, Dolores R. *The Ordinary Way: A Family Spirituality*. New York: Crossroad, 1982.

Leclerq, Jean. "Influence and Noninfluence of Dioysius in the Western Middle Ages." Pp. 25–32 in *Pseudo-Dionysius: Works*. Translated by Colm Luibheid. New York/Mahwah, N.J.: Paulist, 1987.

———. *The Love of Learning and the Desire for God: A Study of Monastic Culture*. Translated by Catharine Mishrai. New York: Fordham University Press, 1982.

Lee, Dorothy. *Transfiguration*. New York/London: Continuum, 2004.

Leech, Kenneth. *Experiencing God: Theology as Spirituality.* San Francisco: Harper & Row, 1985.

———. *Soul Friend: A Study in Spirituality.* London: Sheldon, 1977; San Francisco: Harper & Row, 1980.

———. *True Prayer: An Invitation to Christian Spirituality.* San Francisco: Harper & Row; London: Sheldon, 1980.

L'Engle, Madeline. *A Circle of Quiet.* The Crosswicks Journal, Book 1. San Francisco: HarperSanFrancisco, 1972.

Levinson, Daniel J., et al. *The Seasons of a Man's Life.* New York: Knopf, 1978.

———, with Judy D. Levinson. *The Seasons of a Woman's Life.* New York: Knopf, 1996.

Levy, Charles Eric. "The Experience of Married Love We-Ness: An Empirical Existential-Phenomenological Study." Ph.D. diss., Duquesne University, 1976.

Lewis, C. S. *The Four Loves.* New York: Harcourt, Brace & World, 1960.

———. *A Grief Observed* [by] N. W. Clerk [pseud.]. Greenwich, Conn.: Seabury, 1963.

———. *Perelandra.* New York: Macmillan, 1944.

———. *The Pilgrim's Regress : An Allegorical Apology for Christianity, Reason, and Romanticism.* London: Geoffrey Bles, 1950.

———. *A Preface to Paradise Lost: Being the Ballard Matthews Lectures, Delivered at University College, North Wales, 1941.* London/New York: Oxford University Press, 1954.

———. *The Screwtape Letters.* New York: Macmillan, 1944.

———. *Surprised by Joy: The Shape of My Early Life.* New York : Harcourt, Brace & World, 1955.

———. *Till We Have Faces, A Myth Retold.* London: G. Bles, 1956.

Liebert, Elizabeth. *Changing Life Patterns: Adult Development in Spiritual Direction.* St. Louis, Mo.: Chalice, 2000.

Lonergan, Bernard J. F. *Method in Theology.* New York: Herder & Herder, 1972.

———. "Natural Right and Historical Mindedness." *Proceedings of the American Catholic Philosophical Association* 51 (1977): 132–43.

———. "Reality, Myth, Symbol." In *Myth, Reality, and Symbol.* Edited by Alan M. Olson. Notre Dame, Ind.: University of Notre Dame Press, 1980.

Lösel, Steffen. "Guidance from the Gaps: The Holy Spirit, Ecclesial Authority, and the Principle of Juxtaposition." *Scottish Journal of Theology* 59, no. 2 (2006): 140–58.

Lossky, Vladmir. *The Mystical Theology of the Eastern Church.* London: J. Clarke, 1957.

Luckman, Harriet, and Linda Kulzer, eds., *Purity of Heart in Early Ascetic and Monastic Literature: Essays in Honor of Juana Raasch, O.S.B.* Collegeville, Minn.: Liturgical, 1999.

Luther, Martin. "The Babylonian Captivity of the Church." *Luther's Works.* II. Philadelphia: Muhlenberg, 1943.

———. "The Freedom of a Christian." Pp. 265–316 in *Three Treatises.* Second revised edition. Translated by Charles M. Jacobs et al. Philadelphia: Fortress, 1970.

———, trans. (Franckforter). *The Theologia Germanica of Martin Luther.* Translated by Bengt Hoffman. New York: Paulist, 1980.

Lutheran-Episcopal Dialogue, *Called to Common Mission.* Available at http://www.elca.org/ecumenical/fullcommunion/episcopal/ccmresources/text.html.

The Lutheran World Federation and The Roman Catholic Church, *Joint Declaration on the Doctrine of Justification.* Grand Rapids: Eerdmans, 2000.

Macquarrie, John. *Principles of Christian Theology.* New York: Scribner, 1977.

Marx, Karl, Friedrich Engels, and Dirk Jan Struik. *Birth of the Communist Manifesto, With Full Text of the Manifesto, All Prefaces by Marx and Engels, Early Drafts by Engels and Other Supplementary Material.* New York: International Publishers, 1971.

May, Gerald. *Addiction and Grace.* San Francisco: Harper & Row, 1988

———. *Care of Mind, Care of Spirit: A Psychiatrist Explores Spiritual Direction.* San Francisco: Harper & Row, 1992.

———. *The Dark Night of the Soul: A Psychiatrist Explores the Connection between Darkness and Spiritual Growth.* San Francisco: Harper & Row, 2005.

———. *Will and Spirit: A Contemplative Psychology.* San Francisco: Harper & Row, 1982.
May, Rollo. *Love and Will.* New York: Norton, 1969.
McDonnell, Kilian. *The Other Hand of God: The Holy Spirit as Universal Truth and Goal.* Collegeville, Minn.: Liturgical Press, 2003.
McFague, Sallie. *The Body of God: An Ecological Theology.* Minneapolis: Fortress, 1993.
———. *Metaphorical Theology: Models of God in Religious Language.* Philadelphia: Fortress, 1982.
———. *Models of God: Theology for an Ecological, Nuclear Age.* London: SCM, 1987.
McGinn, Bernard. "Asceticism and Mysticism in Late Antiquity and the Early Middle Ages." In *Asceticism.* Edited by Vincent L. Wimbush and Richard Valantasis. New York/Oxford: Oxford University Press, 1995.
———. *The Flowering of Mysticism.* New York: Crossroad, 1998.
———. *The Foundations of Mysticism.* New York: Crossroad, 1991.
———. *The Growth of Mysticism.* New York: Crossroad, 1994.
———. *The Harvest of Mysticism in Medieval Germany.* New York: Crossroad, 2005.
———. "The Letter and the Spirit: Spirituality as an Academic Discipline." *Christian Spirituality Bulletin* 1, no. 2 (Fall, 1993): 1–10.
———. *The Presence of God: A History of Western Christian Mysticism.* Vols. 1–4. New York: Crossroad, 1991–.
McGonigle, Herbert. *John Wesley's Doctrine of Prevenient Grace.* Lutterworth, England: Wesley Fellowship, 1995.
McIntosh, Mark A. *Discernment and Truth: The Spirituality and Theology of Knowledge.* New York: Crossroad, 2004.
———. *Mystical Theology: The Integrity of Spirituality and Theology.* Malden, Mass.: Blackwell, 1998.
Megyer, Eugene. "Spiritual Theology Today." *The Way* 21 (1981): 55–67.
Merton, Thomas. *Contemplative Prayer.* New York: Herder & Herder, 1969.
———. *Mystics and Zen Masters.* New York: Farrar, Straus & Giroux, 1967.
———. *New Seeds of Contemplation.* Norfolk, Conn.: New Directions 1962.
———. *The Seven Storey Mountain: An Autobiography of Faith.* Orlando, Fl.: Harcourt Brace, 1948.
———. *Zen and the Birds of Appetite.* New York: New Directions, 1968.
Michael, Chester P., and Marie C. Norrisey. *Prayer and Temperament: Different Prayer Forms for Different Personality Types.* Charlottesville, Va.: Open Door, 1984.
Micks, Marianne H. *Loving the Questions: An Exploration of the Nicene Creed.* Cambridge, Mass.: Cowley, 1993.
Milbank, John. *Theology and Social Theory: Beyond Secular Reason.* Signposts in Theology. Cambridge, Mass.: Blackwell, 1991.
———, Catherine Pickstock, and Graham Ward. *Radical Orthodoxy: A New Theology.* London: Routledge, 1999.
Miles, Margaret R. *Carnal Knowing: Female Nakedness and Religious Meaning in the Christian West.* Boston: Beacon, 1989.
———. *Practicing Christianity: Critical Perspectives for an Embodied Spirituality.* New York: Crossroad, 1988.
Miskimin, Harry A. *The Economy of Early Renaissance Europe. 1300–1460 . . .* Cambridge: Cambridge University Press, 1975.
———. *The Economy of Later Renaissance Europe, 1460–1600.* Cambridge; New York: Cambridge University Press, 1977.
———. *Money, Prices, and Foreign Exchange in Fourteenth-Century France.* Yale Studies in Economics 15. New Haven: Yale University Press, 1963.
Moll, Rob. "The New Monasticism: A Fresh Crop of Christian Communities Is Blossoming in Blighted Urban Settings All Over America." *Christianity Today* 49, no. 9 (2005): 38–46

Moltmann, Jürgen. *The Coming of God: Christian Eschatology.* Translated by Margaret Kohl. Minneapolis: Fortress, 1996.

———. *The Crucified God The Cross of Christ As the Foundation and Criticism of Christian Theology.* New York: Harper & Row; London, SCM, 1974.

———. *Theology of Hope: On the Ground and the Implications of a Christian Eschatology.* New York: Harper & Row, 1967.

———. *The Trinity and the Kingdom: The Doctrine of God.* Translated by Margaret Kohl. New York, Harper & Row, 1981.

———, and Robert E. Neale, Sam Keen, David LeRoy Miller. *Theology of Play.* New York: Harper & Row, 1972.

Moody, Raymond A. *Life after Life: The Investigation of a Phenomenon—Survival of Bodily Death.* Harrisburg, Pa.: Stackpole Books, 1976

More, Henry. *Enthusiasmus Triumphatus: Or, A Discourse of the Nature, Causes, Kinds, and Cure, of Enthusiasme.* London: J. Flesher, 1656.

Morrison, Bradley. "Rollo May's Psychotherapy Related to Paul Ricoeur's Language Philosophy" (1993) at http://www.xcelco.on.ca/~btmorrison/ricoeur/Ricoeur&RolloMay.html.

Moseley, Romney M. *Becoming a Self Before God: Critical Transformations.* Nashville: Abingdon, 1991.

Moule, H. C. G. *The Evangelical School in the Church of England: Its Men and Its Work in the Nineteenth Century.* London: James Nisbet, 1901.

———. *Veni Creator: Thoughts on the Person and Work of the Holy Spirit of Promise.* London: Hodder & Stoughton, 1895. Republished as *Person and Work of the Holy Spirit.* Grand Rapids: Kregel, 1977. Page references are to the latter.

Murphy, Nancey C. *Bodies and Souls, or Spirited Bodies?* Current Issues in Theology. Cambridge, U.K.: Cambridge University Press, 2006.

———, and William R. Stoeger. *Evolution and Emergence: Systems, Organisms, Persons.* Oxford: Oxford University Press, 2007.

Niditch, Susuan. "Genesis." In *Women's Bible Commentary.* Expanded edition, with Apocrypha. Edited by Carol A Newsom and Sharon H. Ringe. Louisville, Ky.: Westminster John Knox, 1998.

Niebuhr, H. Richard. *Christ and Culture.* New York: Harper, 1951.

———. *The Responsible Self: An Essay in Christian Moral Philosophy.* New York: Harper & Row, 1963.

Niebuhr, Reinhold. *Moral Man and Immoral Society: A Study in Ethics and Politics.* New York/London: Charles Scribner's Sons, 1941.

Noli, Bishop Fan Sylian, comp. *The Eastern Orthodox Prayer Book.* Boston: Albanian Orthodox Church in America, 1949.

Norris, Richard A. *Understanding the Faith of the Church.* New York: Seabury, 1979.

Norton, David. *Personal Destinies: A Philosophy of Ethical Individualism.* Princeton, N.J.: Princeton University Press, 1976.

Novak, Michael, ed. *The Experience of Marriage: The Testimony of Catholic Laymen.* New York: Macmillan, 1964.

Nygren, Anders. *Agape and Eros.* Translated by Philip S. Watson. Philadelphia: Westminster, 1953.

Oberman, Heiko A. *The Harvest of Medieval Theology: Gabriel Biel and Late Medieval Nominalism.* Cambridge, Mass.: Harvard University Press, 1963.

Ogden, Schubert M. *Is There Only One True Religion or Are There Many?* Dallas: Southern Methodist University Press, 1992.

———. *The Point of Christology.* New York: Harper & Row, 1982.

Olson, Roger E., and Christopher A. Hall. *The Trinity.* Grand Rapids/Cambridge: Eerdmans, 2002.

Origen. *The Song of Songs: Commentary and Homilies.* Translated by R. P. Lawson. Westminster, Md.: Newman, 1957.

Outler, Albert C. *John Wesley [a Representative Collection of His Writings].* Library of Protestant Thought. New York: Oxford University Press, 1964.

———. *John and Charles Wesley: Selected Writings and Hymns.* Edited by Frank Whaling. New York/Ramsey/Toronto: Paulist, 1981.

Packer, J. I. *Alive to God: Studies in Spirituality Presented to James Houston.* Downers Grove, Ill.: InterVarsity, 1992.

———. *Knowing God.* Downers Grove, Ill.: InterVarsity, 1973.

Palmov, Nicholas. *The Assumption of the Religious Dress in Monasticism: Ceremonies for the Assumption of the Dress in the Monasticism of the Greek Church.* Studies in History and Archaeology. Kiev: Tchokoloff, 1914, as reviewd by Aurelio Palmieri, *Harvard Theological Review* 8, no. 2 (April, 1915): 270–72.

Pannenberg, Wolfhart. *An Introduction to Systematic Theology.* Grand Rapids: Eerdmans, 1991.

———, *Systematic Theology.* Translated by Geoffrey Bromiley. Grand Rapids: Eerdmans, 1991–1998.

Peacocke, A. R. *Creation and the World of Science.* Bampton Lectures 1978. Oxford: Clarendon, 1979

———. *God and Science: A Quest for Christian Credibility.* London: SCM, 1996.

Peirce, Charles Saunders. *Collected Papers.* Edited by Charles Hartshorne and Paul Weiss. Cambridge, Mass.: Harvard University Press, 1931–1958.

Peterson, Eugene H. *Christ Plays in Ten Thousand Places: A Conversation in Spiritual Theology.* Grand Rapids: Eerdmans, 2005.

Petipierre, Robert, ed. *Exorcism: The Report of a Commission Convened by the Bishop of Exeter.* London: SPCK, 1972.

Pettersen, Alvyn. *Athanasius.* Harrisburg, Pa.: Morehouse, 1995.

Piaget, Jean. *Growth.* New York: Basic Books, 1958.

Pinnock, Clark. *Flame of Love: A Theology of the Holy Spirit.* Downers Grove, Ill.: InterVarsity, 1996.

Polkinghorne, John. C. *The Faith of a Physicist: Reflections of a Bottom-Up Thinker: The Gifford Lectures for 1993–4.* Princeton, N.J.: Princeton University Press, 1994.

———. "Is Science Enough?" *STR* 39, no. 1 (1995): 11–26.

———. *Science and Creation: The Search for Understanding.* Boston: New Science Library, 1989.

———. "A Scientist's Approach to Belief." *STR* 39, no. 1 (1995): 11–50.

Pourrat, Pierre. *Christian Spirituality.* Vols. I-III. London: Burns & Oates, 1922–24; vols. I-IV. Westminister, Md.: Newman, 1953-58.

Powell, Samuel M. *A Theology of Christian Spirituality.* Nashville: Abingdon, 2005.

Presler, Titus Leonard. *Horizons of Mission.* New Church's Teaching Series 11. Cambridge, Mass: Cowley, 2001.

Principe, Walter H. "Spirituality, Christian." *NDCS*, 931–38.

———. "Toward Defining Spirituality." *Studies in Religion/Sciences Religieuses* 12 (1983): 129–41.

Progoff, Ira. *At a Journal Workshop: The Basic Text and Guide for Using the Intensive Journal.* New York: Dialogue House Library, 1975.

Pseudo-Dionysius: The Complete Works. Translated by Colm Luibheid and Paul Rorem. Classics of Western Spirituality. New York: Paulist, 1987.

Rahner, Hugo, S.J., *The Spirituality of St. Ignatius Loyola: An Account of Its Historical Development.* Translated by Francis John. Chicago: Loyola University Press, 1980.

Rahner, Karl. *The Christian Commitment: Essays in Pastoral Theology.* Translated by Cecily Hastings. New York: Sheed & Ward, 1963.

———. *The Church and the Sacraments.* Translated by W. J. O'Hara. New York: Herder & Herder, 1963.

———. *The Dynamic Element in the Church.* Translated by W. J. O'Hara. Freiburg: Herder, 1964.

———. *Experience of the Spirit: The Source of Theology. TI* 16. New York: Crossroad, 1981.

———. *Foundations of Christian Faith: An Introduction to the Idea of Christianity.* Translated by William V. Dych. New York: Seabury/Crossroad, 1978, 1989.

———. *Hearers of the Word.* New York: Herder & Herder, 1969.

———. *Nature and Grace: Dilemmas in the Modern Church.* New York: Sheed & Ward, 1964.

———. *Sacramentum Mundi: An Encyclopedia of Theology.* New York: Herder & Herder, 1968.

———. *Spirit in the World.* New York: Herder & Herder, 1968.

———. *Theological Investigations.* Translated by Cornelius Ernst. Baltimore: Helicon, 1961-.

———. *The Trinity.* Translated by Joseph Donceel. New York: Herder & Herder, 1970.

Rambo, Lewis R. *Understanding Religious Conversion.* New Haven/London: Yale University Press, 1993.

Ramsey, Arthur Michael. *The Glory of God and the Transfiguration of Christ.* London/New York/ Toronto: Longman's, Green, 1949.

Richard of St. Victor. *The Twelve Patriarchs, The Mystical Ark, Book Three of the Trinity: Richard of St. Victor.* Translated by Grover A. Zinn. Classics of Western Spirituality. New York: Paulist, 1979.

Richards, John. *Exorcism, Deliverance, and Healing: Some Pastoral Guidelines.* Grove Booklet on Ministry and Worship 44. Bramcote: Grove Books, 1976.

Richardson, Herbert Warren. *Toward an American Theology.* New York: Harper & Row, 1967.

Ricoeur, Paul. *The Rule of Metaphor: Multi-disciplinary Studies of the Creation of Meaning in Language.* Translated by Robert Czerney, with K. McLaughlin and J. Costello. Toronto: University of Toronto Press, 1977; original ed., *La metaphore vive.* Paris: Editions du Seuil, 1975.

———. *The Symbolism of Evil.* Translated by Emerson Buchanon. New York: Harper & Row, 1967.

The Rites of the Catholic Church as Revised by Decree of the Second Vatican Ecumenical Council and Published by Authority of Pope Paul VI. Collegeville, Minn.: Liturgical, 1990.

Rogers, Eugene, F. *After the Spirit: A Constructive Pneumatology from Resources outside the West.* Grand Rapids: Eerdmans, 2005.

———. *Sexuality and the Christian Body: Their Way into the Triune God.* Oxford/Malden, Mass.: Blackwell, 1999.

Rougemont, Denis de. *Love in the Western World.* Translated by Montgomery Belgion. Greenwich, Conn: Fawcett, 1966.

Royo Marín, Antonio, and Jordan Aumann. *The Theology of Christian Perfection.* Dubuque, Ia.: Priory, 1962.

Ruether, Rosemary Radford. *Sexism and God-Talk : Toward a Feminist Theology.* Boston: Beacon, 1983, 1993. Page references to the later edition.

Russell, Letty. *Growth in Partnership.* Philadelphia: Westminster, 1981.

Russell, Norman, trans. *The Lives of the Desert Fathers: The Historia Monachorum in Aegypto.* Cistercian Studies Series 34. London: Mowbray, 1981.

Ruusbroec, Jan van. *John Ruusbroec: The Spiritual Espousals and Other Works.* Translated by James A Wiseman, O.S.B. Classics of Western Spirituality. New York/Mahwah, N.J./ Toronto: Paulist, 1985.

Saint Jure, Jean-Baptiste. *L'homme spirituel.* Lyons, Part I 1646; part II 1652. Eng. trans., *The Spiritual Man: Or, The Spiritual Life Reduced to Its First Principles.* Translated from the French of J. B. Saint-Jure . . . by a member of the Order of Mercy. London: Burns & Oates, 1878. Ital. trans., *L'uomo spirituale.* Translated by Maria Pia Ghielmi. Milan: Edizioni Glossa Srl, 2005.

Saliers, Don and Emily. *A Song to Sing, a Life to Live: Music as Spiritual Practice.* San Francisco: Jossey-Bass, 2005.

Sartre, Jean-Paul. *Being and Nothingness: An Essay on Phenomenological Ontology.* Translated by Hazel E. Barnes. New York: Philosophical Library, 1956.

Sayers, Dorothy L. *Are Women Human?* Grand Rapids: Eerdmans, 1971.

Schillebeeckx, Edward. *Celibacy.* Translated by C. A. L. Jarrott. New York: Sheed & Ward, 1968.

———. *Christ the Sacrament of the Encounter with God.* New York: Sheed & Ward, 1963.

Schmemann, Alexander. *O Death, Where Is Thy Sting?* Translated by Alexis Vinogradov. Crestwood, N.Y.: St. Vladimir's Seminary Press, 2003.

———. *The Eucharist: Sacrament of the Kingdom.* Translated by Paul Kachur. Crestwood, N.Y.: St. Vladimir's Seminary Press, 1988.

———. *Sacraments and Orthodoxy.* New York: Herder & Herder, 1965.

Schneiders, Sandra M. "Approaches to the Study of Christian Spirituality." *BCCS*, 15–33.

———. "A Hermeneutical Approach to the Study of Christian Spirituality." *Christian Spirituality Bulletin* 2, no. 2 (Spring, 1994): 9–14.

———. "Spirituality as an Academic Discipline: Reflections from Experience." *Christian Spirituality Bulletin* 1, no. 2 (Fall, 1993): 10–15.

———. "Spirituality in the Academy." Pp. 15–37 in *Modern Christian Spirituality: Methodological and Historical Essays.* Edited by Bradley C. Hanson. AAR Studies in Religion 62. Atlanta, Ga: Scholars, 1990.

———. "The Study of Christian Spirituality: Contours and Dynamics of a Discipline." *Christian Spirituality Bulletin* 6, no. 1 (Spring, 1998): 1–11.

Schrag, Calvin O., and David James Miller, "The Algebra of History: Merleau-Ponty and Foucault on the Rhetoric of the Person." In Ian Angus and Lenore Langsdorf, eds., *The Critical Turn: Rhetoric and Philosophy in Postmodern Discourse.* Carbondale: Southern Illinois University Press, 1993.

Schüssler Fiorenza, Elisabeth. *In Memory of Her: A Feminist Theological Reconstruction of Christian Origins.* New York: Crossroad, 1983.

Segal, Robert A., ed. *The Gnostic Jung.* Princeton, N.J.: Princeton University Press, 1992.

Shapiro, Francine, and Margot Silk Forest. *E.M.D.R. Eye Movement Desensitization & Reprocessing: The Breakthrough Therapy for Overcoming Anxiety, Stress, and Trauma.* New York: Basic Books, 1997.

Sheehy, Gail. *Passages: Predictable Crises of Adult Life.* New York: Dutton, 1976.

———. *The Silent Passage: Menopause.* New York: Random House, 1992.

———. *Understanding Men's Passages: Discovering the New Map of Men's Lives.* New York: Random House, 1998.

Sheldrake, Philip. *Befriending our Desires.* London: Darton, Longman, & Todd, 1994.

———. *Spirituality and History.* Maryknoll, N.Y.: Orbis Books, 1991, 1995, 2001.

———. *Spirituality and Theology: Christian Living and the Doctrine of God.* Maryknoll, N.Y.: Orbis Books, 1998.

Shoemaker, Samuel M. *Realizing Religion.* New York: Association, 1921.

Simeon, Charles. *The Offices of the Holy Spirit: Four Sermons, Preached before the University of Cambridge, in the Month of November, 1831.* New York: Swords, Stanford, 1832.

Singer, June, Robert Segal, Murray Stein, and Robert Moore. *The Cosmology of Inner Space: The Gnostic Vision in Jung's Psychology and the World Today.* Evanston, Ill.: C. G. Jung Institute of Chicago, 1993.

Slocum, Robert Boak, ed. *Engaging the Spirit Essays on the Life and Theology of the Holy Spirit.* New York: Church Publishing, 2001.

———. *A Heart for the Future: Writings on Christian Hope.* New York: Church Publishing, 2004.

Smith, Kenneth L., and Ira G. Zepp. *Search for the Beloved Community: The Thinking of Martin Luther King, Jr.* Valley Forge, Pa.: Judson, 1974.

Society of St. Francis. *Celebrating Common Prayer: A Version of the Daily Office, SSF,* by the European Province of the Society of St. Francis. London: Mowbray, 1992.

Sölle, Dorothee. *Thinking about God: An Introduction to Theology.* London: SCM, 1990.

Solomon, Robert. *About Love: Reinventing Romance for Our Times.* New York: Simon & Schuster, 1988.

Sommerfeldt, John R. *Aelred of Rievaulx on Love and Order in the World and the Church.* New York: Newman, 2006.

Staniloae, Dumitru. *The Experience of God.* Translated by Ioan Ioanita and Robert Barringer. Brookline, Mass.: Holy Cross Orthodox Press, 1994.

———. *Orthodox Spirituality: A Practical Guide for the Faithful and a Definitive Manual for the Scholar.* South Canaan, Pa.: St. Tikhon's Seminary Press, 2002.

Starbuck, Edwin D. "The Varieties of Religious Experience." *The Biblical World* 24, no. 2 (August, 1904): 100–111.

Stendahl, Krister. *Meanings: The Bible as Document and as Guide.* Philadelphia: Fortress, 1984.

Stevenson, W. Taylor. *History as Myth: The Import for Contemporary Theology.* New York: Seabury, 1969.

Suenens, Cardinal Léon Joseph, and Hélder Câmara. *Charismatic Renewal and Social Action: A Dialogue.* Malines Document 3. Ann Arbor, Mich.: Servant Books, 1979.

Sullivan, Michael. *Windows into the Soul: Art as Spiritual Expression.* Harrisburg, Pa: Morehouse, 2006.

Sykes, Stephen. *The Story of Atonement.* Trinity and Truth Series. London: Darton, Longman & Todd, 1997.

Symeon the New Theologian, Saint. *The Discourses.* Translated by C. J. DeCatanzaro. Introduction by George Maloney, S.J. New York: Paulist, 1980.

Tanner, Kathryn. *Economy of Grace.* Minneapolis: Fortress, 2005.

———. *God and Creation in Christian Theology: Tyranny or Empowerment.* Oxford/New York: Blackwell, 1988.

———. *Jesus, Humanity, and the Trinity: A Brief Systematic Theology.* Minneapolis: Fortress, 2001.

———. *Theories of Culture. A New Agenda for Theology.* Minneapolis: Fortress, 1997.

Tanquerey, Adolphe. *Précis de théologie ascétique et mystique.* Eng. trans., *The Spiritual Life: A Treatise on Ascetical and Mystical Theology.* Translated by Herman Branderis. Second and revised edition. Tournai/New York: Desclee, 1961.

Tavard, George H. *Paul Tillich and the Christian Message.* London: Burns & Oates, 1962.

Taylor, John V. *The Go-between God; The Holy Spirit and the Christian Mission.* Philadelphia: Fortress, 1973.

Tazewell, Charles, and Katherine Evans. *The Littlest Angel.* Chicago: Children's Press, 1946.

Teilhard de Chardin, Pierre. *The Divine Milieu: An Essay on the Interior Life.* New York: Harper, 1960.

———. *The Phenomenon of Man.* New York: Harper, 1959.

Temple, William. *Nature, Man and God; Being the Gifford Lectures Delivered in the University of Glasgow in the Academical Years 1932–1933 and 1933–1934.* London: Macmillan, 1935.

Teresa of Avila, Saint. *The Interior Castle.* Translated by Kieran Kavanaugh and Otilio Rodriguez. Classics of Western Spirituality. New York: Paulist, 1979.

Thomas, Owen. *What Is It That Theologians Do, How They Do It and Why.* Lewiston, N.Y.: Edwin Mellen, 2006.

———, and Ellen K. Wondra. *Introduction to Theology.* Third edition. Harrisburg, Pa.: Morehouse, 2002.

Thomas, W. H. Griffith. *The Holy Spirit of God.* London: Church Book Room, 1974.

Thomas à Kempis. *Of the Imitation of Christ: Four Books.* New York: Walker, 1987.

Thompsett, Fredrica Harris. *We Are Theologians: Strengthening the People of the Episcopal Church.* Cambridge, Mass.: Cowley, 1989.

Thornton, Martin. *Christian Proficiency.* London: SPCK, 1959.

———. *English Spirituality: An Outline of Ascetical Theology according to the English Pastoral Tradition.* London: SPCK, 1963.

————. *The Rock and the River: An Encounter between Traditional Spirituality and Modern Thought.* London: Hodder & Stoughton, 1965.

————. *Spiritual Direction A Practical Introduction.* London: SPCK, 1984.

Tillard, J. M. R. *Flesh of the Church, Flesh of Christ: At the Source of the Ecclesiology of Communion.* Collegeville, Minn.: Liturgical, 2001.

Tillich, Paul. *Systematic Theology.* Chicago: University of Chicago Press, 1951–63.

————. *Theology of Culture.* Edited by Robert C. Kimball. New York: Oxford University Press, 1959.

————, and James Luther Adams. *The Protestant Era.* Chicago: University of Chicago Press, 1948.

Tinsley, Lucy. *The French Expressions for Spirituality and Devotion: A Semantic Study.* Washington, D.C.: Catholic University of America Press, 1953.

Tocqueville, Alexis de, and John C. Spencer. *American Institutions and Their Influence.* New York: A. S. Barnes, 1851.

————, and Phillips Bradley, Henry Reeve, and Francis Bowen. *Democracy in America.* New York: Knopf, 1945.

Torrance, James B. *Worship, Community, and the Triune God of Grace.* Downers Grove, Ill.: InterVarsity, 1996.

Tracy, David. *The Analogical Imagination: Christian Theology and the Culture of Pluralism.* New York: Crossroad, 1981.

————. *Blessed Rage for Order: The New Pluralism in Theology.* New York: Seabury, 1975.

Trible, Phyllis. *God and the Rhetoric of Sexuality.* Philadelphia: Fortress, 1978.

Trinkaus, Charles, and Heiko A. Oberman, eds. *The Pursuit of Holiness in Late Medieval and Renaissance Religion.* Leiden: Brill, 1974.

Tuchman, Barbara. *A Distant Mirror.* New York: Knopf, 1978.

Turner, Denys. *The Darkness of God: Negativity in Christian Mysticism.* Cambridge: Cambridge University Press, 1995.

Turner, Philip. "How the Church Might Teach." Pp. 137–59 in *The Crisis in Moral Teaching in the Episcopal Church.* Edited by Timothy Sedgwick and Philip Turner. Harrisburg, Pa.: Morehouse, 1992.

————. *A Rule of Life for Congregations: Based upon the Baptismal Covenant.* Cincinnati: Forward Movement, 1997.

Ulanov, Ann Belford. *Religion and the Spiritual in Carl Jung.* New York: Paulist, 1999.

Underhill, Evelyn. *Letters.* London: Longmans, Green, 1943.

————. *Mysticism: A Study in the Nature and Development of Man's Spiritual Consciousness.* London: Methuen, 1911; New York: Dutton, 1961; and numerous other editions.

————. *Worship.* New York: Harper, 1957.

Van Ackeren, Gerald Van. *Sacra Doctrina: The Subject of the First Question of Summa Theologica of St. Thomas Aquinas.* Rome: Officium Libri Catholici, 1952.

Van Kaam, Adrian L. *The Vowed Life: Dynamics of Personal and Spiritual Unfolding.* Denville, N.J.: Dimension Books, 1968.

Vanier, Jean. *An Ark for the Poor: The Story of L'Arche.* Ottawa: Novalis, 1995.

Vatican Council II: the Conciliar and Post Conciliar Documents. Austin Flannery, general editor. Northport, N.Y.: Costello, 1975 (1987 printing).

Vinck, José de. *The Virtue of Sex.* New York: Hawthorne, 1966.

Vogels, Heinz-Jürgen. *Celibacy, Gift or Law: A Critical Investigation.* Tunbridge Wells, Kent: Burns & Oates, 1992.

Volf, Miroslav. *After Our Likeness: The Church as the Image of the Trinity.* Sacra Doctrina. Grand Rapids: Eerdmans, 1998.

————. "The Final Reconciliation: Reflections on a Social Dimension of the Eschatological Transition." Pp. 233–67 in *A Heart for the Future: Writings on Christian Hope.* Edited by Robert B. Slocum. New York: Church Publishing, 2004.

———. *Work in the Spirit: Toward a Theology of Work.* New York: Oxford University Press, 1991.

von Bertalanffy, Ludwig. *General System Theory: Foundation, Developments, Applications.* New York: G. Brazillier, 1968.

Waaijman, Kees. *Spirituality: Forms, Foundations, Methods.* Translated by John Vriend. Leuven/ Paris/Dudley, Mass.: Peeters, 2002.

Wadell, Paul J. *Becoming Friends: Worship, Justice, and the Practice of Christian Friendship.* Grand Rapids: Brazos, 2002.

Walker, Alice. *The Color Purple.* New York: Harcourt Brace Jovanovich, 1982. Page references to the large print edition, Boston: G. K. Hall, 1986.

Wallis, Jim. *The Call to Conversion.* New York : Harper & Row, 1981.

Walter, Howard A. *Soul Surgery: Some Thoughts on Incisive Personal Work.* New Britain, Conn: Record Press, 1921.

Walton, Brad. *Jonathan Edwards, Religious Affections, and the Puritan Analysis of True Piety, Spiritual Sensation and Heart Religion.* Lewiston/Queenston/Lampeter: Edwin Mellon, 2002.

Ward, Benedicta, trans. *The Sayings of the Desert Fathers: The Alphabetical Collection.* London: Mowbrays, 1975.

Ware, Kallistos. "The Holy Spirit in the Liturgy of St. John Chrysostom." Duquesne Holy Spirit Colloquium, March 23, 2007, publication forthcoming.

———. "The Holy Spirit in the Personal Life of the Christian." Pp. 139–69 in *Unity in the Spirit: Diversity in the Churches.* The Report of the Conference of European Churches' Assembly VIII. Crete, 1979.

———, Introduction to *The Ladder of Divine Ascent: John Climacus.* Translated by Colm Luibheid and Norman Russell. New York: Paulist, 1982.

Weil, Simone. *Waiting for God.* New York: Harper & Row, 1973.

———. "Simone (Adolphine) Weil: (1909–1943) Biographies, Criticism, Journal Articles, Work Overviews." Farmington Hills, Mich.: Gale, 2003.

Weiss, Paul. *History: Written and Lived.* Carbondale: Southern Illinois University Press, 1962.

———. *Modes of Being.* Carbondale: Southern Illinois University Press, 1958.

———. *Nine Basic Arts.* Carbondale: Southern Illinois University Press, 1961.

———. *Religion and Art.* Aquinas Lecture 1963. Milwaukee: Marquette University Press, 1963.

———. *Sport: A Philosophic Inquiry.* Carbondale: Southern Illinois University Press, 1969.

———. *The World of Art.* Carbondale: Southern Illinois University Press, 1961.

———, and Lewis Edwin Hahn, eds. *The Philosophy of Paul Weiss.* Library of Living Philosophers 23. Chicago/La Salle, Ill.: Open Court, 1995.

Wesley, John. *Thoughts upon Slavery.* London: R. Hawes, 1774.

Westerhoff, John H., III. *Will Our Children Have Faith?* New York: Seabury/Crossroad, 1976

White, James F. *Sacraments as God's Self Giving: Sacramental Practice and Faith.* Nashville: Abingdon, 1983.

Whitehead, Evelyn Eaton, and James D. Whitehead. *Seasons of Strength: New Visions of Adult Christian Maturing.* Garden City, N.Y.: Doubleday, 1984.

———. *Shadows of the Heart: A Spirituality of the Negative Emotions.* New York: Crossroad, 1994.

———. *Wisdom of the Body: Making Sense of Our Sexuality.* New York: Crossroad, 2001.

Wigger, J. Bradley. "Face to Face: A Spirituality of Parenting." *Journal of Family Ministry* 14, no. 2 (2000): 17–27.

Wilde, Oscar. *The Picture of Dorian Gray.* London: Ward, Locke, & Bowman, 1891.

Williams, Rowan. *Teresa of Avila.* Guildford: Geoffrey Chapman, 1991.

———. *The Wound of Knowledge: Christian Spirituality from the New Testament to St. John of the Cross.* London: Darton, Longman & Todd, 1979.

Worgul, George S. *From Magic to Metaphor: A Validation of Christian Sacraments.* New York: Paulist, 1980. New edition forthcoming.

Wrenn, Michael J. *Pope John Paul II and the Family: The Text with a Theological and Catechetical Commentary with Discussion Questions on the Apostolic Exhortation of Pope John Paul II on the Role of the Christian Family in the Modern World (Familiaris Consortio).* Chicago: Franciscan Herald, 1983.

Wright, Wendy M. *Introduction to the Devout Life and Treatise on the Love of God.* New York: Crossroad, 1993.

———. *Sacred Dwelling: A Spirituality of Family Life.* New York: Crossroad, 1990.

Wuellner, Flora Slosson. *Heart of Healing, Heart of Light : Encountering God, Who Shares and Heals Our Pain.* Nashville: Upper Room Books, 1992.

Wuthnow, Robert. *After Heaven: Spirituality in America since the 1950s.* Berkeley: University of California Press, 1998.

Yankelovich, Daniel. *New Rules in American Life: Searching for Self-Fulfillment in a World Turned Upside Down.* New York: Random House, 1981.

Yeago, David S. "Martin Luther on Grace, Law, and Moral Life: Prolegomena to an Ecumenical Discussion of *Veritatis Splendor*." *The Thomist* 62 (1998): 163–91.

Yong, Amos. *Beyond the Impasse: Toward a Pneumatological Theology of Religions.* Carlisle, Cumbria, U.K.: Paternoster, 2003.

Zaehner, R. C. *Mysticism, Sacred and Profane: An Inquiry into Some Varieties of Praeter-Natural Experience.* Oxford: Clarendon, 1957.

———. *Our Savage God: The Perverse Use of Eastern Thought.* New York: Sheed & Ward, 1974.

———. *Zen, Drugs, and Mysticism.* New York: Pantheon Books, 1973.

Zizioulas, John D. *Being as Communion: Studies in Personhood and the Church.* Second edition. London: Darton, Longman, & Todd, 2004.

———, and Paul McPartlan. *Communion and Otherness: Further Studies in Personhood and the Church.* London: T&T Clark, 2006.

Index

CPSIA information can be obtained
at www.ICGtesting.com
Printed in the USA
LVOW01s1008260117
522266LV00015B/482/P